Delia Smith's
Complete Cookery Course

Delia Smith's
Complete Cookery Course

BOOK CLUB ASSOCIATES LONDON

Photographs by Bob Komar
Drawings by Ray and Corrine Burrows
Food preparation by Elaine Bastable

Grateful thanks to Linda Blakemore, Susan Goodm
Elisabeth Ingham, Esther Jagger, Alison Leach,
Caroline Liddell, Stuart Morris, Rosemary Oates,
Gwyneth Phillips, Peter Riding and Jenny Rogers
for their help in the preparation of this book

The BBC would like to thank the following London shops
and stores for the loan of equipment and accessories
for the photographs: Debenhams Limited, Oxford Street;
Divertimenti, Marylebone Lane; Selectasine, Bulstrode
Street; Selfridges Limited, Oxford Street

Printed and bound in Great Britain by Mackays of Chatham

Contents

Conversion tables	6
Introduction	7
Equipment	11
Eggs	21
Bread and yeast cookery	41
Pâtés and starters	71
Stocks and soups	89
Fish	113
Meat: roasting and pot-roasting	156
Meat: casseroles and braised dishes	179
Poultry	205
Offal	233
Vegetables	253
Rice and other grains	296
Vegetarian cooking	321
Pulses	339
Pasta and pancakes	357
Herbs	379
Spices and flavourings	403
Sauces	429
Cheese	455
Salads and dressings	479
Barbecues and picnics	499
Cream, ice cream and yoghurt	517
Pastry	539
Cakes	585
Scones and biscuits	616
Fruits and puddings	631
Preserving	664
Left-overs	689
Recommended books	699
Index	701

6

Conversion tables

All these are *approximate* conversions, which have either been
rounded up or down. In a few recipes it has been necessary to
modify them very slightly. Never mix metric and imperial measures
in one recipe, stick to one system or the other. All spoon
measurements used throughout this book are level unless specified
otherwise.

Oven temperatures		
Mark 1	275°F	140°C
2	300	150
3	325	170
4	350	180
5	375	190
6	400	200
7	425	220
8	450	230
9	475	240

Volume	
2 fl oz	55 ml
3	75
5 (¼ pt)	150
½ pt	275
¾	425
1	570
1¾	1 litre

Measurements	
⅛ inch	3 mm
¼	5 mm
½	1 cm
¾	2
1	2·5
1¼	3
1½	4
1¾	4·5
2	5
3	7·5
4	10
5	13
6	15
7	18
8	20
9	23
10	25·5
11	28
12	30

Weights	
½ oz	10 g
1	25
1½	40
2	50
2½	60
3	75
4	110
4½	125
5	150
6	175
7	200
8	225
9	250
10	275
12	350
1 lb	450
1½	700
2	900
3	1 kg 350 g

Introduction

My aim, when I first embarked on the television Cookery Course, was to explain and demonstrate the basic skills and techniques of cooking—not to professional cooks or aspiring *cordon bleu* students, but to men and women who wanted to acquire a sound general knowledge of cooking that would stand them in good stead for a lifetime of family meals, entertaining and personal pleasure. The whole idea is that an absolute beginner to cooking can start here; at the same time I hope that the more experienced cook, too, will find new ideas, even inspiration. Your letters and reactions to the Course—which have been of enormous help to me throughout—suggest that the books and programmes have been of practical value.

That is not to say there isn't plenty left to say on the subject of cooking, of course. It is an endless process: the more one cooks, the more one learns. Personally I have learned a tremendous amount, researching for and writing this book—and one of the most important discoveries, perhaps, is that there is no definitive method of cooking. The Cookery Course, really, is a set of guidelines which I have found work best for me (and I sincerely hope for you too). You'll always find people who say something *must* be done in such-and-such a way and no other; and commercial concerns who say that they make and market the products we want are actually trying to persuade us to want the products they offer. The fact is, there is no scientific substitute for the *experience* of cooking and eating; it may be a hackneyed saying, but the proof of the pudding, or the cake or casserole, really *is* in the eating.

Another conclusion I have drawn from fifteen years of cooking and writing about food is that people are more important than food. It is all very well for chefs in grand kitchens to dedicate themselves to *haute cuisine* and all its complications, because they don't have to serve and eat it later and mingle with the guests. You and I, when we entertain, have to play the dual role of cook and host, and nothing can turn a meal (however good it is) to ashes faster than a flustered cook who transmits his or her panic to the guests. I like to concentrate, therefore, on flavour rather than effect, to serve meals that need as little last-minute attention as possible, and to try to please people rather than to dazzle them.

To that extent the Cookery Course reflects my personal approach to food. I also hope it reflects the changing background to cooking today—our dwindling resources and world shortages which have in turn sent prices on a dizzying climb. The really affluent era of food is passing, and it is an accepted fact that the effects of affluence in the western world are as much to blame for the spread of heart disease as anything, and that our kind of diet is a major factor in this. In view of all this it seems to me to make sense to go back to cooking the basic dishes *well*, and to attempt to set a pattern of more moderate eating overall (rather than to make drastic overnight changes in your diet simply because of the latest theory). We all eat far more than we need to, and this is the root cause. I have sometimes been accused of using too much cream, butter or olive oil in my recipes, but the whole point of cooking recipes is that there are very few of us who actually use a 'recipe' every day. We eat grills, omelettes, salads and other plain foods most of the time: on those occasions when we are going to bother actually to cook a recipe it is worthwhile making the end result as delicious as possible. In short, I don't advocate cream, wine or butter in cooking every day, but rather for special occasions.

Inevitably, I suppose, there will be omissions of some kind in the Cookery Course. Why nothing on freezing, I have been asked. But freezing is not cooking; in fact it is a large and complicated subject on its own—and this book is big enough as it is! Anyway, for the omissions I apologise in advance. But so long as the Cookery Course has proved to anyone that cooking need not be difficult, and that in fact it can be a lot of fun, and if it can help to remove some of the apprehensions from people's minds, then I am happy.

This is the collected edition of the Cookery Course, which was originally published in three separate parts between 1978 and 1981. It contains all the information given in the previous books (plus a bit extra!) and all the recipes; only the format has been altered slightly—inevitably, because the individual books were published to relate closely to the television programmes. I hope that this new layout will make it easier for you to find your way round particular subjects and, through the cross-references, to find specific recipes.

Delia Smith

Equipment

It would be quite unthinkable for a carpenter or a dressmaker or even an amateur gardener to attempt to create anything worth while without the right tools for the job. Yet many people try to cook with second-rate, dilapidated, or sometimes with hardly any equipment at all. Whether you have to cook for a family every day or simply want to cook for pleasure, one thing is certain: good results will be achieved far, far more easily with the right kind of basic equipment.

Good kitchen equipment *is* expensive, but most items last a lifetime and will pay for themselves over and over again. I see so many people attempting to cook with battered saucepans with ill-fitting lids, with blunt knives and makeshift scales—often in the homes of those who have spent a small fortune on the kitchen fixtures. But all the matching units in the world can't compensate for having to peel brussels sprouts with a table knife.

I don't suggest you can go out and equip yourself with all the essentials in one go. But they should be your priorities as and when you are able to add to your stock, and they should be distinguished from the mountain of gadgetry which clutters up the shops in the name of labour-saving: a great many of these supposedly convenient gadgets are often more expensive than the basic tool and a lot less efficient (even when they are not going wrong).

General Cooking

Saucepans Now there's a subject for a start. The market is inundated with them, all shapes, sizes and colours of the rainbow. But they represent a big investment, so how does a beginner know what to choose? I do think some personal preference comes into this, and often what a person is used to is what he or she likes best. It's probably fair to say that no one particular type of saucepan can answer every type of need. I have several different sorts myself, and below are my opinions on them. But first, one important point, how do you prevent cookware sticking? Always follow the manufacturer's instructions on how to season new saucepans, frying-pans and casseroles—this will vary depending on the make, but it makes a world of difference.

Heavy-gauge aluminium These are my personal choice. Not quite so glamorous as the others to look at, they offer all-round reliability and a good, even conducting of heat. They are easy to keep clean— sometimes the aluminium inside them blemishes, but this is easily remedied by boiling up water in them, to which a little lemon juice or vinegar has been added. Very hard-wearing and should last a lifetime. A warning about these saucepans: food should not be allowed to stand too long in them as the metal can react unfavourably on the food.

Enamelled cast ironware These are very heavy and for this reason they hold the heat extremely well—so a much lower heat is needed to keep up a gentle simmer. They come in bright jewel colours and look very attractive. But their heaviness can be a disadvantage: very often two hands are needed to lift a large saucepan full of something. If they are dropped on a hard surface they can chip or even break. I have found that sauces tend to stick and catch if I'm in a hurry and haven't kept the heat as low as it should be. Finally, the inside enamelled surface can become badly stained (though an overnight soak in a biological washing-powder solution does help).

Stainless steel I know one or two professional cooks who prefer these to anything else. I have found, though, that the contents of the pan nearest the edges (say while boiling milk or making a sauce) get hot quicker than the centre, which means that cooks in a hurry will regularly find the edges of the pan are scorched. The advantages, however, are that they are easy to keep clean, look attractive, and are light to handle.

Copper saucepans I have a set of heavy, handsome copper saucepans hanging up on the wall of my kitchen—and that's where they're staying. I know that the great French chefs swear by them, but I couldn't manage them at all. The brass handles become very hot, and it is easy to forget to use a cloth. Also I found the tinned lining wore down quickly, exposing the copper beneath whose qualities make some foods become rancid more quickly.

Non-stick saucepans For my own cooking I find it essential to use metal implements, and for that reason alone I can never recommend non-stick pans—all the ones I have ever used very soon abandoned their non-stick surface.

Frying-pans My choice here is definitely for a heavy, cast-iron pan—there is a particularly good French, imported one which has a matt-black inside coating which remains unharmed by metal utensils. Every cook should have two frying-pans, one with an 8 inch (20 cm) base diameter and another a 10 inch (25·5 cm).

Meat roasting tins Solidity is the important thing here—the cheap thin-gauge metal ones, when exposed to very high temperatures, simply buckle. And once the base of the tin has become uneven you might as well throw it away. Also in this category, it is worth mentioning that the oval cast-iron (shallow) gratin dishes are useful.

Casseroles I would definitely recommend cast-iron enamelled ware. One good 4½–5 pint (2·5–3·1) casserole would be about right for a family of four. The advantage of this kind of casserole is that you can use it on top of the stove as well as inside—and it is attractive enough to be taken straight to the table. The less expensive earthenware casseroles are useful for certain recipes, but these are only suitable for oven cookery.

Baking
For baking you need: a long straight *rolling-pin* (see Pastry section), a *flour dredger* which sprinkles a dusting of flour over a flat surface very evenly, a *pastry brush* (the flat one rather than the round type), and a set of *pastry cutters*. I always use fluted cutters, but plain ones are available, and they come in sets of seven ranging from 1 inch (2·5 cm) to 3½ inch (9 cm) in diameter.

Baking sheets Good, solid and flat, these are a very necessary item as they conduct heat from underneath, so helping to cook the underside of a quiche or tart. Biscuits and scones are also cooked this way.

Patty tins If you are buying these for the first time, make sure you buy tins with a dozen sections and not just nine. If you are slogging through a batch of mince pies you save a lot of time cooking twelve in one go.

Quiche tins Should be as solid as possible, with a loose base. The most useful sizes are 8 inch (20 cm) and 10 inch (25·5 cm).

Pies and tarts For these the old-fashioned enamelled pie-plates are best, because being metal they conduct the heat, and cook the pastry, more evenly. One 8 inch (20 cm) and one 9½ inch (24 cm) plate should cover most needs. A deep-rimmed pie-plate with sloping sides, however, is useful for a recipe that calls for depth (like a lemon meringue pie). Here 8 inch (21 cm) diameter is ideal.

Bread tins come in a bewildering variety of sizes, but except for the most ambitious the old-fashioned bread tins (with pleated corners, rims and double bases) which come in 1 lb (450 g) and 2 lb (900 g) sizes seem to be the most popular. I *do* think a non-stick tin is useful in bread-making. Although it still must be greased, it is much easier to turn the bread out. For a loaf made from 1 lb (450 g) of flour, the base of the tin should be 7½ inches × 3½ inches (19 cm × 8·5 cm).

Whisking and mixing

Whisks One of the prime functions of a whisk is to get air into something, and a balloon whisk (especially with egg whites) will obtain the largest volume of all: it whisks very evenly and can disperse lumps in a sauce in seconds.

Electric hand whisk I have never felt the need to own a free-standing mixer—partly, I think, because I like to get the feel of the ingredients I am mixing. An electric hand whisk allows me to do this, and its other advantage is that it can be used anywhere in the kitchen—in a saucepan or bowl over heat, for instance. A hand rotary whisk is, of course, cheaper, but a lot more hard work.

Kitchen fork I use a wooden kitchen fork for fluffing and separating rice. It is gentler than a metal one, and is also useful for starting off the mixing of bread dough.

Kitchen spoons Apart from the metal teaspoons, dessertspoons and tablespoons which are essential, a cook also needs a variety of wooden spoons, including a very useful one with a pointed edge that can delve into the corners and crannies of a saucepan quickly (e.g. for scrambled eggs). Other handy spoons are: a long-handled draining spoon with perforations in it to separate something solid from its liquid; an unperforated, long-handled spoon which will save you burning your arms when you want to baste something in a hot oven; and a ladle.

Slices and spatulas

Fish slice Something of a misnomer, because this will come in useful when frying all kinds of things. Its flat blade should have plenty of flexibility in it—the rigid ones simply can't slide under such delicate things as fried eggs without damaging them.

Kitchen tongs These will permit you to turn steaks, chops or sausages without piercing them and losing their juices. My husband insists on a pair for his barbecue.

Spatula A flat-edged piece of hard rubber with a wooden handle: it clears a bowl of dough or other mixture in seconds and much more effectively than scraping with a spoon.

Cutting, chopping and grating

Knives A set of good-quality kitchen knives can transform your culinary life overnight—and by this I mean the stainless steel ones with riveted wooden handles (the Swiss make excellent ones). Carbon steel knives are often recommended but are the devil to stop discolouring. There are endless shapes and lengths of knives available, but you can build up your collection gradually with care. My priorities would be a couple of varying cook's knives (see illustration), a small kitchen knife, a small curved paring knife, a potato peeler, a good carving knife with either a serrated or straight edge (and a carving fork), a palette knife for smoothing icing or cream and lifting biscuits from a baking sheet, and a bread knife (though in fact my palette knife has a serrated edge and cuts bread beautifully).

Keeping knives sharp This is vital. They ought to be sharpened regularly: a sharpening steel is best for this, although it requires a little practice. I was hopeless at first. The butcher's tip to sharpen little and often is a good one, and remember always to sharpen the whole length of the blade, not just one section. (If you really can't manage a steel, there are knife-sharpening gadgets available: they just tend to wear out knives rather more quickly, that's all). It also helps to keep knives sharp (and is a lot kinder on the fingers) if you store them on magnetic racks, which can be attached to the wall, rather than in drawers where they can come into contact with other implements. Perhaps even more important, never use your knives on a plastic or laminated surface—both the surface and the knives will be ruined in no time. Good knives need a *wooden chopping board* with a bit of give in it.

Kitchen scissors A good tightly-riveted pair, kept strictly for kitchen use, will come in handy more often than you might imagine. They are so useful for snipping herbs, cutting string on puddings or scaling fish. My pair, made in Finland, are the best I have come across and (rather enterprisingly) they are manufactured for left-handed people as well.

Graters Quite honestly nothing grates as well or as easily as the versatile, four-sided grater with each of its sides offering a different variety of grate. And one of its endearing qualities is that it is so easy to clean. The only other grater I use is a small nutmeg grater, which has a built-in compartment for holding a few whole nutmegs. It hangs on a hook within arm's reach, ready for instant use.

Lemon zester This is a useful, and inexpensive, item which nothing can really replace. It extracts the outer 'zest' from a lemon, leaving the unwanted pith behind, and is so constructed it can get round the awkward curves of a lemon without difficulty.

Grinding and mincing

Mincer The cast-iron kind, with a clamp base, is not really an expensive piece of equipment and is virtually indestructible. These come with three different blades for different coarseness of mince and—as we shall see later—are invaluable for dealing with leftover meat, making hamburgers and a dozen other recipes, including chutneys. I emphasise the clamp-base because suction bases never seem strong enough—but make sure you have a suitable table edge to clamp it to.

Pestle and mortar A mortar is a heavy porcelain bowl and a pestle a rounded porcelain tool that crushes or pounds the substances in the bowl—use it for crushing whole spices or pounding garlic and salt together to a cream. I would not be without mine, and suggest the larger and sturdier kind you can buy the better.

Pepper mill There are plenty of pepper mills around that don't work too well, so it is worth investing in a good, wooden one. The taller it is, the less often you will have to refill it with peppercorns. Elsewhere in the book I have enlarged on the virtues of freshly-ground pepper, so let me only say here that it has a hundred per cent more fragrance and flavour than the ready-ground stuff.

Lemon squeezer In this case, the simpler the better. A strong plastic or a tough glass squeezer will do well: some of the plastic ones have a screw-on cup underneath to catch the juice and separate off the pips—so that they are easier to pour.

Sieving, sifting, straining

Sieves I have three sieves at home. Two of them, in different sizes, are metal ones because I have had to discard so many melted and disfigured plastic ones in the past. The one plastic one I still possess, with its fine mesh, is used almost exclusively for sifting flour.

Colander The same goes for colanders: never get a plastic colander—you are guaranteed a disaster sooner or later when it has been left too near the heat. The small aluminium or enamel ones will be sturdier and safer.

Salad basket Although practically redundant in the winter, my wire salad basket comes into its own in the summer. When salad leaves require washing, you can put them wet inside one of these enclosed baskets then (outdoors) swing the whole thing, using circular movements, and shake off most of the excess water. Then just leave it somewhere to finish drying.

Measuring

Scales If you have cooked for a lifetime with maybe a fairly modest repertoire, then perhaps you don't have to weigh anything—your 'instincts' are well developed. Lucky you. If you're a beginner or, like me, have upwards of 1500 recipes on file and cannot commit even one of them to memory, then you simply *must* weigh everything to be sure of success. My advice is to opt for a proper pair of balance scales (where the weights go on one side, the ingreients on the other): these are far more accurate than the needle-and-spring kind and sturdy enough to outlast you. Look for the largest pair possible. I have some antique balance scales like this that still register perfect balance. You can now buy a set of metric weights, as well as imperial—so the same scales can cope with either.

Measuring jugs A glass measuring jug, with imperial and metric volumes marked on the side, will tell you in seconds what 3 fl. oz is (otherwise it is impossible to know: milk bottles are not advised).

Timing, testing and temperature

Skewers Unassuming little pieces of equipment, but *vital*. Without one I just don't know how to tell if potatoes or vegetables are cooked, but the 'feel' or give of a skewer as it is inserted into the centre is a sure guide. Flat skewers are essential for kebab cookery.

Kitchen timer Very often these are incorporated into modern ovens. But if yours does not have one built in, they can be bought separately. Memories are fallible, and a timer can save a lot of hard work from going out of the window.

Cooking thermometer Sometimes described as a 'sugar thermometer'. Will save a great deal of agonising as to whether the fat is hot enough to put in the chips, or the jam has reached a set. Such information is printed alongside the appropriate temperature on good kitchen thermometers. A *meat thermometer* is a gadget inserted in a joint of meat to help you determine when the joint is ready. However, they can be fallible if they happen to touch and rest against a bone.

There is only one other item I would include in this list. I find my *food processor* does all the work of a mincer and a liquidiser—and more, as it's excellent for shredding, slicing and grating in large quantities. For chopping things evenly, though, I still prefer a wooden board and a sharp knife. I also feel that pastry and cake mixes made in a processor don't incorporate enough air. Otherwise it's very useful. Alternatively a solid 2 pint (1 litre) capacity *liquidiser* will take care of the puréeing part.

Eggs

Including recipes for:
Eggs en cocotte
Omelette savoyard
Egg and lentil curry
Poached eggs with cream and watercress
Eggs and leeks au gratin
Cheese soufflé
Piperade
Chilli eggs
Zabaglione
Lemon soufflé omelette
John Tovey's quick hollandaise sauce

In this book it's the egg—and not the chicken—that comes first. There are good reasons for starting with eggs, not least because they are such a basic ingredient in our cookery and a real understanding of what they are and what they can do is essential before we progress to, say, pastry later.

But there's another reason. Someone who 'can't even cook an egg' is—to the rest of the world—someone who has either despaired of or totally neglected the art of cooking. Yet there is an assumption here that egg cookery is so basic it needs no practice or experience— it's intuitive. I don't believe that. Cooking *can* be easy, but only when you know the proper way to do it. And that's something I hope to demonstrate by starting with eggs. And anyway imagine— if everyone from the age of nine to ninety could make an omelette correctly, they'd never lack for one delicious, interesting and nutritious meal at their fingertips!

What's in an egg?

Eggs are full of life: they provide nutrients, proteins, fats, vitamins and minerals, nearly everything needed for life. One ingredient that may seem less essential, but as we shall see figures pretty largely in the cooking of an egg, is air. It's that tiny pocket of air (see illustration) that is directly related to the age and quality of an egg.

Nature included this air pocket so that the tiny, developing chicks could breathe. However, when eggs are for consumption rather than hatching, they are cooled and stored, and their water content starts to evaporate—and the air pocket gets bigger. It follows therefore that, generally speaking, the larger the air pocket the staler the egg. (I say generally because sometimes a hairline crack, invisible to the human eye, can let air into a very fresh egg: but this is distinctly rare.)

The freshness of an egg is very important in cooking. Stale eggs, with their flat yolks and watery whites, spread themselves miserably to all corners of the frying-pan. Not to mention the ones whose yolks in poaching water completely part company with their whites—while the whites in turn are reducing the water to a mass of foaming bubbles!

Cholesterol

Cholesterol, a by-product of animal fats and dairy foods which has a tendency to build up in our systems, is often cited as a contributory factor in heart disease. Quite apart from the total diversity of opinion among nutrition experts all over the world on the subject, I am certainly not in a position to expound on medical problems. What I can say is that if we only eat what we actually *need* to eat and in a balanced pattern, all the risks of our modern diet are minimised. The root of the problem is that as a (comparatively) affluent nation we have acquired the habit of over-eating and under-exercising. Perhaps the worry ought to be, not am I eating too many eggs or too much butter, but am I eating too much overall? In the end it may be the old answer about moderation being the cure for most ills.

	Size 1 70g or over
Large	Size 2 65-70g
	Size 3 60-65g
Standard	Size 4 55-60g
	Size 5 50-55g
Medium	Size 6 45-50g
Small	Size 7 under 45g

Buying eggs

If there's one thing we can thank our membership of the EEC for, it's the compulsory date-stamp on egg-boxes. Undoubtedly it has meant that fresher eggs are now more widely available, and if the packing-date on the box does happen to say Week 1 and it's already Week 4, you can tell those eggs have been hanging around the supermarket a bit too long. It is not always easy to work out which Week 33 is, in the middle of a crowded supermarket, but if you buy eggs regularly you should be able to check week by week; or you can get little charts from the British Egg Information Service, 37 Panton St., London SW1.

All eggs are classified for quality (A,B or C) at the packing station, by the process called 'candling'—originally quite literally by shining a candle behind the egg to detect defects such as blood spots, cracks and blemishes. Class A and B eggs can be sold in shops. Class A have excellent internal quality; Class B have fair internal quality. Boxes containing Class A eggs could have a red band round bearing the word 'Extra'. This means that the eggs have been packed for less than 7 days (the date of packing must be on the box). Class C eggs are used only for manufacturing.

Then what about all those slightly mysterious numbered codes on the boxes? These designate first the country of origin (the UK is 9), then the region and then the licence number of the packing-station. All this fascinating information would only concern us if we had a complaint to make. More to the point is the continental grading system (size 1–7) which came into force in 1978.

This replaced the original four categories: large, standard, medium and small. Size 1, the largest of them all, doesn't fit into the egg-boxes—and I've got a sneaking feeling there aren't many size 1 hens laying them anyway—so I think that as far as consumers are concerned we can discount that particular size. Sizes 6 and 7 aren't normally available to the public either, because they're far too small (45–50 g or under 45 g respectively). That really leaves us with only four sizes, which is in fact what we had before. I would recommend if you want 'large' eggs you buy size 2, and if you want 'standard' eggs you buy size 3 or 4.

Free-range eggs
Ninety per cent of the eggs sold in Britain are battery-produced. However, if you're lucky enough to live near an old-fashioned farm where the hens scratch about and run free, you probably can get well-flavoured eggs with rich-coloured yolks. A warning though: many farm gates with their Free Range notices are not to be trusted. Many have their own deep-litter units where hens by no means run free. Also the eggs bought there will be ungraded, often with startling degrees of size difference, and blood spots or hairline cracks are all part of the bargain.

Brown or white?
The only difference between brown and white eggs is the colour of the shell. The contents are identical. In this country we tend to find brown eggs aesthetically pleasing and happily pay extra for them. And I admit, if I had a pretty breakfast tray all set with a fine china egg-cup, I would personally choose a brown egg (preferably with speckles) and of course brown bread to match.

How fresh are they?
The best place to buy eggs, at least in a town, is from a supermarket with a quick turnover. But once you've bought your eggs, how do you know if they're fresh or not? One reliable way of telling is to place

one in a bowl of cold water: if it sits on the bottom in a horizontal position as in the illustration, the egg is very fresh. On the other hand, if it tilts to a semi-vertical position, it is less fresh; and stale if it pops up into a completely vertical position.

By breaking one out into a saucer you can tell at a glance. A fresh egg will have a rounded, plump yolk that sits up proudly: the white will consist of an inner gelatinous circle clinging all round the yolk, with a second outer circle of flatter, more liquid white. When an egg is stale the yolk turns flabby and the white loses its gelatinous inner circle—it looks frankly weak and watery. This is what makes eggs more difficult to separate, among other things.

Storing eggs

It's my opinion that eggs stored in a cool place will remain in good shape for two weeks. During the third week of storage I tend to use them only for cakes or sauces. Eggs in any event don't like extremes of temperature: I prefer not to keep mine in the fridge, if only because most recipes call for eggs at room temperature. This helps to avoid curdling in cake recipes and they are less likely to break if you're boiling them. If you have no practical alternative, then keep your eggs in the lowest part of the refrigerator: near the freezing compartment is usually too cold a position (which is unhappily where most manufacturers of fridges tend to put their egg racks). And remember to remove them several hours in advance to allow them to come to room temperature—for breakfast take them out the night before. The general guidelines then are (i) store them in a spot neither too warm nor too cold, (ii) store them thin end down, and (iii) store them away from strong smells, because the shells are porous and can absorb pungent flavours.

Separated yolks and whites can be kept for a day or two. The yolks, if they're unbroken, can be kept in water: if broken, sprinkle some water on top to prevent a skin forming. The container should be covered closely with foil or cling-film and kept in the fridge. It's interesting to note that chilled egg whites when whisked produce a slightly larger volume (though it's up to you to decide if this is any incentive to go to the trouble of separating and chilling the whites first—I know my life is too busy for such refinements!).

Beating egg whites

The secret of beating egg whites is knowing when to stop, because once they're over-beaten they start to collapse. What happens is this: whisking incorporates air into the whites, making them expand

and grow in volume. As you whisk, tiny air bubbles are formed, but like all bubbles (or balloons even) too much air causes them to burst—and naturally with over-beaten egg whites the loss of air will cause a loss of volume.

I find that when you lift the whisk up and the egg stands up in soft peaks, it is time to stop. If you are folding egg whites into another mixture (i.e. for a soufflé or mousse) use just one metal tablespoonful and fold that in first. This slackens the mixture, making it much easier to fold the rest in. For notes on various types of whisk see pages 14 and 15.

Boiled eggs

There seem to be almost as many methods of boiling an egg as there are cooks. The aunt of a friend of mine insists that three verses of 'Onward Christian Soldiers' is the correct timing for a perfect egg (but she takes it a trifle *maestoso*, I think). My recommendations would be rather more precise.

To get the best results the egg should be at room temperature, otherwise the change in pressure within causes them to crack on contact with the heat. (If you find your boiled eggs constantly cracking, try piercing the rounded end first with a needle to release the pressure—it's very easy.) The water for boiling should not be bubbling too fast, just barely simmering. The saucepan should be small enough to prevent the eggs dancing around while cooking. Both these are factors which can also cause cracking.

I have found the most trouble-free method is to carefully lower the eggs (using a tablespoon) into gently simmering water. Simmer for exactly 1 minute, then remove the saucepan from the heat, put a lid on and leave the eggs for a further five minutes for size 4, or six minutes for size 2. This will produce a white that is just set and a soft creamy yolk. If you like them done more or less than this, add or subtract ½ minute from the five or six minutes. This way there's less chance of them cracking by careering about in the bubbling water and less likelihood of overcooking by boiling too fiercely. *Note:* for *really* fresh eggs, that is less than four days old, allow extra cooking time.

Hard-boiled eggs

·Place the eggs in a saucepan of cold water, bring them up to a gentle simmer, and simmer for exactly 7 minutes for size 4 eggs or 9 minutes for size 2 eggs. *Always* cool them under cold running water to prevent them cooking further or developing a dark ring between the yolk and the white. If, for a particular recipe, you need to peel the eggs while they're still warm—tap gently to crack the eggs all over, peel the shells, and rinse off any reluctant pieces of shell under a warm running tap.

Poaching eggs

You could assemble a whole catalogue of 'dos and don'ts' on the subject of poaching if you wanted to. French chefs whisk the water to form a sort of whirlpool before dropping the egg in, which is said to help it keep a good shape. Some say add a little salt to the water: others say never, never add salt. Some add a few drops of vinegar, others pour in as much as 3 tablespoons. Salt and vinegar *do* help the white to coagulate, but the method below has proved 100 per cent satisfactory in my experience.

The most important ingredient is really fresh eggs. Start with a small frying-pan, filled to a depth of approximately 1½ inches (4 cm) barely simmering water. No salt, no vinegar. Keep the heat low enough for there to be just the merest trace of tiny simmering bubbles on the base of the pan, and no more.

Break each egg gently into the water (breaking the eggs into a cup first is all right but unnecessary, I think), and don't attempt to poach more than two at a time unless you're a really experienced hand. Three minutes is just right for size 2 eggs, but you can vary this fractionally according to taste. While they are cooking you can help the tops to cook by basting with the water. To remove, use a slotted spoon and have ready a wad of kitchen paper on which to rest the spoon and egg for a few seconds, to absorb any excess water. Remember to remove the first egg that went in, before the other.

Scrambling eggs

On this I'm a disciple of Escoffier. And what he did was to melt a walnut of butter in a small solid saucepan over a gentle heat, then swirl it around to coat the pan thoroughly. Have ready two large eggs beaten and seasoned, and put them into the foaming butter. (Whatever you do, don't let it brown.) Now with a wooden spoon— preferably one with a point—stir like mad, getting the point right into the corner of the pan to prevent the egg sticking.

Take the pan off the heat while there's still some liquid egg left, then add another knob of butter which will melt into it as it finishes cooking in the heat of the pan. For a touch of luxury you could stir in a teaspoonful of thick cream along with the second lot of butter!

Frying eggs

A very personal thing, how you like your egg fried—but for absolute beginners here is my method, which might prove helpful. For me frying requires a bit more heat than other methods, because I like a faint touch of crispness around the edge of the egg: so—a medium heat, a fresh egg and some hot but not smoking bacon fat or pure lard (butter goes too brown for frying, I think). Let the egg settle in the pan and start to set; then, using a tablespoon, tip the pan and baste the top of the egg with the fat until it's done to your liking. Lift it out carefully with a fish slice.

Baked eggs (eggs en cocotte)

These are deliciously special, and can be cooked with a variety of other ingredients (such as cheese, cream, lightly-cooked chopped vegetables) in the base of the dishes. The most important items are the special dishes in which the eggs are cooked, called ramekins and looking like small ridged soufflé dishes.

The basic method is as follows. Butter the dishes fairly generously and break an egg into each one. Season them with salt and pepper, then put a large knob of butter on top of each yolk. Now stand the dishes in a meat-roasting tin, pour in enough hot water to come halfway up the sides of the dishes, then bake on a high shelf in a pre-heated oven (gas mark 5, 375°F, 190°C) for 15–20 minutes. Then serve straightaway.

Omelettes

Let me say first that the *size* of your frying-pan is as vital for good omelettes as for many other things. Ideally every cook should possess two or three pans of varying size—a two-egg omelette, for instance, needs a 6 inch (15·5 cm) pan, while a four- or five-egg omelette calls for a 10 inch (25·5 cm) pan. Too few eggs in a large pan make a thin, dry (and probably tough) omelette. Too many eggs in a small pan make a thick and uncomfortably spongy one. An omelette pan should be rounded at the sides and, best of all, made in enamelled cast iron or heavy aluminium.

If your omelette is for one person, break two eggs into a basin and on no account over-beat them. This is where so many people go wrong. You don't need an electric whisk or even a hand-whisk— just a large fork or, as I observed a Breton lady demonstrating an omelette French-style once, a knife. She simply stirred the yolks into the whites with the blade of the knife. So—no vigorous beating or whisking.

Next add a seasoning of salt and freshly-milled black pepper.
Now put your omelette pan on a medium heat to warm through,
without anything in it (if you're using butter, this pre-heating the
dry pan prevents the butter being over the heat too long and
therefore browning). When the pan is hot, throw in a good knob of
butter, say ³/₄oz (15g), then turn the heat up to its highest and
swirl the butter round and round so that it coats the base and sides
of the pan completely.

When the butter starts to froth, pour in the eggs and shake the
pan to spread them out evenly, then take a fork or a spoon and
draw the edges of the omelette towards the centre, allowing the
pools of liquid egg on the surface to run into the channels you have
made.

Carry on like this until the omelette is almost set but the surface
still soft and a little liquid (or as the French say, *baveuse*). When it's
ready, take the pan handle in one hand, tilt the pan onto the edge of
a warm plate, then with a fork or spoon in your other hand flip the
edge of the omelette over to the centre. Then let it fold over again as
you turn it out of the pan.

One tip, if you're using butter, is to add a little of the melted
butter to the eggs just before you pour them in. This seems to give
the omelette an extra-buttery flavour. The nicest omelettes of all,
I believe, are the simplest, and if you're adding a filling, use very
little—remembering that the eggs are the most important part.
One favourite variation of mine is an omelette made with a few
fresh herbs (*omelette fines herbes*): use a level tablespoon of very
finely-chopped parsley and a level tablespoon of very finely-
chopped leek, or spring onion or chives. Add the herbs to the two
stirred eggs 30 minutes before you make the omelette, then proceed
as above.

Note: olive oil or a flavoured groundnut oil can be used instead
of butter.

Open-faced omelettes
This is a quite different sort of omelette—it's never folded but
served cut into wedges. In Spain they refer to this as *tortilla* and
in Italy *frittata*. Fillings can be varied: a typical tortilla would
contain potatoes, peppers, onions and slices of spiced chorizo
sausage. In Italy I've eaten it cooked with cubes of cheese and raw
chopped spinach leaves. On the next page is a French version,
sometimes known as *Omelette savoyard*.

Omelette savoyard

(serves 2 people)

4 eggs
1 large onion, chopped
3 rashers of bacon, chopped
2 medium-sized potatoes, peeled and cut into small cubes
2 oz Gruyère cheese (50 g), cut into thin slivers
1 dessertspoon butter
1 dessertspoon olive oil
Salt and freshly-milled black pepper

You'll need a medium-sized frying-pan.

Melt the butter and oil together in the frying-pan. Dry the cubes of raw potato thoroughly in a tea towel, then fry them over a medium heat, tossing them around quite often until they're beginning to turn golden and are almost cooked through (about 10 minutes). Then add the bacon and onion to the pan and continue to cook these for a further 10 minutes or so or until the onion is soft.

Meanwhile pre-heat the grill to its highest setting. Arrange the slivers of cheese over the other ingredients in the pan, then beat the eggs with a fork (gently and not too much); season them with pepper but only a pinch of salt.

Turn the heat right up under the frying-pan and pour in the eggs. Now, using a palette knife, draw the outside of the omelette inward, allowing the liquid egg to escape round the edges. Then place the pan under the grill for a few moments to set the top. Serve cut in wedges with a crisp green salad as an accompaniment.

Note: In the summer this tastes just as good served cold.

Eggs and lentil curry

(serves 3 people)

If I'm in the mood for a curry but a bit short of time, an egg curry always seems to fit the bill.

6 eggs
1 medium onion, roughly chopped
1 large carrot, thinly sliced
2 sticks celery, chopped
1 clove garlic, crushed

1 small green pepper, chopped
3 oz whole lentils (75 g)
2 tablespoons groundnut oil
1 rounded tablespoon flour
1 rounded teaspoon Madras curry powder
½ teaspoon ground ginger
1 level teaspoon ground turmeric
1 pint boiling water (570 ml)
2 tablespoons natural yoghurt
Salt

To garnish:
Chopped parsley and slices of raw onion

First heat the oil in a thick-based saucepan and fry the onion, browning it a little, then add the celery, carrot and pepper, and continue to fry till these have browned a little too (about 5 minutes). Then stir in the lentils and crushed garlic, and after that sprinkle in the flour and spices. Stir to soak up the juices, and keep stirring whilst you gradually add 1 pint (570 ml) of boiling water. Add some salt, then put a lid on and simmer gently for about 35 minutes or until the lentils are soft.

While the sauce is cooking place the eggs in cold water, bring them up to simmering point and then simmer for 7 minutes exactly. Now run some cold water over them until they're cool enough to handle, then peel and slice them in half.

A minute or two before serving, add salt to taste, stir the yoghurt into the sauce and add the halved eggs. Then serve the curry with boiled rice sprinkled with chopped parsley and raw onion slices and have some mango chutney to go with it.

Poached eggs with cream and watercress

(serves 2 people)

The sauce for this recipe is a very attractive speckled pale green colour— and the whole thing goes very well with some plain buttered noodles.

4 fresh eggs
2 bunches watercress, trimmed and chopped
1 oz butter (25 g)

¾ oz plain flour (20 g)
½ pint milk (275 ml)
1 oz mild cheese (25 g), grated
1 level tablespoon Parmesan cheese, grated
2 tablespoons double cream
Lemon juice
½ oz extra butter (10 g)
Salt and freshly-milled black pepper

Make the sauce first by gently melting the 1 oz (25 g) of butter in a
saucepan, stirring in the flour and adding the milk by degrees until
you have a smooth white sauce. Then season, turn the heat to its
very lowest and allow the sauce to cook for about 7 minutes. While
that's happening, trim and discard the watercress stalks and chop
the leaves roughly. Then melt the extra ½ oz (10 g) of butter in a
saucepan, add the watercress and, again with the heat as low as
possible and a lid on, allow the watercress to collapse down into the
butter—this should take roughly 5 minutes.

Now add the watercress and all its buttery juices to the sauce,
adding the grated cheeses. Stir to melt the cheese, then pour the
sauce into a liquidiser and blend it at high speed until you have a
green speckled sauce. Next return the sauce to the saucepan, adding
the cream and a squeeze (½ teaspoonful) of lemon juice and a
seasoning of salt and pepper. Keep the sauce warm whilst you now,
quickly, poach 4 eggs by breaking them into a frying-pan of barely
simmering water and giving them approximately 3 minutes. Lift
them out with a draining-spoon, resting each one on a wad of
kitchen paper to drain. Serve them on a bed of rice or noodles with
the sauce poured over and sprinkled with more grated Parmesan.

Eggs and leeks au gratin

(serves 4 people)

Eggs, leeks and cheese are a really
delicious trio and all this needs to go with
it is crusty wholewheat bread.

8 eggs
4 medium leeks, cleaned and chopped
3 oz strong Cheddar cheese (75 g), grated
1 tablespoon Parmesan cheese, grated
3 oz butter (75 g)
1½ oz plain flour (40 g)

Right: Omelette savoyard, page 30.

| ¾ pint milk (425 ml) |
| Cayenne pepper |
| Salt and freshly-milled black pepper |

| *To garnish:* |
| Some chopped parsley or watercress |

For this you'll need a generously-buttered shallow baking dish.

Select a saucepan that will hold 8 eggs fairly snugly, then cover them with cold water, bring the water to a gentle simmer and allow 7 minutes exactly—then cool them under cold running water.

While the eggs are cooking, make up a sauce using 2 oz (50 g) of the butter and 1½ oz (40 g) of flour, and add the milk gradually till the sauce is smooth. Then leave it to cook very gently for about 6 minutes. (Alternatively, use the all-in-one method, page 434).

Next melt the other 1 oz (25 g) of butter in a saucepan, stir in the chopped leeks and let them sweat gently (with a lid on) for 5 minutes—they should have cooked in that time but still have a bit of 'bite' to them.

Now arrange the leeks over the base of the buttered baking dish and place the peeled halved hard-boiled eggs on top—round side up. Next stir two-thirds of the Cheddar cheese and all the Parmesan into the sauce. Season well and, as soon as the cheese has melted, pour the sauce all over the eggs. Sprinkle the remaining Cheddar on top with a dusting of cayenne, then place the dish under a medium grill until the sauce is bubbling hot and the cheese is nicely toasted. Sprinkle with parsley or garnish with watercress before serving.

Cheese soufflé

(serves 3–4 people)

The one and only secret of success in making a soufflé is to *whisk the egg whites* properly (see page 25). Once you have mastered that, soufflés should never be a problem. But do remember it is in the nature of soufflés to start to shrink straightaway, and always serve them absolutely immediately.

Left: Aduki bean and brown rice salad, page 344; Sausage rolls, page 565; Courgette and cheese quiche, page 560

| 3 oz grated cheese (75 g) (any hard cheese can be used) |
| 3 large eggs, separated |
| 1 oz plain flour (25 g) |
| 1 oz butter (25 g) |
| ¼ pint milk (50 ml) |
| A pinch cayenne pepper |
| ¼ teaspoon mustard powder |
| A little freshly-grated nutmeg |
| Salt and freshly-milled black pepper |

Pre-heat the oven to gas mark 5, 375°F (190°C)

For this you will need a 1½ pint (850ml) soufflé dish or a pie-dish, butter it well.

First of all in a medium saucepan melt the butter, then add the flour and stir it over a moderate heat for 2 minutes.

Gradually add the milk to the saucepan—stirring all the time—and simmer gently for 3 minutes, still giving it an occasional stir. Then stir in the cayenne, mustard, nutmeg and a seasoning of salt and pepper, and leave the sauce to cool a little before stirring in the grated cheese. Beat up the egg yolks thoroughly, then stir them in.

Next whisk the egg whites till they are stiff, take a couple of spoonfuls and beat them into the sauce, then fold in the rest very carefully. Transfer the mixture to the soufflé dish, place on a baking sheet in the centre of the oven and bake for 30–35 minutes. The soufflé is cooked when a skewer inserted into the centre comes out clean.

Piperade
(serves 2 people)

This is the famous egg dish from the Basque region of France, where it's served very often with a thick slice of Bayonne ham. I serve it either just with triangles of fried bread or with grilled gammon steaks.

| 2 green peppers, deseeded and cut into strips |
| 1 lb tomatoes (450 g), skinned, deseeded and chopped |

2 medium onions, chopped small
1 or 2 cloves garlic, crushed (how much is up to you)
½ teaspoon dried basil
4 large fresh eggs
Butter and olive oil
Salt and freshly-milled black pepper

For this you'll need a heavy saucepan.

Melt a knob of butter and a dessertspoon of olive oil in a shallow heavy pan and add the onions, cooking them very gently for 10 minutes without browning. Now add the crushed garlic, tomatoes and peppers, stir everything around a little, season with salt and pepper and basil, and cook without covering for another 20 minutes or so (the peppers should be slightly underdone).

Now beat the eggs thoroughly, pour them into the pan and, using a wooden spoon, stir just as you would for scrambled eggs. When the mixture starts to thicken and the eggs are almost cooked, remove the pan from the heat, continuing to stir, and serve immediately (as with scrambled eggs, do be very careful not to overcook).

Chilli eggs

(serves 2 people)

These are eggs set in a hot spicy tomato sauce. In the summer 1 lb (450 g) of peeled fresh tomatoes would be best, but in the winter the tinned Italian variety have more flavour than imported tomatoes.

4 fresh eggs
3 tablespoons olive oil
1 large onion, chopped
1 green pepper, chopped
2 cloves garlic, crushed
½ teaspoon hot chilli powder
½ teaspoon cumin powder
¼ teaspoon oregano
A few drops of tabasco

14 oz tin Italian tomatoes (400 g)
4 oz Cheddar cheese (110 g), grated
Freshly chopped parsley
Salt and freshly-milled black pepper

A heavy medium-sized frying pan.

Heat the oil in the frying-pan and fry the chopped onion, green pepper and garlic gently for about 10 minutes. Then stir in the chilli and cumin powders and add the oregano along with a few drops of tabasco. Mix thoroughly and then add the contents of the tin of tomatoes.

Turn up the heat a bit and let the mixture cook (uncovered) for about 10 minutes or until the tomatoes have reduced to a thick pulp, then season with salt and freshly-milled black pepper.

Now carefully break the eggs into the pan on top of the mixture. Then sprinkle the cheese all over the eggs, cover the pan with a close-fitting lid or a suitably-sized plate and, lowering the heat, simmer very gently for about 10–15 minutes, or until the eggs are cooked to your liking. Sprinkle with chopped parsley and serve.

Zabaglione

(serves 4 people)

This very famous Italian classic should be made with Marsala wine, which isn't very expensive, but failing that a sweet sherry or Madeira would do.

8 egg yolks
3 fl oz Marsala (75 ml)
4 dessertspoons caster sugar

For this you'll need a medium-sized mixing bowl that will sit comfortably over a saucepan containing barely simmering water.

Into the mixing bowl place the egg yolks and sugar and start to whisk them (not on the heat yet) with an electric hand whisk or a balloon whisk until the mixture is pale and creamy. Then gradually whisk in the Marsala bit by bit.

Now transfer the bowl to the saucepan—keep the heat very low— and continue whisking until the mixture thickens. This can sometimes be rather slow (10–15 minutes), but don't be tempted to turn the heat up because, if the mixture becomes too hot, it will curdle.

When it does thicken, pour it into four warmed wine glasses and serve straight away.

Lemon soufflé omelette

(serves 2 people)

This is a light, foamy, lemony pudding literally made in moments.

3 large eggs, separated
1 lemon
2 dessertspoons caster sugar
Butter

A thick-based frying-pan.

First of all, add the grated rind and the juice of the lemon to the egg yolks, together with the sugar, and whisk until the mixture is slightly thick and creamy. Now start to melt a knob of butter in the frying-pan and turn the heat on the grill to its highest. Whisk the egg whites until stiff, then using a metal spoon carefully fold them into the yolks, lightly and quickly.

Now pour the lot onto the heated butter, then fold and stir a bit to prevent anything sticking to the bottom. After about 10 seconds place the pan under the grill, so that the top can brown nicely. Serve immediately straight from the pan.

If you like to make it slightly more spectacular you can warm a small ladle and pour brandy into it. Set light to the brandy, then carry your omelette to the table, pouring the lighted brandy over just before you get there.

John Tovey's quick hollandaise sauce

This recipe is excellent for using up egg yolks, and is equally delicious with plain grilled fish or meat—or as an accompaniment to vegetables like asparagus and artichokes. (For a more traditional version of this sauce, see page 437).

| 6 oz (170 g) butter |
| 1 tablespoon wine vinegar |
| 2 tablespoons lemon juice |
| 3 egg yolks |
| ½ teaspoon caster sugar |
| A pinch of salt |

Put the butter into a small saucepan and allow it to melt slowly. Place the wine vinegar and lemon juice in another saucepan and bring to the boil. Meanwhile blend the egg yolks, sugar and salt in a liquidiser—then, with the motor still switched on, gradually add the hot lemon juice and vinegar.

When the butter reaches the boil, start to pour this in very slowly in a thin trickle (with the liquidiser motor running all the time) till all the butter is added and the sauce is thickened. To keep it warm, place it in a basin over some hot water till ready to serve.

See also:

Aioli sauce
Alpine eggs
Broccoli cheese soufflé
Crème caramel
Dutch omelette
*Eggs en cocotte with soured cream
    and asparagus*
Eggs Florentine
Ham, egg and cheese risotto
Home-made mayonnaise
Hot chocolate rum soufflé
Lemon meringue pie
Queen of puddings
Sauce rouille
Sauce tartare
Scotch eggs with fresh herbs
*Smoked haddock with cream and
    egg sauce*
Spaghetti carbonara
Spanish tortilla
Welsh rarebit soufflé

Bread and yeast cookery

Including recipes for:
Quick and easy wholewheat bread
Plain white bread
Oatmeal bread
Soured cream soda bread

Quick wheatmeal rolls
Poppy seed rolls
Breakfast baps
Chapattis
Muffins
Bara brith
Hot cross buns
Pizza with salami and mushrooms
Pizza with Mozzarella,
  anchovies and olives
Quick wholewheat pizza
Pissaladière

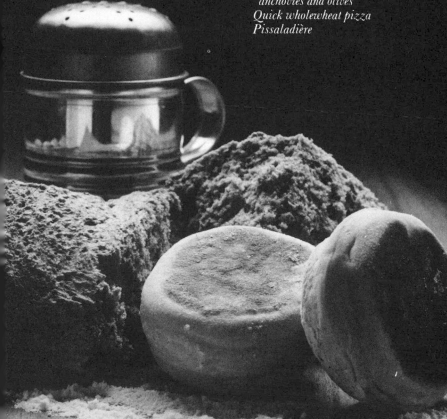

Flour, yeast and breads

You may drive out Nature with a pitchfork, but she will ever hurry back, to triumph in stealth over your foolish contempt.

Horace: *Epistles*

There's a lot of truth in that little Latin quote, and never more so than now when technology tends to dictate, rather than serve, the needs of man. When it comes to the milling of flour and the commercial baking of bread, in this country and others, nature has indeed been driven out, not with a pitchfork but by a mountain of machinery.

In Britain more than 80 per cent of our flour is milled for the convenience of the machines that make factory bread, and not for the pleasure it gives to those who eat it. Alas, the very essence and flavour of the cornfields are contained in that part of the wheat which is discarded by modern millers: even the natural colour of the wheat is bleached out. It's true that the lost nutrients are replaced chemically, but as our modern wrapped-and-sliced white loaf shows only too clearly, nothing can replace the character, texture and flavour of the wheat.

However, it seems that Horace was right—nature is poised for a comeback. It is now quite evident from sound medical opinion the world over that too much 'refined' food isn't very good for us: it lacks the fibre ('roughage') essential to our diet, and it's said to be the cause of serious colonic diseases, not to mention the national preoccupation with constipation. As a result the 'wholefood' movement is losing its cranky image and gathering strength, and more and more people are attempting quite deliberately to adapt to a more wholesome, less refined diet.

First of all we must define what is meant by refined flour as opposed to unrefined 'whole' flour. In the past large bakeries have managed to obscure the real difference: often so-called brown bread has been white with caramel colouring added, and sometimes the odd bit of natural grain was re-incorporated. Now the Trades Description Act stipulates that wholewheat bread *must* be made with 100 per cent wholewheat flour, and so-called 'wheatmeal' bread with 81–85 per cent extraction flour. Nowadays anything brown that is not called either of these is probably of the refined, dyed variety.

A grain of wheat

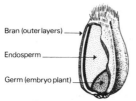

Bran (outer layers)

Endosperm

Germ (embryo plant)

Let us examine a grain of wheat, then, and see how it is milled into the various types of flour. Each grain contains three basic components. There is the *germ* (the part that germinates and grows into a new wheat plant), and this contains proteins, vitamins, oil and much of the flavour. Next there is the *endosperm*, containing starch, and all round both these are the protective layers of *bran*. The germ accounts for 2 per cent of the grain, the bran layers 13 per cent and the starch 85 per cent. In the days when the whole grain was ground by hand on millstones, the bread contained all the properties above.

Milling old and new

Obviously the bread made with these traditional methods was brown. The trouble started, in my opinion, when white flour (at least, whiter) became fashionable on a wide scale in the late 17th century, as a symbol of status and wealth. This 'refined' flour was sifted, or bolted, through a wool-and-linen fabric which got rid of the toughest layer of bran particles: later an even finer flour was obtained by sifting through silk. This fine flour made lighter bread and was of course more suitable for cakes, biscuits and other confections.

By the 1870s the modern mechanical roller-mill had been invented, which automatically separated the bran and the germ from the starch: the starch was then crushed through fine meshes, and finally bleached with chlorine into our modern whiter-than-white flour. The 'status symbol' was available to all, but ironically it is no longer because we want it but because we have to have it. The vast machinery that makes our national loaf can now only cope with this sort of flour (even the bleaching, which helps to mature the flour, is for the benefit of technology rather than taste; it is banned in several countries because it also happens to destroy the vitamin E content—in Britain this is put back synthetically).

To my way of thinking, if we want an alternative to the whole commercial world of the Sliced White, the only really satisfactory alternative we have is to choose our own flour and make our own bread. It may be that you are one of those few, fortunate people who live near a small baker still using select flour and traditional baking methods. If not, I hope to prove to you how uncomplicated

home-baking can be, how even an absolute beginner can produce
a loaf infinitely superior in texture and flavour to any factory bread
on offer. But before embarking on any of the recipes in this chapter,
please read the following notes carefully.

Flour
100 per cent stoneground wholewheat flour (wholemeal)
As the name suggests, this is flour ground on a traditional millstone.
It contains the whole of the grain of wheat. Nothing has been added
and nothing taken away. There has been some confusion as to what
exactly is the difference between *wholewheat* and *wholemeal*.
Whatever terms the millers might use to describe the coarseness of
the grinding, so far as consumers are concerned there is *no*
difference. I have bought various bags of flour, some labelled
wholemeal and others labelled wholewheat: sometimes the texture
of one is coarser than the other, sometimes it's identical. Suffice it to
say that whatever texture you happen to like is right for you.

80–90 per cent extraction flours
These are unbleached flours in which 10–20 per cent of the grain
has been extracted in the milling. Provided these are stone-ground,
they are natural flours with the bran partially removed. This type of
flour is sometimes referred to as 'wheatmeal' and the loaf made from
it is called wheatmeal bread—lighter in texture but still with a
wholewheat-flavour. (If you like making wholewheat bread most of
the time but occasionally want the lighter wheatmeal, you can make
up your own 85 per cent extraction by using half quantity of
wholewheat flour and half of strong white.) *Note:* Unless the
extraction rate is given on the packet and it carries the magic words
'stone ground', the sort of brown flour distributed by some of the
larger firms is usually roller-milled white flour with added colour
and part of what has been extracted put back.

Strong white flour
White flours are normally of 70–72 per cent extraction, with hardly
any traces of bran or germ left and of course bleached (actually an
unbleached variety is available, and this is a pale cream colour).
    All flours vary in strength, according to the amount of *gluten*
(protein) they contain. This will depend on the variety of wheat,
and the type of soil and climate in which it is grown. Strong (or
'hard') wheats are grown in extreme climates, as in Canada or
Russia: in this country our wheat, and therefore our flour, is soft.

The stronger the wheat, the higher the gluten content and (as we shall see) the better a dough will stretch and expand—which is exactly what we need for bread.

Plain flour
Plain household flour is usually a soft flour. It won't give such good results as strong flour for bread, but it is cheaper and quite capable of producing a home-made loaf better than any shop-bought varieties. With less gluten in it, it is the very best type of flour for cakes and short pastries (and, along with self-raising flour, is dealt with in the Pastry chapter).

How to store flour
Flour needs a cool, dry place for storage. That's easier said than done in a modern kitchen, I know, but do try to keep it away from a damp steamy atmosphere: a large and roomy enamelled flour-bin is ideal or, failing that, tightly-lidded storage jars will do. Wholewheat flours have a much shorter shelf-life than white flours, because the wheat germ contains oil which can in time develop a rancid flavour. I think six weeks is the maximum storage time for wholewheat (so buy in small quantities), and three months the maximum for white flour.

Yeast
In her splendid book *English Bread and Yeast Cookery*, Elizabeth David has this to say:

In Chaucer's England one of the names for yeast or barm was goddisgoode 'bicause it cometh of the grete grace of God'. These words simply imply a blessing. To me that is just what it is. It is also mysterious, magical. No matter how familiar its action may become nor how successful the attempts to explain it in terms of chemistry and to manufacture it by the ton, yeast still to a certain extent retains its mystery.

Perhaps one of the reasons yeast seems so mysterious is that it is in fact alive. When we buy it it is alive (one hopes) but inactive: under the right conditions, that is with a little warmth and the addition of some water, it is activated and releases the gas that will raise the dough. All this activity ceases only when the dough is placed in the oven and the extreme temperature kills off the yeast.

Yeast is available in three forms: fresh from some bakers or chemists, and dried (granular) or powdered in tins or packets.

Fresh yeast should look firm and moist, cream-coloured and cool to touch. If it's crumbly, dryish and dark in places it is stale and might not do its work. To use it simply mix the required amount into the liquid and mix into the dough straight away. Fresh yeast can be bought in bulk and stored in a deep freezer in, say, wrapped 1 oz (25 g) portions. It will keep in a freezer for three months, or in a refrigerator for three days.

Dried yeast As supplies of fresh yeast are so unreliable I either use dried yeast, which is reconstituted with warm water and sugar, or easy-blend powdered yeast—which is the easiest of all because you simply sprinkle it evenly into the flour, then add the required amount of water. No mixing, no fuss. Ah, but it's not like the real thing, some people will say. But first of all it *is* the real thing, because dried or powdered it's still yeast. Secondly, I have tasted fresh yeast and dried yeast bread side by side, and really couldn't tell the difference. One word of warning though: dried yeast, just like fresh, does become stale. So dried granular yeast must be stored in an airtight container and used within two months, and if it doesn't produce a 'frothy head' (see page 47) it is not fresh and won't raise the dough. Easy-blend yeast, available in packets, containers and sachets from supermarkets is date-stamped. Please read the note on page 50 before using powdered yeast in the bread recipes below.

Liquid
Water is most commonly used for bread; and occasionally milk or a combination of both. Milk in the mixture gives a softer crust and is better for soft rolls, baps and muffins. Liquid measurements can never be absolutely exact because different types of flour absorb different amounts.

Salt
The quantity of salt you put into bread is determined by two considerations—your own taste, and whether you're in a hurry. Salt does slow down the action of the yeast (too much can actually kill it), so if you want to increase the salt in any of my recipes do allow extra rising time.

Sugar
Sugar is always needed to activate dried (but not fresh) yeast. For dried yeast use brown sugar for wholewheat loaves, and white for

white bread mixes. Molasses is sometimes used to give a different flavour and a moister loaf.

Fats
Adding a small proportion of fat can very slightly enrich a dough and help it to stay fresh longer. Personally I find butter is best of all, but vegetable fat or lard if you prefer can be used instead. Proper enriched doughs are those that have quite a lot of fat in them, sometimes plus eggs and dried fruit (e.g. hot cross buns, malt loaves). The extra fat retards the growth of the yeast, so an extra quantity of yeast is used in this type of recipe.

How a loaf of bread is made
These notes apply to the traditional method of breadmaking. However, later in this chapter, I have also given recipes for quick and simple loaves, dispensing with some of these stages.

Flour should be at room temperature, even slightly warmer, to speed things up. If your flour feels chilly, warm it in a low oven for 10 minutes (and if the bowl it's in gets too hot, tip it into another).

Dried yeast The water for mixing with the yeast should be hand-hot, i.e. you can place your little finger into the water for a few seconds without it hurting. Measure it out and pour approximately one-

third of it into another jug, add the sugar to this, then sprinkle in the dried yeast. Stir once and leave it until it forms a frothy head—this will probably take 10 minutes but might take a little longer. In order to raise the dough it must have at least $^3/_4$ inch (2 cm) of froth.

Mixing Add the salt to the flour and blend it in thoroughly—remember if you add extra salt to allow for extra rising time. Pour the yeast liquid in and mix to a dough, gradually adding the rest of the water, bearing in mind that as flours vary you may not need it all or you may well need a spot more. Add enough to make a smooth dough that will leave the bowl clean. If you've overdone the liquid and it's too slippery it doesn't matter a scrap: just sprinkle in some more flour.

Kneading For bread dough that has to be kneaded, simply place it on a flat work surface then stretch it away from you, using the heel of one hand (see illustration) to push from the middle and the clenched knuckles of your other hand to pull the other half of the dough towards you—both hands should move simultaneously to stretch out the dough. Then lift the edges over and back to the middle. Give it a quarter-turn and repeat the process. It soon becomes a rather rhythmic operation, and the dough will then start to become very elastic. This is the gluten at work. In simple language, the water meets the gluten and what makes it become springy and alive is a good pummelling. That's why if you're feeling angry bread-making can be most therapeutic! One point to bear in mind here is that refined flour has a larger proportion of gluten, so white bread dough will become more elastic and rise much more than a wholewheat dough. A properly kneaded piece of dough will look plump and rounded with a very smooth surface.

Rising This is the period the dough must be left for the yeast to do its work: all yeast doughs need at *least an hour at room temperature* before baking or less in a warm place. I used to think how annoying it was that longer rising times produce better bread, though now I do feel it is sometimes more convenient to go away and leave it for a couple of hours. In the end you will make the sort of bread that fits into your own timetable. To speed up the rising it is best to leave the dough in a so-called 'warm' place. I use the plate-warming compartment of my cooker— but some may be too hot for this and care has to be taken because too high a temperature can kill off the yeast. Always cover the dough, either with a folded damp tea-towel or by completely encasing the bowl inside a polythene bag such as a bin-liner)—put a few drops of oil in the bag first to prevent the dough sticking. The Flour Advisory Bureau recommend that if no suitable warm place is forthcoming you wrap the bowl in a polythene bag, seal it and sit the whole thing in a larger bowl of warm water. (If you don't cover the dough, heat is lost and a skin can develop and, when you knead again, the dough will be lumpy.)

If you have more time to spare, the dough will rise at room temperature and perhaps be the better for it. You can even allow the dough to rise at a cold temperature, in the lower part of the fridge, covered in the same way. This is useful if you want to mix and knead the dough the night before, leave it to rise in the fridge, and shape and bake next morning. Dough, when risen properly, should have doubled in size and should spring back and feel very slightly sticky when lightly touched with the finger. Remember the longer the rising time, the more uniformly the yeast will work and the more evenly textured the finished bread will be.

Knocking down and proving Some recipes call for a second rising or 'proving', which is exactly what it is: the yeast proving it is still alive and active. The experts say that sometimes during the first rise a dough will expand unevenly (with a resulting loaf that is partly too open-textured, partly too close-textured). The proving ensures there will be an even rise. Knocking down is simply punching all the gas out of the dough and bringing it back to its original size, to allow it to rise for a second time in the bread tin.

Baking Bread tins should always be generously greased. I always use butter for this, and a piece of kitchen paper to spread it evenly all round the tins—especially in the ridges and corners. Always bake bread in a hot oven (from gas mark 6, 400°F (200°C) min., to gas mark 8, 450°F (230°C) max.) Bear in mind it's always better to overcook rather than undercook bread: to test if a loaf is cooked, tap it on the under-side with your knuckles and, if it sounds hollow, it's done. If you like very crusty bread, then after you've turned the loaves out of their tins, pop them back in the oven upside down for 5–10 minutes (to bake the underneath and sides). *Always* cool bread on a wire cooling tray, otherwise, on a flat surface, the steam will be trapped and the crust will become wet and soggy.

Storing bread

The best way to store a loaf for any length of time is in the freezer. I have a small 4-star freezing compartment above my fridge and I sometimes freeze bread for as little as three days—because once defrosted it really is fresher than one kept in the bread bin for the same time. Otherwise I would recommend a stainless steel or aluminium bread bin, or roll-top container. But all these must have tiny air holes in them to keep bread for a reasonable period: if the moisture is not allowed to escape, mould can develop.

So much for the essential principles of bread-making, which I hope will answer most everyday queries. At the same time I wouldn't want anyone to be side-tracked into too many paths of perfection. Your loaves, buns and rolls may not win a prize at a Master Bakers' contest (I know mine wouldn't), but the pleasure they will give you and your family will make the small amount of effort worth while.

Important note: When using dried easy-blend yeast in the following recipes, use exactly the same quantity (i.e. 2 teaspoons dried granular yeast equals 2 teaspoons powdered easy-blend yeast), but remember no pre-mixing is required. Simply sprinkle the dry powdered yeast into the flour, then add the water.

Quick and easy wholewheat bread

(makes 1 large or 2 small loaves)

This recipe was inspired by Doris Grant in her excellent book *Your Daily Food*. Although it's quick and easy, I have never found a shop-bought wholewheat loaf nearly as good. For those of us who simply don't have the time for kneading, knocking down and proving, this loaf is an absolute gem and the one that I, personally, make most often.

1 lb stoneground wholewheat flour (450 g)
2 teaspoons salt
Approximately 12–13 fl oz hand-hot water (355–380 ml)
1 teaspoon brown sugar
2 level teaspoons dried yeast (or see note opposite)
A little extra flour

(For 3 lb (1 kg 350 g) flour simply multiply the rest of the ingredients by 3.)

You'll need one 2 lb (900 g) bread tin with a base measurement of 6^1/$_2$ × 3^1/$_2$ inches (16·5 × 9 cm) or two 1 lb (450 g) bread tins 5^1/$_4$ × 3 inches (13·5 × 8 cm). The tin or tins should be buttered fairly thickly.

Begin by weighing the flour and mixing the salt into it so that it is fairly evenly distributed. Then warm the flour slightly in a low oven for about 10 minutes.

While the flour is warming, prepare the yeast by measuring 3 fl oz (75 ml) hand-hot water in a measuring jug. Stir the sugar in and sprinkle in the 2 teaspoons of yeast as well, stir once, then leave for 10–15 minutes until a good 1 inch (2·5 cm) of froth has formed.

Now tip the warm flour into a large mixing bowl, make a well in the centre, stir the yeast liquid once—to make sure it's dissolved—then pour it into the well and, starting with a wooden spoon, begin to mix the yeast liquid into the flour to form a dough, gradually adding the rest of the measured water. Finish off the mixing with your hands until you have a smooth dough that leaves the bowl clean, i.e. no bits of flour or dough remain on the side of the bowl. The exact amount of water you need depends on the flour. You can do the mixing with the dough hook of an electric hand whisk (or even in a mixer).

Now transfer the dough to the tin (or tins) by stretching it out to an oblong and folding one edge into the centre and the other edge over that. Fit the dough into the tin, pressing all round the edges so that the surface will already be slightly rounded. Next sprinkle the surface with a generous dusting of flour. Cover the tin with a damp tea towel and leave it to rise in a warm place for 30–40 minutes or at room temperature for approximately an hour.

Meanwhile pre-heat the oven to gas mark 6, 400°F (200°C), and when the dough has risen to within ¼ inch (½ cm) of the top of the bread tin (or to the very top if you are using a shallower loaf tin), then bake the bread for 45 minutes if it's the large size or 35 minutes for the smaller size. After that turn out the bread and return it to the oven, upside down, for a further 5–10 minutes to crisp the base and sides.

The loaves, if cooked, will sound hollow when tapped underneath. Cool the bread on a wire cooling tray and *never* put it away or freeze it until it's absolutely cold. *Note:* If you want to make a lighter textured loaf by the same method, all you do is use ½ lb (225 g) 100 per cent wholewheat flour and ½ lb (225 g) strong white flour and prepare it in exactly the same way as above.

Plain white bread

(makes 2 loaves)

This is, for those who prefer the lighter texture of a plain white loaf (and indeed most people prefer it for toast), a basic white loaf recipe.

2 level teaspoons dried yeast (or see note on page 50)
¾ pint hand-hot water (425 ml)
1 teaspoon white sugar
1½ lb strong white flour (700 g), warmed slightly
1 level tablespoon salt
½ oz butter
A little extra flour

Two 1 lb loaf tins (450 g), well buttered.

Pour ¼ pint (150 ml) of the hand-hot water into a bowl, then with a fork whisk in the sugar, followed by the dried yeast—and leave this mixture on one side to froth.

Meanwhile sift the flour and salt into a bowl and rub in the butter. When the yeast is ready, pour it into a well made in the centre of the flour, then pour in the remaining ½ pint (275 ml) of warm water. Now mix to a dough, starting off with a wooden spoon and using your hands in the final stages of mixing.

Wipe the bowl clean with the dough—adding a spot more water if there are any dry bits left—and transfer it to a flat work-surface (there shouldn't be any need to flour the surface). Knead the dough for ten minutes or until it develops a sheen and blisters under the surface (it should also be springy and elastic).

You can now either leave the dough on the surface covered by the upturned bowl or return the dough to the bowl and cover with polythene or clingfilm. Leave it until it looks as though it has doubled in bulk—1½ to 2 hours at room temperature or 45 minutes to an hour in a warm place.

After that knock the air out, then knead again for 5 minutes. Now divide the dough in half, pat each piece out to an oblong, then fold one end in to the centre and fold the other end in on top. Put each one into a buttered tin, sprinkle each loaf with a dusting of flour, then place them side by side in an oiled polythene bag until the dough rises above the tops of the tins (30 minutes in a warm place or an hour at room temperature).

Now pre-heat the oven to gas mark 8, 450°F (230°C) and bake the loaves for 35–40 minutes or until they sound hollow when their bases are tapped. Return them, out of their tins, upside down in the oven to crisp the base and side crust. Then cool on a wire rack.

Oatmeal bread

(makes 2 small loaves)

This bread has a lovely wholesome flavour, just the thing for a snack lunch with some strong Cheddar cheese; it also makes delicious bacon sandwiches.

4 oz medium oatmeal (110 g)
½ pint milk (275 ml)
2 teaspoons dried yeast (or see note on page 50)
¼ pint hand-hot water (150 ml)
10 oz wholewheat flour (275 g), warmed slightly
10 oz strong white flour (275 g), warmed slightly
1 dessertspoon salt
1 teaspoon honey
2 oz butter (50 g)
1 teaspoon sugar

A floured baking sheet.

Start this about 4 or 5 hours ahead by combining the oatmeal and the milk in a bowl and leaving them to soak. Then to make the loaves, start by pouring ¹/₄ pint (150 ml) of hand-hot water into a jug. Whisk in the sugar and then the yeast, and leave it for 10 minutes to get a good frothy head.

Then mix the two flours and the salt in a mixing bowl, making sure you mix them together very thoroughly. Then make a well in the centre of the flour.

Next gently warm the butter and honey together in a small saucepan until the butter becomes liquid, then pour this into the well in the flours, followed by the frothed yeast. Finally add the soaked oatmeal mixture, then mix everything together to form a smooth dough that leaves the bowl clean. If it's very stiff you may need a drop more milk. Now transfer the dough to a flat working surface and knead it for about 10 minutes: after that return it to the bowl and cover with a damp cloth or cling-film. Leave it like this until the dough has doubled in bulk (about 90 minutes at room temperature or rather less in a warm place). Then knock and punch the air out and knead again for 5 minutes.

Next, divide the dough in half, and make each half into a round shape. Roll each loaf gently in some wholewheat flour, pressing in a light coating, then place both on a floured baking sheet. Use a sharp knife to make ¹/₄ inch (¹/₂ cm) deep slashes across the top of each loaf.

Place the baking sheet (and contents) inside an oiled plastic bag and let the dough prove for a further 1–1¹/₂ hours (or 45 minutes in a warm place). Bake in a pre-heated oven, gas mark 8, 450°F (230°C), for 10 minutes, then turn down the heat to gas mark 4, 350°F (180°C), and bake for a further 30 minutes.

Soured cream soda bread

(makes 1 loaf)

This is a good loaf to make if you're in a hurry or need some bread unexpectedly. It doesn't need yeast, as the soured cream and soda are the raising agents. It is best eaten slightly warm from the oven.

1 lb wholewheat flour (450 g)
2 teaspoons salt
1 teaspoon bicarbonate of soda

¼ pint soured cream (150 ml)
¼ pint water (150 ml) (plus 2–3 extra tablespoons)

Pre-heat the oven to gas mark 7, 425°C (220°C)

A greased baking sheet.

Begin by mixing the flour, salt and bicarbonate of soda thoroughly in a bowl. Then in a jug whisk the soured cream and water together and stir this mixture into the flour together with 2–3 further tablespoons of water, if it needs it.

Knead the dough lightly (into a round ball) so as to get the surface smooth, then put it onto the prepared baking sheet and cut halfway through the loaf with a sharp knife, one way, then do the same the other way forming a cut cross, which will form the loaf into four crusty sections.

Bake the loaf in the top half of the oven for 30 minutes—covering the top with foil for the last 5 minutes of the baking time, if the crust looks like getting too dark. Cool on a wire rack for a minimum of 15 minutes before eating. This is delicious cut in thick slices, buttered and spread with home-made lemon curd (page 598) or some really good honey.

If you don't like a very crisp crust, wrap the bread in a tea-towel whilst it cools, so that the steam it gives off softens the crust a little.

Note: Soda bread is best eaten as fresh as possible: it's not a keeping loaf at all—though I'm sure there won't actually be any left to keep! If you can't get soured cream use ½ pint (275 ml) milk and 2 teaspoons of cream of tartar.

Quick wheatmeal rolls

(makes 12 rolls)

The quick wholewheat bread on page 50 is not suitable for individual rolls because, without kneading, there's no elasticity in the dough and, during the rising time, it spreads itself out too much. This recipe does require 5–6 minutes kneading but only one rise, so it's still relatively quick.

| 8 oz wholewheat flour (225 g) |
| 8 oz strong white flour (225 g) |
| 1 teaspoon butter |
| 1 level teaspoon brown sugar |
| 2 level teaspoons salt |
| 2 level teaspoons dried yeast (or see note on page 50) |
| ½ pint hand-hot water (275 ml) |
| A little extra flour |

One large or two small well-greased baking sheets.

Measure the flours into a bowl, add the salt and mix thoroughly together. Then warm the flour slightly in a low oven.

To prepare the yeast measure ½ pint (275 ml) hand-hot water in a jug, then pour half of it into another jug or bowl. Sprinkle in the sugar and then the yeast, stir and leave it aside till a good 1 inch (2·5 cm) frothy head has formed.

Now remove the flour from the oven, rub in the fat, then make a well in the centre, stir the yeast liquid and pour it into the well. Pour the other liquid into the yeast jug, to rinse it out, then add this to the flour gradually stirring with a wooden spoon at first and then finishing off with your hands until you have a smooth dough that leaves the bowl cleanly.

Now transfer the dough onto a flat working surface and knead it thoroughly for about 6 minutes, by which time it will have become very elastic and springy.

Next divide the dough into 12 portions to form the rolls. If you want your rolls to be absolutely the same size, you can weigh the dough, divide the total weight by twelve and then weigh each individual piece. Stretch each piece into an oblong and fold one end into the middle and the other end over that. Then, with the folds underneath, slap the roll into a round ball. Place the rolls onto the well-greased baking sheets, cover with a sheet of oiled polythene, or encase the baking sheet inside an oiled pedal-bin liner. Leave the rolls to rise until they have doubled in size: 35–40 minutes in a warm place or 1–1½ hours at room temperature.

Meanwhile pre-heat the oven to gas mark 7, 425°F (220°C). When the rolls have risen, sprinkle them with flour and bake them on a high shelf of the oven for 20–25 minutes. They should sound hollow when you tap them underneath if they are cooked enough. Cool the rolls on a wire cooling rack.

Poppy seed rolls
(makes 16 rolls)

Basically these are the familiar soft Vienna rolls—improved, I think, by a liberal sprinkling of poppy seeds.

1 lb strong white flour (450 g), warmed slightly
2 teaspoons salt
½ pint hand-hot milk (275 ml)
2 teaspoons dried yeast (or see note on page 50)
1 teaspoon white sugar
4 oz butter (110 g) (room temperature)
1 beaten egg
2 tablespoons (approx.) poppy seeds

1 large (or 2 small) baking sheets, well-greased.

Start by pouring ¼ pint (150 ml) of milk into a bowl and whisk the sugar into it with a fork, followed by the dried yeast. Leave this on one side for 10 minutes to froth. Meanwhile sift the flour and salt into a bowl, make a well in the centre, and (when it's ready) pour in the frothed yeast and milk, and the rest of the milk. Mix to form a smooth dough, then turn out onto a flat working surface and knead for 10 minutes.

After that put the dough back in the bowl, cover with clingfilm and leave it to rise until doubled in bulk (which will take 1½–2 hours at room temperature or 45 minutes to an hour in a warm place). Then punch the dough down in the bowl to knock the air out, and then gradually work in the softened butter. The dough will now be very sticky, but ignore this and carry on until the butter is evenly worked into the dough.

Next, turn it out onto a lightly-floured work-surface and knead into a round shape—divide this into sixteen sections. Roll each piece out into a long roll, and literally tie each roll into a knot. Place each roll on the baking sheet and brush with beaten egg. Now pop the baking sheet and rolls into an oiled polythene bag, and leave them to prove until puffy and risen again—about half an hour in a warm place or an hour at room temperature. Pre-heat the oven to gas mark 5, 375°F (190°C), sprinkle the rolls with the poppy seeds and bake for about 20 minutes or until golden brown.

Breakfast baps

(makes 12)

These are indeed good at breakfast; they're also good for hamburgers or for filling and taking on a picnic.

1 lb plain white flour (450 g)
1½ teaspoons salt
2 oz butter (50 g)
¼ pint hand-hot water (150 ml)
¼ pint milk (150 ml)
1 teaspoon granulated sugar
2 teaspoons dried yeast (or see note on page 50)

Lightly grease 2 baking sheets.

Sift the flour and salt into a bowl, and rub the butter in until thoroughly blended. Now blend the water, milk and sugar together in another bowl, whisk in the yeast and leave on one side for 10 minutes to form a good head of froth. Now make a well in the flour, stir the liquid into it until the mixture forms a smooth dough, then turn the dough onto a lightly-floured surface and knead for about 10 minutes—or until the dough is silky smooth and feels very springy and elastic. Return it to the bowl, cover with a damp cloth or cling-film and leave it until it's doubled in bulk (about 1½ hours at room temperature or 50–60 minutes in a warm place).

Then pre-heat the oven up to gas mark 9, 475°F (245°C). Knead the dough lightly and divide it into 12 equal pieces. Form each one into a ball and place them on a baking sheet—you should manage to get six on each baking sheet. Flour your hands and flatten the balls slightly into disc shapes. Then press a deep hole with your thumb in the centre of each bap (this prevents any blistering whilst it's cooking). Now brush each one with milk and sprinkle on a generous dusting of flour. Then put the baking sheets inside large plastic bags for 20–25 minutes to prove. Bake for 10 minutes so they are golden brown under the floury tops. Transfer to a wire rack to cool, and eat them very fresh.

Chapattis
(makes 12)

This is an anglicised version of the flat bread served with curry in India. Don't be put off because it sounds complicated. It's actually much easier and quicker than it sounds.

½ lb wholewheat flour (225 g)
1 teaspoon salt
About ¼ pint cold water (150 ml)
A little lard

A frying-pan or griddle.

Simply mix the flour and salt in a bowl, then gradually add enough water to combine the mixture to a non-sticky dough. Transfer the dough to a work surface and knead for about 10 minutes. Then leave it, covered by the upturned bowl, to rest for 30 minutes. After that pre-heat the grill to high, then break up the dough and roll it into walnut-size pieces. Now roll out each piece on a lightly-floured surface as thin as possible; just less than ¹/₈ inch (3 mm).

Next heat a frying-pan or griddle over a medium heat and grease lightly with a piece of lard paper. Put the pancakes on the hot surface, one at a time, and wait until bubbles start to rise in them, rather like cobblestones. Flip over and cook for about 15 seconds, then transfer each one to cook under the grill about 6 inches (15 cm) from the heat. They should immediately inflate to virtually a round ball. Then, when lightly browned, turn and cook the other side. To serve, as the bread collapses, transfer it to a warmed dish, lined with a napkin. Cover and take to the table.

Each chapatti should take about ¹/₂ minute to cook, so the total cooking time is only about 6 minutes.

Muffins
(makes 12)

Muffins always remind me of fireside teas in the depth of winter. I like to cook them on top of the stove, which is the traditional method, but if you haven't got a griddle, use a heavy frying-pan.

1 lb strong plain flour (450 g)
1 rounded teaspoon salt
8 fl oz milk (225 ml)

2 fl oz water (55 ml)
1 teaspoon caster sugar
2 level teaspoons dried yeast
A little lard

Measure the milk and water in a small saucepan and heat until just hand hot. Pour it into a jug, add the sugar and dried yeast, mix it with a fork and leave it about 10 minutes to get a real frothy head.

Meanwhile sift the flour and salt into a large mixing bowl, make a well in the centre, then pour in the frothy yeast mixture and mix it to a soft dough—it should leave the bowl cleanly, but if it seems a bit sticky add a spot more flour. On the other hand, if it seems a little dry add just a spot more water.

Now transfer the dough to a flat surface and knead it for about 10 minutes, by which time it should be very smooth and elastic. The dough can go back into the bowl now. Just slip the bowl inside a large, oiled polythene bag, and leave it in a warm place until the dough has doubled in size. This will take about 45 minutes or longer, depending on the temperature.

When the dough has risen, lightly flour the work surface, then tip the dough out and roll it out to about ½ inch (1 cm) thick, then using a 3 inch (7.5 cm) plain cutter cut out 12 rounds, re-rolling the dough a couple of times again if it starts to get puffy. Mix the scraps and re-roll to use all the dough up.

Now place the muffins on an ungreased lightly-floured baking sheet, sprinkling them with a little more flour, then leave them to puff up again for about 25–35 minutes in a warm place.

When they are ready to be cooked, grease a thick-based frying-pan or griddle with just a trace of lard. Then heat the pan over a medium heat, add some muffins and cook them for about 7 minutes on each side, turning the heat down to low as soon as they go in. You'll need to do this in three or four batches, but they can be made well in advance.

If you want to serve them in the traditional way, all you do is break them just a little around their waists without opening them, then toast them lightly on both sides. The correct way to eat them is just to pull them apart without cutting and insert a lot of butter. You can store them in an airtight tin for about two days before toasting if you have any left over.

Bara brith

(makes 1 loaf)

There are several different versions of this Welsh 'speckled bread'. Many of them don't contain yeast; but, for me, this version is the nicest and if there's any left over it's delicious toasted.

1 lb strong plain flour (450 g)
4 teaspoons dried yeast
8 fl oz milk (225 ml)
2 oz brown sugar (50 g) plus 1 teaspoon
1 teaspoon salt
3 oz butter or margarine (75 g)
1 standard egg
1 teaspoon mixed spice
12 oz mixed dried fruit (350 g)

A 2 lb (900 g) loaf tin well greased.

First warm the milk in a small saucepan till it's hand-hot, and then pour it into a bowl. Whisk in 1 teaspoon of sugar, followed by the yeast, then leave it in a warm place to froth for about 15 minutes.

Now sift the flour and salt into a large mixing bowl, stirring in the sugar as well. Then rub the fat into the dry ingredients until the mixture looks like fine breadcrumbs. Stir in the mixed spice next, then pour in the beaten egg and frothed yeast, and mix to a dough. Now turn the dough onto a floured surface and knead until smooth and elastic (about 10 minutes), then replace the dough in the bowl and cover with a cloth or some clingfilm. Leave in a warm place to rise until it has doubled in size—about 1½ hours.

After that turn the dough out and knock it down to get the air out, then gradually knead the fruit in and pat out to a rectangular shape. Roll it up from one short side to the other and put it in the loaf tin (seam-side down). Place the tin inside an oiled plastic bag and leave it to rise, until the dough has rounded nicely above the edge of the tin (about 30–45 minutes). Meanwhile pre-heat the oven to gas mark 5, 375°F (190°C).

When the dough has risen and springs back when pressed lightly with a floured finger, remove the polythene bag; transfer the loaf to the oven and bake on the shelf below centre for 30 minutes. Then cover the top of the loaf tin with foil to prevent it over-browning, and continue to bake for a further 30 minutes. Turn the loaf out, holding it in a teacloth in one hand and tapping the base with the other. It should sound hollow—if not pop it back upside down (without the tin) for 5 minutes more. Cool the loaf on a wire rack, and brush the top with clear honey, to make it nice and sticky, before the loaf cools. Slice thinly and serve buttered.

Hot cross buns
(makes about 12)

It's hard to believe the difference in home-made hot cross buns—they really are far better than any bought from a shop and a lot cheaper into the bargain!

1 lb plain flour (450 g)
1 teaspoon caster sugar
¼ pint hand-hot water (150 ml)
1 level teaspoon salt
2 oz cut mixed peel (50 g)
2 oz butter (50 g), melted
1½–2 fl oz warmed milk (40–50 ml)
1 level tablespoon dried yeast
1 rounded teaspoon mixed spice
3 oz currants (75 g)
2 oz caster sugar (50 g)
1 egg, beaten

For the glaze:
2 tablespoons granulated sugar
2 tablespoons water

Pre-heat the oven to gas mark 7, 425°F (220°)

A greased baking sheet.

First stir 1 teaspoon of caster sugar into the ¼ pint (150 ml) of hand-hot water, then sprinkle in the dried yeast and leave it until a good frothy 'beer' head forms.

Meanwhile sift the flour, salt and mixed spice into a mixing bowl and add the sugar, currants and mixed peel. Then make a well in the centre, pour in the yeast mixture plus 1½ fl oz (40 ml) of milk (again hand-hot), the beaten egg and the melted butter. Now mix it to a dough, starting with a wooden spoon and finishing with your hands (add a spot more milk if it needs it).

Then transfer the dough onto a clean surface and knead it until it feels smooth and elastic—about 6 minutes. Now pop it back into the bowl, cover the bowl with a lightly oiled plastic bag (a pedal-bin liner is ideal), and leave it in a warm place to rise—it will take about an hour to double its original size. Then turn it out and knead it again, back down to its original size.

Divide the mixture into 12 round portions, arrange them on the greased baking sheet (allowing plenty of room for expansion), and make a deep cross on each one with a sharp knife. Leave them to rise once more, covering again with the oiled polythene bag for about 25 minutes. Then bake the buns for about 15 minutes.

Then, while they're cooking, melt the sugar and water over a gentle heat, and brush the buns with it, as soon as they come out of the oven, to make them nice and sticky.

Note: If you like you can make more distinctive crosses with strips of dampened shortcrust pastry lightly pressed into each bun before baking.

Pizza

One of the very nicest ways of eating bread is as a 'pizza'—freshly-baked bread dough with delicious fillings melting and bubbling on top. There are, of course, hundreds of variations—tomatoes, cheese, olives, anchovies, chopped peppers, capers, sliced mushrooms, salami—anything and everything can be used. Below is a recipe for a plain pizza dough and then two with my own favourite fillings.

Pizza dough

8 oz plain flour (225 g)
1 level teaspoon salt
¼ teaspoon sugar
1½ teaspoons dried yeast
1 standard egg, beaten
3–4 fl oz water (75–110 ml), hand-hot
1 teaspoon oil

First pour 3 fl oz (75 ml) of hand-hot water into a basin and whisk in the sugar, followed by the yeast; then leave this mixture on one side for about 10–15 minutes until it gets a nice frothy head on it.

Meanwhile sift the flour and salt together in a mixing bowl. Then pour in the frothy yeast mixture and the beaten egg, and mix to a dough. (You may need to add just a spot of extra warm water—it depends on the flour—but, at the end, you should have a soft, pliable dough that leaves the bowl clean.) Then transfer the dough to a working surface and knead for about 10 minutes until it's silky smooth and fairly elastic.

Now replace the dough in the bowl and rub the surface all over with the oil. Then seal the top of the bowl with cling-film—or cover with a clean, damp cloth—and put the dough in a warmish place to rise for about an hour, or until it has doubled in size.

Once the dough has 'proved' (that is, doubled in size), knead it again for about 5 minutes, and then it's ready to use.

Pizza with salami and mushrooms (serves 2–4 people)	
	8 oz (225 g) tin Italian tomatoes, drained
	1 tablespoon tomato purée
	1 teaspoon dried basil
	4 oz salami or Italian pepperoni sausage (110 g)
	1 tablespoon capers
	1 small pepper, deseeded and finely chopped
	2 oz mushrooms, thinly sliced (50 g)
	2 tablespoons grated Parmesan
	Oil
	Salt and freshly-milled black pepper

Prepare the pizza dough as above and line a tin as in the next recipe. Pinch out a narrow border and brush the base with oil.

Pre-heat the oven to gas mark 7, 425°F (220°C).

Now either liquidise the tomatoes or simply rub them through a sieve into a bowl. Then stir in the tomato purée and basil, taste, and season with salt and freshly-milled black pepper. Now pour the mixture on to the pizza base and spread it all over.

Next, skin and thinly slice the salami and halve the slices. Then arrange them over the top of the pizza, sprinkle on the chopped pepper, capers, sliced mushrooms and grated Parmesan, and again trickle a little oil over the top. Leave the pizza on one side for about 10 minutes before baking in the oven for 15–20 minutes.

Pizza with Mozzarella, anchovies and olives

(serves 3–4 people)

Mozzarella cheese, or similar types, are sometimes available at delicatessens and specialised food shops, but if you can't get hold of it, make this with thinly sliced Dutch Gouda cheese.

For the tomato sauce:
2 tablespoons oil
1 Spanish onion, peeled and chopped
2 cloves garlic, crushed
Two 14 oz (400 g) tins Italian tomatoes
¾ teaspoon dried basil (or fresh if you have it)
1 large bayleaf
Salt and freshly milled black pepper

For the garnish:
4 oz Mozzarella cheese (100 g), cut in small pieces
2 oz (50 g) can anchovy fillets, drained and chopped
1 dozen black olives, pitted and halved
1 teaspoon dried oregano
1 tablespoon grated Parmesan
Oil

A shallow oblong tin, 10 × 11 inches (25·5 × 28 cm) ungreased.

First prepare the sauce. Heat the oil and fry the onion until softened and golden; then stir in the remaining sauce ingredients and simmer gently (uncovered) for about an hour, or until the tomatoes have reduced to a jam-like consistency. Then take the pan off the heat, discard the bayleaf and leave the sauce to cool. Now place the dough in the tin and push it out with your hands to line it completely, bringing it up at the edges and pinching it to make a sort of border to contain the filling. If the dough is very springy, be determined with it.

Then brush the base of the dough with oil, cover with the tomato filling and spread it right up to the pinched edge. Next sprinkle the surface with the cheese, anchovies, halved olives, dried oregano and Parmesan, drizzle a tablespoon of oil over the top and leave the pizza at room temperature for 10–15 minutes before baking.

Meanwhile pre-heat the oven to gas mark 7, 425°F (220°C). Then bake the pizza for 15–20 minutes. Check that the bread base is cooked through to the centre by lifting the pizza up with a fish slice and taking a look. It's better to overcook a pizza slightly than undercook it, and always serve it straight from the oven.

Quick wholewheat pizza
(serves 2–4 people)

Wholewheat dough gives a different, somewhat more substantial pizza— every bit as good as the traditional kind.

½ lb wholewheat flour (225 g)
½ teaspoon salt
1 teaspoon yeast
1 teaspoon mixed herbs
6 fl oz hand-hot water (170 ml)
1 teaspoon sugar
Freshly milled black pepper

For the filling:
14 oz tin Italian tomatoes (400 g)
1 tablespoon olive oil
1 large onion, chopped
1 clove garlic, crushed
1 teaspoon dried basil
1 tablespoon tomato purée
3 thinly-pared slices Cheddar cheese
Small tin anchovies, drained
2 oz mushrooms (50 g)
6 black olives
A little more mixed herbs

A well-buttered 8 inch (20 cm) sandwich tin.

Combine the flour, salt, herbs and pepper in a bowl, then in a jug measure 6 fl oz (170 ml) of hand-hot water and whisk in the sugar and yeast. Leave it to get a frothy head (about 10 minutes), then stir the frothed yeast into the dry ingredients and mix to a smooth dough. Then press it down into the well-greased sandwich tin, bringing the dough up the side of the tin. Now leave to rise, covered with a damp cloth, for about 25 minutes.

Right: Soured cream soda bread, page 54; Muffins, page 59; Quick wheatmeal rolls, page 55; Quick wholewheat pizza, this page.

While that's happening heat the oil in a saucepan and soften the onion. Stir in the contents of the tin of tomatoes, followed by the basil and garlic, and simmer (uncovered) for 25 minutes or until the sauce has reduced to a very thick jam-like consistency. Then add the tomato purée.

Now push the dough lightly back up the side of the tin, if it has slipped during the rising, then spread the tomato sauce over the base of the bread. Scatter the thinly-sliced mushrooms over the top; lay the pieces of cheese over the mushrooms, then add the anchovies, making a faint criss-cross pattern. Next, drizzle a little more olive oil over everything and sprinkle with a few more mixed herbs and the olives.

Bake on a high shelf at gas mark 7, 425°F (220°C), for about 20 minutes. Then serve piping hot with a crisp salad and some Italian wine to drink.

Pissaladière

(serves 2–4 people)

Just over the border from Italy, in the south of France, they have their own version of pizza—Pissaladière. In this recipe I have sacrificed total authenticity by using a wholewheat dough (because it's quicker), but you can use a white dough if you prefer.

2 lb large onions (900 g), thinly sliced
4 tablespoons (approx.) olive oil
1 fat clove garlic, crushed
2 oz (56 g) tin of anchovy fillets in oil
1 dozen (approx.) black olives, pitted and halved
1 teaspoon mixed dried herbs
Salt, freshly-milled black pepper

For the dough:
8 oz wholewheat flour (220 g)
1 teaspoon mixed dried herbs
6 fl oz hand-hot water (175 ml)
1 teaspoon brown sugar
1 teaspoon dried yeast
Teaspoon salt
Freshly-milled black pepper

Left: Turkish stuffed tomatoes, page 307; Country pâté, page 82.

Pre-heat the oven to gas mark 7, 425°F (220°C)

A swiss-roll tin 13 × 9 inches (33 × 23 cm) brushed with oil.

Make the filling first by heating the oil in a large saucepan. Stir in the onions and crushed garlic, then cook them over a gentle heat (uncovered) for about 30 minutes, stirring occasionally, or until the onions have just about formed a soft mass and show a tendency to stick to the base of the pan. Then take the pan from the heat and taste and season with salt and freshly-milled pepper.

While the onions are cooking you can combine the flour, salt and herbs, and some freshly-milled pepper together in a bowl. Pour 5 fl oz (150 ml) of hand-hot water into a separate bowl and, using a fork, whisk in the sugar followed by the yeast. Leave on one side for 10 minutes to froth, then pour this into the flour mixture. Add a further 1 fl oz (25 ml) of hand-hot water and mix to form a dough.

Then turn the dough out onto a lightly floured surface and roll out roughly to a shape 13 × 9 inches (33 × 23 cm). Place it in the tin, pushing it up the sides and into the corners with your fingers. Then brush the dough with olive oil, cover with a clean cloth and leave in a warm place for 20–30 minutes to rise a little.

Now spread the cooked onion filling over the base. Drain the tin of anchovies: reserve the oil and slice the fillets in half lengthways. Arrange them in a diamond-shaped pattern (like lattice-work) all over the onion filling, and stud each diamond with a halved, pitted olive. Sprinkle with the herbs and drizzle the reserved anchovy oil over the lot. Bake on a high shelf of the oven for 20–25 minutes. Serve hot or cold.

See also:
Crumpets

Pâtés and starters

Including recipes for:
Charcuterie
Mozzarella and tomato salad
Crudités
Sardine-stuffed tomatoes
Pickled herrings
Russian herring
Fresh fruit and mint vinaigrette
Avocado vinaigrette
Avocado mousse with prawns
  and vinaigrette
Avocado and seafood salad
Marinaded mushrooms
White bean and tuna fish salad
Asparagus and cheese tart
Smoked fish creams
Country pâté
Rillettes de Tours
Chicken liver pâté
Taramasalata
Smoked mackerel pâté
Smoked fish pâté

The whole idea of a first course (or starter, as it's become more popularly known) is that it should encourage the appetite, rather than spoil it. There's nothing worse than having to first struggle through a huge slab of rich pâté (and the bread needed to get it down), and then have to cope with a main course! In fact my enjoyment of special occasions at multi-starred restaurants has often been marred, simply because I couldn't find a plain enough starter to really appreciate the skills lavished on the main course. For me the biggest problem comes when I am confronted with an hors-d'oeuvre trolley.

Hors-d'oeuvre means literally 'outside work', which reflects the attitude of most 19th century French chefs, who preferred to sub-contract the tedious job of preparing it. Most countries have some kind of hors-d'oeuvre: the Scandinavians their *smørrebrød*, the Italians their *antipasti*, the Spaniards their *entremeses*; but it was in France that the hors-d'oeuvre reached epic proportions—and also in Russia, where a separate room was often set aside for it! We still find the legacy of this in some restaurants, where an awesome array of meats, fish dishes, salads, eggs, canapés and so on get trundled in while glazed looks come over the faces of the diners. It is very tempting to load the plate with a selection of everything, and finish up with a complete meal rather than a starter. That, of course, destroys the whole point of a first course, so perhaps it's just as well that it isn't very practical for us to go to such lengths at home.

Now I accept that not everybody will share my simple tastes in food, but I still think it is a safe general rule to have only one rich course in a meal. (In fact I have deliberately made a distinction between pâtés and starters in the title of this chapter because I prefer, on the whole, to serve pâtés on their own for lunch or supper, with plenty of crusty bread, and some pickled gherkins and a side-salad to counteract the richness.)

My own favourite starters send to need little or no cooking: a *Tomato salad* (served in late summer when the tomatoes are red and ripe), with fresh basil, parsley, a little chopped shallot and some good vinaigrette is almost unbeatable. Some thinly sliced *Parma ham*, or salami or mortadella (or a mixture of all three), served with preserved pimentos and French bread spread with unsalted Normandy butter, would also be a real treat. I think it is the salady starters that seem to sharpen the appetite best. *Avocado vinaigrette* is a popular one, but *Asparagus* or *Artichoke vinaigrette* come into the same category. Other firm favourites in our house are *Egg mayonnaise* and

Eggs en cocotte, but since they are slightly richer than some other starters one must take care to serve a portion that won't spoil the main course.

Before giving some recipes for first courses, and a number of pâtés, let me offer some suggestions for starters that are simple to prepare and make no strenuous demands on the appetite.

Soups are dealt with in a separate chapter.

Charcuterie

This is the name given to a whole range of cooked, dried, salted or smoked meats, which can be served either separately or mixed.

Prosciutto (Parma ham) This is the Italian raw cured ham, which is cut into almost transparently thin slices. It is often served with slices of melon, but I prefer it by itself or mixed with other meats.

Salami (salted matured sausage) This comes in many nationalities, Danish, French, German—but for me the best of all is the Italian. If you are fortunate enough to be offered a choice, ask for *Casalinga* which is usually one of the rougher, country varieties.

Mortadella (large smooth boiled pork sausage) Real Italian mortadella is normally 12–18 inches (30–45 cm) in diameter (the smaller kind is not Italian and never as good). It looks like spam; but don't be deceived: its mildly spicy flavour is something quite different.

Mixed together, 4 oz (110 g) of each of the above will serve 6 people as a first course. As an accompaniment I would suggest some preserved pimentoes (bright red and yellow peppers which are sold in jars), black olives, and some Italian mixed pickles, which are usually a selection of preserved carrots, baby onions, cauliflower and celery.

Other forms of charcuterie also make very suitable first course dishes. In the end it's a matter of finding out where they are sold—in Britain usually in delicatessens or specialised food stores—and making your own choice.

Cheese for starters

Cheese is traditionally eaten at the end of a meal in this country, but there are at least two cheeses that make excellent first courses, served as they would be in their country of origin:

Mozzarella fresca (fresh Mozzarella) Originally made from buffalo milk (but now often from cow's milk), this soft white cheese is to be seen in some shops in little plastic bags steeping in a bowl of cold water, which is the way it should also be stored at home in the refrigerator. Serve it cut into slices, with some sliced tomatoes, rock salt and coarsely ground pepper, and a drizzle of olive oil poured over.

Feta This crumbly, creamy-tasting cheese is the basis of a *Greek salad*. The recipe for this delicious salad is given in the Cheese chapter.

Crudités
This is the generic title for various arrangements of raw vegetables or salad ingredients, served with a sauce such as *Aioli sauce* (see page 484) or *Avocado sauce* (page 445). The different vegetables are often cut into long strips, dipped into the sauce, and then eaten with the fingers. An alternative—and perhaps better—arrangement is to shred or grate the ingredients. Grated carrot, shredded raw cabbage, thin slivers of raw fennel, some slices of cucumber, and thin strips of red or green pepper would make an attractive combination. Prepare each ingredient in separate bowls and sprinkle over a little (not too much) vinaigrette. Then arrange a selection of the vegetables in a pretty pattern on each plate, spooning a dollop of *Aioli sauce* or *Avocado sauce* in the centre.

Asparagus and globe artichokes
In their season these make excellent starters. Details for cooking and serving both of them are included in the Vegetables chapter on pages 256 and 270.

Fish
Most varieties of smoked fish and shellfish can be served as starters; apart from the recipes and suggestions here there are others, for fresh fish, in the Fish chapter; see the list at the end of this chapter. Other fish that might be considered are:

Sardines Portuguese are the best and are delicious served with nothing more than a little tomato salad and some crusty bread. Or as a variation you might try the following:

Sardine-stuffed tomatoes
For 4–6 people, mash up the contents of two tins of sardines (oil as well), then add to this 3 inches (7·5 cm) of cucumber finely chopped, half a green pepper finely chopped, 2 tablespoons of mayonnaise,

1 clove of garlic crushed, a generous pinch of cayenne and
2 tablespoons of lemon juice. Season the mixture well, then pack it
into 8 small or 6 largish hollowed-out and well-drained tomatoes.
Serve with some wholewheat bread and butter.

Pickled herrings (rollmops) These can be bought in jars from any
supermarket, and I always find it best to rinse them under a cold tap
then pat them dry with kitchen paper, in case they are too vinegary.
Serve them with sliced pickled dill cucumber, chopped beetroot and
soured cream. A similarly interesting first course is:

Russian herring
Place a slice of buttered rye bread on four small plates, and on top of
each slice arrange one pickled herring folded into three. Top this
with some thinly sliced onion rings. followed by a whole slice of
apple (Cox's are good). Finally cover with a dollop of soured
cream—5 fl oz (150 ml) for four people—and scatter some fresh
snipped chives all over.

A recipe for *Soused herrings* is given on page 129.

Tuna This is very useful. It can be flaked over a *Salad Niçoise* (page
498), which can be served as a first course provided the portions are
not too large; or it goes particularly well with white beans—see the
recipe on page 80.

Anchovies These are always a good standby in the larder, and
especially for making first courses. They can be used as a simple
hors-d'oeuvre accompanied by a few salad ingredients, or if you
want to make *Egg mayonnaise* with bought mayonnaise (salad cream
just *won't* do) add a few strips of anchovy as a garnish.

Melon
There are several types of melon which, if they are bought in good
condition, can make a very nice start to a meal. My complaint is
that in some restaurants the melon is often served over-chilled—or
worse still, it has been kept uncovered in the refrigerator and has
absorbed other flavours! So always store melons in sealed polythene
bags, and remember to bring them out of the fridge in time to reach
room temperature.

To test melons for ripeness, press the opposite end of the fruit
from the stalk with your thumb—if it gives a bit, then the fruit is
ripe. A ripe melon should smell fragrant too.

Although sugar and ginger are traditional accompaniments, in my opinion a good melon doesn't need anything at all to go with it. I once had a beautiful Cantaloupe melon ruined by being drowned in port (all I could taste in the end was the port). However a good summery starter would be a mixture of chopped melon and some halved, de-pipped grapes sprinkled with lots of fresh chopped mint and a dressing (made with one part cider vinegar to four parts oil). Served in glass goblets it does look most attractive.

The most popular varieties of melon are:

Cantaloupe (musk melon) These are usually small and green, with a very rough skin. Inside the flesh is deep orange with a lovely perfumed flavour.

Charentais These too are small melons, with a yellow-green skin and a golden yellow flesh with a distinctive flavour.

Ogen This is another small melon, easily distinguished by its yellow and green striped skin. Inside the flesh is green.

Honeydew These are larger and more commonly available than the others. Sometimes they sport a dark green skin, sometimes a bright yellow one. The flavour depends on their ripeness: a really ripe one will be juicy and fragrant, an under-ripe one watery and tasteless.

Fresh fruit and mint vinaigrette

(serves 6 people)

This is an unusual first course which really sharpens the appetite. I like to serve it in tall, stemmed glasses which makes it look pretty and appealing.

2 dessert apples, cored and diced but with skins left on
2 medium-sized pears, cored and diced but unpeeled
The juice of half a lemon
2 oranges, peeled and cut into chunks
4 oz grapes, halved and de-pipped (110 g)
1 tablespoon fresh chopped mint

For the dressing:
3 tablespoons wine vinegar
6 tablespoons olive oil

1 level teaspoon salt
4 tablespoons double cream

To garnish:
6 springs fresh mint

Dice the apples and pears straight into a bowl, and pour the lemon juice over them to prevent discolouring. Stir gently to coat all the pieces, then add the grapes and orange chunks, stir in the chopped mint, cover the bowl with clingfilm and chill in the fridge for a couple of hours.

To make the dressing, place the salt and wine vinegar in a bowl, leave for a few minutes for the salt to dissolve, then add the olive oil. Whisk well to blend, then stir in the double cream.

When you're ready to serve, divide the fruit among six glasses, pour the dressing over and garnish each with a sprig of fresh mint.

Avocado vinaigrette

(serves 6 people)

This is one of my own favourite first courses, if the avocados are buttery soft and the vinaigrette is well made.

3 ripe avocados
1 quantity of vinaigrette dressing (see page 482), using a large clove of garlic
6 crisp lettuce leaves
1 tablespoon fresh snipped chives

Ideally the avocados shouldn't be halved until just before serving, but if you're at all anxious as to whether they're sound or not then you can halve them and have a look about an hour before serving— but *don't* remove the stone. If they look sound, then just replace the halves together and wrap in clingfilm.

To serve, split the avocados in half and remove the stones. If at all possible, don't do this until *just* before serving because they do tend to discolour quickly. Serve each half on a crisp lettuce leaf (if it won't sit straight, make a depression on the underside with your thumb, and this might help), spoon some of the vinaigrette into the hollows left by the stone and sprinkle with the chives. Have some extra dressing on the table along with some crusty bread and creamy butter.

Avocado mousse with prawns and vinaigrette

(serves 8 people)

This is a delicious, creamy and most attractive starter to a dinner party. But don't make it too far in advance as it tends to lose its beautiful colour.

2 ripe avocados
½ oz powdered gelatine (10 g)
5 fl oz hot chicken stock (150 ml)
The juice of half a lemon
1 clove garlic, finely chopped
5 fl oz double cream, lightly whipped (150 ml)
5 fl oz mayonnaise—see page 483 (150 ml)
3 oz peeled prawns (75 g)
Salt and freshly-milled black pepper
1 quantity vinaigrette dressing (page 482)

8 small ramekins, lightly oiled.

Put 3 tablespoons of the stock and the gelatine in a bowl and stand it in a pan of simmering water. Stir until the gelatine is dissolved, then pour into the goblet of a liquidiser with the rest of the stock. Next skin and stone the avocados, chop the flesh roughly and add it to the liquidiser (include the darker green part that clings to the skin—this will help the colour). Now add the lemon juice and garlic, and blend until it's completely smooth.

Empty the mixture into a bowl and stir in the whipped cream and the mayonnaise very thoroughly, then season with salt and pepper. Spoon the mixture into the lightly-oiled ramekins, cover them with clingfilm and pop them into the fridge to set.

When you're ready to serve, slide a palette knife around the edge of each ramekin and ease the mousse away from the sides. Turn the mousses out onto serving plates, top each one of them with some of the prawns, and sprinkle some vinaigrette over each serving. Have plenty of crusty bread ready to go with this.

Avocado and seafood salad

(serves 4 people)

A distinct improvement on the inevitable prawn cocktail as a starter.

4 oz peeled prawns or fresh crabmeat (110 g)
2 ripe avocados

| 1 quantity of yoghurt seafood sauce (see page 536) |
| A few crisp lettuce leaves, shredded |

| *For the garnish:* |
| Cayenne pepper |
| 4 lemon wedges |
| 4 sprigs watercress or some chopped parsley |

First halve and peel the avocados, removing the stones, then chop the flesh into small (¹/₂ inch, 1 cm) pieces. Now arrange some shredded lettuce in 4 stemmed glasses or bowls, and divide the chopped avocados equally between each one. Next sprinkle the prawns—equally—over the avocado, then spoon the sauce over. Serve each one with a wedge of lemon to squeeze over, a faint dusting of cayenne pepper, and a sprig of watercress or some chopped parsley as a garnish.

Marinaded mushrooms

(serves 4 people)

These have a really delicious flavour and can be made well ahead.

| 8 oz dark-gilled mushrooms, wiped and sliced (225 g) |
| 6 rashers streaky bacon, chopped small |
| 2 cloves garlic, very finely chopped |
| 4 tablespoons olive oil |
| 8 fl oz red wine (225 ml) |
| 2 tablespoons fresh chopped parsley |
| 6 lettuce leaves |
| Salt and freshly-milled black pepper |

Heat the olive oil in a large frying pan, then add the chopped bacon and fry until the fat begins to run. Then add the sliced mushrooms along with the garlic, and cook for another couple of minutes— shaking the pan and stirring the mushrooms around all the time. Now pour in the red wine, turn the heat up high and let it all bubble for a minute or two and reduce a little.

Turn the heat down and cook for a further 4 minutes. Season to taste and transfer to a serving dish. Allow the mushrooms to cool before popping the dish into the refrigerator to chill. Serve on crisp lettuce leaves with some fresh chopped parsley sprinkled on top.

White bean and tuna fish salad

(serves 6 people)

This Italian dish (otherwise known as *Tonno e fagioli*) is one of my husband's favourite first courses—so I have to include it here!

8 oz haricot beans (long variety) (225 g)
1 onion, cut in half
1 carrot, cut into chunks
1 bayleaf
1 sprig of thyme
7 oz tin tuna fish in oil (200 g)
1 Spanish onion, sliced thinly and separated into rings
2 level tablespoons chopped parsley
Salt and freshly-milled black pepper
Crisp lettuce leaves for serving

For the dressing:
1 tablespoon lemon juice
1 teaspoon wine vinegar
1 teaspoon dried mustard powder
1 teaspoon salt
Freshly-milled black pepper
2 cloves garlic, crushed
5 tablespoons olive oil

The beans should be soaked overnight, or else covered with plenty of cold water, brought to the boil, simmered for 5 minutes, then left to soak for two hours. After that add the onion halves, carrot, bayleaf and thyme (but don't add any salt) and simmer the beans again for about an hour—or until they're tender.

While they are cooking make the dressing (directions on page 482). Then as soon as the beans are cooked, drain them thoroughly in a colander, removing the onion, carrot and herbs, and tip them into a large salad bowl. Pour the dressing over them while they are still warm (so they can really soak up all the delicious flavours).

Meanwhile drain the tuna fish and break it up into largish flakes. When the beans have cooled, and you're ready to serve, stir in the onion rings, tuna flakes and parsley. Taste and season with salt and pepper, then arrange on six plates lined with lettuce leaves, and sprinkle more parsley over each serving if you like.

Asparagus and cheese tart

(serves 4–6 people)

For those who don't grow their own asparatus—and have to pay high prices in the market—here is a recipe for a first course that makes a little go a long way.

For the pastry:
4 oz plain flour (110 g)
A pinch of salt
1 oz lard (25 g)
1 oz margarine (25 g)
Cold water, to mix

For the filling:
¾ lb asparagus (350 g), approximately 15 medium-sized stalks
2 large fresh eggs
1½ oz Cheddar cheese, grated (40 g)
1 level tablespoon grated Parmesan cheese
½ pint double cream (275 ml)
Salt and freshly-milled black pepper

Pre-heat the oven to gas mark 4, 350°F (180°C) and pop a baking sheet in to pre-heat as well.

An 8 inch (20 cm) round flan tin, greased.

First of all make up the pastry, then roll it out and line a flan tin with it. Prick the base all over with a fork and cook for 10 minutes, then take it out of the oven and turn the heat up to gas mark 5, 375°F (190°C).

The asparagus meanwhile should be half-cooked (five minutes in a steamer), then cut into 1½ inch (4 cm) lengths. Arrange the asparagus evenly over the pastry base, then sprinkle on the Cheddar cheese. Now whisk the eggs until frothy, and beat them into the cream together with a good seasoning of salt and freshly-milled black pepper. Pour this cream mixture over the asparagus and cheese, and sprinkle the Parmesan on top.

Place the tart on the pre-heated baking sheet in the oven for 40–45 minutes, or until the centre is firm and the filling golden-brown and puffy. This tart is delicious eaten hot or cold.

Smoked fish creams
(serves 8 people)

Serve these light, puffy little creams garnished with plenty of watercress and some *Hollandaise sauce* (page 437) as a sauce. A delicious first course for a special occasion.

10 oz smoked haddock fillets (275 g)
2 eggs, lightly beaten
Whole nutmeg
½ pint double cream (275 ml)
Salt and freshly-milled black pepper

Eight 2½ inch (6 cm) ramekin dishes, well buttered.

Begin by carefully skinning the fish (you should have about 8 oz (225 g) of flesh after this). Cut the fish into pieces about 1½ inches (3·5 cm) square and place them in a liquidiser or food processor, along with a little salt, pepper and some freshly grated nutmeg. Switch the machine on and blend until the fish has turned to a smooth, even pulp. Then blend in the lightly beaten eggs. Transfer the mixture to a bowl, cover with clingfilm and leave it in the fridge overnight, or at least for 6 hours.

When you're ready to cook the fish creams, pre-heat the oven to gas mark 5, 375°F (190°C). Fill a large roasting tin with about 1 inch (2·5 cm) of boiling water and put this on the centre shelf of the oven. Next return the fish mixture to the liquidiser together with the cream, and blend them together thoroughly. Fill each ramekin three-quarters full with the mixture, then place all the ramekins in the tin containing the hot water. Cook for exactly 30 minutes. Serve the creams immediately, either in the ramekins or turned out onto plates (do this by holding each ramekin with a cloth, tipping the creams upside down onto the palm of your hand and then straight onto a plate the right way up).

Country pâté
(serves 10–12 people)

This is a rough well-seasoned pâté—good for outdoor eating or for lunch with lots of crusty bread, a salad and some 'country' wine.

12 oz lean minced beef (350 g)
10 oz lean bacon, chopped small (275 g)
1 lb fat belly pork, minced (450 g)
8 oz pig's liver, minced (225 g)
1 or 2 cloves garlic, crushed
4 fl oz dry white wine (110 ml)
1 fl oz brandy (25 ml)
15 black peppercorns
10 juniper berries
1 rounded teaspoon salt
¼ teaspoon ground mace

A 2 lb (900 g) loaf tin or terrine.

The weight given in the ingredients for the meats is *before* preparing
e.g. removing rinds and bones from the pork and bacon, fat from the
beef and tubes from the liver. If you give your butcher plenty of
notice, he'll probably mince your meats for you. If not, use the
medium blade of a mincer or chop them in a food processor.

To make the pâté, place the meats and bacon in a large bowl and
mix them all very thoroughly. Add the salt, mace and garlic. Crush
the peppercorns and juniper berries on a flat surface using the back
of a tablespoon, then add to the meat.

Now pour the wine and brandy over, have another really good mix,
then cover the bowl with a cloth and leave it in a cool place for a
couple of hours. Before cooking the pâté, pre-heat the oven to gas
mark 2, 300°F (150°C). Then pack the mixture into a loaf tin and
place that in a meat-roasting tin half-filled with hot water. Bake for
about 1¾ hours. By the time it has cooked the pâté will have
shrunk quite a bit. Remove it from the oven and allow to cool
without draining off any of the juices (because when cold, the
surrounding fat will keep the pâté moist).

When the pâté is cold, place a double strip of foil across the top and
put a few weights on to press it down for a few hours—this pressing
isn't essential but it helps to make the pâté less crumbly when you
cut it. Serve with hot toast, crusty bread, or croûtons baked until
crisp in the oven.

Chicken liver pâté

(serves 4–6 people)

This is a fine smooth velvety pâté, which will serve 4 people for lunch or 6 people as a first course.

8 oz chicken livers (225 g)
6 oz butter, room temperature (175 g)
2 extra oz butter, for melting (50 g)
2 tablespoons brandy
2 level teaspoons mustard powder
¼ teaspoon powdered mace
1 level teaspoon fresh chopped thyme, or ¼ teaspoon dried thyme
2 cloves garlic, crushed
Salt and freshly-milled black pepper

Take a good thick frying pan, melt about 1 oz (25 g) butter in it, and fry the chicken livers over a medium heat for about 5 minutes. Keep them on the move, turning them over quite frequently. Then remove them from the pan, using a draining spoon and transfer them to an electric blender, or press them through a nylon sieve.

Now melt the rest of the 6 oz (175 g) butter and add this to the blender. Then pour the brandy onto the juices left in the frying pan (this is to rinse it out), and pour that over the liver. Then add the mustard, mace, thyme and garlic, season well with salt and pepper, and blend till you have a smooth purée.

Next press the whole lot into an earthenware pot, or 6 individual pots, pour the 2 oz (50 g) melted butter over, leave it to get quite cold, then cover with foil or clingfilm and leave it in the bottom of the fridge for a day or two. This is nice served with hot toast, sprigs of watercress, some silver-skinned onions and a few gherkins.

Rillettes de Tours (pork pâté)

(serves 6–8 people)

This is famous around the Loire district of France and sold everywhere in charcuteries—sometimes in thick chunks from a large terrine or packed into little pots. I would recommend this for anyone who doesn't like liver pâtés.

2 lb piece lean belly pork (900 g)—ask the butcher to remove rind and bones for you

8 oz back pork fat (225 g)
4 fl oz dry white wine (110 ml)
½ teaspoon powdered mace
10 black peppercorns
10 juniper berries
2 cloves garlic, crushed
1 dessertspoon fresh thyme (or 1 rounded teaspoon dried thyme)
1 heaped teaspoon salt

Pre-heat the oven to gas mark 1,
275°F (140°C)

A 2 pint (1·25 litre) earthenware terrine.

With your sharpest knife, cut the pork lengthwise into long strips about 1 inch (2·5 cm) wide, then cut each strip across and across again into smaller strips, and place these in the earthenware terrine. Cut the fat into small pieces too, and mix these in (the excess fat will help to keep the pork properly moist during the cooking). Now add the thyme, mace, salt and garlic along with the peppercorns and juniper berries (the last two both crushed with the back of a tablespoon). Then pour in the wine.

Mix everything around to distribute the flavours, cover the terrine, place it in the centre of the oven and leave it there for 4 hours. After that, taste a piece of pork and add more salt (and pepper) if necessary. Now empty everything into a large sieve standing over a bowl and let all the fat drip through (press the meat gently to extract the fat). Leave the drained fat to get cold.

Next take a couple of forks, and pull the strips of meat into shreds (sometimes it is pounded instead, but personally I think it's worth persevering with the fork method). Then pack the *rillettes* lightly into the terrine, and leave to get cold. After that, remove the jelly from the bowl of fat, melt it gently and pour it over the *rillettes*. Then spread a layer of fat over the top to keep it moist. Keep the *rillettes* in a cool place or in the lowest part of the refrigerator (covered with foil or clingfilm) till needed. Serve with hot toast, crusty bread or crisp baked croûtons.

Taramasalata

(serves 8 people)

This is the nicest version of this Greek smoked cod's roe pâté that I've tasted—the recipe comes from Mrs. Neil of Highbullen in North Devon and makes a really delicious first course for 8 people.

½ lb smoked cod's roe (225 g)
½ pint mild olive or groundnut oil (275 ml) —you may need an extra ¼ pint (150 ml)
Juice of half a lemon
1 clove garlic
1 tablespoon fresh chopped parsley
A little boiling water

Before you start, the cod's roe should be soaked in cold water for at least a couple of hours, then rinse and drain it thoroughly before peeling off the skin. Now put the roe in a mixing bowl and mash it first to a pulp using a fork, then, with an electric beater, whisk it at top speed, gradually pouring in the lemon juice.

Now start adding the oil a drop at a time (still whisking as you would when making mayonnaise) and keep adding oil until the mixture becomes solid and dry—forming lumps and working its way up the sides of the bowl. At this stage you can start to beat in a little boiling water, say 2 fl oz (55 ml) or just enough to turn the mixture into a soft mousse. (Don't add the water before the mixture has become solid or it will separate.) Then stir in the chopped parsley and crushed garlic and serve straight away.

Smoked mackerel pâté

(serves 8–10 people)

There was a time when smoked mackerel was a rarity, but now it's become very popular and is almost as widely distributed as kippers. In this recipe, you only need two smoked mackerel to feed 8–10 people as a first course for a dinner party, and the pâté can be made well in advance, so there is no last minute preparation. More information on smoked fish will be found in the Fish chapter.

2 medium smoked mackerel
5 fl oz soured cream (150 ml)
4 oz cottage cheese (110 g)
Juice of half a large lemon
Salt, freshly-milled black pepper and nutmeg

For the garnish:
A large lemon, cut in wedges
1 bunch watercress
Couple of pinches cayenne pepper

First skin the mackerel then carefully remove all the fish from the bones (if the mackerel are already filleted simply scrape the flesh from the skins). Now flake the fish, and place it in the goblet of a liquidiser, then add the cottage cheese, soured cream and lemon juice. Switch on and blend until completely smooth, stopping the motor and stirring the mixture half way through if you need to.

Next, spoon the mixture into a bowl, taste and season with salt and freshly-milled black pepper, a pinch of nutmeg, plus a spot more lemon juice if you think it needs it. Pack into individual dishes, cover with foil and chill for several hours before serving.

To serve, sprinkle on a touch of cayenne pepper, garnish with watercress and lemon wedges and serve with wholemeal toast.

Smoked fish pâté

(serves 8–10 people)

You can use any combination of smoked fish for this delicious first course.

1 medium-sized smoked trout
1 medium-sized smoked mackerel
¼ lb smoked eel (110 g)
¼ lb smoked salmon (110 g) (small, cheaper scraps are perfectly good for this recipe)
½ lb butter, at room temperature (225 g)
1 heaped teaspoon very finely chopped raw onion (optional)
Juice of a small lemon
Nutmeg
Salt and cayenne pepper
Watercress and lemon quarters for garnishing

To make the pâté, skin all the fish and take all the flesh from the bones—this is much easier than it sounds, and you'll find the flesh comes away quite easily. Put the trout, mackerel and eel into a large mixing bowl, and then chop the smoked salmon very finely (in fact chop it in the same way as you would chop parsley—into minute pieces). Now add the salmon to the other fish then, with a large fork, mash thoroughly until you have a fairly smooth paste.

At this point I like to add one heaped teaspoon of very finely chopped raw onion, but you can leave it out if you don't like it. Next, using a fork, mash and blend the whole lot with the butter and lemon juice. Then add about a quarter of a whole nutmeg, freshly-grated, then taste it and season with as much salt and cayenne pepper as you think it needs.

Now pack it into a dish or terrine, cover it well and chill lightly for an hour or two. Serve the pâté with baked croûtons or hot toast, plus a few lemon quarters to squeeze over and a few sprigs of watercress to make it look pretty.

See also:

Alpine eggs
Courgettes and tomatoes au gratin
Dressed crab
Eggs chapter
Eggs en cocotte with soured cream and asparagus
Fillets of sole gratiné
Globe artichokes
Goujons of sole
Guacamole
Hot crab soufflé

Hummus bi tahina
Mixed vegetables à la Grècque
Moules à la marinère
Mussels with garlic stuffing
Potted haddock with capers
Provençal vegetable stew
Risotto alla Milanese
Scallops in the shell
Soused herrings
Stocks and soups chapter
Turkish stuffed tomatoes
Whitebait

Stocks and soups

Including recipes for:
Brown beef stock
Light beef stock
Pressure-cooked beef stock
Chicken giblet stock
Chicken carcass stock
Pressure-cooked chicken stock
Turkey giblet stock
Fish stock
Leek, onion and potato soup
Minestrone soup with rice
Chilled avocado soup
Gardeners' soup
Smoked bacon and lentil soup

Chilled beetroot consommé
Scotch broth
Watercress cream soup
Punchnep soup
Soupe à l'oignon gratinée
Eliza Acton's vegetable mulligatawny
Chilled Spanish gazpacho
Fresh tomato soup with basil
Chinese mushroom soup
Carrot and artichoke soup
Cream of celery soup
Tomato, apple and celery cream soup
Garlicky fish soup

I can recall a time, not so long ago, when home-made soups seemed to be in a period of decline: perhaps the combination of increased affluence after the war and the advent of tinned, dehydrated and instant soups gave us less incentive to make our own. Thankfully I feel that home-made soups are now making a comeback. Where once we could overlook the bland uniformity of a ready-made soup at a price, in these days of world shortages and inflation we've grown more critical. I believe that you can spend either money or time on food, and lately many people have found they have had rather more time than money and that 30 minutes' preparation can produce a soup at half the cost of and with twice the flavour of a tin.

Of course economy is not the only reason for making a proper soup. There's something wholesome and comforting about a soup made with care from fresh, natural ingredients. It is filling, satisfying and above all easy. However I would emphasize the word care, because simply throwing together any old hotch-potch of ingredients—however good they may be individually—can result in no real flavour whatsoever. Dried bean soups, which can be a meal in themselves, are dealt with in the Pulses chapter.

Stocks are the basis of many soups (and indeed casseroles—see the chapter on these). Like soups, home-made stocks have been eclipsed by the huge range of commercial alternatives, and the dilemma facing us is the same. So first let's see what is involved in making stock at home.

Stock

The first thing to say about making basic stock for soups and casseroles is that it is *not* as much bother as it sometimes sounds. For a start a proper stock-pot—the sort that needs endless boiling-up and skimming—isn't really needed in today's family kitchen. What I think is more useful is one occasional stock-making session. Freezer owners can freeze any surplus and use it on another occasion.

All that is actually involved is bones, carcasses or giblets plus a few other ingredients being simmered, totally unattended. A rich brown stock is the only one that requires the bones to be roasted first, and even this doesn't call for any real work. The results will produce goodness and flavour at a minimal cost, and will prove how well spent in these days of chemical flavourings just a few minutes of your own time can be.

Is home-made stock necessary?

Not always. Especially with many vegetable soups, bearing in mind that most vegetables have lots of good fresh flavour of their own, introducing a meat-flavoured stock can conflict with and spoil the original vegetable flavour. On the other hand, a meaty stock makes the world of difference to clear-based soups (like *Soupe à l'oignon* or *Minestrone*), and I nearly always use some sort of stock to give body to soups made with dried vegetables and pulses.

Stock cubes

If you were making a soup containing the delicious juices and flavour of, say, a pound of leeks and the same amount of carrots, would you *really* want (or need) to add ingredients like hydrolised protein, ribonucleotides, and monosodium glutamate? These, and several others, are ingredients to be found in the various stock cubes available, and it is my opinion that they are very often totally opposed to the flavour of natural ingredients. Unless you positively happen to like the taste of stock cubes (which as far as I'm concerned never come close to the chicken, beef or whatever they're supposed to be derived from) then I suggest you don't use them. It has been suggested that because of their overpowering flavour, stock cubes need a lot more watering down than is usually recommended—but then why really bother in the first place?

Some principles of stock-making

Simmering An important word in the vocabulary of stock and soup making. Fast boiling can turn a stock very cloudy and murky, or ruin the delicate flavour of a fresh vegetable soup. So always keep everything at a *gentle* simmer.

Skimming When you're boiling bones, giblets or a chicken carcass, a certain amount of scum inevitably rises to the surface. To get rid of this it's important to skim the surface right away. Quite easy to do: just slide a large spoon horizontally across the surface and gently lift off and discard the scum.

Removing fat Marrowbones, oxtails, neck of lamb etc all give off a certain amount of fat while they're cooking, and there are two ways of dealing with this. First, if you allow the stock or soup to settle for about 30 minutes after cooking, you can skim some of the fat from the surface as above. What is also helpful here is to lay a double sheet of absorbent paper on the surface, to float as it were, and absorb the fat (sometimes it needs two or three lots to remove the fat completely). The other way, and this de-greases *more* thoroughly, is to leave the whole thing to cool overnight, and next morning you'll find the fat has solidified on the top and you can remove it completely.

Reducing If, after straining and de-greasing, you feel your stock needs more concentrated flavour, bring it back to the boil and simmer *without* the lid on so that some of the liquid evaporates. Simmer until the flavour of the stock is as concentrated as you want it to be. One of the great French chefs, Michel Guérard, in his book *Cuisine Gourmande* actually gives some directions for a concentrated jellied fish stock, by reducing 1³⁄₄ pints (1 litre) of liquid down to seven tablespoons!

Brown beef stock

Butchers will chop up and sell you marrowbones for just a few pence.

3 lb beef marrowbones, in pieces, (approx 1·5 kg)
2 onions, peeled and quartered
2 large carrots, peeled and cut into chunks
3 celery stalks, each cut into three pieces
A few parsley stalks
1 bayleaf
8 whole black peppercorns
1 blade mace
1 teaspoon salt
¼ teaspoon dried thyme
4—5 pints cold water (2¼—3 litres)

Pre-heat the oven to gas mark 8, 450°F (230°C)

Begin by placing the bones in a meat roasting tin, tucking the chunks of carrot, quartered onion and celery in amongst them. Now, without adding any fat, just pop the roasting tin onto a high shelf in the oven and leave it there for 45 minutes, basting with the juices now and then. After that both the bones and the vegetables will have turned brown at the edges. Now transfer them all to the very largest cooking pot you own, add enough cold water just to cover everything, add the rest of the ingredients, then as soon as it

reaches boiling point remove the scum and lower the heat. Put the
lid on but not completely (leave a little gap for the steam to escape
thereby reducing and concentrating the stock). Now simmer very
gently for about 4 hours. When the stock is ready, strain it into a
clean pan, leave it to become quite cold, then remove the congealed
fat from the surface. The stock is now ready for use, or for freezing
for later use.

Light beef stock
If you want a pale coloured stock, use the same ingredients as above
and follow the same instructions but leave out the initial roasting of
the bones and vegetables.

Pressure-cooked beef stock

This method, of course, cuts the cooking
time down to an incredible 40 minutes.
You can't make such a large quantity,
but the resulting stock will have a more
concentrated flavour and you can dilute
it afterwards.

2½ lb beef marrowbones, in pieces (approx 1 kg)
2 pints cold water (just over 1 litre)
1 small onion
1 carrot, cut into chunks
1 celery stalk halved (plus leaves)
1 small bunch parsley stalks
1 bayleaf
5 whole black peppercorns
1 small blade mace
1 teaspoon salt

Place the bones in the pressure-cooker along with the water. Bring
to the boil, then remove any scum with a spoon. Now add the
remaining ingredients, put the lid on the cooker and bring to
pressure. Then place the 15 lb weight on and cook for 40 minutes.
Reduce the pressure by allowing the cooker to cool slightly, then
place it under cold running water to release. Strain the stock, leave
to cool, then remove the fat from the surface.

Chicken giblet stock

This stock is useful not only for soups, but also for chicken casseroles, cooking rice, and making gravies and sauces.

12 oz chicken giblets, washed (350 g)
2 pints cold water (1·25 litres)
1 carrot, cut into chunks
1 onion, quartered
1 celery stick, halved
1 leek, sliced
6 whole black peppercorns
¾ teaspoon salt
A few parsley stalks
2 pinches dried herbs (or sprig of fresh thyme)

The general rule is to use 1 pint (570 ml) water per set of giblets, or if you're buying frozen giblets (which are a godsend for stock) use 6 oz (175 g) giblets per 1 pint water. If you are using fresh giblets and don't need the liver for making a stuffing, do add it to the stock as well—I think it adds a real richness of flavour.

Just put everything into a large cooking pot, bring to the boil, skim the surface to remove any scum, then simmer gently with the lid almost on for 2 hours. After that strain the stock, cool it and remove the fat from the surface before using or freezing.

Chicken carcass stock
Use the same vegetables, herbs and flavourings as in the above recipe, adding them to the cooking pot along with the broken-up carcass of the bird (plus any odd bits of bone and skin). Add enough cold water to cover, then proceed as above.

Pressure-cooked chicken stock
Proceed as above with vegetables, herbs and flavourings and either giblets or carcass, plus 2 pints (1¼ litres) of water. Bring to pressure and cook with 15 lb pressure for 30 minutes.

Turkey giblet stock

The giblets (including the liver) and neck of the turkey
1 onion, sliced in half
A few parsley stalks

A chunk of celery stalk and a few leaves
1 bayleaf
6 whole black peppercorns
Salt

Wash the giblets first, then place them in a saucepan with the halved onion, cover with 1½ pints (855 ml) of water and bring to simmering point. Then remove surface scum with a slotted spoon, add the remaining ingredients, half cover the pan and simmer for 1½–2 hours. After that strain the stock, and bring up to boiling point again before using to make the gravy.

Fish stock Use this as the basis for all kinds of fish soup.

1 lb fish trimmings (450 g—whatever your fishmonger can rustle up for you)
1 pint water (570 ml)
1 onion, quartered
2 sticks celery, chopped
A few parsley sprigs
1 bayleaf
¼ teaspoon dried thyme
¼ pint dry white wine (140 ml)
Salt and freshly-milled black pepper

Simply place the fish trimmings in a large pan, with the water, wine and the rest of the stock ingredients, season with salt and pepper, then bring up to simmering point. Simmer for about 20 minutes (without a lid on), then strain and reserve the stock.

Soups
Some principles of soup making
Sweating I have found that a better flavour is produced in vegetable soups if the chopped vegetables are stirred into a little melted butter quite thoroughly until they're all glistening and well-coated. Then, with a little salt added, they are placed over the gentlest heat possible and the pan is covered. The heat then draws out the natural juices and the vegetables become softened before the liquid is added. Care is needed for this, because too much heat will cause the vegetables to brown and spoil: so to prevent this you need to take

off the lid from time to time and just stir them around. This process is called 'sweating'.

Blending and puréeing There are several ways to purée a soup. First of all, a good old fashioned sieve will serve you very well: the contents of a soup pan can be pressed through it in a few minutes. Sieves can be difficult to wash, though, and perhaps a more satisfactory method is to whizz the soup to a purée in an electric liquidiser (blender). If you are using one of these, do remember that liquidising is liable to reduce food to a velvet-smooth consistency. Some people prefer a less uniform texture: this can be achieved if you take care to liquidise food very briefly indeed.

There is also available a gadget called a vegetable or food mill (see illustration). It can be used to purée fruit and vegetables very finely, to medium thickness or quite coarsely. Useful, but I find it needs rather intricate washing and careful drying.

Lastly there is now widely available a machine called a food processor (see page 20).

Rescue operations

Beware of over-seasoning a soup, especially (a) if you are using a stock that's already seasoned and (b) if you are reducing the stock or soup. A concentration of flavour will also mean a concentration of seasoning, and it's very easy to end up with a soup that's too salty. I recommend tasting and seasoning right at the end.

If for these or any other reasons you have *over-salted* a soup, you have two possibilities. One is to add more unsalted liquid to dilute the salty flavour, though this way you risk also diluting the overall flavour. The other is to add a couple of raw potatoes cut in half and allow these to cook gently in the soup. They will absorb quite a bit of saltiness which may put things right. Remember to remove the potatoes before serving.

If a soup is *too thin*, removing the lid and allowing it to simmer gently will reduce and thicken it (as described on page 92). Or, if you're short of time, you can make up a paste by mashing together softened butter and flour (say 1 tablespoon of each) then use a balloon whisk to whisk the paste into the soup; when it comes up to simmering point the soup will have thickened. Alternatively you can use arrowroot. This thickens liquid without clouding it—so it is the best choice for thickening a clear soup (see recipe for *Chinese mushroom soup*, page 108).

Another fast way to thicken anything, when you're in a hurry, is to add some ground rice. What is so good about this is that you can just plonk a couple of tablespoons of ground rice into the hot liquid (it won't go lumpy) and whisk with a balloon whisk till sufficiently thickened—and if not, add a bit more.

If on the other hand your soup is *too thick*, you can thin it down with milk or stock, or even plain water.

Having said all this, let me now reassure you that by following the recipes with care you should have none of these problems!

Leek, onion and potato soup

(serves 4–6 people)

I think this has to be my very favourite soup—if possible garnished with some fresh snipped chives and a swirl of cream.

4 large leeks
2 medium potatoes, peeled and diced
1 medium onion, chopped small
1½ pints light chicken stock or water (850 ml)
½ pint milk (275 ml)
2 oz butter (50 g)
2 tablespoons cream or top of the milk
1½ tablespoons fresh snipped chives (or, if unavailable, chopped parsley)
Salt and freshly-milled black pepper

Trim off the tops and roots of the leeks, discarding the tough outer layer. Now split them in half length-ways and slice them up quite finely, then wash them thoroughly in two or three changes of water and drain well.

In a large thick-based saucepan gently melt the butter, then add the leeks, potatoes and onion, stirring them all around with a wooden spoon so they get a nice coating of butter. Season with salt and pepper, then cover and let the vegetables sweat over a very low heat for about 15 minutes.

After that add the stock and milk, bring to simmering point, put the lid back on and let the soup simmer very gently for a further 20 minutes or until the vegetables are soft—if you have the heat too high, the milk in it may cause it to boil over. Now you can either put the whole lot into a liquidiser and blend to a purée, or else press it all through a sieve.

Return the soup to the saucepan and reheat gently, tasting to check the seasoning, and stirring in the chopped chives and adding a swirl of cream just before serving.

Note: the chilled version of this soup is called *Vichyssoise*.

Minestrone soup with rice

(serves 4–6 people)

This soup is really a meal in itself, especially if you have some home-made wholewheat bread to serve with it and perhaps a lump of cheese to follow.

8 oz leeks, washed and finely chopped (225 g)
2 sticks celery, washed and finely chopped
6 oz carrots, washed and finely chopped (175 g)
6 oz cabbage, washed and shredded (175 g)
2 tomatoes, fresh or from a tin
1 medium onion, finely chopped
2 oz streaky bacon, rinds removed and finely chopped (50 g)
1 tablespoon butter
1 tablespoon olive oil
1 clove of garlic, crushed
2½ pints any good home-made stock (1·5 litres)
1 teaspoon dried basil
2 tablespoons rice
1 dessertspoon tomato purée
2 tablespoons chopped parsley
Salt and freshly-milled black pepper
Lots of grated Parmesan cheese to serve with it

First heat up the butter and oil in a large saucepan, then add the bacon and cook this for a minute or two before adding the onion, followed by the celery and carrots and then the tomatoes, also chopped. Now stir in the crushed garlic and some salt and pepper, then cover and cook very gently for 20 minutes or so to allow the vegetables to sweat—give it an occasional stir to prevent the vegetables sticking.

Then pour in the stock along with the basil. Continue to simmer gently (covered) for about 1 hour. After that add the leeks, cabbage and rice and cook for a further 30 minutes.

Finally stir in the tomato purée, cook for another 10 minutes and, just before serving, stir in the parsley. Serve in warmed soup bowls and sprinkle with Parmesan cheese.

Note: in the autumn finely chopped courgettes—instead of the cabbage—make a nice change.

Chilled avocado soup
(serves 6 people)

This makes a lovely first course at a dinner party at any time of the year. It looks very pretty served in glass bowls to show of its pale pistachio green colour.

2 medium-sized, ripe avocado pears
1 clove garlic, crushed
1 tablespoon lemon juice
½ pint soured cream (275 ml)
1 pint cold chicken stock (570 ml)
Salt and freshly-milled black pepper

First halve the avocado pears, remove the stones and scoop out all the flesh—it's very important that you take care to scrape out all the very greenest part next to the skins, because this is what makes the soup such a lovely colour. Now chop the flesh roughly, and put it into the goblet of the liquidiser with the garlic, lemon juice, half the chicken stock and some salt and pepper.

Blend at high speed for about 15 seconds, then empty the contents into a soup tureen or bowl. Now stir in the soured cream and the rest of the stock, then whisk it a bit to get it all blended evenly. Cover the soup and chill very thoroughly for several hours. Serve it with one or two cubes of ice stirred in at the last minute.

Note: only make this soup on the day you intend to eat it, because if it's kept too long it tends to discolour.

Gardeners' soup

(serves 6–8 people)

This is a soup for autumn when there's nearly always a glut of tomatoes and the over-ripe ones are sold cheaply; or, as the title suggests, it's helpful for the gardeners whose tomato and cucumber crops threaten to overwhelm them.

¾ lb English cucumber, peeled and chopped (350 g)
¾ lb red ripe tomatoes (350 g)
1 medium potato, peeled and chopped
The outside leaves of a lettuce, shredded
1 small onion, finely chopped
1 clove garlic, crushed
1 pint hot water (570 ml) mixed with 1 teaspoon tomato purée
1 teaspoon dried basil
2 teaspoons freshly-chopped parsley
1 dessertspoon lemon juice
Butter
Oil
Salt and freshly-milled black pepper

First drop the tomatoes into boiling water then, after one minute, slip the skins off and chop the flesh roughly. Now in a thick-based saucepan melt one tablespoon of butter with one tablespoon of oil and soften the onion in it for 5 minutes. Next add the garlic, lettuce, cucumber, tomatoes and potato. Stir everything around, add seasoning and lemon juice, then pop the lid on and, keeping the heat low, let the vegetables sweat for a good 15 minutes.

Then add the basil and the hot water mixed with tomato purée, bring it up to simmering point, cover and simmer gently for a further 20 minutes or until the vegetables are soft.

Now pour the soup into a liquidiser, but only liquidise it for 6–8 seconds (the vegetables should be in very fine bits). Then sprinkle with parsley and serve hot with some fresh, crusty bread.

Smoked bacon and lentil soup

(serves 4–6 people)

This is another very substantial soup and, remember, brown lentils don't need any soaking.

6 oz green-brown whole lentils, washed and drained (175 g)
6 rashers smoked, streaky bacon de-rinded and finely chopped
2 carrots, chopped
2 medium onions, chopped
2 celery stalks, sliced
8 oz finely shredded cabbage (225 g)
8 oz tin Italian tomatoes (225 g)
2 cloves of garlic, crushed
3 pints home-make stock (1·75 litres)
1 tablespoon oil
Salt and freshly-milled black pepper
2 tablespoons chopped parsley

Heat the oil in a large cooking pot and fry the bacon in it until the fat begins to run. Then stir in the prepared vegetables (except the cabbage) and, with the heat fairly high, toss them around to brown them a little at the edges. Now stir in the washed, drained lentils plus the contents of the tin of tomatoes followed by the crushed garlic then the stock. As soon as the soup comes to the boil, put a lid on and simmer, as gently as possible, for about 1 hour. About 15 minutes before the end add the cabbage. Taste and season. Just before serving stir in the chopped parsley.

Chilled beetroot consommé

(serves 6 people)

This summer soup requires no fat for cooking and is suitable for slimmers if low fat yoghurt is used at the end. Be sure to use *raw* beetroot.

1½ lb raw beetroot, peeled and chopped (700 g)
10 large spring onions, chopped
2½ pints water (1·5 litres)
1 cucumber
A bouquet garni*
1 tablespoon red wine vinegar
1 tablespoon lemon juice
¼ pint natural yoghurt (150 ml)
2 tablespoons snipped chives to garnish
Salt and freshly-milled black pepper

* Bouquet garni—sprigs of thyme, 1 clove garlic, parsley, bayleaf and 2 strips of orange zest tied up in a piece of gauze.

Put the prepared beetroot in a large saucepan with the chopped spring onions, the water and the bouquet garni. Bring to the boil and simmer gently, uncovered, for about 1 hour. At the end of this time the beetroot will have lost its redness and have a pale look. Now peel and dice the cucumber, add it to the soup and simmer for about 10 minutes. Next, have ready a large sieve set over a suitable bowl: pour the soup through the sieve and leave it to drain through. You should now have a good clear soup. Season to taste and add a tablespoon of vinegar and a tablespoon of lemon juice to sharpen the flavour. Chill well and serve with a marbling of yoghurt and a garnish of snipped chives.

Scotch broth
(serves 6–8 people)

This soup really needs to be made a day in advance—so that the fat can be lifted off the surface easily when the soup is cold. Reheat and you'll have one of the best winter 'stomach warmers' I know.

2 lb neck of lamb, cut into even-sized pieces (900 g)
2 oz pearl barley, rinsed (50 g)
1 large carrot
1 medium turnip
1 medium onion
3 leeks
Half a small white cabbage
Chopped parsley
Salt and freshly-milled black pepper

Place the meat in a deep saucepan together with 3 pints (1·75 litres) cold water. Bring to the boil and skim off any scum which appears on the surface, then add the rinsed barley together with a little seasoning. Put a lid on the pan but tilt the lid slightly so that some of the steam can escape, then simmer, very gently, for about 1 hour.

Meanwhile prepare the vegetables: peel the carrot, turnip and onion and cut into ¼ inch dice (½ cm). Now trim the leeks, cutting off the root and leaving about 2 inches (5 cm) of green at the top. Halve lengthways, cut into small pieces, wash thoroughly, then drain well. Slice the cabbage thinly and wash and drain that well too.

When the broth has been cooking for 1 hour, add the vegetables. Bring to the boil again, half cover the pan with a lid and simmer gently until the vegetables are tender (about 45–60 minutes). Then remove from the heat and set aside to cool slightly.

Using a draining spoon, take out the meat and place it on a plate. Now separate the flesh from the bones, discard any fat and gristle as well as the bones, and return the meat to the pan. Leave until the soup is cold and the fat has solidified on top; scrape off the fat. When required, reheat the broth, season to taste and serve piping hot with a sprinkling of chopped parsley on top.

Watercress cream soup

(serves 4–6 people)

This is excellent at a dinner party and can, if you prefer, be served well chilled.

The white parts of 3 large leeks—approx 1 lb (450 g), washed and chopped
2 bunches watercress, de-stalked and chopped. Reserve 4 sprigs for garnishing
2 medium potatoes, peeled and chopped
2 oz butter (50 g)
1½ pints very light chicken stock (or water) (850 ml)
¼ pint double cream (150 ml)
Salt and freshly-milled black pepper

Melt the butter in a thick-based saucepan, then add the prepared leeks, potato and watercress and stir them around so that they're coated with the melted butter. Add some salt, cover with a lid and let the vegetables sweat over a low heat for about 20 minutes, giving the mixture a stir about halfway through.

After that, add the stock (or water), bring to simmering point and simmer, covered, for a further 10 to 15 minutes or until the vegetables are quite tender. Remove from the heat and when cool liquidise the soup—but not too vigorously. Return the soup to the saucepan, stir in the cream, season to taste and reheat gently. When serving, garnish each bowl with a sprig of watercress.

Punchnep soup

(serves 6–8 people)

Punchnep is a Scottish dish of creamed potatoes and creamed turnips cooked separately then whipped together (see page 293). This soup, based on that dish, has a lovely creamy texture.

1½ lb turnips, peeled and weighed after peeling (700 g)
1 large potato, peeled—about ½ lb (225 g) after peeling
The white parts of 2 leeks
2 oz butter (50 g)
1 pint milk (570 ml)
1 pint hot water (570 ml)
Freshly-grated nutmeg
2–3 tablespoons double cream
Salt and freshly-milled black pepper

First split the leeks in half lengthways and cut into pieces of about ¼ inch (½ cm), wash well in cold water and drain in a colander. Then cut the peeled turnip and potato into cubes.

Next melt the butter in a thick-based saucepan, add the vegetables and stir them around so that they're well coated with the butter. Season with a little salt and pepper, cover with a lid and, keeping the heat very low, cook gently for 15 minutes, stirring from time to time. Now pour in the hot water and milk, bring to simmering point and simmer, again gently, for approximately 15 minutes or so until the vegetables are absolutely tender.

Then liquidise the soup or rub it through a sieve placed over a large bowl. Rinse the saucepan, return the purée to the pan and reheat slowly. Season to taste with salt and freshly-milled black pepper and some freshly-grated nutmeg. Make sure the soup is piping hot then stir in a swirl of cream just before serving.

Soupe à l'oignon gratinée

(serves 6 people)

This is so French that I've kept its original title. It's very filling and warming but remember that only fireproof soup bowls can safely go under the grill. To make croûtons of French bread, cut the bread in diagonal slices and bake in a medium oven for 20–25 minutes until golden and crisp.

2 tablespoons butter
2 tablespoons oil
1½ lb onions, thinly sliced (700 g)
2 cloves garlic, crushed

½ teaspoon granulated sugar
2 pints good beef stock (1·25 litres)
½ pint dry white wine (275 ml)
6 large croûtons of French bread
8 oz Gruyère cheese, grated (225 g)
Salt and freshly-milled black pepper

In a large thick-based saucepan heat the butter and oil together. Add the prepared onions, garlic and sugar and cook over a low heat, stirring occasionally, for approximately 30 minutes or until the bottom of the pan is covered with a nutty brown, caramelized film. (This browning process improves both the colour and flavour.)

Next add the stock and wine, bring to the boil and simmer, covered, over a low heat for about 1 hour. Then season to taste and, if you're feeling in need of something extra specially warming, add one or two tablespoons of brandy.

Now spread the croûtons with butter and place one slice in each fireproof soup bowl. Ladle the soup carefully on top and, when the croûtons float to the surface, sprinkle with the grated cheese. Place under a hot grill and when nicely golden brown and bubbling serve immediately.

Eliza Acton's vegetable mulligatawny

(serves 4 people)

Eliza Acton is one of my very favourite cookery writers and this is a recipe from her cookery book published in 1840.

3 large onions, chopped
4 oz butter (110 g)
1½ lb peeled marrow or unpeeled courgettes (700 g)
½ lb tomatoes, skinned and chopped (225 g)
1 large potato
¾ pint stock or water (425 ml)
1 dessertspoon Worcester sauce
1 teaspoon Madras curry powder
Long grain rice measured to the 3 fl oz (75 ml) level in a measuring jug
Boiling water measured to the 6 fl oz (just over 150 ml) level in a measuring jug
Salt and freshly-milled black pepper

First melt the butter in a large saucepan, add the chopped onions and cook until they're golden brown colour. Meanwhile cut up the marrow into 1 inch (2·5 cm) cubes and peel and dice the potato. Now add these to the onions together with the tomatoes. Season well, then let the vegetables cook (covered) over a low heat until soft—about 20–30 minutes.

In the meantime put the rice in another saucepan with some salt, pour on the measured boiling water, bring to the boil, cover and cook gently until all the liquid is absorbed and the rice is tender.

Next, when the vegetables are cooked, turn them into a liquidiser and reduce to a purée. Then pour the purée back into the saucepan and stir in the cooked rice together with the stock, Worcester sauce and curry powder. This soup should have quite a strong flavour, so season to taste and add more curry powder if you think it needs it.

Reheat gently, cook for about five minutes more, then serve with some crisp croûtons of bread sprinkled in each bowl.

Chilled Spanish gazpacho

(serves 6 people)

This is a truly beautiful soup for serving ice-cold during the summer and it's particularly refreshing when the weather is hot. However, please don't attempt to make it in the winter as the flavourless imported salad vegetables will not do it justice.

1½ lb firm ripe tomatoes (700 g)
4 inch piece of cucumber, peeled and chopped (10 cm)
2 or 3 spring onions, peeled and chopped
Half a large red or green pepper, deseeded and chopped
2 cloves garlic, crushed
4 tablespoons olive oil
1½ tablespoons wine vinegar
1 heaped teaspoon fresh chopped basil, marjoram or thyme (depending on what's available)
About ½ pint cold water (275 ml)
Salt and freshly-milled black pepper

For the garnish:
Half a large red or green pepper, deseeded and very finely chopped
4 inch piece of cucumber, peeled and finely chopped (10 cm)
2 spring onions, finely chopped
1 hard-boiled egg, finely chopped
1 heaped tablespoon fresh chopped parsley
Salt and freshly-milled black pepper
4 ice cubes

Begin by placing the tomatoes in a bowl and pouring boiling water over them; after a minute or two the skins will loosen and slip off very easily. Halve the tomatoes, scoop out and discard the seeds and roughly chop the flesh.

Now place the tomatoes, cucumber, spring onions, crushed garlic and chopped pepper in a liquidiser, adding a seasoning of salt and pepper, the herbs, oil and wine vinegar. Then blend everything at top speed until the soup is absolutely smooth. (If your liquidiser is very small combine all the ingredients first, then blend in two or three batches.) Taste to check the seasoning and pour the soup into a bowl. Stir in a little cold water to thin it slightly—anything from $^1/_4$ to $^1/_2$ pint (150–275 ml)—then cover the bowl with foil and chill thoroughly.

To make the garnish, simply combine all the ingredients together with a seasoning of salt and freshly-milled black pepper, and hand them round at the table together with small croûtons of bread fried till crisp in olive oil, well drained and cooled. Serve the soup with four ice cubes floating in it.

Fresh tomato soup with basil

(serves 4 people)

1½ lb red, ripe tomatoes (700 g), cut in quarters (leave the skins on)
1 medium-sized onion, chopped small
1 medium-sized potato, chopped small
1 clove garlic, crushed
½ pint stock (275 ml)
2 teaspoons fresh, chopped basil
1½ tablespoons olive oil (preferably good quality)
Salt and freshly-milled black pepper

Gently heat up the olive oil in a thick saucepan, then put in the onion and potato and let them soften slowly without browning. This takes 10–15 minutes.

Now add the tomatoes, stir well and let them cook for a minute. Pour the stock over the tomatoes, stir, season with salt and pepper and add the garlic. Cover and allow to simmer for 25 minutes.

When the soup is ready, pass the whole lot through a sieve to extract the skins and pips. Taste to check the seasoning, add the basil, then re-heat and serve with crusty French bread. If the weather is hot, this soup is just as delicious served ice-cold.

Note: if you cannot get fresh basil use 1 teaspoon of dried, adding it at the same time as the tomatoes.

Chinese mushroom soup

(serves 4–6 people)

This needs a really good well-flavoured chicken stock as a base, then it provides a lovely light soup without too many calories.

¾ lb small flat mushrooms, finely chopped (350 g)
2 medium onions, finely chopped
1 tablespoon oil
3 pints good chicken stock (1·75 litres)
2 tablespoons long grain rice
2 dessertspoons arrowroot
4 spring onions, finely chopped
Salt and freshly-milled black pepper

Begin by heating the oil in a large saucepan then add the chopped onions and fry gently for about 10 minutes. Next add the prepared mushrooms, stir them around in the oil and cook for a minute or two. Now pour in the chicken stock, sprinkle in the rice and bring to simmering point, stirring occasionally to prevent the rice from sticking. Simmer gently, uncovered, for approximately 25 minutes.

Meanwhile, in a small basin, blend the arrowroot (which will thicken the soup) with 2 dessertspoons of water until smooth.

When the soup is ready, add the blended arrowroot together with the spring onions and, stirring continuously, bring back to simmering point and simmer for 1 minute. Season to taste and serve very hot.

Carrot and artichoke soup

(serves 6–8 people)

This not only has a delicious, very creamy texture and flavour, but you also have an added bonus because of its beautifully rich saffron colour.

1 lb carrots (450 g)
1½ lb Jerusalem artichokes (700 g)
1 medium onion, chopped
3 sticks celery, chopped
3 oz butter (75 g)
2½ pints light stock (1·5 litres)
Salt and freshly-milled black pepper

Start by peeling and de-knobbling the artichokes and, as you peel them, slice them into a bowl of cold water to prevent them discolouring.

Scrape and slice the carrots. In a cooking pot melt the butter, soften the onion and celery in it for 5 minutes, then stir in the carrots and artichokes. Add some salt and, keeping the heat low, put the lid on and let the vegetables sweat for 10 minutes. Then pour in the stock, stir well, put the lid back on and simmer for a further 20 minutes or until the vegetables are soft.

Now either liquidise the soup or pass it through a sieve. Taste to check the seasoning, reheat and serve.

Cream of celery soup

(serves 4 people)

Try, if possible, to use crisp *English* celery for this recipe because it has a better flavour than the imported kind.

¾ lb trimmed celery stalks, save the leaves (350 g)
¼ lb potatoes, peeled and cut into chunks (110 g)
2 medium-sized leeks (whites only), sliced and washed
1 pint chicken stock (570 ml)
¼ pint single cream (150 ml)
¼ pint milk (150 ml)
¼ teaspoon celery seeds
Salt and freshly-milled black pepper
1 oz butter (25 g)

In a largish pan melt the butter over a low heat. Then chop the celery and add it to the pan with the potatoes and drained leeks. Stir well, coating the vegetables with butter, cover with a lid and cook for about 15 minutes.

Then add the stock with the celery seeds and some salt. Bring to simmering point, cover once more and cook very gently for 20–25 minutes or until the vegetables are really tender. Purée the soup by liquidising or sieving, then return to the pan, stirring in the cream and milk.

Bring the soup back to the boil, check the seasoning, adding more salt and pepper if necessary. Then just before serving, chop the reserved celery leaves and stir them into the soup to give it extra colour.

Tomato, apple and celery cream soup

(serves 4 people)

This is one of John Tovey's famous soups, as served at his hotel the Miller Howe in the English Lakes, and it demonstrates his own method of sweating vegetables tightly sealed with greaseproof paper.

1 pint chicken (or turkey) stock—see recipe page 94 (570 ml)
4 oz onions, finely chopped (110 g)
5–6 oz tomatoes, quartered—use the stalks as well (150–175 g)
5–6 oz apples, quartered—use the cores as well (150–175 g)
5–6 oz celery, cut into 2 inch (5 cm) lengths, plus leaves (150–175 g)
2 oz butter (50 g)
2½ fl oz dry sherry (60 ml)
¼ teaspoon salt
Freshly milled black pepper
Freshly grated nutmeg
1 small pinch ground ginger
Apple slices and snipped fresh chives, to garnish

First melt the butter in a large, heavy pan, then add the onion and cook gently until golden (about 10 minutes), taking care that they don't burn or catch on the bottom. Add the sherry, vegetables, fruit, spices and seasoning to the pan, place a double thickness of greaseproof paper (which has been well dampened with cold water first) over the ingredients, and cover the pan with a lid.

Simmer very gently for 1 hour, checking from time to time that nothing is sticking. After that, add the stock to the contents of the pan (first removing the paper!), and stir everything. Now transfer the soup—in two batches—to a liquidiser and blend, then press through a sieve (to remove pips and stalks), and return to a clean pan. Reheat, check the seasoning, ladle into warmed soup bowls, and garnish each serving with an apple slice and some snipped chives. Serve with croûtons.

Garlicky fish soup

(serves 3–4 people)

This soup always conjures up visions of the south of France for me! You can, of course, cut down the quantity of garlic if you prefer (but don't leave it out altogether).

1 quantity of fish stock (see page 95)
1 lb fish fillets—haddock, cod or whiting, skinned and cut into smallish cubes (450 g)
14 oz tin of Italian tomatoes (400 g)
2 medium potatoes, finely chopped
2 tablespoons fresh chopped parsley
3 cloves garlic, crushed
½ teaspoon dried basil
1 tablespoon lemon juice
2 tablespoons olive oil
Salt and freshly-milled black pepper

In a large, heavy saucepan or flameproof casserole heat the oil and add the diced potato and garlic. Leave to cook for about 5 minutes before adding the fish stock, the cubes of fish and the contents of the tin of tomatoes. Then sprinkle in the basil, add a squeeze of lemon juice, and simmer the soup gently for 15 minutes. After that taste to check the seasoning, and sprinkle in the chopped parsley just before serving.

See also:
Chilled yoghurt and cucumber soup
Italian bean and pasta soup

Scallop cream soup
Thick bean and bacon soup
Thick pea soup

Fish

Including recipes for:
Goujons of sole
Skate with black butter
Italian baked fish
Flaky fish pie
Fisherman's pie ·
Fish kebabs
Halibut with bacon
Baked fish with soured cream
  and capers
Baked fish with mushrooms
Plaice fillet with garlic and herbs
Soused herrings
Stuffed backed herrings
Marinaded mackerel
Deep-fried sprats in mustard sauce
Trout with caper sauce
Foil-baked fresh salmon

Basic fish batter
Grilled kippers
Jugged kippers
Bloater paste
Kipper fish cakes
Smoked haddock with cream
  and egg sauce
Smoked fish pie
Potted haddock with capers
Marinaded kipper fillets
Moules à la marinière
Mussels with garlic stuffing
Scallops in the shell
Scallop cream soup
Spiced prawns with tomatoes
Dressed crab
Hot crab soufflé

Unfortunately one of the really essential ingredients in fish cookery is the one that so often is missing, namely a good fishmonger. In many parts of the country fishmongers of any description have become rather thin on the ground, and to find a really reliable one has grown increasingly difficult. This is partly offset by the ready and regular supply of commercially-frozen fish (which is probably the root cause of our vanishing fishmongers in the first place). However, unlike other types of frozen food, frozen fish has much to commend it: only the best quality is frozen and sub-zero temperatures do not materially affect the flavour—indeed very often rather more fresh flavour is retained by freezing (since it is generally carried out immediately or soon after the fish is caught).

Having said that though, there is nothing to compensate for a trustworthy and friendly fishmonger, who is willing to help and advise. There are two ways to tell a good one: firstly if his shop is busy and attracting a lot of regular custom, and secondly by how much fish there is left on the slab towards the end of the afternoon. If there is a lot then beware, because it's all going to be put away and brought out again the next day. (One of the best fishmongers I ever knew was virtually sold out by two o'clock every day.)

In spite of our proud fish 'n' chip shop tradition and the dreaded, breaded fish fingers, as a nation we don't eat nearly enough fish. I suspect this is because, unlike some other countries, we have always had an over-plentiful supply of meat. Yet fish contains as much protein as meat, is easier to digest, and has one crucial advantage: it can be cooked so quickly. If you don't have a lot of time for cooking, think of fish. It can be grilled, fried, poached or baked to provide a nutritious meal in hardly any time at all.

Buying fresh fish
There is no mistaking really fresh fish. It has a plumpness and firmness about it that proclaims it to be fresh straight away. Scaled fish should have a sequin-like iridescence, and all fishes' eyes look sparkling, almost alert (and in the case of herrings, red). In general the thing to look for is overall brightness: stale fish, however often they are hosed down, look grey, dull and droopy with blurred eyes and flabby flesh.

Preparing fish
All fish, with the exception of sprats and other tiny species, should be gutted by the fishmonger, and all fish, apart from mackerel and

herrings (see pages 128 and 131), should be skinned and filleted—
if that's what is needed—by him. Why struggle at home with
diagrams and blunt filleting knives, when you can have the job done
for you at no extra cost? In fact fish is now so expensive there's all
the more reason to have it prepared for you.

If you want to cook fish on the bone, then just ask to have it gutted
and, where appropriate, scaled (if the fishmonger doesn't make a
proper job of this, you can do it yourself by simply scraping along
the skin with the blunt side of a knife in the opposite direction to the
way the scales are, i.e. from head to tail). If you are lucky enough to
buy your fish straight off a boat or even catch it yourself, then
gutting at home isn't too complicated. You can either remove the
insides through the gill-slits (if the heads are to be left on) by
squeezing and scraping with a teaspoon, or by making a slit along
the belly, opening the fish out and then scraping. If you are cutting
off the heads some of the entrails will come out attached to the gills
(which are bright red flaps underneath openings on each side of the
head, and should also be cut away before cooking). Always wash
away any traces of blood and slime, and then dry the fish as
thoroughly as possible with kitchen paper or a clean cloth.

Storing fish
Like anything else, fish that has been frozen should not be allowed
to thaw out and then be re-frozen—so if you want to freeze some
yourself, check that it is very fresh. The safest rule obviously is to eat
fresh fish as soon as possible, though a day's storage in the
refrigerator isn't going to hurt. One exception to this, and a curious
one, is the Dover sole, which because of a chemical that develops
after death actually improves in flavour a couple of days after it is
caught. How kind of nature to give us at least one variety of fish that
can cope with the time taken up by its journey inland.

The methods of cooking fish
Shallow-frying To shallow-fry a whole, or part of a fish to the best
degree of crispness, use olive oil. If on the other hand you'd like to
get a buttery flavour, then use half oil and half butter (on its own
butter burns too easily and can spoil the flavour). Solid fat is not
very good for fish—except perhaps bacon fat or pure lard for frying
herrings. Have enough oil or fat in the pan to give a depth of
1/8 inch (3 mm) and make sure it is really hot before the fish goes in.
I think it best to thaw frozen fish before frying, whatever it says on
the packet: the coldness of the fish brings the temperature of the fat
down dramatically (and that is what makes food oily). Times for

shallow-frying fish are approximately the same as for grilling (see below).

Deep-frying Olive oil or groundnut oil is to be preferred for this—both can be stored and used several times over, but be careful to label the jar 'fish oil'. Ideally a cooking thermometer should be used to check the correct temperature of the oil (370°F, 187·5°C for fillets, goujons and fish in batter; 375°F, 190·5°C for whitebait, croquettes and fishcakes), and always warm the thermometer in hot water first to prevent the glass cracking. If you have no cooking thermometer, the best way of testing if the oil is hot enough is to throw a small cube of bread into it and if it turns golden-brown in 60 seconds you can go ahead. Do not, however, allow the oil to overheat or the flavour will be spoiled.

The pan needs to be only one-third full of oil—any more than that and there is a danger of it bubbling over when the food goes in. A frying basket isn't necessary—the fish or the batter has a habit of getting stuck in the mesh—just use a draining-spoon with a long handle to get the fish in and out.

Fish destined for the deep-fryer ought to be at room temperature: chilled or frozen fish lowers the oil heat and the food will taste soggy and oily (and in any event try, if you can, to raise the heat under the pan as you lower the fish in, then turn it down again). To tell if the fish is cooked, the batter or coating turning a golden-brown is a good indication. Small fish or pieces of fish rise to the surface when they are cooked. But if in doubt, the best way of all is to try a bit. Always drain fried fish on crumpled greaseproof paper before serving.

Grilling The first tip here is to line the grill pan or grid with foil before you start—this will prevent a fishy flavour lingering in the pan. Pre-heat the grill to high, before placing the fish under it. White fish need to be brushed generously with melted butter before grilling, and basted with the buttery juices when you turn them.

Type and size of fish	Grilling time
Whole Dover sole and plaice	4–6 minutes each side
Fillets of sole or plaice	2–3 minutes each side
Fish steaks (salmon, halibut, cod, turbot, etc.) weighing approx. 6–8 oz (175–225 g)	Allow 5–6 minutes each side, and have extra butter ready for basting during cooking to prevent dryness

Whole mackerel	Make 3 diagonal scores on each side and brush with melted butter. Grill for approx. 6–7 minutes each side for 8 oz (225 g) fish
Herring	For 6–8 oz (175–225 g) fish, score as above and allow 4–5 minutes' grilling on each side

Poaching For poaching you need some form of liquid, though not too much of it: a mixture of white wine (or dry cider) and water with a few herbs, a bayleaf, peppercorns, sliced onion, sliced carrot and a piece of lemon peel is a very suitable poaching liquid. Or for some white fish a mixture of milk and water with flavourings is used. The operative word here is gentle—the liquid should barely simmer, in order not to overcook or break up the fish. Rolled-up fillets of sole or plaice will only need 4–5 minutes' poaching: larger whole fish or pieces weighing 1½–2 lb (700–900 g) will need 7–10 minutes. I have to admit that, on the whole, I think it preferable to cook fish in the oven in foil rather than poach it, as this retains more of the flavour.

Steaming A useful method to know, which offers gentle cooking that safeguards the flavour and juices of the fish. Again foil is useful: just butter a piece of foil generously, lay the fish in it with some seasoning and a squeeze of lemon juice, then wrap it up into a parcel and place in a steamer over boiling water. Depending on thickness it will take 10–15 minutes to cook. (You can save on fuel by placing the steaming fish over the potatoes as they're boiling.)

Baking This way the fish is brushed with melted butter or with oil (maybe with a stuffing added) and then baked in the oven— sometimes open, sometimes lightly covered with a piece of buttered foil for protection. At other times a small quantity of poaching liquid is used, or extra butter for basting: methods of baking vary quite a lot, so see instructions in individual recipes.

In foil or en papillote This is an excellent way to cook fish, because all the essential flavour and juices are retained inside a sealed parcel (which when opened will give off a beautiful, fragrant and appetising aroma). For fish like salmon and salmon trout, which are sometimes served cold, the parcels can be left unopened until just before serving. Various flavourings can be added: lemon juice, wine, butter, slivers of onion, garlic, fresh herbs. In Italy I have eaten sole cooked like this surrounded by fresh mint leaves. For timings, see individual recipes.

Popular varieties of fish
In the British Isles there are five main groups of fish available to us; white fish, oily fish, freshwater fish, smoked fish and shellfish. These last two groups will be dealt with on pages 136–154. Of the others let's look first at some of the most popular varieties of the group known as white fish.

Sole
First—because it is said to have the finest flavour of all—is the *Dover sole*. This is a flat fish, weighing anything from 8 oz up to 2 lb (225–900 g), white on the under-side with its speckled grey camouflage on the upper-side, with a rounded not pointed head. Its flavour is best preserved by serving it simply: brushed with melted butter, grilled in its own juices and served with some parsley butter and lemon juice. I also believe that any fish (like meat) benefits in taste from being cooked on the bone instead of filleted.

Grilled Dover sole on the bone Ask the fishmonger to skin it for you. Then brush it with melted butter, and give it from about 4 to 6 minutes on each side under the hot grill, depending on thickness.

Lemon soles (and *witch soles*) are similar fish, but look rather more pointed. They are certainly cheaper but don't compare in flavour.

Goujons of sole

(serves 2 as a main course or 4 as a first course)

Goujons are small strips of fish coated in egg and breadcrumbs. To make this more economical you could use plaice fillets but, either way, ask the fishmonger to skin them for you.

8 small fillets of sole or plaice
3 level tablespoons of well-seasoned flour
1 large egg, beaten
4 oz fresh white breadcrumbs (110 g)
Some oil for deep frying

To garnish:
Chopped parsley and slices of raw onion

First wipe the fillets and cut them into thinnish strips diagonally across the grain. Roll the strips in the seasoned flour, then dip them first in the beaten egg and then in the breadcrumbs. (Have the breadcrumbs on a flat working surface so that you can roll the strips under the palm of your hand to get them well and evenly coated.)

Next heat the oil in a deep pan to 350°F (180°C)—test the temperature either with a thermometer or drop in a small cube of bread and if it turns golden and crisp in one minute it's hot enough. Then deep fry the fish for 2–3 minutes until golden-brown. You'll probably need to do the frying in 2 or 3 separate lots. When cooked, drain on crumpled greaseproof paper. Serve garnished with chopped parsley and slices of raw onion.

Skate

Swimming in the sea, a skate looks like a cross between Concorde and a space-craft, with its huge wings. The wings are what we buy at the fishmonger, triangular in shape with a pinky flesh (if they are from a small fish they weigh about 8 oz (225 g) each, if from a large fish they are bought cut into pieces). It is a delicious fish: the flesh parts so conveniently from the soft bones, which themselves stay intact, so there is little likelihood of finding any unwelcome, spiky bits of bone. It is hard to beat just washed, well dried, given a light coating of flour, then fried in a mixture of butter and oil till crisp and golden: or else served with browned butter, which adds a lovely buttery flavour as in the next recipe.

A group of white fish belonging to the skate family—and often referred to rather misleadingly as rock salmon—are the *dogfish, huss* or *flake*. In fact they have nothing at all in common with salmon, actually are rather dull (if cheap) and need to be jazzed up a bit with other ingredients.

Skate with black butter

(serves 4 people)

The important thing to remember here is not to overcook the butter—a split second too much and it can be burnt rather than browned.

4 skate wings
3 tablespoons white wine vinegar
1 bayleaf
1 blade mace
A couple of sprigs of parsley

| 1 level tablespoon chopped capers |
| Salt and freshly-milled black pepper |
| 3 oz butter (75 g) |

| *To garnish:* |
| **Lemon slices** |

First of all place the skate wings side by side in a wide pan or a roasting tin. Sprinkle with salt and pepper, then add 2 tablespoons of the wine vinegar, the bayleaf, mace and parsley sprigs. Add enough water to cover, bring slowly to the boil and simmer over a low heat for 10–15 minutes, but be sure not to overcook the fish.

Meantime, slowly melt the butter in a small saucepan, then pour the clear golden butter into another saucepan, leaving the white sediment behind. Heat the butter until it's a rich warm brown, then remove at once from the heat, stir in the remaining vinegar and the capers and season with salt and pepper. Drain the fish well— discard the herbs—and arrange it on a warmed serving dish. Finally pour the butter over and garnish with slices of lemon.

The cod family
There are several branches to this family, varying amongst themselves more in size than in texture or flavour. *Cod* itself is a very firm, flaky fish that can weigh up to 14 lb (6·5 kg) (*codling* is simply a small cod, by the way), but sadly it loses much of its flavour if not eaten very fresh. It is available all through the year. So too is *hake* (except sometimes in the early autumn), which is a similar if elongated version of cod. *Haddock* is another relation, smaller and more finely textured, much of which goes to be smoked. *Coley* is a rather dull cousin, *whiting* a much more succulent one, and Norwegian *red fish* a somewhat ferocious-looking one that surprisingly tastes as good as cod and is in need of more promotion. All these fleshy, firm fish lend themselves to a wide spectrum of seasonings, flavourings and sauces.

Turbot and halibut
These are usually large flat fish, although turbot can be as small as 2 or 3 lb (900 g–1·35 kg) when it can be cooked whole with a stuffing. Halibut can weigh up to 40 lb (18 kg). Both are available all through the year, have a fine flavour, are quite expensive, but are easy to grill, fry, poach or bake in long cutlets on the bone.

Plaice

A fish that does need, I think, some extra flavourings. It is a flat white fish, easily recognisable by the bright orange spots on the upper side. A whole plaice can weigh up to 5 lb (2·25 kg) or be as small as 8 oz (225 g). It is available in Britain all the year round. You can grill it like Dover sole, but you might consider a sauce or flavoured butter to go with it. Deep-fried in a light crisp batter (page 127), it goes well with tartare sauce (page 484). Filleted, it can be used in any sole recipe and the smaller frozen fillets are very good. *Dabs* and *flounders* are smaller, less interesting, versions of plaice.

Italian baked fish

(serves 4 people)

Four pieces of any white fish can be used for this dish in which the fish is baked in a thick tomato sauce.

4 thick pieces of white fish
1 medium onion, finely chopped
1 fat clove garlic, crushed
14 oz (400 g) tin Italian tomatoes
1 teaspoon dried basil
2 tablespoons olive oil
¼ lb mushrooms (110 g), thinly sliced
1 dessertspoon black olives
Juice of half a lemon
Salt and freshly-milled black pepper

Pre-heat the oven to gas mark 5, 375°F (190°C)

Start by making a good thick tomato sauce. Heat the olive oil in a saucepan and fry the onion for about 5 minutes. Now add the garlic and tomatoes. Season with salt and pepper and stir in the dried basil. Bring to simmering point and cook gently—uncovered—for 15 minutes, stirring occasionally. Next add the sliced mushrooms, making sure that they are well stirred in. Simmer for a further 10 minutes until it looks like a thick purée.

Now place the fish in a shallow baking dish or tin, season with salt and pepper and sprinkle a little lemon juice on each piece. Next spoon an equal quantity of the purée onto each piece of fish and arrange a few olives on top. Cover the dish with foil and bake on a high shelf for about 25 minutes, depending on the thickness of the fish. Serve this with brown rice and a tossed green salad.

Flaky fish pie

(serves 4 people)

Any white fish can be used for this—
whiting, coley, etc.—and even if using
the more expensive haddock or cod,
³/₄ lb (350 g) will feed 4 easily.

12 oz any white fish (350 g)
Milk
1 oz butter (25 g)
2 tablespoons flour
1 teaspoon capers, chopped
1 small gherkin, chopped
2 tablespoons chopped parsley
2 hard-boiled eggs, chopped
1 tablespoon lemon juice
Salt and freshly-milled black pepper

For the quick flaky pastry:
8 oz flour (225 g)
6 oz margarine (175 g)
For method see page 565

To glaze:
Beaten egg

First place the fish in a medium-sized saucepan with just enough
milk to cover, bring to the boil, cover and simmer gently for about
5–10 minutes. Now strain off the milk into a measuring jug and,
when the fish is cool enough to handle, flake it into large pieces
(discarding all the bones, skin, etc).

Next, melt the butter in the same saucepan and stir in the flour.
Cook for about 2 minutes over a medium heat, then gradually add
¹/₂ pint (275 ml) of the milk the fish was cooked in, stirring all the
time. Bring the sauce to the boil, simmer gently for 6 minutes, then
take the pan off the heat and add the flaked fish, chopped capers,
gherkin, parsley and eggs. Season with salt and pepper and lemon
juice. Cover and leave until the mixture is quite cold.

When you're ready to cook the pie, pre-heat the oven to gas mark 7,
425°F (220°C). Roll out the pastry to a 12 inch (30 cm) square,
trimming if necessary. Lift the square onto a greased baking sheet,
then place the cold fish mixture in the centre. Glaze around the edge
of the pastry with beaten egg, then pull the opposite corners of the

pastry to the centre and pinch all the edges together firmly, so you
have a square with pinched edges in the shape of a cross. Glaze all
over with beaten egg and decorate with any pastry trimmings.
Glaze these and then bake the pie for about 30 minutes or until the
pastry is well risen and golden.

Fisherman's pie

(serves 4 people)

Whatever white fish is available can be
used for this delicious family recipe.

1½ lb white fish (700 g)
4 oz butter (110 g)
1 pint milk (570 ml)
2 oz plain flour (50 g)
4 oz peeled prawns (110 g)
2 hardboiled eggs (roughly chopped)
1 level tablespoon capers (drained)
3 tablespoons fresh chopped parsley
1 tablespoon lemon juice
Salt and freshly-milled pepper

For the topping:
2 lb freshly-cooked potatoes (900 g)
1 oz butter (25 g)
¼ pint soured cream (150 ml)
A little freshly-grated nutmeg

Pre-heat the oven to gas mark 6, 400°F
(200°C)

Start by arranging the fish in a baking tin and seasoning it well with
salt and pepper. Then pour over ½ pint (275 ml) of the milk, dot
with a few flecks of butter, and bake in the oven for 15 to 20 minutes.
Pour off (and reserve) the cooking liquid, and remove the skin from
the fish, flaking the flesh into fairly large pieces.

Now make the sauce: melt the remaining 3 oz (75 g) of butter in a
saucepan, then stir in the flour and gradually add the fish cooking
liquid—stirring well after each addition. When all the liquid is in,
finish off the sauce by slowly adding the remaining ½ pint
(275 ml) of milk and seasoning with salt and pepper.

Next mix the fish into the sauce, along with the prawns, hardboiled eggs, capers and parsley (taste at this stage to see if it needs any more salt and pepper) and stir in the lemon juice. Now pour the whole mixture into a 2½ pint (1·4 l) baking dish (well buttered).

Next cream the cooked potatoes with the butter and soured cream, add some freshly grated nutmeg, then spread it evenly all over the fish. Bake on a high shelf (same temperature) for about half an hour, or until heated through and browned.

Fish kebabs

(serves 2 people)

This is an unusual and delicious way of serving fish—any white fish, like the thick end of a cod fillet or haddock.

1 lb white fish (450 g)
3 tablespoons olive oil
1½ tablespoons lemon juice
1 tablespoon dry white wine
2 tablespoons parsley, finely chopped
1 medium green pepper, chopped
1 medium onion, quartered
Salt and freshly-milled black pepper
Lemon quarters

First remove the skin from the fish and cut it into 1 inch (2·5 cm) cubes. Next, put in a bowl the olive oil, lemon juice, wine and chopped parsley and seasoning and mix well with a fork to amalgamate thoroughly, then plunge the cubes of fish into it. Now separate the layers of the onion quarters and arrange them evenly over the fish. Put aside in a cool place to marinade for at least an hour.

When you're ready to cook the fish, pre-heat the grill to high and line the grill pan with foil. Then thread the pieces of fish onto skewers, alternating with pieces of onion and green pepper. Place the skewers on the grill pan, brush with the marinade and grill for a minute or two under the high heat. Then turn the heat to medium and cook for a further 4—5 minutes on each side, brushing on more of the marinade before turning.

Serve with savoury rice, the juices from the pan poured over, and lemon quarters. Brown rice looks nice, if you can get it.

*Halibut
with bacon*

(serves 4 people)

This is nicest served with creamy potatoes mashed with soured cream and flavoured with a little nutmeg.

4 halibut steaks (single-portion-sized steaks)
2 carrots, very thinly sliced
1 stick celery, very thinly sliced
4 oz mushrooms (110 g) thinly sliced
4 slices back bacon, rinds removed
1 large onion, finely chopped
2 tablespoons chopped parsley
½ teaspoon dried thyme
4 slices lemon
2 oz butter (50 g)
½ pint dry white wine (275 ml)
Salt and freshly-milled black pepper

Pre-heat the oven to gas mark 7, 425°F (220°C)

Start by laying the bacon slices in a well-buttered baking dish, which is large enough to take the fish steaks. Then sprinkle over the prepared carrots, mushrooms, celery and onion followed by the wine. Cover tightly with foil and bake for 30 minutes.

Next, remove the dish from the oven and arrange the fish steaks on top of the vegetables. Then sprinkle with parsley, thyme, salt and freshly-milled black pepper; place a lemon slice on each steak and dot with flecks of butter. Cover the dish again with foil and bake for a further 15–20 minutes, then serve.

*Baked fish with
soured cream
and capers*

(serves 2 people)

This would be suitable for some thick fish cutlets—cod, halibut or turbot or some thick pieces of fresh haddock.

1 lb fish (450 g)
2 fl oz dry white wine or dry cider (55 ml)
1½ oz butter (40 g)
½ teaspoon dried tarragon leaves
1 chopped white of leek
¼ pint soured cream (150 ml)

| 1 teaspoon flour |
| 2 teaspoons drained chopped capers |
| 1 tablespoon finely-chopped watercress leaves |
| Salt and freshly-milled pepper |

| *To garnish:* |
| Sprigs of watercress |
| Lemon quarters |

Pre-heat the oven to gas mark 5, 375°F (190°C)

Place the pieces of fish in a buttered baking dish just large enough to accommodate them. Add the cider and dot with half the butter. Season with salt and pepper, sprinkle in the tarragon, then cover the dish with foil and bake near the top of the oven for 20 minutes.

Meantime, melt the rest of the butter in a saucepan, add the chopped leek and let it soften gently. Then sprinkle in the flour and, stirring all the time, cook over a low heat for a couple of minutes.

When the fish is ready, lift up a corner of the foil and pour the liquid into a jug. Now add this liquid, a little at a time, to the mixture in the saucepan, stirring after each addition. When it's all added, bring to boiling point and cook for at least a minute. Then turn the heat low and stir in the cream, capers and chopped watercress. When it's heated through, pour it over the fish and garnish with sprigs of watercress and lemon quarters.

Baked fish with mushrooms

(serves 3–4 people)

For this you need 2 large whole plaice or Dover soles, boned, cut into fillets and skinned.

| 4 large plaice fillets, skinned |
| ½ lb dark mushrooms (225 g), finely chopped |
| 1 oz butter (25 g) |
| 1 tablespoon oil |
| 1 small onion, finely chopped |
| Freshly-grated nutmeg |
| Lemon juice |
| 1 tablespoon finely-chopped parsley |

¼ pint milk (150 ml)
2 level tablespoons flour
1 tablespoon thick cream
Salt and freshly-milled black pepper

To garnish:
Chopped parsley

Pre-heat the oven to gas mark 4, 350°F (180°C)

First of all melt half the butter and all the oil together in a pan and fry the onion gently until soft and golden. Add the mushrooms and cook until all the juices have evaporated and the remaining mixture is a dryish, spreadable paste—this will probably take about 20 minutes. Remove from the heat, season with salt, pepper and nutmeg, then transfer all but 2 tablespoons of the mixture to a basin and mix with the parsley.

Next cut the fish fillets in half lengthways and spread an equal quantity of the mushroom mixture on the skinned side of each piece of fish. Roll up the fillets from the head to the tail end and place them closely together in a baking dish. Now pour in ¼ pint (150 ml) water, place a piece of buttered paper directly on top of the fish and bake in the oven for 20 minutes.

Meantime, melt the remaining butter in a saucepan, blend in the flour and cook for 2 minutes, stirring continuously. When the fish is ready transfer it to a warmed serving dish, using a draining spoon; cover and keep warm. Now add the cooking liquid to the butter and flour mixture, beating all the time to get a smooth sauce, and also blend in the milk. Then bring to boiling point, stirring all the time, add the remaining mushroom mixture, season with salt, pepper and a squeeze of lemon juice and stir in a tablespoon of cream. Pour over the fish and sprinkle with parsley before serving.

Plaice fillets with garlic and herbs

(serves 2 people)

For this ask the fishmonger for 2 plaice boned and filleted into 2 flat fillets each, or use frozen fillets (thawed first)

4 plaice fillets
2 tablespoons fresh breadcrumbs
1 clove garlic, chopped very small

| 1 teaspoon dried thyme |
| 1 tablespoon fresh chopped parsley |
| 1 egg |
| 2 oz butter (50 g) |
| 1 tablespoon olive oil |
| 1 small lemon |
| Salt and freshly-milled black pepper |

Melt the butter and oil in your largest frying-pan and, while it's melting, combine the breadcrumbs, garlic, thyme, parsley and the grated peel of the lemon in a shallow dish. Then beat the egg and season it with coarsely-milled pepper and salt. Pat the fillets dry with some kitchen paper and dip them first in the beaten egg, then in the breadcrumbs, making sure they get a good even coating.

Now fry the fillets in the hot butter and oil till golden-brown—about 3 minutes each side or more if they're thick.

Drain on crumpled greaseproof paper and serve with the lemon, quartered, to squeeze over.

These go very well with sauté potatoes and a crisp green salad.

Oily fish
Under this heading come a group of fish which are rich in flavour, but because of their slight oiliness do need to be eaten fresh.

Herrings
A prince of fish, in my opinion, a true delicacy when freshly caught. Yet until recently herring were amongst the cheapest and most abundant of our native fish, and little thought of in consequence. The irony is that present-day intensive fishing (for animal-feed products among other things) has contrived to put the species in jeopardy. It has therefore become scarcer and more expensive—and probably, like the oyster, will become more highly regarded.

It is quite possible you might find yourself faced at some time or another with the prospect of having to bone a herring. It is actually quite easy—more formidable in the anticipation than in practice. First of all ask the fishmonger to clean, scale and trim the fish—that much he must do. Then when you get home, take a pair of scissors and cut each fish along the tummy, turn it over (flesh-side down) on a board, then bash (with a rolling-pin if you like) the fish out to flatten it completely. Now press hard with your fingers all along the backbone, to loosen it from the flesh. Then, turning the fish over, get hold of the backbone at the head and ease it away—it will bring all the little bones with it. If it proves a bit stubborn, use a sharp knife to prompt it a little. Remove any reluctant small bones left behind—and you have now boned a herring.

Soused herrings
(serves 6 people)

These are delicious served with home-made wholewheat bread and a salad, but they do need to be made a couple of days in advance. For 6 pickled herrings you'll need:

1 pint white wine vinegar (425 ml)
1 teaspoon whole allspice berries
1 teaspoon whole coriander seeds
½ teaspoon mustard seeds
1 dried chilli
2 bayleaves
1–2 teaspoons brown sugar
6 freshly filleted herrings (frozen ones are not so good)
1½ tablespoons salt
2 dill pickles
1 Spanish onion, thinly sliced
Some made-up mustard
6 cocktail sticks

First of all make the marinade in a saucepan by combining the vinegar, spices, bayleaves and sugar with ¼ pint (150 ml) water. Bring to boiling point, then simmer very gently for 5 minutes. Remove from the heat and leave until cold.

Next sprinkle the herrings with the salt and let them drain in a colander for about 3 hours. After that rinse off the salt and dry off any excess moisture with kitchen paper. Now cut each dill pickle in three lengthways, spread the filleted side of each fish thinly with mustard and place a piece of dill pickle and some slices of onion horizontally at what was the head end of each fillet. Then roll up the fillets from the head to the tail end—the skin being on the outside—and secure each roll with a cocktail stick. Pack them into an oval casserole and sprinkle the remaining onion on top. Pour over the marinade, cover with a lid, and put them in the lowest part of the refrigerator. They will not be ready for serving for at least 48 hours and, in fact, they will keep well for at least a week.

Stuffed baked herrings

(serves 4 people)

For this you need 4 medium herrings. Ask for the soft roes to go in the stuffing.

4 herrings with roes
1 tablespoon butter
1 small onion, finely chopped
2 hard-boiled eggs, chopped
1 clove garlic, crushed
3 tablespoons chopped parsley
1 teaspoon dried thyme
2 slices white bread (crusts removed)
Milk
1 teaspoon lemon juice
Salt and freshly-milled black pepper
A little butter

Pre-heat the oven to gas mark 5, 375°F (190°C)

You'll need a shallow, buttered baking dish.

When buying the fish ask the fishmonger to remove the heads and to gut and fillet them, if you're not sure how to do this; and make sure you get the roes.

First wash the fish and dry them on kitchen paper. Then heat the butter in a small saucepan and gently fry the onion for about 10 minutes or until soft. Transfer the onion to a bowl and add the chopped hard-boiled eggs, garlic, parsley and thyme. Then soak the bread in milk, squeeze out the excess and shred it into the bowl. Chop the herring roes and stir this into the mixture together with the lemon juice and seasoning.

Next, fill each herring with some of the stuffing, then re-shape them to their original form and lay them in the prepared baking dish. Dot each fish with a generous knob of butter and bake on a high shelf for 30–40 minutes, basting occasionally with the buttery juices.

Mackerel

An under-estimated fish if ever there was one. It has a bad reputation with older generations, who were suspicious of its career as a scavenger (it is all right for humans to eat the flesh of other creatures, but wrong apparently for the poor mackerel). It is a sobering thought, in these days of high prices, to read of Cornish fishermen having to dump mackerel catches back in the sea because nobody will buy them, and a saddening one, because mackerel eaten fresh (which they usually are) are a treat. If they look floppy, grey and dull they should be avoided of course: a fresh mackerel will be stiff and rigid, with a sparkling, positively beautiful rainbow hue.

The smaller mackerel are the best size to buy—working out at one fish per person. Bone them in exactly the same way as herrings (see page 129). They are excellent plainly grilled: make diagonal cuts across the body, season on both sides with salt and pepper, and give them about 5 minutes under a high grill on both sides. They are traditionally—and rightly—served with a sharp purée of gooseberries flavoured with a little nutmeg, or with a purée of rhubarb flavoured with a spot of ginger.

Marinaded mackerel

(serves 3 people)

If you can get your fishmonger to fillet the mackerel for you, so much the better. If not, follow the instructions for boning herring on page 129.

3 large mackerel, filleted
¾ pint dry white wine (425 ml)

1 onion, thinly sliced
1 carrot, thinly sliced
2 tablespoons olive oil
A large bouquet garni*
1 teaspoon brown sugar
Salt

* Bouquet garni—consisting of celery leaves, strips of lemon zest, bayleaf, parsley sprigs, sprigs of thyme, a whole clove of garlic, 10 black peppercorns and 1 seeded chilli—all tied together in a piece of gauze.

Begin by heating the oil in a thick-based saucepan, then add the carrot and onion and stir around. Cover and cook gently for 10 minutes. Next add the white wine, also ¼ pint (150 ml) water and the bouquet garni. Bring to simmering point, cover and cook gently for approximately 30 minutes.

Towards the end of the cooking time arrange the fillets in a single layer, in a roasting tin, then empty the contents of the saucepan over the fish. Bring up to simmering point and simmer for a minute.

Next, using a draining spoon, transfer the fillets to an oval earthenware casserole or dish which accommodates them neatly. Return the pan to the heat and boil the juices for 2–3 minutes or until reduced sufficiently just to cover the fish. Season to taste with salt, add the sugar, remove the bouquet garni, then strain the liquid over the fillets.

Put aside to cool, then cover and chill for at least 12 hours before serving. (They will keep quite well for 3–4 days.)

Whitebait

Whitebait are tiny baby herring, rarely more than an inch long. At one time—more than a hundred years ago—they were caught at the mouth of the Thames, and consumed by Members of Parliament at 'whitebait feasts' in Greenwich at the end of the parliamentary session. Alas, they are almost never sold fresh nowadays—at least I've never seen them—but it doesn't matter too much, because frozen whitebait are perfectly good. They are eaten whole, deep-fried and crisp enough to rustle as they're served on the plate. Let them de-frost first, dry them thoroughly, then coat them with a dusting of flour and deep-fry them for about 3 minutes.

Sprats

Cousins to the herring, only smaller—yet larger than whitebait. Usually they are 2½–3 inches long (6·5–7·5 cm). They are delicious fried or baked, and always a bargain price-wise.

Deep-fried sprats in mustard sauce

(serves 2 people)

Fresh silvery sprats are always an economical fish, and deep-fried and crisp they really are a delicacy.

1 lb sprats (450 g)
Some seasoned flour
Groundnut oil for frying

For the mustard sauce:
1 oz butter (25 g)
½ oz flour (10 g)
½ pint milk (275 ml)
½ small onion, peeled and chopped
2 teaspoons dry mustard
Salt and freshly-milled black pepper
2 teaspoons lemon juice
A generous pinch sugar
2 pinches cayenne pepper

Make the mustard sauce first. Melt the butter in a saucepan and gently soften the onion in it for about 10 minutes. Now blend in the flour and cook very gently for a minute or two before adding the mustard powder. Now add the milk a little at a time, stirring after each addition, and when it's all added, bring the sauce to boiling point and let it simmer very gently for about 3 minutes. Season to taste with salt, pepper, lemon juice and a pinch of sugar, then keep the sauce warm whilst you prepare the sprats.

First make a small incision behind a gill of each fish and gently squeeze the belly up towards the head to eject the gut, but try to keep the head intact. Rinse the fish well and dry off any excess moisture with kitchen paper before tossing in the seasoned flour. Heat the oil in a deep pan to 350°F (180°C)—to test, either use a thermometer or throw in a small cube of bread and if it turns golden in about a minute it's hot enough. Now deep-fry the sprats for about

3 minutes—you'll probably need to do them in 2 or 3 separate lots. When cooked, drain on crumpled greaseproof paper, keep hot and serve as soon as possible sprinkled with a little cayenne pepper and with the mustard sauce poured over.

Freshwater fish
Trout

There are two kinds of trout, the *brown* and the *rainbow trout*: the latter is actually becoming more widely available and less expensive because of notable success up and down the country with commercial fish-farming. These farming methods can produce small trout weighing 6–10 oz (175–275 g), which from frozen will poach in about 10 minutes (6 minutes if fresh). Put some parsley, lemon slices, bayleaf, peppercorns, onion rings and a few herbs in the poaching water, along with a glass of white wine. When cooked, drain the fish and serve with parsley butter. Alternatively they can be fried, dipped first in flour, and with a few capers and lemon juice or white wine added to the pan at the end. Trout also bakes and grills well: it is in fact an excellent all-round fish. *Note:* it is normal to leave the heads on, though the gills should be removed as usual.

Trout with caper sauce

(serves 2 people)

A couple of frozen trout would be all right for this—only let them thaw first.

2 trout, gutted
5 tablespoons oil
1 large clove garlic, crushed
4 oz capers (110 g), drained and coarsely crushed
The juice of a large lemon
Salt and freshly-milled black pepper

A few hours before cooking time, put the oil in a bowl with the crushed garlic and beat in the lemon juice followed by the capers and some salt and pepper. Then leave it aside for the flavour to develop.

When you're ready to cook the fish, remove the grill rack and line the grill pan with foil. Pre-heat the grill and arrange the fish over the foil, after gashing each side of the fish twice in the thickest part of their bodies, and brushing a little oil on both sides. Sprinkle with salt and pepper and pour on the caper sauce. Grill under a high heat so that the skins turn crisply brown—they will need 3–4 minutes on each side. Then serve with all the pan juices poured over and you'll need lots of crusty bread to mop up the liquid.

Salmon

The salmon has a fascinating career. Once matured—anything between 2 and 7 years old—it will always return to the same river to spawn, sometimes to the exact spot where it was itself hatched. Unfortunately once a salmon enters the river it stops feeding and starts to deteriorate in quality. So commercially-sold salmon are always caught in the estuary just as they leave the sea. Their season starts in February and goes on till mid-September: prices (never cheap, regrettably) begin to descend from June when there are more salmon available. One can never afford to buy any but the freshest, and these will have a bright silver belly and flank, an iridescent purple-black back, with peach-coloured flesh that's firm to the touch.

The very best way to cook it is wrapped in buttered foil in the oven. If you are serving it cold, it can stay in the foil to cool and the skin taken off just before serving. A whole, 8 lb (3·5 kg) salmon can feed an entire party, but for a smaller number of people ask the fishmonger for a middle cut.

Foil-baked	**1½ lb middle-cut salmon (675 g)**
fresh salmon	**2 oz butter (50 g)**
	2 bayleaves
(serves 4 people)	**Salt and freshly-milled black pepper**

Pre-heat the oven to gas mark ½, 250°F (130°C)

Start by wiping the fish with some damp kitchen paper, then place it in the centre of a large double sheet of foil. Half the butter and both bayleaves should be placed in the centre cavity of the fish, and the rest of the butter smeared on top. Season well with salt and pepper, then wrap the foil over the salmon to make a loose but tightly-sealed parcel. Put the foil parcel on a heatproof plate and bake in the oven for 1 hour and 10 minutes. The skin will come off very easily once the fish is cooked.

For larger pieces of salmon the cooking times are: for 2 lb (900 g), 1¹/₂ hours; for 3 lb (1 kg 350 g), 2 hours; for 4 lb (1 kg 800 g), 2¹/₂ hours; for 5 lb (2 kg 250 g), 3 hours. Salmon steaks weighing up to 8 oz (225 g) each, cooked in this way, need 20–25 minutes.

Salmon trout
Also called sea trout, though it is not exactly salmon, trout or sea-going. With its firm but delicate pink flesh, it is said to combine all the virtues of trout and salmon. It weighs anything from 1¹/₂ to 4 lb (675 g to 2 kg), and can be cooked in exactly the same way as salmon (see above).

Basic fish batter   I have found this very simple flour-and-water batter the best of all for deep-frying fish, as it really turns out crisp. These quantities should be enough for 4 pieces.

4 oz self-raising flour (110 g)
¹/₂ teaspoon salt
¹/₄ pint (plus 1 scant tablespoon) water (150 ml)

Just sift the flour and salt into a bowl, then gradually whisk in the water till smooth and free from lumps.

Smoked fish
One thing at which the British really excel is smoking fish. Nowhere else in the world can you get juicy kippers, smoked Finnan haddies, or sides of smoked salmon comparable to our own. It is an ancient art but, unlike so many that have died out, this one thrives and many traditional smokehouses have survived to supply a constant demand. Smoking was one of the earliest methods developed by men to preserve the surplus of summer for the lean winter, and it was quite logical really: cooking needed fire, and fire provided smoke. The carbon in the smoke reacted with the oils in the food to create a coating which not only had a preservative effect on the fish (or ham or whatever), but also imparted an interesting smoky flavour. Sometimes resinous woods were thrown on the fire at the end of the process to give the food a final tarry layer—which helped to ward off the flies.

Smoking is in fact the last stage in the preserving process. First comes the salting or brining, which starts to extract moisture from the fish; then comes air-drying or dripping which continues to dry the fish, then smoking which completes the drying and at the same time provides that 'antiseptic' coating. Smoking is only really effective for foods containing plenty of oil, and once again nature has done her bit by supplying just such rich, oily fish as herrings, mackerel and salmon.

Before the days of refrigeration and fast transport fish was much more heavily smoked: nowadays it is only lightly smoked to create flavour rather than to improve the keeping qualities of fish. Lighter smoking also means less natural colour; dyes are often used now to make up for this and help the fish look more like the original heavily smoked product. There are two types of smoking. In cold smoking—at under 85°F—care is taken not to cook the flesh, and this is used for haddock, salmon, bloaters and herring (kippers). With hot smoking the temperature reaches 90°F and the fish is then lightly cooked at 180°F and the results—like Arbroath smokies, mackerel, or buckling—have a stronger, smokier flavour.

While large-scale factory curing and smoking has provided a slightly blander species of smoked fish, at the same time it has put them within the reach of anyone who wants them, and this has kept up a demand. Demand, in turn, has benefited the small traditional smokehouses throughout the country. I am lucky, in this respect, to live near the Pinney family at Butley Creek in Suffolk, where people come in pilgrimage to a tiny restaurant and shop to sample their unique smoked fish. Mr Pinney's patent process uses whole oak logs rather than the conventional sawdust (modern electric saws, he claims, can leave traces of oil in sawdust which sometimes spoils the flavour of the fish). Oak logs, too, need less attention than sawdust fires which, if unattended, have a habit of going out. Anyway the two modest looking wooden ovens provide some of the best smoked fish I've ever tasted.

Smoked salmon

To start with, the king of them all. The best salmon are said to come from the coldest waters, and Scotch and Irish salmon can well claim to be the best in the world. Once smoked, prime Scotch salmon has a firmer flesh than any other, and can be carved by an expert in complete slices from heat to tail, to an almost wafer-like transparency. To enjoy it at its very best (and how else can we afford to at current prices?) it should be carved to order and not pre-sliced left to dry and curl at the edges. If you're buying it to take home, do have it wrapped carefully and eat it as soon as possible. Smoked salmon experts tend to dismiss pepper-mill and lemon wedges when sampling it and, judging from the rare occasions when I have had the opportunity to try really good smoked salmon, I rather agree.

Smoked trout
Smoked trout are delicately flavoured and therefore best served by themselves. To keep succulent, their skins (their 'mackintoshes' as Margaret Costa aptly describes them in her *Four Seasons Cookbook*) should be left on till just before eating. Serve smoked trout with lemon wedges, and a mixture of a little grated horseradish and whipped cream (not too much horseradish or you will mask the fish flavour, and certainly do not use the commercial sauces which contain turnip amongst other odd ingredients).

Smoked eel
A delicacy almost on a par with smoked salmon in my opinion. It's cheaper if bought un-filleted—and better that way because it stays moister. Skinning and filleting at home is very easy. Serve smoked eel in the same way as smoked trout.

Smoked mackerel
Ever since herring fishing has had to be controlled, smoked mackerel has really taken off commercially. It now comes dyed orange and vacuum-packed from supermarkets or, sadly, half defrosted from fishmongers' slabs. The best smoked mackerel is unfrozen and still intact in its skin—worth hunting around for. At Pinneys (see page 137) they serve smoked mackerel with a sweet brown sauce which matches its richness perfectly. At home I like to make it into one of my favourite smoked fish pâtés, (see recipe page 87).

Smoked cod's roe
This is delicious made into the rich, pink paste which is an anglicised version of the Greek taramasalata (usually made in Greece with salted grey mullet roe). It may seem horrifyingly expensive, but a little of it goes a long way—see *Taramasalata* recipe on page 86.

The smoked herring family

Kippers A kipper is a fat, juicy herring which has been split, gutted, salted and smoked. One of the sad things in the history of kippering (a curing process invented in the 1840s by a man called John Woodger) is that since the last war—when some foods were required by weight rather than number—most kippers have been under-cured, because curing removes moisture and therefore weight. Most kippers today are also dyed: this is done to compensate for what would otherwise be their anaemic under-cured appearance. Some undyed kippers are still available from parts of Scotland and the Isle of Man, but they're rather exclusive and mainly available in the north-west.

Look for plumpness, oiliness, a silvery-golden colour and a good smoky smell in a kipper. As I've said before, all fish (and meat) tastes better cooked on the bone, and kippers are no exception. I also think the best way to cook them is under a hot grill.

Grilled kippers
Pre-heat the grill, then line the grill pan with foil (which will stop any kippery smells haunting the pan) and brush the foil with melted butter. Remove the heads and tails from the kippers with scissors, then lay the fish on the foil skin side uppermost. Grill them for 1 minute, turn them over (flesh side uppermost), brush the flesh with melted butter and grill for a further 4–5 minutes until the butter is sizzling. Serve immediately with lemon to squeeze over them and perhaps a dash of cayenne. If you have an aversion to bones, you can of course buy kipper fillets: treat them in just the same way.

Jugged kippers
This is a traditional, and sometimes preferred, way to prepare kippers. All you do is remove the heads, then fold the sides of the fish together and pack vertically in a tall warmed jug. Now pour in enough boiling water to cover the kippers, put a lid or plate on top of the jug, and leave them in a warm place for 6 minutes. Then drain and dry them with kitchen paper, and serve on hot plates with a knob of butter to melt over each fish.

Bloaters These are very popular in East Anglia. Instead of being split like kippers, the herrings are cured and lightly smoked whole (with guts intact!). When I bought my first bloater I thought there had been some mistake but, no, the guts are meant to provide that 'gamey' flavour. So, to cook them, split them and remove the guts, wipe them with kitchen paper and grill them just like kippers. Alternatively you can make a delicious *Bloater paste*, by pounding the flesh together with butter, lemon juice and a pinch or two of cayenne; serve it spread on toast or in brown bread sandwiches.

Smoked buckling These are hot-smoked herrings, which need no further cooking, and are nice and juicy. Serve and eat them in the same way as smoked trout, or else separate them out into fillets (easily done with all smoked fish) and serve with thinly sliced onion rings, chopped dill-pickled cucumbers and soured cream.

Smoked sprats These are young baby herrings, cured and smoked. They're fiddly to deal with but inexpensive and delicious. Skinning and filleting them is time consuming but not difficult. They can be served plain, sprinkled with lemon juice and cayenne.

The smoked haddock family
Finnan haddock Six miles south of Aberdeen there's a village called Findon, where east coast haddock were first smoked over peat (Finnan is a derivative of Findon). Much smoked haddock still comes from the Aberdeen area, but some is also smoked in London nowadays. If you want to know the difference: in an Aberdeen cure the fish is split from head to tail so the backbone lies on the right-hand side of the tail; with a London cure the backbone lies on the left and an extra cut is made so that the flesh stands away from the bone. Finnan haddock is best cooked in the oven with a little milk to provide steam, and a generous amount of butter dotted over.

Arbroath smokies These are young haddock (or occasionally whiting) that have been beheaded and gutted but otherside left whole. They are then smoked to a dark, almost bronze, colour and always sold in pairs. They're usually eaten hot, brushed with butter on the outside and placed in the oven with a good knob of butter pressed down inside. Or, to quote Gerald Watkin (of the Worshipful Company of Fishmongers), they can be 'placed under a slow grill, covered with bacon rashers, so as they warm the bacon fat combines with them to remedy their only deficiency'.

Smoked fillets Usually these *are* haddock, but they can be any white fish (like cod). No smoked fillets have such good flavour as fish smoked on the bone, but they're convenient if you're in a hurry or don't want to be bothered with bones. Good, I think, for poaching, buttering and popping a poached egg on top.

Golden cutlets Also known as block fillets these are small smoked fillets of haddock or whiting—too small really to be of much use, but again suitable for a poached egg topping.

Kipper fish cakes

(serves 4 people)

Kippers, I think, make better fish cakes than ordinary white fish, because they have much more character and flavour.

About 1 lb kippers or kipper fillets (450 g)
1 lb potatoes, scrubbed (450 g)
1 hard-boiled egg, chopped
2 teaspoons English mustard
2 teaspoons grated onion
2 tablespoons chopped parsley
1–2 tablespoons cream, or top of the milk
A little nutmeg and cayenne pepper
Some butter and oil for frying
Watercress and lemon quarters for garnishing

First boil the potatoes in their jackets in salted water until tender, then cool and drain them and peel off the skins. Place the potatoes in a bowl with the egg, mustard, onion, parsley and cream.

Jug the kippers (as described on page 139), then flake the fish, discarding the bones and skin, and add the flesh to the potato mixture. Beat with a fork until everything is well combined then season to taste with cayenne and nutmeg. Heat sufficient butter and oil to cover the base of a thick frying pan. Press the mixture into about 12 small cake shapes, then fry for about 5 minutes on each side until they are a golden brown colour.

To serve: garnish with sprigs of watercress and lemon quarters (for squeezing the juice over the fish cakes) and have more cayenne pepper available for those who like it.

Smoked haddock with cream and egg sauce

(serves 4 people)

Smoked haddock is often served simply with a poached egg, but this recipe with chopped hard-boiled egg in a cream sauce is a delicious alternative.

1½ lb smoked haddock (700 g)
½ pint milk (275 ml)
1 bayleaf
About 2 oz butter (50 g)
1 oz plain flour (25 g)
1 small onion
3 tablespoons double cream
1 hard-boiled egg, chopped
Salt and freshly-milled black pepper

Pre-heat the oven to gas mark 4, 350°F (180°C)

First place the fish in a baking tin, season with freshly-milled black pepper and a little salt, tuck in a bayleaf and add the milk. Dot with flecks of butter and bake, uncovered, for about 20 minutes.

Meanwhile, chop the onion quite finely, melt 1½ oz (40 g) butter in a saucepan and sauté the onion very gently without colouring it. When the fish is cooked, remove it from the baking tin, keep it warm and pour the liquid in which it was cooked into a jug. Stir the flour into the butter and onion mixture, then add the fish liquid a little at a time and blend to a smooth sauce. Cook over a very low heat for approximately 6 minutes then stir in the hard-boiled egg and the cream.

To serve, pour the sauce over the fish and, perhaps, have some creamy mashed potatoes to go with it.

Smoked fish pie

(serves 4 people)

This is a lovely creamy fish pie and, with its soured cream and mashed potato topping, all it needs is a green vegetable or salad to go with it.

1½ lb smoked haddock (700 g)
4 kipper fillets, weighing a total 4–6 oz (110–175 g)

1 pint milk (570 ml)
1 bayleaf
4 oz butter (110 g)
2 hard-boiled eggs, roughly chopped
3 tablespoons fresh chopped parsley
1 tablespoon capers (these can be left out if not available)
1 tablespoon lemon juice
2 oz flour (50 g)

For the topping:
2 lb fresh boiled potatoes (900 g)
1 oz butter (25 g)
¼ pint soured cream (150 ml)
Freshly-grated nutmeg
Salt and freshly-milled black pepper

Pre-heat the oven to gas mark 6, 400°F (200°C)

Arrange the fish in a baking tin, pour ½ pint (275 ml) milk over it, add a few flecks of butter and the bayleaf, then bake in the oven for 15–20 minutes. Pour off and reserve the cooking liquid, then remove the skin from the fish and flake the flesh into largish pieces.

Next make the sauce by melting the remaining butter in a saucepan, then stirring in the flour and gradually adding the fish liquid bit by bit, stirring well after each addition. When all the liquid is in, finish the sauce by gradually adding the remaining ½ pint (275 ml) milk and seasoning with salt and pepper and simmering for 3–4 minutes.

Now mix the fish into the sauce, together with the hard-boiled eggs, parsley and capers, then taste to see if it needs any more seasoning, and stir in the lemon juice. Pour the mixture into a buttered baking dish (about 2½ pints (1·5 litre) capacity).

Next prepare the topping: cream the potatoes, starting off with a large fork, then finishing off with an electric beater if you have one, adding the butter and soured cream. Season the potatoes and add some freshly-grated nutmeg, then spread it evenly all over the fish. Bake on a high shelf in the oven—still at gas mark 6, 400°F (200°C) for about 30 minutes, by which time the pie will be heated through and the top will be nicely tinged with brown.

Potted haddock with capers

(serves 8 people)

This is good as a light lunch with some home-made wholemeal bread or toast.

1 lb smoked haddock fillets (450 g)
½ lb melted butter, unsalted (225 g)
A good pinch of hot curry powder
2–3 tablespoons lemon juice
4 tablespoons drained capers
Salt and freshly-milled black pepper
Watercress or parsley and lemon for garnish

Place the haddock fillets in a pan, cover with boiling water and poach them for about 5 minutes, then remove from the pan and drain thoroughly. Now skin the fish and flake the flesh into the goblet of a liquidiser. Add the melted butter and blend until smooth. Then empty the mixture into a bowl and season—but be sparing with the salt. Stir in the curry powder and lemon juice to taste and fill eight individual dishes with the mixture.

Chop the drained capers and scatter some on the top of each dish. Cover with foil or clingfilm and put the dishes in the refrigerator so that the fish mixture becomes firm before serving. Serve with lemon quarters and sprigs of parsley or watercress.

Marinaded kipper fillets

(serves 4 people)

This dish, if you leave it to marinate long enough, puts kipper fillets in the smoked salmon class.

8 kipper fillets, approximately ¾ lb (350 g)
6 fl oz mild olive oil (175 ml)
2 fl oz wine vinegar (55 ml)
1 dessertspoon brown sugar
2 bayleaves
1 heaped teaspoon mustard powder
1 medium-sized onion, thinly sliced into rings
2 teaspoons crushed coriander seeds
Freshly-milled black pepper
Lemon slices, lettuce leaves and watercress for garnishing

Turn the kipper fillets upside down on a flat surface and, using a sharp knife to help you, take off the skins. Then in a 1½ pint (850 ml) oval dish, layer the fillets with slices of onion and a sprinkling of coriander and freshly-milled black pepper, tucking the two bayleaves here and there. Now in a screw-top jar dissolve the mustard powder and brown sugar in the vinegar and olive oil, screw on the lid and shake vigorously, then pour the mixture over the fillets. Now cook the dish very carefully, with either a lid or a double sheet of foil or clingfilm. Then leave the kipper fillets to marinate in the lowest part of the refrigerator for 4 or 5 days.

To serve, place two fillets on a crisp lettuce leaf for each person. Garnish with lemon slices and watercress, and serve with thinly sliced brown bread and butter.

Shellfish
Mussels

I love the appearance of mussels: a rich saffron colour and they sit so prettily in the blue, boat-shaped shells. To me their aroma and flavour are the very essence of the sea. Some people accuse them of being dangerous to eat, but in fact mussel poisoning (unpleasant though never dangerous) is positively rare. If you know how to buy mussels and how to deal with them the risk is negligible. I would point out, however, that all shellfish is highly perishable. So you should always eat mussels (and any other type of shellfish for that matter) on the day you buy them.

Mussels are at their best in cold weather, so their season is usually from October to March. When you see them in a fishmonger's, a sign of freshness is that most of them are tightly closed: if there are a lot of 'gapers' don't bother. When buying mussels you need to allow at least 1 pint (570 ml) per person for a first course, and 1½–2 pints (about 1 litre) for a main course. That may seem a lot, but some will have to be discarded and, once they are out of their shells, mussels are very small and light.

The ritual of cleaning and preparing them *sounds* more bother than it actually is. When you get them home, dump the mussels straight away into a sinkful of cold water. First of all throw out any that float to the top, then leave the cold tap running over them while you take a small knife and scrape off all the barnacles and pull off the little hairy beards. Discard any mussels that are broken, and any that are open and refuse to close tight when given a sharp tap with a knife.

After you've cleaned each one, place it straight in another bowl of clean water. When they're all in, swirl them around in three or four more changes of cold water to get rid of any lingering bits of grit or sand. Leave the cleaned mussels in cold water until you're ready to cook them. As an extra safety precaution, always check mussels a second time after cooking—this time discarding any whose shells haven't opened.

Moules à la marinière

(serves 4 people as a first course)

This is the most popular of all mussel recipes and, for me, a real treat served with crusty French bread and some chilled white wine.

4 pints cleaned mussels (2·25 litres)
1 wine glass dry white wine
1 clove garlic, chopped
1 onion, finely chopped
2 oz butter (50 g)
3 tablespoons double cream
1 tablespoon freshly chopped parsley
Salt and freshly-milled black pepper

In a wide-bottomed pan melt half the butter and, over a low heat, gently soften the garlic and onion. Then pour in the white wine and, when it comes to the boil, tip in the mussels—which should have been drained and dried a little first. Cover with a lid and leave on a high heat for 4–5 minutes. Then remove the lid and start lifting out the mussels as they open and place them on a warm dish—a draining spoon is best for this. Keep them warm in a very low heated oven. Throw away the empty half shells, and any mussels that haven't opened up their shells during cooking.

Have ready a sieve lined with fine muslin; strain the liquid in which the mussels were cooked through this then return it to the pan. Simmer to reduce by half then add the cream and the rest of the butter. Season with freshly-milled black pepper and, perhaps, a little salt. When the cream has heated and the butter has melted, pour the sauce over the mussels resting in their half shells, and sprinkle on the chopped parsley.

Mussels with garlic stuffing

(serves 4 people)

You *have* to like your garlic for this one and, if you do, be sure to have lots of crusty fresh bread to mop up the juices.

4 pints cleaned mussels (2·25 litres)
4 oz butter, at room temperature (110 g)
1 tablespoon lemon juice
1 heaped tablespoon chopped parsley
2 cloves garlic, crushed
Salt and freshly-milled black pepper

Pre-heat the oven to gas mark 8, 450°F (230°C)

Place the prepared mussels in a wide dry saucepan, cover with a lid and cook over a low heat (there's no need to add any liquid) until they all open. Now remove and discard the empty half shells and throw away any mussels that haven't opened, then arrange the remaining mussels in their half shells in four individual fireproof dishes.

Next, in a basin, combine the butter, lemon juice, parsley and garlic, season with salt and pepper and mix well. Place a small dab of the savoury butter on each mussel then put the dishes on the top shelf of the oven and cook for 5–10 minutes or until the mussels are sizzling noisily. Serve immediately still sizzling and bubbling.

Scallops

Scallops with their bright orange roes come in decorative shells. The fish itself sits on a flat fan-shaped shell and is enclosed by a similar concave one (the one shell scallops are traditionally served in). This curved shell has become a religious and cultural symbol: the shrine of St. James the apostle at Compostella in Spain has adopted the scallop shell as its emblem, and scallops themselves have been named after the saint—hence *Coquilles St. Jacques*. Scallops are a great delicacy, and in fact some of the best scallops in the world come from British waters off the Isle of Man, and the Cornish and Irish coasts.

When you're buying scallops, as with other shellfish, it's obviously best to buy them as fresh as possible (i.e. live in the shell); if their shells are closed you can be sure they're fresh. Don't worry if you're nervous about these things, the fishmonger will open and clean them ready for you. Some shops sell scallops already prepared, in which case you'd do well to make sure they look plump, firm and upright. If scallops look at all sad and soggy, then they've probably been prepared rather too long ago. An acceptable alternative to fresh scallops are the frozen ones—not so good of course but better than none.

Scallops cook very quickly. The corals only take a matter of seconds, so they are usually added to the cooking pan only shortly before serving.

Scallops in the shell

(serves 4 people as a first course)

I think these look very pretty served in the shells, brown and bubbly from the grill. (Ask the fishmonger for 4 deep shells to serve them in.)

8 small, or 4 large cleaned scallops
Half an onion, chopped finely
¼ lb mushrooms, sliced (110 g)
2 oz butter (50 g)
½ pint dry white wine (275 ml)
1½ oz flour (40 g)
¼ pint double cream (150 ml)
2 tablespoons breadcrumbs
A little extra butter
Salt and freshly-milled black pepper

Start by slicing the white part of each scallop into rounds, putting the corals on one side for use later. Then poach the white slices very, very gently in white wine until tender—about 10 minutes. (It's always necessary to cook scallops gently or they can become tough.) When they're cooked, strain them reserving the liquid.

Now melt the butter in a saucepan, add the onion and mushrooms and cook over a low heat for about 15 minutes. Then sprinkle in the flour, and add the scallop liquid very gradually, stirring continuously to obtain a thick smooth sauce. Add seasoning and a little more butter and cook gently for about 6 minutes.

Then remove the saucepan from the heat and stir in the white slices and the coral pieces of scallop, plus the cream. Now heat the mixture through over a very gentle heat, taking great care not to let it boil. Divide the mixture between four buttered scallop shells, sprinkle with breadcrumbs, add flecks of butter and brown under a pre-heated grill.

Scallop cream soup

(serves 4–6 people)

This is very easy and quick to prepare and cook, but tastes as though it has taken ages!

4 very large cleaned scallops (when taken out of their shells the total weight should be approximately ¾ lb or 350 g)
1 medium-sized onion, finely chopped
1 lb potatoes, diced (450 g)
2 oz butter (50 g)
1 pint fish stock (570 g) (see recipe on page 95)
½ pint cold milk (275 ml)
2 egg yolks
3 fl oz double cream (75 ml)
Salt and freshly-milled black pepper

First gently melt the butter in a fairly large saucepan, add the onion and cook it *very* gently without colouring it at all (about 10 minutes). Next add the diced potatoes, mix them in with the butter and onions, and season with salt and pepper. Then, keeping the heat very low, put the lid on the pan and leave the mixture to sweat for another 10–15 minutes.

After that pour in the hot fish stock, give it a good stir, cover the pan again and leave to simmer gently for a further 10–15 minutes.

Meanwhile you can be preparing the scallops: wash and dry them thoroughly and cut off the coral-coloured bits—chop these and keep them on one side on a separate plate. The white parts should be diced roughly, put in a saucepan with the cold milk and a little salt and pepper, then poached very, very gently for 8–10 minutes.

When the vegetables are cooked, transfer them and their cooking liquid to a blender and whisk to a purée (or else press it all through a nylon sieve). Now combine the white parts of the scallops (and the milk they were cooked in) with the potato purée. At this point the pieces of coral roe can be added and the soup gently re-heated.

Finally beat the egg yolks thoroughly with the cream, remove the soup pan from the heat, stir in the egg and cream mixture and return the pan to a *gentle* heat. Cook, stirring, until the soup thickens slightly—but be very careful not to let it come anywhere near the boil or it will curdle.

To serve, pour the soup into a warm tureen and ladle it into warm soup bowls. This really is one of the most delicate and delicious soups imaginable. *Note:* if you want to make this soup in advance, prepare it up to the egg yolk and cream stage. This final stage should only be done at the last minute, just before serving.

Prawns and shimps

If I was ever an aspiring gourmet, time has tempered me. No longer can I be tempted to peel two pints of cooked brown shrimps (a job which used to take all afternoon) to make a tiny amount of shrimp paste—admittedly delicious but consumed, it seemed, in a few seconds. But fresh, fat and juicy prawns, *yes*, I will willingly peel to serve unadulterated—with just some lettuce, a squeeze of lemon or perhaps some home-made mayonnaise. They have to be fresh, native prawns though. For 'prawns' covers a multitude of varieties, many of them from warm foreign waters where they grow fast and often large. Even when unfrozen these lack the firm texture and flavour of our own. If I *have* to buy frozen prawns for cooking, the best I've come across are the Norwegian prawns which the food departments of one quality chain-store sell.

   Just to confuse matters, what we call prawns the Americans call shrimps. But our tiny shrimps are almost a national delicacy when potted in Lancashire with melted butter and spices (one firm in Morecambe Bay, incidentally, operates a mail-order shrimp service). At one time these potted shrimps came in prettily glazed porcelain pots, but now plastic has penetrated here too. One authority suggests that to appreciate the flavour of potted shrimps, they should be gently warmed till the butter just begins to flow. I agree, and certainly I've found that melting the shrimp butter in a saucepan with a couple of tablespoons of fresh cream makes a lovely 'instant' sauce to serve with plain grilled fish.

Scampi, by the way, is the Italian name for what we used to call Dublin bay prawns. They are not in fact prawns but a tiny member of the lobster family (yet another name for this shellfish is Norway lobster). All the meat lies in the tail and scampi are always sold headless, usually already boiled and rubbery and frozen. It seems appropriate that they end up deep-fried in bright orange 'breadcrumbs' to be served as basket meals in pubs.

How to peel prawns
Holding the prawn's head with your left hand and its tail with your right hand, uncurl the prawn and straighten it out as much as possible. Now press the head and tail towards each other in a straight line, and then pull them apart again—the shell should come away in your right hand, leaving the head and body in your left hand. Now simply separate the head from the body.

Spiced prawns with tomatoes

(serves 2–3 people)

I think fresh boiled and peeled prawns are so delicious all they need is lemon juice, seasoning and some wholemeal bread and butter. Frozen prawns, on the other hand, need an imaginative recipe like this one.

8 oz packet frozen prawns (225 g)
1 lb tomatoes, skinned and chopped (450 g)
1 large onion, halved and sliced
2 cloves garlic, crushed
1½ tablespoons groundnut oil
¾ teaspoon coriander seeds
½ teaspoon cumin seeds
1 cardamom pod
½ teaspoon ground ginger
1 rounded teaspoon ground turmeric
½ teaspoon chilli powder
Salt and freshly-milled black pepper

In a large frying pan heat the oil, then add the onion slices and fry gently for approximately 10 minutes or until softened and golden.

In the meantime, grind the whole spices with a pestle and mortar (or this can be done in a small basin using the end of a rolling pin).

Then add all the spices, together with the garlic, to the onion and stir until everything is well heated. Now add the prawns and stir them around too, so that they're evenly coated with the spice mixture, then add the prepared tomatoes and some salt and freshly-milled pepper. Bring to simmering point and cook for about 20–25 minutes, uncovered, by which time a lot of the excess liquid will have evaporated and the tomatoes will have reduced to the consistency of a sauce.

Serve with spiced pilau rice or some nutty-flavoured brown rice cooked with onion.

How to dress crab

If you're not squeamish you can buy fresh, live crab and cook it yourself. I'm afraid I am squeamish and I could no more drop a live crab into boiling water than I could stab it through the head. I'm perfectly happy to leave the boiling to the experts and to find a reliable fishmonger to choose me a good cooked crab.

A good crab full of meat should feel heavy for its size. I bought one recently which weighed just over 1 lb (450 g) and it yielded almost 7 oz (200 g) of meat. From a large 2 lb (900 g) crab you should get about ³/₄ lb (350 g) of meat. Together with some home-made mayonnaise and a salad, 7–8 oz (200 g) of crabmeat is plenty for two people as a main course—or you could stretch it between four for a starter.

The first thing you do is to choose and buy your cooked crab. The fishmonger will pull it slightly open so that you can see it's full of meat and not empty. Back in your kitchen you'll need a

chopping board, two bowls (one for the white meat and one for the dark meat), a small sharp knife, a teaspoon, a metal skewer (preferably flat), and either a small hammer or a pair of nutcrackers.

Put the crab on its back on the chopping board, so that the claws and softer body shell face upwards, then simply twist off the legs and claws (A)—they'll come away very easily— and put them on one side.

A

Now put your thumbs against the hard back shell close to the crab's tail, and push and prise the body section out and away from the hard back shell (B). From the body section you now remove and discard (i) the small greyish-white stomach sac, just behind the mouth and (ii) the long white pointed 'dead man's fingers'. These can be easily distinguished and it is a quick and easy job to remove them (C).

The body shell (and in particular the parts where the legs and claws joined the body) is a mass of tiny crevices, all harbouring delicious meat. Scrape and pick the meat out, dividing it between the bowls according to the colour of the meat. Remove the meat from the hard back shell in the same way (D).

Crack the claws and legs with your hammer or nutcracker then, with a skewer, poke out all the white meat into the appropriate bowl (E).

If you want to serve the crab in the hard back shell, break off the jagged, overlapping rim from all round the edge of the shell, then wash and dry it well, and smear it inside with oil (F).

Then season the white meat with salt, freshly-milled pepper, cayenne and lemon juice (chopping or shredding the meat a little). Now season the brown meat in the same way. Place it down the centre of the shell, and place the white meat on either side. Finally decorate the crab with finely chopped parsley (see the photograph on page 282) and serve with a fresh crisp salad and some home-made mayonnaise (page 483).

Hot crab soufflé

(serves 4–6 people as
a first course)

Crabmeat makes one of the nicest of all
hot savoury soufflés.

The crabmeat from a fresh cooked crab, weighing 1 lb (450 g) or 8 oz (225 g) frozen mixed brown and white crabmeat, thawed
1½ oz butter (40 g)
1½ oz flour (40 g)
¼ pint single cream (150 ml)
¼ pint milk (150 ml)
1 tablespoon grated onion
2 tablespoons grated Parmesan cheese
½ teaspoon English mustard powder
1½ teaspoons anchovy essence
1–2 teaspoons lemon juice
3 tablespoons chopped parsley
5 egg yolks
6 egg whites
Salt and cayenne pepper

Pre-heat the oven to gas mark 6,
400°F (200°C) and put in a baking sheet
on the shelf below centre.

First grease a 4 pint (2·25 l) baking or soufflé dish. Then melt the
butter in a saucepan, stir in the flour and cook for 1–2 minutes.
Then gradually add the cream and milk, a little at a time, stirring
after each addition. Bring to the boil and—still stirring—allow it to
simmer for a minute or two. Now remove the pan from the heat and
stir in the rest of the ingredients, except for the crabmeat and egg
whites.

Next, add the crabmeat and taste the mixture—it should have quite
a strong flavour. If not add some more anchovy essence, salt,
cayenne and lemon juice. Now whisk the egg white until stiff but not
dry and, using a metal spoon, fold them into the crab mixture, then
pour the soufflé into the prepared baking dish. Put the dish on the
pre-heated baking sheet in the oven and bake for 45–50 minutes.
After about 30 minutes, check to see that the top of the soufflé is not
getting too brown—if it is, cover with foil. Serve *immediately* it's
cooked.

See also:

Anchoiade
Avocado mousse with prawns and vinaigrette
Avocado and seafood salad
Baked mackerel with herb stuffing
Brown rice and tuna fish salad
Buttery kedgeree
Fillets of sole gratiné
Fish cakes

Garlicky fish soup
Kipper quiche
Poached trout with herbs
Salade Niçoise
Smoked fish creams
Smoked fish pâté
Smoked mackerel pâté
Taramasalata
Trout with butter, cream and chives
White bean and tuna fish salad

Meat: roasting and pot-roasting

Including recipes for:
Yorkshire pudding
Bœuf en daube
English pot roast
Boiled beef and dumplings
Roast pork with green butter
Stuffed pork tenderloin

Loin of pork Dijonnaise
Bacon pot roast
Sugar-glazed gammon
Stuffed breast of lamb
Shoulder of lamb with rice and kidney stuffing
Baked lamb with coriander

*Never you mind about the pieces of needlework, the maps of the world made
by her needle. Get to see her at work on a mutton chop. . . .*
Cobbett's Advice to a Young Man Getting Married

I think that if we all had to pass an examination in meat cookery
before getting married nowadays, there would be rather a surplus of
spinsters in this country. And the reason would be that the whole
subject of meat cookery—not to mention meat butchery—is
daunting for anyone. Even the cuts of meat vary from region to
region, sometimes from butcher to butcher, and however skilled
you are as a cook you have to have an ally in a helpful local
butcher. I fear my own experience of butchers is that really helpful
ones are few and far between—but then maybe we get what we
deserve, by not asking to see what gets whisked into those plastic
bags before we have time to blink. Now that animal foodstuffs
are getting scarce and expensive, some meat—especially pork—
can be rather tasteless (or worse, tainted by the kind of diet
used). So a good, discerning butcher is vital. Failing that, a
reliable quality supermarket can be better than an unhelpful
butcher.

Pot roasting

The trouble with a straightforward roast, quite apart from
requiring the more expensive cuts of meat, is that the meal as a
whole (including Yorkshire pudding and roast potatoes) can take
up a great deal of your time and attention. Pot roasts on the other
hand leave you in peace. You still get a reasonably-sized joint to
carve and at a cheaper price.

The principle of pot roasting is long, slow cooking of the meat in a
fairly heavy cooking-pot (with a tight-fitting lid) in a small amount
of liquid which can be stock, wine or cider. This creates a steamy
atmosphere inside the closed pot, which keeps the joint moist as it
cooks. Herbs and vegetables may be added too, and sometimes the
meat is marinaded first. The finished dish should be very tender and
succulent.

The medium-priced and cheaper cuts are usually the most
suitable for pot roasts: *silverside* and *top rump* are both good, and so is
chuck and *blade* boned and rolled. My own favourite is *brisket*
(economical and with lots of flavour), but you do need a reliable
butcher to roll it for you, because a lot of excess fat and gristle can be
lurking unseen inside.

Principles of roasting meat

Strictly speaking, roasting means exposing a piece of meat to an open fire, turning it (usually on a spit) so the air circulates around it and each part comes near to the source of the heat and the whole is cooked evenly. True roasting in fact is more like grilling as we know it: the nearest equivalent is the modern spit-roast, which is fitted to some domestic ovens or sold as a separate unit. Still, for most of us, in practical terms roasting means cooking a joint inside an ordinary oven.

Oven roasting

It is best to begin roasting with a very high oven setting (gas mark 9, 475°F, 245°C) and then lower the heat to continue cooking. This blast of heat at the beginning produces a more attractive-looking joint with a tasty outside crust. In order to approximate some circulation of air in an enclosed oven, setting the joint on a roasting rack is often advised. It doesn't make a great deal of difference though, unless you object to the very crusty, well-cooked bit of the meat that sits on the base of the roasting tin. With something like a piece of sirloin or a rib joint on the bone, the bone itself provides a form of built-in rack.

Beef

Scotch beef, bred in the Highlands, grass-fed, mature and well hung, is the best in the world, and in the last couple of years I have also had some very good Irish beef, but I cannot reconcile myself to the immature, barley-fed beef (which is widely sold in my neighbourhood at any rate): an insipid imitation of what good beef should be, it seems to me. I even feel it would be better to have less meat—make a really good piece of beef a treat—so that we would not have to rear it so intensively.

I have heard breeders say that this mass-produced beef is what the housewife wants, that is, lots of it, tender and almost fat-less. But what people so often fail to realise is that fat means flavour: tender lean meat that is lacking the one essential, flavour, is no pleasure at all. Nature has so arranged things that when a good piece of meat with its proper percentage of fat is placed near a fire or in an oven, the heat draws out some of the juices while the fat melts and bastes the meat within as well as outside, keeping the meat succulent (which is why wise old cooks, and wise new ones too, take care to baste the meat as it is roasting). If you can't eat the fat at the end, that doesn't matter; its presence during cooking is the essential thing.

Roasting beef

The cardinal rule here is to buy the right cut in the first place. It's no wonder that letters pour in from people who are unsuccessful in roasting beef when you consider some of the so-called roasting joints on offer—all manner of things get tied up with string and labelled 'roasting'. My advice is to buy an unequivocal, decent-sized piece of *sirloin* for a special occasion, and otherwise a *double rib joint* (which as it happens is next door, anatomically).

Do buy, and cook your joint *on the bone*. You won't be paying any extra, since meat bought on the bone costs less per pound. The bone provides a good conductor of heat inside the joint, thus cooking the meat more evenly with less loss of juices; it also helps to stop the meat disintegrating, which you will appreciate when you come to carve. If you are worried that your family is too small to cope with a large joint, bear in mind that good roast beef is delicious cold with chutney and jacket potatoes, and minced it makes lovely rissoles. However, if you prefer it, both the above joints can be boned and rolled. When you buy a piece of sirloin, make sure it contains the 'eye' or undercut, which some butchers take out and sell as fillet steak (which it is). A decent joint of sirloin on the bone will weigh 4–5 lb (2–2.5 kg). If you choose a wing rib for roasting, then ask for a 'double rib' as a single one is too thin—it looks the same as a sirloin but without the undercut. A more economical roasting joint— which unhappily is not always available unless you order it—is a cut called the *aitchbone*. A whole one is very large, but some butchers will sell part of one. It comes from the pelvic region of the animal, just behind the rump, and as it needs slower roasting it isn't really suitable for eating rare, but its flavour is excellent.

To prepare a joint for roasting Dust the fat-surface with a mixture of flour and dry mustard, and sprinkle with freshly-milled pepper (but no salt, since this encourages the juices to escape). Add a knob of beef dripping to the tin, just to moisten the base, before placing the joint in it. Start by giving it 20 minutes at gas mark 9, 475°F (245°C), then lower the heat to gas mark 5, 375°F (190°C), and cook for 15 minutes per pound (for rare), plus 15 extra minutes (for medium-rare), plus 30 minutes extra (for well-done), and baste the meat by spooning the pan juices over it during the cooking.

Try to plan the meal so that the joint is allowed to 'relax' for about 30 minutes before carving. Keep it in a warm place but don't worry that it will become cold—it will hold its heat for this time.

Removing it from direct heat will firm up the texture, making it easier to carve. This will also permit you to increase the heat in the oven for the roast potatoes and Yorkshire pudding. As the meat relaxes, some of the juices will exude onto the plate: these should be added to the gravy. And while on the subject of carving, may I refer you to my comments on knives on page 16. Carving is only difficult and dangerous when the knife is blunt.

Accompaniments to beef

Grating fresh *horseradish* is a tiresome job: the fumes cause tears and discomfort. It is possible, though, to buy preserved grated horseradish, which you can combine with cream to make your own sauce—or else stir in a little grated horseradish to some commercially bottled horseradish sauce to give it an extra kick. Whether it is on its own or mixed with cream, horseradish is very strong—so be warned. *Mustard* is the other traditional accompaniment, and should be made up ten minutes, at least, before it is needed. *Yorkshire pudding* was originally served as a first course, to temper the appetite and make the meat go further. But crisply-made Yorkshire pud is now—and with every reason—something of a delicacy. There are just a few rules: for a successful pudding you must (i) have the oven very hot, (ii) use a metal container, and (iii) always use plain flour rather than self-raising.

Yorkshire pudding (for 4 people)	**3 oz plain flour (75 g)**
	1 egg
	3 fl oz milk (75 ml)
	2 fl oz water (50 ml)
	Salt and freshly-milled pepper
	2 tablespoons beef dripping (for the roasting-tin)

Pre-heat the oven to gas mark 7, 425°F (220°C)

To make the batter, sift the flour into a bowl, make a well in the centre, break an egg into it and beat it, gradually incorporating the flour, milk, water, and seasoning (an electric hand-whisk will do this in seconds). You don't have to leave batter to stand, so make it when you're ready. About 15 minutes before the beef is due to come out of the oven, increase the heat to gas mark 7, 425°F (220°C), and place an oblong tin 11 × 7 inches (28 × 18 cm) on a baking-sheet on a free shelf, adding the dripping to the tin. After 15 minutes remove the meat and leave on one side to rest, then place the tin over direct heat while you pour the batter into the sizzling hot fat. Then return the tin to the baking sheet on the highest shelf (or second highest, if you have roast potatoes on that one). The pudding will take about 25–30 minutes to rise and become crisp and golden. Serve as soon as possible, as it loses its crunchiness if it has to wait around too long.

Bœuf en daube	3–3 ½ lb top rump of beef (1 kg 350 g to 1 kg 750 g), tightly rolled and tied
(serves 6 people)	About 4 tablespoons beef dripping
	1 tablespoon flour
	½ pint stock (275 ml)
	4 tomatoes, peeled and quartered
	2 oz dark gilled mushrooms (50 g) sliced
	1 rounded tablespoon flour, worked to a paste with a tablespoon of butter
	Freshly-milled black pepper
	For the marinade:
	½ pint red wine (275 ml)
	2 tablespoons olive oil
	2 tablespoons red wine vinegar
	2 onions, halved and sliced
	2 carrots, sliced in rounds
	A bouquet garni*
	2 teaspoons salt

* Bouquet garni—consisting of a bayleaf, a strip of orange zest, ½ teaspoon dried thyme, ½ teaspoon black peppercorns, 6 all spice berries, 2 large unpeeled cloves, garlic, halved lengthways—all these tied together in a little piece of gauze.

First prepare the marinade by combining all the ingredients in a bowl, then put in the meat. Cover with a cloth, then put in a cold place for at least 12 hours, and during that time, turn the meat over occasionally.

When you wish to begin cooking, pre-heat the oven to gas mark 1, 275°F (140°C). Remove the meat from the marinade and dry it thoroughly on kitchen paper.

Now heat the dripping in a thick cooking pot which will take the meat neatly and, when the fat is hot, add the meat and sear it all over—it should be a nutty brown colour. Then transfer to a plate, and pour off all but about 1 tablespoon of the fat from the pan.

Next, remove the vegetables from the marinade with a draining-spoon, reserving the liquid. Dry them on kitchen paper, then tip them into the cooking-pot and fry them until they are lightly browned. Then stir in the flour and brown this slowly, but be careful it doesn't burn. Now stir in the reserved marinade liquid, the bouquet garni, stock, tomatoes and mushrooms, add the meat and season with freshly-milled black pepper.

Bring to simmering point, cover with a piece of foil and a tight-fitting lid, then place the pot in the centre of the oven and let it cook slowly for about 3 hours. To test if the meat is fully cooked a skewer should go into the meat easily.

When ready, remove the meat and keep warm. Tip the contents of the pot into a sieve placed over a bowl and press the vegetables against the side of the sieve to extract all the juices. Return the liquid to the pan and boil quickly to reduce and concentrate the flavour. Now add the butter and flour mixture and whisk, with a balloon whisk, until the sauce thickens.

Season to taste with salt and pepper. Carve the meat, pour over some of the sauce and pour the rest into a warmed sauce boat.

English pot roast

(serves 4–6 people)

The root vegetables in this seem to absorb the meat flavour, which makes them extra good.

2½ lb rolled brisket (1 kg)
4 small whole onions, peeled
4 smallish carrots, peeled
4 sticks celery cut in three
½ large swede, peeled and cut in chunks
Some beef dripping
¼ lb dark gilled mushrooms (110 g)

½ pint hot stock (or hot water enriched with ½ teaspoon Worcester sauce and 2 teaspoons mushroom ketchup)
A sprig of thyme
A bayleaf
1 tablespoon flour and 1 tablespoon butter worked to a paste
Salt and freshly-milled black pepper

Pre-heat the oven to gas mark 1, 275°F (140°C)

First melt the dripping in a thick cooking-pot and, when it's hot, put in the meat and sear and brown it all over, then transfer it to a plate. Next lightly brown the onions, carrots, celery and swede, then remove them temporarily to the plate too.

Next, empty all the fat from the pot, then replace the brisket and arrange the vegetables and mushrooms around the meat. Add the hot stock, bayleaf and thyme and a little salt and pepper. Cover with foil and a tightly-fitting lid and as soon as you hear simmering, place in the centre of the oven and leave for about 3 hours.

When ready, place the meat and vegetables on a warmed serving dish, then bring the liquid to the boil and boil briskly until reduced slightly. Add the butter and flour paste and whisk until the sauce thickens. Serve with the meat and some sharp English mustard.

Boiled beef and dumplings

(serves 6 people)

Salted silverside would do for this, but salted brisket is even better.

3 lb joint boned, rolled brisket (1 kg 350 g), salted (ask your butcher if it needs soaking or not)
1 sprig thyme
1 bayleaf
A few parsley stalks
5 medium carrots
5 small onions
2 turnips, quartered
2 celery stalks, cut into 1 inch (2·5 cm lengths)
Salt and freshly-milled black pepper

Right: Minestrone soup, page 98; Quick and easy wholewheat bread, page 50; Vegetarian goulash, page 328; Watercress cream soup, page 103.

For the dumplings:
4 oz self-raising flour (110 g)
¼ teaspoon salt
2 oz suet (50 g)
¼ teaspoon dried mixed herbs
Salt and freshly-milled black pepper

Place the meat in a deep saucepan and cover it with cold water.
Add the herbs, some salt and pepper, and bring slowly to the boil.
Cover and simmer for about an hour, skimming the surface to
remove any scum halfway through. Then add the vegetables, cover
and simmer gently for another hour or until tender.

To make the dumplings, mix the flour, salt and pepper in a bowl.
Stir in the suet and herbs and add just enough water to make a soft
but not too sticky dough. Shape it into 8 small dumplings.

Next remove the meat from the pan and keep warm. Pop the
dumplings into the pan, cover, and cook for 20–25 minutes.
Slice the beef and serve it surrounded by the vegetables and
dumplings with a little of the broth as gravy and plenty of mustard.

Pork

The pig has long played an honourable part in the British diet.
Every part of him can be consumed: even his skin translates into
crisp, crunchy crackling and his fat is rendered down into pure lard.
Before the Enclosure Acts and the industrial revolution, almost
every cottage kept its pig which was consumed by the family in the
seasons when there was an R in the month (this was before the days
of refrigeration). Winter sealed the fate of the cottage pig; the
dressed boar's head was a festive Christmas dish, and the salting,
lard-making and preserving of the pork were all done in the coldest
weather. Even the pig-sty was cleansed by the sharp January frosts,
ready for the young porker to be moved in in the spring and be
fattened up for the next winter. By a happy coincidence a cottage
would often have a small orchard attached, where in autumn the
windfall apples provided a succulent addition to the pig's diet (so
apple sauce became a natural environmental accompaniment for
him when he got served up on the plate).

Today pork is reared fairly intensively. Again our modern
preoccupation with leanness has taken its toll on character and
flavour. For good, well-flavoured pork it is essential to shop around
for a reliable butcher who buys in turn from a reliable farmer.

Left: Fish kebabs, page 124; Italian baked fish, page 121; Soused herrings, page 129.

Pork cuts for roasting

Leg of pork is the most popular roasting joint, but because if its size it mostly has to be sold in two or else boned and rolled without the knuckle. This cut promises the most lean meat but not, I think, such a sweet flavour as others.

Loin of pork is also a prime roasting joint, equivalent in the anatomy of the animal to the sirloin and ribs of beef. This is best bought on the bone, but the butcher *must* chine it for you—that is, loosen the bone yet leave it attached so it can easily be cut away before carving.

Blade bone This comes at the top of the foreleg, so could be more accurately described as a piece of the shoulder. The meat has an excellent flavour when cooked on the bone. Alternatively it can be boned for you and stuffed before roasting.

Spare rib Like loin, this is sometimes sold as individual chops. It is actually the collar of the animal and, when roasted, full of flavour.

Hand and spring This is the curious name for the upper part of the foreleg of the pig, which happens to be well endowed with crackling and can be boned, stuffed and then roasted.

Belly of pork Sometimes sold in rashers as streaky pork, but the thick end (i.e. the leanest end) can be bought as a roasting joint. It has much to recommend it, good crackling, a sweet flavour, and not least it is the most economical joint.

Fillet and tenderloin These on the other hand are among the most expensive, but they are lean cuts without any wastage. In my opinion they need other flavours and ingredients with them to create interest.

Roasting pork

If you want to serve genuinely crisp crackling, ask the butcher to score the skin well (if you have to do it yourself, use the tip of a sharp knife and cut down the skin with quick, jerky movements). Then sprinkle the scored surface quite generously with salt to give it a thin coating—on no account put any fat near the crackling.

For a touch of extra flavour you can insert a few slivers of garlic into the flesh (make a small incision first) and sprinkle some thyme or rosemary over the joint. Place it on its own in a roasting tin—there is fat enough in the meat to lubricate it while it's cooking—

and give it 20 minutes in the oven at gas mark 9, 475°F (245°C), then lower the heat to gas mark 5, 375°F (190°C), and continue roasting for 35 minutes to the pound for leg or loin of pork. For other joints mentioned above lower the heat to gas mark 4, 350°F (180°C), and allow 45 minutes per pound.

What goes wrong with crackling Several things can turn the skin into tough old leather instead of crackling. One is using too deep a roasting tin, where that part of the crackling inside does not get proper exposure to the heat. Another reason could be that the skin was wet and soggy (especially if the meat has been frozen): to get good crackling it has to be dried thoroughly before salting and cooking. Another mistake is to plaster fat on the surface before cooking.

Roast pork with green butter

(serves 6 people)

Ask the butcher—giving him a bit of notice—to bone out a hand and spring of pork for this recipe.

5–5½ lb hand and spring of pork (2·25–2·5 kg)
Salt

For the butter:
1 tablespoon chopped parsley
1 tablespoon chopped watercress
1 teaspoon rock salt
1 teaspoon black peppercorns
1 teaspoon juniper berries
1 clove garlic
The grated rind of 1 lemon
The juice of ½ lemon
1½ oz butter (40 g)
Some white wine

Pre-heat the oven to gas mark 8, 450°F (230°C)

First of all, using a pestle and mortar or a bowl and the end of a rolling-pin, grind down the rock salt, peppercorns, juniper berries and garlic. Then add them to the butter with the lemon juice and rind, the chopped parsley and watercress, and mix thoroughly. Next, lay the boned joint, rind side down, on a flat working surface, wipe it with kitchen paper, then spread the butter mixture carefully all over it. Now tie it with string in several places so that it has the appearance of a long, roundish sausage, then transfer it to a roasting tin and sprinkle with salt.

Roast the joint in the top half of the oven for 20 minutes, then move it down to the centre of the oven and bake for a further 2 hours. To make sure that the meat is cooked, test with a skewer—the juices should be yellowy without any trace of pinkness. Remove the string before carving and use the pan juices and a dash of white wine to make a gravy to serve with it.

Stuffed pork tenderloin

(serves 4 people)

This is a good recipe for a dinner party, as it's easy to carve and serve. To serve 8 just double the ingredients and use 2 tenderloins.

1 pork tenderloin (weighing about 1 lb (450 g)
3–4 rashers streaky bacon, rind removed
½–¾ oz butter (10–15 g)

For the stuffing:
1 oz butter (25 g)
1 medium onion, finely chopped
¼ teaspoon thyme
¼ teaspoon sage
3 oz mushrooms (75 g), finely chopped
4 oz fresh breadcrumbs (110 g)
4 tablespoons chopped parsley
The grated rind of a lemon
2 teaspoons lemon juice
1 egg, beaten with 2 tablespoons cream or top of the milk

For the gravy:
1 tablespoon brown flour
About ½ pint dry white wine or dry cider (275 ml)
Salt and freshly-milled black pepper

Pre-heat the oven to gas mark 4, 350°F (180°C)

Leave the fat on the tenderloin, as this will help to keep it moist. With a sharp knife, split it in half lengthways and, using a rolling-pin, batter the two halves to flatten and widen them slightly. Season with salt and freshly-milled black pepper.

To make the stuffing, melt the butter in a pan and fry the onion and herbs gently for about 10 minutes, then add the mushrooms and raise the heat slightly. Cook for a further 3–4 minutes or until the juices from the mushrooms have almost evaporated, then empty the contents of the pan into a bowl and add the rest of the stuffing ingredients. Fork the mixture together lightly, then season to taste.

Next spoon the stuffing into one half of the tenderloin, patting it down to firm it slightly, then place the other half on top. Smear with some butter and season with freshly-milled black pepper. Cover the top of the fillet with the rinded bacon and tie with string at about 2 inch (5 cm) intervals to keep it neat and tidy, then transfer, carefully, to a buttered roasting tin. Bake near the top of the oven for 1 hour, then place on a serving dish and keep warm.

To make the gravy, stir the flour into the pan juices, add the wine and some seasoning and let it bubble until syrupy.

To serve, carve the meat into thick slices and pour over the gravy. A garnish of fried apple rings would go well with it.

Loin of pork Dijonnaise

(serves 6 people)

This has a lovely golden crust and the crackling is cooked separately to go with it.

1 piece loin of pork with crackling approximately 3 lb (1 kg 350 g) in weight
3 level tablespoons breadcrumbs
3 level teaspoons Dijon mustard
1 heaped teaspoon whole peppercorns
1 heaped teaspoon dried sage
Salt
3 small Cox's apples
Some butter
½ pint dry cider (275 ml)

Pre-heat the oven to gas mark 7, 425°F (220°C)

Start by scoring the skin of the pork with the tip of a sharp knife. Then take off the skin, together with about half the layer of fat underneath—in one piece if possible. Place this on a shallow baking tray and put it on the highest shelf of the oven for 15–20 minutes. At the end of this time it will be a very crisp and crunchy piece of crackling to accompany the meat. When you remove it from the oven, pour the fat into a bowl to use later for frying, etc.

Meantime, place the breadcrumbs in a mixing bowl, crush the peppercorns with a pestle and mortar or using the back of a tablespoon, and add them to the breadcrumbs together with the sage and about ¹/₂ teaspoon salt.

Next spread the mustard all over the layer of fat left on the pork, then press the breadcrumb mixture firmly all over, making sure that it is well coated. Transfer the joint to a roasting tin and place a square of foil lightly on top. Place the meat on a high shelf in the oven, reduce the heat to gas mark 5, 375°F (190°C), and roast the pork for about 2 hours, basting occasionally, and removing the foil for the last 30 minutes. When the pork is cooked, leave it in a warm place to relax, then spoon off the fat from the roasting tin, sprinkle a little flour into the juices and make some gravy with the cider.

Core the apples and cut into rings—but do not peel—and fry gently in butter till tender.

Serve the pork cut in slices with the gravy and garnished with the fried apple rings.

Ham, gammon and bacon
Each of these are terms used to describe meat from the pig that has been cured, i.e. preserved and flavoured in several different ways, either by salting, smoking or being steeped in brine (or molasses or honey). There are hundreds of refinements of the curing process used throughout the world: the wafer-thin Parma ham or *prosciutto* is a great delicacy in Italy, and in France the raw ham from the Bayonne district in the Pyrenees is smoked with aromatic herbs. In this country we have our own specialities:

York ham is the most famous. It is dry salt-cured and lightly smoked with a mild flavour. A similarly mild cure is the *Wiltshire cured ham*. For those who like a stronger, smokier flavour there is the *Suffolk cure*, which is prepared in molasses which adds a sweetness to the flavour. *Bradenham ham*, very expensive, is also steeped in molasses, which turns the skin completely black.

Soaking Whole hams need long soaking, not just to remove the saltiness from them but also to replace some of the moisture lost during the curing. Whole hams should always carry the specific curer's soaking and cooking instructions. For smaller gammon and bacon joints the modern curing methods are far less salty than they used to be, and soaking is not so essential. The ideal would be to cover them with water overnight, but, failing that, a joint can be immersed in cold water and brought up to the boil. This water should then be thrown out and the cooking started with fresh water.

Cuts The best cuts for boiling, braising or half-braising/half-roasting are *middle-cut gammon* (the leanest and best), *bacon collars, corner gammon* or *gammon slipper*. If you want to eat a joint of gammon or bacon cold, it is a good idea to give it 15 minutes less cooking time and leave it to cool in its cooking water, which will keep it extra moist. Or if you're serving it hot, keep it in the water for 15 minutes after it comes off the heat. In general the cooking time for joints is 25 minutes per pound (450 g), and for whole hams 15–20 minutes per pound.

Bacon pot roast

(serves 6–8 people)

In this recipe the bacon is half simmered, then finished off as a pot roast on a bed of vegetables.

3 lb collar of bacon (1 kg 350 g)
1 small potato, peeled
1 small onion (stuck with a few cloves)
1 bayleaf
6 black peppercorns
½ pint dry cider (275 ml)
For the pot roasting:
1 small swede, cut into chunks
2 carrots, sliced
1 onion, sliced
3 sticks celery, cut into chunks
2 oz butter (50 g)
Freshly-milled black pepper

Begin by placing the joint in a suitably-sized saucepan along with the potato (to take care of any saltiness), the onion, bayleaf and peppercorns. Pour in the cider and top up with enough cold water just to cover the bacon. Then cover with a lid and simmer the joint for 45 minutes. Towards the end of that cooking time, pre-heat the oven to gas mark 4, 350°F (180°C).

Meanwhile fry the prepared vegetables in the butter to tinge them with colour, then arrange them in the bottom of a casserole. Season with some pepper, and when the 45 minutes are up, remove the bacon from its liquid, cut off the skin with a sharp knife, and place the joint on top of the vegetables in the casserole. Pour in enough of the cooking liquid just to cover the vegetables, season only with pepper, put a lid on and place the casserole in the oven for a further 45 minutes. Serve the bacon cut in slices, with the vegetables and some of the juice spooned over.

Sugar-glazed gammon

(serves 6 people)

I think this is one of the nicest ways to cook gammon—half in liquid and then finished off in the oven with a mustard and sugar glaze.

1 piece of middle-cut gammon, rolled, approx. 3½ lb (1 kg 75 g)
1 onion peeled and stuck with a few cloves
A bayleaf
1 pint dry cider (570 ml)
2 dozen cloves
½ teaspoon of black peppercorns
2 tablespoons dark brown sugar
1 tablespoon made-up English mustard

Place the gammon joint in a saucepan that will take it comfortably, cover it with cold water, bring it up to the boil, then throw out the water. Now add the bayleaf, peppercorns and onion, and pour in ³/₄ pint (425 ml) of cider and enough water to cover. Bring this to the boil and simmer gently for an hour. Then remove the gammon, let it cool a little, then with a sharp knife cut off the string and remove the skin. Pre-heat the oven to gas mark 6, 400°F (200°C).

Now stand the gammon up (fat side uppermost) and score the fat diagonally first in one direction, then the other, so that it stands out in a diamond-shaped pattern. Into each diamond insert a clove, then spread the mustard all over the joint and press the brown sugar all over too (it is easiest to do this with your hands). Put the joint into a roasting tin with the remaining ¼ pint (150 ml) of cider in the bottom, place in the oven and bake for 45 minutes, basting it now and then with the cider and juices. Serve cut into slices with some *Cumberland sauce* (see page 442).

Lamb
If Scotland has the finest beef, then I think Wales has the best lamb—even the sheep in the hills seem to look more attractive, whiter and woollier than elsewhere. Even so, all lamb in Britain is extremely good, since it has the advantage of living happily in its natural habitat—in other words being completely free-range. It therefore has a natural seasonal cycle, which is at its peak in June, July and August (in fact it progresses from West Country lamb which is available by April to Scottish lamb which reaches the shops in August). New Zealand lamb starts to arrive in December. There is nothing to beat fresh lamb in June, when all the young spring vegetables are in season: tiny melt-in-the-mouth peas, baby carrots tossed in herb butter and fresh Jersey potatoes.

Roasting cuts
Leg and shoulder of lamb are the commonest, most popular cuts. Shoulder is more economical and has the sweetest meat of the two, because it is interlaced with layers of fat which melt and keep it moist during the cooking. Some people are averse to shoulder because they think it is hard to carve, though I feel a really sharp knife solves most problems.

Best end of neck is another joint that can be roasted. But it is extremely fatty and as the inside should conventionally be slightly pink and underdone, the result is that the layers of fat don't have time to melt. So often have I eaten this in a restaurant where it has arrived surrounded by an unappetising layer of undercooked fat. My own preference would be to slice it into cutlets and grill them to crisp up the fat.

Breast of lamb when rolled and stuffed makes an economical roast.

To roast a shoulder or leg of lamb, pre-heat the oven to gas mark 8, 450°F (230°C), give it 30 minutes, then turn down the heat to gas mark 4, 350°F (180°C), and time it for 30 minutes to the pound thereafter. (If you like the flavour of garlic, a few slivers inserted here and there won't go amiss.)

Accompaniments to lamb

In the summer *mint sauce* is a favourite accompaniment. Be
careful—strong malt vinegar can mask all the flavour of the meat.
Better, I think, to use a milder wine vinegar and even dilute it with
water. Use 3 tablespoons of chopped mint, 1 tablespoon of wine
vinegar and about 3 tablespoons of water. Some very finely-
shredded lettuce and one spring onion, also very finely chopped, are
nice additions.

Redcurrant jelly goes equally well with lamb. But do make sure it's
a really authentic one that is actually based on redcurrants.

My own favourite accompaniment, however, is a combination of
both these: *Redcurrant, orange and mint sauce* (see page 443).

*Stuffed breast
of lamb*

(serves 2 people)

This needs a large breast of lamb. Ask
the butcher to remove the bones for you,
but if you don't have this done by him,
you'll find them quite easy to remove
provided you have a sharp knife.

A large breast of lamb
2 oz fresh breadcrumbs (50 g)
Grated rind of ½ lemon
¼ whole nutmeg, grated
1 tablespoon freshly-chopped mint
1 tablespoon freshly-chopped parsley
1 medium onion, very finely chopped
1 teaspoon finely-crushed rosemary
1 small egg, beaten
Salt and freshly-milled black pepper

Pre-heat the oven to gas mark 4, 350°F
(180°C)

First of all, in a mixing bowl put the breadcrumbs, onion, parsley,
mint, grated nutmeg, rosemary and lemon rind, and season well
with pepper and salt. Mix thoroughly, then stir in the beaten egg to
bind the mixture together.

Now spread the stuffing evenly over the breast of lamb. Roll it up
gently but not too tightly, tuck the flap end over, then tie
securely with string in three places—again not too tightly. Tuck in
any bits of stuffing that fall out. Wrap the meat in foil, set in a
roasting tin and cook for 1½ hours. At the end of this time unwrap

the foil, baste with the juices and let it brown for a further half hour.

Serve the meat cut into thick slices with a thin gravy made with the pan juices and some redcurrant jelly.

Shoulder of lamb with rice and kidney stuffing

(serves 4–6 people)

This, again, is an excellent dinner-party recipe. It's easy to carve and serve, doesn't mind waiting around and tastes absolutely delicious.

3½–4 lb shoulder of lamb (boned but not rolled) (1·75–2 kg)
½–1 oz butter (10–25 g), softened
Salt and freshly-milled black pepper

For the stuffing:
1 onion, finely chopped
2 oz butter (50 g)
1 clove garlic, crushed
2 oz long grain rice (50 g)
¼ pint stock (150 ml)
½ teaspoon dried thyme
4 lambs's kidneys

First prepare the stuffing. Heat 1 oz (25 g) butter in a small saucepan and gently fry the onion in it until softened and golden. Then stir in the garlic, the rice and thyme and cook for a further 2 minutes before pouring in the stock. Now bring it all up to simmering point, cover and cook gently for about 15–20 minutes (by which time the rice should have absorbed all the liquid and be just tender). Pre-heat the oven to gas mark 5, 375°F (190°C).

Meanwhile, heat the rest of the butter in another saucepan. Core and slice the kidneys and toss them in the hot fat for a minute over a fairly high heat, then stir the kidneys into the cooked rice. Now lay the meat, skin-side down, on a board and pack the stuffing into all the pockets and crevices left after boning. Roll the joint up and tie it into a neat shape with string. Place it in a meat-roasting tin, smear it with softened butter and season with salt and pepper, then bake in the oven for 1½–2 hours.

Make a thick gravy from the pan juices to go with the lamb.

Baked lamb with coriander

(serves 4 people)

If you don't want to spend too much time but would like to cook lamb a little differently, then this is a good recipe.

½ **leg of lamb—fillet end**
2 cloves garlic
1 heaped tablespoon coriander seeds, crushed
Dripping
A little wine

Pre-heat the oven to gas mark 5, 375°F (190°C)

First, with the point of a sharp knife make 6–8 evenly-placed incisions in the meat, and put slivers of garlic and the crushed coriander seeds in these cuts. (If you haven't a pestle and mortar to crush the seeds, use the back of a tablespoon.) Double these quantities if you are cooking a whole leg or shoulder. Personal taste will dictate the amount of garlic you use—I suggest either 1 large clove or 2 small ones.

Place the meat in a roasting tin together with a knob of dripping and cook in the pre-heated oven for 30 minutes to the pound. When the lamb is cooked, transfer to a warmed serving dish, tip off fat from the roasting tin and if possible add a little wine to the remaining juice to make a gravy.

To serve, carve it in thick slices. Redcurrant jelly goes well with it.

See also:
American hamburgers
Beefsteak and kidney pie
Beefsteak and kidney pudding
Bœuf en croûte
Cevapcici (Yugoslav kebabs)
Country pâté
Ham, egg and cheese risotto
Indian kebabs
Lamb kebabs
Leg of lamb baked with butter and herbs

Meat loaf
Mustard-glazed lamb cutlets
Old English rabbit pie
Pork chops with cream and mushrooms
Pork chops with sage and apples
Pork spare ribs in barbecue sauce
Rillettes de Tours
Rissoles
Special cottage pie
Steak au poivre
Turkish stuffed peppers

Meat: casseroles and braised dishes

Including recipes for:
Beef in beer
Simple Stroganoff
Hungarian goulash
Bœuf Bourguignonne
Braised steak and onions in stout
Stewed shin of beef with
  mushroom dumplings
Irish stew with parsley dumplings

Traditional Lancashire hotpot
Ragoût of lamb
Normandy pork with cream and apples
Pork with apples and cider
Spanish pork with olives
Ossobuco
Sausages braised in red wine
Braised meatballs with peppers
  and tomatoes

Stews, casseroles, ragoûts, hotpots, carbonnades, navarins . . .
there are any number of names for what is essentially the same
method of cooking meat. All of them spring from that momentous
(though unrecorded) moment in history when someone discovered
that they could protect their meat from the fierce direct heat of a fire
by insulating it in a clay pot. The advantages were soon obvious,
I'm sure: the pot could also contain liquid and vegetables and
flavouring which the meat could absorb, and the longer slower
cooking made the meat more tender, no matter what part of the
animal it came from. Nothing has really changed today, except
perhaps for the clay pot, which has been replaced by decorative
oven-to-table casseroles.

We tend to lump together all recipes that are cooked in a pot and
call them casseroles. But strictly speaking, there is a difference.
Stewing is done on the top of a cooker with heat being applied
directly to the underneath of the pot; while *casseroling* takes place
inside the oven with heat circulating all around the pot. In both
cases the meat is cut up fairly small and cooked in a liquid (stock,
wine, water, cider or whatever).

Braising, like casseroling, is done in the oven, but the meat is
cooked in much larger pieces and only a minimum of liquid is added,
so that the meat actually cooks in the steam for the most part.

The numerous other names given to meat cooked in a pot refer to
specific recipes, or types of recipe (e.g. the hallmark of a good hotpot
is a layer of crunchy golden potatoes over the top).

But whatever names we choose to give it, I now feel that the
casserole has become one of the cornerstones of British family
cooking. What with inflation and more women devoting their time
to careers, feeding families of four or more with expensive steaks or
chops is not a very practical proposition. Casseroles on the other
hand can be prepared (even cooked) ahead. They can be left to
simmer slowly without attention from the cook, and costs can be
kept down quite a lot by stretching the meat with the addition of
vegetables and pulses.

It is for these reasons that it's helpful to have a good collection of
casserole recipes, that range from the everyday to those suitable for
entertaining. Here is a selection of my own tried and trusted
favourites, showing, I hope, how with a little bit of imagination a
couple of pounds of stewing meat can be transformed into
something really delicious and special.

This chapter, incidentally, covers all kinds of meat except
poultry, which is dealt with in the following chapter.

Choosing the right cuts

It is the forequarter meat on an animal (see chart on page 182) that's usually the most suitable for stewing and braising— everything from the waist up. Without becoming too technical, it is the front portion that initiates the movements of the animal and therefore works harder than the back portion. This means there is more muscle there, and more of something called connective tissue, a gelatinous substance which builds up as the animal matures. Conveniently, there is also rather more fat marbling the forequarter meat, so that during the longer, slower cooking that's needed for these cuts, there is a gradual rendering-down of the connective tissue (which provides flavour and body to the sauce), and at the same time an internal basting of the meat fibres by the marbling of fat. This does a splendid job of keeping the meat succulent, and (because there's a good deal of flavour in the fat itself) explains why forequarter meat *develops* flavour as it cooks.

In short, these factors perhaps explain why so often the cheaper cuts of, say, beef, given longer cooking have a beefier flavour than the more expensive hind-quarter cuts: why, for instance, a slow-cooked piece of shin can compare so well in flavour with a grilled fillet steak.

I find certain cuts of so-called stewing steak better for some dishes than for others, so that in all my recipes I name the cut—and suggest you always ask for it by name too. Unidentified stewing, or braising, steak can often be a mixture and can cook unevenly, I've found. Below is a list of the cuts that are suitable for braising and stewing; as you can see from the illustration these cuts are always from the same part of the animal's anatomy but, confusingly, the *way* they're cut varies from region to region. The names vary even more—in fact one cut (I call it thick flank) has some 27 different names up and down the country!

Braising beef

My own favourite cut for braising is no. 9 on the chart. Where I live in East Anglia, this is called *chuck* and *blade steak*. In other regions it can be called *shoulder*, which as you can see from the diagram is exactly where it is.

If you want large pieces of meat rather than cubes, *thick flank* (no. 4) is suitable: actually from the hind-quarters and called *round* or *flesh end* in Scotland or *bedpiece* elsewhere.

Beef skirt is not shown on the chart because its position is internal—below the diaphragm of the animal. It is however an

Beef

Lamb

scrag end of neck

best end of neck

shoulder and middle neck

Pork

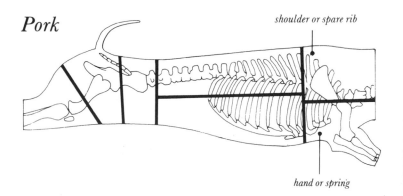

shoulder or spare rib

hand or spring

excellent cut for braising and one end can even be grilled if scored across the grain and tenderised by marinating before cooking.

Stewing beef

Next come stewing cuts from the *neck* (no. 12) and *clod* (no. 13). These are accorded some undignified titles such as *sticking*, or in Scotland *gullet*, or in the North *vein* or *sloat*! Also suitable for stewing is *thin flank* (no. 7) sometimes just called *flank*.

Both the *leg* (no. 1) and the *shin* (no. 14) provide excellent stewing meat, with an exceptionally good flavour. But because of the extra amount of connective tissue these cuts need much longer stewing than any of the other cuts of beef I have mentioned, and they are not suitable for braising.

Lamb

For stewing, *middle neck* or *scrag end of neck* are generally used as the bones impart delicious juices to the liquid. Also *best end of neck chops* are ideal for braising (as in *Lancashire hotpot*). In Scotland these are called *single loin chops* and in the Midlands simply *cutlets*. Both these shoulder cuts will also roast (see page 168).

Pork

Pork for braising usually comes from the region of the shoulder. The upper part is called either *shoulder* or *spare rib*. The lower part of the shoulder is known as *hand and spring*.

The principles of casserole cookery

Trimming and size of meat pieces One thing that's often disappointing with cuts of braising steak (and this is especially true of the packaged meat found in supermarkets) is that they are sliced too thinly. For braising in whole slices, cuts of $1/2$–$3/4$ inch thick (1–2 cm) are all right, but for many casseroles the ideal sized pieces are $1^1/2$ inches (4 cm) square and $1^1/4$ inches (3 cm) deep. Therefore it is preferable to buy a piece and cut it up yourself. Trim off *excess* fat and gristle before using, but remember that some connective tissue and marbling will add richness to the finished dish.

How much per person? This depends on all sorts of things—how much the meat needs to be trimmed, what extra ingredients go into the casserole, what other dishes you plan to serve at the same meal and so on—but, on average, I find that 8 oz (225 g) of meat per person is needed if someone has a large appetite, like my husband. For a normal appetite 6 oz (175 g) per person is usually adequate.

Browning the meat Most, though not all, meat benefits from being seared in hot fat before the liquid is added. I have found that searing meat at a *high* temperature, as compared with browning it over a *medium* heat, results in far less visible loss of juices. Meat fibres contract when heat is applied, squeezing out juices from inside: but if the heat is high enough these juices will be burnt into a crust on the meat instead of being lost in the cooking fat. I would also add that this dark, mahogany-coloured crust on the outside of the pieces of meat gives a richer, better flavour to a casserole.

One important point, if you're browning meat in batches and removing it to a plate, is to make sure that whatever juices do run out are re-incorporated into the casserole and not lost. And one final point: never overcrowd the pan during the browning. If you do, there will be too much steam rushing out and the meat will never brown because it will have become damp. So remember, brown only a few pieces at a time.

Liquid for casseroles The liquid in a casserole, mingling with the meat juices that do escape, provides the finished sauce. *Bone stock* is good for beef casseroles, but failing that plain hot water enriched with a few drops of Worcester sauce and mushroom ketchup makes a handy instant stock. Red or white *wine* will add extra flavour of its own, and its acidity will actually help to tenderise the meat as it cooks. *Beer* (pale or brown ale, or stout) makes a deliciously rich sauce: the long slow cooking transforms it completely, leaving no trace of its original bitterness. *Tomatoes*—fresh peeled or tinned Italian plum tomatoes—also give body and flavour to certain casseroles, like *Goulash* (see page 189). A good alternative is hot water enriched with tomato purée. *Cider* is also delicious in casseroles—but it must be dry cider.

Thickening casseroles Some casserole recipes call for the liquid to be thickened, and this can be done in various ways. The most popular way is to add some flour to the casserole after the meat has been browned (so that it can mingle with the juices and fat in the pan) and before the liquid is added. It is exactly the same principle as for the thickening of a white sauce (described on page 433). Another way to thicken a casserole is to toss the meat in seasoned flour before browning it (see recipe for *Braised steak and onions in stout*, page 191). Alternatively, when the casserole has completed cooking, the liquid can be strained off and simmered until slightly reduced and thickened. Or a flour and butter paste can be whisked into the liquid at the end of cooking time.

Vegetables If vegetables are to be included along with the meat in a casserole, the main consideration is not to cut them too small. This is a common mistake and results in the vegetables disintegrating under the strain of the long cooking. This applies particularly to onions, which if sliced too small can collapse altogether. It's far nicer, I think, to be able to discern slices of onion that have retained their shape. Vegetables that cook quite quickly (such as green peppers and mushrooms) are usually added to a casserole halfway through or towards the end of cooking time.

Cooking temperatures and times Slowly, slowly is the word that needs to be emphasised here. It is said that the correct simmering temperature is reached when the liquid shows the barest shimmer of movement and an occasional bubble breaks the surface. I have found that, using a heavy flameproof casserole, the ingredients for a beef casserole can be brought slowly up to simmering point on top of the stove, then transferred to the middle or low shelf of a pre-heated oven. Gas mark 1, 275°F (140°C) is gentle enough to produce the very best results. But ovens vary and different types of cooking pots will affect temperatures too, so you may have to adjust the oven temperature accordingly.

The time a casserole takes to cook will vary from 2–2½ hours for chuck, blade and thick flank, up to 4 hours for shin, leg and neck. Pork cuts for braising and casseroling normally take 1½–2 hours, and lamb much the same.

Skimming If a fair amount of fat has come out of the meat during the cooking, it will settle on the surface and can be removed by tilting the casserole slightly and spooning off with a large kitchen spoon. And if there's still some left, another tip is to float two or three pieces of absorbent kitchen paper on the surface—this should soak up any fat remaining. Of course, if you've had time to make the casserole in advance, the fat on the surface will solidify as it cools and can then just be lifted off. Which brings me to:

Reheating Many casseroles seem to improve in flavour if kept overnight (cool them quickly and keep them in a refrigerator, by the way, once they're cold). This means it's quite possible to make two casseroles while the oven is in full swing, and keep one for the next day. The reheating must be done very thoroughly, though, either on top of the stove over a very low heat or in an oven heated to gas mark 3, 325°F (170°C). Either way, the food must come up to a gentle simmer and maintain that temperature for 30 minutes in order to kill off any harmful bacteria.

Notes on cooking casseroles

Cooking pots and casseroles I've found the most useful type of casserole is the heavy cast-iron kind with enamelled lining. It isn't the cheapest *but* it does conduct the heat evenly and has the advantage of being suitable for cooking on top of the stove and inside the oven. It is also attractive enough to take to the table.

A 4½ pint (2½ litre) capacity casserole is the average family size, but you might also find a smaller size (3 pint or 1¾ litre) useful at times and a larger one (6½–7 pint or 4 litre) for entertaining. What one's aiming for is a pot that contains the ingredients comfortably without leaving masses of empty space. Well-fitting lids are *very* important, because they minimise the loss of liquid by evaporation during the cooking. If you happen to have a lid that doesn't fit too well, then cover the casserole with foil first to make it fit more snugly. And it follows that you should leave it be: too many peeps and stirs will let some of the flavour out as effectively as an ill-fitting lid.

Electric slow cookers These are self-contained cooking pots which are sometimes called crockpots, with their own electric element which is geared to producing the slow continuous heat needed for casseroles. It uses very little electricity, and is useful for those who are out at work all day since it can be left unattended quite safely. On a high setting a casserole will take around 5 hours; on a low one it will take an average of 8 hours, and won't come to any harm if left for 10!

If you're not at home all day, to use one of these effectively you must of course prepare everything before you go and allow 20 minutes or so for the casserole to pre-heat. If you're considering buying one, ask yourself if you are the sort of person who is organised enough to see to all this before you go out.

Pressure cookers Pressure cooking can cut down the time needed for casseroles to about one-third of normal. So speed, and the consequent saving in fuel costs, are the self-evident advantages of this method. It has also been pointed out that because everything is locked away from the air, and cooked for a shorter time, losses of vitamins and minerals are reduced to a minimum. Pressure cookers can be transported easily and used on any sort of cooker, so they're ideal to take on self-catering or camping holidays.

Those are the pluses, but there are also disadvantages: (i) as I have explained, the flavour of the cheaper cuts develops with long slow cooking—so a certain amount can be lost with speedier cooking under pressure; (ii) the liquid content in pressure cookers has to be a minimum of ³/₄ pint (425 ml), and I often find I want to use less than this. Also no thickening can be added till after the pressure cooking, so this has to be a separate process at the end.

In my experience many busy people swear by their pressure cookers and use them whenever possible: others (like myself) use them very rarely. In the end it's a matter of personal preference, so if you are wondering whether or not to invest in one yourself, do get a book on pressure cooking from the library and study the facts for yourself first.

Beef in beer

(serves 6–8 people)

This is an old Flemish recipe often known by its original name *Carbonnades de boeuf à la flamande*. Sometimes large baked croûtons sprinkled with grated cheese are arranged on the top of the cooked beef and the dish is then popped under the grill until the cheese is bubbling. Whether you do this or not, this recipe has a beautiful rich sauce and is one of my firm favourites.

2 lb chuck steak (900 g), cut into 2 inch (5 cm) squares
³/₄ lb onions, peeled, sliced in quarters then separated into layers (350 g)
1 fat clove garlic, crushed
1 tablespoon olive oil
1 sprig fresh thyme or ½ teaspoon dried thyme
1 bayleaf
1 well-heaped tablespoon plain flour
½ pint pale ale (275 ml)
Salt and freshly-milled black pepper

Pre-heat the oven to gas mark 1, 275°F (140°C)

Heat the oil in a large flameproof casserole until sizzling hot then sear the meat in it—just a few pieces at a time—till they become a dark mahogany brown all over. As the pieces brown, remove them to a plate, then add the onions to the casserole and, with the heat still high, toss them around until brown at the edges. Now return the meat to the casserole together with any juices. Add the flour, turn the heat down, and using a wooden spoon stir it around to soak up all the juices. It will look rather stodgy and unattractive at this stage but that's quite normal.

Next gradually stir in the pale ale and, whilst everything *slowly* comes up to simmering point, add the thyme, bayleaf, crushed garlic, and some salt and frshly-milled black pepper.

As soon as it begins to simmer, stir thoroughly, put on a tight-fitting lid and transfer the casserole to the middle shelf of the oven.

Cook at a gentle simmer for 2½ hours. Don't take the lid off and have a taste halfway through because, early on, the beer hasn't had time to develop into a delicious sauce; the beautiful aroma will make you very hungry, but please leave it alone!

Simple Stroganoff
(serves 4–6 people)

The classic recipe for Stroganoff is made with thin strips of fillet steak, cooked and served very quickly; it needs rather exact timing. This version, however, is made with strips of chuck steak, which costs less, has more flavour, and can be cooked slowly on top of the stove demanding no particular skill.

1½ lb lean chuck steak (700 g)
1 lb mushrooms, sliced (450 g)
2 large onions
½ pint dry white wine or dry cider (275 ml)
3 oz butter (75 g)
½ pint soured cream (275 ml)
Nutmeg
Salt and freshly-milled black pepper

First trim the meat and cut it into thin strips, about ¼ inch (½ cm) wide and no more than 2½ inches (6 cm) long.
The onion should be peeled, cut in half, then each half sliced and the layers separated out into half-moon shapes.

Now melt the butter in a thick-based saucepan or flameproof casserole and gently soften the onion for 5 minutes or until it has turned pale gold. Then, with a slotted spoon, remove it to a plate.

Next, turn the heat up high, add the pieces of meat to the casserole (a few at a time) and brown them. Then reduce the heat, return the onion and all the meat to the pan, season with salt and pepper and pour in the wine or cider. Bring to simmering point, cover and let it cook very gently on top of the stove for 1½ hours—stirring it just now and then.

When the time is up stir in the mushrooms (which will add a lot of juice in case you think it seems a little dry), put the lid back on and leave to cook for a further 30 minutes or until the meat is tender.

Then taste to check the seasoning, and stir in the soured cream with a good grating of fresh nutmeg. Let the cream heat through (but not boil) and serve the Stroganoff with plain boiled rice.

Hungarian goulash

(serves 4 people)

This makes a fairly economical dinner party dish: it is very easy to prepare and won't mind hanging around if your guests are late. It also goes very well with braised red cabbage (see recipe on page 262).

1½ lb chuck steak (700 g) trimmed and cut into 1½ inch (4 cm) cubes
2 large onions, roughly chopped
1 clove garlic, crushed
1 tablespoon olive oil
1 rounded tablespoon plain flour
1 rounded tablespoon Hungarian paprika
14 oz tin Italian tomatoes (400 g)
1 medium-sized green or red pepper
5 fl oz carton soured cream (150 ml)
Salt and freshly-milled black pepper

Pre-heat the oven to gas mark 1, 275°F (140°C)

Begin by heating the oil in a flameproof casserole till sizzling hot. Then brown the cubes of beef on all sides, cooking a few at a time and transferring them to a plate as they brown.

Now, with the heat turned to medium, stir in the onions and cook them for about 5 minutes or until they turn a pale golden colour. Then add the crushed garlic and return the meat to the casserole.

Sprinkle in the flour and paprika and stir to soak up the juices. Next, add the contents of the tin of tomatoes, season with salt and pepper and bring everything slowly up to simmering point before covering with a tight-fitting lid and transferring the casserole to the middle shelf of the oven. Cook for 2 hours.

Prepare the pepper by halving it, removing the seeds and cutting the flesh into 2 inch (5 cm) strips. Then, when the 2 hours are up, stir the chopped pepper into the goulash, replace the lid and cook for a further 30 minutes.

Just before serving, stir in the soured cream to give a marbled, creamy effect, then sprinkle a little more paprika over, and serve straight from the casserole, with some rice (or vegetables).

Boeuf Bourguignonne
(serves 6 people)

This is my adaptation of the famous French classic: beef braised in Burgundy, garnished with cubes of bacon, button onions and mushrooms. If you want to cut the cost then try using dry cider, which gives different results but is every bit as good.

2 lb chuck steak (900 g), cut into 2 inch (5 cm) squares
½ lb smoked or green streaky bacon, bought in one piece then cut into cubes (225 g)
¾ lb small onions (350 g)
1 medium sized onion, sliced
2 cloves garlic, chopped
2 sprigs fresh thyme or ½ teaspoon dried thyme
1 bayleaf
1 heaped tablespoon plain flour
¾ pint red Burgundy (425 ml)
¼ lb dark flat mushrooms, sliced (110 g)
3 tablespoons olive oil
Salt and freshly-milled black pepper

Pre-heat the oven to gas mark 1, 275°F (140°C)

Heat two tablespoons of oil to sizzling point in a large flameproof casserole and sear the chunks of beef—a few pieces at a time—to a rich, dark brown on all sides. Using a slotted spoon, remove the meat as it browns to a plate. Next add the sliced onion to the casserole and brown that a little too. Now return the meat to the casserole, sprinkle in the flour, stirring it around to soak up all the juices, then gradually pour in the Burgundy—stirring all the time. Add the chopped garlic and herbs, season with salt and pepper, put the lid on and cook in the oven for 2 hours.

Then, using a bit more oil, fry the button onions and cubes of bacon in a small frying pan to colour them lightly, and add them to the casserole together with the sliced mushrooms. Put the lid back on and cook for a further hour.

This is nice served with buttered noodles or onion-flavoured rice.

Braised steak and onions in stout

(serves 2 people)

For this recipe you'll need four pieces of braising steak—chuck or blade.

1 lb braising steak, cut into four pieces (450 g)
2 largish onions, halved and sliced
5 fl. oz stout (150 ml)
½ teaspoon Worcestershire sauce
Oil
Some seasoned flour
Salt and freshly-milled black pepper

Pre-heat the oven to gas mark 1, 275°F (140°C)

Melt a tablespoon of oil in a flameproof casserole and, when it's sizzling hot, coat the meat in seasoned flour and brown the pieces on both sides till they're a good rich brown colour. Lift them out of the casserole and reserve on a plate.

Now fry the onions to brown them well at the edges, then arrange the meat on top (plus any juices that are on the plate) and season with salt and pepper. Next pour in the stout and Worcestershire sauce. Then put the lid on and transfer the casserole to the oven. Cook for approximately 2½ hours or until the meat is tender.

Note: if you like you could braise the steak on top of the stove using a very low heat but, because this method seems to cause a bit more evaporation, add one extra fluid ounce (25 ml) of stout.

Stewed shin of beef with mushroom dumplings

(serves 4–6 people)

For years I never bought shin of beef because it looked so unappealing, but I missed out because those sections of connective tissue melt down during the long, slow cooking and provide extra flavour and enrichment to the sauce. Now, if I want an old-fashioned brown stew, I wouldn't use anything else.

2 lb shin of beef, cut in bite-sized cubes (900 g)
¾ lb onions, cut into quarters (350 g)
2 large carrots, scraped and cut into large chunks
1 bayleaf
1 sprig fresh thyme or ½ teaspoon dried thyme
1 heaped tablespoon flour
15 fl oz hot beef bone stock (400 ml)—or hot water enriched with 1 teaspoon Worcester sauce
2 teaspoons mushroom ketchup
Beef dripping
Salt and freshly-milled black pepper

For the dumplings:
4 oz self-raising flour (110 g)
2 oz shredded suet (50 g)
1 onion, finely grated
2 oz mushrooms, very finely chopped
Salt and freshly-milled black pepper

Pre-heat the oven to gas mark 1, 275°F (140°C)

In a flameproof casserole melt about 1 tablespoon of beef dripping and, when it's smoking hot, brown the pieces of beef—a few at a time—to a really dark rich brown colour. As the pieces brown remove them to a plate using a slotted spoon. Next fry the onions and carrots so that they turn dark at the edges. Now spoon off any excess fat, turn the heat down, return everything to the casserole and sprinkle in the flour, stirring it in well to soak up the juices. Next, gradually stir in the hot stock and the mushroom ketchup, add the thyme, bayleaf and seasoning and bring everything slowly up to simmering point. Then put on a very well fitting lid, using foil if you need to. Now transfer the casserole to the lowest shelf of the oven and cook for 3 hours or until the meat is tender.

Towards the end of cooking time make the dumplings. Sift the flour into a mixing bowl, add some pepper and a pinch of salt, then stir in the suet, the chopped mushrooms and the grated onion. Add enough cold water to bring it all together to make a fairly stiff but elastic dough that leaves the bowl cleanly. Divide the dough into 8 pieces and roll each portion into a dumpling shape.

When the stew is ready, using a draining spoon, take out all the meat and vegetables and put them on a large warm serving dish. Cover with foil and keep warm in the bottom of the oven.

Season the liquid to taste, then bring it up to a very fast boil. Put the dumplings into the bubbling liquid, cover and cook for 20–25 minutes, making sure they don't come off the boil. When the dumplings are ready put them all round the meat and vegetables, pour over some of the gravy and serve the rest in a sauce boat.

Irish Stew with parsley dumplings

(serves 4 people)

I don't make any claims about this so far as its Irish authenticity is concerned, but it does taste very good.

2½ lb lean middle neck and scrag-end of mutton or lamb (1 kg)
¾ lb onions, sliced (350 g)
½ lb carrots, sliced (225 g)
2 medium-sized leeks, washed and sliced
1 large potato, peeled and sliced
1 tablespoon pearl barley
2 tablespoons seasoned flour
Hot water
Salt and freshly-milled black pepper

For the dumplings:
4 oz self-raising flour (110 g)
2 oz shredded suet (50 g)
1 tablespoon fresh parsley, chopped (if fresh is not available make plain dumplings)
Salt and freshly-milled black pepper

First wipe the pieces of meat and cut away excess fat, then dip them in the seasoned flour. Now put a layer of meat in the bottom of a large saucepan, followed by some onion, carrot, leek and potato and season with salt and pepper. Then put in some more meat and continue layering the ingredients until everything is in.

Now sprinkle in the pearl barley followed by approximately 2 pints (1·25 litres) hot water and bring to simmering point. Spoon off any scum that rises to the surface, then cover the pan with a well-fitting lid and leave to simmer over a low heat for about 2 hours.

About 15 minutes before the end of cooking time, make the dumplings. Mix the flour, salt, pepper and parsley in a bowl. Then mix in the suet—but it mustn't be rubbed in. Add just sufficient cold water to make a fairly stiff but elastic dough that leaves the bowl cleanly. Shape it into 8 dumplings.

When the stew is ready, remove the meat and vegetables with a slotted spoon onto a large warm serving dish. Cover with foil and keep warm.

Season the liquid to taste, then bring to a brisk boil. Put the dumplings in, cover and cook them for 20–25 minutes, making sure that they don't come off the boil.

Serve the meat surrounded by the vegetables and dumplings, with some of the liquid poured over and some in a gravy boat.

Traditional Lancashire hotpot

(serves 4 people)

This has acquired its name from the time when it was baked at home, then wrapped in blankets to keep hot and provide lunch for a day at the races.

4 lambs' kidneys, cored, skinned and chopped
2 lb best end and middle neck of lamb (900 g)
Dripping
1 pint hot water (570 ml) mixed with ½ teaspoon Worcestershire sauce
1 bayleaf
2 sprigs fresh thyme (or ½ teaspoon dried)
2 lb potatoes (900 g), cut into ¾ inch (1·5 cm) slices

¾ lb onions, roughly chopped (350 g)
1 tablespoon flour
A little butter
Salt and freshly-milled black pepper

Pre-heat the oven to gas mark 3,
325°F (170°C)

In a large frying pan heat some dripping until it is smoking hot, then brown the pieces of meat 2 or 3 at a time until they all have a good brown crust. As they cook, remove them to a wide casserole. Brown the pieces of kidney too, and tuck these in amongst the meat.

Next fry the onions—add a little butter to the pan if you need any extra fat—cooking them for about 10 minutes till they turn brown at the edges. Now stir in the flour to soak up the juices, then gradually add the hot water and Worcestershire sauce, stirring or whisking until flour and liquid are smoothly blended. Season with salt and pepper and bring it up to simmering point, then pour it over the meat in the casserole. Add the bayleaf and thyme, then arrange the potato slices on top, in an overlapping pattern like slates on a roof. Season the potatoes and add a few flecks of butter here and there. Cover with a tight-fitting lid and cook near the top of the oven for 1½ hours, then remove the lid and cook for a further 50 minutes.

I sometimes finish off the hotpot under the grill. If you brush the potatoes with a little more butter and place the casserole under a hot grill they crisp up and brown beautifully. Alternatively, if you think they're not browning enough during cooking, you can turn the heat in the oven right up during the last 15 minutes.

Ragoût of lamb

(serves 2–3 people)

Neck of lamb isn't cheap any more but it is less expensive than many other cuts and, because of the bones, always gives the maximum amount of flavour. This, I think, is an excellent summer casserole.

2 lb neck of lamb, either middle neck or scrag end or a mixture of both (900 g)
1 tablespoon oil
2 medium-sized onions, roughly chopped

1 sprig fresh thyme (or ½ teaspoon dried)
1 bayleaf
2 cloves garlic, crushed
1 heaped tablespoon flour
1 pint boiling water (570 ml)
¾ lb new potatoes, scraped (350 g)
4 medium-sized tomatoes, peeled
Salt and freshly-milled black pepper

Pre-heat the oven to gas mark 1,
275°F (140°C)

First trim any excess fat from the meat, wipe each piece and season
it with salt and freshly-milled pepper. Then heat the oil in a largish
flameproof casserole, and brown the meat a few pieces at a time.
When they're nicely brown transfer them to a plate, using a
draining spoon.

Now gently fry the onions in the fat left in the pan—this will take
about 10 minutes or so. Then, when the onions are softened and
browned a little bit round the edges, add the garlic. Next stir in the
flour, to soak up the juices, and gradually pour in the hot water,
stirring to make a sort of gravy.

When simmering point is reached, return the pieces of meat to the
casserole and add the thyme, bayleaf and seasoning—it won't look
much at this point, but not to worry.

As soon as it comes back to simmering point, put the lid on and
transfer the casserole to the oven. Cook it for about 1 hour, then add
the scraped potatoes and peeled tomatoes. Put the lid back on and
cook for a further 45 minutes, or until the potatoes are cooked.

*Normandy pork
with cream
and apples*

(serves 4 people)

This is quite rich and special. It needs a
lightly cooked green vegetable or a crisp
green side salad to go with it.

4 medium-sized pork spare rib chops or loin chops
2 oz butter (50 g)
1 medium cooking apple
1 large Cox's apple
1 large onion, cut into thin rings

1 clove garlic, crushed
¾ teaspoon dried thyme
¼ pint dry cider (275 ml)
3 tablespoons double cream
Sugar
Salt and freshly-milled black pepper

Pre-heat the oven to gas mark 5,
375°F (190°C)

Begin by melting half the butter in a thick frying pan and frying the
pork chops on both sides to a nice crusty golden colour. Then, using
a draining spoon, transfer them to a suitably sized casserole and
sprinkle with thyme.

Now add the remaining butter to the pan and fry the onion and
garlic for 5 minutes to soften. Meanwhile, core the apples and cut
them into rings, leaving the peel on as this gives extra flavour. Next
transfer the softened onion and garlic to the casserole, then fry the
apple rings in the same fat just for a few seconds on each side and
transfer them to the casserole as well, sprinkling on about a
teaspoon of sugar.

Next, spoon off any fat still left in the pan and then pour in the cider.
Bring it up to simmering point and pour it into the casserole and
season with salt and freshly-milled black pepper. Now put a lid on
and then place the casserole into the oven, and cook for about 30–40
minutes or until the chops are cooked. Then to finish off, pour in the
cream, stir it into the juices and serve immediately.

*Pork
with apples
and cider*

(serves 4 people)

This is a hearty winter dish that can be
left on its own for three hours if you plan
to be out. You could also leave some red
cabbage to braise in the oven with it and
return to a complete meal.

4 thick lean belly pork strips or spare rib chops
6 rashers unsmoked streaky bacon
1 large cooking apple, peeled, cored and sliced
2 medium-sized onions, chopped small
¼ pint dry cider (150 ml)

2 cloves garlic, finely chopped
6 juniper berries, crushed with the back of a spoon
1½ lb potatoes, peeled and thickly sliced (700 g)
Olive oil
A little butter
Salt and freshly-milled black pepper

Pre-heat the oven to gas mark 1,
275°F (140°C

If the pork is very fatty, trim away the excess. Heat some oil in a frying pan and brown the pork on both sides, then transfer to a wide shallow casserole. Next, in the same pan, fry the bacon rashers a little until the fat starts to run. Then, using a draining spoon, place the bacon on top of the pork and season, but be careful with the salt as there'll be some in the bacon.

Now sprinkle over the juniper berries and garlic, then spread the slices of apple and onion on top. Add the cider and cover with a layer of overlapping potatoes. Finally, put a few dabs of butter on top, cover the dish first with greaseproof paper or foil, and then with a close-fitting lid. Transfer to the oven and cook for 3 hours.

Toward the end of the cooking time, pre-heat the grill to its highest setting. When the oven time is completed, place the dish, uncovered, under the grill so the potatoes become brown and crispy.

Spanish pork with olives

(serves 4–6 people)

This casserole has what I'd call a rich Mediterranean flavour. Nice served with *Saffron rice* (page 305).

2 lb shoulder of pork, trimmed and cut into bite-sized cubes (900 g)
2 tablespoons olive oil
1 rounded tablespoon plain flour
2 medium-sized onions, sliced
2 cloves garlic, crushed
1 teaspoon dried basil
1 lb tomatoes, peeled and chopped (450 g), or 14 oz (400 g) tin of tomatoes
6 fl oz red wine (175 ml)
1 green pepper, deseeded and chopped

Right: Spanish pork with olives, this page

2 oz Spanish pimento stuffed olives, sliced (50 g)
Salt and freshly-milled black pepper

Pre-heat the oven to gas mark 1,
275°F (140°C)

Begin by heating the oil in a large flameproof casserole, then add the cubes of pork and brown them on all sides. Cook only a few cubes at a time and remove them to a plate as they're done. Then add the onions to the casserole and brown them for a few minutes before returning the meat to the pan and sprinkling in the flour.

Stir everything well and add the chopped tomatoes—pour boiling water over fresh tomatoes first to help get the skins off. Pour in wine, add the garlic, basil and a seasoning of salt and pepper. Stir, bring slowly to simmering point, then cover with a tight-fitting lid.

Transfer the casserole to the centre shelf of the oven and cook for 1¹/₂ hours. After that add the chopped pepper and sliced olives, cover again, then cook for a further 30 minutes. This is delicious served with rice and a crisp green salad.

Ossobuco

(serves 4 people)

This is a famous Italian casserole: shin of veal cooked in white wine with tomatoes. Try to buy the pieces of shin about 2 inches (5 cm) thick.

4 large pieces shin of veal
½ pint dry white wine (275 ml)
¾ lb tomatoes, peeled and chopped (350 g)
1 tablespoon tomato purée
1 large clove garlic, finely chopped
The grated rind of 1 small lemon
2 heaped tablespoons fresh chopped parsley
Butter
Salt and freshly-milled black pepper

You'll need a wide, shallow flameproof casserole that can hold the pieces of veal in one layer.

In the casserole melt 1 tablespoon of butter and fry the pieces of veal, to brown them lightly on both sides, keeping them arranged

Left: Roast duck, page 225, with Morello cherry sauce, page 444; Chicken with whole spices, page 220; Spiced pilau rice, page 305.

upright in the pan. Then pour over the wine, let it bubble and reduce a little before adding the tomatoes, tomato purée and a seasoning of salt and freshly-milled black pepper.

Then cover the casserole and leave it to cook gently on top of the stove for about 1 hour. After that, take off the lid and let it cook for another half an hour or so or until the meat is tender and the sauce reduced. Before serving, mix the chopped garlic, parsley and lemon rind together, then sprinkle this all over the meat. Serve this with rice (preferably *Risotto alla Milanese*, see recipe page 309)—and don't forget to dig out the marrow from the centre of the bone, it's delicious.

Sausages braised in red wine
(serves 3 people)

This is best made with very good quality pork sausages, preferably the spicy, herby sort that some butchers make themselves.

1 lb pork sausages (450 g)
½ lb lean streaky bacon in one piece, then cut into cubes (225 g)
½ lb small button onions (225 g)
½ teaspoon dried thyme
1 bayleaf
1 clove garlic, crushed
1 heaped teaspoon flour
½ pint red wine (275 ml)
6 oz mushrooms, sliced if large (175 g)
Lard
Olive oil
Salt and freshly-milled black pepper

Take a large flameproof casserole, melt a little lard in it and brown the sausages all over. Then, using a slotted spoon, remove them to a plate whilst you lightly brown the bacon cubes and onions. When they're done, sprinkle in a heaped teaspoon of flour to soak up the juices, then gradually stir in the wine. Now pop the sausages back in, plus the garlic, bayleaf, thyme and a little seasoning. Put the lid on when simmering point is reached, turn the heat as low as possible and simmer very gently for 30 minutes.

Meanwhile brown the mushrooms in a little olive oil in a frying pan. Then, after the sausages have been cooking for the 30 minutes, stir the mushrooms into the casserole and continue to cook for a further 20 minutes—this time with the lid off.

Serve with what else but a pile of creamy mashed potato!

Braised meatballs with peppers and tomatoes

(serves 4–6 people)

This is another economical but really delicious recipe, probably best made in the autumn when there's a glut of tomatoes and green peppers.

1 lb best quality minced beef (450 g)
½ lb good pork sausage meat (225 g)
Half a green pepper, deseeded and finely chopped
1 egg, beaten
1 medium onion, minced or very finely chopped
1 large clove garlic, crushed
¾ teaspoon dried mixed herbs
1 tablespoon freshly chopped parsley
2 slices bread
1 dessertspoon tomato purée
Flour, for coating the meatballs
Oil, for frying the meatballs
Salt and freshly-milled black pepper

For the sauce:
14 oz tin Italian tomatoes (400 g) or 1 lb ripe tomatoes (450 g)
1 small onion, chopped
1 clove garlic, crushed
Half a green pepper, deseeded and chopped
1 teaspoon dried basil

Begin by making the meatballs: cut the crusts off the bread, then mash it to crumbs with a fork and, in a large mixing bowl, mix it together very thoroughly with the rest of the meatball ingredients and salt and pepper, using your hands.

Now take pieces of the mixture—about a tablespoon at a time—and roll each into a small round. You should get about 16–18 altogether.

Coat each one lightly with flour, then brown them in the oil in a large frying pan.

Meanwhile pre-heat the oven to gas mark 5, 375°F (190°C). When the meatballs are browned transfer them to a casserole and, in the juices remaining in the frying pan, prepare the sauce by softening the onion and green pepper for 5 minutes before adding the tomatoes, garlic and basil, then simmer for a couple of minutes. Taste and season, then pour the sauce over the meatballs in the casserole and cook, with a lid on, in the oven for 45 minutes. After that take off the lid and cook for a further 15–20 minutes.

This is nice served on a bed of buttered noodles, with a crisp green salad.

See also:
Beef curry with whole spices
Braised steak with green peppercorn sauce

Cassoulet
Chilli con carne
Marinaded pork with coriander
Moussaka

Poultry

Including recipes for:
*Traditional roast chicken
  with stuffing*
Creamed chicken with avocado
Coq au vin
Chicken in the pot
*Fried-mustard-and-
  herb-coated chicken*
Chicken with lemon sauce
Chicken in barbecue sauce
Chicken with whole spices
Cold chicken pie

Chicken with grape stuffing
Roast duck
Pork, sage and onion stuffing
Chestnut and apple stuffing
Traditional roast turkey
*Roast stuffed goose with
  prune and apple sauce*

Chicken

Once upon a time chicken was a luxury, an expensive family treat for a special occasion. Now we have moved to the other extreme: chickens are available absolutely everywhere. They are threaded onto rotisseries in shop windows in every high street, there are chains of take-away chicken shops, freezer centres are full of them. Any part or portion of a chicken can be bought separately. It is a credit to our farmers that they have put chicken within the reach of everyone at what, in these days, is a very reasonable price.

At the same time a question remains, one which in our passion for progress I hope we won't overlook. The question of flavour—a word which I fear is too rarely mentioned in our modern chicken production industry. Loss of flavour is the price we seem to have paid for our abundance of chickens. So what's happened and where has the flavour gone? Let's consider our chickens' progress to the table from scratch, as it were.

Rearing To produce today's enormous quantity of chicken, speed is the one thing that's necessary. And what farmers have done is to speed up growth and development so that the ubiquitous broiler of 1½–3 lb (700 g–1.35 kg) in weight is ready for cooking in eight weeks or so. Such a chicken is already at a disadvantage, as lack of maturity also means lack of flavour. To speed up growth sufficiently, first-class protein of animal and vegetable origin has to be used for part of the feeding. In some cases where this type of feed is not correctly controlled it is sometimes possible for the chicken's flesh to be impregnated with a foreign flavour! (I should also add that a code of practice for the poultry industry has been established since 1969 and, although there may be exceptions—as in any industry—it is generally followed. And one popular misconception that needs to be cleared up is the belief that chickens produced for the table are reared in battery cages. They're not, they are actually reared in deep litter (soft shavings) in well-ventilated houses and should—according to the code—have plenty of room to move about.)

Production When a chicken is killed in a factory it is immediately eviscerated and very quickly moves on to the next stage, the cooling. Now the fastest cooling process is by water, which is fine for a quick turnover but, from the point of view of the consumer, means that the cooling chickens can—and do—absorb quite a bit of water. Up to 7.4 per cent of its weight is the permitted level, but in some chickens it is even more. In some instances the birds are injected with a chemical called polyphosphate, which encourages water absorption. Producers claim this makes the flesh moist: I would claim it makes it watery. (You do have a choice here— polyphospate-injected chickens have to be labelled as such.) Our water-logged chickens then move along in sub-zero temperatures to be deep-frozen (water and all).

What's wrong with freezing? Not a lot, provided (a) the chicken has not absorbed nearly 10% of its weight in water, (b) the process of rigor mortis has been completed, and (c) some maturation has been allowed to take place before freezing so that flavour has a chance to develop (as it does naturally if a bird is hung). The trouble with the freezing of most chickens is that none of the above happens and— quite apart from flavour—if a bird is frozen within 6 or 8 hours of killing and rigor mortis is not complete, the flesh becomes tough and chewy. Equally, when the birds are frozen the process must be done quickly or else large ice crystals can form which penetrate the flesh and cause the texture to be stringy.

Alternative chicken

Free-range is one alternative to frozen chicken, but it's only fair to point out here that the free farmyard type of chicken is not necessarily always better: hens scratch about and can eat all sorts of undesirable things which could taint the flesh. Also it is simply unrealistic to supply our size of population with free-range chickens. However it's not all gloom:

Chill-fresh One quality chain store with branches throughout the country has pioneered a method of chicken production which, although the cost is higher, now supplies the country with some half a million fresh chickens each week, not just production-line broilers but mature chickens. (In fact they handle the largest number of 4–5 lb, 1·8–2·25 kg birds in Britain.) These are reared on some 450 selected farms spread over the country, where the chickens can feed and take water ad lib, and stress and crowding are avoided (a good-tasting chicken, it seems, has to be contented!). After they're killed these birds are cooled by air; rigor mortis occurs naturally and, by enzyme action, there is a certain amount of maturation and flavour development under correct temperature control.

New York dressed This is the name given to fresh chicken which is hung, so that flavour matures. In this case the bird is eviscerated only at the point of purchase.

The choice for us We can choose the quality of chicken we want to eat. First, from a reliable poulterer, who knows his source of supply is of high quality and whose poultry is eviscerated only at the point of purchase. Secondly we can choose a fresh, chilled chicken that has not been subjected to water-cooling (water-cooled chicken looks very pale and white, air-cooled chicken has a healthy, pinkish tone). Or we can choose frozen chicken from a good supplier. I have outlined the hazards of freezing broilers above, but with correct and careful freezing quality *can* be achieved. My suggestion is to use frozen chickens for casserole cooking (because the water content can cause them to steam rather than roast).

Choosing the right chicken

Chickens are sold in various categories of size and weight and, obviously, you need to select the right chicken for the right recipe. There are four principal ways of cooking chicken, (i) roasting (ii) pot-roasting and casseroling (iii) shallow and deep-frying (iv) grilling and barbecuing. Here is the range of chickens, and notes as to what each is suitable for:

Poussins and double poussins These are baby chickens weighing up to 2 lb (about 1 kg) each, with not a lot of flavour to them. But split in half and marinaded overnight they make very good barbecue food.

Broilers are the uniform immature birds which weigh in at $2^{1}/_{2}-3^{1}/_{2}$ lb ($1.13-1.68$ kg). If good quality, what they lack in flavour is made up for in tenderness. So, jointed, they're suitable for any recipe that calls for chicken to be grilled or fried.

Roasting chickens These are the 4–5 lb birds ($1.8-2.25$ kg). Their extra age and development means more chicken flavour, and they can take the longer cooking time needed for roasting. I also think these are the best for casseroles too.

Boiling fowl It is said that chickens (as opposed to capons) weighing from 6 to 8 lb ($2.7-3.15$ kg) are only suitable for slow casserole cooking or stock-making, yet I have given an $8^{1}/_{2}$ lb (3.8 kg) bird exactly the same type of cooking as turkey (see page 229) and found it superbly rich in flavour. If you plan to roast a boiling fowl, however, you must be sure of your supplier.

Capons I'm not at all keen on chickens being injected in the neck with hormone capsules which de-sex (caponise) them. True, they will have an enlarged breast, but an abnormal one. Capons are usually sold at Christmas and claim only 1–2% of the market.

Storing fresh chicken

If you buy a fresh chicken, try to get it home as soon as possible. Then remove the wrapping and, most important, the giblets if they are tucked inside. Place it on a plate, cover loosely and put it in the lowest part of the fridge, where it will keep for three days.

Storing and thawing frozen chicken

If you're tackling a frozen chicken, the most important rule is that the bird must be completely and thoroughly de-frosted before it is cooked. Food poisoning can occur if you begin to cook the bird while it is still partly frozen, becaue this creates the semi-warm conditions in which food bugs thrive and multiply. The thawing times below are produced by the Poultry Information Service.

Size of bird	2 lb (900 g)	3 lb (1·35 kg)	4 lb (1·8 kg)	5 lb (2·25 kg)	6 lb (2·7 kg)	7 lb (3·15 kg)
Thawed at room temperature 65°F (16°C)	8 hrs	9 hrs	10 hrs	12 hrs	14 hrs	16 hrs
Thawed in a refrigerator 40°F (4°C)	28 hrs	32 hrs	38 hrs	44 hrs	50 hrs	56 hrs

Frozen chicken can be stored in the freezer for up to nine months, or up to 1 month in the frozen food compartment of a refrigerator (depending on the star rating of your model), but once thawed should not be re-frozen.

Boning chickens

I'm afraid this is something that goes against the grain with me. I was brought up to believe that bones in the meat during cooking enhance flavour (you can test this yourself: eat that little piece of chicken that adheres to the wing bone, and you can really taste the concentrated chicken). Boning a chicken may indeed make it easier to carve—but what about the trouble of boning it in the first place! I can't help thinking that sheer theatrical effect is the reason for some people producing something resembling a stuffed rugby ball in the name of chicken.

Jointing chickens

This is nothing to be afraid of. First of all, if you're buying chicken from a butcher or poulterer, you can ask him to joint it for you

A

B

C

D

E

(everything costs so much these days, we should get all the value we can). If you need to do it yourself at home, there are really only two requirements: a really sharp knife and perhaps a pair of good kitchen scissors (or poultry shears). Follow the diagrams and instructions, and don't worry too much if the joints aren't perfectly neat. Once the chicken is cooked no-one will know.

First, cut through the parson's nose, (A), then stand the chicken in a vertical position (neck end down). Insert the knife into the cut you've already made, and cut straight down the back of the chicken (B). Place it skin-side down, open it out flat, and cut right through the breastbone (C). Now turn the two halves of the chicken skin-side up, stretch out the leg as far as you can, then cut through the natural line dividing the leg from the breast (D). For six portions turn the legs over, find the thin white line at the centre of the joint, and cut through it (E).

Stuffing for chickens

Stuffing was invented for a very good reason. In the case of roasting chicken, where the flesh is very lean and could easily dry out if the fire was fierce, the stuffing provided lubrication—a sort of internal basting to give extra juiciness, particularly to a large bird needing long cooking. A chicken stuffing should have a fair amount of juicy ingredients, like minced pork sausage meat or a generous quantity of butter.

Trussing chicken

I am happy to say we can all abandon our needles and thread. In all the

A

B

C

research I've done over the years I can find no reason for trussing other than the neat appearance it gives a bird, and the supposed ease of carving. A well-cooked bird which has not been trussed is, in fact, quite simple to carve, and neat appearances don't really matter if you are going to carve in the kitchen—which is always the most suitable place to carve in any case.

Carving chicken

As.always, the cardinal requirement is a sharp knife, then it's easy (see the illustrations). And the same rule applies to chicken as to other roast meats and poultry, and that's to allow a good 10–15 minutes between completion of cooking and carving. This lets the juices which have welled up to the surface during cooking seep back into the flesh to keep it succulent. It also makes carving neat slices much easier.

Secure the chicken with a fork, insert knife between leg and body and remove thigh and drumstick in one piece (A). Remove the wing on the same side, then slice the breast (B). Repeat this on the other side of the bird. Lastly, divide the thigh and drumstick, cutting through the joint to obtain two leg portions (C).

Traditional roast chicken with stuffing

As you've probably gathered, I'm a traditionalist and one of the pleasures of the table for me is the aroma of a carefully roasted chicken with crisp brown skin and sizzling juices underneath. Perfect accompaniments would be a stuffing of pork flavoured with sage and onion, a few crisp pieces of bacon (which protected the breast during roasting), a jug of creamy bread sauce, and a gravy made with chicken juices and stock. In this age of fast, convenience living it can be a real therapy to lavish care and thought on cooking something simple really well.

A 4½–5 lb roasting chicken, including neck and giblets (2–2·25 kg)
3 oz butter (75 g)
6 rashers fat, streaky bacon
Salt and freshly-milled black pepper

For the stuffing:
½ lb minced pork or good quality pork sausage meat (225 g)
2 oz fresh breadcrumbs (50 g)
1 smallish onion, very finely chopped or grated
1 dessertspoon dried sage
Salt and freshly-milled black pepper

Pre-heat the oven to gas mark 5, 375°F (190°C)

In advance make up a strong, reduced giblet stock according to the instructions on page 94. Then to prepare the chicken for the oven you first need to make the stuffing.

Stuffing Here I part company with many other cooks and follow my mother's advice, which is to place some stuffing inside the body cavity as well as the breast (which provides moisture and flavour to permeate the inside of the whole bird during cooking). It also means there's some stuffing left over to go with the cold chicken the next day! You can of course make a smaller quantity of stuffing and just use it for the breast if you prefer.

The stuffing is made simply by combining all the ingredients thoroughly in a bowl, and seasoning well. To stuff the breast: at the neck end you'll find a flap of loose skin, and if you gently loosen this you'll eventually be able to make a triangular pocket between the breast and the skin. Pack about one-third of the stuffing in as far as you can, but not too tightly (or it might swell and burst during cooking) then pat it down to make a nice rounded shape. Now tuck the neck flap under the bird's back and secure it in place with a small skewer. Then place the rest of the stuffing inside the body cavity.

The chicken Next smear the butter generously over the bird (if the skin was at all damp, dry it first) and tuck an extra lump of butter at the points where the thighs join the body. Season with salt and pepper, then place the bacon strips in a row—slightly overlapping each other—all along the breast.

Lay the chicken on its back in a roasting tin on a highish shelf in the oven, then calculate the cooking time which will be 20 minutes to the pound and *sometimes* 20 minutes over. It is this final 20 minutes that has to be flexible because larger birds don't take as long as might be expected, and also because ovens vary.

Every 20 minutes or so during roasting baste the bird thoroughly with the buttery juices to keep it moist, and after 1 hour remove the now-crisp bacon slices and reserve them in a warm place for serving; 20 minutes before the end of the cooking time increase the heat to gas mark 7, 425°F (220°C) just to give the skin a final crisping.

Is it cooked? The all-important question. There are three tests I use. (1) If you pierce the thickest part of the thigh with a thin skewer, the juices running out should be golden and clear. If they're pink it is not ready. (2) If the juices were golden and clear, then test the leg by tugging it gently away from the body. If you feel it give, it is ready. (3) (This is if a chicken is not stuffed.) Tip the chicken up and examine the juices running out of the body cavity—they should be golden and clear, and not at all pink.

When it's cooked, set the chicken on a hot dish in a warm place and leave it to 'relax' for 10–15 minutes. Meanwhile spoon or pour off any excess fat from the corner of the tin, stir a little flour into the juices and make a gravy with the giblet stock, simmering to reduce and concentrate the flavour. Carve the chicken, and serve with the stuffing, bacon pieces, gravy and creamy bread sauce (page 441).

Creamed chicken with avocado

(serves 4 people)

This recipe is a delicious way to use left-over cooked chicken or, if you have to work all day and prepare supper when you get home, it's a quick and easy way to jazz up some ready-cooked chicken from a quality chain store.

1 lb cold cooked chicken meat cut into small strips (450 g)
2 oz butter (50 g)
2 oz plain flour (50 g)
½ pint milk (275 ml)
¼ pint chicken stock (150 ml)
½ pint single cream (150 ml)
1 tablespoon dry sherry
Some lemon juice
2 ripe avocados
1 oz mild cheese, grated (25 g)
Salt and freshly-milled black pepper

Pre-heat the oven to gas mark 6, 400°F (200°C)

Begin by melting the butter in a medium-sized saucepan, add the flour and blend to a smooth paste. Cook for 2 minutes then gradually stir in the milk, stock and cream and, stirring all the time, bring to simmering point and cook very gently for 2 or 3 minutes. Then remove the pan from the heat and add the chicken pieces, sherry, salt, pepper and lemon juice to taste.

Now halve and quarter the avocados and, having removed the stone and skins, slice the flesh thinly and cover the base of a casserole with the slices. Sprinkle over a little lemon juice, spoon the chicken mixture on top and, finally, add the grated cheese. Transfer to the pre-heated oven and bake for 20–25 minutes or until the sides start to bubble. A crisp, green salad is a nice accompaniment.

Coq au vin

(serves 6 people)

A truly authentic *Coq au vin* is made, obviously, with a cock bird, and some of the blood goes into the sauce, which by the time it reaches the table, is a rich, almost black colour. In Britain we make

a less authentic adaptation, but it makes
a splendid dinner party dish.

A large 4–5 lb chicken, cut into 6 joints (1·8– 2·25 kg)
½ lb unsmoked streaky bacon, in one piece (225 g)
16 button onions
½ lb dark-gilled mushrooms (225 g)
2 cloves garlic, crushed
2 bayleaves
2 sprigs of fresh thyme
1¼ pints of red wine (725 ml)
1 tablespoon butter
1 tablespoon oil
A butter and flour paste made with 1 rounded tablespoon softened butter and 1 tablespoon plain flour
Salt and freshly-milled black pepper

A large flameproof pot, wide and
shallow to take the joints in one layer.

Melt a little butter and oil in a frying pan, and fry the chicken joints,
skin side down, until they are nicely golden; then turn them and
colour the other side. You may have to do this in three or four
batches—don't overcrowd the pan. Remove the joints from the pan
with a draining spoon, and place them in a large cooking pot. The
pot should be large enough for the joints to be arranged in one layer
yet deep enough so that they can be completely covered with liquid
later. The pot must also be flameproof.

Now de-rind and cut the bacon into fairly small cubes, brown them
also in the frying pan and add them to the chicken, then finally
brown the onions a little and add them too. Next place the crushed
cloves of garlic and the sprigs of thyme among the chicken pieces,
season with freshly-milled pepper and just a little salt, and pop in a
couple of bayleaves.

Pour in the wine, put a lid on the pot and simmer gently for 45
minutes to 1 hour or until the chicken is tender. During the last 15
minutes of the cooking, add the mushrooms and stir them into the
liquid.

Remove the chicken, bacon, onions and mushrooms and place

them on a warmed serving dish and keep warm. (Discard the bay leaves and thyme at this stage.)

Now bring the liquid to a fast boil and reduce it by about one third. Next, add the butter and flour paste to the liquid. Bring it to the boil, whisking all the time until the sauce has thickened, then serve the chicken with the sauce poured over. If you like, sprinkle some chopped parsley over the chicken and make it look pretty.

Note: the results are different but every bit as delicious if you use cider instead of wine, but it must be *dry* cider.

Chicken in the pot

(serves 4 people)

This is the *poule au pot* associated with Henri IV of France, whose ambition was that every family in his kingdom might be able to afford to eat this dish every Sunday.

1 freshly drawn chicken with giblets, weighing about 3½ lb (1½ kg)
½ lb unsmoked streaky bacon in one piece (225 g)
3 tablespoons olive oil
4 medium-sized carrots, cut in 1 inch (2·5 cm) chunks
4 small turnips, quartered
1 clove garlic, crushed
½ pint dry white wine (275 ml)
¾ pint chicken stock, made with the giblets (425 ml)
12 button onions
½ lb mushrooms, sliced (225 g)
1 small bunch parsley stalks
A few celery leaves (if you have them)
1 bayleaf
2 sprigs of fresh thyme (or ¾ teaspoon dried thyme)
Salt and freshly-milled black pepper
A paste made with 1 rounded tablespoon softened butter and 1 tablespoon plain flour

Pre-heat the oven to gas mark 6, 400°F (200°C)

First heat the oil in a large flameproof casserole, then cut the bacon into chunks and fry it a little with the peeled button onions. When the bacon and onions have coloured a little, remove them with a slotted spoon and keep them on one side.

Now, with the oil fairly hot, fry the chicken whole (as you would a piece of meat for a pot roast), turning it several times to brown evenly all over, then remove it from the casserole. Next fry the carrots, turnips and crushed garlic for about 5 minutes, stirring them all around so that they brown slightly. Now put the bacon and onion back in the pan. Push everything to the sides and sit the chicken in the centre. Next pour in the wine and stock, add the parsley and celery leaves tied in a bundle, plus the thyme, bayleaf and salt and pepper. Bring to simmering point, then transfer the casserole to the oven (the casserole should be without a lid, but place a piece of foil over the chicken breast) and let it cook for 30 minutes, uncovering and basting the chicken breast now and then with the surrounding stock.

After 30 minutes remove the foil, add the sliced mushrooms, then bake for another 30 minutes, again basting fairly often with the juices. When the chicken is cooked, take the casserole from the oven, remove the chicken, drain it well and put it on a warmed serving dish. Surround it with the well-drained vegetables and bacon, and discard the bayleaf and herbs.

Now place the casserole over a direct heat and boil the liquid fiercely to reduce it by about a third. Then whisk in the flour and butter paste, and bring back to the boil, whisking continuously until the sauce thickens. Now taste to check the seasoning, then carve and serve the chicken and vegetables with the sauce poured over them.

Fried mustard-and-herb-coated chicken

(serves 4 people)

This is a very good recipe for jazzing up the mass-produced chicken drumsticks or thighs that come in packets.

8 small chicken joints
1 tablespoon Dijon mustard
2 tablespoons made-up English mustard
2 egg yolks
2 tablespoons double cream

| 5 oz breadcrumbs (150 g) mixed with 2 teaspoons mixed dried herbs |
| Plain flour |
| Salt and freshly-milled black pepper |
| Groundnut or olive oil |

First remove the skins from the chicken joints. Then in a small basin mix the two mustards, egg yolks, and cream until well blended and smooth. Then place the breadcrumb and herb mixture on a square of greaseproof paper and some flour on another piece. Season each chicken joint with salt and pepper and dust with flour, then dip in the mustard mixture to coat it evenly, and finally roll the joint in the breadcrumbs and pat the coating on firmly. Chill the joints for 3 or 4 hours so that the mustard flavour can develop and the coating become firm.

Then in a very large frying pan (or two smaller ones) heat about an inch (2·5 cm) of oil to the point where a small cube of bread froths on contact. Then fry the chicken joints over a medium heat, turning them from time to time, until they're crisp and golden—about 20 minutes. Drain the chicken joints on crumpled kitchen paper and serve hot.

Chicken with lemon sauce

(serves 4 people)

This is a light, summery recipe with a sharp lemon sauce.

| A 4 lb chicken with giblets (1·8 kg) |
| 3 oz softened butter (75 g) |
| 1 dessertspoon lemon juice |
| ¼ teaspoon dried tarragon |
| 1 lemon, quartered |
| Salt and freshly-milled black pepper |

| *For the sauce:* |
| 2 oz butter (50 g) |
| 1 tablespoon flour |
| ¼ pint stock, made with the giblets (150 ml) |
| 1 tablespoon lemon juice |
| ¼ pint double cream (150 ml) |

Pre-heat the oven to gas mark 6, 400°F (200°C)

Make the giblet stock as described on page 94, then reduce it down to ¼ pint (150 ml) to give a concentrated flavour.

Prepare the chicken for roasting by mixing the 3 oz (75 g) of butter with ¼ teaspoon of salt, some freshly-milled pepper and a dessertspoon of lemon juice. Add the tarragon, then spread this mixture evenly all over the chicken. Now cut the lemon into quarters and place these inside the chicken. Next place the chicken in a roasting tin and cover the breast with buttered foil. Roast for 1¼–1½ hours, basting the chicken quite often with the buttery juices. Remove the foil from the breast during the last half hour.

While the cooked chicken is 'relaxing' in a warm place, make the sauce. Melt the butter in a small saucepan, blend in the flour, then gradually stir in the chicken stock and lemon juice. Bring to the boil, stirring all the time, simmer for 2 or 3 minutes, then add the cream and some of the juices from the roasting tin. Carve the chicken and serve on a bed of rice with the sauce poured over.

Chicken in barbecue sauce

(serves 4 people)

If you can, buy fresh chicken drumsticks or thigh joints—you could use chicken breasts, but cut them in half. This is one of the easiest supper dishes I know.

8 small chicken joints
For the sauce:
1 medium onion, chopped small
5 tablespoons dry cider (or wine)
5 tablespoons soy sauce
1 heaped tablespoon tomato purée
1 heaped teaspoon mustard powder
1 fat clove garlic, crushed
1 tablespoon soft brown sugar
Olive oil
Freshly-milled black pepper

Pre-heat the oven to gas mark 6, 400°F (200°C)

First of all, make sure the chicken joints are absolutely dry by patting them with kitchen paper. Then rub each joint all over with olive oil and season with freshly-milled pepper (but no salt because of the sauce). Now pop them into a shallow roasting tin, tucking the chopped onion in amongst them and sprinkling them with a few drops of oil. Place the tin on the highest shelf in the oven and let them cook for about 30 minutes.

Meanwhile make up the barbecue sauce simply by crushing the garlic clove, then adding all the rest of the ingredients to it and whisking with a fork until blended thoroughly.

When the chicken has been cooking for 30 minutes, pour off any excess oil from the roasting tin, then pour the barbecue sauce over the chicken and cook for a further 25 minutes, basting frequently.

This is nice served with a brown pilau rice and a salad.

Chicken with whole spices

(serves 4 people)

This dish is made with crushed whole spices and tastes authentically Indian. If you enjoy it, try also the recipe for *Spiced chicken* on page 420.

3¾ lb chicken, cut in 8 pieces (about 1·6 kg)
2 tablespoons groundnut oil
1 tablespoon butter
2 onions, very finely chopped or minced
1 medium green pepper, finely chopped
2 dried red chillies, deseeded and very finely chopped
2 cloves garlic, crushed
¾ teaspoon whole cumin seeds
1 teaspoon whole coriander seeds
8 whole cardamom seeds
1 teaspoon ground ginger
2 teaspoons ground turmeric
1 bayleaf, crumbled
¼ pint natural yoghurt (150 ml)
2 fl oz hot water (55 ml)
Salt and freshly-milled black pepper

Prepare the chicken a few hours before cooking. Arrange the pieces in an oblong meat-roasting tin. In a small bowl mix together the crushed garlic, ground ginger and turmeric with 1½ tablespoons groundnut oil. Now, with a sharp knife, make several incisions in the chicken, season, then coat them as evenly as possible with the oil and spice mixture. Leave in a cool place (but not in the fridge) so that the flavour penetrates.

When you're ready to cook the chicken, pre-heat the oven to gas mark 6, 400°F (200°C). Place the tin on the highest shelf, uncovered, and cook for about 20 minutes or until the chicken pieces are a nice golden colour.

Meanwhile, prepare the whole spices by grinding them and crushing finely, either with a pestle and mortar or on a flat surface using the back of a tablespoon. Next, melt the butter and remaining $1/2$ tablespoon of oil in a frying pan. Add the onion and green pepper, and cook for 5 minutes. Now add the crushed spices, chillies and crumbled bayleaf, stir and cook for a further 5 minutes. Take the pan off the heat, stir in the yoghurt and water and add a little salt.

Now pour this mixture all over the chicken pieces, cover the tin with a double sheet of foil and bake for 30 minutes with the heat reduced to gas mark 4, 350°F (180°C), then remove the foil and let it cook for approximately a further 10 minutes.

Serve with pilau rice and mango chutney.

Cold chicken pie

(serves 8 people)

This is a delicious centrepiece for a picnic, or any sort of lunch out of doors.

For the pastry:
2 oz lard at room temperature (50 g)
2 oz butter at room temperature (50 g)
8 oz plain flour, sifted (225 g)
Cold water
Beaten egg, to glaze

For the filling:
A 4½ lb chicken (2 kg)
1 lb pork sausage meat (450 g)
1 teaspoon mace
6 spring onions, finely chopped
The rind and juice of half a lemon
1 teaspoon fresh thyme (or ½ teaspoon dried thyme)

| 1 tablespoon fresh chopped sage (or ½ tablespoon dried sage) |
| 2 tablespoons double cream |
| Salt and freshly-milled black pepper |

Pre-heat the oven to gas mark 6, 400°F, (200°C)

A round, 8 inch (20 cm) diameter pie tin with rim and sloping sides which is 2 inches (5 cm) deep.

First make up the pastry, by rubbing the fats into the sifted flour till the mixture resembles fine breadcrumbs, then adding just enough water to make a dough that leaves the bowl clean. Rest the dough in a polythene bag in the fridge for half an hour, then use half the dough to line the pie-tin.

Next, with the help of a sharp knife, strip all the flesh you can off the chicken and cut the meat up into ½ inch (1 cm) pieces. Place them in a bowl, sprinkle in the mace and season well.

Now, in a separate bowl, combine the sausage meat with the spring onions, the thyme and sage, the lemon rind and 2 teaspoons of the lemon juice. Pour in the cream and mix everything together well to make a soft mixture (rather like a cake mix)—if necessary, add a little more cream. Next put one-third of the sausage meat mixture in the bottom of the pastry-lined tin and spread it flat. Now put half the chicken pieces on top and sprinkle in any remaining lemon juice, then add another layer of one-third of the sausage meat, followed by the rest of the chicken and a final layer of sausage meat.

Roll out the rest of the pastry and use it to cover the pie—which will be well piled up, dome-like, by now. Seal the edges well, glaze with some beaten egg and bake on a baking sheet in the oven for 30 minutes. Then reduce the heat to gas mark 4, 350°F (180°C) and cook for a further 1¼ hours.

Chicken with grape stuffing
(serves 4 people)

Here's a nice recipe for serving in the summer, when the seedless grapes are in season.

| 4 lb roasting chicken with giblets (1·8 kg) |
| 2 oz butter at room temperature (50 g) |

Salt and freshly-milled black pepper
Giblet stock (see page 94)
4 tablespoons dry white wine
A little plain flour

For the stuffing:
3½ oz butter (85 g)
1 medium-sized onion, finely chopped
4 oz fresh breadcrumbs (110 g)
4 cloves garlic, crushed
1 tablespoon freshly chopped parsley
½ teaspoon dried tarragon
6 oz seedless grapes, or halved and deseeded grapes (175 g)
Salt and freshly-milled black pepper

Pre-heat the oven to gas mark 5,
375°F (190°C)

First make the stuffing. Melt ½ oz (10 g) of butter in a small
saucepan and cook the finely chopped onion for about 6 minutes or
until softened, then add the remaining butter and allow it to melt.
Now transfer the onion and the buttery juices to a bowl, add the
breadcrumbs, then stir in the crushed garlic, chopped parsley,
tarragon and grapes. Taste and season with salt and pepper.

Next loosen the breast skin of the chicken a little to make a pocket
for the stuffing. Place the stuffing in the pocket but don't overfill—if
you do, the skin will burst when cooking. Secure the skin flap
underneath with a small skewer. Season the chicken all over with
lots of salt and pepper, then rub it all over with the softened butter,
and cover the breast with buttered foil.

Place the chicken in a roasting tin and cook for approximately
1 hour 20 minutes, basting the meat with the buttery juices every
20 minutes or so. Remove the foil half an hour before the end of
the cooking time to brown the breast.

Meanwhile make some giblet stock (see page 94), then boil it,
without a lid, to reduce it and concentrate the flavour. To test if the
chicken is cooked, pierce the thickest part of the thigh with a thin
skewer: if cooked, the juices will run golden and clear. Drain the
chicken thoroughly and keep warm while you make the gravy.

Carefully tilt the roasting tin and pour off some of the excess fat.

Then put the tin over direct low heat and blend in a little flour.
Keep stirring and allow the flour to brown before gradually adding
the wine and sufficient strained giblet stock to make a thin gravy.
Taste and season with salt and pepper. Carve the chicken and serve,
passing the gravy round separately.

Duck

Whatever mass-produced chicken lacks in character and flavour,
our duck makes up for, I think. Perhaps that's because we eat
relatively little duck in this country: if demand increased no doubt
we'd have another plentiful but uniform bird. In the meantime
duck, though comparatively expensive, makes a superb choice for
a dinner-party. In the first place you'll be serving something
special; secondly duck has the advantage of needing no attention
whatsoever while it's cooking; and thirdly, if your guests happen
to be late, your duck will happily wait for them without being
spoiled.

Buying duck

If possible, try to get a fresh duck. If you can't a frozen one will do,
so long as you bear in mind one important point: ducks are very
fatty birds and sub-zero temperatures do not prevent rancidity
developing. So while a duck that's been frozen for three months will
be perfectly good, after that it will begin to deteriorate. A duck
frozen for a year will not be very good at all. (Let's hope we'll get
date-stamping on poultry soon!) It is of course essential that frozen
duck is completely defrosted before cooking.

The weight of a duck is very important, because to get a crisp,
fat-free finish it needs long, slowish cooking—and that means the
weight of the bird will be considerably reduced by the end of the
cooking time. So to serve four people, buy a 5 lb or preferably a 6 lb
bird (2·25 or 2·7 kg); to serve six or eight people you'll need two
ducks of this size.

Drying duck

To cook a duck to a lovely crisp finish, it has to be fairly dry before
it goes into the oven. If it has been frozen (or even if it's a fresh
duck which came wrapped in a polythene bag) and the skin looks
damp, dry it thoroughly with a clean tea-cloth or some absorbent
kitchen paper. It is also a good idea to check that the inside of the
duck is dry too. Then leave the bird in a cool dry place for several

hours for the air to dry it as well. The Chinese hang theirs up on lines in a draughty place and one typical 'colour supplement' article once recommended drying a duck with a hair-drier! I can assure you, you don't need to resort to such measures to get a crisply cooked duck.

Stuffing duck
Personally I never put stuffing inside a duck, because (i) duck meat doesn't need lubricating, and (ii) the stuffing tends to absorb too much of the duck fat. But if you like you can prepare some *Pork, sage and onion stuffing* (see recipe on page 227), roll the mixture into little balls, flour them and fry them to serve with the finished duck. That's especially nice if the duck is served with an apple sauce.

Cooking times for duck
In France duck is often served pink and underdone, or sometimes the skin and bones are removed and only the breast is cooked. Also pressed duck is considered a delicacy, though it's not to my taste. In England we tend to prefer our duck cooked whole and for quite a long time, so that the high proportion of fat can be rendered down and run out, leaving moist flesh and a mahogany-coloured crisp skin (rather like crackling); 30 minutes per pound (450 g) is a general guideline. This longer style of cooking does mean that the wings and part of the legs are frazzled, but believe me, the rest is so good that it's worth the small loss. However if you prefer duck in the French manner, you can cut down the cooking time.

Roast duck	**1 duck, weighing 6 lb (about 2·75 kg)**
(serves 4 people)	**Salt and freshly-milled black pepper**
	1 bunch of watercress, for garnishing

Pre-heat the oven to gas mark 7, 425°F (220°C)

The golden rule is never to put any sort of fat near a duck, because it has more than enough of its own. Just place the bird in a roasting tin, then prick the duck skin all over—going deep into the flesh— with a skewer (to leave little escape routes for the fat to run out). Season the duck quite liberally with salt and pepper, then place the tin on a highish shelf in the oven (see note at end).

After 20 minutes turn the heat down to gas mark 4, 350°F (180°C), then basically all you have to do is leave it alone for 3 hours—just once or twice pouring off the fat that has collected in the roasting tin. Pour the fat into a bowl—don't throw it away, it is lovely for roasting or sautéing potatoes.

When the cooking time is up, remove the duck from the tin, first tipping it up to let excess fat drain out of the body cavity, and place it on a carving board. Leave it to 'relax' for 5 minutes, then divide it into portions: all you need do is cut the bird in half lengthways (i.e. along the length of the breast and through the backbone) with a sharp knife, then cut the halves into quarters—you may need the help of some kitchen scissors here. Leaving any escaped pieces of bone behind, sit the quarters up together on a warm serving dish and garnish with watercress.

Note: it is best to place the duck on a rack in the roasting tin. If the rack from your grill pan will fit into the oven, you can use that.

Sauces for duck
To make a gravy, simmer up some stock with the duck giblets (as for *Chicken giblet stock*, page 94). Pour off the fat from the roasting tin and, over direct heat, add some flour to the juices that are left and stir it around. Now blend in the giblet stock (plus some wine if you feel like it) and simmer gently to thicken slightly.

Alternatively you can serve it with *Morello cherry sauce* or *Bitter orange sauce* (pages 444–445), which are my own favourites.

Turkey
I come from a long line of turkey cooks and, throughout my life once a year, I have enjoyed the annual ritual of feasting not just on turkey but also on all the favourites that traditionally go with it.

Fashions in cooking turkey have come and gone, but ever since kitchen foil was introduced I have stood firm and stuck to the method which, in our family, has always been a hundred per cent successful (which is to say, cooking in foil). I can honestly say we've never had a turkey that's too dry, so we've never become bored with it cold. On the contrary, our enthusiasm for turkey lasts down to the jelly and dripping—delicious on toast for breakfast—and to the beautiful soup you can make from the carcass. I offer you here the family recipe for roast turkey with all the trimmings, but first a few words about buying a turkey.

Buying turkey

Try if possible to get a fresh bird, and remember to order it in plenty of time. If you can only buy a frozen bird, or it's more convenient, try to buy one that has been frozen without added water, then don't forget to allow plenty of time for it to de-frost slowly and *completely*. Always remove the giblets as soon as you can—with a fresh bird immediately you get home, with a frozen one as soon as it has thawed.

Important points

Let the bird come to cool room temperature before you cook it (i.e. remove it from the refrigerator, cold garage, shed or wherever the night before if you plan to eat your turkey dinner in the middle of the day). Also make the stuffing the night before, but *don't* yet stuff the turkey—it is important to let the air circulate round the inside of the bird. Stuffing made in advance also needs to be taken from the fridge the night before. The point is that if everything is chilled when it goes into the oven, it upsets the cooking times. Also remove and discard the trussing strings if there are any—they are not needed (see page 210). The stuffing for the turkey and the giblet stock can be prepared the day before.

Pork, sage and onion stuffing

(for a 12–14 lb turkey, about 6 kg)

As I said earlier in connection with chicken, I believe a stuffing is a good means of providing some lubrication and juiciness inside a lean-meated bird while it's cooking. Minced pork or good pork sausage meat used as a base to a stuffing provides this lubrication.

2 lb pork sausagemeat (900 g)
1 heaped dessertspoon dried sage
1 large onion, grated or chopped very finely
4 heaped tablespoons white breadcrumbs
2–3 tablespoons boiling water
Salt and freshly-milled black pepper

First combine the breadcrumbs with the onion and sage in a large mixing bowl, then stir in a little boiling water and mix thoroughly. Next work the sausagemeat into this mixture and season with salt and pepper. If (like me) you prefer your stuffing crumbly when it's cooked, leave it as it is. If you like to carve it in slices, then add a beaten egg to bind it all together.

Chestnut and apple stuffing

(for a 12–14 lb turkey, about 6 kg)

This stuffing is also delicious but Christmas, with all the extra work involved, is not the time to be peeling and skinning chestnuts—a beastly job at the best of times. As they are going to be mashed anyway, I really think a tin of whole or puréed natural chestnuts (unsweetened) will do fine.

1 lb tin of natural chestnuts (450 g)
1½ lb pork sausagemeat (700 g)
1 lb cooking apples, peeled, cored and finely chopped (450 g)
1 medium-sized onion, finely chopped
1 beaten egg
Salt and freshly-milled black pepper

Drain the chestnuts into a large bowl, and mash them almost to a pulp with a fork. Combine them with the rest of the ingredients (except the egg) and mix thoroughly. Then add the beaten egg to bind everything together.

Now for the turkey

Size A good size of turkey for the average family is 12–14 lb (about 6 kg). This is oven-ready weight—which is equivalent to 14–16 lb (around 7 kg) New York dressed weight. But below you'll find cooking times for varying sizes of turkey.

A note for beginners Cooking a turkey for the first time at Christmas, when in-laws and other guests are probably milling around, can be quite a traumatic experience. I think the secret of success is to give the turkey a good blast of heat to begin with, and once you've got it going (i.e. the heat has penetrated right through) you can then turn the oven down and let the turkey cook through more gently. It is also a good precaution to calculate your starting time so that the bird should complete cooking at least 30 minutes before you plan to sit down to eat. That way it has a chance to 'relax' so that the flesh can re-absorb the juices that have bubbled to the surface; it also allows sufficient time to give the turkey another 10 minutes' or so cooking time if it needs it.

Timing It might be helpful to beginners if I give you an account of the exact timings of a recent turkey of mine. The turkey (14 lb oven-ready weight) went into the oven, pre-heated to gas mark 7, 425°F (220°C), at 8.15 am. The heat was lowered to gas mark 3, 325°F (170°) at 8.55. The foil came off and the heat was turned up to gas mark 6, 400°F (200°C) at 12.30. Then with lots of basting it was cooked by 1.15 and served by 1.45.

Here are the cooking times for other sizes of turkey:

8–10 lb turkey: (3·5–4·5 kg)	30 minutes at the high temperature, then 2½–3 hours at the lower temperature, then a final 30 minutes (uncovered) at gas mark 6, 400°F (200°C).
15–20 lb turkey: (7–9 kg)	45 minutes at the high temperature, then 4–5 hours at the lower temperature, then a final 30 minutes (uncovered) at gas mark 6, 400°F (200°C).

Please bear in mind that ovens, and turkeys themselves, vary and the only sure way of knowing if a bird is ready is by using the tests described in the recipe.

Traditional roast turkey

1 turkey, about 14 lb oven-ready (6 kg)
6 oz softened butter (175 g)
½ lb very fat streaky bacon (225 g)
Salt and freshly-milled black pepper
1 quantity of pork, sage and onion stuffing (or chestnut and apple stuffing)

Pre-heat the oven to gas mark 7, 425°F (220°C)

1 packet of extra-wide foil.

Begin, on the morning of cooking, by stuffing the turkey. Loosen the skin with your hands and pack the stuffing into the neck end, pushing it up between the flesh and the skin towards the breast (though not too tightly because it will expand during the cooking). Press it in gently to make a nice rounded end, then tuck the neck flap under the bird's back and secure with a small skewer. Don't expect to get all the stuffing in this end—put the rest into the body cavity.

Now arrange two large sheets of foil across your baking tin—one of them widthways, the other lengthways. Lay the turkey on its back in the centre, then rub it generously all over with the butter, making sure the thigh bones are particularly well covered. Next season the bird all over with salt and pepper, and lay the bacon over the breast with the rashers overlapping each other.

The idea now is to wrap the turkey up in the foil. The parcel must be firmly sealed but roomy enough inside to provide an air space around most of the upper part of the turkey. So bring one piece of foil up and fold both ends over to make a pleat along the length of the breast-bone—but well above the breast. Then bring the other piece up at both ends, and crimp and fold to make a neat parcel.

Place the roasting tin on a low shelf in the oven and cook at the initial high temperature for 40 minutes.

After that lower the heat to gas mark 3, 325°F (170°C) and cook for a further 3 hours for a 12 lb bird (around 6 kg), or 3½ hours for a 14 lb bird (around 7 kg). Then tear the foil away from the top and sides of the bird and remove the bacon slices to allow the skin to brown and crisp. Turn the heat up to gas mark 6, 400°F (200°C) and cook the turkey for a further 30 minutes. The turkey will need frequent basting during this time, so the whole operation will probably take nearer 40–45 minutes.

To test if the bird is cooked, pierce the thickest part of the leg with a thin skewer: the juices running out of it should be golden and clear. And the same applies to any part of the bird tested—there should be no trace of pinkness in the juices. You can also give the leg a little tug, to make sure there is some give in it.

Then remove it from the roasting tin (using a carving fork and fish slice) and transfer it to a warm carving dish. If you can engage someone's help while lifting it, it's a good idea to tip the turkey to let the excess juice run out. Leave the turkey in a warmish place for 20–30 minutes to 'relax' before carving: provided it's not in a draught it will stay hot for that length of time, and it will give you a chance to turn the heat up in the oven to crisp the roast potatoes (you'll find my recipe for *Roast potatoes* on page 278).

Meanwhile to make the gravy: tip all the fat and juices out of the foil into the roasting tin. Spoon off all the fat from the juice in a corner of the tin, then work about 2 tablespoons of flour into the remaining juices over a low heat. Now, using a balloon whisk, whisk in the giblet stock (see page 94) bit by bit, until you have a smooth gravy. Let it bubble and reduce a bit to concentrate the flavour, and taste and season with salt and pepper. (And when you have carved the turkey, pour any escaped juices into the gravy.)

Goose
Try to get a fresh goose, but if you can only get hold of a frozen one, remember to defrost it very thoroughly and dry well.

Roast stuffed goose with prune and apple sauce

(serves 8 people)

1 young goose with giblets, weighing 10–12 lb (4·5–5·4 kg)

Flour

For the stuffing:

½ lb fresh white breadcrumbs (225 g)

½ lb onion, finely chopped (225 g)

1 dessertspoon sage

1½ oz butter (40 g)

2 eggs

The goose liver, finely chopped

Salt and freshly-milled black pepper

For the sauce:

½ lb prunes (225 g), soaked in ½ pint (275 ml) dry cider for about 6 hours

½ lb cooking apples, peeled and chopped (225 g)

Half an onion, chopped

¼ teaspoon powdered cloves

2 pinches powdered mace

2 tablespoons caster sugar

For the stock:

The giblets

1 onion

| A bayleaf |
| 1 pint water (570 ml) |

Pre-heat the oven to gas mark 7,
425°F (220°C)

First make the stuffing by melting the butter in a saucepan and
softening the onion in it for 5 minutes, then add the chopped goose
liver, stir and cook for a further 5 minutes. Now empty the contents
of the saucepan into a bowl, add the breadcrumbs and sage, and
mix thoroughly. Season very well with salt and freshly-milled black
pepper, then bind the mixture together with two well-beaten eggs.
Stuff the tail-end of the bird with this mixture, and secure the gap
with a small skewer.

Place the goose in a roasting tin—on a rack if you have one—then
prick all the fleshy parts with a skewer. Season well and dust it all
over with flour. Put it into the pre-heated oven, cook for 30 minutes
then lower the temperature to gas mark 4, 350°F (180°C) and cook
for a further 3½ hours, pouring the excess fat out of the roasting
tin several times during that time. While the goose is cooking, make
some stock by simmering the giblets with an onion, a bayleaf,
seasoning and 1 pint (570 ml) of water for about 1 hour.

Next prepare the sauce: put the prunes and a ¼ pint (150 ml) of
the cider in which they were soaked into a pan. Simmer them till
they're soft, then chop them up into small pieces, throwing away the
stones. Now soften the onion in a saucepan with 1 tablespoon of
goose fat (taken from the roasting tin), then add the chopped apples
and simmer until they're soft and fluffy. Now stir in the chopped
prunes, caster sugar and spices. Taste to see if you need a little more
sugar or spice, and reheat gently just before serving.

To serve the goose, drain it well and place it onto a hot serving dish.
Drain off the fat from the tin and make some gravy from the
remaining juices and giblet stock. Give each person a little of the
stuffing, and serve the gravy and sauce separately. The nicest
vegetable accompaniments would be some crisp roast potatoes and
spicy baked red cabbage.

See also:
Chicken liver pâté
Chicken paprika
Chicken salad with tarragon and grapes

Creamy chicken curry
Pheasant with cream and apples
Spiced chicken

Offal

Including recipes for:
Peppered liver
Paprika liver
Liver in yoghurt and juniper sauce
Ox liver and bacon hotpot
Faggots and peas
Lambs' kidneys in red wine
Kidneys in fresh tomato sauce
Curried lambs' kidneys
Kidneys in jacket potatoes

Curried ox kidneys
*Pork kidneys in mushroom and
 onion sauce*
Pork kidneys in chilli sauce
Cold, pressed ox tongue
Lambs' tongue casserole
Oxtail with haricot beans
*Sweetbreads with soured cream and
 onion sauce*
Tripe and onions

One of my favourite cookery writers, Margaret Costa, once called a chapter on offal 'awful offal'. Not that offal is awful, she explains, but the *name* sounds awful. I agree with her, but find the various alternatives (like 'spare parts') equally off-putting. In fact the whole subject can be discouraging to some people not just because of its anatomical origins—the word itself is derived from those parts that 'fall off' or are rejected when a carcass is dressed—but because so often the meat has been neither sensitively nor imaginatively cooked. Lumps of semi-boiled watery kidney in a steak-and-kidney pie, or unevenly cut paving-slabs of over-cooked liver, these are the real culprits. In working on, and testing for, this chapter I have actually converted several people to offal who would otherwise never have considered eating it!

Offal really has an important place in our diet. Not only can it supply a generous amount of essential nutrients, but it does so at a very economical price. Being rich and concentrated in flavour means a little goes a long way, and items such as ox kidneys and liver, or pork kidneys, provide relatively cheap and quite delicious meals, as I hope the recipes in this chapter will show. But first let's consider some of the items in question.

Liver

Rich in iron and many vitamins, so most nutritionists would have us all eat liver at least once a week. In cooking it there are two important considerations. One is to try to persuade an obliging butcher to slice the liver *thinly* and *evenly* for you. And having achieved that, your next objective is to cook it carefully and, if frying or grilling it, quickly. If you cook it too long, it will be tough and dry.

Calves' liver This is the most expensive and said to be the finest flavoured. Serve it thinly sliced and lightly fried (so that it's still slightly pink) in butter, with some crisp fried bacon to go with it.

Ox liver This is the cheapest, but excellent braised with lots of onion and a thick gravy. With its rather coarser texture it isn't suitable for frying or grilling.

Lambs' liver My own favourite. Properly cooked it can be meltingly tender with a delicious flavour. If you're unable to buy it thinly sliced, try cutting it up into evenly-sized strips, as in *Liver in yoghurt and juniper sauce* (page 239).

Pigs' liver This is extremely strong-flavoured and, in my opinion, not suitable for grilling, frying, or even casseroling. However, it is just the thing for pâtés and terrines and the recipe for *Faggots and peas* (page 241).

Notes on frying and grilling liver

Always wipe the liver as dry as possible with kitchen paper first. Only calves' and lambs' liver are suitable for grilling or frying.

To fry Lightly dust the pieces with seasoned flour and fry in hot butter or oil over a medium heat. It's important to get a good brown crust on the meat, and then only turn once after 3–4 minutes (or when you can see tiny droplets of blood beginning to form on the uncooked surface). Cook for a further 3–4 minutes.

To grill Brush the liver with oil or butter and give it a minute longer on both sides than for frying.

Kidneys

These too are packed full of nutrients. All types of kidneys are excellent for cooking, given the appropriate treatment for the right recipe. One point to remember is that kidneys do not have such a good flavour if stored too long. It's best to cook them really fresh, preferably on the day of purchase. If that's not possible, keep them until the next day but no longer.

Veal kidneys These are very expensive and, outside large cities, not easy to come by. They need gentle cooking and are usually served plain or with a light sauce.

Ox kidney This is an essential ingredient for steak-and-kidney pudding or pie (see pages 561 and 562)—no other type of kidney will give the proper, traditional flavour. Ox kidney is cheap and, though it is not recommended for grilling or frying, it is excellent stewed, braised, or especially curried (see page 245). Should you want to grate your own suet, by the way, the fat around an ox kidney is the best for this.

Lambs' kidneys I'm particularly fond of plump, juicy lambs' kidneys which are available through the spring and summer months, when home-grown lamb is in its peak season. Frozen or imported they are never quite as good, so if you buy these in the winter, they do need a good-flavoured sauce to go with them. If you can, buy lambs' kidneys still encased in their own fat, which seems to keep them fresher. It peels off easily, and if you place the fat in a meat roasting-tin in a low oven, it will render down to a bowlful of the most delicious cooking fat (which will have cost you nothing).

Pork kidneys In the past cooks have tended to subject pork kidneys to various periods of pre-soaking and blanching, to tone down what used to be a rather strong flavour. Nowadays, with more intensive meat production, we're eating blander, younger pork and I think this is the reason why the kidneys are milder, tender and quite delicious. They can therefore be cooked without any special treatment and, if you like their flavour, it may be useful to know that pork kidneys can be sliced and used as an alternative in any of the lambs' kidney recipes in this chapter.

Preparation of kidneys
To prepare lambs' or pork kidneys, first remove the skins, then slice the kidneys in half lengthwise. Now use a pair of kitchen scissors to snip out the cores (which look like solid fatty lumps)—simply pinch the cores between your fingers and snip all around them with the scissors. With ox or calves' kidneys the process is just reversed: instead of cutting the core away from the kidney, you snip the lobes of kidney away from the core. (If I'm making a steak-and-kidney pudding, I sometimes pop the cores plus any little piece of kidney still attached into a pan with an onion, carrot and herbs and boil up some stock, which after skimming makes a delicious gravy for serving with the pudding.)

Tongue
Ox tongue Salting improves the flavour of an ox tongue and so (especially around Chistmas or party-time when there's a house full of people to feed) a salted tongue is the best kind to buy. Cooked and pressed and served cold, it goes well with *Cumberland sauce* (page 442) or *Spiced plum chutney* (page 669). For its preparation and cooking details see page 248.

Lambs' tongues These are nicest braised until the skins slip off easily (which is done by slitting the underside of each tongue and then carefully peeling away the skin), then sliced, reheated gently and served with a hot *Parsley sauce* (page 436) or in a casserole (see page 249).

Oxtail
There is something about the flavour and aroma of an oxtail braising in the oven that's very comforting on a bitter cold winter's

day. Choose an oxtail that clearly has plenty of flesh around the
bone: one complete oxtail will serve 3–4 people. The recipe on page
250 is particularly good with haricot beans, which seem to absorb so
much of the flavour.

Heart

Invariably when I attempt to write about cooking heart, I find the
description and detail end up sounding comical. Facts like 'a heart
is heavy in proportion to its size' or 'long slow cooking makes a heart
tender' almost seem like something out of a romantic novel!
Anyway lambs' hearts, in my opinion, are the nicest. Allow one per
person, wash in cold water, then use a pair of kitchen scissors to cut
out all the tubes and the dividing wall in the centre. You then have a
convenient cavity for a stuffing (which I think is really essential).

Sweetbreads

I am often asked what exactly *are* sweetbreads? In fact they're
glands, more specifically the thymus and pancreas glands of the
animal. They are—rightly—considered to be a great delicacy and
are not readily available without pre-ordering. Ox sweetbreads are
fairly tough and they need long, slow cooking; calves' sweetbreads
are rare and much more tender; but best of all are lambs'
sweetbreads. For the last two the preparation is the same. Pre-soak
the sweetbreads in cold water for 1–2 hours; then boil in fresh water:
5 minutes for lambs', 10 minutes for calves'. Cool them in a colander
under cold running water then, using a sharp knife, remove any
gristle, skin and veins.

Tripe

Tripe is the stomach of an ox. It has to be treated by blanching and
pre-soaking, and this is done by the supplier or the butcher. It's this
initial treatment that gives tripe its bleached white appearance.
Honeycomb tripe—which a friend of mine describes as having the
feel and texture of slithery knitting!—is very good when cooked
with love and, judging by its regular appearance in supermarkets, is
still popular. Normally it needs about an hour's further cooking at
home, but this can vary so check cooking times with your supplier.
If it is over-done it becomes limp, when ideally it should still have
some 'bite' to it.

Peppered liver

(serves 2 people)

This is more or less the same as *Steak au poivre* but quite a bit cheaper and—if you like liver—every bit as good.

12 oz lambs' liver (350 g) **—ask the butcher to cut it into the thinnest slices possible**
2 teaspoons whole black peppercorns
1 tablespoon flour
1 tablespoon olive oil
1 teaspoon butter
5 fl oz red (or white) wine (150 ml)
1 level teaspoon salt

You'll need to crush the peppercorns first, and this can present one or two problems. If you've got a pestle and mortar you're home and dry; if you haven't, then the best way to crush them is by exerting a lot of pressure on the back of a tablespoon with the peppercorns underneath it. This last method can often result in one or two peppercorns escaping and rolling off onto the floor, if you're not careful. So be warned.

When you've got the peppercorns coarsely crushed, add them to the flour with a level teaspoon of salt. Then dip the pieces of liver in it, pressing the pepper in a bit on both sides. Now in a large heavy-based frying pan heat the oil and butter to the foamy stage, then put the liver slices in and cook them gently for a minute or two. As soon as the blood starts to run, turn them over, and gently cook them on the other side for slightly less time.

Whatever you do, don't overcook the liver or it will be dry and tough. Transfer the slices onto a warm serving dish, add the wine to the pan, let it bubble and reduce, then pour it over the liver and serve immediately.

Paprika liver

(serves 3–4 people)

This is one of my favourite recipes for liver—quick, simple and quite delicious.

1 lb lambs' liver (450 g), cut into narrow strips about 2½ inches (6 cm) long
1 large onion, very finely chopped
1 green pepper, deseeded and cut into narrow strips about 1½ inches (4 cm) long

5 fl oz soured cream (150 ml)
3 oz butter (75 g)
5 fl oz red wine (150 ml)
1 level tablespoon Hungarian paprika
Salt and freshly-milled black pepper

First melt 2 oz (50 g) of the butter in your largest frying pan, add the onion and green pepper and soften them over a gentle heat for about 7 or 8 minutes. Then transfer the vegetables to a plate using a draining spoon. Now with the heat fairly high, melt the extra butter and add the slices of liver. Let them cook and brown, and when the blood starts to run turn them over and cook them for just another minute or so before adding a seasoning of salt and pepper, the paprika and the vegetables. Then pour in the wine and let it bubble and reduce slightly (for about 2 minutes). Then—off the heat—stir in the soured cream until you have a nice smooth sauce. Serve the liver straight from the pan onto pre-heated plates, with the onion, pepper and sauce spooned over it. This is delicious served with brown rice and some fried shredded cabbage.

Liver in yoghurt and juniper sauce

(serves 4 people)

1 lb lambs' liver (450 g)—ask the butcher to slice it very thinly
1 largish onion
1 clove garlic, crushed
2 oz butter (50 g)
1 teaspoon olive oil
1 heaped teaspoon juniper berries, crushed
5 fl oz natural yoghurt (150 ml)
Salt and freshly-milled black pepper

First prepare the liver by cutting it into very thin strips, about 1½ inches (4 cm) long. The onion should be peeled, cut in half and then sliced thinly and the slices separated into little half-moon shapes. Now take a thick frying pan, melt the butter and oil together over a low heat until foaming, then add the onion, juniper and crushed garlic.

Cook them gently, without browning, for about 10 minutes. Now add the pieces of liver, increasing the heat, and brown them quickly and evenly by turning them—be careful not to overcook them. When they're browned, turn the heat right down again, take the pan off the heat and add the yoghurt—stirring it down into the pan juices—then return to the gentle heat and let it all simmer very, very gently for about 5 minutes. Taste, season with salt and freshly-milled black pepper, then serve the liver and sauce with rice and a side-salad.

Note: the cooked yoghurt sometimes takes on a slightly separated appearance but this is normal and in no way affects the flavour.

Ox liver and bacon hotpot

(serves 4 people)

This is another economical family supper dish—just 1 lb (450 g) of ox liver will be plenty for four people.

1 lb ox liver (450 g), cut into slices no more than ¼ inch (½ cm) thick
4 oz streaky bacon, rind removed and cut into small pieces (110 g)
1 medium-sized carrot, peeled and cut into chunks
1 celery stalk, cut into chunks
2 oz swede, peeled and cut into chunks (50 g)
3 fairly big onions, peeled and sliced
2 lb potatoes, peeled and cut into fairly thick slices (900 g)
1 heaped tablespoon seasoned flour
1 level teaspoon dried sage
1 teaspoon Worcestershire sauce
Stock or water
A little beef dripping
Salt and freshly-milled black pepper

Pre-heat the oven to gas mark 3, 325°F (170°C)

First of all, toss the slices of liver in the seasoned flour to coat them well, then arrange them in a good-sized casserole and sprinkle in any left-over flour. Then add the bacon and sliced onion, together with the chunks of carrot, celery and swede. Add the sage and a good seasoning of salt and pepper. Next pour in just enough stock or water barely to cover the ingredients in the pot—probably about 1 pint (570 ml)—then add the Worcestershire sauce. Finally, cover the top with a thick layer of potatoes, overlapping each other, then season again with salt and pepper. Cover the casserole and cook in the oven for 2 hours. After that, take the lid off and cook for a further 30 minutes.

When the time's up, brush the potatoes with a little melted beef dripping or butter and pop the casserole under a pre-heated hot grill to get a nice crusty top to the potatoes.

Faggots and peas

(serves 4 people)

A real old-fashioned treat—traditionally served with 'mushy' peas.

4 oz unsmoked bacon (110 g), bought in one piece, then cut into 1 inch (2·5 cm) cubes
1 lb pig's liver (450 g) cut into 1 inch (2·5 cm) cubes
6 oz fat belly pork (175 g), cut into 1 inch (2·5 cm) cubes
2 medium-sized onions, quartered
15 fl oz stock (425 ml)
¼ teaspoon dried thyme
¾ teaspoon dried sage
¼ teaspoon powdered mace
2 oz fresh white breadcrumbs (50 g)
Salt and freshly-milled black pepper

For the mushy peas:
12 oz green split peas (350 g)
1 onion, quartered
1¼ pints water (725 ml)
1 teaspoon Worcestershire sauce
1 teaspoon tomato purée
1 dessertspoon mushroom ketchup
2 oz butter (50 g)
Salt and freshly-milled black pepper

Pre-heat the oven to gas mark 5, 375°F (190°C)

First of all, place the cubes of bacon, liver and pork in a casserole along with the quartered onions, then pour in the stock. Cover the casserole and cook in the centre of the oven for 45 minutes, then drain the meat and onions in a sieve (reserving the liquid). Next, using the fine blade of a mincer, mince the meat and onions into a mixing bowl, then add the breadcrumbs, herbs and spice. Season with salt and pepper, and mix to combine everything thoroughly. Next use your hands to shape the mixture into 8 good-sized balls.

Grease a shallow baking dish, and arrange the faggots in a single layer in it. Pour over ¹/₂ pint (275 ml) of the reserved liquid, and bake (uncovered) on a high shelf of the oven for 45 minutes.

To cook the peas: mix the tomato purée. Worcestershire sauce and ketchup with the water, and pour this into a pan, adding the onion quarters. Bring to the boil, then add the split peas and bring back to the boil. Now turn the heat down, cover the pan and simmer gently for ³/₄–1 hour, or until the peas are absolutely tender. After that, mash the butter into them, along with a seasoning of salt and pepper. If they seem a bit on the dry side, you can mix them with a bit of the stock left over from the faggots. Serve the peas with the faggots, and the juices poured over.

Lambs' kidneys in red wine

(serves 2 people)

6 small lambs' kidneys
1 large onion, chopped
12 oz dark-gilled mushrooms (350 g)
4 rashers unsmoked bacon, chopped
1 clove garlic, crushed
1 level tablespoon flour
¹/₂ teaspoon fresh chopped thyme (or ¹/₄ teaspoon dried)
¹/₂ pint red wine (275 ml)
2 oz butter or dripping (50 g)
Salt and freshly-milled black pepper

Begin by melting the fat in a pan and softening the onion and garlic in it for 5 minutes. After that add the chopped bacon and the mushrooms, and cook for a further 10 minutes. Meanwhile prepare the kidneys: cut them in half and remove the skins, then snip out the cores with a pair of kitchen scissors.

Now add the halved kidneys to the pan and cook them to colour a little, stirring them around the pan. Next sprinkle in the flour and stir it to soak up the juices, then add the thyme and pour in the red wine. Bring the whole lot to simmering point; season with salt (not too much, because of the bacon) and pepper. Then cover the pan and simmer gently for 15 minutes. Then remove the lid and simmer for a further 10 minutes.

Kidneys in fresh tomato sauce

(serves 2 people)

These are nice served with hot, buttery noodles and a green salad.

6 lambs' kidneys
12 oz ripe, red tomatoes (350 g)
1 medium onion, chopped
1 clove garlic, crushed
1½ teaspoons fresh chopped basil (or ¾ teaspoon dried)
1 level tablespoon tomato purée
1 level dessertspoon flour
1½ tablespoons olive oil
Salt and freshly-milled black pepper

Prepare the kidneys by peeling off the skins, cutting them in half and snipping out the white cores with some scissors. It's important to take out the cores—if you don't, the kidneys will be tough.

In a medium-sized saucepan, cook the onion gently in the olive oil for 6 minutes or so. Meanwhile pour boiling water over the tomatoes, slip the skins off and chop up the flesh roughly. Now add the kidneys to the onion, turn up the heat a little and let the kidneys brown, stirring them and turning them around. Next sprinkle in the flour and cook it for a minute or two, then add the chopped tomatoes, tomato purée and garlic. If you are using dried basil add it now, but if it's fresh keep it on one side. Have another good stir, season with salt and pepper, cover the saucepan and let it simmer over a gentle heat for about 20 minutes. Stir in the fresh chopped basil just before serving.

Curried lambs' kidneys

(serves 2 people)

This can be made with 2 pork kidneys, chopped, instead of lambs' kidneys.

6 lambs' kidneys
1 level teaspoon ground ginger
1 clove garlic, crushed
½ teaspoon chilli powder
1 level teaspoon turmeric
1 level teaspoon ground cumin
1 level teaspoon ground coriander
1½ tablespoons groundnut oil
1 large onion, very finely chopped

1 dessertspoon tomato purée
5 fl oz water (150 ml)
2 rounded tablespoons natural yoghurt
Salt and freshly-milled black pepper

Begin by snipping the skin off the kidneys, then halve them lengthwise and cut out the white cores using some kitchen scissors. Now cut each kidney half into three or four pieces. Then, in a bowl, mix the garlic and all the spices together, add the kidney pieces and stir to coat them well. Cover the bowl with foil and leave to stand for an hour or so at room temperature.

After that, heat the oil in a wide, solid-based saucepan and soften the onion in it until it just begins to brown; then turn the heat right up, add the kidney pieces and toss them around to brown quickly. Next mix the tomato purée with the water and gradually stir this into the kidney mixture. Then season with salt and pepper, cover the pan and simmer very gently for 30 minutes, stirring once or twice. When the cooking time is up, taste to check the seasoning. Beat the yoghurt until smooth, and stir it into the kidney mixture over a gentle heat. Leave on the heat just long enough to heat the yoghurt through, then serve with spiced pilau rice and chutney.

Kidneys in jacket potatoes

(serves 4 people)

This is a lovely combination of kidney and bacon juices soaked into the potato.

4 large potatoes
4 lambs' kidneys, skinned and cored
8 rashers streaky bacon
A little made-up English or Dijon mustard
2 oz butter (50 g)
Oil
Salt and freshly-milled black pepper

Pre-heat the oven to gas mark 5, 375°F (190°C)

Clean the potatoes by wiping them with a damp cloth—or if they're very dirty by scrubbing them. Then dry them as well as possible (if you wash them sufficiently early, you can leave them to dry for an hour or two). Rub the lightest film of oil into the skins of the potatoes (this makes them crisp), then bake them in the oven for 1–1½ hours, depending on their size. Test with a skewer to see if they're cooked.

When the potatoes are cooked, remove them from the oven and turn up the heat to gas mark 6, 400°F (200°C). Holding them in a cloth (they're very hot!) make an incision with a knife lengthwise and crosswise, and lift the four corners of skin up and pull them back a bit. Now make a depression in the centre of each potato, using a tablespoon. Season well with salt and pepper and add a knob of butter to each one. Then spread the rashers of bacon with mustard and wrap two round each kidney. Lay one in each potato and return to the oven for 30 minutes. Serve immediately, with a green salad on the side.

Curried ox kidneys
(serves 6 people)

Another very economical, yet rather special, curry.

2 lb ox kidneys (900 g)
2 large onions
2–3 tablespoons groundnut oil
1 tablespoon tomato purée
1 dessertspoon ground coriander
1 teaspoon ground turmeric
1 teaspoon cumin seeds
5 fl oz natural yoghurt (150 ml)
½ pint water (275 ml)
2 fat cloves garlic, crushed
About ½ teaspoon crumbled dried chillies, deseeded
Salt

Begin by cutting the kidneys into pieces about 1 inch (2·5 cm) square, removing all the fat and cores as you do so. Then halve and thinly slice the onions (although this may look an awful lot of onion, it reduces to about half its initial volume).

Now heat the oil in a largish pan and, when it's sizzling hot, brown the kidneys, removing them to a plate afterwards with a slotted spoon. Stir in the onions and cook until they are golden brown, adding a little more oil if necessary. Now add the coriander, turmeric and cumin seeds and cook for a minute or two before stirring in the yoghurt and tomato purée, water and crushed garlic. Finally add the chillies and the kidneys. Season with salt, bring to simmering point, then cover and simmer gently for about an hour. Then take the lid off and continue to cook gently for a further 30 minutes or until the kidney is tender and the sauce thickened. Then serve on a bed of spiced rice, with an onion and tomato salad and some chutney.

Pork kidneys in mushroom and onion sauce

(serves 4–6 people)

1 lb (450 g) pork kidneys will serve 4–6 very economically, especially in this recipe which has lots of delicious sauce.

1 lb pork kidneys (450 g)
(4–6 kidneys depending on size)
6 rashers streaky bacon, chopped
A little oil for frying

For the sauce:
1½ oz butter (40 g)
1 oz plain flour (25 g)
15 fl oz cold milk (425 ml)
8 oz mushrooms (225 g), very finely chopped
2 onions, very finely chopped
An extra 1½ oz butter (40 g)
Nutmeg
Salt and freshly-milled black pepper

Start by making the sauce. Melt the butter in a saucepan, then add the chopped onion and cook for 5 minutes to soften. Next add the chopped mushrooms, stir them in and cook—gently—for about 30 minutes without a lid or until the mixture is reduced to a pulp (give it an occasional stir to prevent it sticking).

Meanwhile make the white sauce by combining the butter, flour, milk and some seasoning in a saucepan and whisking it over a medium heat until it starts to bubble and thicken. Stir it (with a wooden spoon to get right into the corners), whisk again very thoroughly, then turn the heat down as low as possible and cook the sauce gently for 6 minutes.

When the mushroom mixture is ready, gradually stir the white sauce into it. Check the seasoning, add a good grating of whole nutmeg, then leave it on one side while you prepare the kidneys.

First halve them, then using a pair of scissors snip out the cores and slice the kidneys across into bite-sized pieces. Now heat a little oil in a frying pan and add the chopped bacon and kidneys. Fry them over a medium heat until the kidneys are lightly browned (don't overcook them or they will get tough—there should be just a hint of pink in the centre). Then stir the bacon and kidneys into the mushroom sauce. Reheat gently, check the seasoning and serve with brown rice and a green vegetable.

Pork kidneys in chilli sauce

(serves 4 people)

The robust flavour of pork kidneys is well suited to a spicy sauce, like the one in this recipe.

6 pork kidneys
2 medium-sized onions, roughly chopped
1 large green pepper, deseeded and chopped
1 clove garlic, crushed
½ teaspoon dried chilli, crushed
1 tablespoon tomato purée
1 dessertspoon flour
14 oz tin Italian tomatoes (400 g)
3–4 tablespoons olive oil
Salt and freshly-milled black pepper

First prepare the kidneys by skinning them, halving them lengthwise and removing the core, then slicing them across into pieces about ¼ inch (½ cm) thick.

How heat 3 tablespoons of olive oil in a good-sized casserole and brown the kidneys quickly over a high heat, then remove them to a plate. Next add the onion and green pepper to the oil left in the pan (you can add a little more oil if needed), and soften them for 5 minutes or so. Then stir in the garlic and the crushed chilli and cook for a minute or two more before returning the pieces of kidney to the pan.

Stir in the flour to soak up the juices, then pour in the contents of the tin of tomatoes, and add the tomato purée. Season well with salt and pepper, then simmer gently over a low heat for about 20–25 minutes without a lid. This is nice served with some rice and a salad.

Cold pressed ox tongue

To press a pickled ox tongue yourself may sound a bit daunting but it's much easier than it sounds.

A pickled ox tongue, approximately 4–4½ lb (2 kg)
1 large onion, quartered
2 leeks, split and washed
2 carrots, cut into chunks
A few parsley stalks
6 peppercorns
A bayleaf
1 clove garlic, peeled
2 teaspoons gelatine powder
2 tablespoons port

A 5–6 inch deep cake tin
or soufflé dish (13–15 cm)

When you get the tongue home, scrub it well with a stiff brush then soak it for about half a day in cold water. Throw the water away and place the tongue in a deep pot, cover with 6–7 pints (3.5–4 litres) of fresh cold water and bring it to the boil. Now skim away all surface scum before adding the prepared vegetables, garlic, herbs and peppercorns. Simmer very gently for about 3½–4 hours.

The tongue will be ready when the skin along the surface is blistered and the 'T'-shaped bone at the root of the tongue comes away easily when pulled. Take the tongue out of the pot, then douse it with cold water and strip away all the skin. Trim the ragged and gristly bits of the meat at the root and underneath the tongue to neaten it, then curl the tongue round and fit it into the tin or dish.

Now boil the cooking liquor briskly, to reduce it and concentrate the flavour a bit. Then sprinkle the gelatine into a little cold water in an old cup, melt it over simmering water until absolutely clear before straining it into ½ pint (275 ml) of the cooking liquor. Add the port and pour the mixture over the tongue. Put a saucer over, weight it heavily, then leave until cold and set. Serve the tongue with some chopped jelly as a garnish. This is delicious with pickles and chutneys or *Cumberland sauce* (page 442).

Lambs' tongue casserole

(serves 6 people)

Lambs' tongues make an excellent family casserole.

For the casserole:
2 lb lambs' tongues (900 g)
1 oz lard (25 g)
10 button onions, peeled but left whole
8 carrots, halved across
2 slices streaky bacon, chopped and rinds removed
4 oz mushrooms, halved if large (110 g)
1 oz plain flour (25 g)
½ pint stock—see below (275 ml)
½ pint dry cider (275 ml)
4 tablespoons fresh chopped parsley
Salt and freshly-milled black pepper

For the stock:
1 medium-sized carrot
1 medium-sized onion
1 stalk celery
1 bayleaf
1 bunch parsley stalks
6 peppercorns
Water

First of all, rinse the lambs' tongues in cold water, then place them in a large saucepan together with the vegetables and herbs for the stock (see ingredients). Season with just a little salt and pour over enough cold water to cover. Bring to the boil, cover the pan then simmer gently for 1½ hours. After that time, remove the lambs' tongues from the pan and continue to boil the stock—without a lid so that it can reduce. When the tongues are cool enough to handle, strip the skins from them and trim the bases (the discarded bits and pieces can go back into the pan while the liquid is reducing).

At this stage, pre-heat the oven to gas mark 3, 325°F (170°C). When the liquor has reduced to about ½ pint (275 ml), strain it into a measuring jug and make it up to 1 pint (570 ml) with cider.

Now heat the lard in a casserole, cut the tongues into slices about ¼ inch (½ cm) thick and fry these in the lard until browned— then remove them to a plate with a draining spoon. Stir the halved carrots and button onions into the fat remaining in the pan and let these brown before adding the bacon and mushrooms. Cook them a little and return the slices of tongue to the pan.

Sprinkle in the flour, give it a good stir and cook for another couple of minutes before adding the stock and cider mixture. Bring it all up to simmering point, put a lid on the casserole and then cook in the oven for 1 hour. Taste and season if necessary, and just before serving sprinkle in the chopped parsley.

Oxtail with haricot beans

(serves 4 people)

This is, I think, one of the best ways of cooking an oxtail as the beans absorb all the delicious flavour.

8 oz haricot beans, the long type (225 g)*
1 large oxtail cut into joints
2 medium-sized carrots, cut in chunks
2 medium onions, sliced
1 medium turnip, cut into longish chunks
2 large sticks celery, chopped
¾ teaspoon dried thyme, or a sprig of fresh thyme
¾ pint hot stock (425 ml)
¾ pint red wine (425 ml)
1 rounded tablespoon flour
2–3 oz beef dripping (50–75 g)
Seasoned flour
Salt and freshly-milled black pepper

* The beans should be either soaked overnight or covered with plenty of water, brought to the boil, simmered for five minutes then left to soak for 2–3 hours.

Pre-heat the oven to gas mark 2, 300°F (150°C)

Melt the dripping in a large frying pan until sizzling hot. Coat each piece of oxtail with seasoned flour and fry them to a really good nutty brown colour—then place them in a casserole. Next, fry the vegetables—adding more dripping to the pan if you need to—until they're nicely tinged with brown at the edges. Now add the vegetables to the oxtail along with the drained beans, stirring everything round a bit and adding the thyme.

Stir the flour into the juices left in the frying-pan and gradually add the stock a little at a time, followed by the wine (stirring constantly to prevent lumps). Season the sauce with freshly-milled pepper, but no salt as it can toughen the beans. Pour the sauce over the rest of the ingredients, put on a close-fitting lid and cook in the oven for 3 hours.

Before serving, spoon off any surface fat and season with salt, tasting as you do so. This is very good with braised red cabbage.

Sweetbreads with soured cream and onion sauce

(serves 4–6 people)

2 lb calves' sweetbreads (900 g)
½ teaspoon salt
1 tablespoon lemon juice

For the sauce:
½ pint water (275 ml)
2 large onions, sliced very thinly
2 oz butter (50 g)
¾ oz flour (15 g)
½ teaspoon mustard powder
5 fl oz soured cream (150 ml)
Salt and freshly-milled black pepper
A squeeze of lemon juice

To garnish:
Fried croûtons
Chopped parsley

First, soak the sweetbreads in cold water for about 2 hours, changing the water fairly frequently. Then drain and place them in a saucepan with a further 2 pints (1·25 litres) of fresh cold water, and add the lemon juice and salt.

Now bring to the boil, reduce the heat to give a gentle simmer and cook for about 15 minutes. Drain the sweetbreads and douse with cold water. Now split them into pieces, removing any bits of tubes and tough outer membrane that you may come across. Then cover them and put them on one side.

Now to make the sauce: melt the butter in a large saucepan. When it is frothy, stir in the sliced onions and cook them over a very low heat for about 15 minutes until the onions are soft without being coloured. Then stir in the flour and mustard and cook for about 2 minutes before stirring in (gradually) the water. Bring to the boil, still stirring, then cover and simmer gently for 15 minutes.

Rub the contents of the pan through a sieve (or liquidise). Now return the sauce to the rinsed-out pan, and stir in the cream. Return the sweetbreads to the pan and reheat, very gently or the cream will separate. Taste and season. Pour into a warmed serving dish, surround with croûtons and garnish with chopped parsley.

Tripe and onions	
(serves 2–3 people)	2 lb tripe (900 g)
	2 pints (approx.) light stock or water (1·25 litres)
	1 large carrot, cut into chunks
	1 whole onion stuck with a clove
	2 stalks celery, cut into chunks
	Bouquet garni*
	1½ lb Spanish onions, thinly sliced (700 g)
	2 oz butter (50 g)
	1 tablespoon oil
	1–2 tablespoons cider vinegar
	Chopped parsley, to garnish

* Bouquet garni: 1 sprig parsley, 1 sprig thyme, 1 bayleaf and 6 whole peppercorns tied up in a bag of muslin or double gauze.

First place the tripe in a large saucepan and pour in enough stock (or water) to cover, then add the carrot, whole onion and celery stalks, pop in the bouquet garni, bring up to boiling point, then cover and simmer for 30 minutes to an hour (this depends on how much blanching the tripe has had—your butcher should be able to tell you. It should still be a bit chewy after it has been simmered). Meanwhile cook the sliced onions in 1 oz (25 g) butter and 1 tablespoon of oil in a large frying pan until golden but still slightly crisp. Scrape into a warmed serving dish and keep hot.

Next drain the cooked tripe, dry it as much as possible then cut it into roughly 1 inch (2·5 cm) squares—discard the vegetables etc. Heat the remaining butter and fry the tripe until golden and lightly crisped. Cover the onions with the tripe, then pour the vinegar into the frying pan and swirl it round, scraping the base and sides of the pan—then pour the vinegar over the tripe. Sprinkle with the parsley and have extra vinegar on the table.

See also:
Beefsteak and kidney pie
Beefsteak and kidney pudding
Chicken liver pâté

Risotto with chicken livers
  and mushrooms
Shoulder of lamb with rice and
  kidney stuffing

Vegetables

Including recipes for:

Baked aubergines with tomatoes
Broad bean purée
Baby broad beans in parsley sauce
Broccoli fritters
Fried cabbage with bacon
Cabbage with garlic and juniper
Braised red cabbage with apples
Spring carrots with tarragon butter
Carrots with spring onions and cream
Cauliflower with garlic and bacon
Braised celery with cheese and
  onion sauce
Courgette fritters
Courgettes and tomatoes au gratin
Braised fennel
Buttered leeks
Baked marrow with tomatoes and
  coriander
Duxelles
Mushrooms in hot garlic butter
Crisp-fried onion rings
Creamed parsnips

Creamed potatoes with soured cream
  and chives
Creamed potatoes with nutmeg
Crunchy roast potatoes
Jacket potatoes with soured cream
  and chives
Stuffed potatoes with garlic and herbs
Potatoes boulangère
Gratin dauphinois
Sauté potatoes Lyonnaise
Sauté potatoes Niçoise
New Jersey potatoes with fresh
  herb butter
Braised peas with lettuce and
  spring onions
Baked spinach with brown rice
  and cheese
Eggs Florentine
Mashed swedes with crispy bacon
Turkish stuffed tomatoes
Buttered turnips
Punchnep
Glazed baby turnips

In this country meat-eating has been virtually part of our heritage: apart from periodic shortages during wars or depressions the British have been renowed for their huge consumption of meat and game. And as a nation entirely surrounded by sea, our fish intake has been pretty high too. It's not surprising then that vegetables have not featured largely in the history of our cooking—their role has been to help the meat go down, rather than as things to be enjoyed in their own right.

Now that meat is so expensive, however, I think vegetable eating (and growing) is at last coming into its own. Here education is of paramount importance. I have seen—and it's a sad reflection on our past attitudes—the winner of First Prize for aubergines in a local Horticultural Show giving away his whole crop because his wife had not the faintest idea how to cook them!

There is one important point to make before we discuss the cooking of vegetables. If we want to get the very best out of them, we have to be familiar with their various seasons. In this modern jet-age the natural seasons of our home-grown vegetables have become obscured by the mountains of imports flown in from all round the world; and deep-freezing, which makes it possible to eat in December what was grown in June, has furthered the confusion. I firmly believe that part of the boredom attached to the daily round of wondering what on earth to cook today is caused by the continuous availability of absolutely everything. Nature has provided us with a perfectly varied diet on its own, which Progress has helped us to lose sight of.

Without being extremist about this (in fact I'm delighted we can nowadays literally shop around the world) I do feel that with the disappearing seasons some of the joy of food has been lost. For me looking forward to something is part of the pleasure—those first tiny peas of early June, or the heightened flavour of compact brussels sprouts after a sharp November frost. And there's one other point. Out-of-season vegetables inevitably cost more, so that imported tomatoes in January are not only tasteless but far more expensive. It's true that someone with a large garden can grow and freeze large crops and therefore save quite a bit of money; but then it's also true that smaller crops of a wider variety will also save money *and* provide something fresh in the kitchen garden every single month of the year.

In the notes which follow I have recommended some varieties of different vegetables. These suggestions are largely for the benefit of the home-grower. Unfortunately, they may not all be readily

available in the market at present. Once again this is something
that only we, the consumers, can do anything about, by insisting
that we want the vegetables that *taste* best.

Vegetables, like most fresh foods, are best eaten when they are in
season. Here is a quick checklist of what it makes sense to buy when.

Summer	**Winter**
Asparagus	Aubergines
Beans: broad, dwarf, runner	Broccoli
Cabbage	Brussels sprouts
Carrots	Cabbage
Cauliflower	Red cabbage
Celery	Carrots
Corn-on-the-cob	Cauliflower
Courgettes	Jerusalem artichokes
Fennel	Leeks
Globe artichokes	Onions and shallots
Mange tout	Parsnips
Marrow	Potatoes
Mushrooms	Swedes
New potatoes	Turnips
Peas	
Spinach	
Tomatoes	

A final note before going on to the preparation of vegetables: an
important part of your kitchen equipment is—a plain thin skewer.
Sliding a skewer into a potato or brussels sprout to test for
tenderness is still the easiest way to see if vegetables are cooked.

Asparagus

Asparagus (or 'grass' as it's known in the trade) is a very regal vegetable. While the carefully graded bunches of matching spears might sometimes seem an expensive luxury, the loose ungraded asparagus can be reasonable at the height of the (short) season. I'm no gardener, but some time ago I planted some 2-year-old crowns and now asparagus obligingly appears in profusion during May and June all by itself. Those few stalks that are really too thin to be picked up with the fingers can be used in a quiche or with *Eggs en cocotte with soured cream and asparagus* (see page 579).

To cook asparagus Steaming is the only way to cook asparagus—its flavour is so delicate I'm absolutely against ever putting it into water. You can buy specially shaped asparagus steamers, but I find it hard to justify the expense. An ordinary steamer (as used for steamed puddings) will do very well. Trim the stalks down to a reasonable length, 8–9 inches (20–23 cm), fit them inside the steamer and sprinkle them with salt. Place the steamer over a saucepan of boiling water and let the asparagus cook for 8–12 minutes, depending on the thickness of the stalks. Meanwhile heat up some butter in a pan to the frothy stage, and when the asparagus is ready serve it on hot plates with the butter poured over (and some crusty bread to mop up the juices afterwards). Alternatively you can serve it with *Hollandaise sauce* (see page 437), which will keep warm in a bowl over a pan of barely simmering water. Don't forget the napkins and finger bowls.

Note: 2 lb (900 g) of asparagus is a generous serving for 4 people.

Aubergines

Aubergines are extremely beautiful vegetables, dark, shiny, rich maroon. Some are long—rounded at one end and thinner at the other—with a cap of green leaves and a stalk. Others are round and squat-looking. Inside they are all cream-coloured, with a flavour quite unlike that of any other vegetable (the peel itself has a lot of flavour). Because they contain a great deal of water it is always best to sprinkle the insides or the cut slices with salt—which will draw some of the excess water out. Place the salted aubergines in a colander, put a plate on top and weight it down, and in half an hour or so a lot of the surplus moisture will drain out. Then dry them in a cloth and they're ready to be cooked.

Baked aubergines with tomatoes

(serves 4 people)

Cooked like this aubergines can make a good accompaniment to lamb, or even be eaten as a lunch dish on their own.

4 aubergines—approx. 1¾ lb (800 g)
4 tablespoons oil
1 large onion, peeled and finely chopped
6 largish tomatoes, skinned and chopped
2 cloves garlic, crushed
2 tablespoons finely-chopped parsley
A good pinch each of ground allspice, cinnamon and caster sugar
Some butter
Salt and freshly-milled black pepper

For the topping:
2–3 tablespoons dry white breadcrumbs
1 tablespoon grated Cheddar cheese
1 tablespoon butter

First prepare the aubergines: cut each one into smallish pieces, pile them all in a colander, sprinkle with salt (2 heaped teaspoons), then place a plate on top of them. Weight it down with a scale-weight and leave to drain for 1 hour.

When you're ready to cook, pre-heat the oven to gas mark 5, 375°F (190°C), and butter a shallow baking dish generously. Drain the aubergines and dry them thoroughly on kitchen paper, then heat the oil in a frying-pan. Add the aubergines to the pan and fry to a pale-golden colour, then add the chopped onion and carry on cooking until that has softened a bit.

Next add the tomatoes, garlic and parsley, the spices and sugar, and season with salt and pepper. Let everything simmer gently for about 5 minutes, stirring occasionally. Then transfer the mixture to the baking dish, sprinkle the top with a mixture of the cheese and breadcrumbs, and dot the surface with flecks of butter.

Bake near the top of the oven for about 30 minutes, or until browned and bubbling on top.

Beans

Broad beans These are the first beans of spring and are at their best, I think, when they're young and tender. So many people claim not to like them because they have only tasted the old (probably over-boiled) toughies. On one memorable occasion I ate them in a Chinese restaurant filleted, with the skins peeled off. Now I would never have the patience to do that, but for those who grow their own I would recommend that they harvest some of the immature pods (not more than finger-thick) and try cooking them whole—see the recipe on the next page. Shelled broad beans need very light cooking, just 6–8 minutes, and are delicious served tossed in *Herb butter* (page 450) or else in a salad with bacon (see page 497).

For a lovely *Broad bean purée:* for 2–3 people shell 2 lb (900 g) beans, and cook them for 6–8 minutes in salted water. Drain them well, then place them in the goblet of a liquidiser together with 1 oz (25 g) butter, 2½ fl oz (65 ml) single cream, some pepper and nutmeg and whizz them to a purée. Taste to check the seasoning, and serve with a few snipped chives sprinkled over. These go very well with pork sausages.

Dwarf beans These are sometimes called *haricots verts* (tiny flat baby beans) or Bobby beans (which are actually rounder and larger). Top and tail them with scissors, and cook in boiling salted water for about 4–6 minutes if they're really tiny, 8–12 minutes if larger. I like to drain them, put them back in the pan and toss with olive oil, a little crushed garlic and pepper and salt before serving.

Runner beans Is there anyone who doesn't love these? They are, in my opinion, superior in flavour to any of the other beans, and for that reason I would supplement them with nothing more than salt and pepper, and perhaps a little butter. To prepare them, use a sharp paring knife to top and tail them, and pare away the stringy edge along the seams of each bean. Slice them thinly, diagonally (an operation which, I've come to the conclusion, is really done best with a bean slicer—the kind with a handle). Boil them in salted water for 5 minutes or so, depending on their age.

Baby broad beans in parsley sauce

This recipe is for gardeners who can pick their broad beans very young—no more than finger thick—and cook them, chopped, in their pods.

(serves 4 people)

1 lb young broad beans (450 g)
2 oz butter (50 g)
1½ oz flour (40 g)
½ pint milk (275 ml)
4 tablespoons fresh chopped parsley
An extra ½ oz butter (10 g)
1 teaspoon lemon juice
Salt and freshly-milled black pepper

First wash, top and tail the beans, then cut them into ½ inch (1 cm) lengths. Place them in a saucepan, pour in enough boiling water just to cover, and add some salt. Cover, and when they come to the boil, simmer them for about 10 minutes.

Meanwhile start to make the sauce by melting the butter in a small saucepan, add the flour and beat until smooth. Then gradually add the milk, beating until smooth after each addition. Allow the mixture to cook for a few minutes over a gentle heat. Now when the beans are cooked, strain the cooking liquid into a jug. Drain the beans well and place them in a warm serving dish.

Then quickly beat 5 fl oz (150 ml) of the cooking liquid into the sauce—again gradually. Season to taste with salt, pepper and lemon juice, then throw in the parsley and stir in the extra ½ oz (10 g) of butter. Serve the beans with the sauce poured over.

Broccoli
Sprouting broccoli—purple or white—and calabrese, which is the wider curly-headed variety, can be used in precisely the same way as cauliflower (see for instance, *Sautéed cauliflower with coriander*, page 427). The leafy sprouting heads can be either boiled or steamed briefly then finished off by tossing in butter with salt and pepper. For a light, wafer-crispness, try deep-frying the small heads—as in the following recipe.

Broccoli fritters

(serves 2–3 people)

You could, in fact, also use thinly sliced courgettes in this recipe for crisp fritters.

8 oz small broccoli sprigs (225 g)—if you buy 1 lb (450 g) you should be able to pick off the correct weight of sprigs
2 egg whites
2 level tablespoons plain flour
Oil for frying—ideally olive oil, otherwise groundnut oil

To serve:
1 teaspoon crushed sea salt and coarsely ground black pepper

Fill a deep fryer or else a largish saucepan to one-third of its capacity with oil, and start to heat it up to 360°F (185°C)—or until a cube of bread turns golden in 60 seconds. Meanwhile crumple some greaseproof paper and lay it in a serving dish, and keep this warm. Now whisk the egg whites to the stiff peak stage, then coat the broccoli sprigs, first in the flour, then in the beaten egg white. Deep-fry them—in two batches—shaking the pan gently and using a knife to stir the sprigs around and separate them; 2–3 minutes for each batch should be enough, so the whole operation is fairly quick. Then drain them on the crumpled greaseproof paper, sprinkle with crushed sea salt and coarse pepper and serve immediately or they'll lose their crispness.

Brussels sprouts

My advice is to ignore totally those pale (and highly expensive) sprouts that turn up at the end of August in the shops. More than any other vegetable, brussels sprouts need a sharp frost on them to heighten the flavour (and what need of sprouts have we in August, with so many other vegetables and salads in season?). The best-quality brussels are like tight round buttons: take off the damaged outer leaves, make a cross-wise incision at the stalk end (to enable it to cook as evenly and quickly as the leaves), then pour just enough boiling water over to cover. Simmer gently for 5–8 minutes, depending on their size. Test them with a skewer, and try not to overcook them—they should be still firm and bright green. Then drain, season and serve in butter. Even better, boil them for a little less time, have some melted butter ready in a frying-pan quite hot and frothy, and toss them quickly in that over a gentle heat.

Cabbage

I'm pleased to say that cabbage has come on a lot. At one time (at least when I was at school) it was a sadly misunderstood vegetable—too much stalk, too much water and far too much cooking. No wonder so many people opted out of cabbage for life.

In a way I think the Chinese cook cabbage best, simply by stir-frying it—tossing shreds of cabbage in oil over a very high heat for the minimum time, and not so much as threatening it with any water. This way it retains its crispness and flavour. If, however, you want to cook plain boiled cabbage (any variety): cut it into quarters, discarding the tough outer leaves and cutting away the ribs, then shred it finely and pack it tightly into a saucepan. Add some salt and enough boiling water (straight from the kettle) to come halfway up, then cover with a tight-fitting lid. Boil it till tender but still retaining some 'bite' (about 10 minutes). Stir it and turn it over halfway through to make sure it cooks evenly. Drain it in a colander, pressing and squeezing out the excess moisture, season with pepper and toss in some butter before serving.

There are many varieties of cabbage available throughout the season, and for the recipe below any variety can be used—including the hard, white drumhead varieties.

Fried cabbage with bacon

(serves 2 or 3 people)

This is good enough for a meal on its own, and excellent with sausages and jacket potatoes.

1 lb shredded cabbage (450 g)
2 streaky bacon rashers, chopped
1 clove garlic, crushed
1 medium onion, chopped small
2 tablespoons olive oil
Salt and freshly-milled black pepper

Take a large frying-pan and begin by frying the onion and bacon together in olive oil for about 5 minutes. Then add the crushed garlic and cook for another 2 or 3 minutes. Now stir in the shredded cabbage (which will seem rather bulky at first, but as the heat gets to it it will start to collapse) and keep stirring it now and then so it cooks evenly. Season with freshly-milled pepper, but taste before adding salt because of the bacon. The cabbage should cook in about 10 minutes and still retain its crispness, but if you prefer it softer put a lid on the frying-pan—which will give it some steam.

Cabbage with garlic and juniper

(serves 2–3 people)

This recipe, gleaned from the famous Miller Howe hotel in the English Lakes, is one of my favourite vegetable dishes.

1 lb cabbage (any) (450 g), prepared and shredded
½ medium onion, finely chopped
1 clove garlic, crushed
6 juniper berries
2 tablespoons olive oil
Salt and freshly-milled black pepper

In a good solid saucepan or flameproof casserole, gently heat the olive oil and soften the onion in it for 5 minutes. Meanwhile crush the juniper berries (either with a pestle and mortar, or by placing them on a flat surface and crushing them with the back of a tablespoon). Then add these to the onion along with the crushed garlic. Fry for about 1 minute longer, then add the shredded cabbage. Stir it around until it's all glistening with oil, season with salt and pepper, then put a lid on and let it cook in its own juice for 10 minutes—stirring once or twice so that it cooks evenly.

Red Cabbage

There was a time when red cabbage was confined to a lethal dose of malt vinegar inside a pickle jar. But now it's becoming much more popular as a delicious vegetable. Braised slowly in the oven with apples and spices, it really is the perfect accompaniment to pork or pork sausages and is very good served with *Cassoulet* (see page 349).

Braised red cabbage with apples

(serves 4 people)

2 lb red cabbage (900 g)
1 lb onions (450 g), chopped small
1 lb cooking apples (450 g), peeled, cored and chopped small
3 tablespoons wine vinegar
3 tablespoons brown sugar
1 clove garlic, chopped very small
¼ whole nutmeg, freshly grated
¼ level teaspoon ground cinnamon
¼ level teaspoon ground cloves
½ oz butter (10 g)
Salt and freshly-milled black pepper

Pre-heat the oven to gas mark 2, 300°F
(150°C)

Discard the tough outer leaves of the cabbage, cut it into quarters
and remove the hard stalk, then shred the cabbage finely.

In a fairly large casserole, arrange a layer of shredded cabbage
seasoned with salt and pepper, then a layer of chopped onions and
apples with a sprinkling of garlic, spices and sugar. Continue with
these alternate layers until everything is in.

Now pour in the wine vinegar, add a knob of butter, put a lid on the
casserole and let it cook very slowly in the oven for about 2½–3
hours, stirring everything around once or twice during the cooking.
Red cabbage, once cooked, will keep warm without coming to any
harm. It will also reheat very successfully—so it can be made in
advance if necessary. Serve it with sausages, or pork dishes, or
Lancashire hotpot.

Carrots
The young carrots of spring and early summer, sold still in bunches,
are sweet, tender and delicious. We grow a variety called Early
Nantes, which have the sweetest flavour and fragrance. When
you're buying 'bunch' carrots your supplier may offer to cut off the
tops, but I think these are better left on until you're ready to cook
them (somehow this seems to keep them fresher). Don't scrape new
carrots—just rinse each one under a cold tap—and when you're
cooking them, pour boiling water over (but not too much), add
some salt, then watch them like a hawk for 10–20 minutes,
depending on their thickness. Test them with a skewer—they
should be tender but under no circumstances soggy. I like to toss
them in a little *Herb butter* (page 450) or use one of the recipes below.

Spring carrots with tarragon butter
Use 1 teaspoonful of chopped tarragon leaves to 3 oz (75 g) butter,
add some salt and freshly-milled pepper, mix together thoroughly,
then melt this over 1 lb (450 g) carrots just before serving.

Carrots with spring onions and cream
Finely chop 3 spring onions and add them to 2 tablespoons of cream
(single or double) together with some seasoning. Toss the hot,
drained carrots in this mixture just before serving.

Maincrop carrots, I have found, taste better if you manage to buy them with the earth still clinging to them—scrubbing and packing them in polythene bags may be convenient but not the best thing for them. To cook: scrub and scrape the skins (even older carrots don't need peeling), and if they are large, tough and woody then cut them in quarters vertically and excise any of the hard centre core. Cook them in very little boiling salted water (just enough to cover) with ¼ teaspoon of sugar added. They will take from 8 to 10 minutes to cook, depending on size. Then drain them and toss in butter or bacon fat before serving.

Cauliflower

Whatever did cauliflowers do to deserve their overboiled, watery-white-sauce image? They have far more potential than that, as I hope the recipes here show. Since I've been growing them in my garden I've come to the conclusion that bleached whiteness is not necessarily the hallmark of a good cauliflower: my home-grown caulis have all been creamy-yellow and quite delicious. Tightness and fresh-looking leaves are what to look for when buying.

One of the nicest ways to cook cauliflower is to separate it first into largish florets, then pack them upright (i.e. stalk downward) in a large, wide saucepan. Tuck in a bayleaf, season with salt and pepper and a little freshly-grated nutmeg, then pour in just about 1½ inches (4 cm) of boiling water. Cover with a lid and simmer for about 5–6 minutes—this way the stalks will cook in the water, and the florets in the steam. Afterwards drain them and toss them in butter before serving.

For a spicier recipe see *Sautéed cauliflower with coriander* (page 427).

Cauliflower with garlic and bacon

(serves 3–4 people)

In this recipe the sprigs of cauliflower are first blanched and then finished off in the oven.

1 medium cauliflower
2 rashers streaky bacon, chopped
1 clove garlic, crushed
1 small onion, finely chopped
2 oz butter (50 g)
2 tablespoons olive oil
1 tablespoon freshly-chopped parsley

| 2 tablespoons fresh breadcrumbs |
| Salt and freshly-milled black pepper |

Pre-heat the oven to gas mark 5, 375°F
(190°C)

Begin by dividing the cauliflower into walnut-sized florets; place
them in a saucepan and just cover them with boiling water. Add
salt, bring up to the boil, simmer for 2 minutes, then drain well in a
colander.

Next, using the same saucepan, melt half the butter together with
the oil and cook the onion and garlic for about 5 minutes to soften
them, then add the bacon and cook for another 5 minutes. Now add
the rest of the butter and, when it's melted, stir in the breadcrumbs
and parsley and cook for a further minute or two. Then place the
drained cauliflower either in a meat-roasting tin or a gratin dish and
spoon the breadcrumb mixture evenly on top.

Bake in the oven for 10–15 minutes and, after about 5 minutes of the
cooking time, baste with the buttery juices. When ready the
cauliflower should be tender but still firm. Before serving, sprinkle
on some freshly-milled black pepper.

Celery

I never buy imported celery out of season because it never tastes
anywhere near the same as our own. I think it's at its best after a
good November frost, and Fenland celery is particularly delicious
when the black earth still clings to it and the stalks are white all the
way up to the leaves. If you scrub the stalks under cold running
water and dry them with a cloth they'll stay crisp stored in a plastic
bag in the lowest part of the fridge for several days, but remember to
seal the bag well. Home-made bread, good cheese and crisp celery
are one of the nicest instant meals I know. However, it's just as
delicious cooked, as in the following recipe.

*Braised celery
with cheese and
onion sauce*

(serves 4 people)

| 1 large or 2 small heads of celery |
| 1 oz butter (25 g) |
| 1 tablespoon oil |
| 1 carrot, thinly sliced |
| 1 onion, thinly sliced |

¼ pint chicken stock (150 ml)
¼ teaspoon celery seeds
Salt and freshly-milled black pepper

For the sauce:
Milk
1 oz butter (25 g)
1 smallish onion, finely chopped
½ oz flour (10 g)
3 oz Cheddar cheese, grated (75 g)
1 egg yolk

Pre-heat the oven to gas mark 4, 350°F (180°C)

For this you'll need a large flameproof casserole.

Prepare the celery by breaking off the stalks and, using a bristle brush, clean each one under the cold running water. Trim off the leaf and base of each stalk and cut in half.

Next blanch the celery by putting it in boiling salted water for about 5 minutes, then drain well.

Now in a flameproof casserole, heat the butter and oil, add the prepared carrot and onion and cook for about 5 minutes. Add the drained celery and the chicken stock. Sprinkle with the celery seeds and season with a little salt and pepper. Place the casserole in the oven and bake, covered, for 30 minutes or until the celery is tender.

When ready transfer the vegetables to a serving dish, using a slotted spoon. Empty the cooking liquid into a measuring jug and make it up to ½ pint (275 ml) with milk.

To make the sauce, heat the butter in a saucepan and fry the finely-chopped onion until golden, then blend in the flour and cook for a couple of minutes before adding the milk mixture a little at a time, stirring well after each addition. Bring to simmering point, still stirring, and simmer gently for a minute or two, then remove from the heat and beat in the cheese and egg yolk. Pour the sauce over the vegetables and bake in the oven for a further 20 minutes or until you're sure it's all piping hot. Served with rice this makes a complete and delicious meal for two—even without meat.

Corn-on-the-cob

This is something I've never grown myself, but a more green-fingered neighbour always lets me have some of his surplus cobs, and once a year we have a feast (on our own, getting faces and fingers smothered in butter and sharing a damp tea-towel). On the streets of Istanbul, I recall, every corner seemed to have corn-on-the-cobs being grilled over open charcoal fires, and groups of people standing round munching their way through them!

At home we boil the cobs. First remove the husks and fibrous bits, then wash the cobs and plunge them into boiling water (10 minutes is usually sufficient). Test the kernels for tenderness with a skewer, then drain well and have some hot melted butter and hot plates handy. Pour some butter over each cob, and season well with salt and coarsely-ground black pepper. They are easiest to eat if you stick small skewers or forks into each end, and use these to hold them. And if you want to be more refined than us, have some finger-bowls and linen napkins on the table.

Courgettes

Courgettes (or zucchini) are the easiest vegetables in the world to grow—and perhaps the hardest to stop growing! If you don't inspect them every day during their season you will end up with mature marrows, rather than baby ones (which is what courgettes really are). Like their elders, they do contain a fair amount of water and sometimes this can be bitter. So if you have the time, prepare them by slicing them thinly into rounds (always leaving the skin on), then layer them in a colander, sprinkling each layer with salt, and place a suitably-sized plate on top. Weight this down with a heavy object (like scale weights), and after 30 minutes quite a bit of water will have been drawn out. Dry them really thoroughly in a clean cloth, and then they're ready to cook. I prefer not to put any water near them—just fry them in a mixture of butter and olive oil for about 7 minutes (rather like sautéed potatoes), so that the edges turn crisp and golden.

Courgette fritters

For these, cut the courgettes into 2 inch (5 cm) lengths (skins on), then cut each length in half horizontally, and cut each half into chip-like lengths. Salt and drain these as above, dry well, then cook in exactly the same way as *Broccoli fritters* (see page 260).

*Courgettes
and tomatoes
au gratin*

(serves 2–4 people)

This is a very quick and easy supper dish for 2 people, especially good if you grow your own tomatoes and courgettes and have a glut to use up. You could also serve it as a 'starter' for 4 people.

4 medium courgettes, sliced but *not* peeled
2 tablespoons olive oil
4 large tomatoes, skinned and sliced
1 large clove garlic, crushed
1 rounded teaspoon dried oregano
4 level tablespoons Parmesan cheese, grated
4 oz Cheddar cheese, grated (110 g)
Salt and freshly-milled black pepper

Pre-heat the oven to gas mark 5,
375°F (190°C)

If you have the time salt, drain and dry the sliced courgettes as described above. Heat the oil in a frying pan large enough to hold the courgettes in one layer (otherwise do them in two batches), add the crushed garlic and sauté the courgette slices to a nice golden colour on each side. Next arrange layers of courgettes and the skinned and sliced tomatoes in a heatproof gratin dish, sprinkling each layer with grated Parmesan, oregano and salt and freshly-milled pepper. Finish with a layer of the tomatoes, sprinkle the Cheddar cheese all over, and bake on a high shelf in the oven for 30 minutes. Serve this with lots of crusty wholemeal bread and butter and a crisp lettuce salad.

Fennel
This is dealt with primarily in the chapter on Salads (see page 486), but it is also extremely good served as a vegetable. When cooked the aniseed flavour is definitely less pronounced.

Braised fennel

(serves 4 people)

This is a vegetable that's served both raw in salad and cooked as a vegetable in Italy. In the 18th century it was used quite a lot in English cooking, so let's hope it will become popular here again.

4 bulbs fennel, uniform size if possible
2 slices streaky bacon, rind removed
1 oz butter (25 g)
1 carrot, sliced
Half an onion, sliced
5 fl oz cooking water (150 ml)
Chopped parsley
Salt and freshly-milled black pepper

First trim the green shoots from the tops of the fennel bulbs and shave off the bases. Then peel off any outer layers if they seem brownish, and halve the bulbs across their widest part. Put them into a large saucepan of boiling water, bring to the boil again and blanch for 3 or 4 minutes. Then drain them—reserving 5 fl oz (150 ml) of the water.

Now fry the bacon in the butter in a large saucepan or casserole, stir in the sliced vegetables and cook for a few minutes before pouring in the reserved water and adding some salt and freshly-milled black pepper. Arrange the fennel in the base of the pan, bring to simmering point, cover and cook gently for about 45 minutes, turning the fennel occasionally.

When cooked, transfer to a serving dish along with the vegetables, bacon and some of the juices. Sprinkle with parsley and serve.

Globe artichokes

If would be hard to find a prettier vegetable than this: its aesthetic presence animates any table display. Although they were once very popular in Britain, the biggest crop now comes from Brittany in the late spring. It may be, with the waning of their popularity, that people do not know how to prepare and eat them. So first let me explain that globe artichokes are—as indeed they look—large members of the thistle family, and have three distinct parts. There are the leaves (the bottom parts of which are edible), the choke (which is inedible) and the heart which is very edible.

How to prepare and cook artichokes First remove about four of the toughest outer leaves, then place the artichoke at the edge of a table so that the stalk overlaps the edge. Grasp the stalk and snap away the stem, removing also some of the tough fibres running up into the base. Now remove the inedible choke: carefully spread the leaves apart until you come to the central cone of thinner, lightly-coloured leaves. Then pull this cone out in one piece and underneath it you'll find the hairy 'choke'—scrape this all out of the heart with a teaspoon, and add a little lemon juice to stop the inside discolouring. Now rinse out the artichokes and leave them upside down in some cold water to which some more lemon juice has been added (about 1 tablespoon to 2 pints (1·25 l) of water), until you are ready to cook them.

Don't boil artichokes in iron or aluminium pans, as this can discolour them. Have your chosen pan ready filled with salted boiling water with a tablespoon of lemon juice (or white wine vinegar) added. Gently boil the artichokes, uncovered, for about 30–40 minutes or until one of the outer leaves pulls away easily and the bases feel tender when tested with a skewer. Then drain the artichokes upside down in a colander, shaking them to get rid of the excess water.

How to eat artichokes This does have its comic side, with ever-mounting piles of discarded leaves scarred with rabbit-toothed marks! Artichokes can be served cold or, perhaps better, just tepid. Tear off one leaf at a time, dip it into the sauce (see below), and eat the tender rounded part at the base. When you arrive at the heart, cut it into sections with a knife and fork and eat with the rest of the sauce. Don't forget to have plenty of napkins, some finger bowls, and a large plate for the discarded leaves.

Sauces for artichokes To serve warm, I would recommend *Quick Hollandaise* (page 39) or *Hot lemon butter*, which is simply the juice and grated rind of a lemon plus 6 oz (175 g) butter, melted together until bubbling and poured immediately into the cavity of each artichoke. For serving cold, I suggest either *Vinaigrette* (page 482) or some *Home-make mayonnaise* with garlic (page 483).

Jerusalem artichokes

These are vegetables with a distinctive flavour and are another neglected delicacy. Although they're cheap and couldn't be easier to grow, they are largely ignored. My guess is that this is because of their ugliness: the tubers do look most misshapen, covered with daunting knobbly bits. There's no need to be daunted. If you're prepared to buy slightly more than you actually need, you can soon cut off (and discard) the knobbles, which makes life a lot easier. They are then easy to peel, but as they discolour quickly pop them straight into cold water as you peel. As a vegetable they can be roasted like potatoes or sautéed, or cooked as in *Potatoes boulangère* (page 283) with leeks substituted for the onions, or made into a cream purée. Best of all, I think, they make a really delicious soup with a truly creamy texture (*Carrot and artichoke soup*, page 108).

Leeks
There is a period, from about the end of January to the end of March, when fresh vegetables seem a bit thin on the ground. But nature hasn't let us down: it provides an abundance of leeks throughout the winter and these two months are the time to make the most of them. Having said that, though, leeks are best served in the simplest possible manner—no water, no white sauce, just a little seasoning.

Sometimes leeks can arrive rather dusty, so care is needed when preparing and cleaning them. The best way is to cut off all but about 1½ inch (4 cm) of the green part, and trim off the root end. Then, using a small sharp knife, make a vertical slit down two-thirds of each leek. Now you can hold each leek under a cold running tap, spreading the layers out in a fan shape to wash out any hidden dirt.

Buttered leeks
(serves 4 people)

1½ lb leeks (700 g), trimmed and washed
2 oz butter (50 g)
Salt and freshly-milled black pepper

Chop the cleaned leeks into roughly 1½ inch (4 cm) pieces. Then melt the butter in a thick-based saucepan, and add the slivers of leek, stirring them around thoroughly. Season with salt and freshly-milled pepper, and let them sweat in their own juices for 6–8 minutes, or until they're cooked to your liking.

Mange tout
These are a real summer delicacy—tiny under-developed peas that are cooked and served in their pods. In cooking them there are two important points to bear in mind: on no account should they be overcooked—the end results should be really crunchy, and they should not be allowed even a sniff of water. Top and tail the pods. Melt 2 oz (50 g) of better in a wide, shallow saucepan (or

a frying pan), stir in 1 lb (450 g) of mange tout gently to get each one coated in the butter, add some salt, and then just toss them around over a medium heat. You'll find they cook very quickly, in just 1–2 minutes.

Marrow

If you grow courgettes then you're bound to find that some have remained hidden from view under the large flat leaves—and before you know it you have a young marrow on your hands. If so, then pick it immediately because the older monsters aren't much good for anything. If you are buying a marrow the same rule applies: small is beautiful, not more than 1½–2 lb (700–900 g). The way to tell a young marrow—apart from its size—is to look for a shiny skin, and when you press along one of the ridges with your thumb, it should leave an impression.

Young marrows should be cut up into large 1½ inch (4 cm) cubes (with the skin left on) and cooked, sprinkled with salt, in a steamer over simmering water until tender. Serve it with a *Herb butter* (see page 450) or, better still, as in the following recipe.

Baked marrow with tomatoes and coriander

(serves 4 people)

If, like me, you've sometimes suffered from rather too many home-grown marrows, do try this way of cooking them—which also takes care of any tomatoes that are too ripe for a salad.

1½ lb young marrow (700 g)
8 oz red ripe tomatoes (about 4 medium-sized ones), skinned and chopped (225 g)
Half a medium-sized onion, chopped
1 clove garlic, crushed
½ teaspoon whole coriander seeds, crushed in a pestle and mortar or with the back of a tablespoon
1 dessertspoon fresh chopped basil (or 1 level teaspoon dried)
Oil
Salt and freshly-milled black pepper

Pre-heat the oven to gas mark 3, 325°F (170°C)

Melt a tablespoon of oil in a flameproof casserole, add the onion and garlic, and soften them over a gentle heat for 5 minutes. Stir in the chopped tomatoes and cook for a further 5 minutes.

If the marrow is young and fresh it won't need peeling: just cut it into approximately 1½ inch (4 cm) chunks. Add them to the tomatoes and onions along with the crushed coriander seeds. Then add the basil if it's dried (if you're using fresh basil, add it at the end), and season with salt and pepper. Stir everything around well, put a lid on, and place the casserole in the oven to cook for 1 hour or until the marrow is tender. About 10 minutes before the end of the cooking time, put the casserole back on the top of the stove and simmer without a lid to reduce some of the liquid.

Note: this is equally good served cold—or reheated the next day.

Mushrooms

The best mushrooms I've ever tasted were those gathered on early-morning walks through the mountains of Wales, as a small child. My grandfather seemed able to spot a field mushroom from dozens of yards away, and I would run and pick them—some small, round and delicate with pink gills, others large and flat and velvet-brown. Back at home they would sizzle in bacon fat for breakfast, with plenty of bread to mop up the last traces of juice.

Field mushrooms are still a delicious, if rare, treat. Cultivated mushrooms are not quite the same, but at least they are plentiful, always available and not too expensive. I rarely use the 'button' variety, which I find rather tasteless. I much prefer the fully-opened caps with pink or brown gills. One of the nicest mushroom-flavoured recipes is *Marinaded mushrooms* (see page 79), which makes a very good first course. For a really concentrated mushroom flavour—for sauces, stuffing or quiches—make what the French call *Duxelles* (see, for instance, *Boeuf en croûte* on page 566 and *Cheese tartlets with mushroom pâté* on page 473).

Duxelles

Heat 1 oz (25 g) butter in a saucepan, stir in 1 medium-sized onion very finely chopped, and cook for 5 minutes. Chop 8 oz (225 g) mushrooms very finely, add these to the pan, and cook gently for 30 minutes (uncovered) so that all the liquid evaporates and the mixture becomes a thick paste. Season with salt, pepper and a grating of nutmeg.

Mushrooms in
hot garlic butter

(serves 4 people)

This recipe is for people who, like me, love the sizzling garlic butter that goes with snails but cannot eat the snails.

1 lb mushrooms (450 g)
6 oz butter, at room temperature (175 g)
2 large cloves garlic, crushed
1 tablespoon lemon juice
1–2 tablespoons freshly chopped parsley
Salt and freshly-milled black pepper

Pre-heat the oven to gas mark 7, 425°F (220°F)

Begin by preparing the mushrooms simply by wiping them with kitchen paper, then pull off the stalks—but don't discard them. Now, in a small basin, combine the crushed garlic with the butter, and stir in the parsley and lemon juice. Season the mixture with salt and freshly-milled black pepper.

Next arrange the mushroom caps, skin side down, in a gratin dish or roasting tin, with the stalks arranged among them. Place a little of the garlic butter mixture into each cap, and spread whatever remains over the stalks as well.

Now place the dish on the top shelf of the pre-heated oven, and let them cook for 10–15 minutes or until the butter is sizzling away and the mushrooms look slightly toasted. Serve straight from the oven with lashings of crusty bread to mop up the garlicky juices.

Onions (and shallots)

On the subject of preparing onions, I would like to say that in my 17 years of cooking I have been regaled with countless theories on how not to cry. None of them have worked! I do now own a food-processor, which chops onions finely, so perhaps I don't weep as much as I used to. The mildest onions are the large Spanish type, and these are good for slicing and eating raw in salads. It is the medium-sized home-grown variety that are the real tear-jerkers.

Shallots—I grow the purple shallots—keep very well through the winter if stored correctly. Usually they are mild flavoured, and especially good for cooking whole in a number of recipes. I make a habit of pickling some shallots for Christmas—and the recipe for that is on page 675.

Crisp-fried onion rings
First you need to heat some oil in a deep-fryer to 350°F (180°C).
Slice 2 onions into thinnish rings and separate out the rings. Beat up
1 large egg white to the stiff peak stage, then dip the rings first into
seasoned plain flour, then into the egg white. Deep-fry them a few at
a time until crisp and golden (1–2 minutes). Drain on some
crumpled greaseproof paper, and serve as soon as possible. These
are lovely served with steak or liver.

Parsnips

This is another vegetable that needs a good sharp frost to really
sharpen up its flavour; and since there are so many other vegetables
about in the autumn, it is best to wait till the end of October or into
November if you want to eat them at their best. Peel them thinly,
quarter them lengthways, and cut out the woody core before
cooking. They can be plain boiled in salted water, but are even
better baked.

Baked parsnips (For these, follow the method for blanching and
roasting potatoes (page 278), but place them on a lower shelf in the
oven and give them slightly less cooking time.

Creamed parsnips

(serves 4 people)

Even people who think they don't like
parsnips usually have to admit that they
like this.

1 lb parsnips (450 g)
¾ pint hot water (425 ml)
¼ pint single cream (150 ml)
Freshly-grated nutmeg
Salt and freshly-milled black pepper

Peel the parsnips and cut out the woody centre bits, then cut them
up into small cubes. In a saucepan bring the hot water to boiling
point, add the cubed parsnips and simmer—covered—for
approximately 10 minutes or until tender when tested with a
skewer.

When ready, place a colander over a bowl and drain the parsnips, reserving the liquid. Now, either purée them with the cream in a liquidiser or sieve them and beat in the cream a little at a time with a fork. Taste and season with freshly-grated nutmeg, salt and pepper and, if you think the mixture is too dry, mix in 1 or 2 tablespoons of the reserved liquid.

Potatoes

Potatoes are the most important source of vitamin C in our diet—it was only when potatoes became one of our staple foods in the 18th century (we now eat approximately 6 oz (175 g) per head a day) that diseases like scurvy began to die out. The protein value of potatoes is higher than in most other plant foods. Per ounce, of course, an orange will give you more vitamin C, but whereas we don't all eat an orange a day most of us do eat potatoes. Having said that, it is also a fact that careless preparation and cooking can destroy much of their goodness as well as flavour—I'd go so far as to say that learning to cook potatoes so that they really taste like potatoes is one of the most important lessons in cooking.

Buying and storing potatoes

If you have the storage space it's obviously cheaper and more convenient to buy old potatoes in bulk. I buy mine in ½-cwt bags which, provided they are closed properly each time they're opened, protect the potatoes adequately from the light. It is light that causes damage and turns them green (so it is odd that the small supermarket packs should be transparent and expose their contents to the full glare of the light). Nor do potatoes that have been scrubbed keep so well—so for small quantities my advice is to buy them loose with the earth still clinging to them. New potatoes should always be eaten as fresh as posible and not stored: a sign of their freshness, when you're buying them, is that the skin slips off easily when rubbed with the thumb. Also the earth around them should look moist.

Preparation

That part of the potato directly beneath the skin is richest in nutrients, so peeling needs to be done with a certain amount of care. Ideally they should not be peeled at all. New potatoes taste better with their skins left on, and maincrop potatoes too are better just scrubbed, then boiled or steamed with the skins on, and peeled afterwards. When the actual skins are eaten (as with jacket potatoes) they provide fibre, another valuable item conspicuously lacking in our modern diet. Where a potato obviously has to be peeled, to preserve the best part beneath the skin it is preferable to use a good potato peeler that pares off the thinnest amount of peel.

Varieties of potato
So far as new potatoes are concerned none can compare for flavour with the kidney-shaped Jerseys that arrive in the shops in June, so delicious I could eat them just on their own, steamed in their skins with chopped mint and melted butter! Now that we can choose which variety of potato we buy (since it has to be described on the packet or counter), my pesonal choice for an early potato would be Pentland Javelin, and for a good all-round, well-flavoured maincrop variety—Red Desirée, which is my favourite both for buying and (depending of course on regional variations in soil) for growing. It stays firm when boiled, fluffs nicely around the edges for roasting, and makes very good chips.

Boiling or steaming
First, new potatoes. Here opinion is unanimous that they should be started off in boiling water—so they can be cooked in as short a time as possible and so retain most of their flavour. With maincrop potatoes it is said that putting them in cold water and bringing them up to the boil helps them absorb some of the water and become juicier (new potatoes contain more water and have no need of this), and that this also helps prevent them breaking up.

My own opinion is based on the idea that in general water is the enemy of flavour (with potatoes as with all root vegetables): so I prefer to add boiling water to maincrop also, so they spend less time in contact with the water, and breaking is never a problem with a good quality variety like Red Desirée. At all events the heat, once they have returned to the boil, should be gentle; and to stop the water evaporating too fast a well-fitting lid is essential.

To steam potatoes—which is the best way of preserving nutrients and flavour—place them in a steamer over a saucepanful of boiling water, sprinkle them with salt, cover the steamer with a lid and steam until tender. How much salt? This really depends on who is going to eat them, but a rough guide is 1 rounded teaspoon to each 1 lb (or 500 g) of potatoes. To serve: once the boiled potatoes have been drained, place a clean cloth over the saucepan instead of the lid. This will absorb some steam and give them a floury edge.

Mashed or creamed potatoes

How you mash or cream potatoes can be a personal thing: my mother won't use anything but a large kitchen fork, while several friends of mine swear by their potato mashers. Inclined to laziness myself, I use my electric hand-whisk. But whichever implement you use, make sure your saucepan is big enough to give you plenty of mashing room. Drain the potatoes first, add a little salt and freshly-milled pepper, a good knob of butter— 1 oz (25 g) per 1 lb of potatoes, and preferably cream or top of the milk (2 tablespoons per pound)—failing that, milk will do. Then whisk, beat or mash until the potatoes are soft, creamy and free from lumps. Here are a few variations:

Creamed potatoes with soured cream and chives Soured cream is delicious with potatoes—a ¼ pint (150 ml) carton for 2 or 3 lb of potatoes. Whisk it in with the butter, along with 3 tablespoons of freshly-snipped chives.

Creamed potatoes with nutmeg Again use soured cream or fresh natural yoghurt (if it's not *fresh*, yoghurt will be too acid for this) to whisk into the potatoes, then finish off with about a quarter of a whole nutmeg, freshly grated.

Crunchy roast potatoes

I've deliberately added the word 'crunchy' to this section because I believe properly-cooked roast potatoes are a rare delicacy, and it is crunchiness that is so often missing. The first essential ingredient is a good, solid roasting tin with a really sound base—the cheap, tinny ones that buckle in a hot oven are useless. For the sake of flavour the best sort of fat to use is the same as the meat with which the potatoes will be served (i.e. beef dripping for beef, lamb dripping for lamb, lard for pork), and if you're roasting the joint in the oven you can probably spoon off enough fat from that for the potatoes; the best alternative to these is pure lard.

Because the fat for roasting needs to be *really* hot, it is not a good idea to roast the potatoes around the meat (besides, if you have a large family, there simply won't be room). The oven temperature should be gas mark 7, 425°F (220°C). If the joint is still roasting, remove it to a lower shelf: if it is cooked, take it out of the oven (a joint will hold the heat for about 40 minutes, in a warm place, and, as I have said elsewhere, is all the better for 'relaxing' before it is carved).

Place the roasting tin to pre-heat with about 2 oz (50 g) of fat per pound of potatoes. Then peel and cut the potatoes into even sizes, pour boiling water over them, add some salt, and simmer for 10 minutes—then drain (reserving the water for gravy). Now put the lid back on the saucepan and shake it vigorously up and down: what this does is roughen the edges of the potatoes and make them floury, giving a crispier surface.

Make sure the fat in the roasting tin is really hot when the potatoes reach it: if it is, the outsides of the potatoes will be immediately sealed; if it isn't, they will stick or become greasy. As you add the potatoes to the tin, the temperature of the fat will come down—so what you do is remove the tin from the oven (closing the door to keep the heat in) and place it over direct heat, medium should be enough to keep the fat sizzling. Then spoon in the potatoes, tilt the pan (holding it with a thick oven glove) and baste each one with a complete covering of hot fat. Now transfer them to the highest shelf of the oven, and roast for 45–55 minutes. Turn them over at half-time. *Note:* roast potatoes don't take kindly to being kept warm, so serve them as soon as possible.

Jacket potatoes

One of the nicest and most nutritions ways of eating potatoes (I love the crisp skins dipped in home-make chutney!). Maris Piper, King Edward, and Desirée are all good varieties for serving in their jackets. If you can, scrub and thoroughly dry them in a cloth well in advance as this will help to crisp the skins. Before baking, pre-heat the oven to gas mark 7, 425°F (220°C), prick the potato skins in several places (to prevent splitting), then rub the skins with a smear of olive oil all over and a little bit of salt as well. Large potatoes will take about 1–1½ hours to bake through. To speed up the cooking time, you can insert metal skewers through the potatoes, but in fact a lower temperature (gas mark 5, 375°F, 190°C) and longer cooking will give you a tougher, more crunchy skin. To test if they are done, push a skewer into the thickest part of the flesh; then slit them open and serve with a generous knob of butter and some seasoning. And here are a few alternative fillings:

Jacket potatoes with soured cream and chives For 3–4 potatoes, mix ¼ pint (150 ml) of soured cream with a bunch of freshly-snipped chives and a seasoning of salt and freshly-milled pepper. When the potatoes are cooked, hold them with a cloth and make a slit lengthways across the top and then widthways: then lift up the four flaps of skin and make a depression in the potato. Add a good knob of butter to each one, and pour in the cream-and-chive mixture.

Stuffed potatoes with garlic and herbs For 3 large jacket potatoes you'll need: a 5 oz (150 g) packet of Boursin cheese (or any other cream cheese containing garlic and herbs—you can even make up your own combination), 2 oz (50 g) of butter, 2 oz (50 g) of grated Cheddar cheese. When the potatoes are cooked, slice them into halves, then, holding each half in a cloth, scoop out the cooked potato into a bowl. Combine the potato with the cream cheese and butter, and season to taste. Pile the mixture back into the empty potato shells. Sprinkle each half with the grated Cheddar, and pop them under a grill until they're brown and bubbling.

For a complete meal try *Kidneys in jacket potatoes* (page 230).

Chips

A perfect chip should be (i) crisp on the outside, (ii) soft, almost melting, in the middle, and (iii) dry, which is to say not greasy, oily or soggy. It is relatively easy to cook soggy chips, but far more difficult to produce a beautifully dry, crisp and melting chip.

To start with you need the right kind of potato. New potatoes—apart from being too small to chip—ought only to be cooked in their skins. Of the maincrop potatoes the best are the mealy-textured varieties like King Edward and Desirée (both reds), or Majestic and Maris Piper (whites). Once peeled you could slice up the potatoes with a chip-cutter, though that always seems to require a great deal of strength. I prefer to use a small sharp knife, slicing the potatoes first across, at intervals of just less than ½ inch (1 cm), then slice into chips the size of my little finger.

If you have time at this stage to soak the chips for half an hour—to reduce their starch content and swell them with water—all well and good: if not, make sure you rinse them well under cold water. Most important of all, dry them *thoroughly* in a clean tea-towel.

To fry them you can use either lard or oil, but if it is oil I do advise a good-quality groundnut oil (because there are so many nasty cooking oils on the market which will impregnate your chips with their unwelcome flavour). Fill the chip-pan, or at least a wide, thick-based saucepan, only one-third full of oil or lard—any more than that and it will very likely bubble over the top when the chips go in. The temperature of the oil/lard is all-important. It should have reached 375°F, 190°C before the chips go in, and the only accurate way to tell is by using a cooking thermometer (and place it in the pan at the beginning, to eliminate any danger of it cracking in the hot fat). In the absence of a thermometer you can

Kidneys in fresh tomato sauce, page 243.

test the temperature by dropping in a cube of bread: if it browns within 1 minute, the chips can go in.

The safest way to lower the chips in gently is to use a chip-basket, and be ready to pull it out if the fat erupts too violently (which probably means the chips were not dry enough). Fry the batch for 4–5 minutes and then remove them—you can hang the basket on the lip of the pan in fact. The temperature of the fat will now have dropped dramatically, and it must be reheated to 390°F, 195°C for the final browning—which will take just 1 or at the most 2 minutes. Watch the chips very carefully at this stage and lift them out as soon as they are golden-brown—any longer and they will turn hard.

Now transfer the chips to a warmed serving dish lined with some crumpled greaseproof paper, to remove any vestiges of fat. Then remove the paper, crush some flaky sea salt and some coarsely-ground pepper over them and take them straight to the table. Chips *cannot* be kept hanging round or even kept warm successfully: within no time at all they will start to go soggy, no matter how crisp they were when they came out of the pan.

Potatoes boulangère

(serves 4–6 people)

This French method of cooking potatoes gets its name from the bakeries where villagers, short of fire fuel, would take their pots of potatoes along to cook in the bread ovens. This is a particularly good dish to serve at a dinner party as it needs no last-minute attention and will wait quite happily if you're running late.

2 lb potatoes (900 g)
1 largish onion
¼ pint hot stock (150 ml)
¼ pint milk (150 ml)
2 oz butter (50 g)
Salt and freshly-milled black pepper

Pre-heat the oven to gas mark 4, 350°F (180°C)

The best cooking utensil for this recipe is either an oblong meat-roasting tin or a wide, shallow baking dish. Butter it generously (all

Left (from top to bottom): Scallops in the shell, page 148; Marinaded kipper fillets, page 144; Dressed crab, page 152.

over the sides as well), then peel the potatoes and cut them into thinnish slices. Peel the onion and chop it finely.

Now arrange a layer of potatoes over the base of the tin, followed by a sprinkling of onion and a seasoning of salt and freshly-milled black pepper. Continue with another layer of potatoes, and so on until everything is in and you finish up with a layer of potatoes (seasoned) at the top. Pour in the stock and milk, and fleck the surface all over with dots of butter.

Place the tin on the highest shelf of the oven, and leave it there for about 45 minutes or until the potatoes are cooked and the top layer is nicely golden-brown.

Note: For a change, use a chopped leek instead of an onion.

Gratin dauphinois

(serves 3–4 people)

This is one of the greatest potato dishes I've ever tasted. I know it does seem extravagant to use ¼ pint (150 ml) cream for 1 lb (450 g) potatoes, but I would forgo a pudding with cream once in a while in order to justify it.

1 lb good-quality potatoes (Edwards or Desirée) (450 g)
1½ oz butter (40 g)
¼ pint double cream (150 ml)
¼ pint milk (150 ml)
1 small clove garlic, crushed
Whole nutmeg
Salt and freshly-milled black pepper

Pre-heat the oven to gas mark 2, 300°F (150°C)

A *shallow* gratin dish well buttered.

First, peel the potatoes and slice them very, very thinly (a wooden mandoline is excellent for this operation, if you have one), then plunge the potato slices into a bowl of cold water and swill them round and round to get rid of some of the starch. Now dry them very thoroughly in a clean tea-cloth. Then in the gratin dish arrange a layer of potato slices, a sprinkling of crushed garlic, pepper and salt and then another layer of potatoes and seasoning.

Now mix the cream and milk together, pour it over the potatoes, sprinkle with a little freshly-grated whole nutmeg, then add the butter in flecks over the surface, and bake on the highest shelf in the oven for 1¹/₂ hours.

Note: Sometimes cheese is added to this, but I think it masks the potato flavour too much.

Sauté potatoes Lyonnaise

(serves 2 people)

This is the basic method for making sauté potatoes, but if you prefer them plain, simply leave the onion out. The secret of really crisp sauté potatoes is, first of all, to use olive oil if at all possible and, secondly, to use two or three frying-pans so that the potatoes can cook in a single layer and not overlap each other.

2 lb potatoes (Red Desirée) (900 g)
4–5 tablespoons olive oil
1 small onion, finely chopped
Some coarse rock salt and freshly-milled black pepper

Have ready a warm serving dish with some crumpled greaseproof paper placed in it.

First thinly peel the potatoes and cut them into even-sized pieces—but not too small. Put them in a saucepan, cover them with boiling water, add some salt, bring to simmering point and cook for 15 minutes. Then drain them, arrange them on a wooden board and slice them thinly and evenly.

For the next stage you need two medium-sized frying-pans and a small saucepan. Heat a tablespoon of olive oil in the saucepan, add the onion and fry gently. Now heat 2 tablespoons of oil in each frying-pan and when it begins to sizzle add the potatoes, dividing them between the pans so that they don't overlap. Fry them over a high heat, turning them after 5–7 minutes to cook on the other side until they are golden brown and crisp all over. Then, using a slotted spoon, transfer them to the crumpled paper to drain and scatter on the fried onion. Loosen the top of the pepper-mill a little to get a really coarse grind and sprinkle over the potatoes; crush some rock salt between your finger and thumb and sprinkle on.

Lastly pull out the paper from underneath and serve at once—if you delay the potatoes will go soggy.

For *Sauté potatoes Niçoise* cook half a finely-chopped green pepper and a crushed clove of garlic with the onion, then stir the mixture into the potatoes and sprinkle with freshly-chopped herbs or parsley before serving.

New potatoes
Around April we begin to get the first imported new potatoes, by which time the old ones are looking decidedly wrinkled and sprouty. However these very early imported potatoes are often disappointing in flavour, and it's only when our home-grown varieties start to make an appearance that their true delicacy can be appreciated— and that goes especially for the Jersey Royals.
Freshness is the key to buying new potatoes. Pick one up before you buy and rub your thumb along it—if the skin slips away with your thumb, you can be sure the potatoes are really fresh.
To prepare them, all you actually need to do is to rinse them clean under a cold tap. Don't scrape or peel them, because the skins are full of flavour and nutrients.
New potatoes also deserve careful cooking: what I do is place the largest ones on the base of the pan, with the smaller ones on top. Add some salt, and pour in enough boiling water to come not more than three-quarters of the way up (so that, in effect, the smallest potatoes are cooked in the steam and will be ready at about the same time as the larger ones). Use a tight-fitting lid, and test with a skewer to see if they are cooked after about 20 minutes.

New Jersey potatoes with fresh herb butter

(serves 4 people)

No new potatoes can ever taste as good as Jersey Royals in my opinion—they're so good I could eat them just by themselves. Because they're rather expensive they need careful cooking, and this is a delicious way to serve them.

2 lb Jersey potatoes (900 g)
1 sprig fresh mint
3 oz butter (75 g)
1 tablespoon fresh chopped parsley
2 tablespoons fresh chopped mint
1 tablespoon fresh snipped chives
Salt (ideally rock salt) and freshly-milled black pepper

Wash, but don't scrape, the potatoes as there are a lot of nutrients as well as flavour in the skins. Place the larger ones over the base of the saucepan and pop the smaller ones on top. Pour in enough boiling water to not quite cover, add some salt and a sprig of mint. Cover with a tight-fitting lid, and simmer gently for about 20–25 minutes. Test them with a skewer, and remember they must be tender but still firm—overcooking really does spoil them.

Meanwhile mix the butter and herbs thoroughly together with some pepper. Then drain the cooked potatoes, add the herb butter, put the lid back on and swirl the pan around to get each one thoroughly coated. Remove the lid and just savour the delicious aroma for a couple of seconds before you dish them out!

Peas

I hear some people now saying they actually prefer frozen peas to fresh peas, because those bought in the pods from supermarkets are so often hard and old. It's quite true that growers—and I live among many of them—have found the demand from freezing companies more lucrative, and growing peas to sell fresh has become uneconomical. But nothing will convince me that the uniform frozen peas can ever compare with those freshly-picked, mouthwateringly tender and sweet. The answer, as always, is for us to keep asking for fresh peas, and then they will come back.

The best way to cook them is briefly. Pour boiling water into the pan to reach halfway up the peas, add some salt, cook and in just a couple of minutes, your peas will be ready. I don't find it necessary to add mint or butter, or anything to add to their flavour. If the peas you have grown, or bought, happen to be getting on a bit, the following recipe is good for braising them into tenderness.

*Braised peas
with lettuce and
spring onions*

(serves 4 people)

This is a very good recipe for using fresh shelled peas that are not so young.

| 2 lb peas (900 g), freshly shelled (weight before shelling) |
| 6 lettuce leaves |
| 8 spring onions |
| 2 oz butter (50 g) |
| 4 tablespoons water |
| A pinch of sugar |
| 1 level teaspoon salt |

Trim the onions—you only need the bulbous white part—and break the lettuce leaves into wide strips. Then melt the butter in a thick-based saucepan, add the onions, lettuce and peas. Stir well, then add the water, sugar and salt. Bring to simmering point, then cover the saucepan and let it cook over a very, very gentle heat for about 20–25 minutes (keeping an eye on the pan, and shaking it now and then to prevent the vegetables sticking). Add just a little more water if you think it needs it.

Spinach

A very versatile vegetable, spinach—and there's something very wholesome about it when the leaves are young, fresh and squeaky. Fresh spinach can be rather dusty or muddy: the best way to deal with this is to fill the sink with cold water, pick out any damaged or brown leaves and remove any tough stalks, then plunge the rest in the water and swirl them around. Do this in 2–3 changes of water, then let it all drain in a colander, shaking it well over the sink. Young spinach leaves can be wiped and used raw in a delicious salad (see page 489). When cooked, spinach loses roughly half its weight—so 1 lb (450 g) of spinach is only enough for 2 people.

Spinach has plenty of moisture in it, so it needs no water at all for cooking. For 1 lb (450 g) of spinach leaves, melt 1 oz (25 g) butter in a thick-based saucepan, then, keeping the heat at medium, pack the spinach leaves in. Add some salt, put on a tight-fitting lid, and let it cook for about 30 seconds. Then take the lid off and you'll find the spinach has collapsed down into the butter. Give it a stir so that the top leaves get pushed down to the base of the pan, replace the lid and give it another 30 seconds or so, shaking the pan a couple of times—I find the whole operation takes less than 2 minutes. Next drain the spinach in a colander, pressing it well with a saucer to get rid of any excess water. You can now return it to the pan, and season with freshly-milled pepper and—best of all—nutmeg. Add a bit more butter or, if you like, a tablespoon of fresh cream.

For a delicious sauce to accompany fish or rice dishes see *Spinach and cheese sauce* (page 436).

Baked spinach with brown rice and cheese

(serves 2–3 people)

For this meatless supper dish you can use either fresh or frozen spinach.

1 lb fresh spinach leaves, washed and chopped, (450 g) or ½ lb frozen spinach, thawed (225 g)
Brown rice measured to the 8 fl oz level in a measuring jug (220 ml)
16 fl oz hot water
1 onion, finely chopped
1 tablespoon oil
1 teaspoon butter
4 oz grated Cheddar cheese (110 g)
2 large eggs, beaten
2 tablespoons chopped parsley
2 tablespoons wholewheat breadcrumbs
1 tablespoon melted butter
Couple of pinches cayenne
Nutmeg
Salt and freshly-milled black pepper

Pre-heat the oven to gas mark 4, 350°F (180°C)

Melt the butter and oil in a saucepan and soften the onion in it, then stir in the rice to get it nicely coated with oil. Add the hot water, stir once, and simmer gently with a lid on for 40 minutes or until the liquid has been absorbed and the grains are tender.

As soon as the rice is cooked, cool it in a bowl, then combine it with the grated cheese, and stir in the eggs and parsley followed by the chopped spinach. Season well and add a good grating of nutmeg.

Now place the mixture into a large oiled pie dish, mix the breadcrumbs with the melted butter and cayenne and sprinkle that over the top. Bake in the oven for about 35 minutes.

Eggs Florentine

(serves 2 people)

This is a very quick supper or lunch dish for 2 people. Some recipes call for hard-boiled eggs but I think they taste far nicer baked in with the spinach.

1 lb fresh spinach, cooked (450 g) or 8 oz frozen spinach, thawed (225 g)— either should be well drained
4 large fresh eggs
1 oz plain flour (25 g)
1½ oz butter (40 g)
½ pint milk (275 ml)
2 tablespoons double cream
3 oz grated Lancashire cheese (75 g)
1 oz grated Parmesan cheese (25 g)
Salt and freshly-milled black pepper
Nutmeg
A little extra butter

Pre-heat the oven to gas mark 5, 375°F (190°C)

First butter a large shallow baking dish generously, arrange the cooked spinach over the base, season with pepper, a little salt and freshly grated nutmeg. Then sprinkle 1 tablespoon of cream over and pop the dish in the lower part of the oven to heat through.

Now place the butter, milk and flour in a saucepan and whisk over heat to make a smooth white sauce. Then stir in the grated Lancashire cheese and cook the sauce for 3 minutes over a very gentle heat—stirring now and then.

Now take the baking dish out of the oven, make four depressions in the spinach and gently break the eggs into each one (I like to sprinkle just a little salt and pepper onto the yolks.) Stir the remaining tablespoon of cream into the cheese sauce and pour it over the eggs to cover everything completely. Sprinkle with Parmesan, add a few flecks of butter here and there and bake on a high shelf in the oven for 15–20 minutes.

Swedes

Like all root vegetables, swedes store well and are perfect for long, slow cooking in stews and casseroles, where they can extend the meat considerably as well as add character of their own.

Mashed swedes	2 lb swedes (900 g)
with crispy bacon	6 rashers bacon, chopped small
	2 oz butter (50 g)
(serves 4–6 people)	2 tablespoons single cream
	Salt and freshly-milled black pepper

Start by peeling the swedes and cutting them into smallish cubes. Put them in a saucepan and just cover them with water. Add salt, bring to simmering point and cook gently for 20–30 minutes or until the swedes are tender when tested with a skewer. Then tip them into a colander to drain thoroughly.

Return the saucepan to the heat, add a knob of butter and fry the chopped bacon until it begins to crisp. Now return the swedes to the saucepan, add the remainder of the butter and the cream and mash well to a creamy consistency. Season well with salt and freshly-milled black pepper and pile onto a warmed dish to serve.

Tomatoes

Here I would like to make a personal plea to tomato-growers. Please could we have some choice of variety? And—just as potatoes now have to be labelled according to variety—could not tomatoes be identified also? The growers have always claimed that the average consumer, whoever that is, wants a uniform size (i.e. eight toms to the pound); and since boring old 'Moneymaker' and similar varieties obligingly conform to this, that's what we get. In fact I can hardly believe this premise to be true—after all what is the difference between two large tomatoes cut into quarters and four small ones halved?

There's another problem too. Most commercial tomatoes are harvested before they have fully ripened, and therefore tend to become pithy and woolly inside. It's no wonder that people who travel to the continent take on a wistful look when speaking about

French or Italian tomatoes. (Mind you, I would point out that just because a tomato is large and misshapen, it is not automatically better: it depends on the variety and the soil in which it is grown.)

At home we have grown a small outdoor bush variety called Little Pixie, which produces very sweet tomatoes (and you don't have to pinch out the leaves). I have even seen these grown in window boxes and grow bags. For more experienced home tomato-growers, I would recommend a variety called Ware Cross (which my grandfather used to grow)—lovely deep red fruits with sweet green centres. For the shop-bought varieties you need a well-flavoured salad dressing (see *Tomato salad*, page 488) or when cooking them a gutsy, well-seasoned recipe. *Note:* if you have a lot of green tomatoes at the end of the season, see *Spiced green tomato sauce* (page 445) and *Green tomato chutney* (page 668).

Turkish stuffed tomatoes
(serves 4–8 people)

These are good for a light lunch-time dish with salad for 4 people, or this quantity will also serve 8 people as a 'starter'.

8 really large ripe tomatoes
Italian rice, measured to the 5 fl oz level in a measuring jug (150 ml)
1 small onion, finely chopped
1 clove garlic, crushed
1 tablespoon pine nuts (available at Greek or healthfood shops)
1 tablespoon currants
1 teaspoon fresh thyme
1 teaspoon ground cinnamon
10 fl oz hot stock or water (275 ml)
Olive oil
Some sugar
Salt and freshly-milled black pepper

Pre-heat the oven to gas mark 4, 350°F (180°C)

Begin by cooking the rice: fry the onion in a tablespoon of olive oil in a saucepan until softened, then add the crushed garlic and pour in the rice. Add the cinnamon, pine nuts and the currants and give everything a good stir to get it well coated. Then season with some salt and pepper and pour in the hot stock. Stir just once, cover with a lid and let it simmer gently for 15–20 minutes or until all the liquid has been absorbed and the grains of rice are tender. Then remove the rice from the heat, add the thyme and fluff it with a skewer.

Prepare the tomatoes by slicing off a little of the round end and scooping out all the core and seeds—trying to leave as much of the actual flesh as possible. Put a pinch of sugar into each hollowed-out tomato, then pack each one with the rice mixture and replace the lids. Place the tomatoes in a meat roasting tin with a little water in the bottom, drizzle a few drops of olive oil over each one and bake for 25–30 minutes. They are lovely eaten hot or cold. There is a photograph of them on page 68.

Turnips

I think turnips are much under-estimated—probably because they have been too often badly cooked in the past, boiled to death and waterlogged. Just cut into chunks, browned in dripping and added to stews and casseroles they're marvellous, or sliced in a *Cornish pasty pie* (page 557). A more sophisticated way to serve them would be *Turnips and leeks boulangère*. Follow the recipe on page 283 for *Potatoes boulangère*, but using instead of potatoes and onions the equivalent quantities of turnips and leeks.

In Scotland turnips are whipped to a purée—bashed neeps—and in Wales they serve punchnep, a delicious combination of creamed potatoes and turnips whipped to a smooth purée, which Dorothy Hartley in her excellent book *Food in England* describes as looking like 'hot alabaster'. To prepare turnips, peel them as thinly as possible and keep them in cold water till ready to cook, to prevent them browning.

Punchnep

(serves 4 people)

Although it might seem unnecessary, the secret of this to get the right flavour is to boil the vegetables separately.

1 lb turnips (450 g), peeled and cut into chunks
1 lb potatoes (450 g), peeled and cut into chunks
3 oz butter (75 g)

| 3 fl oz single cream (75 ml) |
| Salt and freshly-milled black pepper |

Put the potatoes in one saucepan and the turnips in another and cover both with boiling water. Season with salt and simmer—covered—until the vegetables are tender. (You'll find the potatoes will be ready about 5 minutes before the turnips.)

Meanwhile warm a shallow oval serving dish and, when the vegetables are ready, drain off the water, then combine them in one saucepan. Next pour the cream into the empty saucepan and warm it over a gentle heat. Add the butter to the vegetables, season well and mash thoroughly. Now empty the mixture into the warmed dish, then, using a skewer or similar implement and a circular movement, make several holes in the vegetables and pour the hot cream into the holes. Serve immediately.

Buttered turnips
Peel 1 lb (450 g) turnips and dice them into fairly small cubes. Now blanch them in boiling water for 3 minutes, drain well, then finish off by tossing them in 3 oz (75 g) melted butter in a large frying pan—keeping the heat fairly gentle so they don't brown (5 minutes should be long enough). Serve them sprinkled with snipped chives or chopped parsley.

Glazed baby turnips

(serves 4 people)

| 2 lb young turnips (900 g) |
| Some light stock |
| 1 teaspoon Dijon mustard |
| 2 tablespoons dry white wine or dry cider |
| 1 level teaspoon sugar |
| Chopped parsley |
| Salt and freshly-milled black pepper |

Baby turnips about the size of golf balls are creamy white with leafy green tops, and usually sold in bunches in the summer, when they are in season.

First of all prepare the turnips by peeling them carefully, then put them into a saucepan of boiling water and boil for 3 minutes. Next drain in a colander and then return them to the saucepan. Now add just enough stock to cover the turnips, bring this to the boil and simmer (uncovered) for about 10 minutes, or until the turnips are tender. Use a draining spoon to remove the turnips, place them in a warmed serving dish and keep hot while you make the glaze.

Next blend the mustard with a little of the white wine and add to the stock in the saucepan with the remainder of the wine and the sugar. Reheat, taste and season with salt and freshly-milled pepper. Simmer rapidly (without a lid) until the liquid has reduced to a syrupy consistency, then pour this syrup over the turnips, sprinkle with plenty of chopped parsley and serve.

See also:

A risotto for spring
Asparagus and cheese tart
Baked stuffed courgettes
Broccoli cheese soufflé
Brown rice, lentil and mushroom salad
Brown rice with vegetables and cheese sauce
Bubble and squeak
Buckwheat and vegetable pie
Cabbage leaves stuffed with rice
Courgette and cheese quiche
Cucumber with soured cream and dill
Dolmades (stuffed vine leaves)
Hazelnut and vegetable burgers
Italian stuffed aubergines
Kidneys in jacket potatoes
Marinaded mushrooms

Mushroom and onion quiche
Non-meat loaf
Onion rice
Piperade
Provençal vegetable stew
Rice with mushrooms
Rice with peppers
Risotto with chicken livers and mushrooms
Sautéed cauliflower with coriander
Sautéed mixed vegetables
Spinach and cream cheese quiche
Spinach pasties
Thick onion tart
Turkish stuffed peppers
Vegetarian goulash
Vegetarian shepherd's pie

Rice and other grains

Including recipes for:
Perfect rice
Onion rice
Rice with peppers
Rice with mushrooms
Rice with herb butter
Spiced pilau rice
Saffron rice
Brown rice, lentil and
  mushroom salad
Turkish stuffed peppers
Risotto with chicken livers and mushrooms
Risotto alla Milanese
A risotto for spring
Buttery kedgeree
Brown rice pudding with prunes and apricots
Home-made muesli
Traditional oatmeal porridge
Buckwheat and vegetable pie

Without cereals (which for our purposes means rice, wheat, oats maize, rye, barley, buckwheat and millet) man would not have got very far on this planet. Their cultivation goes back at least to the Stone Age, and every great civilisation since then has relied on one or other of them. Even today, rice is still the staple food for half the world's population, and very efficient it is too, being a good source of the proteins and vitamins essential to health—at least in its natural form. For here is a certain irony: for a long time now all our energy and ingenuity has been directed towards transforming our cereals into forms far removed from their natural state—refining and whitening our wheat flour, polishing our rice grains, creating new breakfast cereals. The result of course has been a loss in nutrients, and flavour. I touched on the problem—in so far as it concerned wheat—in the chapter on Bread, but the situation is much the same for most of our grain products, and rice in particular.

As it happens, I think the pendulum is swinging back. The encouragement of 'natural' cereals is one of the main aims of the wholefood movement, and more and more people are now discovering for themselves the versatility of grains and grain products. I hope this section will offer a few ideas on these lines; but first let's look at the most adaptable of all the grains, rice, and see what happens to it in its preparation.

What's in a grain of rice?

If you were able to magnify a rice grain, when it's first harvested and cleaned of mud, leaves and stem, what you would see is something rather like a nut with an outer inedible shell, which has to be removed and discarded. Inside that would be the outer casings (again just like nuts—think of unblanched almonds): these are bran layers, a brown outer layer and a whiter inner one. Beyond these is the starchy centre (endosperm) which also contains the embryo (or germ). It so happens that this starchy kernel is one of the most easily-digested of all available foods, taking about half the time to be digested that most other foods require.

How rice is treated

In poorer countries rice is still pounded by hand, either with pestle and mortar or between grinding stones, to remove the inedible husk. In industrialised countries (like America where much of our rice now comes from) this is done in large, modern rice mills where the grain is not only cleaned and hulled by machine, but also 'polished' to remove the bran layers and germ and to scour the grain down to a translucent white, refined, purified endosperm—in other words the end product is depleted of a lot of its original vitamins and minerals.

Grades of rice
Rice is produced, in most major growing countries, in three sizes of grain, each one suitable for different kinds of dish:

Short grain Often simply called pudding rice in Britain, this is a quick-growing rice (which is why it is the cheapest). The grains are fat and almost round, with barely more length than width. They are also rather chalky, which makes them sticky when cooked and are therefore best suited to rice puddings—they cook to a lovely creamy consistency in the milk.

Medium grain A sort of halfway rice, neither as sticky when cooked as short grain nor as cleanly separate as long grain. It isn't widely available in this country, but when it is, it should be used for croquettes, rice moulds or some risottos.

Long grain These grains are four or five times as long as they are wide, with scarcely any chalkiness (which means they are fluffy and separate when cooked). To buy good quality long grain you should look for really fine, needle-pointed ends and, with white rice, a certain translucence.

Then, apart from the shape of the grain, rice also reaches the shops in different degrees of preparation, which affect both the cooking and the taste:

Prepared rice
Brown rice This is the whole natural rice grain, with only the inedible outer husk removed: the bran layers and germ are left intact. It comes in the three sizes mentioned above, and is a rather appealing mixture of green and brown in colour. Personally I think long grain brown rice is the nicest of all rices, and for two reasons: (i) it contains the highest percentage of fibre, natural vitamins and minerals, and (ii) it has most flavour and 'bite' to it after it's cooked. It takes longer to cook than white rice and, paradoxically, it is more expensive to buy (considering it has gone through fewer processes). But it stores well and I try to balance out the cost by buying in bulk.

White (polished) rice This is the refined one that has had all but the starchy endosperm removed. It is pearly white and comes in all three grain sizes, the long grain type being the most commonly available rice in shops and supermarkets.

Easy-cook rice This white rice is so-called because it has been treated by a special steaming process (rather like pressure cooking) *before* milling. It is claimed by the manufacturers that this processing helps the grain to retain much of its nutritional content, and hardens it so it becomes less starchy and remains separate in the cooking—although it needs a little more cooking time than ordinary polished white rice. (However, I tested a batch of easy-cook rice alongside some ordinary long grain white rice, both of them American, and found that using the *Perfect rice* method given on page 303, the ordinary long grain was every bit as easy—and 25% cheaper! Still, if you feel safer using easy-cook then just allow ten minutes' extra cooking.)

Pre-cooked rice sometimes described as pre-digested! This is polished white rice which is cooked or half-cooked after milling, then dried so all it needs is to re-absorb the water it lost in the drying. My own opinion of it is—like my opinion of sliced white bread—blotting paper!

Some regional varieties

Finally, rice is sometimes described by names which refer to the countries or regions where it was grown. Here are some of them:

Patna rice A generic term used to describe the long grain rice grown all round the world. The name derives from the days when it was first grown in Patna (an area of north-east India) and exported to Europe. Since most of our long grain rice now comes from America, the Americans are slightly puzzled as to why we should still refer to their rice as 'Patna'!

Basmati This is a very fine quality rice with a superb flavour, and does in fact come from India. Usually only available in Indian provision stores and, in my opinion, the best sort to serve with a curry. I used to find it quite tricky to cook until I used Elizabeth David's method, given in her book *Salts, Spices and Aromatics*, and have never had a failure since.

Carolina A general word to describe rice, referring to the region in America where rice was first planted in 1694. In actual fact most rice production in America has now shifted to other states.

Arborio (Italian) rice This is the rice that's grown in northern Italy.
Its quality is superb and I think it has the best flavour of all. The
grains are rounder and much plumper than long grain, and if you
rub a grain of it between your fingers, you can see clearly an outer
translucent edge and a white core in the centre. To make a true
risotto you need arborio rice—it takes longer and in this case it's not
meant to be fluffy and separate, but because it's stirred quite
frequently it cooks to a rather creamy consistency (see recipes for
Risotto alla Milanese and *Risotto with chicken livers and mushrooms*, pages
308 and 309).

There are two types available: one is very white and the grains
look chalky. The other is browny-yellow and has a more polished
look. This latter kind is treated to make the grains firmer and more
separate (presumably because that is what the export market wants
rather than the true risotto).

If you can get hold of the so-called 'easy-cook' Italian (one
quality supermarket chain now sells it), then as an all-purpose rice
it does have a better flavour and texture, I think, than ordinary
long-grain white rice—and can be cooked exactly as in the *Perfect
rice* recipe.

Other rice products
When rice is milled, some of the grains are broken and these are
used to make *rice flakes*, which are used for puddings, and *rice flour*
which is used for confectionery and cooking, and makes a good
thickening agent. One tablespoon of rice flour per ½ pint
(275 ml) of liquid will thicken a soup or stew beautifully: just whisk
it into the liquid and bring to simmering point.

Do not be afraid!
So many people have told me they can't cook rice, and yet (rather
like omelette-making) there's nothing intrinsically difficult about
it: once it has been explained, you should be well away. So if
you're one of those people who live in fear of cooking rice, here is a
complete guide to trouble-free rice cookery. The following points
apply to long grain white and brown rice but not to Italian
rice—for which guidelines are given in the recipe for *Risotto alla
Milanese*.

(1) First of all buy good quality long grain rice. My white rice comes
from a reliable supermarket chain who market it under their own
name. My long grain brown rice comes from a wholefood shop

where I can buy it in 7 or 14 lb (3 or 6 kg) packs, which reduces the price per pound considerably.

(2) Don't wash rice (except Basmati). All other rice is thoroughly cleaned at the milling stage, and washing it later removes some of the nutrients (anyway the high temperature of the cooking will purify it).

(3) Always measure rice and liquid by *volume* and not by weight. Cups and mugs are often recommended, but I find they vary so much it's impossible to gauge whether a certain cup will be enough for such and such a number of people. So I now always measure both rice and cooking liquid in a glass measuring jug. I find that filling the jug with rice up to the 5 fl oz level gives enough for 2 people (up to the 10 fl oz level for 4 people and so on) and this provides fairly generous portions. Then I empty the rice out of the jug and measure into it exactly *twice* that amount of liquid (i.e. up to the 10 fl oz level for 2 people, up to the 20 fl oz level for 4 people and so on).

(4) Please leave rice alone while it's cooking! Lack of confidence in the kitchen always manifests itself in over-handling, and it is the nervous cooks who are forever peeping, prodding and stirring and that, so far as rice is concerned, is a disaster. Why? Because rice grains are delicate and easily broken: if you start to stir them while they're cooking, they break, releasing the starch inside and turning them sticky.

(5) Use a thick-based saucepan or flameproof casserole, and be gentle. Once boiling point has been reached turn the heat down to the barest simmer. Try not to lift the lid: I think rice should be cooked as briefly as possible, and each time the lid is lifted steam and heat escape and the cooking time is unnecessarily prolonged.

(6) Timing *is* important and it remains the same regardless of the quantity of rice you are cooking. For long grain white rice I find 15 minutes is just enough. When the time is up, tip the pan to one side and check there is no liquid left unabsorbed—if there is, give the rice a couple of minutes more.

(7) The way to test rice is to bite a couple of grains: they should be tender but firm. Then tip the rice into a warm serving bowl—if you leave it in the pot it will go on cooking. Then fluff the grains with a skewer (lots of cooks say with a fork, but I find a skewer separates them more efficiently).

(8) It is inadvisable to keep rice warm for long but it will keep for 10 minutes without coming to harm if you put it in a bowl placed over a saucepan of barely simmering water. Cover the bowl with a clean tea towel but don't put a lid on top.

(9) Cooked rice keeps well (even up to a week) in a bowl covered with clingfilm in the refrigerator. To reheat it, just place it in a thick-based saucepan with a couple of tablespoons of water, cover and warm it gently, shaking the pan from time to time. It will only take a couple of minutes.

(10) All the above information applies also to the cooking of brown rice, except that this takes 40–45 minutes to cook instead of 15 (extra time that's easily warranted by the character and flavour of brown rice).

Liquid for cooking rice

Plain salted water is fine for cooking savoury rice. The liquid should be boiling (to save time I always pour it into the measuring jug straight from a boiling kettle). Stock is an excellent alternative particularly if the rice is to be served with chicken (use chicken stock) or beef (use beef stock). I don't recommend stock cubes, as I find them too strong, masking the delicate flavour of the rice.

Perfect rice

(serves 2 people)

A friend of mine swore she'd *never* be able to cook rice: she had tried—she said—every sort of rice and every kind of method, only to be teased so much by her family that she gave up completely. Now I'm happy to report she has been persuaded to follow the method below and has had perfect rice evey time. What is perfect rice? Simply this, that when it's cool enough to handle you can pick up a handful that will run through your hands in a stream of perfectly separate grains. So here goes. You will need:

Long grain white or brown rice measured to the 5 fl oz level in a glass measuring jug
Boiling water or stock, measured to the 10 fl oz level in a glass measuring jug

1 dessertspoon oil, or ½ oz (10 g) butter
Salt

One small, solid based saucepan or flameproof casserole and a shallow serving dish, warmed.

Begin by heating the oil or butter gently, just to the melting stage, then add the rice and, using a wooden spoon, stir the grains to get them all thoroughly coated and glistening with fat.

Now add the boiling stock or water and salt, stir just once as the liquid comes up to simmering point, then put on a tight-fitting lid. Turn the heat down to keep the gentlest simmer—then go away and leave it completely alone. Don't take the lid off and, above all, don't stir it. After exactly 15 minutes, if the rice is white (40 if it's brown), I give you permission to have a look and test a few grains. If they're tender, and, when you tilt the pan almost on its side, you can see no trace of liquid left, the rice is cooked.

Now tip it out into a warmed serving dish, using a rubber spatula to dislodge any grains that refuse to leave the base. Lightly fluff the grains with a skewer. Serve immediately. Or if you need to keep it warm—say for up to 10 minutes (no longer)—cover the bowl with a tea cloth (which will absorb the steam and help to keep the grains separate) and place it over a pan of barely simmering water.

Note: I find a wide, shallow serving dish makes it easier to fluff the grains, as they can be spread out more easily.

This method of cooking rice can be used with all kinds of other flavourings. Here are some suggestions. The quantities given will be sufficient to flavour rice for 4 people.

Onion rice
Cook 1 finely chopped medium-sized onion in the oil or butter for 5 minutes before stirring in the rice. Then proceed as above.

Rice with peppers
Cook half a chopped onion and half a chopped green or red pepper in the oil or butter before stirring in the rice.

Rice with mushrooms
Cook half a chopped onion and ¼ lb (110 g) chopped mushrooms in the oil or butter before stirring in the rice.

Rice with herb butter
When the rice is cooked, add a knob of herb butter (see page 450) so it melts into the rice as you fluff it.

Spiced pilau rice

(serves 4 people)

This fluffy yellow rice, fragrant with spices, is lovely to serve with curries.

Long grain white rice measured up to the 10 fl oz level in a glass measuring jug
Boiling water measured up to the 20 fl oz level in a glass measuring jug
2 oz butter or oil (50 g)
1 small onion, finely chopped
1 inch whole cinnamon stick (2·5 cm)
¾ teaspoon cumin seeds, crushed
1 bayleaf
2 cardamom pods, crushed
1 dessertspoon ground turmeric
Salt

Melt the butter or oil in a thick-based saucepan and soften the onion in it for about 3 minutes. Then stir in the spices, bayleaf and salt and allow a minute or two while the heat draws out their fragrance. Next stir in the measured rice, and when it's well coated with oil and spices, pour in the boiling water. Stir once, put on a tight-fitting lid, and simmer gently for 15 minutes or until the rice is tender. Tip into a serving dish straightaway, fluff with a skewer and remove cinnamon before serving.

Saffron rice

(serves 4 people)

I buy saffron from a large chain-store chemist and crush the strands with a pestle and mortar.

Long grain white rice, measured up to the 10 fl oz level in a measuring jug
Boiling water or chicken stock, measured up to the 20 fl oz level in a measuring jug
1 small onion, finely chopped
1 tablespoon butter
1 tablespoon olive oil
½ teaspoon saffron
Salt

Begin by softening the onion in the oil and butter for 5 minutes, then stir in the powdered saffron and allow 1 minute for the heat to draw out the flavour before adding the rice. Stir to get the rice nicely coated with the oil and butter then add the boiling water or stock. Stir again once and add salt.

Then, when it comes to the boil, cover with a lid and leave it to simmer very gently for 15 minutes or until all the liquid has been absorbed. Don't stir it or peek, but leave it alone until the 15 minutes are up. Then taste a grain without stirring the rice and tilt the pan a little to check that the liquid has been absorbed.

When the rice is cooked tip it onto a warm, shallow serving dish and fluff with a fork before serving.

Brown rice, lentil and mushroom salad

(serves 4–8 people)

This recipe is enough for four people as a main course or for eight as a side salad.

Brown rice, measured to the 8 fl oz level in a measuring jug
Boiling water, measured to the 16 fl oz level
8 oz whole brown lentils (225 g)
½ oz butter (10 g)
Some salt
4 oz mushrooms, thinly sliced (110 g)
8 spring onions, thinly sliced—green tops as well
Half a large green pepper, chopped small
1 tablespoon finely chopped walnuts
One 6 inch piece unpeeled cucumber, chopped (15 cm)

For the dressing:
5 dessertspoons oil
1 dessertspoon wine vinegar
1 rounded teaspoon mustard powder
1 clove garlic, crushed
Salt and freshly-milled black pepper

To garnish:
A few crisp lettuce leaves

2 heaped tablespoons chopped parsley
Sliced tomatoes

Begin by cooking the lentils in plenty of (unsalted) boiling water for about 30–40 minutes or until they're *just* soft but not mushy. Meanwhile, in another saucepan melt the butter, stir in the rice to get it nicely coated, then pour in the boiling water. Stir once, cover and simmer very gently for 40–45 minutes until the rice is tender and has absorbed all the liquid.

Whilst the lentils and rice are cooking, prepare the dressing by mixing together in a bowl the oil, vinegar, mustard, garlic, salt and some freshly-milled pepper.

Then drain the lentils, combine them with the cooked rice in a salad bowl, and while they're still warm pour on the dressing. Mix well and leave to cool. Then stir in the rest of the ingredients and serve on a bed of crisp lettuce leaves. Finally garnish with sliced tomatoes and fresh chopped parsley.

Turkish stuffed peppers

(serves 4 people)

This is one of the nicest recipes for using left-over cooked lamb or beef and making it into something really special.

Long grain white rice, measured to the 8 fl oz level in a measuring jug
Boiling water measured to the 16 fl oz level
4 medium sized green or red peppers
¾ lb (approx) cooked lamb or beef cut up into very small pieces (350 g)
2 medium onions, peeled and chopped
2 cloves of garlic, finely chopped
14 oz tin Italian tomatoes (400 g)
4 teaspoons tomato purée
2 tablespoons currants
½ teaspoon ground cinnamon
½ teaspoon marjoram
2 dessertspoons pine nuts, if available (most health food shops stock them)
Olive oil
Salt and freshly-milled black pepper

Pre-heat the oven to gas mark 5, 375°F (190°C)

Begin by melting some oil in a saucepan, then stir in the rice. When it is well-coated with oil, pour in the boiling water and add a sprinkling of salt. Put a lid on and simmer for approximately 15 minutes, or until all the liquid has been absorbed.

Meanwhile fry the onions and garlic in a little more oil for a couple of minutes, then add the meat together with the currants and pine nuts. Season well with salt and pepper, stir in the cinnamon, marjoram and two of the tomatoes plus a tablespoon of juice from the contents of the tin, then turn the heat very low and leave to simmer very gently.

Now prepare the peppers by slicing off the stalk ends and pulling out the core and the seeds. Run each one under cold water to make sure all the seeds are gone, then sit them upright in a small casserole (just so there's not too much room for them to keel over). When the rice is cooked, add it to the pan containing the meat and stir well to combine everything. Taste to check the seasoning at this point.

Now spoon the mixture into each of the peppers: pack it down well to get as much in as you can, and put the rest of it all around the base of the peppers. Finally, put a teaspoon of tomato purée on top of each stuffed pepper and pour the rest of the tin of tomatoes all around the peppers.

Cover the casserole, and cook in the oven for 45–50 minutes or until the peppers are tender when tested with a skewer.

Risotto with chicken livers and mushrooms

(serves 2–3 people)

If you're using frozen chicken livers—the sort that come in 8 oz (225 g) cartons—do make sure they are thoroughly defrosted before you start.

3 oz butter (75 g)
2 medium onions, one thinly sliced, the other chopped
2 oz streaky bacon, chopped (50 g)
Italian rice, measured to the 8 fl oz level in a measuring jug
¼ pint dry white wine (150 ml)
1½ pints boiling chicken stock (875 ml)
½ lb chicken livers cut into lobes (225 g)

| ½ lb mushrooms, sliced (225 g) |
| A bayleaf |
| 1 heaped tablespoon tomato purée |
| 1 teaspoon dried basil |
| 1 oz freshly-grated Parmesan cheese (25 g) |
| Salt and freshly-milled black pepper |

The risotto and sauce are made in separate saucepans, but need to be cooked at the same time. For the sauce, put half the butter in a fairly large saucepan and sauté the sliced onion until soft and golden. Add the bacon and cook for a further 2 or 3 minutes.

Now melt the rest of the butter in a bigger saucepan and cook the chopped onion until softened. Stir in the rice and cook until slightly browned. Next add the wine and continue to cook, uncovered, over low heat until it has all but evaporated. Then add a generous half pint (275 ml) of the boiling chicken stock. Cover and cook over a gentle heat for approximately 20 minutes. Then add a ladleful of stock and when that is absorbed continue to add a ladleful at a time, as and when the rice requires it—it will probably take 1¼ pints (725 ml) in all.

While the rice is cooking you can go back to the sauce: turn the heat up high under the pan and add the chicken livers and, when they've turned a rich brown, stir in the mushrooms. Let them cook for 2 or 3 minutes before adding ¼ pint (150 ml) chicken stock, the bayleaf, tomato purée and basil. Season and cook gently for 10 minutes until the mixture is reduced to a good sauce consistency. Keep the sauce warm and, when the rice is ready, serve the risotto with the sauce spooned on top and sprinkle with freshly-grated Parmesan cheese.

Risotto alla Milanese

(serves 4 people as a main course)

This recipe is only suitable for Italian rice, which needs quite different treatment from long grain rice. A high proportion of liquid is used, the rice is cooked in an uncovered pan, and a good deal of stirring is necessary—particularly towards the end of cooking. It's a relatively simple dish but absolutely beautiful if made properly. You can either serve it on its own as a first course or it's very good served as an accompaniment to *Ossobuco* (page 201).

½ teaspoon powdered saffron
4 tablespoons butter
1 medium-sized onion, chopped
2 tablespoons bone marrow (from an obliging butcher)
Italian rice, measured to the 12 fl oz level in a measuring jug
5 tablespoons dry white wine
Approximately 2 pints boiling chicken stock (1·25 litres)
4 tablespoons of, if possible, freshly-grated Parmesan cheese
Salt and freshly-milled black pepper

Begin by melting 2 tablespoons of butter in a heavy-based saucepan, add the saffron and allow 1 minute for the heat to draw out the flavour. Then add the chopped onion and bone marrow and cook, over a low heat, for about 10 minutes until softened.

Stir in the rice and cook for a minute or two before adding the wine and some salt. Stir gently once, then simmer over a low heat, without a lid, until the liquid has been absorbed (about 10—15 minutes). Now put in a ladleful of the boiling stock and again let it simmer until the stock has nearly all been absorbed but the rice is still moist. Continue adding the boiling stock a ladleful at a time until the rice is tender but still firm and creamy rather than mushy. Stir as necessary to prevent the rice from sticking to the bottom of the pan—particularly towards the end.

When the rice is cooked, remove the pan from the heat, stir in the remaining butter and Parmesan cheese. Cover and leave to stand, off the heat, for 5 minutes before serving. Season to taste then serve with lots more freshly-grated Parmesan cheese on the table.

A risotto for spring

(serves 4–6 people)

This sounds almost like a musical composition but is a good description, I think, for this dish of brown rice, cheese and lightly sautéed green vegetables.

Long grain brown rice, measured up to the 15 fl oz level in a measuring jug

1½ pints boiling water (850 ml)
1 small onion, chopped
3½ tablespoons olive oil
2 leeks, cleaned and chopped into ½ inch (1 cm) pieces
1 small cauliflower, divided up into thumbnail-sized florets
1 lb broccoli (pick off and use the heads only) (450 g)
½ lb fresh spinach, washed, dried and shredded (225 g)
4 oz strong Cheddar cheese, grated (110 g)
2 tablespoons freshly-grated Parmesan cheese
1 tablespoon butter
Salt, cayenne and freshly-milled black pepper

For the garnish:
4 spring onions, very finely chopped, including the green parts

Begin by heating 1½ tablespoons of the olive oil in a medium-sized, thick-based saucepan and frying the onion for 5 minutes. Next, add the rice and stir it around so that the grains are well coated with oil. Now add the boiling water and some salt, stir once, then bring to simmering point. Cover and let the rice simmer very gently for 40 minutes or until the grains are tender.

About halfway through the cooking time, melt the 2 remaining tablespoons of oil with the butter in a very large frying pan (or divide between two medium-sized pans); add the cauliflower, broccoli, leeks and some seasoning. Then, over a medium heat, move the vegetables around until they have browned a little but still retain their crispness—say for about 8 minutes. Now add the spinach; it will appear somewhat bulky to begin with but will soon collapse. Cook, stirring occasionally, for about 5 minutes. Meanwhile turn the grill on to high.

When the rice is cooked put it into a shallow heatproof serving dish and fluff it. Add half the Cheddar cheese and half the Parmesan and stir them in. Add the vegetables and stir again. Then sprinkle the remaining Cheddar and Parmesan cheese on top, together with a pinch or two of cayenne.

Now place the dish under the grill and let the cheese topping melt and brown. Garnish with the spring onions.

Buttery kedgeree

(serves 4 people)

This was a typical breakfast dish in the days when grand Victorian breakfast dishes were spread out on handsome Victorian sideboards. Nowadays it is a very good lunch or late supper dish.

1½ lb thick smoked haddock fillets (700 g)
3 oz butter (75 g)
1 onion, chopped
Long grain white rice measured up to the 8 fl oz level in a measuring jug
Boiling liquid measured to the 16 fl oz level (see recipe method)
¾ teaspoon hot curry powder (Madras)
3 hard-boiled eggs, chopped
3 heaped tablespoons fresh parsley, chopped
1 tablespoon lemon juice
Salt and freshly-milled black pepper

First place the haddock fillets in a saucepan and cover them with 1 pint (570 ml) cold water. Bring to the boil, put on a lid, and simmer gently for about 8 minutes. Then drain off the water into a measuring jug. Transfer the haddock to a dish, cover with foil and keep it warm.

Now, using the same saucepan, melt 2 oz (50 g) butter and soften the onion in it for 5 minutes. Next stir in the curry powder, cook for half a minute, then stir in the measured rice and add 16 fl oz (450 ml) of the haddock cooking water. Stir once then, when it comes up to simmering point, cover with a tight-fitting lid and cook, very gently, for 15 minutes or until the rice grains are tender.

When the rice has been cooking for 10 minutes, remove the skins from the fish and flake it. Then, when the rice is ready, remove it from the heat and fork in the flaked fish, hard-boiled eggs, parsley and lemon juice and the remaining 1 oz (25 g) of butter.

Now cover the pan with a folded tea towel and replace it on very gentle heat for five minutes. Then tip the kedgeree quickly onto a hot serving dish, season to taste and serve.

Brown rice pudding with prunes and apricots

(serves 4–6 people)

This is a pudding for wholefood-minded people, deliciously different from the traditional rice pudding.

Brown rice, measured to the 10 fl oz level in a measuring jug
Milk, measured to the 20 fl oz level
4 tablespoons dark brown sugar
1 egg, beaten
½ teaspoon ground cinnamon
Quarter of a nutmeg, grated
4 oz dried apricots (110 g) and 6 oz prunes (175 g) both soaked overnight then drained and chopped
5 fl oz yoghurt (150 ml)

In a thick-based saucepan bring the milk to the boil and sprinkle in the rice. Stir, then cover and cook over a very low heat for about 50 minutes or until the rice is tender. Keep an eye on it or the milk may boil over and, towards the end of the cooking time, have a peep as you might need to add a drop more milk. Then take it off the heat and stir in 3 tablespoons of the sugar, the beaten egg, cinnamon and nutmeg.

Next, butter a 4 pint (2 litre) casserole, spread half the rice mixture in it and top this with half the fruit. Spread the rest of the rice on top and cover this with the remaining fruit. Cover the casserole with a lid and bake in a pre-heated oven for 30 minutes at gas mark 4, 350°F (180°C).

At the end of the cooking time, remove the pudding from the oven, spread the yoghurt over the top and sprinkle with the remaining tablespoon of sugar.

Note: this is just as delicious served cold, if you have any left over.

Other cereal grains

Not long ago I attended a lecture by Prof. Kenneth Mellanby on the subject 'Can Britain feed herself?'. I am happy to report that if Britain were to *decide* to feed herself—or had to under siege conditions—we could all live quite happily on a perfectly balanced diet. Of course we couldn't rely on as much meat as we used to, and the proposition assumed that we would have to increase our cereal production and consumption quite considerably.

That wouldn't be a bad thing in any event. Meat *is* becoming less affordable, and perhaps that's nature's way of enticing us away from excessive consumption of animal fat and towards an increased awareness of the nutritional advantages of natural cereals. But first, there is a distinction to be made. There are two kinds of cereal available: whole natural cereals, and refined cereals.

Although we eat far more of the latter—millions of pounds' worth of advertising has persuaded us to do so—we might do better to choose for ourselves. Examine the packets: among the details of free tea-towels and cut-out speed boats you will find that many cereals have been re-fortified, even 'enriched', with the vitamins lost in the refining process. What is rarely replaced is the fibre that was contained in the bran and germ. However there are breakfast cereals which are made from 100% wholewheat, and say so on the packet. My advice is to choose these: they contain the whole grain, fibre and all, and have no need of added vitamins.

Whole grain cereals

Packaged breakfast foods are by no means the only way to consume cereals. A whole variety of grains come to us (as rice does) in several guises. The uses of some may be unfamiliar; but if they are natural whole grains as opposed to refined ones, what they all have in common is real nutrition and flavour.

To be sure that the grains you buy are whole grains, it makes sense to go to a wholefood shop—because the grains sold in grocers and supermarkets are often refined.

Barley A great deal of our barley, of course, finds its way into beer, but the grain is also sold—most often as *pearl barley*, which is the refined variety, or as *pot barley*, which is the whole grain with only the inedible husk removed, and is found in healthfood shops. Both these are good additions to stews or soups (see recipes for *Irish stew*, page 193, and for *Scotch broth*, page 102). *Barley flakes* are the grains mechanically rolled into flakes, and an excellent use for these is in *Muesli* (see page 318).

Rye is more commonly milled into various grades of flour for bread-making—*coarsely-milled rye*, for instance, is used in the production of Pumpernickel bread: and *rye flour* (because of its quick fermentation) is often added to wheat flour to give bread a slightly 'sour' flavour. Like other grains, *flaked rye* can be bought in healthfood shops.

Right (from top to bottom): Lamb kebabs, page 506; American hamburgers, page 502; Rice salad, page 490; Bacon and egg pie, page 511.

Wheat We've already examined all the different varieties of wheat flour in the section on Bread, but the grain itself—or parts of it—has many other applications. *Wholewheat grains* can be soaked for a few hours, then cooked in the same way as rice (but it takes longer): the result is chewier, and some people prefer to combine the wholewheat grains with some rice or beans. *Wholewheat flakes* are good in *Muesli* (see page 318). *Cracked wheat* (which is simply the whole grain lightly crushed) is sometimes sprinkled on bread before baking, or included, as in granary loaves, in the dough itself. *Wheatgerm* is the embryo of the grain, and contains a very high proportion of vitamins, minerals and oils: it is sold separately and a few teaspoons sprinkled on your yoghurt, porridge or fruit salad is a good way of upping your vitamin intake for the day! *Wheat bran* is the layer that lies just below the inedible outer husk of the wheat grain. If you're living on a diet that contains about five slices of wholewheat bread a day plus fresh fruit and other wholefoods, you'll probably be getting enough dietary fibre. On the other hand if you prefer white bread and other refined foods, it might be a good idea to incorporate some wheat bran into your diet. The best way to do this, I think, is to sprinkle it onto ordinary breakfast cereals and pour on some milk so that it slips down almost unnoticed. *Semolina* is also made from wheat grain: basically it's the starchy part of hard wheat in granular form, before it has been finely milled.

Oats Much used in biscuit-making—see the Scones and biscuits chapter for the different grades of *oatmeal* (milled oats) and varieties of *oat flakes*. In F. Marian MacNeill's charming book *The Scots Kitchen*, oats are referred to as 'the flower of the Scottish soil', so it's not surprising that some of the best recipes for using oats come from Scotland, and the pride of them all is *Porridge* (see recipe, page 319).

Buckwheat This is strictly speaking not a grain, but its use and preparation are much the same. *Buckwheat flour* is traditionally used for the Russian type of pancakes known as blinis, and for the Breton version known as *galettes* (see Pasta and pancakes chapter). The *whole buckwheat* seeds can be bought roasted—in which case they're sometimes called *kasha*—or in their natural state. They have a delicious and distinctive grainy flavour, cook very much like rice, and combine beautifully with vegetables for a savoury dish like the one on page 319.

Left: Roman gnocchi, page 465; Spaghetti alla carbonara, page 364.

Home-made muesli   If you've not yet made its acquaintance, this is a mixture of whole cereal grains with the addition of fruit, nuts and other things ad lib. Its ancestor was a Swiss peasant dish, but it became world famous after it had been adapted as part of a health diet at the Bircher-Benner Clinic in Switzerland. Very soon the cornflake brigade cashed in and now any number of versions appear in the supermarkets. My quarrel with the branded mueslis is that they usually contain rather a lot of dried milk powder (which is not really something I want to eat in spoonfuls) plus the inevitable sugar, making most of them too sweet. If you have a wholefood shop within easy distance you can probably buy an unsweetened mueseli base, or you can do what I do: buy the grains and other ingredients and make it at home.

½ lb wholewheat flakes (225 g)
½ lb rye flakes (225 g)
½ lb whole oat flakes (225 g)
½ lb barley flakes (225 g)
¾ lb roasted peanuts (350 g) (you can roast these yourself under a medium grill), chopped
1 lb sultanas (450 g)
½ lb raisins (225 g)

This is a basic mixture, but there are 101 variations—the nuts for instance could be roasted hazelnuts, brazils, walnuts, or, if you're feeling rich, slivered roast almonds with the skins left on. The fruit too can be varied: chopped dates, dried apricots or figs, or chopped dried apple rings. Personally I think the proportions of fruit here make the addition of sugar unecessary, but if it isn't sweet enough for you add some more dried fruit. When serving muesli you can sprinkle in some bran, which will slip down unnoticed among all the other good things. Wheatgerm too (see page 317) can be added and fresh fruits in season. Milk is always poured over and, if you're trying to cut down on fats, skimmed milk is fine.

Traditional oatmeal porridge

(serves 2 people)

Traditions surrounding porridge-making are legion: sometimes the oats were added in batches, some at the beginning, some halfway through, and some at the end—the undercooked ones giving a contrast in texture and a nuttier flavour. Salt wasn't added till halfway through, in case it should toughen the grains before they cooked: today the Scots still make their porridge well salted.

1 pint water (570 ml)
2½ oz medium oatmeal (60 g)
1 teaspoon salt
To serve: ¼ pint single cream (150 ml)

In a medium-sized saucepan, bring the water up to a fast boil, then sprinkle in the oatmeal slowly whisking it in with a balloon whisk. Carry on whisking until the mixture returns to the boil, then reduce the heat, cover the pan and let the porridge cook very gently for 10 minutes. After that add the salt, whisk it in, cover again and cook gently for a further 15 minutes or so.

The traditional way to eat porridge is without sugar, and with an individual bowl of cream. But if you have a sweet tooth, sprinkle dark brown sugar over the porridge, let it melt a little, then pour in the cream so that it mingles with the sugar and marbles the surface.

Buckwheat and vegetable pie

(serves 3–4 people)

Buckwheat has a distinctive flavour of its own, and baked in the oven with vegetables it makes an excellent vegetarian main course.

8 oz roasted buckwheat (225 g)
1 oz butter (25 g)
1 pint boiling water (570 ml)
1 tablespoon tomato purée
1 large onion, chopped
1 green or red pepper, deseeded and chopped

8 oz mushrooms, sliced if large (225 g)
14 oz tin tomatoes (400 g)
1 clove garlic, crushed
1 rounded teaspoon dried oregano
1½ oz grated cheese, any sort will do (40 g)
1 oz wholemeal breadcrumbs (25 g)
2 tablespoons oil
Cayenne pepper
Salt and freshly-milled black pepper

Pre-heat the oven to gas mark 5, 375°F (190°C)

First combine the boiling water with the tomato purée; next melt the butter in a saucepan. Add the buckwheat and stir until it is thoroughly coated with fat. Then pour in the liquid, bring up to simmering point, stir once and add some salt, then put the lid on and cook gently for about 10 minutes.

Meanwhile, heat 2 tablespoons of oil in a frying pan and cook the onion and pepper in it for 5 minutes to soften but not to colour them. Add the mushrooms and cook gently for a further 5 minutes. Then stir in the garlic and oregano, season with salt and pepper and add the contents of the tin of tomatoes. Stir well, then leave to simmer gently without a lid so that the liquid reduces slightly.

Stir the cooked buckwheat into the vegetable mixture, then transfer the contents of the pan to a lightly buttered 2½ pint (1·5 litre) pie dish. Scatter the grated cheese and breadcrumbs over the surface, and a sprinkling of cayenne if you like. Place the dish in the centre of the oven and bake for 20–30 minutes or until the topping is golden and bubbling.

See also:

Aduki bean and brown rice salad
Baked spinach with brown rice and cheese
Brown rice and tuna fish salad
Cabbage leaves stuffed with rice
Cider baked apples with toasted muesli
Dolmades (stuffed vine leaves)

Eliza Acton's rich rice pudding
Green herb and rice salad
Ham, egg and cheese risotto
Rice salad
Shoulder of lamb with rice and kidney stuffing
Turkish stuffed tomatoes

Vegetarian cooking

Including recipes for:
Spinach pasties
*Brown rice with vegetables
  and cheese sauce*
Curried nut roast
Hazelnut and vegetable burgers
Vegetarian goulash
Dolmades (stuffed vine leaves)
Sautéed mixed vegetables

Cucumber and yoghurt salad
Toasted sesame and sunflower seeds
Cabbage leaves stuffed with rice
Mixed vegetables à la Grècque
Scone pizza
Non-meat loaf
Provençal vegetable stew
Thick onion tart

Interest in vegetarian food has quickened considerably over the last couple of decades, hand in hand with the wholefood movement. Vegetarians used to have a crusading image, forever prophesying doom to the meat-eaters. But now—thanks to better communication, imaginative cookery books, and a number of thriving vegetarian restaurants up and down the country—the whole idea of vegetarianism seems much less esoteric to people. I'm glad of this, if only because I think that our traditional belief in this country that a main course without meat (or at least fish) isn't a main course at all is nonsense.

Personally I couldn't, and wouldn't want to, become a vegetarian, but I do have a deep interest in vegetarian food—and for two main reasons. The first is that I am convinced that the diet of the future will have to be much less meat-centred than it is at present—simply because the world's grain supply (upon which the meat supply depends) gets scarcer as the world's population gets higher. Intensive cattle farming means intensive feeding, and it takes 10 lb of grain in feed to provide 1 lb of meat. With two-thirds of the world living at or below subsistence level, while the rest suffer the effects of diseases directly attributable to over-consumption, it doesn't need a crystal ball to predict that there must be some change. And isn't it better to have a little of something really good rather than a lot of something bland and boring? Polyphosphate-injected chicken, chemically cured bacon, water-pumped ham, and barley-fed beef are all meat products that I can easily live without.

The other reason for my interest is that vegetarian cooking is challenging and stimulating. It is actually very *satisfying* to be able to produce a delicious meal that contains no meat—you discover that when people are enjoying what they're eating it doesn't occur to them that it includes no meat until you actually tell them! Vegetarian cooking opens up new horizons, and explores a whole new range of ingredients—many of them very economical.

Since the meat versus vegetarian controversy is based on a number of misconceptions on both sides, let's dispose of them first.

Vegetarians are cranky? Yes, some of them are—as in any other section of society—but the majority are not. Some vegetarian and healthfood shops do have their weird corners full of pills and potions and plant milk, but many young people now live quite normally and unobtrusively on a healthy diet of eggs and dairy produce, vegetables, fruits, grains, nuts, seeds and plant protein.

Vegetarian myths Vegetarians themselves have been known to make rash claims, such as that vegetarians are slimmer, healthier, and less aggressive than carnivores. Rubbish. I know a number of rather plump vegetarians who are subject to the same bouts of 'flu or rheumatism as the rest of us (for that matter I also know slim meat-eaters who seemingly never have a day's illness!). The facile connection between eating meat and aggression (a theory derived, I believe, from a comparison between the fierce meat-killing lions and tigers and the peace-loving, plant-eating elephants) does seem to crumble when you consider that the most aggressively-minded man of recent history, Hitler, was—guess what—a vegetarian.

The protein question The proteins in our food are essential for health, though to judge from some current advertising campaigns, which glorify products as being 'rich in protein' or 'high-protein', you might be forgiven for thinking that we need all the body-building ingredients that we can possibly push down our throats. The truth is that an average adult has a minimum protein requirement of 45 grams a day, and can do very nicely on 75 grams. This is a target that non-meat eaters can reach comfortably, with the only reservation being that they must find a *balance* of foods in their diet.

First- and second-class proteins Without getting over-scientific, proteins themselves are made up of what are called 'amino acids', eight of which are essential to our health. First-class proteins contain all eight essential amino acids, and these are found in meat and fish, poultry, eggs, cheese, milk and so on. But (as some meat-eaters point out) nuts and beans are second-class proteins, which is to say they are deficient in at least one of these amino acids.

That is not to say that eating only second-class protein foods cannot provide a balanced diet, however. Nature, as she usually does, has arranged things perfectly adequately by ensuring that the amino acid lacking in one plant food is supplied by another. A good example of plant foods complementing each other to provide the eight essential amino acids is beans on toast!

Should you wish to embark, full-time or part-time, on a non-meat diet, what you require to eat is a balanced selection of cheese, milk, cream, butter, eggs, pulses, nuts, wholewheat bread, grains, fresh vegetables and fresh or dried fruit.

One of the positive aspects of a vegetarian diet is that it actually provides plenty of variety, whereas meat-eaters can be inclined to stick endlessly to a meat-and-two-veg routine. A typical day's meals which provide all the necessary nutrients (and amino-acids) for a vegetarian could be: breakfast of muesli with milk, wholewheat toast and coffee. Lunch something like cheeses, salad and wholemeal bread with fresh fruit to follow. And for dinner perhaps curried nut roast with vegetables, and yoghurt to follow. To me that sounds as delicious and appetising as any meat-centred diet.

But it is not the purpose of this chapter to convert anyone to vegetarianism, nor indeed to perpetuate the unnecessary distinctions between 'us' and 'them'. It is intended to offer a collection of delicious meatless main courses, which are both interesting and easy on the pocket.

Spinach pasties

(makes 6)

These are very easy to make and you can use either a packet of frozen puff pastry or the *Quick flaky pastry* given on page 565.

1 oz butter (25 g)
2 oz cottage cheese (50 g)
1½ oz freshly-grated Parmesan (40 g)
1 small clove garlic, finely crushed
¼ teaspoon dried dillweed
Some freshly-grated nutmeg
Lemon juice to taste
Salt and freshly-milled black pepper
Beaten egg to glaze
8 oz ready-made puff pastry (225 g) or quick flaky pastry made with 6 oz (175 g) flour and 4 oz (110 g) margarine
8 oz cooked spinach, fresh or frozen (225 g). If you use fresh you'll need 1 lb (450 g) to make 8 oz (225 g) cooked weight

Heat the oven to gas mark 7, 425°F (220°C)

A baking sheet, lightly greased.

Cook the spinach over a gentle heat until all the excess moisture has evaporated, then remove from the heat, beat in the butter, cheeses and all the rest of the ingredients apart from the egg and pastry and season generously. Leave on one side to cool.

Roll out the pastry fairly thinly, then, using a small saucepan lid or saucer, cut out six rounds about 6 inches (15 cm) in diameter. It will be necessary to re-roll the pastry scraps to get 6 rounds. Then put about a tablespoon of the cooled spinach mixture on one half of each pastry circle.

Brush the pastry edges with beaten egg, then bring one half of a pastry circle over to cover the spinach filling on the other half, pressing the edges together to seal well and form the pasty. Repeat this with the other five circles. Glaze with beaten egg, then place the six pasties on the greased baking sheet.

Make a small ventilation hole in the centre of each one and bake on the second shelf from the top of the oven for about 15 minutes or until the pasties have risen nicely and are golden brown.

Brown rice with vegetables and cheese sauce

(serves 2 people)

This is a really delicious supper dish for two people. The different textures and flavours of the vegetables, coupled with the firm 'bite' of the rice moistened with a cheese sauce all add up to proof that economy and simplicity can still come up trumps!

For the rice:
Long grain brown rice measured to the 8 fl oz level in a measuring jug
Boiling water measured to the 16 fl oz level
1 carrot, cut into ¼ inch (½ cm) chunks
1 large celery stalk, cut into ¼ inch (½ cm) chunks
1 medium-sized onion, roughly chopped
1 tablespoon oil
½ oz butter (10 g)
Salt

For the garnish:
4 oz cauliflower, divided into 1 inch (2·5 cm) florets (110 g)
4 oz Chinese leaves (or white cabbage) shredded into wide strips (110 g)
Oil

For the cheese sauce:
½ pint cold milk (275 ml)
1 oz butter (25 g)
1 oz flour (25 g)
½ teaspoon mustard
2 pinches cayenne pepper
3 oz strong Cheddar cheese, grated (75 g)

Start off in a thick-based saucepan by heating the butter and oil together then add the onions, carrots and celery and soften them all for about 5 minutes. Next stir in the rice and, when it's all nicely coated with fat, add salt and boiling water. Put on a tight-fitting lid and cook gently, undisturbed, for 45 minutes.

Meanwhile make the sauce simply by placing all the ingredients (except the cheese) in a pan and whisking them over a medium heat until the butter has melted and the sauce has thickened and come to the boil. Simmer gently for about 8 minutes, then stir in half the grated cheese and set the pan aside whilst it melts.

Next, about 10 minutes before the rice is ready, heat some oil in a frying-pan and sauté the cauliflower for 5 minutes, tossing it around to get it nicely toasted. Then add the shredded cabbage to the frying pan and sauté it for 5 minutes or until it's cooked but still with some 'bite'.

Finally, pile the rice mixture into a large heatproof serving dish, followed by the fried vegetables; pour the cheese sauce over, then sprinkle the remaining grated cheese on top. Place the dish under a pre-heated grill for just as long as it takes to get the topping golden and bubbling.

Curried nut roast

(serves 4 people)

This is the perfect recipe to serve to anyone who feels that vegetarian food might be boring—it's never failed to please. Meat eaters are always amazed that anything that doesn't contain meat can taste so good!

½ lb hazel or Brazil or walnuts, finely chopped (225 g)
½ lb fresh tomatoes, peeled and chopped (225 g)

1 medium-sized green pepper, deseeded and finely chopped
2 medium-sized onions, finely chopped
3 oz wholewheat breadcrumbs (75 g)
1 clove garlic, crushed
1 teaspoon dried mixed herbs or 2 teaspoons fresh mixed herbs
1 tablespoon mild curry powder (or a heaped teaspoon of hot Madras curry powder)
1 egg, beaten
Cooking oil
Salt and freshly-milled black pepper

Pre-heat the oven to gas mark 7, 425°F (220°C)

One 7 inch (18 cm) square cake tin, greased.

Begin by gently frying the onion and chopped pepper in a little oil until they're softened—about 10 minutes.

Meanwhile, mix the nuts and breadcrumbs together in a large bowl, adding the garlic, herbs and curry powder. Then stir in the onion, pepper and tomatoes, mix very thoroughly and season. Now add the beaten egg to bind the mixture together. Finally, pack the mixture into the prepared tin and bake for 30–40 minutes until golden.

This can be served hot with spiced pilau rice, yoghurt, mango chutney, or a fresh tomato sauce. It's also very good served cold with a salad.

Hazelnut and vegetable burgers

(serves 4 people)

Many of the so-called beefburgers of today taste of anything but beef—and those that include TVP (Textured Vegetable Protein) can be a very rubbery consistency. By contrast, these made with nuts and vegetables are simple, honest and quite delicious.

2 medium-sized carrots, grated
2 celery stalks, finely chopped
1 medium-sized onion, finely chopped

2 tablespoons finely chopped cabbage
2 tablespoons brown breadcrumbs
2 oz hazelnuts, ground (50 g)
2 tablespoons wheatgerm
A couple of pinches of cayenne pepper
A pinch of ground mace
½ teaspoon dried mixed herbs or 1 teaspoon of fresh mixed herbs
1 egg
1 tablespoon tomato purée
1 tablespoon yoghurt
Salt and freshly-milled black pepper

For the coating:
1 beaten egg
About 4 oz dry wholewheat breadcrumbs (110 g)

These are quite simple to make. Having done the chopping, grating and grinding, put all the ingredients (down to and including the herbs) in a bowl and mix well. In another bowl place the egg, tomato purée and yoghurt and whisk, then add this mixture to the vegetable mixture and season to taste.

Next form the mixture into eight small patties. Cover and chill for a few hours in the refrigerator. This will help to firm up the patties and prevent them breaking during cooking.

Shortly before you are ready to cook the burgers, heat the oven to gas mark 4, 350°F (180°C). Then dip each one into the beaten egg first, then into the wholewheat breadcrumbs, and place on a well-oiled baking sheet. Bake for 15 minutes then turn the burgers over with care and bake for a further 15 minutes.

Serve with a home-made tomato sauce or plain yoghurt and some brown pilau rice.

Vegetarian goulash

(serves 4 people)

This is nicest made with summer vegetables.

2 tablespoons olive oil
2 medium onions, sliced
1 rounded dessertspoon wholemeal flour

1 heaped tablespoon Hungarian paprika
14 oz tin Italian tomatoes (400 g)
½ pint hot water enriched with 1 teaspoon tomato purée (275 ml)
½ lb cauliflower sprigs (i.e. half a medium-sized cauliflower head) (225 g)
½ lb new carrots, cut in chunks (225 g)
½ lb courgettes, cut in chunks (225 g)
½ lb new potatoes, cut into halves (225 g)
Half a green pepper, deseeded and chopped
¼ pint soured cream or yoghurt (150 ml)
A couple of pinches of cayenne pepper
Salt and freshly-milled black pepper

Pre-heat the oven to gas mark 4, 350°F (180°C)

Start by heating the oil in a flameproof casserole; fry the onion until softened, then stir in the flour, most of the paprika and the cayenne pepper. Cook for a minute, then stir in the contents of the tin of tomatoes, and the water. Bring the sauce up to boiling point, stirring all the time, then add all the vegetables. Season with salt and freshly-milled black pepper, cover, then transfer to the pre-heated oven and bake for 30–40 minutes.

Finally stir in the soured cream or yoghurt, scatter the rest of the paprika on top and serve. Buttered brown rice goes well with this.

Dolmades (stuffed vine leaves)

(serves 6 people as a first course or 4 as a lunch dish)

This is one of the nicest vegetarian dishes I know. If you live in an area where there are Greek or Cypriot shops, you should be able to get hold of some vine leaves. If not, use raw spinach leaves or the blanched inside leaves of young spring cabbage.

12 fresh large vine leaves, approximately 2 oz (50 g)
Long grain rice measured to the 3 fl oz level in a measuring jug
1 lb tomatoes, peeled and chopped (450 g) or 14 oz tin of tomatoes (400 g)

2 teaspoons tomato purée
1½ teaspoons oregano
¼ teaspoon ground cinnamon
1 tablespoon chopped fresh mint
1 tablespoon chopped fresh parsley
1 small onion, chopped
3 small cloves garlic, crushed
1½ tablespoons olive oil
1 oz pine nuts (25 g)
The juice of half a lemon
Salt and freshly-milled black pepper

Bring a frying pan of water to boiling point, then add the vine leaves all in one bunch and blanch them for about 1 minute, turning the bunch over after 30 seconds. Then empty them into a colander, rinse under cold running water and, when drained, spread out each leaf flat—vein side uppermost.

For the filling: cook the rice in double its volume of boiling salted water until tender. Heat the oil in a frying pan and fry the onion and pine nuts to colour them, then tip in the cooked rice together with one-third of the tomatoes, the tomato purée, half a teaspoon of oregano, the mint, parsley, cinnamon and 2 cloves of crushed garlic. Stir well, cook for a couple of minutes, then, removing the pan from the heat, add the lemon juice, salt and pepper.

Now spoon a dessertspoonful of the rice mixture onto the stalk end of a vine leaf and fold the leaf over once, squeezing and pressing the filling to a sausage-shape. Then tuck in the sides of the leaf and continue to roll up to make a tight, neat, cylindrical parcel.

When all the vine leaves are filled, spoon half the remainder of the tomatoes into the base of a small flameproof casserole or heavy saucepan. Now pack the dolmades in tightly and spoon the remaining tomatoes, garlic and oregano on top. Add a seasoning of salt and pepper. Now press a suitable sized plate over the dolmades to prevent them unrolling during cooking, cover the casserole with a lid, and simmer very, very gently on top of the stove for 2 hours.

Serve the dolmades hot or cold with the juices spooned over them.

Sautéed mixed vegetables

(serves 4 people)

Kate Bush—whose performances both singing and dancing project a tremendous amount of energy—is a vegetarian. This recipe and the two that follow it are some of her favourites. They were devised by her sister-in-law Judith and make up a complete meal. It has become a firm favourite for supper in my home.

½ lb onions, roughly sliced (225 g)
6 oz green peppers, cut into ½ inch strips—approx. 2 small peppers (175 g)
6 oz carrots, sliced—approx. 3 small carrots (175 g)
½ lb mushrooms, sliced (225 g)
¾ lb tomatoes, quartered (350 g)
2½ tablespoons sunflower seed oil
Salt and freshly-milled black pepper

Begin by heating the oil in a large saucepan with a lid (or a shallow casserole). Add the onions and soften them for a minute or two before adding the carrots. Cook for a further couple of minutes, then add the mushrooms, pepper and tomatoes. Stir and season, then put the lid on and, keeping the heat fairly low, leave the vegetables to steam in their own juice for 20–25 minutes. Serve with brown rice (see page 303). The vegetables can be varied according to season.

Note: curry spices can be added to this dish while the oil is heating in the pan. A good combination is: 2 crushed cardamom pods; ¹/₂ teaspoon crushed cumin seeds; ¹/₄ teaspoon crushed, dried chilli; 1 teaspoon fresh, chopped ginger (or ¹/₂ teaspoon dried ginger powder); 1 teaspoon turmeric; 1 chopped clove garlic.

Serve the vegetables, spiced or otherwise, with rice and the following two side dishes.

Cucumber and yoghurt salad

4 inches unpeeled cucumber, thinly sliced then cut into strips (10 cm)
½ pint natural yoghurt (275 ml)
The juice of ½ lemon

1 large clove garlic, crushed
1 tablespoon snipped chives
Salt

Simply combine all the ingredients in a bowl. Serve with the rice
and vegetables with a sprinkling of toasted seeds (below).

Toasted sesame and sunflower seeds

2 oz sesame seeds (50 g)
2 oz sunflower seeds (50 g)
1 dessertspoon soy sauce

In a shallow heatproof dish, mix the two lots of seeds together, then
sprinkle in the soy sauce and mix thoroughly. Now spread them out
evenly and place the dish under a hot grill to toast them for
4 minutes—shaking the dish a couple of times to even them out.
When they are cool, store them in a screw-top jar.

Cabbage leaves stuffed with rice

(serves 2 people)

You can make all sorts of stuffings for
cabbage leaves if you follow this basic
recipe—you could use lentils or chopped
nuts or whatever ingredients happen to
be handy.

1 smallish head of spring cabbage
¾ lb ripe tomatoes, peeled and chopped (350 g)
1 medium-sized onion, chopped
Half a green pepper, deseeded and finely chopped
Long grain brown rice measured up to the 5 fl oz level in a measuring jug
Boiling water measured up to the 10 fl oz level in a measuring jug
2 tablespoons olive oil
2–3 spring onions, finely chopped
Salt and freshly-milled black pepper
A pinch of cayenne

Cook the rice first of all: heat the oil in a saucepan and fry the onion
and pepper in it for 5 minutes, then add the rice, give it a stir, and
pour in the boiling water. Season with salt, cover and simmer for

about 45 minutes or until all the liquid has been absorbed and the grains are tender. Then turn the cooked rice into a bowl and leave it to cool a little.

Meanwhile prepare the cabbage, discarding the tough outer leaves, then carefully peeling off about six or seven whole leaves. In each one of these make a V-shaped cut with a sharp knife to snip out the hard stalky bits. Next chop up the heart of the cabbage and bring a large saucepan of water to the boil. Blanch the whole leaves and chopped cabbage by cooking them in the boiling water for 5 minutes.

Then drain the cabbage in a colander, rinse in cold water and drain again. Shake off as much moisture from the leaves as you can and wrap them in a cloth or paper towel to dry.

Now heat the oven to gas mark 4, 350°F (180°C). Then add the chopped spring onions and the chopped cabbage to the cooled rice, with a generous pinch of cayenne and some salt and pepper.

Now take a heaped tablespoon of the rice-and-chopped-cabbage mixture and wrap it in one of the prepared leaves—squeezing gently until you have a neat, firm package.

Fill and roll the remaining cabbage leaves with the rest of the stuffing, then pack the parcels closely together in a casserole. Season with salt and pepper, pour the chopped tomatoes over the parcels, cover and bake for 1 hour in the oven.

Mixed vegetables à la Grècque

(serves 2–4 people)

This can be a main course if served with a brown rice salad mixed with fresh herbs, or a first course if simply served on crisp lettuce leaves.

6 button onions
4 oz cauliflower (110 g) broken into 1 inch (2·5 cm) florets
4 oz small to medium-sized mushrooms, halved (110 g)
2 oz dry weight kidney beans (50 g), soaked and cooked as described on page 343
1 medium-sized onion, finely chopped
1 fat clove garlic, crushed
2 tablespoons wine vinegar

1 lb tomatoes, skinned and quartered (450 g), or 14 oz tin Italian tomatoes (400 g)
1 teaspoon oregano
1 heaped teaspoon whole coriander seeds, crushed
8 black peppercorns, lightly crushed
4 tablespoons olive oil
Juice of 1 medium-sized lemon
2 fl oz water (55 ml) mixed with 1 heaped teaspoon tomato purée
2 spring onions (including green tops), finely chopped
2 tablespoons chopped fresh parsley
Salt and freshly-milled black pepper

Heat 2 tablespoons of the olive oil in a heavy-based pan and soften the onion for 5 minutes. Then add the garlic, wine vinegar, tomatoes, oregano, coriander, peppercorns, lemon juice, water and tomato purée, and some salt. Bring to the boil and stir in the button onions. Now cover the pan and simmer for 20 minutes.

Then add the cooked and drained beans, the cauliflower and mushrooms, cover the pan again and simmer for a further 20 minutes, stirring the vegetables round once or twice during the cooking time. After 20 minutes test the vegetables with a skewer, they should be tender but still firm. Taste and check the seasoning.

Pour the contents of the pan into a shallow dish and leave to cool. I think this dish is best left overnight but a few hours will do. To serve, sprinkle the vegetables with the rest of the olive oil, then scatter the chopped parsley and spring onions on top.

Scone pizza

(serves 2 people)

This recipe was given to me on the programme *Multi-Coloured Swap Shop* by Heather Carey, then aged 12. It's very easy and quick to make and absolutely delicious.

4 oz self-raising flour (110 g)
1 oz margarine (25 g)
2 oz hard cheese, grated (50 g)
½ teaspoon salt

1 teaspoon dried mixed herbs
2 tablespoons milk mixed with 2 tablespoons water
3 mushrooms, thinly sliced
2 tinned tomatoes, drained and mashed together with 1 teaspoon tomato purée
Half an onion, very finely chopped
Salt and freshly-milled black pepper

Pre-heat the oven to gas mark 7, 425°F (220°F)

A baking sheet, well greased.

First of all sieve the flour into a bowl, add the salt then rub in the margarine. Next *gradually* add the milk and water to mix the ingredients to a soft dough—you may not need all the liquid.

Now roll out the dough to a circle approximately ½ inch (1 cm) thick and place it on the baking sheet. Spread it with the mashed tomato, sprinkle the grated cheese on top of that, then decorate with the chopped onion and sliced mushrooms, and season it with the mixed herbs and some salt and pepper. Then pop it into the oven to bake for 15–20 minutes or until golden brown and bubbling on top. A few chopped olives would make a nice addition to the topping or, for non-vegetarians, you could use a few anchovies.

Non-meat loaf

(serves 4 people)

This is delicious hot with a home-made tomato sauce or cold with pickles and salad.

6 oz green or brown lentils (175 g)
4 oz split peas (yellow or green) picked over and rinsed (110 g)
1 pint vegetable stock or water (570 ml)
2 tablespoons butter or margarine
1 medium-sized onion, chopped
Half a green pepper, deseeded and chopped
2 carrots, scraped and chopped
2 sticks celery, chopped
1 fat clove garlic, crushed
1 egg, beaten
¾ teaspoon dried mixed herbs

¼ teaspoon cayenne pepper
¼ teaspoon powdered mace
2 tablespoons chopped parsley
Salt and freshly-milled black pepper

One 1 lb (450 g) loaf tin, well greased.

Start by bringing the stock or water to boiling point, stir in the split peas and simmer, covered, for about 5 minutes. Then add the lentils and herbs and continue to simmer, with the lid on, for a further 25–30 minutes or until all the liquid has been absorbed and the lentils and peas are soft; then take off the heat.

Now heat the oven to gas mark 5, 375°F (190°C).

Heat the butter in another pan, add all the prepared vegetables and the garlic and fry for 10 minutes or until golden. Now stir the vegetables into the lentil mixture together with the cayenne, mace, beaten egg, herbs and parsley, mix well then season to taste.

Spoon the mixture into the prepared tin, cover with foil and bake for 40 minutes. When it's cooked, slip a knife around the inside edge of the tin and turn the loaf out onto a warmed serving dish.

Provençale vegetable stew (ratatouille)

(serves 4 people)

This famous French recipe is best made in the autumn when the vegetables needed for it are cheap and plentiful.

2 medium-sized onions
3 medium-sized courgettes
2 large aubergines
4 large tomatoes (or you can use a 14 oz (400 g) tin of Italian tomatoes well drained)
2 red or green peppers
2 cloves garlic, crushed
1 teaspoon dried basil
4 tablespoons olive oil
Salt and freshly-milled black pepper

This can be a most attractive dish—but not if it ends up mushy. So to avoid this, make sure you don't cut up the vegetables too small (they must retain their individuality), and also make sure you get rid of the excess moisture in the courgettes and aubergines by draining them at the start.

Begin, then, by wiping the aubergines and cutting them into 1 inch (2·5 cm) slices, then cut each slice in half; the courgettes should be wiped as well and cut into 1 inch (2·5 cm) slices. Now put the whole lot into a colander, sprinkle generously with salt, press them down with a suitably-sized plate and put weights (or other heavy objects) on top of the plate. Let them stand for about 1 hour—the salt will draw out any bitterness along with excess moisture.

Meanwhile chop up the onion roughly, deseed and core the peppers and chop these up too. Skin the tomatoes (plunging them into boiling water for a couple of minutes is the best way to loosen the skins), then quarter them and take out the seeds.

To cook the ratatouille: fry the onions and garlic in the oil gently in a large saucepan for a good 10 minutes, then add the peppers. Dry the pieces of courgette and aubergine in kitchen paper, then add them to the saucepan. Next add the basil and a seasoning of salt and pepper, stir once really well, then simmer very gently (covered) for 30 minutes. After that time add the tomato flesh (roughly chopped), taste to check the seasoning and cook for a further 15 minutes with the lid off.

Thick onion tart

(serves 4–6 people)

The secret of this tart, with its wholewheat cheese pastry, is to cook the onions until they almost caramelise so they form a lovely thick, brown layer over the base.

For the pastry:
2 oz self-raising flour (50 g)
2 oz wholewheat flour (50 g)
A pinch of salt
½ teaspoon mustard powder
2 oz margarine (50 g)
1½ oz grated Cheddar cheese (40 g)

For the filling:
1½ lb onions chopped fairly small (700 g)
2 tablespoons butter
2 eggs
4 fl oz milk (110 ml)
1 tablespoon grated Cheddar cheese
Salt and freshly-milled black pepper

Pre-heat the oven, and a baking sheet,
to gas mark 4, 350°F (180°C)

An 8 inch (20 cm) fluted flan tin, greased.

First make the pastry by sifting the flours, salt and mustard powder
into a mixing bowl, then rubbing in the margarine until the mixture
becomes crumbly. Then stir in the grated cheese, and add enough
cold water to make a dough that leaves the bowl clean. Wrap the
dough in a polythene bag and leave to rest in the fridge for half an
hour. Meanwhile you can be preparing the filling.

Melt the butter in a thick-based saucepan, then add the chopped
onions, stir to get them well coated in the butter, and cook them
(uncovered) over a medium heat for about half an hour until they
have reduced and turned a deep brown. Give them a stir from time
to time to prevent them catching on the bottom of the pan and, if at
the end of the time they haven't turned almost mahogany-brown,
turn the heat up and cook for a further 10 minutes.

Then roll out the pastry to line the flan tin, prick the base with a
fork, place it on the pre-heated baking sheet, and bake in the centre
of the oven for 15 minutes. After that remove from the oven and
brush the inside of the pastry case with a little beaten egg (from the
filling), and return to the oven for another 5 minutes.

Then spread the onions all over the base of the flan, beat the eggs
together with the milk and some seasoning, and pour as much of this
mixture over the onions as possible (depending on how much the
onions have reduced, there may be a tiny spot left over—though
probably not). Finally sprinkle the cheese over the top, return the
flan to the oven and bake for 30 minutes till the filling is puffy and
golden-brown.

**Many of the recipes in this book
are suitable for vegetarians, but
see especially:**
A risotto for spring
Brown rice, lentil and mushroom salad
Buckwheat and vegetable pie
Courgette and cheese quiche

Egg and lentil curry
Hummus bi tahina
Italian bean and pasta soup
Minestrone soup with rice
Mushroom and onion quiche
Vegetarian shepherd's pie

Pulses

Including recipes for:
Aduki bean and brown rice salad
Thick pea soup
Chilli con carne
Italian bean and pasta soup
Lentil, bean and anchovy salad
Cassoulet
Chilladas
Vegetarian shepherd's pie
Thick bean and bacon soup
Red bean salad
Hummus bi tahina
Spiced lamb with chick peas
Pease pudding

With our food there seems to be an inexorable process at work: yesterday's poor-man's diet is today's luxury. It's hard to believe you could once buy oysters, fifty of them, for a shilling; or that the fish-porters at Billingsgate once went on strike because they were getting too much salmon for lunch! The plain fact is, of course, that over the past century our consumption has far outstripped our resources, except in one rather neglected area—pulses (that is to say, the family of beans, peas and lentils). Pulses for thousands of years have been the staple diet of poor countries all over the world, from China to Mexico.

Sadly, that is still their image. It must be rather humiliating to be a bean: a 'bean-feast' was a meal judged fit only for workmen, and if you 'hadn't got a bean' you really had not got anything at all. Yet ancient peoples were far more respectful than we are: some appointed a god in charge of beans, and others never buried their dead without a supply of beans to take them into the other world.

Doubtless it will be pointed out that we still consume beans in Britain in absolutely vast quantities. I recall a cartoon at the time when de Gaulle was objecting to this country joining the Common Market: it showed the General recoiling from a report on how many million tons of baked beans the British consumed in a year. *Mon Dieu!* was his reaction. As well it might have been, when you think that out of the great range of beans available (kidney, haricot, butter, lima, broad . . . and so on) in this country beans means just one bland, processed variety.

Nutritional value for money

I believe that our attitudes to pulses are gradually changing, in fact. There is no doubt about their nutritional value: according to a recent report by the Consumers Association they took four of the top ten places in the list of vegetable proteins—with dried peas, for instance, you get over 8 g of protein for 1p. (Vegetable proteins, are, as already mentioned, called 'second-class proteins' because they lack the important amino-acids that are found in meat, fish, dairy foods, etc.; but this is not to undermine their value—the missing amino-acids are found in flour or rice or pasta, so a plateful of beans-on-toast will provide you with the same amount of protein as beefsteak.) Soya beans are the most nutritious of all the pulses. Their yield, in the countries where they're grown, is so enormous compared with the acreage involved that ecologically the soya bean seems set to figure very largely in the future of this small planet with its ever-growing population. There cannot be much argument about the need to create a new balance in our present-day way of eating. The meat-based diet we have been used to is rapidly disappearing out of reach of many people's pockets: the need to 'stretch' the meat we can afford is becoming an economic necessity. The food technologists' answer to this problem has been to come up with the meat-substitutes, textured vegetable proteins (TVP) masquerading as mince.

I find this quite extraordinary—pretending we've got meat when we haven't. The commercial giants responsible for its manufacture claim it is to extend meat rather than replace it, but then so will beans, peas and the rest of the pulses on their own, without the cost of refining and disguising them, and far more pleasantly. On the Continent, where they have always been less meat-conscious, pulses have long been used with imagination to extend a meat-ration. They are *not* dull or unattractive, and I hope the recipes here will prove my point.

Varieties of pulses

First let us run through the commoner types of pulse—there are so many varieties it would be tedious to include them all. People who live alongside immigrant communities will doubtless find some pulses not mentioned here, but those described below can be found on some supermarket shelves or in specialised food shops.

Butter beans These are large, flat beans, cream in colour. Boiled on their own (as I remember them at school) they do tend to be dull: but they make a good thick soup, and are useful if haricot beans are unavailable as they respond well to a well-flavoured vinaigrette dressing with lots of chopped shallots and parsley strewn over.

Haricot beans There are two main types of haricot bean: the long, thin, shiny-ivory one which the Italians call *fagioli*. These are delicious in salads, stews, and Tuscan bean and pasta soup; they are also the kind used in France, cooked in the Breton way and served with mutton and lamb. The other type of haricot is the small round one of tinned baked bean fame. In my opinion they are inferior to, and lack the flavour of, their handsomer cousins.

Red kidney beans Not surprisingly, these shiny-polished beans are both red and kidney-shaped. They have a delicious flavour, a must for *Chilli con carne* (page 346). They make a good salad and will adapt themselves to any recipe for bean soup. Remember, they must always be boiled for at least 10 minutes.

Soya beans Smallish, round, and a pale yellow/cream colour. They need careful soaking and long cooking, and are rather mealy-textured when cooked. For me their flavour and texture are not up to that of white haricots.

Aduki beans These are tiny, red-brown beans with a little white thread down one side. Because of their size they make perfect partners to brown rice, to give a good protein balance (see recipe page 344).

Chick peas Light brown, nutty-looking beans, which need careful soaking (definitely overnight) and as much as 3 hours' cooking. But they are worth it in my opinion with their lovely nutty flavour. They can be made into cutlets, soups, salads, or puréed with oil and lemon to a paste to make what the Greeks call *Hummus* (page 354).

Split peas These halved dried peas can be deep green or golden-yellow. I think the green ones are superior in flavour, but both are suitable for thick, warming pea soups, or for purées or cutlets.

Whole died peas The ones used to make 'mushy peas'. They are delicious, with more character than tinned or frozen peas. Especially good with pork or boiled bacon, or made into the traditional *Pease pudding* (page 356).

Lentils There are in fact over sixty varieties of lentil. But as far as whole lentils are concerned there are three main types that concern us. Most popular are the green-brown variety (as I call them since they're usually a mixture of both colours) that look like little pills. I love their flavour, and if I never had any more meat I'd be content with a plentiful supply of these around. There is a smaller version, sometimes called Chinese lentils, which are more red-brown and also rarer and more expensive. The French *lentils du pays* are slate-grey and, if you can find them, have a very superior flavour.

Split lentils These are literally filleted lentils, with the skins removed and split naturally into two halves. They cook to a mush very quickly and are suitable for thick purées and soups.

Other varieties of pulses are much rarer over here, though they play an important part in the cooking of other countries. The white, flat *Lima beans* are used in America for soups and salads, and *black-eyed beans* (cream with a 'black eye') are served with ham. In the Caribbean *black beans* are served spiced or in a sauce as a side-dish.

as are *Egyptian beans* (round and brown) in the Middle East. The beautiful pale-green *flageolets* in France are a high-class variation of the haricot, and quite delicious.

Buying and storing pulses

Although British farmers are experimenting with growing different types of pulse, most of them are imported at the moment. The vegetables are harvested annually and dried in the autumn, so the year's crop usually begins to reach us around November. Obviously one of the big advantages of dried vegetable pulses is that they do store easily and—provided suitable soaking time is taken into consideration—can be used fairly spontaneously.

However, it is wrong to think that, for cooking, pulses keep indefinitely. After about a year they start to harden to such an extent that sometimes no amount of cooking will soften them. Therefore it is important to buy them from somewhere reliable (and if you do get landed with a batch that is more ancient than it should be, take them back and complain). Also if your memory is as bad as mine, place a little sticker on the storage jar—I use large glass ones—to remind you when you actually purchased the contents. I've found that a year or even 18 months can slip by almost unnoticed in the larder.

Soaking

Most, though not all, dried vegetables have to be soaked to replace the moisture lost in the drying process. Overnight soaking may seem a long time: in fact I once mentioned it on a radio programme, and one listener wrote insisting that beans should never be soaked that long or they would be likely to ferment. (Just for the record—I checked with Queen Elizabeth College of Nutrition, who confirmed that they would have to soak under normal conditions for 36–48 hours before fermentation.)

So, if it's convenient, overnight soaking is perfectly all right except for chick peas, soya beans and red and white kidney beans. For these, you will need to cover with cold water, bring to the boil, boil for 10 minutes, then leave to soak for up to 2 hours depending on the type of bean. You usually need about 4 pints (2·25 l) of soaking water for every ½ lb (225 g) of beans.

Cooking

Most pulses except split peas and lentils need rather long cooking: 1½–3 hours according to variety. Perhaps the most important rule is *not* to add any salt until the end of the cooking, which is quite logical really: salt draws out moisture (to extract moisture from vegetables like courgettes you sprinkle salt on them), so even a small amount of salt in the soaking or cooking water will simply retard the process. Adding salt at the end makes them taste just as good, I find, but you should taste carefully to add just the right quantity. Pressure-cooking can cut down the cooking times for pulses drastically, especially for soups. However, since pressure-cooking requires a certain amount of unthickened liquid, it is not always suitable for all recipes. And pressure-cookers themselves vary, making it impossible to provide general guidelines: to cook pulses in them, therefore, consult the manufacturers' booklets, which should also provide information on soaking times.

Digesting pulses

Dried vegetables in the past have acquired a somewhat bad reputation, and are said to cause flatulence. This shouldn't be the case if the beans are properly soaked and carefully cooked. There is some evidence that throwing away the soaking water and using fresh for cooking helps to eliminate the problem. So if you suffer from bean side-effects I suggest you do just that.

Aduki bean and brown rice salad

(serves 6 people)

Aduki beans go very well with brown rice, especially in a salad.

1 mugful brown rice
2 mugs boiling water
4 oz aduki beans (110 g), soaked overnight
1 large green pepper, deseeded and chopped
2 stalks celery, finely chopped
½ cucumber, diced—leave the peel on
6 spring onions, finely chopped—including the green parts
Salt

For the dressing:
4 fl oz olive oil (110 ml)
1 tablespoon wine vinegar
1 fat clove garlic, crushed
1 teaspoon mustard powder
1 teaspoon salt

| 2 tablespoons finely-chopped parsley |
| 2 tablespoons finely-chopped celery leaves |
| Freshly-milled black pepper |

First put the beans in a saucepan together with the water in which they were soaked (no need to add salt), bring to the boil and cook for 45 minutes to 1 hour or until the beans are tender.

Meantime, place the rice with some salt in another saucepan, and add the boiling water. Bring to the boil, cover and simmer very gently for about 40 minutes or until the rice is tender and all the water absorbed.

Next, put all the ingredients for the dressing in a salad bowl and whisk together. Then while the cooked rice and the beans (drained) are still warm, empty them into the salad bowl and mix everything together lightly with a fork. Leave the salad till cold, then add the chopped vegetables, mixing them in lightly. Taste, and season again if it needs it. Serve sprinkled with chopped parsley and celery leaves.

Thick pea soup

(serves 6 people)

This needs some crisp fried croûtons of bread to sprinkle over just before serving.

| 3½ pints basic stock (2 litres) |
| ¾ lb split peas (yellow or green) (350 g) |
| 2 oz butter (50 g) |
| 4 thick rashers bacon, diced |
| 1 medium onion, roughly chopped |
| 1 celery stalk, chopped |
| 1 large carrot, sliced |
| A little extra stock, if needed |
| Salt and freshly-milled black pepper |

First strain off 3½ pints (2 litres) basic stock into a large saucepan then bring just up to simmering point, add the split peas, cover and simmer very gently for about 30 minutes (there is no need to soak the split peas first).

Meanwhile, heat 1 oz (25 g) butter in another saucepan and add the prepared vegetables and the bacon; cook them over a medium heat until softened and nicely golden—this will take about 15 minutes.

Add the softened vegetables to the stock and split peas, season lightly with salt and freshly-milled black pepper, then cover and simmer very gently for a further 40–50 minutes.

When the soup is ready, either press the whole lot through a sieve or liquidise in an electric blender. Now return it to the saucepan, taste to check the seasoning, and add a little more stock if it seems to need thinning a bit.

Before serving, melt the remaining butter into it.

Chilli con carne

(serves 4 people)

This is very often made with minced beef, but I think it's far nicer made with chuck steak cut into very small pieces. It's medium hot as it is, so if you like things hotter or milder you can adjust the quantity of chilli, but this dish should be hot and spicy, and in my opinion cutting down the spiciness simply reduces it to an ordinary stew. So go carefully with the chilli by all means, but don't relegate it out of existence.

1 lb chuck steak (450 g), cut into very small pieces
2 medium onions, chopped
1 fat clove garlic, crushed
1 pint hot stock (570 ml)
2 heaped tablespoons tomato purée
Salt
1 rounded tablespoon flour
½ lb red kidney beans (available from wholefood shops) (225 g)
1 large green pepper, deseeded and chopped
1 level teaspoon crushed dried chilli or chilli powder
Beef dripping or oil

First of all start with the beans. Cover them with cold water, bring them to boiling point and boil for 10 minutes. Then turn the heat out and let them soak for an hour. Towards the end of the soaking time, pre-heat the oven to gas mark 2, 300°F (150°C).

Now in a flameproof casserole melt about a tablespoon of beef dripping and gently cook the onion and garlic in it for about 6 minutes. Then turn the heat up, add the beef and brown it well, stirring it around a bit.

Next sprinkle in the flour, stir it in to soak up the juices, then combine the tomato purée with the hot stock and add it gradually to the meat and onion.

Now add the chilli, drain the red beans thoroughly, add them, and bring to simmering point. Put a lid on, then transfer the casserole to the oven and cook for about 1½ hours. When the time's up remove the lid, stir in the chopped pepper, cover again and cook a further 30 minutes. Add salt as necessary before serving.

Italian bean and pasta soup

(serves 4–6 people)

This is a beautiful thick Tuscan peasant soup hardly needing anything more to follow it.

½ lb white haricot beans (225 g)
¼ lb small-cut macaroni (110 g)
2½ tablespoons tomato purée
1 teaspoon dried basil
1 large onion, chopped small
2 cloves garlic, crushed
2 oz grated Parmesan cheese (50 g)
2 tablespoons olive oil
Salt and freshly-milled black pepper

Place the beans in a saucepan, then add 3 pints (1·75 litres) cold water to them, bring them to the boil, boil for 1 minute, then turn the heat out and let them soak for 2 hours.

Now gently fry the onions in olive oil together with the garlic for about 10 minutes. Then add the tomato purée and basil, stir for a minute, and pour in the beans and the water they were soaking in. Now bring the soup up to simmering point, cover and simmer gently for about an hour. When the time's up season with salt and pepper, then put half the soup either through a sieve or blend in a liquidiser. Return the puréed half to the pan, bring to simmering point, then add the macaroni and simmer for a further 10–12 minutes, stirring from time to time. Serve the soup with lots of freshly-grated Parmesan cheese to sprinkle over.

Lentil, bean and anchovy salad

(serves 4 people)

This is a really delicious salad and substantial enough to serve as a main course for lunch.

8 oz whole lentils (brown) (225 g)
8 oz white haricot beans (225 g)
Salt and freshly-milled black pepper

For the dressing:
8 tablespoons oil
1 tablespoon wine vinegar
1 tablespoon lemon juice
1 small onion, peeled and finely chopped
1 clove garlic, crushed
1 heaped teaspoon mustard
4 tablespoons finely-chopped fresh parsley
2 oz (50 g) tin anchovy fillets

To garnish:
2 hard-boiled eggs, chopped
1 oz small black olives (25 g)
A few crisp lettuce leaves

Prepare the beans in advance by putting them in a saucepan and covering with cold water. Bring to boiling point and boil for 2–3 minutes, then remove from the heat and let the beans soak for about an hour. After that boil them again for about another hour until *just* soft.

About half an hour before the beans are ready pick over the lentils (there's no need to soak them); wash them and boil in plenty of water until *just* soft.

Meanwhile mix together in a bowl all the ingredients for the dressing and add the oil from the tin of anchovies. Chop the anchovies and put on one side.

When the beans and lentils are cooked, drain them, tip them into a bowl and, while they're still warm, pour in the dressing. Mix well so that they are well coated and leave to cool.

Before serving, taste and season the salad well with salt and freshly-milled black pepper, then place some crisp lettuce leaves on 4 plates and arrange the mixture on top. Finally garnish with the chopped hard-boiled eggs, chopped anchovies and olives.

Cassoulet

(serves 6 people)

Although this was originally a French peasant dish, I think it's particularly good for entertaining in winter because it's all done in advance and doesn't mind waiting in the oven if you want to eat a bit later than planned.

¾ lb white haricot beans (350 g)
½ shoulder of lamb—the inside half, not the leg half, and ask the butcher to take out the bone for you
1 lb belly of pork (450 g), boned and cut into strips
½ lb streaky bacon in one piece (225 g)
½ lb garlic sausage in one piece (225 g)
4 juniper berries
2 medium onions, chopped
A bayleaf
2 cloves garlic
A sprig of thyme
A small sprig of rosemary
A few parsley stalks
5 oz fresh white breadcrumbs (150 g)
Salt and freshly-milled black pepper

It's not necessary to soak beans overnight, but wash them well in about two changes of water before placing them in a saucepan with about 3 pints (1·75 litres) of cold water. Bring to simmering point and after about 2 minutes put aside and leave for an hour for the beans to soak in the liquid.

Meanwhile prepare the other ingredients by first of all trimming any really excess fat off the lamb and cutting the meat into very large chunks. Then, using a sharp knife, pare the rind as thinly as possible from both the bacon and the pork, and chop the rinds into very small pieces.

Leave the pork slices whole, but chop the bacon into 6 chunks, also peel and chop the garlic sausage into largish pieces. Now tie in a little bunch the thyme, rosemary, parsley stalks and bayleaf, then skin and crush the cloves of garlic; also crush the juniper berries using either a pestle and mortar or the back of a tablespoon.

When the beans have finished soaking drain them in a colander, throw away the water, then put them in a large saucepan together with the bacon, chopped bacon and pork rinds, garlic sausage, onions, garlic, juniper, bunch of herbs and some freshly-milled black pepper, but no salt as there will be some in the bacon. Cover with about 2¹/₂ pints (1·5 litres) cold water, bring to simmering point and simmer gently for 1¹/₂ hours.

Halfway through the cooking time pre-heat the oven to gas mark 3, 325°F (170°C), and roast the lamb and pork for 45 minutes.

When the meat is cooked the bean mixture will also be ready, so empty the contents of the saucepan into a sieve or colander placed over a bowl, let it drain, reserve the liquid and remove the herbs. Then in a buttered 5 pint (3 litre) earthenware casserole arrange half the bean mixture over the base, placing the pieces of lamb and pork on top. Season with salt and freshly-milled black pepper, then add the rest of the bean mixture. Now add to the casserole ³/₄ pint (425 ml) of the bean cooking liquid, cover the surface entirely with the breadcrumbs and cook in the oven—uncovered—for 1¹/₂ hours.

Chilladas

(serves 8 people)

These lightly-spiced lentil cakes flavoured with green peppers really are just as good as having meat.

1 lb green or brown whole lentils (450 g)
1¹/₂ pints hot water (845 ml)
4 oz butter (or vegetable margarine) (110 g)
2 onions, peeled and finely chopped
2 small green peppers (or 1 large), deseeded and chopped small
2 carrots, scraped and finely chopped
1 teaspoon mixed herbs
¹/₂ teaspoon powdered mace
1 teaspoon cayenne pepper
4 teaspoons tomato purée
2 cloves garlic, crushed
Salt and freshly-milled black pepper

For the coating:
Dry fine breadcrumbs
1 egg, beaten
Groundnut oil for shallow frying

Wash the lentils and place them in a saucepan with 1½ pints (845 ml) of hot water. Let them come to the boil, then cover and simmer very gently for about an hour or until all the liquid has been absorbed and the lentils are mushy. Towards the end of their cooking time, heat the butter in a frying-pan and soften the onion, garlic and carrot in it for 5 minutes, then add the chopped peppers and cook for a further 5–10 minutes.

Next, season the lentils and tip them into a bowl to mash them to a pulp with a fork—though not too smooth. Now mix in the softened vegetables together with the cayenne, mace, herbs and tomato purée—then divide the mixture and shape it into 24 small rounds. To cook them, dip them first into beaten egg, then into the bread-crumbs, and shallow-fry them in about ¼ inch (½ cm) of groundnut oil till golden on both sides. Drain on kitchen paper, and serve with a home-made tomato sauce (see page 363).

Vegetarian shepherd's pie

(serves 4 people)

If you're not a vegetarian shepherd don't worry, I still think you'll find this recipe quite delicious and far better than many of the minced meat versions.

6 oz whole brown/green lentils (175 g)
4 oz split peas—green or yellow (110 g)
1 pint hot water (570 ml)
1 medium onion, peeled and chopped
½ green pepper, chopped
2 carrots, chopped
2 sticks celery, chopped
1 clove garlic, crushed
½ teaspoon dried mixed herbs
2 pinches ground mace
¼ teaspoon cayenne pepper
Butter or margarine

For the topping:
½ lb tomatoes (225 g), peeled and sliced
1½ lb cooked potatoes (700 g)
3 oz Cheddar cheese (75 g), grated
1 small onion, chopped
2 oz butter or margarine (50 g)

2 tablespoons top of the milk
Salt and freshly-milled black pepper

Begin by washing the lentils and split peas, then put them in a saucepan with the hot water and simmer gently, covered, for approximately 45–60 minutes or until the peas and lentils have absorbed the water and are soft. Pre-heat the oven to gas mark 5, 375°F (190°C).

Meantime, melt some butter in a frying-pan, add the celery, onion, carrots and chopped pepper, and cook gently until softened, then add these to the cooked lentil mixture after mashing it a little first. Add the seasonings and salt and pepper to taste, then spoon the mixture into a large pie-dish (3 pint or 1·75 litre) and arrange the sliced tomatoes on top.

Next, prepare the topping by softening the onion in butter in a small pan, then mash the potatoes, add the cooked onion, butter, top of the milk and grated cheese, and mix thoroughly. Season well, then spread on top of the ingredients in the pie dish. Bake for about 20 minutes or until the top is lightly browned. Home-made tomato sauce (page 363) is a delicious accompaniment.

Thick bean and bacon soup

(serves 6 people)

8 oz dried butter beans (225 g)
2 pints water (1 litre)
1 bayleaf
4 oz streaky bacon (or offcuts) (110 g)
2 tablespoons oil
1 oz butter (25 g)
1 onion, finely chopped
1 leek, cleaned and finely chopped
1 large clove garlic, crushed
2 smallish stalks celery, finely chopped
About ¼ pint milk (150 ml)
2 tablespoons chopped parsley
Salt and freshly-milled black pepper

First put the butter beans and water in a saucepan and bring them to the boil, then boil for a minute, cover and leave on one side for about an hour. Now add the bayleaf and any bacon rinds you may have to the pan, bring to the boil again, cover and simmer for 45 minutes (removing the bayleaf and rinds at the end).

Meanwhile heat the butter and oil in a large saucepan, add the chopped vegetables, then chop up the bacon small and add that too. Stir to coat everything with butter and oil, and cook over a low heat for about 10 minutes.

Now tip the cooked beans and their cooking liquor into the pan containing the bacon and vegetables, add the garlic, cover and continue simmering for a further 20 minutes or until the beans and vegetables are soft. Then mash them against the sides of the pan with a large fork, and thin down the soup with milk. Reheat, add the chopped parsley, taste to check the seasoning and serve.

Red bean salad

(serves 4 people)

A red bean salad always looks so good, as the beans are such a lovely colour, and it's always an attractive one to put in amongst other salads to provide a contrast.

12 oz dried red kidney beans (350 g)

For the vinaigrette dressing:
1 tablespoon wine vinegar
1 teaspoon mustard
1 teaspoon salt
2 cloves garlic, crushed
6 tablespoons olive oil
Freshly-milled black pepper

To finish off:
1 green pepper, deseeded and finely chopped
1 medium onion, finely chopped
2 drops tabasco sauce

First rinse the beans with cold water and then place them in a saucepan. Cover with plenty of water, bring up to the boil for 1 minute, then leave them for 2 hours.

Next pour off the water and cover with fresh cold water. Bring them up to the boil and boil gently for about $1^{1}/_{2}$–2 hours or until the beans are tender.

Meanwhile prepare the vinaigrette by combining all the ingredients in a bowl. Then, as soon as the beans are tender, drain them and toss them in the vinaigrette while they are still warm. Leave them to cool before adding the chopped onion, green pepper and tabasco.

If possible leave the salad to marinade for several hours before serving on crisp lettuce leaves.

Hummus bi tahina

(serves 6 people)

If you want to make the proper authentic version of this you'll need to hunt out some tahina paste, which is available at specialist food shops and health food shops.

4 oz chick peas (110 g)
Juice of 2 lemons
¼ pint tahina paste (150 ml)
2 fat cloves garlic
4 tablespoons olive oil
Cayenne pepper
Chopped parsley
Olive oil
Salt

To begin with put the chick peas in a saucepan and cover them well with boiling water, then put on one side to soak for 2 hours.

Next bring them to the boil, cover and simmer gently for approximately 1½–2 hours until the chick peas are tender. Then drain them—reserve the cooking liquid—and put the chick peas into a blender together with the lemon juice, garlic, olive oil and ¼ pint (150 ml) of the cooking liquid. Switch on and blend, adding the tahina paste to the mixture as the blades revolve. (It will probably be necessary to stop the blender every now and then to push the mixture down into the goblet.) The consistency should be something like a mayonnaise and, if you think it's too thick, add a little more of the cooking liquid. Taste and season with salt and cayenne pepper.

Place in a serving bowl and garnish with a thin layer of olive oil, some chopped parsley and a pinch or two of cayenne pepper. Have plenty of fresh, hot, crusty bread as an accompaniment.

Spiced lamb with chick peas

(serves 4–6 people)

If you can't get fresh chillies or root ginger for this recipe, you can use 1 level teaspoon of chilli powder and 2 level teaspoons of ground ginger instead.

6 oz chick peas (175 g)
2 lb boned shoulder of lamb (900 g)
4 tablespoons groundnut oil
1 aubergine (about ¾ lb, i.e. 350 g), unpeeled and cut into small chunks
1 teaspoon powdered turmeric
1 teaspoon garam masala
1 lb tomatoes, peeled and thickly sliced (450 g)
3 fresh chillies, halved, deseeded and finely sliced
2 cloves garlic, crushed
2 tablespoons finely-chopped mint
1 tablespoon finely-chopped root ginger
¼ pint natural yoghurt (150 ml)
1 Spanish onion, thinly sliced

First of all place the chick peas in a saucepan, cover with 2 pints (about 1 litre) boiling water, put a lid on and leave on one side for 3 hours. Then bring to the boil, and boil, covered, for approximately 1 hour or until the peas are really tender, and put them on one side once again.

Next cut the meat into 1 inch (2 cm) cubes, trimming off excess fat. Now heat the oil in a thick-based saucepan, add the cubes of meat (a small quantity at a time) and fry over a high heat, removing the meat to a plate, using a draining spoon, when nicely browned.

Then add the onion and aubergine to the pan, stirring them around in the fat, and fry until coloured before adding the turmeric and garam masala. Cook for another minute, then add the tomatoes, chillies, garlic, ginger and mint. Drain the chick peas, reserving the liquid, then return the meat to the pan together with the chick peas and about ³/₄ pint (425 ml) of their cooking liquor.

Bring up to simmering point, cover and cook very gently for 30 minutes, then take off the lid and continue cooking for approximately three-quarters of an hour or until the meat is really tender and the sauce thick. Lastly stir in the yoghurt and, when all is well heated through, serve with *Spiced pilau rice* (page 305).

Pease pudding
(serves 6–8 people)

A real old-fashioned pease pudding is sometimes made in a cloth but more conveniently, I think, in a basin like this:

1 lb whole dried peas (soaked overnight) (450 g)
Generous pinch of thyme
1 bayleaf
1 small onion, quartered
2 oz butter (50 g)
1 large egg, beaten
Salt and freshly-milled black pepper

Put the peas, herbs and quartered onion together in a saucepan and cover with plenty of cold water. Bring to the boil, cover and boil gently for 2 hours or until the peas are tender (a sign that they are ready is that they start splitting their skins). Then drain the peas in a colander and discard the bayleaf—the onion can stay in.

Now mash the peas to a pulp. Beat in the butter and egg and, when the butter has melted, taste and season with salt and freshly-milled black pepper. Pack the pea purée into a well-buttered 2–2½ pint (1·25–1·5 litre) pudding basin. Put a sheet of greased foil over the top and secure with string. Then steam the pudding over boiling water for 1 hour. Uncover and turn it out onto a warmed plate. Cut in wedges like a steamed pudding to serve.

Pease pudding can be served with boiled bacon or boiled beef and any leftovers can be fried in butter the next day.

See also:
Brown rice, lentil and mushroom salad
Chick pea salad
Haricot bean and salami salad

Non-meat loaf
Oxtail with haricot beans
Smoked bacon and lentil soup
White bean and tuna fish salad

Pasta and pancakes

Including recipes for:
Fresh tomato sauce
Tomato chilli sauce
Ragù Bolognese
Spaghetti alla carbonara
Spaghetti with anchovies, mushrooms and olives
Lasagne al forno
Baked meat and macaroni pie
Macaroni with leeks and bacon
Wholewheat macaroni cheese
Basic pancakes
Crêpes Suzette
Pancake cannelloni
Spinach-stuffed pancakes with cheese sauce
Cheese soufflé pancakes
Apple and cinnamon crêpes

Pasta

If I were asked to choose between a meal in a multi-starred French restaurant or with an Italian family at home, without hesitation I'd choose the latter. Marcella Hazan, in one of my favourite Italian cookbooks, describes the experience beautifully. The whole country, she says, shuts down at midday for this two-hour event and 'there probably has been no influence, not even religion, so effective in creating a rich family life, in maintaining a civilised link between the generations, as this daily sharing of a common joy'.

She says so much more, and so could I, about the Italian way of eating. But let me just commend its simplicity: it is never lavish, vulgar or pretentious. The Italians are not a nation who rely heavily on freezers or canned foods, but manage on very little meat and plenty of seasonal vegetables and fruit. Butter is something of a luxury—in my experience served with bread only at breakfast—and in passing it's interesting to note that, despite their rather obese image, the Italians have one of the lowest incidences of heart disease in the world: so perhaps their use of olive oil in place of butter and their enthusiasm for lots of fresh fruit and salads shows that 'preventative' eating need not be as dull as is sometimes suggested.

However this part of the chapter is concerned with just one item that the Italians have made famous, namely pasta, which is one thing that I think should be a permanent resident in any larder or storecupboard. The marvellous thing about pasta is that, with a little imagination, this one basic ingredient can be made into a whole range of different dishes.

What is pasta?

When I was a child, just after the war, spaghetti was something that came out of a tin in a bright orange sauce, and was usually served on toast, sometimes with a poached egg on top! Later on it began to appear in the shops in its natural state, though in quite unmanageable packets, as I recall, at least a yard long. In those days it was dismissed, at any rate by the elderly, as 'foreign', but nowadays foreign holidays and a steady flow of cookbooks have helped to establish it on supermarket shelves, in quite a number of its infinite varieties.

Pasta is simply the Italian word for dough, and in particular a dough made from durum (or hard) wheat. When hard wheat is first ground it produces not flour, but semolina, and this is used—with hard wheat flour and water—to produce pasta. The dough is then moulded or stamped into the appropriate shape by machine and (unless it is to be sold immediately as fresh pasta) it is then dried. Once it was dried in the back gardens of Naples by the Mediterranean breezes, but now technology has reproduced this wonder of nature.

Egg pasta Most commercial pastas are purely wheat-and-water but sometimes you come across egg pastas, in which eggs have been added to the basic dough (as they are in home-made pasta). Egg pasta is rich, more filling and quite delicious—and if the packet is printed in Italian it will be described as *pasta all'uovo*.

Green pasta (pasta verde) is just pasta into which spinach has been worked at the dough-making stage. This is done, I suspect, more for the sake of colour than for flavour, but it does look most attractive in dishes like lasagne.

Wholewheat pasta It's hard to imagine that we, the British, actually export pasta to Italy, but we do! The Italians are now buying wholewheat pasta that's made here. I was a bit hesitant about it at first, but I was wrong to think that because of its pale brown colour it would taste very different from ordinary pasta. It doesn't, and now I use it quite often.

Home-made pasta If you're within easy reach of London's Soho, or anywhere else where there is an Italian community, you might be lucky enough to buy home-made fresh pasta. It's certainly worth seeking out as it is nicer than the dried sort. Failing that, you could make it at home yourself, but be warned—it is very hard work kneading pasta, and then you are faced with a lump of very resilient, elastic dough which needs to be rolled and stretched out to a transparent thinness! It can be difficult, too, to obtain the correct ingredients (although a strong flour will do). If you want to get really serious about home-made pasta you could, of course, invest in a pasta machine which costs upwards of £30. It's a sort of mangle which can be adjusted to different pasta shapes, and it squeezes and presses the pasta out thinly, which does eliminate a lot of the hard work. However if, like me, you're not an absolute perfectionist, a good quality packaged pasta will probably suit you well enough.

Pasta shapes
There are literally hundreds of different pasta shapes, which may seem a bit daunting. But it needn't be: for one thing, there is no

definitive list—manufacturers can and do add further shapes from time to time. And in fact there are only five basic types:

(1) First there are the tiny decorative shapes that go into soups *(pasta in brodo)* and sometimes into puddings: they can be stars, flowers, letters of the alphabet, little animals . . . the list is endless.

(2) Then there are the solid spaghetti-type pastas, long and thin. *Spaghetti* itself is cylindrical and usually about 10 inches (25·5 cm) long; it has a thinner cousin, called *spaghettini*. In this group I would also include the long, noodle varieties—*tagliatelle* which is flat rather than cylindrical, enriched with eggs, and dried in bunches rather than lengths. It too has a thinner cousin, *linguine*.

(3) Next are what I'd call the *macaroni* group or tubular pastas. Some are cut short or curled slightly: some have pointed ends *(penne)*, some are ribbed *(rigatoni)*.

(4) The fancy shapes—bows, shells, twists, wheels, frills and the rest of them—are intriguing to look at but all taste the same in the end. Like the pastas in groups (2) and (3) above, these are usually served with a sauce.

(5) Finally there are the pastas which are stuffed or can be bought ready-stuffed. The very large sheets of *lasagne*, and big tubular *cannelloni*, are both meant to be stuffed and baked. Ready-stuffed pasta are usually only available at Italian shops—*ravioli* are little square packages with a stuffing inside: *tortellini* are similar but curled in shape.

This list is strictly a basic grouping of variations. My own larder collections consists of spaghetti, tagliatelle, a short-cut macaroni for soups, and a standard macaroni. I find I sometimes buy odd shapes but I can't see any particular advantage in them. On the contrary, the cooking time can be rather uncertain if the shape is thick—and beware of pasta 'shells' in which the boiling water can become trapped, only to escape at the table when it's too late!

Cooking pasta

First let's discuss what pasta *should* be like when cooked. The now-familiar Italian words *al dente* appear frequently on packets and in many recipes to describe the approved texture of cooked pasta. Translated literally they mean 'to the teeth' which clearly suggests that pasta must have some bite to it.

If it's over-cooked all the guts will have gone out of it, and you'll only have a soggy, sticky mass. As an experienced pasta consumer I have found that, over the years, I have come to cook pasta in less and less time, and I now give ordinary supermarket spaghetti only 8 minutes' boiling. In the end there's only one way for you to tell, and that's to bite a bit and see if it's to your liking. I find that macaroni, spaghetti and lasagne take 8–10 minutes to cook, but if you're using a thick variety it might need a couple of minutes more. These suggested timings are for dried (packet) pasta. Fresh or home-made pasta is quicker to cook.

How much pasta?
Pasta isn't quite as fattening as some people imagine. Of course if it is baked with a rich ragù and covered in a melted cheese sauce, then it can be extremely high in calories; but served with a fresh tomato sauce (or with any sauce which only calls for 2 tablespoons of olive oil for four people) it can be much lower in calories than many meat dishes.

If you are serving a layered pasta dish or pasta that is stuffed and baked, you'll only need quite a small quantity of pasta. If you are serving spaghetti or any other type of pasta just with a sauce, then you'll need more, and I recommend 8–10 oz (225–275 g) of pasta— dry weight—between two people for a main course, or 4–6 oz (110–175 g) as a starter. Mind you, it all depends on your appetites: I have to confess we often get through 12 oz (350 g) between two in our house when we're really hungry!

Notes on ingredients
One of the best reasons for eating pasta is that, in 15 minutes from start to finish, you can provide yourself with a complete meal—and all from a collection of ingredients that are common to most kitchen cupboards. The following are what I'd consider essential items to keep handy.

Olive oil For pasta I *do* think this is essential. Whereas for other types of cooking I might substitute groundnut oil, with pasta olive oil seems a must and well worth the slight extra expense. If I can I buy pure olive oil in 5-litre drums (from Italian shops), which works out very much cheaper than buying several small bottles. Alternatively, the 5-litre containers of blended olive oil sold by a well-known chain of chemists are also very good value.

Basil Tomatoes are one of the principal ingredients of pasta dishes in Italy, and basil has a strong affinity with tomatoes. Even in its dried form it is very useful for cooked tomato (and other) sauces, and it's the one herb I always make sure to have in stock.

Parmesan cheese Grated and sprinkled over soups and pastas, this cheese is used almost like seasoning in Italy. It is a hard cheese, said to need 2–3 years' ageing to reach maturity (and some of the more expensive ones have had 5 or more years'). The preservative used in the packaged, ready-grated Parmesan gives the cheese an alien taste, I think, and I go out of my way to buy whole pieces of the cheese in delicatessens or Italian shops. It keeps beautifully in a sealed polythene bag in the lowest part of the refrigerator, and this way you can grate it as and when you need it.

Tomatoes So far as tinned tomatoes are concerned, I always buy Italian. They really are the best and very useful indeed for all sorts of cooking purposes when fresh tomatoes are out of season. Tomato purée (or tomato paste as it is sometimes called) is very concentrated in flavour. Useful though it would be to make it oneself when there is a glut of tomatoes in the garden, so far as I am aware it is impossible to make it at home.

How to boil pasta
The number one rule is always to have plenty of boiling water. If too little water is used, the pasta clogs together in a mass and some of it may not cook at all. So allow 4 pints (2¼ litres) of water for each 8 oz (225 g) of pasta.

Always add some salt to the water—about 2 teaspoons for 4 pints (2¼ litres) plus a few drops of olive oil, which will help to keep the strands separate. Have the water boiling rapidly and keep the heat high while you add the pasta (if it's spaghetti, you'll need to push it down gradually into the pan and the water will soften it as it goes down). The water should, if the heat is high enough, come to the boil again very quickly; then give the pasta one really good stir, turn the heat down and let is simmer gently for the required time. *Don't* put a lid on—there's no need to and, if you do, you risk having the water boil over.

When the pasta is cooked to your liking, pour it into a colander sitting in the sink and allow most of the water to drain off. If the sauce is to be served separately, then place the colander over the saucepan in which you cook the pasta (the heat of the pan will help to keep the pasta hot while you serve) and dish up directly in the kitchen. Serve each helping onto a plate that has been nicely warmed—large soup plates would be ideal because that little bit of depth helps to conserve the heat. Speed is now the important factor (*presto pronto!* as the Italians say), because there is nothing worse than eating pasta that is the wrong side of tepid.

To serve spaghetti Use two instruments (a large spoon and a fork) to extract a quantity of spaghetti, lifting it as high as possible above the colander, and it will separate from the rest with perfect ease.

To eat spaghetti The big mistake here is trying to wind too much onto the fork at once. Select just two or three strands with your fork and coax them over to the rim of the plate. Then, holding the fork at a right angle to the plate, simply wind the fork round and round, so that those few strands extricate themselves from the rest and are twisted round the fork in a little bite-sized bundle. Easier said than done, you're thinking? But remember two things—practice makes perfect and the Italians themselves always wear little napkins tucked neatly under their chins!

Fresh tomato sauce

(serves 2 people)

This sauce is good to serve with almost any kind of pasta—and it's also useful for using up those slightly over-ripe tomatoes at the end of the season.

1 lb ripe tomatoes, skinned and chopped (450 g)
1 small onion, finely chopped
1 clove garlic, crushed
1 teaspoon tomato purée
1 dessertspoon fresh chopped basil (or ½ dessertspoon dried)
Olive oil
Salt and freshly-milled black pepper

To peel the tomatoes pour some boiling water over them and let them stand for a minute or two; then you'll find the skins slip off very easily. Chop up the flesh quite small.

Heat 1 tablespoon of olive oil in a saucepan, and soften the onion and garlic in it for 5 minutes without letting them brown, then add the tomatoes, tomato purée, basil and a seasoning of salt and pepper. Give everything a good stir then cover the pan and simmer gently for 15 minutes. After that uncover the pan and simmer for a further 10–15 minutes for the sauce to reduce slightly. It can either be served as it is, or liquidised a little first.

Tomato chilli sauce
Make the sauce as above but add ¼ teaspoon chilli powder, in which case it would be a good accompaniment to sausages, rissoles or hamburgers.

Ragù Bolognese

This is really the all-purpose Italian pasta sauce: it can form the basis of *Lasagne* or *Baked meat and macaroni pie* (see recipes), or served with spaghetti it is enough for 4 people.

6 oz lean minced beef (175 g)
3 oz chicken livers, chopped small (75 g)
2 rashers unsmoked streaky bacon, finely chopped
1 teaspoon dried basil
1 small onion, very finely chopped
1 fat clove garlic, crushed
8 oz tin Italian tomatoes (225 g)
4 tablespoons red wine
2 heaped tablespoons tomato purée
1½ tablespoons olive oil
Salt and freshly-milled black pepper

Heat the oil in a thick-based saucepan, then gently soften the onion, bacon and garlic in it for 5 minutes. Now turn the heat up, add the chicken livers and minced beef, and brown them, keeping the ingredients on the move with a wooden spoon. When the meat has browned, pour in the contents of the tin of tomatoes, plus the tomato purée, wine, basil and some seasoning. Put a lid on and simmer gently for 20 minutes, then take the lid off and simmer gently for a further 20–25 minutes to get a nice concentrated sauce.

Spaghetti alla carbonara

(serves 2 people)

This doesn't have to be spaghetti—you can use tagliatelle or macaroni. It's a very simple dish of pasta with a bacon and egg sauce which I must admit tastes far nicer than it sounds.

½ lb spaghetti (225 g)
4 oz streaky bacon, de-rinded and chopped (110 g)
2 large eggs
1½ tablespoons olive oil
1 tablespoon Parmesan cheese, grated
Salt and freshly-milled black pepper
Extra Parmesan cheese for serving

To cook the pasta, place it in a very large saucepan of boiling salted water to which ½ tablespoon of olive oil has been added to prevent the spaghetti sticking together. It will need 8–10 minutes from the time it comes to the boil. Meantime, heat 1 tablespoon of olive oil in a saucepan and fry the bacon till the fat starts to run. While all this is happening, whisk the eggs in a bowl, adding some freshly-milled black pepper and a tablespoon of Parmesan cheese.

As soon as the pasta is cooked drain it in a colander then return it to the hot saucepan—away from the heat though. Now, quickly and deftly, stir in the beaten eggs and the bacon (plus the oil it was cooked in) and keep stirring to coat the pasta with liquid egg, which will soon cook from the heat of the saucepan and turn slightly granular. Serve on really hot plates with lots of Parmesan cheese to sprinkle over.

Note: if you would like to vary the above recipe slightly, you could add a chopped onion or a crushed clove of garlic to cook with the bacon. Another nice addition is to beat 2 tablespoons of double cream into the eggs, which gives a lovely cream finish to the sauce.

Spaghetti with anchovies, mushrooms and olives

(serves 2 people

If you like lots of 'gutsy' flavour in food, you'll like this delicious recipe.

½ lb spaghetti (225 g)
3 tablespoons plus 1 teaspoon olive oil
8 oz fresh mushrooms, thinly sliced (225 g)
2 onions, thinly sliced
2 cloves garlic, crushed
5 anchovy fillets, snipped in half
3 rashers lean bacon, de-rinded and roughly chopped
6 Spanish stuffed olives, sliced

| 2 tablespoons chopped parsley |
| 2 tablespoons grated Parmesan cheese |
| Salt and freshly-milled black pepper |

In a heavy-based frying-pan heat the 3 tablespoons of oil, then gently cook the mushrooms, onion, and bacon for about 10 minutes, stirring them around occasionally. Then add the garlic, anchovy fillets, parsley and olives and let them heat through. Season to taste.

In the meantime, cook the spaghetti for 8–10 minutes in boiling salted water to which 1 teaspoon of oil has been added. When cooked, drain in a colander, pile it onto a warmed serving dish, pour the savoury mixture on top and sprinkle on the Parmesan cheese.

Lasagne al forno

(serves 6 people)

For me, this is the supreme pasta dish— wafer-thin leaves of green pasta, layered together with a filling of thick ragù Bolognese and surrounded by a nutmeg-flavoured cream sauce, hot and bubbling. It isn't something you can dash off in a hurry but it's a superb dinner-party dish, and once made it's very easy just to pop in the oven and serve without any last-minute fuss.

| 1 quantity of ragù Bolognese (see page 364) |
| ½ lb lasagne verdi (green spinach lasagne) 225 g |
| Freshly-grated Parmesan, to finish |

| *For the cream sauce:* |
| 3 oz butter (75 g) |
| 2 oz plain flour (50 g) |
| 1½ pints milk (850 ml) |
| ¼ pint single cream (150 ml) |
| Salt and freshly-milled black pepper |
| Freshly-grated nutmeg |

A roasting tin, measuring about 7 × 9½ inches (18 × 24 cm), well-buttered.

First make up the cream sauce by placing the milk, butter and flour in a thick-based saucepan. Put it over a gentle heat and whisk continuously with a balloon whisk until the sauce comes to simmering point and thickens. Now, with the heat as low as possible, continue to cook the sauce for 10 minutes.

To cook the lasagne (½ lb will be about 16 sheets, each measuring 7 × 3 inches or 18 × 7·5 cm), have ready a large saucepan of salted, boiling water to which a little oil has been added. Drop in 8 sheets, one at a time. If it is fresh pasta cook them for 3 minutes or until they float to the top: if they're dried cook them for about 8 minutes—but make sure you don't overcook, or they will be soggy. When cooked transfer them immediately, using a fish slice, to a bowl of cold water (which will prevent them sticking together). Repeat this process with the remaining sheets.

Next sieve the white sauce into a bowl, beat in the cream, season with salt and pepper and grate in about a quarter of a whole nutmeg. Now spread about a quarter of the ragù over the base of the prepared roasting tin. Cover this with approximately a quarter of the sauce, then arrange a single layer of the drained and dried lasagne over the top. Repeat this process, finishing off with a final layer of cream sauce. Cover the top with a good sprinkling of grated Parmesan cheese—and the lasagne is ready for the oven. All this preparation can be done well in advance. When required, bake in a pre-heated oven, gas mark 4, 350°F (180°C) for 30–35 minutes.

Baked meat and macaroni pie

(serves 4 people)

The large, ribbed type of macaroni, sometimes called *rigatoni*, or the un-ribbed *penne* are best for this dish. But ordinary macaroni will do.

1 quantity of ragù Bolognese (see page 364)
¾ lb macaroni (350 g)
Olive oil
1 clove garlic, crushed
2 oz grated Cheddar cheese (50 g)

For the sauce:
1½ oz butter (40 g)
1 oz plain flour (25 g)

¾ pint cold milk (425 ml)
Nutmeg
Salt and freshly-milled black pepper

Pre-heat the oven to gas mark 4, 350°F (180°C)

First make up the white sauce by placing the butter, flour and milk together in a pan over a medium heat and whisking until the sauce starts to bubble and thicken. Stir with a wooden spoon to get right into the corners of the pan, then whisk again thoroughly. Turn the heat down as low as you can and cook the sauce gently for 6 minutes, then grate in a quarter of a whole nutmeg.

Meanwhile cook the macaroni in plenty of boiling salted water (with a few drops of oil added) for 8–10 minutes—make sure you don't overcook it. When cooked, drain it well in a colander, then in a dry saucepan heat one tablespoon of oil, add the crushed garlic, return the macaroni to the pan and toss it around well.

Next butter a baking dish or casserole, add the macaroni to it, then pour in first the ragù Bolognese followed by the white sauce. Stir everything thoroughly so the macaroni gets properly coated with both sauces. Finally sprinkle the grated Cheddar cheese over the top, then bake in the oven for 30–40 minutes.

Macaroni with leeks and bacon

(serves 4 people)

Again, I think this is nicest made with the larger type of pasta called *penne* but supermarket macaroni is almost as good.

¾ lb macaroni (350 g)
3 small leeks, cleaned and chopped
6 oz streaky bacon, de-rinded and chopped (175 g)
2 oz butter (50 g)
Olive oil

For the sauce:
2 oz butter (50 g)
1½ oz plain flour (40 g)
1 pint milk (570 ml)
6 oz Cheddar cheese, grated (175 g)

3 fl oz double cream (75 ml)
Salt, freshly-milled pepper and freshly-grated nutmeg

For the topping:
2 tablespoons Parmesan cheese
1 tablespoon breadcrumbs
2 pinches cayenne pepper

A 2½ pint (1·5 litre) pie-dish, well buttered.

Start by bringing a large saucepan of water to simmering point, add some salt and a few drops of olive oil, then bring the pasta back to the boil and cook for 10 minutes exactly. Then turn it into a colander and, to prevent it cooking any further, rinse it under the cold tap.

Whilst the pasta's cooking, melt 2 oz butter (50 g) in a pan and soften the leeks and bacon over a gentle heat and, in another pan, make the white sauce with the butter, flour and milk and leave it to simmer very gently.

Now turn the pasta, leeks and bacon into the prepared pie dish and mix them well together. Next stir the grated cheese into the sauce, season to taste with salt, pepper and nutmeg and, finally, add the cream. Then pour the sauce over the ingredients in the pie dish, sprinkle the top with the Parmesan, breadcrumbs and cayenne pepper.

This is a dish which can be prepared well beforehand then, when it's needed, put into an oven pre-heated to gas mark 4, 350°F (180°C) for 30–40 minutes till the top is nicely browned and the sauce bubbling.

Wholewheat macaroni cheese

(serves 2 people)

This is a basic macaroni cheese with a few other goodies added for extra texture and flavour.

4 oz wholewheat macaroni (or any macaroni will do) (110 g)
2 pints water (1·25 litres)
2 oz butter (50 g)
1½ oz plain flour (40 g)

1 teaspoon dried mustard
¾ pint milk (425 ml)
6 oz Cheddar cheese, grated (175 g)
4 rashers streaky bacon, de-rinded and chopped
2 oz mushrooms, sliced (50 g)
1 medium onion, chopped
A little extra butter
Salt, freshly-milled black pepper and freshly-grated nutmeg
2 tomatoes, cut into small pieces

A 2 pint (1·25 litre) baking dish, buttered

In a large saucepan put 2 pints (1·25 litres) of water and 1 teaspoon salt, bring to the boil, add the macaroni and boil, uncovered, for 8–10 minutes. Meanwhile melt 2 oz (50 g) of butter in another saucepan then blend in the flour and mustard, add the milk a little at a time to make a white sauce and cook for about 6 minutes. Then stir in half of the grated Cheddar cheese and let it melt gently into the sauce, adding a seasoning of salt and pepper and a grating of nutmeg.

Now melt a little butter in a small frying-pan and gently fry the onion, bacon and mushrooms together for about 6 minutes or until soft. Next drain the macaroni in a colander, combine it with the sauce and the onion, bacon and mushroom mixture and turn it all into the prepared baking dish. Sprinkle the remainder of the cheese on top together with the pieces of tomato. Finally, place the dish under a pre-heated hot grill until golden brown and bubbling.

Note: this is a dish which can be made well in advance as it can be reheated in an oven pre-heated to gas mark 6, 400°F (200°C) in about 15–20 minutes.

Pancakes

Pancakes turn up all over the world in various forms. Here in England we have our annual ritual of tossing them out of frying-pans for one reason or another. In Russia they turn up as blinis, made with yeast and served topped with soured cream and caviare. The Jews have blinzes, the nicest of which are those stuffed with cream cheese and cinnamon, folded into parcels, then crisply fried.

The Chinese make theirs into little parcels too, crunchy rolls stuffed with vegetables. In Brittany almost every other eating-place is a *crêperie*, or pancake-shop, where their *galettes* and *crêpes* can accommodate an apparently limitless selection of ingredients, both sweet and savoury.

To make a pancake is not difficult, but to make a good *thin* pancake takes a bit of practice. A beginner using the recipe below will probably end up with 12 pancakes, but in no time at all they'll be able to get 14 or even 16 out of the same mixture.

Choosing the right pan

To make perfect pancakes, you need a good heavy frying-pan not more than 7 inches (18 cm) in diameter—that's the inside base measurement. A larger pan would make the batter difficult to spread out and you'd end up with pancakes with ragged edges. The pan needs to be hot and lightly greased. The idea is simply to lubricate the pan enough to prevent the pancake from sticking. Too much fat will make the pancake fry—which is all wrong. I think that using butter is best—and remember you will need to regrease and reheat the pan between each pancake.

Keeping pancakes hot and reheating them

Pancakes are best eaten as soon as cooked but they can be made well ahead, laid flat, wrapped and refrigerated, then reheated next day. Reheat them by stacking them onto a warm plate—cover the stack with foil and set the plate in a warm oven. Alternatively (and this is the usual way to keep freshly-cooked pancakes warm while you make the rest of the batch) set the foil-covered plate on top of a pan of simmering water.

Basic pancakes

(makes 12–14)

This basic batter is one I have arrived at after many experiments: I think it's light, it does *not* need to stand, and (dare I say it?) it is pretty foolproof.

4 oz plain flour (110 g)
A pinch of salt
2 large eggs
7 fl oz milk (200 ml) mixed together with 3 fl oz water (75 ml)
2 tablespoons melted butter
A little extra butter for cooking the pancakes

First sieve the flour and salt into a large mixing bowl, holding the sieve up high to give the flour an airing. Then make a well in the centre of the flour and break the two eggs into it. Now start to whisk the eggs (with an electric or any sort of whisk, or even a fork), beginning to incorporate bits of flour from around the edges as you do so. Then start to add small quantities of the milk-and-water mixture gradually—and ignore any lumps because they'll eventually disappear as the whisk gets to them. When all the milk-and-water has been added, slide a rubber spatula around the edge of the bowl to bring any elusive bits of flour into the centre of things. Then whisk once more till the batter is smooth and the consistency of thin cream.

When you're ready to cook the pancakes, add the 2 tablespoons of melted butter to the batter and stir it in. Then melt about a teaspoon of butter in the pan then swirl it all round to get the whole of the pan thoroughly lubricated. Now tip the excess butter onto a saucer (remember that the pan needs to be coated with butter but the pancakes should not be cooked in fat). Next get the pan really hot, then turn the heat down to medium, and to start with do a test pancake to determine whether or not you're using the correct amount of batter. I find 2 tablespoons about right.

As soon as the batter hits the hot pan, tip it around from side to side to get the base evenly coated with batter. It should take only half a minute or so to cook: you can lift the edge with a palette knife to see if it's tinged gold as it should be. If the pancake is thin enough there is no need to turn it over—it will be cooked through (and when it's rolled up with sugar and lemon or a stuffing, the paler coloured inside will not be visible). Just slide each pancake, when it is cooked, out of the pan onto a warm plate. Cover it with foil and put the plate over a pan of simmering water to keep the pancake warm while you cook the next.

Lemon pancakes
Sprinkle each pancake with freshly squeezed lemon juice and caster sugar, fold in half, then in half again to form triangles. Serve sprinkled with a little more juice and extra sections of lemon.

Strawberry jam pancakes
Have some warmed strawberry jam ready, put a dessertspoonful in the centre of each pancake, then roll it up, folding the ends inwards like a parcel. Serve with pouring cream.

Honey or syrup pancakes
Warm some maple syrup or runny honey. Brush each pancake with it, then fold into triangles (as *Lemon pancakes*), and have more syrup or honey in a jug on the table.

Buckwheat pancakes
Buckwheat flour is available from healthfood shops, and is used to make several varieties of pancake, most famous of them the Breton *crêpes*. I think the best results of all are obtained by using half buckwheat flour and half plain (as all buckwheat tends to give them a slightly rubbery texture).

Crêpes Suzette
(serves 4–6 people)

In restaurants, these tend to be produced like a cabaret act, which put me off them for a time. However, I was asked for a recipe, so I made some and discovered how delicious they are.

For the crêpes:
Make up the basic batter (as given on page 371), adding to it the grated zest of 1 medium-sized orange and 1 tablespoon caster sugar

For the sauce:
The juice of 3–4 medium-sized oranges— you need 5 fl oz (150 ml) altogether
The grated rind of 1 medium-sized orange
The grated rind and juice of 1 small lemon
1 tablespoon caster sugar
3 tablespoons Grand Marnier, Cointreau or brandy
2 oz unsalted butter (50 g)

Make the pancakes *(crêpes)* stacking them as described on page 371. Ideally, they should be thinner than those in the basic recipe, so use only 1³/₄ tablespoons of batter for each *crêpe*. This should give you at least 16.

When you have cooked and stacked the *crêpes*, mix together all the sauce ingredients (except the butter) in a bowl, and warm the plates on which the *crêpes* are to be served. Take a large frying-pan— preferably 10 inch (25·5 cm)—and melt the butter in it, add the sauce ingredients and allow them to heat very gently.

Place the first *crêpe* in the pan, give it time to warm through, then fold it in half and half again, to make a triangle shape. Slide it to the very edge of the pan. Tilt the pan slightly so that the sauce runs back into the centre, then add the next *crêpe*, and continue until they are all reheated, folded and soaked with the sauce.

If you want to be dramatic, you might at this point heat a tablespoon by holding it over a gas flame or resting it on the edge of a hotplate. Then, away from the heat, pour a little liqueur or brandy into the spoon, return it to the heat to warm the spirit, then set light to it. Carry the tablespoon of flames to the table along with the pan, and pour the flames over the *crêpes* before serving.

Pancake cannelloni

(serves 4 people)

This is one of my own favourites. In Italy they make large round tubular pasta called cannelloni, which can be stuffed with a filling, or they roll up sheets of pasta round a filling. I've adapted this to suit pancakes, which are then baked in a creamy sauce and topped with cheese. Lovely!

1 quantity of basic pancakes (see page 371) (approximately 12)
1 quantity of ragù Bolognese (see page 364)

For the sauce:
1½ oz butter (40 g)
1 oz plain flour (25 g)
¾ pint cold milk (425 ml)
Freshly-grated nutmeg
Salt and freshly-milled black pepper

For the topping:
2 heaped tablespoons grated Parmesan cheese
A few drops olive oil

Pre-heat the oven to gas mark 6, 400°F (200°C)

A shallow gratin dish or baking tin, well-buttered.

To make the sauce place the cold milk, flour and butter together in a saucepan and whisk over a medium heat until the sauce begins to bubble and thicken. Then reduce the heat as low as possible and allow the sauce to cook gently for 6 minutes. Season with salt and freshly-milled pepper and a good grating of whole nutmeg.

Now spread the pancakes out, place an equal quantity of ragù Bolognese on each one, roll them up tightly and fold in the ends. Then tuck them side by side into the prepared gratin dish, pour the sauce over, sprinkle with the Parmesan cheese and drizzle about one teaspoon of olive oil over the surface. Bake on a high shelf for 30 minutes.

Spinach-stuffed pancakes with cheese sauce

(serves 4 people)

In the summer months, instead of using frozen spinach these can be made with 2 lb (900 g) of fresh spinach cooked with butter and salt (no water), in its own steam in a lidded saucepan, for about 5–7 minutes.

1 quantity of pancake batter (page 371), made with half wholewheat flour and half plain flour
2 × 8 oz packets frozen spinach (2 × 225 g)
2 oz butter (50 g)
¹/₈ pint double cream (about 75 ml)
1½ oz strong Cheddar cheese, grated (40 g)
1 oz Parmesan cheese, grated (25 g)

For the sauce:
2 oz butter (50 g)
1½ oz plain flour (40 g)
¾ pint milk (425 ml)
¹/₈ pint double cream (about 75 ml)
1½ oz strong Cheddar cheese, grated (40 g)
Salt, freshly-milled black pepper and freshly-grated nutmeg

Pre-heat the oven to gas mark 6, 400°F (200°C)

A shallow baking dish or tin, well-buttered.

Allow the spinach to defrost in a colander placed over a plate, so that the excess liquid drains out of it.

Make up 12 pancakes according to the basic recipe and stack them on a plate (there's no need to keep them warm).

Then make up an all-in-one cheese sauce: place the butter, flour and milk in a saucepan and whisk over a medium heat till thickened. Stir in the cheese, the cream, and season with salt, pepper and nutmeg.

Next, press the excess liquid out of the spinach, melt 2 oz butter (50 g) in a saucepan and stir in the spinach followed by the cream. Continue to stir, preferably with a wooden fork, to break up the spinach. Cook gently until the spinach has absorbed the cream and is a nice soft consistency. Now taste it and season with salt, pepper and a little grated nutmeg.

Next, place about a tablespoonful of the spinach mixture on each pancake and roll each up, folding in the ends. Now pack them side by side in the baking dish or tin. Then pour over the prepared sauce, sprinkle with the Cheddar and Parmesan cheeses and bake on a high shelf for 25 minutes or until it's browned and bubbling.

Note: this dish can be prepared well in advance and just popped into the oven to reheat 30 minutes before you need it.

Cheese soufflé pancakes

(serves 4 people)

I first ate these in Italy where they were called *Crespollini Amalfitan* and this version is, I think, exactly the same.

12 thin pancakes (made as on page 371)
2 oz butter (50 g)
2 oz plain flour, sifted (50 g)
4 tablespoons milk (warmed and infused with a bayleaf, a slice of onion and a few peppercorns for 30 minutes)
2 oz strong Cheddar cheese, grated (50 g)
½ teaspoon mustard powder
2 pinches cayenne pepper
3 large eggs, separated
1½ tablespoons grated Parmesan cheese
Extra butter
Salt and freshly-milled black pepper

Pre-heat the oven to gas mark 6, 400°F (200°C)

A shallow baking-dish or tin, buttered.

First melt the butter in a saucepan, add the flour and mix to a smooth paste. Then blend in, a little at a time, the flavoured and strained milk and cook over very gentle heat for 5 minutes. Next stir in the grated Cheddar cheese, the mustard powder and cayenne pepper, and add salt and freshly-milled pepper to taste.

Now turn the mixture into a bowl, beat the egg yolks, and very carefully incorporate them with the mixture. In another bowl whisk the egg whites to the soft peak stage: stir 1 tablespoon into the cheese sauce, then gently fold in the rest, using a metal spoon.

Now spoon a generous portion of the mixture onto one half of each pancake and fold the other half over like a Cornish pasty. Place them side by side in the buttered baking dish, sprinkle with Parmesan cheese, put a few dabs of butter on top, and bake in the centre of the oven for approximately 10–15 minutes.

Apple and cinnamon crêpes

(serves 2–3 people)

These are the French type of pancakes, served flat and made with buckwheat flour; if you can't get any, use wholewheat flour instead.

2 oz plain flour, sifted (50 g)
1 oz buckwheat flour (25 g)
1 large egg
4 fl oz milk (110 ml) mixed with 2 fl oz water (55 ml)
¼ teaspoon vanilla essence
¼ teaspoon ground cinnamon
2 small Cox's apples, peeled and cored
3 tablespoons dry cider
Butter
Caster sugar
Chilled pouring cream

Begin by mixing the flours together in a bowl, then make a hollow in the centre and break the egg into it and whisk it into the flour together with the milk-and-water mixture, added a little at a time.

Beat until you have a perfectly smooth batter, then add the cinnamon and vanilla essence. Next grate the peeled and cored apples straight into the batter.

At this stage put some plates in the oven to warm and also put the cider in a small saucepan to heat.

Now melt a generous piece of butter in a 7 or 8 inch (18 or 20 cm) frying-pan and, when hot, rotate the pan so that the sides as well as the base are well-coated with the butter. Pour off any excess into the batter.

Now drop 2 tablespoons of batter into the hot buttery frying-pan and shake and ease the mixture to spread all over the pan base— using a palette knife if necessary.

Cook until the *crêpe* becomes crisp at the edges and is a lovely golden colour underneath, then, using a fish slice, knife or spatula, toss or turn the *crêpe* over and cook the other side until crisp and golden too. Serve the *crêpes* flat on warmed plates, sprinkled with a little of the hot cider, some caster sugar and some chilled pouring cream.

Note: this quantity of batter should make 7 *crêpes*. If you want to keep them warm between cooking and serving, lay them flat on top of each other between two warmed plates either in a warm oven or on top of a saucepan of simmering water.

See also:
Pesto alla Genovese
Roman gnocchi

Herbs

Including recipes for:

Green herb soup
Carrot and tarragon soup
Spring sauce for lamb
Pesto alla Genovese
  (fresh basil sauce)
Green herb and rice salad
Nine herb salad of Hintlesham
Chicken salad with tarragon
  and grapes

Poached trout with herbs
Trout with butter, cream and chives
Baked mackerel with herb stuffing
Cucumber with soured cream and dill
Pork chops with sage and apples
Leg of lamb baked with butter and herbs
Cream cheese with herbs

Writing in the 16th century the East Anglian farmer Thomas Tusser listed over fifty herbs that he considered *essential* in every kitchen garden, and at one time—in fact until just over 200 years ago—London's Leadenhall had its very own herb market. The fact that it closed down is probably a sad reflection on the decline of the use of herbs in English cooking. And not just cooking, for every cook book right up to the last century contained its own batch of herbal healing remedies for a whole litany of ailments, from toothache to gout!

I suppose the decline of herbs ran parallel to the decline of our cooking, at the time the industrial revolution enticed people off the land. But now, two centuries later, I think nature is luring us back from our modern technology to consider what the earth gives— fresh natural foods and fresh natural flavours, and not least the enormous variety of fragrant and fresh-tasting herbs. Living in the country I am fortunate enough to have room for a fairly large herb garden, but even in the cities more and more people have recently set up their window boxes or growbags to plant a few fresh herbs to enliven their cooking.

Even if that isn't possible, fresh herbs can now be purchased in some shops and supermarkets. There are quite a number of herb farms which send them out by post (which is a slightly extravagant way of acquiring them, since it involves ever-increasing postal charges). But if we keep on pestering those greengrocers who don't yet stock a decent range of fresh herbs, we will eventually get a steadier and more reliable supply of them.

Storing herbs

For those who have to buy fresh cut herbs, do *not* store them stuck in a jar of water on a window sill. Sunlight ruins cut herbs, so tie them loosely but securely in polythene bags and park them in the lowest part of the refrigerator (i.e. a vegetable drawer). In this way I have kept cut chives, tarragon and chervil for up to a week, mint for a fortnight, and thyme, sage and rosemary even longer.

Freezing herbs

I have found that the best way to freeze them for my own use is actually to make herb butter (either of mixed herbs or individual ones, see page 449). A good way to do this is to press the butter into ice-cube trays, and slip the trays into polythene bags before putting back in the freezer. This makes it very convenient to use just one or two blocks for melting over steaks, fish or vegetables.

Chopping herbs
There are plenty of little gadgets on the market for chopping herbs, but none as good as a sharp knife and wooden chopping board. The trouble with many of these gadgets is that they squash—rather than chop—the herbs and make them mushy (they also require tedious and intricate cleaning afterwards!).

Ideally you need a good-sized cook's knife, with a 7 inch (18 cm) blade that is slightly curved. Arrange the herbs on the chopping board by spreading them out, then rest the blade of the knife horizontally on the board at the edge furthest away from you. Hold the pointed end between the finger and thumb of one hand to steady it, take the handle in the other hand, and make sharp cutting movements swinging the handle towards you as you chop—so that the blade swivels in a fan shape across the herbs, and back again. Your reward, I promise, will be a deliciously aromatic, herb-scented kitchen.

Chives are an exception as they are far easier snipped with kitchen scissors. I have also heard it said (and I pass it on to you) that basil should have its leaves torn rather than chopped: this apparently is the best way to retain all the fragrant oils.

Cooking with fresh herbs
In some recipes whole sprigs of herbs are added to the pot at the beginning of the cooking, so that their flavour can truly permeate the food, but this depends entirely on the nature of the dish and the herb itself. There are times (especially when making sauces or soups) when it is far better to add the herb at the very end, just before serving, so that none of the freshness or fragrance is lost. Examples of this would be chives in leek soup, parsley in parsley sauce, and basil in tomato sauce.

Dried herbs
For home drying of herbs I would point you in the direction of the book list at the end of this book, since this is something that requires care and expertise. However, commercially dried herbs are very useful in the kitchen at certain times of the year. Some cooks despise the use of dried herbs altogether—and I would agree that some herbs like chives, parsley and particularly mint lose all their charm and flavour when dried. Nevertheless there are those that deserve their place in the kitchen, and in my notes on the varieties of herbs beginning on the next page I have indicated which these are.

Basil

In my kitchen basil reigns supreme
(appropriately enough, since its name is
derived from the Greek word *basileus* for
king!). It is used extensively in Italian
and Provençal cooking, has a warm
pungent scent and—to me—a taste of
the sun. It is lack of sun that makes it
difficult to grow here if we have a cold
summer, yet I've always managed to
grow some in a pot on my kitchen
window-sill. Provided the white flowers
are pinched off all the time, it goes on
producing leaves right through until the
end of October.

The fresh leaves are quite delicious,
chopped and sprinkled over a tomato
salad, or added to sauces and soups just
before serving. Anything that has tomato
in it will be improved with the addition of
basil—the two have a great affinity.
Dried basil has nowhere near the
character and flavour of the fresh
leaves—but dried basil is better than no
basil at all, and it's fine in soups and
sauces through the winter.

Bayleaves

Bay trees, with their glossy green leaves,
can be quite prolific. I have one about
2 feet (60 cm) high, which gives me all
the bayleaves I need. Fresh bayleaves,
however, can impart a slightly bitter
flavour, so this is a herb which is far
better used dried. To dry them is easy:
just hang a branch in an airy spot and the
leaves will dry in a couple of weeks.

They are used probably more than any
other herb, to flavour stocks, sauces,
casseroles and marinades. One unusual
idea you might like to try is to place a
bayleaf in about 2 inches (5 cm) of

boiling water, add some salt, then sit a whole prepared cauliflower in the water to cook with the lid tightly closed. When it's tender (about 10 minutes), drain, melt some butter over the cauliflower, and sprinkle on a little nutmeg.

Chervil

This herb is used quite a lot in French cooking, but rather less in this country where we tend to prefer the more pungent flavour of parsley. Chervil in fact has a more subtle, delicate flavour, and it is quite easy to grow. Along with a few chives and chopped tarragon, it's delicious in an *Omelette aux fines herbes* (page 29). It can be used in sauces too, but (like parsley) should be added at the last moment if it is to make any sort of impression. Chervil is not good dried.

Chives

I wouldn't be without my chives—a very easily grown perennial that adds interest to a whole variety of dishes from early April right through to October.
Although a member of the onion family, chives have a sweet flavour entirely their own. A catalogue of how to use them would be endless: they turn up in very many dishes all through the Cookery Course, but one of my favourite ways of serving them is to add a couple of heaped tablespoons to 5 fl oz (150 ml) of soured cream, and to pour this over halved jacket potatoes.

Don't chop chives—keep them in bunches and use scissors to snip them in small pieces. They can be deep-frozen for the winter by placing them in a sieve, pouring boiling water over to blanch them, then cooling them under a cold tap. Dry them as thoroughly as possible and freeze in sealed polythene bags.

Dried chives don't work at all, but if you can get hold of a clump (or seeds) of Welsh onion, scallion or green onion (which all look like spring onion tops) you'll find these go on all through the winter. Although they have a slightly stronger flavour, they're suitable for any recipe that calls for chives.

Dill
This herb is best-known for its use in commercially pickled cucumbers, where the leafy heads and the seeds are used. The seeds have to be planted annually, but grow very easily; the feathery leaves have a sharp, aromatic flavour. Chopped, they are good in sauces for fish, or added to butter to melt over. Dill goes particularly well with soured cream dressings or sauces, and has a great affinity with cucumber: add 2 tablespoons chopped to *Cucumber sauce* (page 439), or try the recipe for cucumber cooked with dill on page 399. I find dried dill can be used successfully if you infuse the leaves in warm water for a few minutes, then drain and use as fresh.

Fennel
Garden fennel is a fern-like green herb with quite a pronounced aniseed flavour (just as strong as that of bulb fennel described in the Vegetable chapter, page 253). It's good in sauces or stuffing for fish. An interesting variation on the *Italian baked fish* recipe (page 121) is to add a dessertspoon of chopped fennel leaves to the tomato sauce before pouring it over the fish for baking.

Garlic

I think of garlic (strictly a member of the onion family) as an essential seasoning. I am often teased about my constant use of garlic, but remain unrepentant: you can, if you truly dislike it, always leave it out, but time and again I have heard from other cooks that garlic has often been added to dishes served to garlic-haters and they've been none the wiser! If like me you happen to love it, did you know it's very easy to grow? All you do is separate the cloves (individual sections) from the bulb, and plant them 2 inches (5 cm) deep and about 2 inches (5 cm) apart in early spring. Then in August you can harvest your own crop, which will be firm, juicy and tasting so much better than imported garlic bought from a shop.

One way to crush garlic—a question I'm asked all the time—is to place the clove on a board, set the flat side of a small knife on top and press with your thumb until you have squashed it to a pulp. You could invest in a proper garlic crusher, though these are tiresome things to clean. Probably the best way is with a pestle and mortar: add a little salt as this helps to reduce the garlic to a smooth paste. And one tip for peeling garlic—place the unpeeled clove on a flat surface and simply press it with your thumb. This breaks the skin all over, and it peels away very easily.

Lovage

This is a herb that hardly ever crops up in recipes, yet proliferates in (almost dominates) herb gardens. It has a strong flavour which I can only describe as a sort of pungent, aromatic celery. It's worth growing to make into a lovely green, summery soup, or you can use the leaves in stocks, sauces or anything else that requires a little celery flavour.

Marjoram

There are three different varieties of this plant. Pot marjoram is a perennial herb which is inclined to spread itself all over the space that is allocated to it. Sweet marjoram is a half-hearted perennial (because it won't survive a hard winter). And there is wild marjoram, which is Greece is called rigani and in Italy oregano. I grow the first type, because I'm not organised enough to sow a new batch each year. I use it, along with other herbs, for herb butters, herb omelettes and herb-flavoured dressings for salads. Fresh pot marjoram can be used for any recipe that calls for oregano, but for winter use I would strongly recommend dried oregano.

Mint

Mint comes in a whole range of varieties that can be used for cooking, and when I first started a herb garden I found myself the proud owner of several kinds. However I gradually came to realise that spearmint was the one I used most, and now grow only that. This is the one used for mint sauce, and for cooking new potatoes. When it's being chopped the kitchen is filled with the most fragrant aroma; and a couple of sprigs added to boiling new potatoes will also permeate the room with an appetising smell too. In the summer it is, like chives, a herb I use frequently, and it's included in several recipes that follow.

One unusual application I discovered in the Amalfi area of Italy is to place fresh mint leaves in the belly of fish before baking, grilling or frying them.

One word of warning about mint: never use it dried—it loses all its flavour and becomes very musty and lifeless.

Parsley

What needs to be said about the most universal and widely-used herb of all? No garden or window-box should be without it. The leaves can be used to flavour and enliven the appearance of many, many dishes. The stalks may be added to stocks, while sprigs of parsley are the most ubiquitous garnish of the lot. To keep a good supply going, it's best to sow some seeds in late spring and again at the end of summer, as the plant is a biennial.

Rosemary

The ancient Greeks said that rosemary was good for the brain—a theory that persisted through the centuries (so we find Ophelia presenting it to Hamlet 'for remembrance'). Be that as it may, the Italians love its strong spicy flavour in the kitchen, and make no excuses for using it. The French are more subtle with it, but there are many countries that hardly use it at all.

There are those who say that rosemary can be unpleasant if it gets stuck between the teeth—but this doesn't happen if the needle-like leaves are stripped from their stems and then chopped before using. It has a strong affinity with both pork and lamb, and can be chopped and sprinkled over joints and chops before baking (you'll find you can make a lovely rosemary-flavoured sauce with the juices left in the tin with some stock and a little red or white wine).

Rosemary grows very easily into a sturdy bush, and can be used fresh all through the winter. Dried rosemary is all right, but I would recommend that it be chopped as finely as possible since it's much more spiky when dried.

Sage

Sage has always been one of the great healing herbs: its name comes from the Latin *salvere* (to save). Its culinary use is largely despised by the French, but much favoured by the British and Italians. It is a very strongly-flavoured herb, so has to be used with caution. Delicious in stuffings for all poultry and pork (see the recipe on page 227), and especially good in pork sausages.

It is easy to grow, though as with mint there are many varieties. I grow the broad leaf sage. This is a herb that does dry well, without losing much flavour at all.

Sorrel

Much-loved and used for sauces and soups in France, but not so widely known here. Yet it's easy to grow and well worth including in a herb garden. It has leaves similar in appearance to spinach, and indeed tastes like a sharper version of spinach. Because of this sharpness very little of it is needed—a couple of handfulls, about 1½ oz (40 g) is enough to make a delicious soup.

Right: Pork chops with sage and apples, page 400.

Tarragon

If the king of herbs is basil, then I would like to nominate tarragon as the queen. It's a sophisticated herb, highly prized in French cooking and an essential ingredient in their famous *Béarnaise sauce* (see page 440). It goes well in veal and poultry dishes, and is often included in mixed herb dishes. It is, however, a strongly flavoured herb, so always be sparing with it. A sprig or two preserved in some white wine vinegar will help to give a subtle flavour of tarragon to salad dressings all through the winter.

You can only grow it from cuttings, and if you buy a plant (one will be enough) do make sure the label says it's French tarragon. There is a Russian variety which grows up to 5 feet (1·5 m) high, but has nowhere near the flavour of the French. Dried tarragon is useful—if you steep it in warm water for a minute or two before using.

Thyme

A bush of garden thyme will be a good friend to any cook, as it provides fresh leaves all the year round. It has a really strong, warm resinous flavour, and needs to be used sparingly if it is not to overpower other tastes. A teaspoonful of chopped thyme added to a salad dressing is a good idea, and I use little branches of thyme in my stocks and casseroles—and always add some to beef stews. You'll find it in many recipes in the Cookery Course, and as it is a herb that dries well, it's useful for flat dwellers and non-gardeners.

Left: Crêpes Suzette, page 373.

Green herb soup

(serves 4–5 people)

This soup adapts to any combination of fresh herbs—mint, sage, lovage, thyme, rosemary, sorrel or any others that are available.

1 oz butter (25 g)
6 thick spring onions (and their green tops), thinly sliced
6 oz potatoes, scraped and cubed (175 g)
5 oz outside lettuce leaves, or spinach leaves, de-stalked and shredded (150 g)
2 rounded tablespoons chopped fresh herbs
15 fl oz light stock (425 ml)
5 fl oz single cream (150 ml)
A generous squeeze of lemon juice
Salt and freshly-milled black pepper

Melt the butter in a medium-sized pan, and stir in the thinly sliced spring onions and the cubed potatoes. Stir and cook over a gentle heat so the vegetables soften gently without browning.

Now stir in the shredded lettuce. Get it all nicely coated with butter. Then add the stock, bring to simmering point, cover and cook gently for about 10 minutes or just long enough for the potatoes to soften.

Next pour the contents of the saucepan into a liquidiser. Add the chopped fresh herbs and the cream and blend until smooth. Return the purée to the pan and reheat, tasting and flavouring with the lemon juice, salt and pepper. Serve piping hot with some fresh, crusty wholewheat bread.

Carrot and tarragon soup

(serves 4–6 people)

This is a delicious, summery soup, but it can be made in the winter with 2 finely chopped leeks instead of the lettuce leaves and some dried tarragon instead of fresh.

12 oz carrots (350 g)
The outside leaves of a lettuce (or 2 finely chopped leeks)
1 small onion

| 2 sprigs fresh tarragon, or ¼ teaspoon dried |
| 1½ pints boiling water (850 ml) |
| 2 oz butter (50 g) |
| 3 tablespoons double cream |
| 1 teaspoon sugar |
| Salt and freshly-milled black pepper |

First wash and scrape the carrots and slice them thinly, then chop the onion and lettuce fairly small. In a thick-based saucepan gently melt the butter and soften the onion in it for a minute or two, then add the carrots and lettuce, stirring to get a good coating of butter. Now put a lid on and let the vegetables gently 'sweat' for 10 minutes. Next, strip the leaves from the tarragon, pop them in, then add the boiling water, the sugar and a seasoning of salt and pepper. When it returns to simmering point, put a lid on and simmer very gently for 25 minutes. Now either liquidise or sieve the soup, taste to check the seasoning and reheat gently, stirring in the cream just before serving.

Note: don't be tempted to use stock, as this detracts from the fresh flavour of the carrots.

Spring sauce
for lamb

(serves 6 people)

I always part company with mint sauce if it's made with malt vinegar which completely overpowers the flavour of the lamb, but the following sauce—which my grandmother always served with lamb—is made with wine vinegar diluted with an equal quantity of water, so it's much milder.

| 2 tablespoons fresh chopped mint |
| 2 spring onions very finely chopped |
| 2 lettuce leaves finely shredded and chopped |
| 3 tablespoons wine vinegar |
| 3 tablespoons cold water |

Simply combine all the above ingredients and place in a sauce-boat for everyone to help themselves.

Pesto alla Genovese (fresh basil sauce)

(serves 3 people)

This is a sauce which, freshly made, will throw any pasta lover into transports of delight. The flavour of the fresh basil combined with olive oil and garlic is out of this world!

2 oz fresh basil leaves (50 g)
1 large clove garlic, crushed
1 tablespoon pine kernels
6 tablespoons olive oil
1 oz grated Parmesan cheese (25 g)
Salt

If you have a blender, then put the basil, garlic, pine kernels and olive oil together with some salt in the goblet and blend until you have a smooth purée. Then transfer the purée to a bowl and stir in the grated Parmesan.

If you don't have a blender, use a large pestle and mortar to pound the basil, garlic and pine kernels to a paste. Slowly add the salt and cheese followed by the very gradual addition of the oil until you obtain a smooth purée.

The above quantities will make enough sauce for serving with 12 oz (225 g) of pasta, which is sufficient for 3–4 people.

Green herb and rice salad

(serves 8 people)

This is an excellent way to serve rice, cold at a buffet party or warm with barbecue food.

Brown rice measured to the 12 fl oz (300 ml) level in a glass measuring jug
24 fl oz boiling water or stock (670 ml)— double the volume of rice
1 teaspoon salt
2 oz prepared spinach leaves (50 g)
8 spring onions including the green tops
2 heaped teaspoons chopped herbs (thyme, rosemary, sage, savory, marjoram, tarragon)
2 dessertspoons oil
The grated rind of half a lemon

For the dressing:
½ teaspoon black peppercorns
1 clove garlic
1 teaspoon rock salt
1 teaspoon mustard powder
1 tablespoon wine vinegar
5 tablespoons olive oil

Heat the two dessertspoons of oil in a pan, stir in the rice, then pour in the boiling water or stock. Add 1 teaspoon of salt, stir once and allow it to come back to the boil. Cover, then reduce the heat to give a bare simmer. Cook gently for 40–45 minutes or until all the liquid has been absorbed and the rice is just tender.

Next chop up the spinach leaves and spring onions very finely, and fork into the rice along with the herbs and grated lemon rind. Cover the pan with a folded cloth and leave aside for 10 minutes.

Make the dressing by crushing the salt, peppercorns and garlic together with a pestle and mortar. Add the mustard, vinegar and olive oil, then shake the whole lot together in a screw-top jar.

Tip the salad ingredients into a bowl, pour the dressing all over and fluff it with a skewer. Serve the salad warm or cold.

Nine herb salad of Hintlesham

(serves 4–6 people)

These are the ingredients used by Robert Carrier at his famous restaurant at Hintlesham Hall in Suffolk. For those who can't get hold of the particular kinds of lettuce, he says other types of green salad vegetable will do. Indeed, I have made this salad successfully using watercress and chopped spinach leaves. And, of course, if you can't get certain herbs, use what's available.

1 salad bowl lettuce
1 Cos lettuce
1 Lamb's lettuce (Mâche)
12 sprigs tarragon
12 sprigs basil
12 sprigs purple basil

12 sprigs pourprier (purslane)
12 sprigs roquette
12 sprigs flat-leafed parsley
Coarsely chopped fennel
Coarsely chopped chives
Coarsely chopped parsley

1 quantity vinaigrette dressing (page 482)

Prepare the various lettuces, and cut the fresh herbs (tarragon, basil, purple basil, pourprier, roquette and flat-leafed parsley) into tiny sprigs about 1 inch (2·5 cm) long. Combine the lettuce leaves with the sprigs of herbs and arrange them in a salad bowl. Pour over the dressing, sprinkle with the coarsely chopped fennel, chives and parsley. Toss well before serving.

Chicken salad with tarragon and grapes

(serves 4–6 people)

This is the perfect main course salad for a warm day, with perhaps some brown rice salad to go with it.

1 cooked chicken about 3 lb (1·35 kg) or 3¾ lb (1·7 kg) raw weight
5 fl oz home-made mayonnaise (150 ml), (see page 483)
3 fl oz double cream (75 ml)
4 oz green grapes, halved and de-pipped (110 g)
1 heaped teaspoon chopped tarragon—if you can't get hold of fresh tarragon, use ½ heaped teaspoon of dried, soaked in warm water for 5 minutes, then squeezed dry in kitchen paper
3 spring onions
A few sprigs watercress
1 small lettuce
Salt and freshly-milled black pepper

Remove the skin from the chicken and slice the flesh into longish pieces where possible. Remove all the chicken from the bones and place all the meat in a bowl, seasoning with salt and pepper.

In a separate bowl mix the mayonnaise thoroughly with the cream, adding the chopped tarragon and finely chopped spring onions. Now pour the sauce over the chicken, mix it well so that all the chicken pieces get a good coating, then arrange it on a plate of crisp lettuce leaves and garnish with green grapes and a few sprigs of watercress.

Poached trout with herbs

(serves 4 people)

This is very light and a good recipe for slimmers if the parsley butter isn't used for serving.

4 trout, weighing approximately 6 oz each (175 g), cleaned
Salt
6 whole peppercorns
4 bayleaves
1 small onion, peeled and cut into rings
1 lemon
1 sprig fresh thyme, or 1 teaspoon dried thyme
3 tablespoons fresh parsley, finely chopped
2 tablespoons fresh snipped chives
4 fl oz dry white wine (110 ml)
3 oz butter (75 g)

Place the trout in a large frying-pan or a thick-based roasting tin. Now sprinkle a little salt over them and throw in the peppercorns. Next add the bayleaves, one in between each trout. Lay onion rings over the top, cut half the lemon into slices and arrange them here and there. Add the thyme and sprinkle a tablespoon of chopped parsley over everything. Finally add the wine and enough cold water just to cover the fish. Bring it to the boil on top of the stove and let it simmer gently, uncovered, for 6 minutes if the trout are fresh or 20 minutes if they are frozen.

Mix the remaining parsley and chives with the butter in a small basin, then divide the mixture into four portions. When the trout are ready, carefully lift them out with a fish slice, allowing each one to drain for a few seconds, and serve with the parsley butter and the other half of the lemon cut into wedges.

*Trout with
butter, cream
and chives*

(serves 2 people)

This recipe is a good one for anyone who
has to work and then prepare a meal
quickly—the whole thing takes little
more than 30 minutes.

2 medium trout, 6 or 7 oz each (175 or 200 g), cleaned
1 oz butter (25 g)
3 fl oz double cream (75 ml)
2 tablespoons fresh snipped chives
A little extra butter, melted
1 bayleaf
Salt and freshly-milled black pepper

Pre-heat the oven to gas mark 7,
425°F (220°C)

First line a roasting tin with foil and brush it with a little melted
butter. Then wash the trout and dry them very thoroughly. Now
place them in the roasting tin, brush each one with a little melted
butter and season with salt and pepper. Bake them, on a high shelf
in the oven, for about 10–15 minutes.

While that's happening empty the cream into a saucepan, add the
bayleaf and bring it up to boiling point. Then stir in the chives and
the butter, season with salt and pepper, and pour this mixture into a
warm jug. Serve it with the fish, some buttered new potatoes and a
green salad or some fresh cooked spinach.

*Baked mackerel
with herb
stuffing*

(serves 2 people)

Mackerel need to be very fresh so try to
buy bright, stiff-looking fish rather than
flabby, tired-looking ones.

2 mackerel, gutted and heads removed
2 oz white breadcrumbs (50 g)
1 oz butter (25 g)
3 large spring onions, chopped
The grated rind of half a lemon
2 teaspoons lemon juice
1 tablespoon fresh chopped parsley
1 tablespoon snipped chives

1 teaspoon finely chopped fresh tarragon (or ½ teaspoon dried)
½ teaspoon dried thyme
5 fl oz yoghurt (150 ml)
Salt and freshly-milled black pepper
Oil

Pre-heat the oven to gas mark 5, 375°F (190°C)

Wash and dry the mackerel thoroughly. Start by melting the butter and gently frying the chopped spring onions for about 2 minutes, then combine in the breadcrumbs, lemon rind and juice and half the whole quantity of herbs. Season well with salt and pepper and pack an equal quantity of the mixture into the belly of each fish. Brush the fish with oil and season with salt and freshly-milled pepper. Place them in a foil-lined baking tin and bake in the top half of the oven for 25 minutes.

Stir the remaining herbs into the yoghurt and season with salt and freshly-milled pepper. Pour over the fish and bake for 5 minutes, then serve with some buttery potatoes and a crisp green salad.

Cucumber with soured cream and dill

(serves 2–3 people)

Dill goes well with all cucumber or soured cream recipes. This combines both, and is a marvellous accompaniment to fish.

1 lb cucumber (450 g), cut into ½ inch (1 cm) cubes with the skin left on
1½ oz butter (40 g)
2 spring onions, chopped—including the green tops
1 teaspoon fresh chopped dill or ¼ teaspoon dried dill
2½ fl oz soured cream (65 ml)
1 dessertspoon lemon juice
Salt and freshly-milled black pepper

Heat the butter in a smallish pan and stir in the chopped spring onions. Cook for 2 minutes before tipping in the cucumber. Now give them a good stir to coat with the butter, sprinkle with the dill, then cover and cook over a medium heat for about 8 minutes.

Shake the pan now and then to make sure none of the cucumber catches on the base of the pan.

As soon as the pieces are just tender (but still with a bit of 'bite' to them), turn the heat down, stir in the soured cream and a little lemon juice, and season with salt and pepper before serving.

Note: this is also good made with some small, young courgettes.

Pork chops with sage and apples

(serves 4 people)

This is an excellent recipe and a very easy one. There is a photograph on page 389.

4 lean pork chops
4 tablespoons dried white breadcrumbs
3 level dessertspoons very finely chopped fresh sage or 3 teaspoons dried
1 small egg
1 medium-sized onion, peeled and sliced into rings
1 large cooking apple, peeled and sliced into rings
1 tablespoon butter
2 tablespoons oil
Salt and freshly-milled black pepper
Extra butter and oil

First of all mix the sage and breadcrumbs together and season well with coarsely ground black pepper and salt. Then beat up the egg and dip the pork chops first in the egg, then into the breadcrumb and sage mixture, pressing firmly all round so that the chops get a really good even coating.

Now heat the oil and butter together in a frying-pan and, first of all, brown the chops quickly on both sides with the fat fairly hot, then lower the heat and let them gently cook through (it will take around 25–30 minutes depending on the thickness of the chops).

While that's happening, melt a little more butter and oil in another frying-pan and fry the apple and onion rings. Drain everything on crumpled greaseproof paper before serving.

*Leg of lamb
baked with
butter and herbs*

(serves 4–6 people)

This is a favourite—delicious with
Redcurrant, orange and mint sauce, page 443.

1 leg of lamb weighing about 4 lb (2 kg)
3 oz butter at room temperature (75 g)
1 teaspoon finely chopped rosemary
2 tablespoons fresh chopped mint
2 tablespoons fresh chopped parsley
1 teaspoon fresh chopped thyme
1 clove garlic, crushed
Salt and freshly-milled black pepper

For the gravy:
1 dessertspoon plain flour
3 fl oz dry red or white wine (75 ml)
Approx. ½ pint (275 ml) vegetable stock
Seasoning

Pre-heat the oven to gas mark 5,
375°F (190°C)

Mix the butter, herbs and garlic together, adding a level teaspoon of
salt and some freshly-milled black pepper. Stab the joint in several
places with a skewer, and rub the herb butter all over the upper side
(these stabs with the skewer will allow the butter to run into the
joint during the cooking).

Now wrap the joint loosely in foil, sealing well. Place it in a meat
roasting tin and cook it for 2 hours, then open out the foil and cook it
for a further 30 minutes to brown nicely. With these cooking times
the lamb will be slightly pink. If you like it well done give it a little
extra time in the foil before opening it out. Remove the joint to a
warm serving dish in a warm place while you make the gravy.

Empty the juices from the foil into the roasting tin, then tilt it
slightly. You will see the meat juices and the fat separating, so spoon
off most of the fat into a bowl and leave the juices in the tin. Now
place the tin over a medium heat, and when the juices start to
bubble, sprinkle in the flour and work it to a smooth paste using a
wooden spoon, then cook it for a minute or so to brown. Now pour in
the wine and stock by degrees, stirring continuously and adding just
enough stock to make a thin gravy. Taste to check the seasoning,
pour into a jug and serve with the lamb.

Cream cheese	6 oz cream cheese (175 g)
with herbs	2 spring onions, very finely chopped
	2 tablespoons fresh chopped parsley
(serves 4 people)	1 tablespoon fresh snipped chives
	1 level teaspoon chopped tarragon
	1 level teaspoon chopped thyme
	1 clove garlic, crushed
	Freshly-milled black pepper and salt (if it needs it)

Combine all the above ingredients together in a basin, then form the cheese into a round cake-shape, and serve it for lunch with lots of fresh crusty bread and a crisp salad.

Many other recipes contain some herbs, but in those below herbs play a prominent part:
Aioli sauce
Cabbage with garlic and juniper
Cheese and herb sausages
Fresh tomato sauce
Fresh tomato soup with basil
Fried mustard-and-herb-coated chicken
Garlic butter
Herb butter
Hot herb and garlic loaf
Jacket potatoes with soured cream and chives

Liver in yoghurt and juniper sauce
Marinaded mackerel
Mushrooms in hot garlic butter
New Jersey potatoes with fresh herb butter
Piperade
Place fillets with garlic and herbs
Rice with herb butter
Roast pork with green butter
Sauce rouille
Sauce tartare
Scotch eggs with fresh herbs
Spring carrots with tarragon butter
Stuffed baked herrings
Stuffed potatoes with garlic and herbs

Spices
and flavourings

Including recipes for:
Steak au poivre
Braised steak with green peppercorn sauce
Indian kebabs
Beef curry with whole spices
Spiced chicken
Chicken paprika
Marinaded pork with coriander
Moussaka
Guacamole
Sautéed cauliflower with coriander
Spiced pears in cider

Countries have grown rich, gone to war, built empires on spice. It was the trading currency of the medieval world, its value greater than gold and precious metals. So it is curious to find, in medieval cookery books, so many different spices competing (and in such prolific amounts) in a single recipe. In one I have in front of me a humble pike is treated to no less than eight different flavourings. Such abandon with precious spices was commonly supposed to disguise the taste of not-very-fresh food. And no doubt it was in many cases, but I also think there was an element of status-seeking in it as well. The cookery-books that have survived, after all, were those compiled by master-chefs for grand households. When—in the 17th century—spices became more widely available and cheaper in England, they began to be used with much more discretion and English cooking improved in consequence (the 'best in the world' according to Defoe at the time).

With our conquest of India, the British became even more spice-conscious as exotic curry flavourings were added to the repertoire, along with the already traditional taste of pickles, relishes and preserves. The Victorians in particular were very partial to a whole range of weird and wonderful compounds of spices, which were commercially produced under names like Harvey's Sauce: some of the better ones have survived to the present day (like Worcestershire sauce and tomato ketchup). I have the feeling that we are still suffering a bit from the legacy of the Victorians in this: there is a tendency to prefer to add flavourings to our food in the form of bottled sauces at the table, rather than incorporate them more discriminatingly in the cooking.

However, the range of spices available, even in local supermarkets, is now more impressive. They open up a whole world of recipes, and there is no excuse for our cooking horizons to be bounded by plain fried fish or grilled lamb chops (excellent though they are). All that is required is the confidence to go out and buy them and to experiment—not like a medieval alchemist throwing anything and everything together in a hotch-potch of flavours, but with restraint, allowing the flavour of the spices to enhance and complement the flavour of the food. The recipes in this section (and elsewhere in the book) are designed to demonstrate the balanced use of individual spices in recipes, and the combinations that have been shown to work through experience.

It is impossible to describe the flavour of each spice with any meaning—only testing them for yourself can be any guide—but the list below offers some explanation of their origin and possible uses. I have included in this section some equally important seasonings and flavourings which are normally lumped together under the ungainly title of condiments, and whose proper use is vital to good cooking. Garlic, however, is dealt with in the Herbs chapter.

Salt
It's amazing the difference salt makes to food, almost magically bringing out the flavour of a soup or sauce that may have seemed quite bland. Just how much salt you should or should not use has always been a subject for debate: some 'connoisseurs' even suggest that to add additional salt at the table is an insult to the chef. I believe that's nonsense. Each individual's capacity for salt is different, and what may be enough for the chef may not be enough for his diners. At the same time it could be true that adding more salt to food is a matter of acquired habit rather than need (as with sugar), which is why tinned baby foods now do not contain any salt—so at least our babies are not forming the habit! Others argue the health aspect, maintaining that salt—although a mineral essential to life—can in too high quantities exacerbate (not cause) hypertension and high blood pressure, which are themselves contributory factors to heart disease. This, I think, is an argument only for discretion, which is fundamental to all cooking anyway. If you discover that you *have* oversalted a dish with liquid ingredients, you can rescue it by putting in a peeled potato or two, which will absorb some of the salty flavour.

Types of salt
First of all it's as well to discount the snob element. Since the vogue for kitchen shops there's a lot of rock/sea/Mediterranean/crystal salt around. My advice is never to buy it from fancy packets. It is true that pure, unrefined salt is better than refined because it's saltier and you need less, but you can buy it from chemists, delicatessens and health food stores without paying for the packaging.

Basically there are two kinds of salt. For cooking and the table there is common salt mined from rocks or extracted from sea water. The other kind is saltpetre, which comes out of the earth and is used for curing and pickling. The sea salt I use comes from Maldon; it is packaged in ordinary boxes and, although it is too expensive to use exclusively for cooking, there are certain things I invariably serve it with: chips, sautéed potatoes, fritters and other deep-fried food taste so much better with crushed Maldon salt and coarse pepper over them. Unlike other unrefined salts—such as crystal salt which needs to be crushed first with a pestle and mortar—Maldon comes in tiny flakes and at table can easily be crushed between the fingers. Beware of salt mills, by the way. For grinding salt crystals I have found them quite useless: it is never fine enough and the salt either descends in a rush or not at all.

For everyday use the bulk of our salt comes from rock-deposits in Cheshire. Our so-called 'table salt' is very finely grained and has a chemical (magnesium carbonte) added to make it free-running. Personally I use what is termed 'cooking salt', which has fractionally larger grains, is cheaper and available at supermarkets. Even for the table I can't see the point of paying more for finer grains, particularly using a salt-cellar and spoon rather than a sprinkler.

Pepper

Pepper in my opinion is the most important spice in the kitchen. The one way in which beginners can instantly improve the character and flavour of their cooking and eating is to invest in a pepper-mill. *Freshly-ground* pepper has a fragrance and flavour that the dusty ready-ground stuff cannot approach. This is partly due to the fact that any spice once ground immediately starts to lose its essential flavour, and partly to the fact that most pepper-pots find their way to the table containing ready-ground 'white' pepper. Both black and white pepper come from the berries of the same tree, called *Piper nigrum*, but let us see where the difference lies.

Black pepper Black peppercorns are the whole immature berries. The berries themselves are made up of a white inner kernel and a black outer husk. The white is the hottest part of the berry and when used on its own is distinctly fiery. It is the black outer part that has the aromatic fragrance that really enhances the flavour of food. And this part is included in black pepper, where the berries are gathered while still green, then dried whole in the sun until they turn black.

White pepper For this the berries are allowed to mature fully before they are harvested. The husks are then split and discarded, and the white kernels are dried to become white peppercorns.

Stored whole, the dried berries will retain their taste and aroma almost indefinitely. But by the time they have been powdered to dust in a factory, stored in a shop and lain about in a pepper-pot it is not surprising the result bears no comparison to the fresh and delicate flavour you can keep locked up in your pepper-mill (and unlike salt-mills, pepper-mills do work).

Black pepper I always use this, freshly milled, in my cooking. There is a school of thought that objects, aesthetically at any rate, to finding black speckles in a white sauce. I can only say that knowing what they are all my family and friends have grown quite used to them and don't give it a second thought. (Curious, isn't it, that everyone expects grated nutmeg to look brown and speckled on food and raises no objection, perhaps because there is no such thing as white nutmeg?)

Green peppercorns This variety of pepper has only reached us in the last few years. These are the young, soft berries harvested before they have even developed separate husks and kernels. They are not dried, but retain their moisture and are preserved in small tins or jars. Deliciously aromatic—but still with a peppery fragrance—so far they are only available in specialised food shops. So it is worth keeping a few in hand, if you can find them.

Capsicums
Under this heading come a bewildering variety of the pepper family—red, green, chilli, sweet, paprika, cayenne. Not least are they bewildering because at times their power (i.e. lethal or mild) can only be identified by one means, and that is by tasting.

Fresh chillies These look like small fresh green peppers: sometimes they are long, finger-thin and somewhat crooked and at other times they are shiny-smooth like small rounded carrots. Treat them with respect for the reason above. If they are hot, take the precaution of discarding the really hot seeds and core, and use just the chopped flesh, which is less ferocious (a little chilli powder can always be added to increase the hotness, but there is little that can be done to subdue it afterwards). However, provided this warning is observed, fresh chillies—plentiful where there are immigrant communities—really give an authentic taste to Indian dishes and curries.

Whole or crushed dried chillies: chilli powder Whole dried chillies are useful when there are no fresh ones available. Again, exercise caution. A good compromise is to remove the seeds and use only the outer paper-like casing. Crushed dried chillies (skins and seeds) are good for a dish like chilli con carne, but should be used more sparingly than powdered ones, being definitely more pungent. Chilli powder is the most widely available chilli for the kitchen, if stored too long it will lose some of its character, if not heat. All the above are used mostly in curries and chilli sauces. Sometimes, however you will find a spice labelled 'chilli con carne seasoning': this is usually a blend of half chilli and half ground cumin, so is 50 per cent less powerful. I think chilli con carne tastes better with pure chilli.

Cayenne pepper The difference between this and chilli powder is not always clear, because both can be made from varieties of the same capsicum family. Cayenne is finer and more suitable for sprinkling on food. It is also a very fiery spice, so caution is needed, but it certainly adds zest to smoked fish pâtés in particular and cheese dishes, cheese scones and biscuits (for a cheese topping on any baked dish, mix some grated cheese with breadcrumbs and a couple of good pinches of cayenne pepper).

Tabasco sauce This is a commercially-prepared chilli sauce: very hot, only the merest drop or two is needed at any one time. It is used in much the same way, and in the same dishes, as cayenne pepper.

Paprika A spice made from the ground seeds of sweet peppers (pimentoes as they are sometimes called). It has the flavour of sweet pepper too, and none of the penetrating hotness of chilli. Of all ground spices paprika seems to lose flavour the fastest, so buy in small quantities, and if you haven't used it all after a few months, start again. I actually only use paprika for Hungarian goulash and *Chicken paprika* (page 421), and always buy Hungarian in preference to Spanish. If you see the words 'hot' or 'mild' on a jar, don't take too much notice because it is never a hot spice (to give an edge to it in a goulash I add just a pinch of chilli).

Mustard
Commercially speaking, mustard has run riot recently. Where once the supermarket stocked only the familiar canary-yellow English mustard powder, nowadays the shelves display at least half a dozen—often more—imported varieties or at least home-made imitations of them. They are even turning up in tourist gift shops in pretty pottery jars. Wider choice is always to be welcomed of course, but personally I have always preferred my mustard to be pungent and, well, mustardy, which is why I still think our own

home-grown mustard from East Anglia qualifies as the best. But what are its rivals, and how do they differ from it?

English mustard is made basically—as it has been for over two hundred years—by the milling and blending of two different mustard seeds, the brown (confusingly sometimes called black) and the white (sometimes known as yellow). It is the brown seed that provides the pungency, the white, flavour: but both only come to life when the resulting powder is mixed with water (see below). It is now possible also to buy English mustard ready made-up—which is fine if the lid is replaced firmly and quickly each time, as mustard exposed to the air loses its kick very rapidly.

Dijon mustard is the main mustard of France. It is the nearest to our own, though less ferocious. As the name implies it is made in and around Dijon in Burgundy, and there are any number of local variations. In some the mustard seed is mixed with spices and the acid juice of unripe grapes (verjuice), in others with diluted vinegar; yet others are blended with various white wines of the region. Like nearly all foreign mustards it comes not in powder form but already made-up, since it contains liquid.

Bordeaux mustard This is what we tend to call French mustard over here. It is much darker, and because it also contains the husk of the mustard seed, it is milder and distinctly aromatic. Packed as it is with vinegar, sugar, spices and tarragon it can tend to compete with rather than enhance the flavour of some food, and it should be used very selectively.

Among the other mustards that adorn our shelves, one might take note of the sweet-sour *German mustard*, dark and not dissimilar to the Bordeaux: it goes admirably with German sausage but otherwise should be used with discretion. *American mustard* is much the same colour as ours, but is positively sweet and strictly for hot dogs. For most requirements in cooking (as opposed to using it as a condiment) our English mustard, and Dijon, are more than adequate.

How to make mustard
It's amazing, but even a simple little task like mixing mustard needs a bit of thought. It is the essential oils in mustard that give it its power and pungency, but these are not developed in the whole mustard seed or in the dry milled powder. What is needed for the flavour to emerge is a chemical reaction brought on by the

addition of a little water, and even then it needs a good 10–15 minutes for the flavour to develop fully (so always make up mustard well in advance of using it). The water, too, must be cold—hot water can cause a rather different reaction, which may provide a bitter flavour. Mixing vinegar or salt with dry mustard can also cause bitterness (once the mustard is made up they can be added without any ill-effect). So when making mayonnaise add the vinegar at the end, and with vinaigrette dressing it is best to use mustard that has been made up for at least 10 minutes. Mustard is a very good emulsifier. Apart from the flavour it can add, it does a good stabilising job in something like mayonnaise, and can provide a slight thickening to vinaigrette or to *Cumberland sauce* (see recipe, page 442).

Vinegar

Originally sour wine (which is the precise meaning of the French *vin aigre*), but now the name embraces all similar sour liquids: wine vinegar, cider vinegar, malt vinegar and so on. It is created by an entirely natural process in which alcohol is turned into acetic acid. The bacteriological processes need not concern us overmuch, but the differences between the various vinegars—and the uses they can be put to—are most important.

Wine vinegar, like the wine it is made from, can be either red or white. The best comes for Orleans in France, where it is produced slowly and in oak casks—so look out for that name on the label when you're buying. This is the vinegar to use where it is important that the flavour does not dominate or overwhelm other ingredients, for instance in salad dressings or sauces.

Malt vinegar In England vinegar has traditionally been made from beer rather than wine. The resulting malt vinegar is dark coloured and powerfully flavoured. Indeed in cooking it can only too often be a flavour-killer, masking everything else in the vicinity. It is best confined to pickling and chutneys and those recipes that are intended to have a pronounced vinegary flavour (and *never* used for mint sauce).

Cider vinegar, self-evidently made from cider. Healthy it may be (as some food theorists maintain), but it has its own distinctive taste, and is not an automatic substitute for other vinegars. Use it only where a recipe actually specifies it.

Distilled vinegar is colourless, strong and popular in Scotland. Because it is stronger (up to 12 per cent acetic acid) it has excellent preserving powers, and is used for pickling.

Flavoured vinegars containing fruit, herbs or spices can be bought in some shops. Their uses are limited and, anyway, you can quite easily make your own. Tarragon vinegar, for instance, is made simply by steeping a bunch of tarragon in wine vinegar for a time, then straining the liquid if necessary.

Allspice
It is not, as the name would suggest, a combination of spices. Bought whole (which is to be recommended) it looks like a smoother version of peppercorns, but is in fact the dried berry of an evergreen. It got its name because it is supposed to have the flavour of three spices: nutmeg, cloves and cinnamon. However, the flavour is not really like any of these. It is used in pickling quite a lot, also for marinades for dishes like soused herring or mackerel. If a recipe calls for ground allspice, it is best to grind it with a pestle and mortar yourself as and when you need it.

Capers
I have included capers—not strictly a spice—here because I look on them as such important store-cupboard ingredients. A few capers can jazz up many otherwise ordinary dishes, like plain grilled fish, or sprinkled on pizzas or to add an extra dimension to sauces. I have seen caper bushes, with their very pretty pink flowers, growing out of the rocks along the Amalfi coast in Italy, where they are used extensively in the local cooking—especially *Salsa verde* (see page 444). What they are in fact are the buds of the plant, picked and pickled. Even once the jar is opened they keep their sweet-sharp flavour for some time, provided they remain covered by the pickling liquid. Ideally this should be white wine vinegar, though unfortunately some British firms subject them to our lethal malt vinegar, from which their flavour never quite recovers even when you rinse them under the cold tap. In Italian shops, particularly in London, capers can be bought loose.

Caraway seeds
These, with their nutty toasted flavour, are not much favoured in our cooking nowadays except in old-fashioned seed cake (loved or hated, depending on one's upbringing—I well remember a

schoolfriend trying to pick out all the seeds before eating it!). In Austria and Germany they are used quite a lot in various types of sausage, goulash and cabbage dishes.

Cardamom

An eastern spice, the sun-dried pods are pale green-grey, revealing inside the tiny, black, highly aromatic seeds. It is quite expensive, as spices go, but a little goes a long way. One pod crushed and added (add both pod and seeds) to pilau rice will impart a delicious flavour, recognisable even to those unfamiliar with the look of cardamom. It is used widely in curry dishes, occasionally in sweet recipes, and should never be bought ready-ground.

Cinnamon

This is a spice made from the inner bark of a tree belonging to the laurel family, which is what the pale-brown and hollow cinnamon sticks look like. Break pieces off to add in cooking, then extract them, like bayleaves, at the end. British cooks are familiar with it as a pudding spice and for use in cakes (for this it must be bought ready-ground as it's impossible to grind it at home). It is worth noting that its strength can vary enormously, so shop around for a brand that is reliable and buy in small quantities. One of the best flavour tips I've picked up is from Greek cookery, where a hint of cinnamon is often used in savoury dishes. A little added to the meat in a moussaka gives the dish an authentic Greek flavour, and I've even taken to adding it to shepherd's pie.

Cloves

Cloves look like tiny wooden nails, and their aroma is dark, pungent and exotic. Those who were subjected to the highly-concentrated 'oil of cloves' as a toothache remedy understandably find their flavour intolerable, but for others cloves can enhance all sorts of dishes, from mince pies and Christmas pudding to bread sauce and baked gammon. Unlike other spices, ground cloves seem to taste stronger than whole ones (perhaps because so little is needed, one tends to add too much). A little ground cloves always goes into my spiced red cabbage. Others like the flavour of cloves in an apple pie—where I think just two or three whole ones are better than adding ground cloves, although consumers have to be diligent in seeking them out!

Coriander
I'm particularly fond of coriander: the tiny, round seeds crush easily and give off an aromatic, almost scented flavour sometimes said to be reminiscent of roasted orange peel (in fact Margaret Costa in her *Four Seasons Cookbook* suggests tying the crushed seeds in muslin and adding them to the fruit for marmalade). Coriander turns up in the cooking of countries all over the world. In India it is an important curry spice and the leaves—quite different in flavour—are used a great deal as a herb. Spanish, Portuguese, Arab, Turkish and Greek cuisines all rely on coriander: in fact any recipe *à la grècque* includes it. A lovely way to serve olives with aperitifs is to toss them first in a mixture of crushed coriander seeds, crushed garlic and a little vinaigrette dressing. It quickly loses flavour once ground. Buy it whole, it's so easy to do yourself.

Cumin
Although this turns up in quite a few Mexican dishes, this is a spice I associate with curries. It looks like—and indeed is—long, tiny seeds, which are very easy to grind with a pestle and mortar. Sometimes whole seeds are added to pilaus and, with their strong piquant flavour, they are an essential curry spice.

Curry powder and garam masala
Curry powder—that is to say a ready-made blend of powdered Indian spices—is always to hand in my kitchen, though by no means always for curries. I sprinkle it onto cheesy biscuits, into sauces, and even like to add some to kedgeree. Unfortunately there is no uniformity among commercial curry powders, and some are a good deal hotter than others. The secret is to know your brand of curry powder, and to try and use a little of a hot one rather than a lot of a mild one. Sometimes Indian recipes call for garam masala, which is a blend of spices.

Curry paste can be used instead of curry powder and is particularly useful for marinades and kebabs. It is a blend of spices preserved in oil with sometimes a smaller amount of vinegar added. Like curry powder these pastes can be of varying strength—from very hot to fairly mild. They are particularly useful for marinading or coating as in the recipe for *Indian kebabs* (see page 418).

Ginger

One of the most widely-used spices of all, which comes to us to use fresh, dried, powdered, preserved in syrup and crystallised: a very versatile spice. In this country we are partial to ginger in our gingerbread, cakes, puddings and pickles—not forgetting the ginger beer which in its heyday came in those beautiful stoneware bottles, now collectors' items. If you can get hold of fresh root ginger, it really does add a clean fresh taste, as well as spiciness, to curries. It looks just like a knobbly, misshapen root and it can be stored in the freezer wrapped in freezer-foil and unpeeled. (Elizabeth David says that, peeled and sliced, it stores well in a small jar covered with sherry.)

Lumps of dried ginger are used in making up pickling spices for chutneys and pickles. Preserved ginger is expensive, though less so if you buy it in plain jars (some supermarkets have good stocks around Christmas): chopped up it adds a touch of luxury sprinkled with some syrup over ice-cream, or added to rhubarb fool—in fact ginger has a great affinity with rhubarb—or adorning the top and inside of a preserved ginger cake. Ginger is most commonly found, and used, in its powdered form: check that it is spicy and fresh-tasting, and not musty and stale.

Juniper

These are purple-black, rather wrinkled berries, most notorious as a basic ingredient in gin. But juniper is very much a cooking spice as well, especially with game and pork dishes (perhaps because it grows wild in hill-country where animals and birds feed on the autumn-ripened berries). For cooking, the berries are dried and always crushed before using. Their flavour seems to have a special sympathy with garlic, and if you want to try out juniper for the first time, I suggest you try the cabbage recipe on page 262, which is really delicious. Juniper berries are not as widely available as some other spices, sadly. So the more we pester our suppliers for them, the more plentiful they'll become.

Mace and nutmeg

These two spices belong together, because they come from the same source. *Mace* is part of the outer covering of the nutmeg—resembling a thick-meshed cage—which is removed and dried to become brittle and pale orange in colour. It is sold either in pieces (blades) or ready-ground. With a stronger, much more concentrated flavour than nutmeg it has to be used with care.

Ready-ground it can eventually get stale, but that is a built-in handicap because the brittleness of the spice makes it impossible to grind at home. It has been used extensively in English cooking in the past, for such recipes as potted meats and fish pâtés. If not available, nutmeg can always be used instead.

Nutmeg Another favourite of mine: I always keep it within arm's reach in the kitchen, in a special compartment in its own grater. It's always been a popular spice in this country— 18th-century gentlemen wore miniature graters containing a nutmeg on a chain round their necks, so they could grate some over their hot mulls and toddies at a moment's notice. It's said to be good for sleep and to increase the potency of alcoholic drinks—but I leave you to judge that for yourselves!

It is an important spice for cakes and puddings: all milk puddings should have a dark, caramelised nutmeg crust, and it gives an attractive freckled effect to egg custards and custard tarts. Although the French rarely use it, the Italians accord it great importance— and rightly so, as it contributes a subtle flavouring to cheese dishes, vegetables like spinach, creamy white sauces, meat fillings for ravioli and so on. If I had the power I would ban the sale of ground nutmeg as it's quite useless. If your local grocer or supermarket does not stock whole nutmegs, try a chemist.

Mixed spice
Usually a made-up combination of nutmeg, cinnamon, cloves and allspice. Most useful for puddings and cakes, but buy it in small quantities and shop around a little for one you like, as they can vary quite a lot in composition.

Saffron
The most expensive spice of all. It comes from the dried stigmas of a variety of crocus, and is used for its deep yellow colouring as well as for flavour. Being so costly it's as well that very little—just a few strands—is needed to colour and flavour something like a Spanish paella or an Italian risotto. It is also used in the South of France in fish stews and soups, and turns up here in Cornish saffron cake. If a recipe calls for it and you don't have any, a teaspoonful of turmeric will give you the authentic colour (though obviously a different flavour). To use saffron, you can crush it and mix it with a small amount of water or stock before adding it to the other ingredients.

Turmeric

This is a spice originating from a plant of the ginger family, and it is a bright orange-yellow colour. For all its flamboyance it's a mild spice, and is used freely in curries where its colour is more robust than its flavour (I also add turmeric to rice for the same reason). It can only be bought ready-ground (be careful with it: it can stain hands and clothes rather badly).

Vanilla

There is a marked difference between pure vanilla essence and vanilla flavour essence. The former is extracted from vanilla pods (from a species of climbing orchid): the latter is made from a substitute.

Whole dried vanilla pods, long, thin, dark and rather wrinkled, are useful to have in the kitchen. I think the flavour they provide is better than from essence: if you have time, warm the milk (for, say, a custard) and allow the vanilla pod to infuse into it for a short while. A single pod will last for ages, and can be wiped and dried after use, then stored in a jar for the next time. Another tip is to keep a pod buried in the jar containing caster sugar—then when you make a custard or a sweet sauce, the sugar will already have its own vanilla flavouring.

Steak au poivre

(serves 2 people)

In restaurants this is sometimes served swimming in a sickly cream and brandy sauce. Personally I think the combined flavours of the peppercorns and the steak need nothing else but a glass of wine to rinse out the pan at the end.

2 entrecôte (sirloin) steaks, or you could use rump steak if you prefer, weighing 6–8 oz each (175–225 g)
2 heaped teaspoons whole black peppercorns
2 tablespoons olive oil
¼ pint red wine (150 ml)
Salt

First crush the peppercorns very coarsely with a pestle and mortar (or use the back of a tablespoon on a flat surface). Pour the olive oil into a shallow dish, then coat each steak with the oil and press the crushed peppercorns onto both sides of each steak. Then leave them to soak up the flavour in the dish for several hours—turning them over once in that time.

When you're ready to cook, pre-heat a thick-based frying-pan (without any fat in it) and when it's very hot sear the steaks quickly on both sides. Then turn down the heat and finish cooking them according to how you like them (a medium-rare entrecôte will take about 6 minutes and should be turned several times during the cooking). One minute before the end of the cooking time pour in the wine, let it bubble, reduce and become syrupy. Then sprinkle a little salt over the steaks and serve immediately with the reduced wine spooned over. These are delicious served with *Gratin dauphinois* (page 284).

Braised steak with green peppercorn sauce

(serves 2 people)

This has a lovely piquant flavour. If possible try to get two whole slices of braising steak weighing ½ lb each; failing that cubes of steak will do.

1 lb braising steak (450 g)
1 large onion peeled and sliced
1 tablespoon beef dripping
4 fl oz dry white wine (or dry cider) (110 ml)
3 teaspoons green peppercorns
1 teaspoon tomato purée
1 heaped teaspoon flour
1 clove garlic
1 sprig thyme
Salt and freshly-milled black pepper

Pre-heat the oven to gas mark 2, 300°F (150°C)

Start by melting the dripping in a frying-pan till it is nice and hot, then pop the pieces of steak in and sear them till brown on both sides. Then remove them to a casserole, with the aid of a draining spoon. Now to the fat left in the pan add the onion slices, and brown these, then spoon them over the meat. Next spoon off any excess fat from the pan—tilting it to one side will help—and to the juices that remain add the wine; bring it up to simmering point, at the same time scraping the base and sides of the pan.

Pour the wine over the meat, and add the thyme and clove of garlic (crushed slightly) and a little seasoning. Cover the casserole, then braise the steak in the oven for 2 hours. After that, pour all the juices and the garlic clove into the goblet of a liquidiser and (keeping the onions and meat warm meantime) add the flour, tomato purée and two teaspoons of the green peppercorns to the juices. Blend at top speed until smooth, then pour the sauce into a saucepan with the remaining teaspoon of peppercorns. Bring up to simmering point, and pour it over the meat before serving. *Note:* This could be braised on top of the stove over a very low heat, provided it is covered with a well-fitting lid closely covered in foil.

Indian kebabs

(serves 4 people)

These spicy kebabs are first marinaded, then coated with a curry paste before being grilled.

1½ lb fillet end of leg of lamb (675 g), cut into cubes
2 tablespoons olive oil
1 small green pepper
4 firm tomatoes
1 medium onion
1 large lemon
¼ pint natural yoghurt (150 ml)
1 small piece root ginger
2 teaspoons mild curry powder
2 teaspoons curry paste
Salt and freshly-milled black pepper

First of all—4 hours or so before you cook—place the cubes of lamb in a wide shallow dish, season with salt and pepper, then pour in 2 tablespoons of olive oil. Leave the meat to soak up the oil for about 2 hours, turning the pieces over once or twice.

Cut the onion into quarters, split the quarters into pieces and add these to the meat: also cut the tomatoes into quarters and the pepper into 1 inch (2·5 cm) pieces and add these to the marinading meat. Now in a small basin mix the curry powder, curry paste, lemon juice and yoghurt together and pour this mixture over the meat, etc. Stir and mix everything around well, then leave for another 2 hours in a cool place.

To cook the kebabs: pre-heat the grill, then peel and slice up a 1 inch (2·5 cm) piece of ginger. Now onto four long flat (rather than rounded) skewers thread the meat, onion, tomato and pepper alternately with a little slice of ginger here and there. Pack everything up tightly together, and grill the kebabs under the grill for about 15 minutes, turning them frequently and basting occasionally with the marinade. Serve on rice with the juices spooned over.

Beef curry with whole spices

(serves 3 people)

Good as real Indian curries often are in restaurants, it is possible—using the proper spices—to make them as well if not better at home.

1½ lb chuck steak (675 g), cut into cubes
2 large onions, sliced
2 fresh green chillies, deseeded and chopped
1 piece fresh root ginger (about 1½ inch long), grated or very finely chopped (4 cm)
2 level teaspoons coriander seeds, crushed
1 teaspoon cumin seeds, crushed
1 level tablespoon turmeric powder
2 cardamom pods, crushed
¼ pint natural yoghurt (150 ml)
2 fl oz water (50 ml)
2 cloves garlic, crushed
Some groundnut oil
Salt

Start by browning the cubes of meat in oil in a flameproof casserole, then transfer them to a plate. Add the onions to the pan and fry that for about 5 minutes, before adding all the spices and the garlic—continue to cook for a further 5 minutes to draw out the flavours from the spices, before returning the meat to the pan.

Now gradually stir in the yoghurt and water, and add some salt. Cover the casserole and keep the heat at the lowest possible simmer for 2 hours, stirring everything around a few times.

After 2 hours, take the lid off and continue to cook for a further 15 minutes to reduce the sauce slightly. Serve this with pilau rice, Indian pickles and mango chutney. *Note:* If you can't get fresh root ginger, use a dessertspoon of ground ginger.

Spiced chicken
(serves 4 people)

I would definitely put this amongst my top ten: it's easy to prepare, convenient to serve, and always tastes delicious.

1 chicken weighing 3½ lb (1 kg 600 g), (cut into 4 pieces)
2 medium onions, chopped small
1 level dessertspoon ground ginger
1 level dessertspoon turmeric
1 level teaspoon Madras curry powder
1 clove garlic, crushed
1 tablespoon groundnut oil
1½ oz butter (40 g)
5 oz carton of natural yoghurt (150 g)
5 oz carton of single cream (150 g)
Salt and freshly-milled black pepper
A few sprigs of watercress, to garnish

A few hours before you eat, arrange the pieces of chicken in a large shallow casserole with a lid (or a meat roasting tin covered with foil—the chicken pieces must be side-by-side in a single layer).

Season the chicken with salt and pepper, then mix the powdered spices together and sprinkle approximately 1 heaped teaspoonful over the chicken. Now put a little piece of the crushed garlic into each section of chicken, then drizzle some oil over and, using your hands, rub the spices, oil and garlic into the chicken flesh. Pierce each portion with a skewer in several places, so that the flavours can penetrate. Leave the chicken in a cool place for several hours.

When you're ready to cook, pre-heat the oven to gas mark 4, 350°F (180°C). Pop a fleck of butter on each chicken joint and place the casserole in the oven (uncovered) for half an hour.

Meanwhile fry the onions in a little butter and oil over a low heat for 10 minutes to soften, and mix the remaining spices together with the yoghurt and cream.

When the 30 minutes are up, take the chicken out of the oven, spoon the onion over them, then pour the yoghurt mixture all over. Put on the lid (or cover with foil) and return the chicken to the oven for another 30–45 minutes—or until the joints are tender—basting with the juices once or twice during the cooking.

Garnish with a few sprigs of watercress, and serve with spiced rice and mango chutney. *Note:* There are always rather a lot of juices left over with this dish, but this is unavoidable—so just spoon a little over the chicken before you serve and discard the rest.

Chicken paprika

(serves 4 people)

This is nice served with some well-buttered noodles and a crisp green salad.

1 chicken weighing about 3 lb (1 kg 350 g), cut into 4 quarters
2 medium onions, chopped
1 medium green pepper, deseeded and cut into small strips
1 lb tomatoes (450 g), skinned and chopped (alternatively a 14 oz (400 g) tin of Italian tomatoes)
¼ pint chicken stock (150 ml)
1 dessertspoon flour
1 heaped tablespoon paprika (preferably Hungarian)
5 oz carton of soured cream (150 g)
Oil, for cooking
Salt and freshly-milled black pepper
2 good pinches of cayenne pepper

Pre-heat the oven to gas mark 3, 325°F (160°C)

Begin by heating a little oil in a frying-pan and gently frying the chicken joints to a golden colour. Then use a draining spoon to transfer them to a casserole, and season them with salt and pepper.

In the oil left in the pan fry the onions gently for about 10 minutes to soften. Now stir the flour, cayenne and paprika into the pan, with a wooden spoon, to soak up the juices before adding the chopped tomatoes. Stir them around a bit, then add the stock.

Bring everything up to simmering point, then pour over the chicken in the casserole, put a lid on and bake in the oven for 45 minutes. After that stir in the chopped pepper, replace the lid and cook for a further 30 minutes. Just before serving spoon the soured cream all over, mixing it in just to give a marbled effect, then sprinkle on a little more paprika.

Marinaded pork with coriander

(serves 3 people)

The Greeks call this traditional dish Afelia. If you have time to leave the meat to steep overnight and for the flavours to develop, so much the better.

1 pork fillet, cut into bite-sized cubes
1 lemon
2 heaped teaspoons coriander seeds
1 fat clove garlic, crushed
3 tablespoons olive oil
½ pint dry white wine (or dry cider) (275 ml)
Salt and freshly-milled black pepper

Place the pieces of pork in a shallow dish and season them with salt and freshly-milled pepper. Next, crush the coriander seeds, either with a pestle and mortar or with the end of a rolling-pin in a basin.

Now pour the oil over the pieces of meat, followed by the juice of the lemon and 2 tablespoons of the white wine. Then sprinkle in the crushed coriander seeds and the garlic, and mix everything together. Cover the dish with a cloth and leave it all to marinade overnight—or as long as possible—stirring now and then.

To cook the pork: melt a little oil in your largest frying-pan and when it's fairly hot add the cubes of pork and cook them over a medium heat, turning them and keeping them on the move. When they have browned a little, pour in the rest of the white wine, let it bubble and reduce to a syrupy consistency. The pork will take approximately 10–15 minutes to cook altogether. Serve with a little rice and a salad.

Moussaka

(serves 4 people)

The small amount of cinnamon gives it a really authentic Greek flavour.

1 lb minced lamb or beef (450 g)
8 oz onions, peeled and sliced (225 g)
2 cloves garlic, chopped
3 medium aubergines, cut into rounds about ½ inch (1 cm) thick
2 tablespoons tomato purée
3 fl oz wine (red or white) (75 ml)
1 teaspoon ground cinnamon

Right: Spiced chicken, page 420.

1 tablespoon fresh chopped parsley
Oil
Salt and freshly-milled black pepper

For the topping:
3 oz plain flour (75 g)
3 oz butter (75 g)
1 pint milk
2 oz Cheddar cheese, grated
2 eggs
Salt, pepper and freshly-grated nutmeg

Pre-heat the oven to gas mark 4, 350°F (180°C)

First of all prepare the aubergines. They should be sliced and packed into a colander, then sprinkled with salt. Then place a plate on top of them and a heavy weight on top of that, and leave them for half an hour. This is to drain off some of their excess moisture. Meanwhile fry the onions and chopped garlic in some oil (preferably olive oil) for about 5 minutes, then add the minced meat to the pan to brown—stirring it to break up any lumps. In a basin mix together the tomato purée, wine, cinnamon and parsley, season it all with salt and pepper, then pour the mixture over the onions and meat when it has browned. Stir well, and leave on a gentle heat to simmer quietly.

Now back to the aubergines: heat some olive oil in another frying-pan, dry the aubergine slices in kitchen paper, then fry each one to a golden-brown on both sides. When they are browned leave them on kitchen paper to drain (aubergines eat up cooking oil!). When the aubergines are done, take a casserole and arrange some of them in it. Spread part of the meat mixture on top, followed by another layer of aubergines—until everything is incorporated.

Next make up the topping for the moussaka. Melt the butter in a saucepan and stir in the flour until smooth, then add the milk gradually, stirring vigorously with each addition until you have a smooth white sauce. Next stir in the grated cheese, followed by a seasoning of salt, pepper and freshly-grated nutmeg. Allow the sauce to cool, then whisk up the 2 eggs, first on their own and then into the sauce. Pour the sauce over the meat and aubergines, then bake (uncovered) for an hour until the top is fluffy-golden.

Left (from top to bottom): Hot herb and garlic loaf, page 504; Salade Niçoise, page 498; Chinese beansprout salad with soy dressing, page 495.

Guacamole

(serves 4 people)

This recipe is originally from Mexico. If you like spicy food, it makes an ideal first course.

2 medium avocados
1 clove garlic, crushed
½ medium onion, grated
2 large tomatoes
½ teaspoon chilli powder
A dash of tabasco sauce
The juice of a medium lemon
Salt and freshly-milled black pepper

Skin the tomatoes to start with—if you pop them in a basin, pour boiling water over them and leave for a few minutes, you'll find they slip off quite easily. Then cut the tomatoes into quarters, scoop out and discard the seeds, then chop the flesh into fairly small pieces.

Now halve the avocados and remove their stones. Place each half skin-side up on a wooden board and, with a sharp knife, make an incision down the centre of the skin of each one. Peel the skins off. Chop up the avocado flesh and transfer it to a fairly large mixing bowl, and straightaway pour the lemon juice over it to help stop it discolouring. Now with a teaspoon scrape off from the under-side of the skins all that very green avocado flesh still clinging to them: this is what gives the guacamole a really good green colour. Add this to the bowl, then mash all the avocado with a large fork almost to a purée (it doesn't matter if there are a few little lumps).

Now add the tomatoes, grated onion and garlic to the avocado, season with salt and pepper, and finally stir in the chilli powder and tabasco. Taste it at this stage to check the seasoning (it does need a fair amount of salt to bring out the flavour) and add more chilli if you think it needs it. Cover the bowl with clingfilm and keep in a cool place—best in the lowest part of the refrigerator—until needed.

Serve in individual dishes with some hot crusty bread or slices of thin toast. *Note:* Don't make this too far ahead, because avocado does tend to discolour. If that happens just give the guacamole a good stir—the taste won't be affected.

Sautéed cauliflower with coriander

· (serves 2 people)

Cauliflower florets, just tossed in oil and fried quickly, seem to retain their crunchiness and flavour—which they can so easily lose when cooked with water.

1 smallish cauliflower
½ onion, finely chopped
1 level teaspoon whole coriander seeds
1 small clove garlic
2 tablespoons olive oil
1 knob of butter
Salt and freshly-milled black pepper

First prepare the cauliflower, by separating it into fairly small florets (about an inch long, including the stalk). Wipe them but don't wash them—they'll be cooked anyway at a fairly high temperature. Now heat the oil in your largest frying-pan and soften the onion in it for 5 minutes. Meanwhile chop the peeled clove of garlic finely and crush the coriander seeds with a pestle and mortar (or use the end of a rolling-pin and a small bowl).

When the onion is softened, turn the heat right up, and add the cauliflower. After a minute or two toss the pieces over by shaking the pan then add the coriander seeds and continue to cook the cauliflower for about 5 minutes, seasoning it with a sprinkling of salt and pepper. Finally add the butter and chopped garlic to the pan and cook for a further minute—by which time the cauliflower will have turned an attractive nutty-golden colour, but still retain some bite. Serve straight away.

Spiced pears in cider

(serves 6 people)

For this you need to get hold of really hard pears. After long cooking they will turn a lovely glazed amber colour, most attractive in a glass serving bowl.

6 large hard pears
1 pint dry cider (570 ml)
4 oz sugar (110 g)
1 vanilla pod
2 whole cinnamon sticks

| 1 level dessertspoon arrowroot |
| Some toasted flaked almonds |
| ¾ pint double cream (150 ml) |

Pre-heat the oven to gas mark ½,
250°F (130°C)

Peel the pears but leave the stalks on them, then lay them in a large casserole. Then in a saucepan bring the cider, sugar and cinnamon to the boil, add the vanilla pod to the mixture and pour the whole lot over the pears. Cover the casserole, and bake very slowly for about three hours, turning the pears over halfway.

After the three hours transfer the pears to a serving bowl to cool, and pour the liquid back into a saucepan (you can discard the vanilla pod and cinnamon sticks now).

In a cup mix the arrowroot with a little cold water till you have a smooth paste, then add this to the saucepan with the liquid. Bring to the boil, stirring till the mixture has thickened slightly to a syrup. Then pour it over the pears, allow to cool a little and baste each pear with a good coating of the syrup.

Place in the fridge to chill thoroughly, and serve sprinkled with toasted flaked almonds and thick whipped cream.

Many other recipes contain some spice or flavouring, but in those below these ingredients play a prominent part:

Baked lamb with coriander
Baked marrow with tomatoes and coriander
Buttery kedgeree
Chicken with whole spices
Chilli con carne
Chilli eggs
Creamed potatoes with nutmeg
Creamy chicken curry
Crisp cinnamon flan
Curried lambs' kidneys
Curried nut roast
Curried ox kidneys
Damson (or plum) and cinnamon crumble
Egg and lentil curry
Eliza Acton's vegetable mulligatawny
Fried mustard-and-herb-coated chicken

Gingernuts
Honey and spice cake
Hungarian goulash
Linzertorte
Paprika liver
Peppered liver
Pork kidneys in chilli sauce
Red cabbage and coriander salad
Rhubarb and ginger crumble
Saffron rice
Sautéed mixed vegetables
Spiced apple and onion sauce
Spiced apple and raisin crumble
Spiced fig pudding with rum butter
Spiced green tomato sauce
Spiced lamb with chick peas
Spiced pilau rice
Spiced plum chutney
Vegetarian goulash

Sauces

Including recipes for:
Basic white sauce
Béchamel sauce
Mustard sauce
Cheese sauce
Spinach and cheese sauce
Parsley sauce
Hollandaise sauce
Buttery onion sauce
Leek cream sauce
Celery sauce
Cucumber sauce
Sauce béarnaise
Spiced apple and onion sauce
Traditional bread sauce
Cumberland sauce
Redcurrant, orange and mint sauce
Bitter orange sauce
Morello cherry sauce
Spiced green tomato sauce

Italian green sauce (salsa verde)
Avocado sauce
Proper custard sauce
Sauce sabayon
Butterscotch sauce
Port wine sauce
Rum or brandy sauce
Herb butter
Anchovy butter
Hot lemon butter
Brandy butter
Old-fashioned gravy

It's the one subject that strictly divides us from our cousins on the other side of the English Channel, *sauces*. In France there are literally hundreds: over here (according to the French) we have only one, and that's custard. Of course we do have more than one, but the chauvinists are for ever arguing that the quality of our meat, fish and game is so superior that it has no need of clever sauces to enhance the flavour! Be that as it may, every honest cook will have to admit that—superior meat or not—the British are tireless consumers of bottled commercial ketchup, salad creams, gravy powders, instant packet sauces and even tinned custard.

It seems to me it's not so much that we despise sauces, but rather than as a nation we have never properly acquired the techniques of making them. So, when a housewife hurries out to the supermarket to buy her packet cheese sauce or gravy mix, what is it she's afraid of making at home? There may be an understandable fear of the unknown (for without experience how can anyone *know* anything), but usually there are more practical barriers—like the age-old problem of:

Lumps

The very first thing to know, if you're going to master the art of sauce-making, is that lumps simply *don't matter*. If a sauce goes lumpy all you do is whisk the lumps out of it or pass it through a sieve—that's precisely what sieves are for. You can even pop the offending sauce into a liquidiser, if there's one handy. This is not to say that a lump-free sauce isn't preferable in the first place: but don't let the problem cause you a moment's concern.

Curdling

Another headache, when it comes to the more advanced butter-and-egg based sauces, is curdling. But again it needn't be a problem. In the first place a beginner (or indeed anyone who's not an absolute purist) can use a little stabiliser—such as cornflour—to help things along. Or, if the sauce has curdled, it *can* be remedied. With egg yolk sauces such as hollandaise the remedy is to use a fresh egg yolk and start again, adding the curdled ingredients to it. With proper custard a teaspoon of cornflour will prevent curdling happening in the first place. Let's begin by examining the basic ingredients of a sauce and what they are doing in it.

Flour
In a basic white sauce and all the others that are derived from it flour is what thickens the liquid. As we have already seen (page 43), little granules of starch are present in wheat flour, and when these become wet and hot they burst as boiling point is reached: the granules collapse and spread, becoming gelatinous. Whisking then distributes this throughout and the sauce is thus thickened. (In this context I have found that self-raising flour is more inclined to go lumpy than plain flour, so I don't use it for sauces.)

Cornflour
This is pure starch separated from the rest of the flour, which does the thickening job very efficiently. But unfortunately it does not make a sauce with either the character or creamy texture that comes from white flour. Although I never make sauces with cornflour, I find it very useful for adding to egg-based sauces (especially 'proper' custard) to prevent the eggs from curdling—but only in a *small* amount so as not to affect the flavour.

Arrowroot
This is an edible starch which comes not from corn but from a plant root grown in the West Indies, which is ground down to a fine powder. As a thickening it is excellent for making a glaze for, say, a fruit flan because, unlike cornflour, it will thicken fruit juices and keep them clear and transparent at the same time. To use it, you need about 1 rounded teaspoon for every ¼ pint (150 ml) of liquid, and it has to be added to a little cold water first before being mixed with your liquid and being brought up to boiling point (at that stage remove it from the heat straight away, as over-boiling can cause it to liquify and lose its thickening power).

Liquid
The liquid base for a sauce can be almost anything: light home-made chicken or bone stock, the stock from boiling vegetables (especially if the sauce is to be served with those vegetables), sometimes milk, other times a mixture of milk and stock. Both wine and cider are particularly good for gravies or sauces to accompany meat or fish.

Whenever expert cooks continually disagree on a finer point of cookery it usually means it's not that important. So it is with the question of the temperature of liquid being added to a sauce. There are those who swear it must be hot, and those who insist it should be cold: in my humble opinion it doesn't matter one scrap. If it happens that the liquid you're adding is hot from the stock-pot, fine. On the other hand, if it's cold milk from the fridge, that's fine too. But one exception I must state now—and this is when you are making an *all-in-one sauce* (see page 434): for this the liquid you start off with should be cold.

Butter and fats

Butter is what makes a sauce creamy and rich, and as a rule is added in the same proportion as the flour. For extra creaminess the amount of butter can be increased, or else cream or soured cream added. Soured cream needs careful attention, though, because boiling can cause it to curdle: whereas ordinary cream *won't* hurt if it comes to the boil. Dripping, pork fat and lard are sometimes used in place of butter to make a brown roux.

What is a roux?

To make a classic béchamel 'white' sauce, the first process is to combine melted butter with an equal quantity of flour. The result is called a *roux*: the basis into which the required amount of liquid is worked to make the finished sauce.

In this cookery course we need never actually bother with the word roux, because when a recipe requires an equal quantity of butter and flour mixed together, it will say that. However, roux is the term used in French classic cookery to describe the base of three different types of sauce: *roux blanc* (white base), *roux blond* (pale-cream roux), and *roux brun* or brown roux where the fat and flour are allowed to go on cooking longer—up to 30 minutes—to brown and give the finished sauce a nutty flavour. It is quite a tricky operation to perfect, rarely needed except in advanced cooking.

You may have heard that it is possible to make up a batch of butter-and-flour and store it in the refrigerator ready for use. But it will only keep for about 4 weeks (and anyway only takes a few seconds to mix) so I don't really see the point. I know I can never tell how much I might need in the space of 4 weeks—if any.

How long should a sauce be cooked?

White sauces, when they're first made, can have a rather 'raw' flavour—which means that not all the starch granules have burst and disintegrated into the sauce. For that reason they have to be 'cooked', that is to say left over the gentlest possible heat for about

6–10 minutes. During this cooking process a thin layer of skin may form on the surface. I find this can usually be whisked back into the sauce quite happily, but you can actually prevent this skin forming by keeping back 1 or 2 tablespoons of liquid and 'floating' it on top at the end, without stirring it in. Then whisk it in normally after the sauce has cooked.

Keeping a sauce warm
The only acceptable way to keep a sauce warm, or reheat it, is to place the saucepan in another larger saucepan or pot of gently simmering water (to provide heat all round and not just underneath).

Basic white sauce: traditional method

We've considered the basic ingredients: now they have to be combined correctly. Here are the standard proportions for a pouring sauce—badly-made sauces are often too thick and pasty, so do measure quantities carefully.

For 1 pint (570 ml)
1½ oz plain flour (sifted) (40 g)
2 oz butter (50 g)
1 pint milk or half milk, half stock (570 ml)
Salt and pepper

For ¾ pint (425 ml)
1 oz sifted plain flour (25 g)
1½ oz butter (40 g)
¾ pint milk or half milk, half stock (425 ml)
Salt and pepper

The basic procedure is to (a) melt the butter over a medium heat, (b) stir in the flour off the heat, and (c) back on the heat, add the liquid bit by bit until it has all been incorporated and the sauce is smooth and glossy.

Have the liquid ready in a measuring jug, then melt the butter in a small saucepan very gently—it must not brown or it will affect the flavour and colour of the finished sauce. Take it off the heat as soon as the butter has melted and stir in the sifted flour. Stir to form a smooth glossy paste, then return the saucepan to a medium heat and start to add the milk—about 1 fl oz (25 ml) at a time—stirring quite vigorously with a wooden spoon as you pour, to incorporate each bit of liquid thoroughly before adding the next. If you're conscientious about the stirring you won't get any lumps: if you do, then either whisk them away with a wire- or rotary-whisk or sieve the finished sauce.

When all the milk has been incorporated, turn the heat to its lowest possible setting and let the sauce cook for 6–10 minutes. Then taste and season as required. *Note:* I always use freshly-ground black pepper because I don't mind the little dark speckles, but if you do then use freshly-ground white. For extra creaminess beat in an extra knob of butter at the end or else a couple of tablespoons of thick cream.

Béchamel sauce

When a plain white sauce is called for, you can give it extra flavour by *infusing* the milk beforehand for about 30 minutes. For this you need:

For ¾ pint milk (425 ml):
1 small piece of carrot
½ smallish onion
2 inch piece of celery (5 cm)
6 whole peppercorns
1 blade of mace
½ bayleaf

Place the above ingredients in a saucepan with the ¾ pint (425 ml) of milk, and then bring it to the boil very slowly. After that, remove from the heat and allow it to infuse for 20 minutes. Then strain the milk into a jug and proceed to make the sauce following the method described above. Alternatively you can let it cool for 45 minutes, and carry on with the all-in-one method below.

Basic white sauce: all-in-one method

This speeded-up version is even easier than using a packet! All you need is a balloon whisk (or a coil wire- or rotary-whisk) and a wooden spoon. It is suitable for all sauces except those where a vegetable has to be 'sweated' in butter first. *But* the liquid you add to this one must be cold: the dreaded lumps will form if the flour goes straight into hot liquid.

1½ oz butter (40 g)
1 oz plain flour (25 g)
¾ pint cold milk (or half milk, half stock) (425 ml)
Salt and pepper

Simply place all the ingredients in a saucepan, put the saucepan on a medium heat and whisk until the sauce starts to bubble and thicken. Then stir with a wooden spoon, to get right into the corners of the pan, and whisk again thoroughly. Turn the heat down as low as possible and cook the sauce gently for 6 minutes.

These first three recipes are the basis for a whole range of sauces; on their own they would be rather dull of course, but so many other ingredients can be used for flavouring. Here first are three variations on the all-in-one method, bearing in mind that the infused milk or stock must be cooled for a minimum of 45 minutes (if you're in a hurry, use the traditional method). Cream is used here to add a touch of luxury, but if not available it can be replaced by the same quantity of milk.

Mustard sauce This is a good sauce which is often served with herrings.

½ pint milk (275 ml)
1 small onion, halved
1½ oz butter (40 g)
1 oz plain flour (25 g)
2 rounded teaspoons mustard powder
¼ pint single cream (150 ml) or use all milk
1 teaspoon lemon juice
Salt and cayenne pepper

Bring the halved onion and the milk slowly to the boil, then remove from the heat and let it infuse until cooled. Now place the strained infused milk together with the butter, flour, mustard powder and cream in a saucepan, and bring to the boil, whisking continuously. Then cook the sauce gently for 5 minutes. Taste and season with salt, cayenne and lemon juice.

Cheese sauce

This is a basic cheese sauce which can be used in a wide variety of dishes. Grated Gruyère cheese could be used instead of Cheddar here, for a spot of refinement.

½ pint milk (275 ml)
½ pint single cream (275 ml) or use all milk
1 level teaspoon mustard
1 oz plain flour (25 g)
1½ oz butter (40 g)
2 oz strong Cheddar cheese, grated (50 g)
1 oz grated Parmesan cheese (25 g)
A pinch of cayenne pepper
½ teaspoon lemon juice
Salt and freshly-milled black pepper

Place the first five ingredients in a saucepan and whisk over the heat till smooth and thickened. Now add the cheeses, stir to melt them in, then cook the sauce *gently* for 5 minutes. Season to taste with salt, pepper, cayenne and lemon juice.

Spinach and cheese sauce

This is a delicious, colourful sauce to pour over halved hard-boiled eggs on a bed of brown rice, or to accompany any grilled or fried fish. Cook 8 oz (225 g) fresh spinach leaves as on page 288, then place them in a liquidiser with a cheese sauce made with 2 oz (50 g) butter, 1 oz (25 g) plain flour, ½ pint (275 ml) milk, 3 oz (75 g) grated cheese, and 2 tablespoons double cream. Liquidise until you have a pale green, speckled sauce. Season with salt, pepper and freshly grated nutmeg, and reheat before serving.

Parsley sauce

I like parsley sauce best with baked fish cutlets of various kinds: it's also very good with boiled gammon.

½ pint milk (275 ml)
¼ pint single cream (150 ml) or use all milk
1½ oz butter (40 g)
1 oz flour (25 g)
3 tablespoons finely-chopped parsley
1 teaspoon lemon juice
Salt and freshly-milled black pepper

Place the first four ingredients in a saucepan, and whisk them over the heat till smooth and thickened. Then cook for 5 minutes, add the parsley and lemon juice, and season to taste. *Note:* For extra flavour you can infuse the milk with the parsley stalks first—but let it get absolutely cold before using it for the all-in-one method.

*Hollandaise sauce**

This adaptation of one of the famous French butter sauces goes particularly well with vegetables, like fresh artichokes or new season's asparagus.

For the reduction:
2 tablespoons white wine vinegar
3 tablespoons water
1 slice of onion
1 blade of mace
½ small bayleaf
6 black peppercorns

For the sauce:
1 tablespoon water
3 egg yolks
6 oz unsalted butter (room temperature) (160 g)
Lemon juice to taste
Salt and freshly-milled black pepper

Place the first six ingredients together in a small saucepan and simmer gently (uncovered) until the mixture is reduced to about 1 tablespoon—keep your eye on it because it can boil away before you know it! Then strain the reduced mixture into a bowl, add a further tablespoon of water and a little seasoning. Whisk in the egg yolks.

* See page 39 for a simpler version of this sauce.

Next place the bowl over a pan of *barely* simmering water, and add
$^1/_2$ oz (10 g) of the butter, whisking until it has melted and the
mixture has thickened slightly. Carry on adding lumps of butter—
approx. $^1/_2$ oz (10 g) at a time—and allow the butter to melt
and the mixture to thicken before adding any more.

When all the butter is in, carry on whisking and cooking gently for a
further 2 minutes. Then remove the bowl from over the water, taste,
and add lemon juice and seasoning as required. If the mixture
curdles (which it will only do if overheated) place a fresh egg yolk in
a clean bowl and gradually whisk in the curdled mixture to bring
it back.

Buttery onion sauce

(serves 4 people)

A lovely sauce, this one, to serve with
lamb in the late autumn.

1½ oz butter (40 g)
1 oz flour (25 g)
½ pint milk (275 ml)
¼ pint stock or water (150 ml)
1 large onion, chopped small
Salt, pepper and a scraping of nutmeg
An extra ½ oz butter to stir in at the end (10 g)

Since the onion needs to 'sweat' in the butter first to release its
juices, it is best to use the traditional white sauce method for this
recipe.

Start off by melting the butter in a saucepan, then keeping the heat
very low allow the onion to cook for about 10 minutes without
colouring. Stir it around from time to time. Then add the flour and
stir to a smooth paste.

Now gradually incorporate the milk and cream, a little at a time,
whisking or stirring vigorously after each addition till you have a
smooth sauce. Turn the heat down to its absolute minimum setting,
and let the sauce cook for 6 minutes. Season with salt, pepper and a
scraping of nutmeg—and finish off by stirring a lump of butter in
just before serving.

Leek cream sauce A delicious sauce to serve with a boiled bacon joint; this can be made by using the previous recipe, replacing the onion with 2 medium leeks, cleaned and chopped.

Celery sauce For serving with chicken or boiled bacon, this sauce is ideal.

6 oz celery stalks (160 g), cut into ¼ inch (½ cm) pieces
1½ oz butter (40 g)
1 oz flour (25 g)
¼ pint chicken stock (150 ml)
¼ pint milk (150 ml)
1 teaspoon lemon juice
Salt, pepper, nutmeg

First place the celery in a saucepan and pour boiling water on it, add some salt and simmer for 10 minutes. Then drain the celery and, in the same saucepan, melt the butter and fry the celery in it for a further 10 minutes with the lid on. Then uncover, stir in the flour until smooth, and gradually beat in the milk and chicken stock, a little bit at a time. Cook for 2 minutes, then liquidise the sauce to a purée: return it to the saucepan to reheat, and season with salt, pepper, lemon juice and a sprinkling of nutmeg.

Cucumber sauce This is the sauce to serve with fish, say fillets of brill or even salmon if the season (and the price) are right.

1 firm young cucumber
2 fl oz dry white wine (50 ml)
1½ oz butter (40 g)
1 oz flour (25 g)
¼ pint single cream (150 ml)
½ teaspoon lemon juice
Salt and freshly-milled black pepper

Pare off the peel of the cucumber, preferably with a potato peeler as it is important (for the colour of the sauce) to leave some of the green. Then divide the cucumber in half and liquidise one half together with the white wine (this should yield about ½ pint (275 ml) of liquid). Now chop the other half of the cucumber into small dice and sweat them gently with the butter in a covered saucepan for 10 minutes. Next stir in the flour, beat till smooth, then add the cucumber liquid and cream—bit by bit—whisking all the time until you have a smooth sauce. Cook gently for about 5 minutes, taste, and season with salt, pepper and lemon juice.

Sauce béarnaise

This is one of the great French butter sauces. It is tricky to make because it can curdle or—if you really overheat it— even scramble! However, if you're careful, and add a little mustard powder to help stabilise it, you should have no problems. It is delicious with any plain meat or fish, and especially with *Bœuf en croûte* (page 566).

1 tablespoon coarsely-chopped fresh tarragon (or ½ teaspoon dried)
1 tablespoon coarsely-chopped parsley
1 tablespoon chopped shallot (or spring onion)
6 black peppercorns, crushed
2 tablespoons white wine vinegar
¼ pint dry white wine (150 ml)
3 egg yolks
1 teaspoon mustard powder
1 oz butter (room temperature) (25 g)
6 oz melted butter (175 g)
Salt

Start off in a small saucepan by boiling the herbs, shallot, peppercorns, wine vinegar and white wine together until the mixture has reduced by about a third—in other words there should be about 3 tablespoons of slightly syrupy liquid left in the pan. Now whisk the egg yolks and mustard together in the top of a double saucepan.

Strain the vinegar mixture through a fine sieve onto the egg yolks, add a tablespoon of water and beat over hot (but not boiling) water, using a wire whisk. Next beat in the solid butter, about ½ oz (10 g) at a time, then gradually add the melted butter, a drop at a time—still whisking after each addition until all the butter is in and the sauce has thickened. Taste and season with salt and keep warm over the hot water till needed.

Spiced apple and onion sauce

(serves 4 people)

An apple sauce—with a little onion added—goes well with most pork dishes. If you don't like cloves, you can leave them out of this recipe.

½ **medium onion, finely chopped**
1 tablespoon lard or butter
1 dessertspoon sugar
2 cloves
2 medium cooking apples, peeled and thinly sliced
2 tablespoons water or dry cider
A little freshly-grated nutmeg

Begin by melting the fat in a thick-based saucepan, soften the chopped onion in it for 5 or 6 minutes, then add the slices of apple. Give them a good stir before adding the cloves and the water (or cider) and sugar. Stir again, cover the saucepan and leave the apples to cook down to a fluff (about 10 minutes). When they're cooked remove the cloves, beat the apples down to a smooth sauce, grate in a little nutmeg and pour into a jug to serve.

Traditional bread sauce

(serves 5–6 people)

This is my favourite sauce for serving with roast turkey, chicken or pheasant. Don't be put off by some of the restaurant or packet varieties because home-made it is deliciously light and creamy.

3 oz freshly-made white breadcrumbs (75 g) (a 2-day-old white loaf with the crusts removed will be stale enough to grate, but the best way to do this is in a liquidiser, if you have one)
¾ pint milk (425 ml)
1 medium onion
1 bayleaf
15 whole cloves
6 black peppercorns
2 oz butter (50 g)
2 tablespoons double cream
Salt and freshly-milled black pepper

A couple of hours before you need the sauce, cut the onion in half and stick the cloves in it. How many cloves you actually use depends on you, but I, personally, like a pronounced flavour; if you really don't like cloves, you can use some freshly-grated nutmeg instead.

Place the onion, bayleaf and the 6 black peppercorns in a saucepan with the milk and put this to infuse in a warn place for about 2 hours. Then, over a very low heat, bring the milk slowly to the boil, which should take about 15 minutes. Next, remove the onion, bayleaf and peppercorns and keep on one side.

Stir the breadcrumbs into the milk and add 1 oz (25 g) of the butter and some salt. Leave the saucepan on a very low heat (stirring now and then) until the crumbs have swollen and thickened the sauce. Now replace the clove-studded onion and again leave the saucepan in a warm place until the sauce is needed.

Just before serving, remove the onion and spices, beat in the remaining butter and the cream, and taste to check the seasoning.

Cumberland sauce

This is, perhaps, my favourite English sauce—delicious at Christmas with hot or cold gammon or tongue, and it stores in a screw-top jar for several weeks in a cool place.

4 large tablespoons authentic redcurrant jelly*

4 tablespoons port
1 medium orange
1 medium lemon
1 heaped teaspoon dried mustard powder
1 heaped teaspoon powdered ginger

*** I suspect some commercially-made
redcurrant jellies are not exactly authentic,
so read the labels carefully and go for a make
that guarantees a high fruit content.**

First, thinly pare off the rinds of both the lemon and the orange
(either with a very sharp paring knife or a potato peeler) then cut
them into very small strips, about ½ inch (1 cm) in length and
as thin as possible. Boil the rinds in water for 5 minutes or so to
extract any bitterness, then drain well in a sieve.

Now place the redcurrant jelly in a saucepan with the port and melt
them together over a low heat for about 5 or 10 minutes. The
redcurrant jelly won't melt completely, so it's best to sieve it
afterwards to get rid of any obstinate little globules.

In a serving bowl mix the mustard and ginger with the juice of half a
lemon till smooth, then add the juice of a whole orange, the port and
redcurrant mixture and finally the little strips of orange and lemon
peel. Mix well—and it's ready for use. Cumberland sauce is always
served cold.

*Redcurrant,
orange and
mint sauce*

(serves 6 people)

I think the vinegar in mint sauce is far too
strong for the delicate flavour of lamb in
the peak of summer and that this sauce is
a far nicer one.

4 tablespoons authentic redcurrant jelly (one with a high fruit content)
The grated zest of 1 orange
1½ tablespoons fresh chopped mint

Place the jelly in a small basin, break it up with a fork, then mix in
the orange zest and the mint—and that's it. It must be one of the
quickest sauces in the world, and it's absolutely delicious.

Bitter orange sauce

The bitterness of Seville oranges gives a delicious edge to this sauce which is one of my favourites to serve with duck. If they're out of season and you're using sweet oranges, add a tablespoon of lemon juice to the orange juice to give it sharpness.

2 fairly small Seville oranges
½ pint of stock made from the duck giblets, (275 ml) (see chicken giblet stock, page 94)
4–5 tablespoons port
3 heaped teaspoons brown sugar
1 level tablespoon plain flour
Salt and freshly-milled black pepper

First of all, take off the outer rinds of the oranges with a peeler or zester, then cut the rinds up finely into very thin shreds. Pop them into some boiling water and blanch for 5 minutes, then drain well. Next, squeeze the juice from the oranges and keep it on one side.

When the duck is cooked, transfer it to a serving plate to 'relax' and keep warm, then spoon out the excess fat from the roasting tin and sprinkle the flour into the juices that remain. Stir it in well to form a paste and cook over a medium heat, for a couple of minutes to brown slightly—as you do this, scrape the base and sides of the tin with a wooden spoon. Next add the stock gradually, stirring to make a smooth sauce, then add the sugar. Cook for a minute or two more before adding the orange juice and rind and a seasoning of salt and pepper. Just before serving, stir in the port, then pour the sauce over the duck and serve straightaway.

Morello cherry sauce

This is my other favourite to accompany duck. I know it sounds a bit unlikely, but it really is delicious and it takes no time at all to make. There's one vital point, though, and that's that the main ingredient must be *morello* cherry jam and no other kind (there are several brands on the market: one made by a

Polish firm and another by an English firm well-known for high quality jams and preserves). The reason it's so good is that morello cherries are bitter, and any sharp fruit can better hold its own when combined with the large amount of sugar needed to make a preserve.

6 oz morello cherry jam (175 g)
¼ pint red wine (150 ml)

Simply combine the jam and the wine in a saucepan, and simmer without a lid for 10 minutes. This is enough for 4 people and can be made well in advance and re-heated just before serving.

Spiced green tomato sauce

(serves 4 people)

If you're likely to have a crop of tomatoes that will never ripen, fear not, because this sauce is a real winner and really delicious with good pork sausages.

½ onion, chopped
½ green pepper, chopped
½ fresh green chilli, deseeded and chopped
1 tablespoon oil
1 lb green tomatoes (450 g), coarsely minced or very finely chopped (you needn't skin them)
1 large clove garlic, crushed
½ teaspoon whole cumin seeds, crushed
Salt and freshly-milled black pepper

Using a thick-based saucepan, fry the onion, pepper and chilli in the oil over a low heat for about 10 minutes. Now add the tomatoes, garlic, crushed cumin seeds and seasoning, and bring to simmering point. Cover and simmer for 15 minutes with the lid on and for a further 10 minutes without the lid, which will allow some of the excess liquid to reduce.

This sauce also goes very well with some fleshy fish, such as turbot or mackerel.

*Italian
green sauce
(salsa verde)*

(serves 2 people)

This is a strong-flavoured, quite garlicky sauce, which does wonders for plain mackerel fillets or some grilled trout.

2 tablespoons fresh parsley, chopped
1 tablespoon fresh basil, chopped (or 1 teaspoon dried)
4 anchovy fillets, drained
1 tablespoon capers
1 small clove garlic, crushed
1 level teaspoon English mustard powder
1½ tablespoons lemon juice
6 tablespoons olive oil
Salt and freshly-milled black pepper

To start with chop the anchovy fillets as small as possible and crush them to a paste in a mortar (if you haven't a mortar a small bowl and the end of a rolling-pin will do).

Put the capers in a small sieve and rinse them under cold running water to remove the vinegar they were preserved in. Dry them on kitchen paper and chop them as minutely as you can and add them to the anchovies.

Next add the mustard, garlic, lemon juice and some freshly-milled black pepper and mix well. Now add the oil, mix again and check the taste to see how much salt to add.

Just before serving, sprinkle in the chopped herbs and again mix thoroughly so that all the ingredients are properly combined.

Note: This behaves rather like a very thick vinaigrette and, before each serving, always needs to have another mix.

Avocado sauce

(serves 4 people)

This pale-green pistachio-coloured sauce is delicious with cold salmon in the summer or for use as a dip with lots of thin slivers of raw vegetables.

1 small or ½ fairly large avocado pear
5 oz carton soured cream (150 g)

1 tablespoon fresh lemon juice
½ clove garlic, crushed
Salt and freshly-milled black pepper

Scrape the avocado flesh away from the skin into a bowl, making sure you scrape away the very green bit next to the skin as this is important for the colour of the sauce. Then mash it to a purée together with the lemon juice, garlic and seasoning, and combine it with the soured cream, mixing thoroughly until you have a smooth, pale-green, creamy sauce. Cover the basin tightly with cellophane wrap to stop the avocado discolouring and chill in the refrigerator till needed. Do make this sauce the same day as it's required, since it does tend to discolour if left too long.

Proper custard sauce

(serves 4 people)

Packet custard is very popular, but if you want to serve a pudding for a special occasion a *real* custard with it is incomparably nicer. I'm afraid I do admit to cheating a little here, by using 1 teaspoon of cornflour. But in my experience, it saves an awful lot of anxiety by stabilising the sauce and preventing it from curdling.

½ pint double (or single) cream (275 ml)
3 egg yolks
1 level tablespoon caster sugar
1 level teaspoon cornflour
2 drops of pure vanilla essence

First heat the cream in a small saucepan up to boiling point; and while it's heating thoroughly blend the egg yolks, cornflour, sugar and vanilla together in a small basin. Then pour the hot cream in—stirring all the time—and return the mixture to the saucepan. Heat very gently (still stirring) until the sauce has thickened, which should only take a minute or two.

If it does overheat and start to look granular, don't worry. If you remove it from the heat and continue to beat it *will* become smooth again as it cools—because the small addition of cornflour does a very efficient stabilising job. Serve the custard warm or, with a hot pudding or pie, chilled.

Sauce sabayon

(serves 4 people)

This is a sweet sauce for serving with hot puddings like a Spotted Dick or light lemony sponge. It's also very good with a bread and butter pudding.

3 large egg yolks
2 oz caster sugar (50 g)
¼ pint dry white wine (150 ml)

Start by placing a small saucepan of water on a low heat, and heat the water to just below simmering point.

Now put the egg yolks and sugar into a pudding basin and whisk until the mixture starts to thicken. Next sit the basin over the saucepan of simmering water and, keeping the heat low and continuing to whisk, add the wine slowly, a little at a time. When you've added all the wine, continue whisking until the egg yolk has cooked and thickened to a fairly thick fluffy sauce.

Serve the sauce warm from a warmed jug or serving bowl.

This could be made with dry cider instead of wine, in which case it would go very well with an apple pudding.

Butterscotch sauce

People never fail to drool over this lovely, thick, butterscotch sauce—delicious poured over ice-cream just by itself, or with chopped bananas or fresh sliced peaches.

2 oz butter (50 g)
3 oz soft brown sugar (75 g)
2 oz granulated sugar (50 g)
5 oz golden syrup (150 g) (that's approximately one-third of a 1 lb (450 g) tin)
4 fl oz double cream (110 ml)
A few drops vanilla essence

First of all, place the butter and both the soft brown and granulated sugars in a medium-sized, thick-based saucepan together with the syrup. Heat slowly, and once the ingredients have completely melted and the sugar dissolved and formed a liquid, continue to heat gently for about another 5 minutes. Then turn off the heat underneath the saucepan.

Now gradually stir the double cream into the sauce, followed by a few drops of vanilla essence. Stir for a further 2 or 3 minutes, or until the sauce is absolutely smooth.

That's it; serve it hot or cold. If you want to keep it, it will store well for several weeks in a cool place in a screw-top jar.

Port wine sauce

This puts a steamed pudding into the dinner-party class and is especially good with the raisin pudding on page 652.

5 fl oz ruby or tawny port (150 ml)
Grated zest of 1 Seville orange (but an ordinary orange will do)
2 oz caster sugar (50 g)
5 fl oz water (150 ml)
½ nutmeg, freshly grated
1 tablespoon Seville orange juice
1 oz unsalted butter (25 g)
1 teaspoon flour

Begin by gently boiling the orange zest, water and sugar in a thick-bottomed saucepan for 15 minutes.

Meanwhile, mix the butter into the flour and divide it up into about 6 pieces, adding them to the syrup at the end of the cooking time, followed by the port, nutmeg and orange juice. Boil the mixture for 1 minute over a gentle heat, stirring continuously, then serve immediately.

Note: The sauce can be prepared in advance, except for the butter and flour part, which should be added just before serving.

Rum or brandy sauce

(serves 4 people)

I always think a pouring sauce is best with a rich Christmas pudding—I happen to prefer it with rum, but if you prefer brandy the quantities you use are the same. However if you prefer *Brandy butter* the recipe is on page 452.

1½ oz butter (40 g)
2 level tablespoons plain flour
1½ tablespoons caster sugar
¾ pint milk (425 ml)
2–3 tablespoons rum (or brandy)

First of all slowly melt the butter in a small saucepan.

Now work the flour into the melted butter, using a wooden spoon, until the mixture is fairly smooth. Then gradually add the milk and stir well after each addition to keep the mixture free from any lumps. When all the milk is added and you have a smooth creamy sauce, stir in the sugar, and let it cook over a very low heat for 10 minutes, stirring it slowly all the time to prevent it sticking. Then add the rum, and taste to check if more sugar or rum is needed before serving.

Flavoured butter
These can be used instead of sauces for all sorts of dishes. They are a lot quicker to make and add interest to something plain.

Herb butter

(serves 6 people)

You can serve this with chops, steaks or fish or simply swirl it around some hot cooked vegetables such as carrots, new potatoes, courgettes or cauliflower. You could also stir some into a vegetable soup or a sauce at the last minute.

6 oz butter (room temperature) (175 g)
4 tablespoons chopped parsley
1½ tablespoons snipped chives
1 teaspoon chopped tarragon or thyme
1 large clove garlic, crushed
1 dessertspoon lemon juice
Salt and freshly-milled black pepper

Combine all the above ingredients together. Store, covered with foil, in the refrigerator in small 2 oz (50 g) portions.

This can also be a good way of storing fresh herbs if you have a freezer (or a 4-star freezing compartment).

Anchovy butter   This can be served spread on wholemeal toast sprinkled with cayenne pepper. You can also serve it melted over plain grilled fish fillets.

5 oz unsalted butter (room temperature) (150 g)
2 oz (50 g) tin anchovy fillets in oil
1 teaspoon lemon juice
¼ teaspoon anchovy essence
Some cayenne pepper
½ teaspoon grated onion
1 clove garlic, crushed

First drain the anchovy fillets, then pat them as dry as possible with some kitchen paper. Then place the butter in a bowl and beat it with a wooden spoon till it's light and creamy—then add the anchovies after pounding them to a pulp. Stir in the garlic, anchovy essence, onion and lemon juice, then taste it and season with cayenne pepper (it should be fairly piquant). Now pile the butter into a bowl, cover and chill for an hour or two before serving.

Note: If you like, you can make this by just placing everything in a liquidiser and blending until smooth—only if you do, use fewer anchovies (about three-quarters of the above) as liquidising them seems to make them taste stronger.

Hot lemon butter   This can be served as a quick accompaniment to asparagus, globe artichokes or fish.

4 oz (110 g) salted butter
1 tablespoon lemon juice
Grated zest of ½ lemon
Salt
Freshly-milled black pepper

Heat the butter, lemon juice and zest in a small saucepan. As soon as the butter melts and starts to sizzle, season with the salt and pepper and serve it very hot.

Brandy butter

3 oz unsalted butter (75 g)	
3 oz caster sugar (75 g)	
1½ tablespoons brandy	
1 teaspoon lemon juice	

Make sure that the butter is at room temperature before you begin, then beat, using a wooden spoon, until white and creamy.

Add the sugar a little at a time and beat well after each addition. Continue until all the sugar is in, then gradually work in the brandy a few drops at a time, still beating. Lastly, beat in the lemon juice and, when everything is thoroughly amalgamated, transfer the butter to a suitable dish and chill for 2–3 hours before serving.

Gravy
I see from the *Oxford Dictionary* that gravy is supposed to be 'the fat and juices which exude from flesh in cooking' or a dressing for meat and vegetables made from these. Well, if you were roasting a baron of beef in the 18th century no doubt enough juices would exude from it to provide sufficient gravy. Nowadays our more modest joints need a little help with the gravy, if there's to be enough to go around.

First of all I would like to say quite emphatically that commercially-produced gravy mixes, highly-flavoured beef extracts, meat cubes or stock cubes are *not* needed. Their chemical flavours will not enhance the meat at all: on the contrary they only compete with it. So what is needed? Quite simply the meat roasting tin containing its fat and juices—or the pan in which the meat has been browned. The additional liquid can be wine, dry cider, stock or even water. There are two ways to make gravy:

Deglazing method
This is useful when just a little thin gravy is required. Most of the fat (if any) is spooned out of the pan, then with a wooden spoon you scrape all the crusty bits that cling to the base and sides of the pan (this is deglazing). Then to these and the juices, add either wine, stock or water: boil briskly for a few seconds to form a sauce.

Good old-fashioned gravy

For this—the familiar thicker gravy that goes with a roast joint—the principles are as follows. First make sure you're using a good thick-based roasting tin, then when the meat comes out of the oven, lift it onto a plate and leave it to 'relax' before carving (see page 160). Now tilt the roasting tin, and you will see quite clearly the actual meat juices down in the corner and the fat, separately, settling on top of the juices. Take a large tablespoon and spoon most of the fat off into a bowl—leaving behind 2–3 tablespoons, depending on how much gravy you need.

Now place the roasting tin over direct heat (turned fairly low), and when the juices start to sizzle sprinkle in some flour—about 1 level tablespoon to each ½ pint (275 ml) of liquid to be used. Next, with a wooden spoon quickly work the flour into the fat, using circular movements all over the base of the tin. Then when you have a smooth paste, begin to add the liquid gradually, keeping up the vigorous stirring all over the base of the tin. Carry on like this until all the liquid has been added and you have a smooth sauce (if it's too thick, add a little more liquid). If you have already added too much liquid by mistake, just boil briskly for a minute or two and the sauce will reduce and thicken again. Taste and season the sauce, and add a few drops of gravy browning if it needs it. Before serving, pour the gravy into a warm jug.

Instant gravy

There will be times when you want to make some gravy from scratch, without the benefit of any meat juices. All you need do for this is melt 1 oz (25 g) of dripping or lard in a small saucepan and fry ½ finely-chopped onion in it. Keep the heat high and let the onion turn really brown. Then stir in 1 oz (25 g) of flour and gradually whisk in ¾ pint (425 ml) of stock (or hot water flavoured with ½ teaspoon of Worcestershire sauce and 1 dessertspoon of mushroom ketchup). Simmer for 5 minutes and season to taste, adding a few drops of gravy browning if it needs it.

Notes on gravy ingredients

Stock can be meat of chicken giblet stock or some sort of vegetable stock—potato water and so on. If you are just using boiling water you can enrich it with a few drops of Worcestershire sauce and a dessertspoon of mushroom ketchup.

Wine can be useful for gravies if there's some around. Just a couple of tablespoons can really enrich the flavour. Dry cider is a good alternative, and much more economical.

Gravy browning Commercial gravy browning is simply a concentrated caramel (burnt sugar). It doesn't have the chemical flavours of gravy-mixes and is invaluable for enhancing the colour of gravy. If you don't have, or don't want to use gravy browning, then slice ½ onion and place it in the meat roasting tin along with the meat: it will turn jet black and caramelise during the roasting, and colour the gravy for you.

Flour I always use plain flour for gravy, having found in the past that self-raising tends to go lumpy.

See also:

Aioli sauce
Baby broad beans in parsley sauce
Braised celery with cheese and onion sauce
Chicken in barbecue sauce
Chicken with lemon sauce
Coeur à la crème
Cranberry and orange relish
Deep-fried sprats in mustard sauce
Eliza Acton's English salad sauce
Fresh tomato sauce
Home-made mayonnaise
John Tovey's quick hollandaise sauce

Pesto alla Genovese (fresh basil sauce)
Ragù Bolognese
Redcurrant jelly
Roast stuffed goose with prune and apple sauce
Sauce rouille
Sauce tartare
Spiced fig pudding with rum butter
Spring sauce for lamb
Tomato chilli sauce
Trout with caper sauce
Yoghurt seafood sauce

Cheese

Including recipes for:
Cheese and onion quichelets
Pan-fried pizza
Cheese and herb sausages
Roman gnocchi
Spinach and cream cheese quiche
Toasted cheese with ale
Welsh rarebit soufflé
Fillets of sole gratiné

Greek salad
Dutch omelette
Broccoli cheese soufflé
Alpine eggs
Cheese tartlets with mushroom pâté
Orange cheesecake
Curd cheesecake with fruit topping
Fresh lemon cheesecake with frosted grapes
Cœur à la crème

Cheese is one of the very few foods which has the distinction of providing one complete course of a meal on its own, without any other preparation or adornment. This makes it one of the best friends of a harassed hostess: an imaginative cheese board with a small selection of water biscuits (like Bath Olivers, if you want to be really posh), crisp celery and some fresh fruit is a very good alternative to a dessert when you're pushed for time. But a good cheeseboard can be something of an adventure too. Over the centuries the art of cheese making has produced an incredible range of textures and flavours, and over the last few years more and more of them have become available in our shops. So try to offer guests a good variety, say some Stilton, Cheddar, Brie or Camembert, and perhaps a goat's cheese. With a little bit of experimenting you can come up with all kinds of different combinations of your own.

In this section we are also concerned with the uses of cheese in cooking—and they are many. Cheese is used in sauces, pastry, fondues, omelettes, for toasting, gratining (i.e. browning the top of a dish under the grill after sprinkling with grated cheese), grating onto soups or pasta, in salads and in cheesecakes. Here, too, care must be taken to choose the right kind of cheese for the right kind of cooking. So first of all let's look at the various methods of cheese-making and the results they produce.

Cheese-making

All cheese is made from milk—mostly cow's milk, sometimes goat's and occasionally ewe's—and the basis of all cheese-making is the separation of the solids (curds) from the liquids (whey) in the milk. From then on a whole variety of processes may take place, depending on the nature of the finished cheese—cutting, stirring, scalding, salting, moulding, pressing, ripening and so on.

There are literally thousands of different cheeses, the character of each one dependent not only on its method of production but also on unique local conditions, such as the nature of the grazing for the dairy herds. However, broadly speaking, one can distinguish certain 'families' of cheese:

Soft paste cheeses These are the ones with the floury (unwashed) rinds and very soft creamy centres, of which Brie and Camembert are perhaps the most famous. Slightly firmer, but similar in texture, are those cheeses whose rinds are regularly washed while they're ripening (to keep the moisture needed for fermentation): Pont l'Evêque is a well-known example. Also in the category of 'soft paste' come the goat's cheeses, although in practice the range of textures in goat's cheese is huge.

Blue-veined cheeses These are cheeses which have been injected with a penicillium mould, which creates the characteristic blue veins. Unlike other cheeses they ripen from the inside out and have to be perforated with special needles to aerate them and encourage the mould. In France Roquefort is the prince of the blue cheeses, in England Stilton.

Pressed uncooked cheeses These cheeses are bandaged with a cloth, placed in a mould, then kept under pressure for up to 24 hours. Most of our English cheeses are of this kind, though the degree of pressing (and therefore the texture) varies. Caerphilly, for instance, is a lightly pressed cheese while Cheddar is hard-pressed.

Hard-pressed cooked cheeses To make these cheeses the curds are 'cooked' at 60°C before being put into moulds and very firmly pressed. During the maturing period (up to six months) fermentation occurs internally, creating the holes which are characteristic of such cheeses as Gruyère and Emmenthal.

In addition to these four 'families' of cheese, we can also buy processed cheese, which has little connection with the natural cheeses from which it is processed. The product is made by grinding down a cheese (e.g. Cheddar), mixing it to a paste, flavouring it, then packing it into small portions—and I can't see much point in it.

Finally there is a group of cheeses generally known as fresh unfermented cheeses, sometimes (incorrectly) called cream cheeses; these are soft cheeses, which are made from naturally soured milk, whole or skimmed milk, or cream. Their fat content, and their flavour, varies a great deal. They have varied uses in cooking—cheesecakes for instance, or cheese spreads or salads—but they should all be used as fresh as possible.

Cottage cheese is made from pasteurised skimmed milk. The regulations state that it must contain less than 2% milk fat, and it is therefore often recommended for those on a diet, though on its own the flavour is really rather bland.

Curd cheeses These have a more pronounced flavour, and the curds are formed by the natural action of lactic acid in milk. The fat content of curd cheese varies depending on the degree, if any, to which the milk has been skimmed.

Cream cheeses As the name suggests these are made from cream (single and double) rather than milk, and as a result they have a higher fat content. In this country cream cheeses are sold unripened; they have a buttery texture and a rich, faintly acid, flavour.

Farmhouse or factory?

Some time ago I spent a delightful day on a farm—Chewton Dairy farm at Chewton Mendip to be precise—watching a real expert assessing and grading Cheddar cheese. Just by pressing his thumb on top of one and gauging the amount of 'bounce' under pressure, he could tell both the age and quality of a cheese. In his grandfather's day, he said, this test was carried out by standing on the huge cheeses and bouncing from one to the other! He then proceeded to insert a cheese iron into the Cheddar, to twist it sharply then withdraw it, extracting a small quantity of cheese from the centre. The 'bloom' on the back of the iron told him the smoothness and fat content of the cheese, and then by rubbing a small piece of the cheese between thumb and forefinger he could check the texture. A good cheese, I was informed, should 'feel like a well-nourished dairy-maid'!

This farm is one of only a few which continue to make traditional Cheddars. A small quantity of Cheshire cheese, and even less of Lancashire, is also still made on farms. Altogether about 10% of our English cheese is 'farmhouse' and it's the best you can buy. It is made from the finest quality milk that the dairy herds produce and is well-matured—always worth looking out for. The rest of our cheese is now made in factories—or 'creameries' as they prefer to be called. Modern economics have made this inevitable and even in France, where they are particularly choosy about their cheese, the same trend is happening. Factory cheese, however, is subject to the same stringent standards of classification as farmhouse, and can be excellent.

Grading In the case of farmhouse cheese, the very finest quality cheese is graded and labelled as *superfine*, and good quality cheese as *fine*. The equivalent grades for factory-made cheeses are *extra selected* and *selected*. In both cases, the rest of the cheese which is saleable in spite of having some fault is simply called *graded*.

Buying and storing cheese

Since most of us buy our cheese in relatively small quantities—
either pre-packed or sliced off a whole cheese—the complex
business of caring for a whole cheese (damp wrapping, polishing,
and humidity control) need not concern us too much, though there
are some shopkeepers and restaurateurs who could certainly do
some homework on the subject.

If you are buying portions from larger cheeses, look out for any
that are cracked or look sweaty: it means they have been exposed
to shop temperature for too long and are in the process of drying
out. In the case of soft paste cheeses, check that they are springy
to the touch and (unless you want to eat them immediately) not *too*
runny.

At home the best place to store your cheese is at the bottom of the
refrigerator or, failing that, some other *cool* place. At all events wrap
each piece tightly in foil, with no little tears or gaps to let the air in.
Those china cheese dishes or domes, however attractive they may
be, are not the place to store cheese since they offer no protection
from the air.

Most cheeses however have best flavour and texture if they are
brought to room temperature about 1 hour before eating.

British cheeses

They are—if you don't include the elusive Blue Vinney (said to be
made secretly in Dorset) and the very local Yorkshire cheeses—ten
major British cheeses. All are made from cow's milk, and their very
names are evocative of the dairy pastures where, for the most part,
they are still produced.

Cheddar One of the most imitated of cheeses, and understandably
so: we import Cheddars from all kinds of places like New Zealand
and Ireland, but the original English Cheddar is still the best—
and in particular Farmhouse Cheddar, which is well-matured
(anything up to nine months) and stronger than the mild, younger
Cheddars that are widely available. A good Cheddar cheese
should look amber yellow and fresh, without a greasy shine, and it
should feel firm but not hard. Its clean and mellow flavour makes it
very suitable for cooking, toasting, topping, for cheese sauces or
simply for serving with pickled onions and beer for a ploughman's
lunch.

Cheshire Said to be the oldest of English cheeses, it comes in red,
white or blue—very patriotic! The red Cheshire, which has been

artificially coloured, is milder than the white, which ideally should be flaky and slightly salty (though this will depend on its age). Both red and white Cheshire are good melting cheeses. The blue-veined variety (sometimes artificially produced, sometimes not) has a distinctive ripe, salty flavour.

Double Gloucester A bright orange (artificially induced) colour, but with a mature, creamy and delicate taste. It's best eaten, I think, just with biscuits and celery. It is called 'double' because when it's whole it's twice the size of a single Gloucester (which is not sold now anyway). The variety which includes chives is known as Cotswold cheese.

Caerphilly Another eating, rather than cooking, cheese. It's a quick ripener, ready for eating after only two weeks, which makes it white, mild and semi-soft.

Wensleydale From Yorkshire as the name implies, this comes in two varieties. The young white Wensleydale is mild and very slightly salty; the blue-veined Wensleydale has been allowed to mature for some six months, is soft and flaky in texture and rich, almost sweet, in flavour.

Lancashire A white mild cheese, with a fairly soft and crumbly texture which is supposed to make it 'spreadable', but certainly makes it an excellent toasting cheese.

Derby Mild, hard and honey-coloured when at its best, which is at about four to six weeks. A standard variation is the sage Derby, which is flavoured with chopped sage leaves and coloured green with spinach.

Leicester This is red and crumbly with a medium-strong flavour when it has fully matured after three months. It's good for toasting.

Stilton Named after the village on the Great North Road where it was sold to coach travellers, who spread its fame all over the country. A whole Stilton is 9 inches high and 8 inches across with a crinkly brown rind. The habit of spooning the cheese out of the centre and then pouring port in to keep it moist still persists. In my opinion this ruins the flavour and texture of the cheese, which really ought to be firm and creamy white with a clean network of blue veins. It is far better to slice Stilton horizontally and to keep it wrapped, in the fridge. At full maturity (six months) Stilton should be rich and mellow with a sharp, salty aftertaste. The young version, white Stilton, has not been left to develop a mould and is mild and crumbly.

Dunlop It might be described as the national cheese of Scotland, where indeed it is mainly found nowadays. It is a smooth, creamy white cheese with a mild, occasionally slightly sourish, flavour. It is named after the town of Dunlop in Ayrshire.

Continental cheeses

Once you could only find these—or at least a reasonable selection of them—at specialised cheesemongers or delicatessens, but nowadays many supermarkets carry quite an adventurous stock of them. They are always worth trying out for yourself, so here's a list (by no means exhaustive) of some you might come across.

France

France is *the* country for cheese-making: there are many hundreds of cheeses which are purely local specialities (and if you're ever in a particular region, do ask to sample the local cheese—it may be the only chance you ever get!). Some of course have become world famous. Of the soft paste cheeses *Brie* is widely exported in its traditional disc shape, with a downy white rind and a faintly straw-coloured interior. It should be springy to the touch, creamy and fairly mild in flavour. Rather tangier and fruitier is the famous *Camembert*, which to me is the very essence of the rich dairy lands of Normandy. Also worth trying, if you want a stronger spicy soft cheese, is its neighbour *Livarot* or, from the Alsace region, *Munster*.

The greatest of the French blue-veined cheeses (called *bleus*) is *Roquefort*, a ewe's milk cheese. To qualify for the name, the cheese has to mature only in the humid natural caves of Roquefort. Rather expensive, it's often used in recipes for quiche or salad dressing, but really deserves to be eaten on its own to appreciate its strong, distinctive taste. Other French *bleus* are available over here, such as *Bleu de Bresse* which is somewhat milder than Roquefort.

A proper catalogue of French pressed cheeses would be almost endless, but among those that find their way over here I'd mention *Saint-Paulin* from Brittany, mild and velvety and useful in cooking (also *Port Salut* which is a Saint-Paulin relative, made in a local monastery). *Reblochon* from the Savoy region is also mild and creamy; *Cantal* from the pastures of the Auvergne is a firm, nutty-flavoured cheese.

Goat's cheeses are something of an acquired taste, I'd say, and not all that easy to find in Britain, but they can be absolutely delicious and they come in all shapes and sizes. *Saint-Maure* for example is cylindrical, firm to the touch and full-flavoured. *Valençay* is shaped like a sawn-off pyramid, its rind is dusted with charcoal, and it tastes mild and slightly nutty. *Banon* (from Provence) is disc-shaped and comes wrapped in chestnut leaves.

Switzerland

Best known of the Swiss cheeses are the hard, cooked varieties: the yellow-amber *Gruyère*, with its pock-marking of little holes, has a distinct fruit flavour. So does the ivory-coloured *Emmenthal*, which has a slightly firmer, oilier texture and rather larger holes distributed throughout it. Both are good melting and toasting cheeses, and the basis of several traditional fondue recipes.

Holland

Both the semi-hard Dutch cheeses, the firm yellow *Gouda* and the mild red-rinded *Edam*, have long been familiar over here. Both look good on a cheese-board and are useful in recipes.

Italy

The Italian repertoire of cheeses is extensive, and the Italians make good use of their cheeses in cooking. *Parmesan*, a hard brittle cheese, is indispensable for grating over soups, pasta and other dishes. It is widely sold here ready-grated, which means it has lost a good deal of its flavour: do try to get hold of a whole piece of it and grate it yourself when needed—it keeps very well. *Mozzarella*, a very white soft cheese (occasionally found made from buffalo's milk) comes in little plastic bags which should be stored in water. It is the traditional cheese for cooking on pizza, with a nice elastic texture, and when really young and fresh it is delicious with a little olive oil in a salad. For the end of a meal creamy *Bel Paese* and pungent, almost runny blue *Gorgonzola* make a good contrast.

Greece

Greek cheeses, unfortunately, are usually only to be found in Greek or Cypriot shops in Britain, but *Feta* (soft ewe's milk cheese) is delicious, when very fresh, in a salad; and the hard salty *Kefalotyri* is excellent fried.

*Cheese and
onion quichelets*

(makes 10)

The name sounds odd but it describes
these little cheese tarts perfectly. Serve
them on picnics or car journeys or at
buffet parties when you need food that
can be picked up easily.

For the pastry:
2 oz wholewheat flour (50 g)
2 oz self-raising flour (50 g)
1 oz margarine (25 g)
1 oz lard (25 g)
Salt and freshly-milled black pepper

For the filling:
1 large egg, beaten
3 fl oz milk (75 ml)
¼ teaspoon mustard powder
1½ oz strong Cheddar cheese, grated (40 g)
1 onion, finely chopped
½ oz butter (10 g)
Cayenne pepper

Pre-heat the oven to gas mark 4,
350°F (180°C)

First make up the pastry: combine the flours and add some
seasoning, then rub in the fats until the mixture is crumbly; add
enough cold water to make a dough that leaves the bowl clean. Place
the dough in a polythene bag and leave to rest in the fridge for
30 minutes. Then roll out the dough and, using a 3¼ inch (8 cm)
plain cutter, cut out rounds. Use the rounds to line a patty tin.

Next, for the filling, melt the butter in a small saucepan and soften
the onion in it over a low heat for 10–12 mintues. Leave to cool, then
put a little onion in the base of each tartlet and a little grated cheese
on top. Now whisk together the milk, egg and mustard powder and
season to taste, then spoon some of the liquid carefully into each
tartlet.

Bake in the centre of the oven for about 30 minutes, then top with a
light sprinkling of cayenne pepper. These little tarts can be served
hot or cold.

Pan-fried pizza
(serves 4 people)

This is an extremely quick and easy way to make a pizza, without having to bother with making a bread dough.

8 oz self-raising flour (225 g)
½ teaspoon salt
Freshly-milled black pepper
4–5 tablespoons olive oil
4 generous tablespoons tomato purée
14 oz tin Italian tomatoes, drained and chopped (400 g)
About 5 oz Saint-Paulin or Port Salut cheese, cut into small cubes (150 g)
1 dozen black olives, pitted and chopped
1 teaspoon dried mixed herbs
1¾ oz tin anchovy fillets in oil (45 g)

First sieve the flour, salt and freshly-milled black pepper into a bowl. Make a well in the middle and pour in 2 tablespoons of olive oil, then 4 tablespoons of water. Now mix to a soft, though not sticky, dough—you may find you have to add a further tablespoon or so of water to get the right consistency. Prepare a floured surface, turn the dough out onto it and knead lightly. Now roll out a round to fit the base of a 9–10 inch (23–25 cm) frying pan.

Next heat 1 tablespoon of olive oil in the pan, place the circle of dough in the pan and cook over a low heat for about 5 minutes or until the base is lightly brown.

Have ready an oiled plate and turn the pizza base out onto it. Then, after heating a further 1 tablespoon of oil in the pan, slide the pizza base back in, and cook the reverse side for 5 minutes.

During this time, spread the tomato purée over the surface of the pizza base, together with the drained tomatoes. Next scatter over the cubed cheese, chopped olives and herbs. Finally, arrange the anchovy fillets on top in a criss-cross pattern and drizzle on the oil from the tin.

To see if the underside of the pizza base is cooked you can lift up a corner with a palette knife and have a look. When it's cooked, transfer the pan to a pre-heated grill for 2 or 3 minutes to melt the cheese and heat the topping.

Serve straight away with a mixed salad.

Cheese and herb sausages

(serves 3–4 people)

This is adapted from a traditional Welsh recipe called Glamorgan sausages. They really are lovely—we like them served with fried broccoli and red tomato chutney.

5 oz fresh breadcrumbs (150 g)
4 oz strong Cheddar cheese, grated (110 g)
1 medium-sized onion, grated
1 egg yolk
1 teaspoon dried mixed herbs or 2 teaspoons fresh chopped mixed herbs
¾ teaspoon mustard powder
Salt and freshly-milled black pepper

For coating and frying:
½ oz breadcrumbs (10 g)
½ oz grated Parmesan cheese (10 g)
1 egg white, lightly beaten
Oil

Place the breadcrumbs in a large mixing bowl together with the grated onion, Cheddar and herbs; add the mustard powder and a seasoning of salt and pepper. Then add the egg yolk and stir to bind the mixture together. Now divide it into 12 or 14 small portions and, using your hands, roll each piece into a sausage shape, squeezing it to hold it together.

Before frying them, mix the breadcrumbs reserved for coating with the Parmesan cheese and dip each sausage first into the egg white and then into the breadcrumb and cheese mixture and coat evenly.

Fry in hot shallow oil till crisp and golden. Drain on crumpled kitchen paper before serving.

Roman gnocchi

(serves 3–4 people)

These are little fingers made with cheese and semolina, then baked in the oven with butter. Simple, inexpensive but really good. They *can* be served with a fresh tomato sauce, but I don't think they necessarily need it.

½ pint milk (275 ml)
5 oz semolina (150 g)
3 oz butter (75 g)
2 eggs, beaten
Freshly-grated nutmeg
5 oz freshly-grated Parmesan cheese (150 g)
Salt and freshly-milled black pepper

Put into a saucepan the milk, semolina and ½ pint (275 ml) of water together with a good grating of nutmeg and a little salt and pepper, and bring it all to the boil, stirring all the time. Let the mixture boil for about 4 minutes (still stirring) until it is thick enough to stand a spoon up in. Then remove the pan from the heat and beat in 1 oz (25 g) of butter, 3 oz (75 g) of the Parmesan cheese and both the beaten eggs. Check the seasoning, then spread the mixture in a small Swiss roll tin or something similar (approximately 11 × 7 inches, 28 × 18 cm), lined with oiled greaseproof paper. Leave to cool or refrigerate—overnight if possible.

When you're ready to cook the gnocchi, pre-heat the oven to gas mark 6, 400°F (200°C).

Then cut the cheese and semolina mixture into 'fingers' (you should get about 24–27) or use a pastry cutter for round shapes (see photograph, page 316) and peel away the greaseproof paper. Place them, slightly overlapping, in a shallow buttered baking dish, then dot the top of the gnocchi with the remaining 2 oz (50 g) of butter and bake for 10 minutes.

Then baste the gnocchi with the melted butter and sprinkle the remaining 2 oz (50 g) of Parmesan over them. Replace the dish on an upper shelf of the oven and bake for a further 30 minutes or until the whole thing is golden brown and bubbling nicely.

Spinach and cream cheese quiche

(serves 4–6 people)

Fresh spinach would be best for this quiche, but 1 lb (450 g) of frozen spinach (so long as it's well drained) would do as an alternative.

2 lb fresh spinach (900 g)
1 oz butter (25 g)
½ lb cream cheese (225 g)

3 eggs, beaten
¼ pint milk (150 ml)
Freshly-grated nutmeg
2 tablespoons grated Parmesan
A squeeze of lemon juice
Salt and freshly-milled black pepper
Wholewheat shortcrust pastry made with 3 oz wholewheat flour (75 g) and 3 oz self-raising flour (75 g) (see recipe page 548)

Pre-heat the oven to gas mark 4, 350°F (180°C) and pop in a baking sheet.

First make the pastry and use it to line a 10 inch (25 cm) flan tin. Prick the pastry base all over with a fork, and bake on the pre-heated baking sheet for 15 minutes. Remove the flan tin from the oven and brush the pastry all over with some of the beaten egg from the filling ingredients. Return the flan tin to the oven and cook for a further 5 minutes to allow the egg to set.

Set the flan tin on one side, but leave the baking sheet in the oven and increase the heat to gas mark 5, 375°F (190°C).

Now prepare the filling. First wash the spinach, discarding any coarse stalks or damaged leaves. Drain the leaves thoroughly and place them in a heavy-based saucepan together with the butter and some salt and pepper (there is no need to add any water). Cover and cook the spinach for about 7 minutes, giving the pan a shake occasionally, until the spinach collapses down into the butter.

Then drain the spinach thoroughly in a colander, pressing out any excess moisture. Now place the cream cheese in a bowl and beat it, gradually adding the milk followed by the remaining beaten eggs, Parmesan cheese and a seasoning of salt, pepper and nutmeg. Chop up the drained spinach with a sharp knife, and stir it into the cream mixture, adding a squeeze of lemon juice and (if it needs it) a little more seasoning.

Pour the whole mixture into the flan case and place the flan tin on the hot baking sheet in the upper part of the oven. Bake for 40 minutes, or until the filling is puffy and golden on top.

Note: this is also very nice made with a cheese shortcrust pastry, using 3 oz (75 g) each of wholewheat and self-raising flours, 3 oz (75 g) of fat and 2 oz (50 g) grated Cheddar cheese.

*Toasted cheese
with ale*

(serves 4 people)

This is a lovely sort of toasted cheese,
good for a really speedy supper.

8 oz strong Cheddar cheese, grated (225 g)
2 oz butter (50 g)
4 tablespoons brown ale
1 tablespoon mustard powder
Salt and freshly-milled black pepper
Cayenne pepper
4 thick slices bread

First melt the butter in a saucepan. Then add the mustard, brown
ale, grated cheese and some seasoning and, with a wooden spoon,
stir continuously until the mixture looks creamy and the cheese has
almost melted—but it's important that you don't let the mixture
boil.

Then remove the saucepan from the heat and quickly toast the
bread slices on both sides until they're nice and crisp. Pour the
cheese mixture over each piece of toast, sprinkle with cayenne
pepper then place them under the grill until hot and bubbling.
Serve immediately with, perhaps, some more brown ale to drink
with it.

*Welsh rarebit
soufflé*

(serves 3 people)

This, if you've got the time, is a Welsh
rarebit with a difference. It's rich golden
brown, light and puffy.

½ oz butter (10 g)
½ oz flour (10 g)
6 tablespoons milk
1 teaspoon French mustard
A dash of Worcestershire sauce
A little cayenne pepper
2 eggs, separated
1 oz strong Cheddar cheese, grated (25 g)
1 oz Parmesan cheese, grated (25 g)
6 slices white bread (cut medium thick) from a small loaf
Salt and freshly-milled black pepper

First melt the butter in a small saucepan, blend in the flour and
cook for a minute or two before adding the milk very gradually.

stirring all the time. Let the mixture bubble for 2 minutes, take the saucepan off the heat and stir in the mustard, Worcestershire sauce, a little cayenne, some salt and freshly-milled pepper. Next beat the egg yolks, stir them into the sauce and leave it on one side to cool for a minute.

Now toast the bread on one side. Then beat the grated cheeses into the sauce mixture. Whisk the egg whites until stiff and, using a metal spoon, carefully fold them into the cheese mixture. Cover each slice (on the untoasted side) liberally with the cheese mixture. Pop the slices under a medium grill and when the tops are golden brown, light and puffy, serve at once.

Fillets of sole gratiné

(serves 4 people as a starter or 3 as a main course)

This, like all the best recipes in the world, is unbelievably simple and tastes really good. You can use Dover sole, lemon sole or even plaice fillets.

6 fillets of sole
8 oz stale beadcrumbs (225 g)
3 oz grated Cheddar cheese (75 g)
2 tablespoons fresh chopped parsley
4 oz melted butter (110 g)
6 lemon quarters
Salt and freshly-milled black pepper
A little extra melted butter

Pre-heat the grill to its highest setting.

Mix the breadcrumbs, grated cheese and parsley with 4 oz (110 g) of melted butter. Line the grill pan with foil and paint the foil with melted butter. Lay the sole fillets on it and season them with salt and freshly-milled black pepper, cover them with the breadcrumb mixture and pour over a little more melted butter. Cook under the hot grill for about 5 minutes until the crumbs have turned a rich brown and the fish is cooked. Serve garnished with lemon.

Greek salad

(serves 2–3 people as a lunch dish)

This should, authentically, have crumbled pieces of Greek Feta cheese mixed in with the salad ingredients, but white Stilton would be an alternative.

6 oz Feta cheese, chopped in small pieces (175 g)
6 ripe, firm tomatoes cut in quarters then in eighths
Half a small young cucumber or a whole ridge cucumber cut into $^1/_8$ inch (3 mm) thick slices, the slices then halved
1 medium-sized onion cut in thin rings, then the rings halved
2 oz small firm black olives (50 g)
4 tablespoons olive oil
1 small lemon, quartered
Salt and freshly-milled black pepper

Simply mix the cheese, tomatoes, cucumber, onion and olives together in a salad bowl. Season with salt and freshly-milled black pepper, then pour the oil all over everything just before serving. Garnish with lemon quarters for squeezing over the salad.

Dutch omelette

(serves 1 person)

This is an omelette made with Dutch Gouda cheese, which is placed in the centre then melted under a hot grill so that the omelette itself is finally wrapped round a lovely, creamy, stretchy mass of cheese.

2 large fresh eggs
2 oz Gouda cheese (50 g)
1 tablespoon snipped chives (or very finely chopped spring onion tops)
1 oz butter (25 g)
Salt and freshly-milled black pepper

Pre-heat the grill to a high heat.

Break the eggs into a small basin and, using a fork, mix them lightly together, season, and add the snipped chives. Now cut the cheese, with a sharp knife, into thin slices.

Then over a fairly high heat melt the butter in a 7 inch (18 cm) frying-pan. When the butter starts to froth, swirl it round so that the pan base and sides are well coated, then pour in the eggs. Now quickly lay the slices of cheese all down the centre of the omelette and, after cooking the base of the omelette for a few seconds, transfer the pan to the hot grill. Leave it there until the cheese just melts (it will overcook if left too long).

Have a hot plate ready and fold the omelette into three: tilt the pan, flip the edge of the omelette nearest you over the centre part, then roll that over the far side of the omelette and turn the whole lot over again and out onto a plate.

Eat the omelette absolutely immediately with some crusty bread and a garlicky salad.

Broccoli cheese soufflé

(serves 4 people)

This always looks so beautiful. It's a pale green colour with a golden brown crust on top.

1 lb fresh broccoli (450 g)
2 large eggs
2 extra egg whites
2 oz Cheddar cheese, grated (50 g)
1 oz butter (25 g)
2 tablespoons plain flour
5 fl oz milk (150 ml)
A pinch of cayenne pepper
Freshly-grated nutmeg
1 tablespoon grated Parmesan cheese
Salt and freshly-milled black pepper

Pre-heat the oven to gas mark 6, 400°F (200°C)

A 1³/₄ pint (1 litre) soufflé dish, well buttered.

If you've never made a soufflé before, don't worry because this is a fairly easy one, and no soufflé is ever *all that* difficult once you've mastered the art of whipping egg whites to the right stage and, having got them to the right stage, the art of folding them in properly.

Having turned on the oven, take a large meat-roasting tin, big enough to hold the soufflé dish, then fill it with 1¹/₂ inches (4 cm) of hot water and put that in the over to pre-heat as well.

Now start to prepare the broccoli by trimming off the very stalky bits, then place the rest in a saucepan with a little salt and about 6 fl oz (175 ml) of boiling water. Put a lid on and simmer it gently for about 10–15 minutes or until the broccoli has softened and most of the water has disappeared.

Now drain the broccoli well, then transfer to a largish mixing bowl and, using a large fork, mash it to a pulp. Get it as pulp-like as possible, but don't worry too much about getting rid of all the fibrous pieces of stalk.

Next melt 1 oz (25 g) of butter in a saucepan and stir in 2 level tablespoons of flour. Then when it's smooth gradually add the milk, stirring vigorously after each addition. When all the milk is in you should have a thick glossy paste and now you can mix in the cheese, keeping the pan over the lowest heat possible. After that, empty the cheese mixture into the bowl containing the broccoli pulp, then mix everything together thoroughly. Do a bit of tasting, add salt if it needs it and also some freshly-milled pepper, a pinch of cayenne and about a quarter of a whole nutmeg freshly-grated.

Now for the egg bit. Separate the eggs, add the two yolks to the broccoli mixture and mix them in fairly thoroughly. (All this, by the way, can be done well in advance.) For the whites, take a very large mixing bowl—making sure it's completely dry and free from grease, and you'll need a whisk which is the same. Whisk the egg whites until they stand up in peaks when you lift the whisk, but be careful not to overdo it, or they'll start to flop a bit and go watery.

As soon as they're ready carefully fold the egg whites into the broccoli mixture, using a metal spoon. Turn the bowl round as you fold, adding about a quarter of the mixture at a time. (When you're folding the egg whites in, the most important thing to remember is that you don't want to lose all the air you've whisked into them.)

Now spoon the mixture into the prepared soufflé dish, sprinkle with a dusting of Parmesan cheese, place the dish in the roasting tin, and cook the soufflé for 30–35 minutes. When it's done, it should be nicely risen and beginning to crack on the surface—but be careful not to overcook; it should be soft and moist inside. And, needless to say, serve immediately.

Note: this is equally good made with 1 lb (450 g) cooked cauliflower or courgettes mashed to a pulp.

Alpine eggs

(serves 3 people)

This is a recipe I have given many times before, but I don't apologise for including it here again because it never fails to please and is the quickest supper dish for any number of people— including one.

6 large fresh eggs
¾ lb grated Cheddar (or Lancashire) cheese (350 g)
Approximately 1 oz butter (25 g)
Salt and freshly-milled black pepper
1 dessertspoon freshly-snipped chives, if available

Pre-heat the oven to gas mark 4, 350°F (180°C)

Butter a shallow oval baking dish quite generously, then cover the base with half the grated cheese. Now carefully break 6 eggs onto the cheese, season well with salt and freshly-milled black pepper, then sprinkle the rest of the cheese over the eggs, covering them completely.

Dot with a few flecks of butter here and there, then bake in the centre of the oven for 15 minutes, by which time the cheese will be melted and bubbling, and the eggs just set. Just before serving sprinkle the chives over, and serve with crusty fresh bread and a crisp green salad.

Note: for a special occasion serve Alpine eggs as a first course. Use individual dishes (buttered) with 1 egg per person and 2 oz (50 g) grated Gruyère cheese per person. Prepare and cook in exactly the same way as above.

Cheese tartlets with mushroom pâté

(makes about 24)

These are made with a really crisp cheese pastry and filled with a mushroom and onion pâté.

For the pastry:
4 oz wholewheat flour (110 g)
4 oz self-raising flour (110 g)
1 teaspoon mustard
Pinch of salt

2 oz margarine (50 g)
2 oz lard (50 g)
3 oz Cheddar cheese, grated (75 g)
Some cold water to mix

For the filling:
1 oz butter (25 g)
6 oz flat mushrooms, finely chopped (175 g)
1 small onion, finely chopped
2 eggs
4 fl oz milk (110 ml)
1 tablespoon grated Parmesan cheese
Nutmeg
Salt and freshly-milled black pepper

Begin by making the pastry: sieve the flours, salt and mustard into a large mixing bowl, add the bran remaining in the sieve, rub in the fats until the mixture is crumbly, stir in the cheese, and add sufficient water to make a dough that leaves the bowl clean. Wrap the pastry in a polythene bag and chill it in the refrigerator for about 30 minutes.

Now melt the butter in a small pan and sauté the onion in it until soft—about 5 minutes. Then stir in the mushrooms and continue to cook gently, uncovered, for 30 minutes, stirring occasionally. The mixture should now have formed a sort of paste. Taste and season.

Pre-heat the oven to gas mark 5, 375°F (190°C) and put a baking sheet in near the top.

Next, on a floured board, roll out the pastry fairly thinly and use a 3 inch (7·5 cm) cutter to cut out pastry rounds. Ease these into greased 2½ inch (6 cm) patty tins, prick the bases then put on the baking sheet in the oven and cook for 5 minutes. Now beat the eggs lightly, take the pastry out of the oven and brush each tart with a little egg, then return to the oven for a further 5 minutes.

Now whisk the milk, some seasoning and nutmeg into the beaten eggs. Put a little of the mushroom and onion mixture in the base of each tartlet and, very carefully, pour on some of the egg mixture. Sprinkle with Parmesan, return to the oven for 30 minutes until the mixture is set.

Finally, leave in the patty tins to cool for about 15 minutes.

Orange cheesecake
(serves 8 people)

This is unbelievably easy, it doesn't need any cooking and can be made well in advance.

4 oz wheatmeal biscuits, crushed to fine crumbs with a rolling pin (110 g)
2 oz butter (50 g)
1½ lb cream cheese (700 g)
3 fl oz concentrated orange juice, thawed (75 ml)
2 oz caster sugar (50 g)
The grated zest of 1 orange, boiled in water for 5 minutes, then drained

Begin by melting the butter in a saucepan, but do not let it brown. Then stir in the biscuit crumbs and mix well. Now press the mixture into a lightly oiled 8 inch (20 cm) cake or flan tin with a loose base and leave in a cool place, or in the refrigerator, to harden a little.

When it has firmed, beat the cream cheese, orange zest and sugar together very thoroughly, add the thawed orange juice and continue beating until you have a smooth mixture, then pour it into the biscuit-lined tin. Cover with foil and chill thoroughly.

If you wish, the cheesecake can be decorated with segments of fresh orange (carefully peeled, skinned and well drained) or, in the summer, whole strawberries make it particularly delicious—but don't decorate with either fruit until just before serving or it will soak into the filling.

Curd cheesecake with fruit topping
(serves up to 12 people)

This is a large cheesecake which will serve up to 12 people. The fruit you use can be whatever is in season—in summer I think the nicest topping of all is a mixture of ½ lb (225 g) strawberries and ¼ lb (110 g) each of redcurrants and raspberries.

For the base:
8 oz wheatmeal biscuits (225 g)
4 oz butter (110 g)

For the filling:
1½ lb curd cheese (700 g)
8 oz sugar (225 g)
3 eggs
1 teaspoon vanilla essence

For the topping:
½ pint double cream, whipped (275 ml)
Icing sugar
Fresh fruit (as above)

Pre-heat the oven to gas mark 2, 300°F (150°C)

A 9 inch (23 cm) tin about 2–3 inches (5–7·5 cm) deep with a loose base.

Gently melt the butter in a small saucepan, without letting it brown. Crush the biscuits to fine crumbs with a rolling pin, then stir them into the melted butter. Transfer the biscuit mixture into the cake tin and press it down evenly all over to form a base. Now combine the curd cheese, eggs and sugar together in a mixing bowl and beat to form a smooth, thick cream—an electric mixer is best for this. Then mix in the vanilla essence and pour the mixture over the biscuit base, smoothing it out evenly.

Cook the cheesecake for 30 minutes on the centre shelf, then turn the oven off and leave it to get quite cold in the oven. It should then be chilled for at least 2 hours, or preferably overnight. To turn the cheesecake out of the tin, rinse a clean dishcloth in hot water: hold it around the tin for a few seconds, then push up the base very gently. Just before serving, top the cake with the whipped cream, the fresh fruit and a dusting of icing sugar.

Fresh lemon cheesecake with frosted grapes

(serves 6–8 people)

This is fresh-tasting and lighter than the other cheesecake recipes given in this book, and looks attractive with clusters of frosted grapes on top.

For the base:
4 oz digestive biscuits, crushed into crumbs (110 g)
2 oz butter (50 g)

For the filling:
2½ oz caster sugar (60 g)
12 oz cottage cheese (350 g)
2 large egg yolks
The grated rind and juice of 2 lemons
½ oz powdered gelatine (10 g)
5 fl oz double cream (150 ml)

For the topping:
4 oz seedless grapes (110 g)
1 egg white
Caster sugar

An 8 inch (20 cm) flan tin or sponge tin with a loose base, lightly oiled.

First prepare the base of the cheesecake by melting the butter in a small saucepan, then mix the melted butter with the biscuit crumbs in a bowl. Spoon the mixture into the prepared tin and press it well down all over as evenly as possible.

Now put the gelatine, along with 3 tablespoons cold water, into a small cup and stand this in a small saucepan of barely simmering water. Leave it for about 10 minutes or until the gelatine looks clear and transparent. Then put it on one side.

Now put the egg yolks, sugar and cheese in a liquidiser, blend for about one minute, then add the lemon juice and rind plus the gelatine (pour the gelatine through a strainer). Blend again until everything is thoroughly mixed and the mixture absolutely smooth. Now whip up the cream until you get a 'floppy' consistency, pour this into the liquidiser and blend again for just a few seconds. Next pour the whole mixture over the biscuit base, cover with foil and chill for a minimum of three hours.

Meanwhile whisk up the left-over egg whites. Break the grapes into little clusters of 2 or 3 grapes each and dip each bunch first in the egg white, then in a saucer of caster sugar. Leave them spread out on greaseproof paper for a couple of hours before using them for decoration.

Cœur à la crème
(serves 4 people)

This lovely cream mixture—ideal for serving with soft summer fruits—was originally served in heart-shaped dishes (hence the name). But small ramekins will do for the less romantic!

8 oz unsalted cream cheee (225 g)
½ pint soured cream (275 ml)
2 level tablespoons caster sugar
2 large egg whites
4 tablespoons double cream

Quite simply combine the cream cheese, soured cream and sugar thoroughly in a mixing bowl. Then whisk the egg whites until they are stiff and fold them carefully into the cream mixture. The whole lot now needs to be drained—overnight—in a cool place, and this is done by placing the mixture in a suitably-sized square of muslin, and placing this in a sieve over a bowl. When it has drained completely, pile the mixture into small dishes or ramekins, arrange your fruit on top, then pour a tablespoon of cream over each serving.

See also:

A risotto for spring
Asparagus and cheese tart
Baked spinach with brown rice and cheese
Braised celery with cheese and onion sauce
Brown rice with vegetables and cheese sauce
Cheese sauce
Cheese savouries
Cheese soufflé
Cheese soufflé pancakes
Cream cheese and herb filling for vol-au-vents
Cream cheese with herbs
Eggs and leeks au gratin
Eggs Florentine
Gougère with cheese
Ham, egg and cheese risotto
Home-made curd cheese
Italian stuffed aubergines
Mozzarella and tomato salad
Omelette savoyard
Richmond maids of honour
Scone pizza
Spinach-stuffed pancakes with cheese sauce
Wholewheat cheese-crusted scones

Salads and dressings

Including recipes for:
Vinaigrette dressing
Home-made mayonnaise
Aioli sauce
Sauce tartare
Sauce rouille
Eliza Acton's English salad sauce
Green salad
Tomato salad
Green winter salad
Red spinach and watercress salad
Rice salad
Brown rice and tuna fish salad
New potato salad with mint and chives
Red cabbage and coriander salad

Chick pea salad
Haricot bean and salami salad
Chinese beansprout salad with
 soy dressing
Four star salad
Broad bean salad
Salade Niçoise

I think it would be true to say that salads in this country were not all they should have been for a very long time; largely, I suspect, for the same reason our vegetable cooking lacked imagination: namely that our meat and fish were so good and plentiful that any other additions to the table took second place. Over a hundred years ago, a Victorian food writer described our lack of skill with salads as 'a defect in our national character'. He put it down to our obsession with pickles, and I think he had a point. Perhaps our delicious chutneys and pickles *are* to blame for that all-too-familiar sight a few years ago: wet lettuce leaves, tomato quarters and perhaps a radish presented alone and undressed, with only a bottle of the dreaded factory-made salad cream for company.

Well, times have changed and so have salads. They have been enlivened by the growth of foreign travel and a wider knowledge of and interest in good food. Even stubborn grandmothers who swear they couldn't eat anything 'oily' will enjoy a really well-dressed salad (provided you don't tell them about the oil!).

Salad dressings

The two most widely-used salad dressings are mayonnaise and vinaigrette, and indeed most other dressings are derived in some way from these two. It's the job of a good dressing to complement a salad rather than disguise it, and that's why the right ingredients are so important. This needs to be emphasised because the lack of them is the reason why so many dressings in so many restaurants are abysmal. So let's have a look first at the essential ingredients.

Vinegar As far as I'm concerned, malt vinegar should never find its way anywhere near a salad—its strong taste is too overpowering for delicate salad vegetables (I'm not decrying it: for pickling onions or sprinkling over fish and chips I wouldn't use anything else!). Salads need the much milder *Wine vinegar*, preferably the kind made by the slow Orleans method (see page 410). The disadvantage of wine vinegar is of course its price, but *Cider vinegar* is also suitable for dressings and is less expensive.

You can also make your own *Flavoured vinegars* by adding sprigs of fresh herbs to steep in the vinegar. Tarragon is perhaps the best herb to use—and this is also a good way of conserving it for the winter, when a few drops of tarragon vinegar will give a dressing a nostalgic summery flavour.

Oil Olive oil is obviously the best choice, though its cost seems to get increasingly prohibitive. What few people realise, though, is the enormous saving that can be made by buying olive oil in bulk. It can be widely bought in 3, 4 or 5 litre cans (or polythene packs) which will save you pounds if you've been in the habit of buying small bottles from supermarket shelves.

Olive oil The best-quality olive oil comes straight from freshly cold-pressed ripe olives—this is called 'first pressing'. After that, there is usually a second pressing where the olives are heated in order to extract every last drop. The first pressing gives a fruity but mild taste: the second a stronger, often rather harsh one (sometimes if the olives were over-ripe it is too strong, and the oil has to be what one might call de-flavoured).

The only way to find an olive oil that suits you is to experiment. I have found that a good Italian olive oil is what I personally like best (the most famous is the kind produced in Lucca), though I've also had very good Greek olive oil made from olives from the Calamata region. Both of these can be purchased at Italian or Greek shops. When I can't get to one of them, I buy—again in bulk—a blended olive oil from a national chemist's chain-store, where the olive oil is now sold primarily for culinary rather than medical use, and has greatly improved.

Groundnut oil is always my second choice for salad dressings and, in fact, for mayonnaise it is my first choice. It is rich without having a pronounced flavour, but you do need to hunt around for it in specialised food shops or delicatessens. Maybe it will become more widely available if we keep nagging retailers for it!

Sunflower, soya and all other culinary oils can be used in salad dressings. These are strictly a matter of personal preference: when used for cooking some of them have a quite distinctive flavour, but when used cold are much milder and do not compete with the other flavours in a dressing. They are, for the most part, more economical than olive oil and therefore worth experimenting with.

Lemons Lemon juice, if liked, can be used instead of vinegar in a dressing. I once had a lovely salad in Greece made from olives, tomatoes, cucumber and Feta cheese, with fresh lemon juice squeezed straight on with a drizzle of olive oil. The combination was just right for that salad, though on the whole I have to admit that wine vinegar is preferable.

Vinaigrette dressing
The recipe I give, let me say straightaway, is a guideline rather than a rule. Not only do individual tastes differ, but the ingredients can

vary too. Sometimes a sharper dressing is what's required, sometimes a milder one. However I usually stick to the old saying: 'Be a counseller with the salt, a miser with the vinegar, and a spendthrift with the oil.' This is good advice—the most common fault (especially in restaurants) is over-enthusiasm with the vinegar; and even worse I think, is the addition of sugar to counteract it. Anyway, my version is as follows:

Vinaigrette dressing	
	1 level teaspoon salt (English rock salt, crushed, is best for this)
	1 (or ½) clove garlic (according to taste)
	1 rounded teaspoon mustard powder
	1 tablespoon wine (or cider) vinegar
	Freshly-milled black pepper
	6 tablespoons olive oil

I like to start off with a pestle and mortar: first of all crush the flakes of rock salt to a powder, then add the peeled clove of garlic and pound that together with the salt—which will immediately bring out its juices and turn it into a smooth paste. Next add the mustard powder, vinegar and some freshly-milled pepper, and mix thoroughly until the salt dissolves. Finally add the olive oil, and just before dressing the salad, pour everything into a screw-top jar and shake vigorously to get it thoroughly blended.

I think salad dressings should be made as fresh as possible. So if you happen to have some left over, use it the next day but don't keep it any longer.

Note: there are any number of variations on this theme. For a *Vinaigrette with herbs*, for instance, add a teaspoon each of freshly chopped chives, tarragon and parsley just before serving.

Mayonnaise

No commercially-made mayonnaise, or short cut home-made version, can beat the thick, shining, wobbly texture of a proper mayonnaise you make yourself. For me, it's one of the true luxuries of the kitchen. Making mayonnaise for the first time can be a daunting experience, but *only* if the process is not explained properly. The following method is the traditional one and, I can assure you, pretty foolproof if you follow the instructions to the letter. At first it may seem a bit stupid to be adding the oil, literally drop by drop, and you'd be forgiven for thinking you're going to be there all night. The temptation to add more will be great. Don't, because the fact is, this method actually only takes 7 minutes from start to finish (yes . . . I've timed myself with a stopwatch).

Home-made mayonnaise (makes ½ pint or 2·75 ml)	2 large egg yolks
	1 level teaspoon salt
	1 heaped teaspoon mustard powder
	1 clove garlic, crushed
	½ pint groundnut oil (275 ml)
	White wine vinegar .
	Freshly-milled black pepper

A 1½ pint (850 ml) basin, an electric mixer (or balloon whisk if you need the exercise), plus a damp tea-cloth for standing the basin on to keep it steady.

Begin by putting the egg yolks into the basin, then add the crushed garlic and sprinkle in the mustard powder, salt and a few twists of freshly-milled pepper: mix all these well together. Now with the groundnut oil in a jug in one hand, and your mixer or whisk in the other, add *one* drop of oil to the egg mixture, and whisk that in. However daft it sounds, this is the key to success—whisking each drop of oil in thoroughly, before adding the next. It's *not* going to take all day, because in a few minutes—after you've added several drops of oil—the mixture will begin to thicken. At that stage—and only then—you can begin to add the oil in larger drops (when the mixture has started thickening, the critical point is past).

When about half the oil is in, add about a teaspoon of vinegar to thin the mixture down. Now you can begin pouring the oil in a thin, steady trickle—whisking the whole time. When it's all in, taste and season with salt and pepper and, if it needs it, a little more vinegar.

Curdling occurs if you add the oil too fast at the beginning. If that happens, don't despair. Simply put a fresh egg yolk into a clean basin, add the curdled mixture to that (drop by drop), then carry on with the remainder of the oil as if nothing had happened. Mayonnaise should be stored in a screw-top jar in a cool place—the bottom of the fridge if you like—for no longer than a week.

Quick mayonnaise

For a quick (though not so thick) version of mayonnaise: place two *whole* eggs in a food processor or liquidiser and blend with the mustard, salt, pepper and garlic (as in the previous recipe). Then with the motor turning, pour in all the oil in a steady stream. Taste and add vinegar at the end.

Mayonnaise forms the basis for a number of other sauces.

Aioli sauce

This is one of the best-known, and often served with fish or vegetables in the South of France. Follow the method above precisely, using 4 cloves of garlic instead of one (or more if you're a garlic addict!).

Sauce tartare

This is served with grilled or fried fish. Stir into the finished mayonnaise 2 finely chopped gherkins, 2 level teaspoons chopped capers, and 2 level teaspoons chopped parsley (or tarragon).

Sauce rouille

This is sometimes spread on baked croûtons of French bread and eaten with fish soups, or else stirred into the soup itself. It's also good served with any fried fish, or used as a dip for fried prawns for a first course. Make up half the quantity of *Quick mayonnaise* (see above), adding 2 crushed gloves garlic, 2 dessertspoons lemon juice (instead of the vinegar), 2 heaped teaspoons tomato purée, 2 level teaspoons paprika and 1 pinch cayenne pepper.

Eliza Acton's English salad sauce

(serves 4–6 people)

This sauce made with fresh cream and some cooked egg yolks makes a lovely dressing for potato, or for any other vegetable salad; it's good served with cold chicken, eggs or even fish; and with a little curry powder added it is ideal for a macaroni salad. The recipe comes from *Modern Cookery for Private Families* (modern, that was, in 1845).

The yolks of 3 hard-boiled eggs
5 fl oz double cream (150 ml)
4 teaspoons white wine vinegar
1 tablespoon cold water

| 2 pinches cayenne pepper |
| ¼ teaspoon salt |

Bring the eggs to the boil in plenty of cold water (they must be completely covered) and give them 9 minutes exactly from the time it starts boiling. Then run them under the cold tap to cool them—and stop them cooking any further. Peel away the shells and the whites, and place the yolks only in a mixing bowl.

Add the tablespoon of cold water and pound the yolks to a smooth paste with a wooden spoon. Then add a couple of pinches of cayenne plus the salt, and stir in the cream, bit by bit, mixing it smoothly as you go. When it's all in, add the vinegar and taste to check the seasoning. If you think the mixture's far too runny at this stage, don't worry. Cover the bowl and leave it for a couple of hours in the refrigerator, after which time it will have thickened (it should, in any case, have the consistency of thickish cream rather than mayonnaise).

Salad ingredients and their preparation

Lettuce I could never recommend one particular kind of lettuce, because I like to ring the changes in my salads, and each variety has a different charm of its own. However I do have firm opinions on how a lettuce should be treated, whatever the variety.

First of all I've found the best way to store lettuces is to remove the root but otherwise leave them whole, and enclose them in a polythene bag in the lowest part of the fridge. I believe washing should be avoided if possible, as once the leaves are wet it is so difficult to get them dry again. What I prefer to do is take a damp piece of kitchen paper and wipe each leaf, removing any specks of dust (and crawly things)—this way the lettuce leaves remain dry and can more easily be coated with dressing. Now I realise many people will not agree with me here and will want to wash the leaves: in that case plunge the separated leaves briefly into cold water and place them in a salad basket (see illustration on page 19), then either hang them up after a good shaking or else swing the basket round and round out-of-doors. Finish off by drying the leaves carefully with kitchen paper. Never use a knife when you prepare lettuce, because cutting tends to brown the edges of the leaves. Breaking up the leaves too soon can cause them to go limp quickly, so always leave them whole, if possible, until you're ready to serve the salad (and even then use your hands rather than a knife).

Chinese leaf This looks like a cross between a cabbage and a head of celery—thick white ribs edged with a green leaf. It is marvellous for winter salads when imported lettuces are thin and travel-weary. Just slice it whole, horizontally, as and when you need it, storing the rest in a polythene bag. The very stalky bits at the base, in fact, are delicious lightly fried and served as a vegetable.

Chicory These are tight little buds of very crisp leaves (sometimes white, sometimes a reddish colour). Since light spoils the leaves they are usually wrapped in tissue paper, and are best kept in this until needed. They can be braised and cooked as a vegetable, but I think are best sliced horizontally and used to give a salad extra crunchiness. The leaves are slightly bitter-tasting and therefore need a well-flavoured dressing.

Beetroot This is a salad vegetable that suffers either from having no flavour if it's served alone, or from being totally overpowered by malt vinegar. I prefer to buy it cooked, chop it up with a generous sprinkling of raw shallot or onion and serve it in a vinaigrette dressing. If you want to cook it yourself, it needs washing before boiling for 1¹/₂–2 hours with root, skin and a little of the stalk intact (as it's important not to let any of the juice 'bleed' out). It's ready when the skin slips off easily.

Cabbage Most varieties of cabbage make good salad ingredients if the stalks are removed and leaves are very finely shredded. See *Red cabbage and coriander salad* on page 492.

Fennel A bulbous-looking vegetable, similar in texture to celery but with a distinctive aniseed flavour. Sliced raw and separated into strips in a salad it responds beautifully to a well-flavoured olive oil dressing or some very garlicky mayonnaise.

Cucumber There's nothing nicer than a firm, young cucumber eaten the day it's picked with its flower still intact at the end. However if you're obliged to buy a plastic-wrapped one, do try to feel whether the stalk end is soft—if it is, that cucumber's past its peak. I never peel cucumbers because, as with many other vegetables, I like the appearance and flavour of the skins. If you prefer to peel them, use a potato peeler (which will only pare off the outer skin). Ever since I discovered them on holiday in Greece I've loved the crunchiness of *Ridge cucumbers*. These are shorter and fatter than ordinary cucumbers with little prickles along the ridges. The tough skins of this variety do have to be peeled.

Spring onions Finely chopped (including most of the green parts as well) these are the best onions for salads—or whole, to be taken on picnics and dipped in salt. Welsh onion—which resembles the green part of spring onion—grows happily in our herb bed through the winter, too. It has a stronger flavour than chives but, finely chopped, it makes an excellent winter substitute for chives.

Watercress I love watercress in a green salad, and now that it can be bought ready picked-over and vacuum-packed, it saves such a lot of time (even if it is a little more expensive). Inside the unopened pack, watercress will keep for about 5 days, but once exposed to the air it wilts extremely quickly. For this reason, if you use it for a salad or garnish, don't put it on until the last moment. Watercress bought in bunches should be first picked over and de-stalked, then stored upside down with the leaves submerged in cold water.

The well-dressed salad

I really wouldn't suggest that the French have the last word on everything in the kitchen, but when it comes to dressing a salad properly, we can certainly learn from them. In Italy a haphazard sprinkling of some vinegar, followed by the same of oil with no particular regard for proportions, has killed off many a salad I would have otherwise enjoyed there. (I once read of the owner of a taverna on one of the Greek islands who, with the aid of a sprinkler fixed to the top of a bottle, could aim the dressing for a salad from a distance of four tables away!) In England we have a chemical-tasting oddity called salad cream which often lurks amongst the naked ingredients.

The French, on the other hand, dress their salads with a lot of care—and care is the operative word. A green salad will be given a wide bowl, with ample room for tossing, so that each leaf will be coated and glistening. A tomato salad will be presented on a wide, shallow plate so that the slices don't overlap each other and become damp and woolly. The tradition at 18th century French dinner parties was for the salad to be dressed at table by the hands of the most beautiful lady present. And therein lies the secret of the well-dressed salad—not looks, but *hands*. I'm convinced this is the only way to dress a leafy green salad really well.

So a few points to remember: always have a roomy bowl with space to toss the salad well, sprinkle in a little dressing at a time—never pour it so that one leaf gets totally drenched, and toss the leaves with your hands gently and carefully, so they get evenly coated but never soggy. Use *only* enough dressing to achieve this: if you finish up with pools at the bottom of the bowl, you have failed.

Green salad

The nicest green salads are the simplest, those with the least ingredients: crisp, dry lettuce leaves alone, or perhaps with some watercress, a little finely-chopped spring onion (or shallot) and a plain vinaigrette dressing. Or possibly one with a few fresh chopped herbs added.

Tomato salad

A tomato salad needs careful preparation and, properly made, it makes a good starter before a meal served with some crusty French bread and fresh butter. Choose firm but ripe tomatoes. Pour some boiling water over them and in a minute or two the skins will slip off very easily.

Never prepare a tomato salad too far in advance, because once you slice tomatoes they go a bit woolly. Another important point is that you should use a large flat plate for them—or else smaller individual plates—becaue the slices shouldn't overlap each other, another thing that causes sogginess.

For my tomato salad I like to sprinkle on some very finely chopped raw onion and lots of fresh chopped parsley and perhaps a mere trace of sugar—and some fresh chopped basil leaves would be a luxurious addition. Do not dress the salad until the last minute before serving.

Green winter salad

(serves 4–6 people)

Crisp chicory and Chinese leaves with winter lettuce and an avocado make a delicious salad for the winter months when there is a shortage of fresh greens.

1 small lettuce
1 head chicory
Half a head Chinese cabbage
1 small onion
1 ripe avocado

For the dressing:
2 cloves garlic
1 level teaspoon mustard powder

1 level teaspoon salt
1½ tablespoons wine vinegar
4½ tablespoons olive oil

Select only the crispest leaves of the lettuce, wipe them and
arrange them in a salad bowl. Discard any bruised leaves and hard
stalk of the chicory, then slice it directly into the bowl in about
¼ inch (½ cm) slices (separating the slices). Now slice the
cabbage in the same way, chop the onion fairly finely, and add them
too. The avocado should be cut from top to bottom, opened up and
the stone removed. Now cut each half in half again, and with a sharp
knife you should find the skin will peel away whole if the avocado's
ripe. Then chop the flesh into ¾ inch (2 cm) squares and add to
the salad. Toss it well.

Then make up the dressing: place the peeled garlic cloves, salt and
mustard powder in a mortar and crush to a paste. Next stir in the
wine vinegar, followed by the oil, then transfer to a screw-top jar
and shake vigorously to amalgamate everything. Pour the dressing
over the salad, mix to give it all a good coating and serve.

Raw spinach and watercress salad

(serves 4 people)

This salad is a meal in itself and makes a
change from the inevitable lettuce.

8 oz young spinach leaves (225 g)
1 bunch watercress
2 hard boiled eggs, chopped
4 slices bacon, grilled until crisp

For the dressing:
4 tablespoons dry sherry
3 tablespoons olive oil
3 tablespoons wine vinegar
1 teaspoon lemon juice
Salt and freshly-milled black pepper

Wash the spinach and watercress leaves thoroughly first, and
discard the stalks and any damaged leaves. Then dry them carefully
in a clean tea towel (or salad basket)—do this a few hours ahead of
time if you can, to be sure of getting them quite dry.

To make the dressing, whisk all the ingredients together in a basin,

using a fork, or shake them together in a screw-top jar, then taste
and season to your liking.

To make the salad, tear the spinach leaves into manageable pieces
and place in a salad bowl with the watercress leaves. Pour the
dressing over and toss the leaves thoroughly. Then garnish with the
chopped eggs and the bacon crumbled into small pieces, and eat
straightaway.

Rice salad

(serves 4–6 people)

This can, of course, also be made with
white rice—in which case the rice needs
to be cooked for just 15 minutes.

Brown rice, measured to the 10 fl oz level in a glass measuring jug (275 ml)
1 pint boiling water (570 ml)
1 dessertspoon oil
3–4 tablespoons vinaigrette dressing (see page 482)
3 spring onions, very finely chopped
2 inches cucumber, unpeeled and finely chopped (5 cm)
2 large tomatoes, skinned and finely chopped
Half a red or green pepper, deseeded and finely chopped
1 red dessert apple, cored and chopped with the skin left on
1 oz currants (25 g)
1 oz walnuts, finely chopped (25 g)
Salt and freshly-milled black pepper

Heat the oil in a saucepan, then stir in the rice to get the grains
nicely coated. Add some salt, pour the boiling water over and bring
back to the boil. Stir once, place the lid on and simmer the rice
gently for 40 minutes or until all the liquid has been absorbed (tilt
the pan slightly to check if there's any water left).

Now empty the rice into a salad bowl, fluff it up with a fork and then
pour the dressing over while it's still warm. Leave it to get cold, then
mix in all the other ingredients, adding a little more dressing if you
think it needs it, and tasting to check the seasoning. Keep in a cool
place until needed.

Brown rice and tuna fish salad

(serves 3–4 people)

This is a salad I serve for lunch with plenty of crusty bread to go with it.

Long grain brown rice measured to the 8 fl oz (225 ml) level in a glass measuring jug
Boiling water measured to the 16 fl oz (450 ml) level
1 oz butter (25 g)
½ teaspoon salt
7 oz tin tuna fish (200 g)
1 tablespoon capers, drained
1 tablespoon fresh chopped parsley
1 teaspoon grated lemon rind
The juice of half a lemon
1 dessertspoon wine vinegar
1 teaspoon mustard powder
3 tablespoons olive oil
A few drops tabasco sauce
A 2 inch piece unpeeled cucumber, finely chopped (5 cm)
Salt and freshly-milled black pepper

Melt the butter in a medium-sized pan, then stir in the rice so that it gets nicely coated with butter. Add the boiling water and salt, stir once only, then cover and simmer gently for 40 minutes. When the time's up, check that the rice is tender and there is no water left in the pan. Now tip the cooked rice into a wide shallow bowl and fluff it up with a skewer.

Next, in a screw-top jar, combine the oil, vinegar, mustard and lemon juice by shaking vigorously, pour it all over the rice while it is still warm, then leave to cool. Meanwhile drain the tuna in a sieve set over a bowl, and break the fish into small flakes. When the rice is cool, add the tuna (plus one tablespoon of its oil), together with all the remaining ingredients. Mix thoroughly, taste and season well.

Serve this on crisp lettuce leaves, and have some lemon quarters to squeeze over and some cayenne pepper on the table.

New potato salad with mint and chives

(serves 4—6 people)

This potato salad is so good it's almost best to eat it on its own.

2 lb small new potatoes (900 g)
2 sprigs mint
8 medium-sized spring onions, very finely chopped
3 tablespoons fresh chopped mint
2 tablespoons fresh chopped parsley
2 tablespoons fresh snipped chives
Vinaigrette dressing (see page 482)
Salt and freshly-milled black pepper

Wash the potatoes but *don't* scrape them (there's a lot of flavour in the delicate skins of new potatoes). Place them in a saucepan with salt and a couple of sprigs of mint, then pour onto them enough boiling water to come about halfway up. Put on a tight-fitting lid and simmer them until tender, being very careful not to overcook. About 20—25 minutes should be enough: test them with a skewer—they should be tender but firm. Overcooking will make them watery and mushy.

Drain them in a colander, then put them in a salad bowl. Chop them roughly with a knife, and pour on the dressing while they're still warm. Mix thoroughly. When the potatoes have cooled, mix in the fresh herbs and chopped spring onions. Taste, to check the seasoning, and keep the salad in a cool place until needed.

Red cabbage and coriander salad

(serves 6—8 people)

This is an ideal winter salad and a good one for help-yourself parties.

8 oz red cabbage (225 g)
1 medium-sized Cox's apple
1 onion, finely chopped
2 sticks celery, finely chopped
For the dressing:
2 tablespoons wine vinegar
2 tablespoons olive oil
2½ fl oz natural yoghurt (75 ml)
½ teaspoon salt

| ½ teaspoon mustard powder |
| 1 clove garlic |
| ½ teaspoon coriander seeds, crushed |
| Freshly-milled black pepper |

First of all, cut the cabbage into quarters; remove the ribby parts, then shred the rest as finely as possible directly into a large mixing bowl. Then grate the apple (leaving the skin on) into the cabbage, and add the chopped onion and celery. Stir it around and get everything evenly distributed before making the dressing.

For the dressing, crush the garlic together with the salt, mustard powder and some pepper with a pestle and mortar (or in a basin using the end of a rolling pin), then pour in the oil and vinegar. Give it a good stir, then add the yoghurt and crushed coriander. Now mix vigorously with a fork to amalgamate everything, pour the dressing onto the salad and toss well.

Note: you can make and dress this salad well in advance as it keeps well in a polythene box stored in the refrigerator.

Chick pea salad
(serves 4–6 people)

Chick peas are nutty and slightly crunchy in a salad but you have to plan this one in advance because they must be soaked overnight.

| 8 oz chick peas, soaked overnight (225 g) |
| 8 oz haricots verts, (thin green string beans) (225 g) |
| 5 fl oz garlic-flavoured mayonnaise (150 ml)—see page 483 |
| 1¾ oz tin anchovy fillets, drained and finely chopped (45 g) |
| 6 spring onions, finely chopped |
| 2 tablespoons capers, drained and chopped |
| 2 tablespoons finely chopped parsley |
| Lemon juice to taste |
| A dozen black olives, pitted and halved |
| A few crisp lettuce leaves |
| Salt and freshly-milled black pepper |

Bring the chick peas to the boil and simmer until tender (about 1¼ hours). Don't salt the water though, or the chick peas will never soften! The topped and tailed green beans will need 3 or 4 minutes in boiling salted water, then tip them into a colander, rinse them with cold water, drain well and cut each bean in half.

Combine the mayonnaise, anchovy fillets, spring onions, capers, chopped parsley and a good seasoning of salt and pepper. Then fold the well drained and cooled chick peas with the green beans and black olives into the mayonnaise mixture. Taste, and add a little lemon juice and more seasoning if necessary. Serve piled on a bed of crisp lettuce leaves.

Haricot bean and salami salad

(serves 2 people)

Not simply a side-salad this one, but a pretty substantial lunch (or supper) dish on its own. The haricot beans I recommend for this are the long, thin variety (rather than the small 'baked bean' type).

8 oz dried haricot beans (225 g)
1 small onion stuck with 2 cloves
A few parsley stalks
1 bayleaf
1 clove garlic, crushed
¼ teaspoon dried thyme or a sprig of fresh thyme
2 oz Italian salami, finely diced (50 g)
1 small onion, chopped
2 tablespoons fresh parsley, chopped
Freshly-milled black pepper

For the dressing:
1 tablespoon red wine vinegar
1 teaspoon mustard powder
1 heaped teaspoon salt
1 clove garlic
5 tablespoons olive oil
Freshly-milled black pepper

First place the beans in a saucepan, add about 4 pints (2·25 litres) cold water, cover with a lid and bring to the boil. Then turn off the heat and leave the beans to soak for 1 hour. After that, add the onion stuck with cloves, the parsley stalks, bayleaf, garlic, thyme and a few twists of pepper. Bring the beans back to the boil and simmer gently, uncovered, for 1–1½ hours or until tender.

While the beans are cooking, prepare the dressing. Crush the garlic in the salt (with a pestle and mortar), and then mix in the mustard powder and some pepper, followed by the vinegar and the oil. Transfer the dressing to a screw-top jar and shake vigorously to blend the ingredients. (If you have neither a pestle and mortar nor a garlic press, place the peeled clove on a hard surface and crush it with the flat blade of a knife.)

When the beans are cooked, drain them and discard the onion, bayleaf and parsley stalks. Tip the beans into a large bowl. Pour over the dressing, then add the diced salami, onion and chopped parsley—mix gently to avoid breaking the beans. Taste and season, and leave to cool before serving.

Note: if you can't get Italian salami, use another kind.

Chinese beansprout salad with soy dressing

(serves 4–6 people)

This is a very bright and beautiful salad to look at and the unusual dressing makes it really different.

8 oz fresh beansprouts (225 g)
1 small red pepper, deseeded and chopped
About 6 inches unpeeled cucumber (15 cm), diced
Half a bunch watercress
1 small onion, thinly sliced and separated into rings

For the dressing:
½ teaspoon ground ginger
½ small onion, finely chopped
6 fl oz olive oil, or for economy groundnut oil (175 ml)
2 fl oz red wine vinegar (55 ml)
2 fl oz cold water (55 ml)
2 tablespoons soy sauce
1 small stalk celery, chopped
2 teaspoons tomato purée
2 teaspoons lemon juice
Salt and freshly-milled black pepper

In a good roomy bowl combine the beansprouts, chopped pepper, diced cucumber and sliced onion. Pick over the watercress, selecting the best leaves, and add them to the salad. Cover the bowl with clingfilm and chill in the refrigerator while you make up the dressing. For this, all you do is simply place all the dressing ingredients in a liquidiser, and blend until smooth. Taste, and season the dressing as required.

For this salad I would suggest you serve the dressing separately in a jug, for people to help themselves.

Note: if you don't have a liquidiser, then combine the dressing ingredients by shaking them together in a screw-top jar.

Four star salad

(serves 4 people)

This salad is a meal in itself. The 'stars' in question here are avocado, garlic sausage, mushroom and lettuce, with a lovely, garlicky, soured cream dressing.

2 ripe avocados
4 oz small pink-gilled mushrooms (110 g)
8 oz French garlic sausage, in one piece (225 g)
2 cloves garlic, crushed
1 tablespoon lemon juice
2 tablespoons mayonnaise
2 tablespoons olive oil
1 tablespoon wine vinegar
1 teaspoon mustard powder
1 medium-sized lettuce
4 spring onions, finely chopped
5 fl oz soured cream (150 ml)
Salt and freshly-milled black pepper

Begin by combining the soured cream with the garlic, mayonnaise and mustard powder. Then mix together the oil, vinegar and lemon juice and gradually add these to the soured cream mixture, tasting and seasoning with some salt and pepper. Now slice the garlic sausage into $^{1}/_{2}$ inch (1 cm) slices and then cut these slices into $^{1}/_{2}$ inch (1 cm) strips. Next break up the lettuce leaves and arrange them in a salad bowl: wipe and thinly slice the mushrooms (don't take the skins off) and add these to the lettuce pieces.

Finally prepare the avocados by removing the stones and peeling them, then cutting them into ¹/₂ inch (1 cm) cubes. Add these to the lettuce and mushrooms along with the strips of garlic sausage. Mix it all together gently, then add the dressing and toss again very gently. Sprinkle the chopped spring onions all over the surface and serve straightaway. This is nice served with *Home-made granary bread* which can be made by using the *Quick wholewheat bread* recipe (page 50), made with half wholewheat flour and half granary flour.

Broad bean salad
(serves 2 people)

I devised this recipe when I had a glut of broad beans in the garden—now it's a firm favourite.

1¹/₂ lb broad beans (700 g), the weight before shelling
2 rashers lean bacon, rinded
1 tablespoon fresh chopped herbs (I use a mixture of tarragon, marjoram and parsley)
4 spring onions, finely chopped
For the dressing:
1 small clove garlic, crushed
1 teaspoon English mustard powder
1 dessertspoon lemon juice
1 dessertspoon wine vinegar
1 level teaspoon crushed rock salt
Freshly-milled black pepper
4 dessertspoons oil

First cook the bacon until it's really crisp, then drain it well and crumble it into very small pieces. Next make the dressing by dissolving the salt in the lemon juice and vinegar for a few minutes, then shake it with the rest of the ingredients in a screw-top jar to get everything thoroughly amalgamated.

Now cook the shelled beans in a very little salted water for about 5 minutes—it's very important not to overcook them or they'll lose their colour and go mushy. Drain them thoroughly and toss them in the dressing while they're still warm. When they're cool, toss in the finely chopped spring onion, the bacon and the chopped herbs. Serve the salad on some crisp lettuce leaves.

Salade Niçoise
(serves 4–6 people)

This is a favourite summer lunch dish in our house, served with *Hot herb and garlic loaf* (see page 504), but it also makes a nice refreshing and light first course.

1 lettuce
4 oz cooked new potatoes, sliced (110 g)
4 oz cooked French beans (110 g)
Half a small young cucumber, peeled and cut in smallish chunks
12 oz firm ripe tomatoes, skinned, deseeded and quartered (350 g)
2 oz black olives (50 g)
2 hard-boiled eggs, peeled and quartered
7 oz tin tuna fish, well drained (200 g)
1 tablespoon finely chopped onion, or spring onions
1 tablespoon fresh chopped parsley
1¾ oz tin anchovy fillets, well drained (45 g)
Vinaigrette dressing with garlic and herbs (see page 482)—you won't need the full quantity of vinaigrette

First arrange lettuce leaves around the base of a large salad bowl and sprinkle on a little vinaigrette dressing. Then arrange the tomatoes and cucumber in layers with a little more dressing, then add the onion, slices of potatoes and French beans. Now place the quartered hard-boiled eggs on top with the tuna fish, which should be broken up into chunky flakes. Finally decorate the salad with the strips of anchovy fillet, making a latticed effect (or whatever you like), then sprinkle on the black olives, the fresh chopped parsley and the rest of the dressing. Serve as soon as possible.

See also:
Aduki bean and brown rice salad
Chicken salad with tarragon and grapes
Cucumber and yoghurt salad

Greek salad
Lentil, bean and anchovy salad
Nine herb salad of Hintlesham
Red bean salad

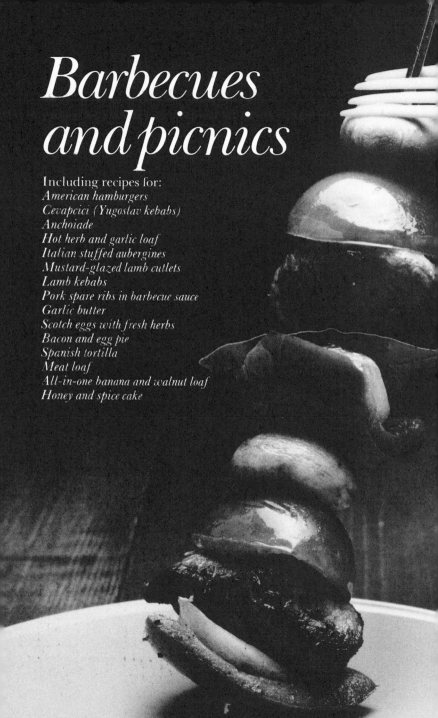

Barbecues and picnics

Including recipes for:
American hamburgers
Cevapcici (Yugoslav kebabs)
Anchoiade
Hot herb and garlic loaf
Italian stuffed aubergines
Mustard-glazed lamb cutlets
Lamb kebabs
Pork spare ribs in barbecue sauce
Garlic butter
Scotch eggs with fresh herbs
Bacon and egg pie
Spanish tortilla
Meat loaf
All-in-one banana and walnut loaf
Honey and spice cake

Eating out of doors is a bit of a hit-and-miss affair in this country
for obvious reasons (such as getting only one week of sunshine in
any one summer, for instance). If that sounds tongue in cheek, it's
meant to because I feel the whole subject of outdoor eating in
Britain should be approached with a sense of humour and with a
certain flexibility.

Not that I'm a pessimist. Each spring I look at patio furniture in
glossy magazines, and I dream dreams. These include candle-lit
geraniums, the sizzling of charcoal-cooked food, the tinkle of ice-
filled glasses, and all the rest. Such dreams never include the Suffolk
winds that blow the smoke back in the direction of the guests, their
eyes getting steadily redder, their coughs louder. Nor do they
include what to do with fifty sausages (that fitted so well on the
barbecue) having to go eight at a time under the grill in the kitchen
because it's pouring! Even the most enthusiastic books on
barbecues finish up with realistic advice, including among the
recommended accessories bug-repellent sprays and burn lotions.

As picnickers, too, we display the same kind of grim, resolute
determination. In French films picnics are all about rivers and
willows and punts, or fields of red poppies and buzzing bees. In
Britain the hot tarmac of the zoo car-park will do, or a patch of grass
with four lanes of traffic on either side. I have even seen a man and
his wife, in a remote part of the Lake District, clad in sou'westers
eating their lunch with plates perched on the car bonnet as the rain
bucketed down! We all have our funny picnic stories, I'm sure.
Nevertheless eating outdoors *is* fun and, if only to avoid eating in
those motorway cafés, picnics are necessary.

Eating al fresco
The number one requirement for food in the open air is that it
should have lots of gutsy flavour. Delicate, subtle dishes can easily
lose their identity outside. Simple food—and lots of it—is the best,
I've found: even the humble British banger is quite transformed
with a smoky, crispy barbecued skin. Remember, too, that appetites
mysteriously increase out of doors and people can eat more if the
food is simple than if it's very rich.

Barbecues
If you're planning to improvise your own barbecue—or at the
other end of the scale have ambitions for a built-in garden
barbecue—then you should refer to one of several specialised
books on the subject. For those of us in the middle who are content

with a ready-made barbecue, however, there is a wide range of equipment and accessories to suit every taste and occasion. Basically there are only two kinds of barbecue: the brazier-type with a shallow bowl, where the air flows *over* the burning charcoal, and the grill-type with built-in air vents, where the air flows up and through the charcoal. All manner of attachments can be bought— hoods, spits, windshields, warming ovens—but none of these affects the basic operation.

Charcoal This is the commonest form of fuel, and comes either in pre-formed briquets (which are more efficient) or as lumpwood (which is cheaper). Hardwood can be used for large barbecues, but is quite impractical for the normal commercial makes.

Laying the fire On the brazier type of barbecue I think it is a good idea to line the bowl first with a sheet of aluminium foil (shiny side upwards), which will help to reflect the heat. Then lay a fire-bed of medium-sized gravel all over the base, so the air can circulate round the charcoal and help it to 'breathe'. Cover the fire-bed with a generous layer of charcoal, making sure it covers the whole area rather than just the centre and is not packed too tightly.

Lighting-up At home we use methylated spirit to get the charcoal alight—but it needs to be done with care. Sprinkle some all over the charcoal, then *wait* for a few minutes for it to get absorbed. Fire-lighters (broken up into smaller pieces and scattered among the charcoal) can be used, but don't start cooking until all the pieces are completely burned out, or the smoke will include some unpleasant fumes. In any case it is pointless to start cooking before the charcoal is properly and evenly alight, and that can take anything from 20 to 30 minutes. At night you can easily tell because the charcoal will glow pink: during the day the pieces will start to turn white.

Cooking on charcoal Try to set your barbecue where it will get sufficient draught but is not directly in the wind. Most barbecues have a grill that can be adjusted to different heights above the fire, which will control the speed of cooking, but sooner or later fat from the food will drop onto the coals and make them flare up. So have a jug of water handy and sprinkle a little onto the fire with your hands—just enough to douse the flame, but not so much that you stop the coals burning.

For that extra smoky flavour you can add small chips of aromatic wood to the fire (such as hickory or apple-wood), but these chips should be well soaked in water before use, unless you buy specially prepared packets of 'smoke chips'. Fresh herbs, such as rosemary, also add an interesting flavour to the smoke: these should be sprinkled on the fire towards the end of the cooking.

Equipment Experience has taught me that implements with very long handles are what are called for in tending barbecue food! Long-handled tongs and fork (for turning the food) will keep your hands a safe distance from the heat and a pair of oven gloves will give added protection. For kebabs, thread the meat etc onto *flat* skewers rather than round ones (which tend to turn themselves without turning the meat).

American hamburgers

(serves 2 people)

In this country the word hamburger conjures up all sorts of dubious images of frozen and packaged discs of meat and greasy griddles. The real hamburger is something else: 100% pure ground beef cooked, if possible, over charcoal to give it a charred, smoky crispness at the edges with a juicy medium-rare centre. All it needs then is a jacket potato brimming with soured cream and chives, and a selection of relishes and ketchup. This recipe will make 4 hamburgers to serve in buns, or two half-pounders (which may need a few more minutes cooking, depending on how you like them).

1 lb chuck steak, about 80% lean meat and 20% fat (450 g)
2 level teaspoons salt
Coarsely ground black pepper
A little oil

To prepare the meat you can either pass it through the fine blade of the mincer twice (which tenderises it), ask the butcher to do it for you, or you can grind the meat finely in a food processor.

To make the hamburgers, place the meat in a bowl and sprinkle in the salt and a good seasoning of coarsely ground black pepper.

Mix this in thoroughly, then divide the mixture into four portions. Take each portion in your hands and shape it into a ball, then place the ball on a flat surface and press to flatten it into a hamburger shape about ³/₄ inch (2 cm) thick.

Now brush each hamburger with very little oil and grill under a pre-heated grill set to high, or over hot charcoal, giving them 4–6 minutes on each side depending on how you like them. Serve in bap rolls (toasted on cut side only), and spread with slivers of raw or fried onion, relish and tomato ketchup.

Cevapcici (Yugoslav kebabs)

(serves 3–4 people)

These are delicious little minced sausages threaded onto skewers.

8 oz chuck steak (225 g)
8 oz lean belly pork or spare rib (225 g)
2 cloves garlic, crushed
1 teaspoon paprika
1 tablespoon finely chopped mint
Cayenne pepper
Salt and freshly-milled black pepper

For the sauce:
Approximately 4 inches (10 cm) cucumber, chopped into small cubes
5 fl oz natural yoghurt (150 ml)
2 teaspoons fresh chopped mint
1 clove garlic, crushed
Salt and freshly-milled black pepper

First the meats should be put through the finest blade of the mincer or chopped finely in a food processor. Then place them in a mixing bowl along with the garlic, paprika, a pinch of cayenne and a good seasoning of salt and pepper. Stir in the chopped mint and mix thoroughly to amalgamate everything. If possible, leave the mixture in a cool place for a while to allow the flavours to develop, then mould the mixture into about 9 little sausage shapes, about 2 inches (5 cm) in length. Thread these onto skewers—the flat kind are best—and cook over hot charcoal or under a pre-heated grill for 10–20 minutes, turning them frequently.

Serve them with a yoghurt sauce, made by simply combining all the sauce ingredients in a bowl.

Anchoïade

(serves 3–4 people)

This is a delicious snack to serve out of doors, either as a first course at a barbecue or for lunch with some 'salady' things to go with it. If it pours with rain, it can double up as a TV snack!

1¾ oz tin anchovy fillets in oil (45 g)
1 large or 2 small cloves garlic, crushed
8 black olives
1 small onion, finely chopped
A few drops wine vinegar
1 tablespoon chopped parsley
1 ripe tomato, skinned and chopped
2 heaped teaspoon tomato purée
1 rounded teaspoon dried oregano or 2 teaspoons fresh chopped marjoram
8 × 1 inch (2·5 cm) thick slices of day-old French bread cut diagonally
Some olive oil
Freshly-milled black pepper
Extra chopped parsley for garnishing

Begin by pounding the anchovies (with their oil) to a pulp, either using a pestle and mortar or a basin and the end of a rolling-pin. Then pit the olives, chop their flesh up finely and add this to the anchovy mixture along with the chopped onion, tomato and a few drops of wine vinegar. Stir thoroughly, then add the crushed garlic, tomato purée, oregano, parsley and some freshly-milled pepper, and stir again.

Now lightly toast the French bread slices on one side only, then spread the mixture on the untoasted side. All this can be done in advance. Then to finish off, pour a few drops of oil over each slice, place them under a pre-heated medium grill for 5 minutes to heat through, and sprinkle with chopped parsley before serving.

Hot herb and garlic loaf

This is perfect for a barbecue or party when lots of salads are being served.

1 French stick loaf
3 oz butter, room temperature (75 g)
2 cloves garlic, crushed

2 tablespoons fresh chopped herbs (parsley and chives with a little tarragon and thyme if available) or 1½ teaspoons dried mixed herbs

Pre-heat the oven to gas mark 6,
400°F (200°C)

First mix the butter, garlic and herbs together. Using a sharp knife, make diagonal incisions along the loaf, as if you were slicing it—but not slicing right through. The loaf should stay joined at the base. Now spread each slice with butter on both sides (it's easiest to do this with your hands) and spread any remaining herb butter along the top and sides of the loaf. Wrap the loaf in foil and bake it in the oven for about 10–15 minutes, and serve hot.

Italian stuffed aubergines

(serves 3–6 people)

These are good to serve as a first course at a barbecue for six people or for lunch in the garden on a hot day for three people with a salad and cold drinks.

3 medium aubergines
1 onion, chopped
2 tablespoons olive oil
1 large clove garlic, crushed
About 6 oz Italian Mozzarella cheese (175 g)—or, failing that, Gouda cheese—cut in thin slices
6 drained anchovy fillets, chopped
1½ tablespoons drained capers, chopped a little
3 largish tomatoes
2 teaspoons fresh chopped basil (or 1 teaspoon of dried basil)
A little additional oil
Salt and freshly-milled black pepper

Trim the green stalks from the aubergines and slice them in half lengthwise. If you have a grapefruit knife use that, or otherwise a teaspoon, to get out the pulpy centres of the aubergines leaving a shell not less than ¼ inch (½ cm) thick. Sprinkle the shells liberally with salt and leave upside down to drain for 45 minutes. Meanwhile chop the pulp.

Now heat the oil in a saucepan and gently fry the onion until softened. Stir in the chopped pulp, crushed garlic and half the basil. Season with salt and pepper and cook over a low heat for about 10 minutes, stirring now and then.

Next wipe the aubergine shells with kitchen paper and arrange them in a small oiled roasting tin or baking dish. Spoon the onion/pulp mixture into the shells, then arrange 2 slices of cheese on top of each aubergine half and sprinkle with the chopped capers and anchovies. Slice the tomatoes and arrange 4–5 slices on each aubergine. Finally sprinkle with the remaining basil and dribble a little more olive oil over each. Season and bake (uncovered) at gas mark 4, 350°F (180°C) in the top of the oven for 40 minutes.

Mustard-glazed lamb cutlets

(serves 4 people)

These are best of all barbecued, but still taste very good grilled and they provide a special supper very quickly.

8 lamb cutlets
2 tablespoons made-up mustard (English or Dijon)
3 rounded tablespoons demerara sugar
Salt and freshly-milled black pepper

Pre-heat the grill to a high setting.

Wipe the cutlets first with some absorbent kitchen paper to dry them, season them with salt and pepper, then spread both sides of each cutlet with mustard. Now dip them in sugar, making sure they get an even coating, and grill them for about 5 minutes on each side—or more or less, depending on their thickness.

Lamb kebabs

(serves 4–6 people)

These are perhaps the nicest barbecue food of all but, if the weather is against you, fear not, they're almost as good when grilled indoors.

1½ lb fillet end of leg of lamb, or pieces from a boned-out shoulder (700 g)
6 tablespoons olive oil
1 medium-sized onion

2 large lemons
2 teaspoons dried oregano
6 small bayleaves
1 small green or red pepper, deseeded
4 small tomatoes
2 cloves garlic, crushed
12 small mushrooms
Salt and freshly-milled black pepper

Start by preparing the meat: cut it into small bite-sized pieces (leaving some of the fat on the cubes as this helps to keep them juicy). Place the meat in a bowl, and then season it with salt and freshly-milled black pepper. Now add the bayleaves (snipped in half), crushed garlic and oregano. Peel the onion and cut it into quarters, then separate the quarters into layers and add these to the meat together with the green or red pepper cut into $\frac{1}{2}$ inch (1 cm) pieces.

Pour over the juice of one lemon, followed by the olive oil, and leave the meat to marinade (covered with a cloth) for several hours or overnight, stirring the ingredients and turning the meat cubes over now and then.

When you are ready to grill the kebabs, get your charcoal hot (or pre-heat your grill), then take a skewer—preferably a flattened one rather than a twisted or round one—and start by threading one mushroom and half a tomato (rounded end towards the handle of the skewer), then alternate a piece of meat, half a bayleaf, a piece of onion and a piece of pepper.

When everything is threaded onto the skewers, finish off with the other half of the tomato and the other mushroom. Push gently at both ends, because it's important for everything to be packed as tightly as possible. Grill the kebabs, basting them from time to time with the oil marinade and turning them over. They'll take about 15–20 minutes to be charred nicely on the outside and pink and juicy within. Serve with the other lemon cut into quarters.

Pork spare ribs in barbecue sauce

(serves 4 people)

Pork spare ribs (the actual rib bones) or lean pork slices are both good coated and flavoured with a barbecue sauce.

12 spare ribs

For the sauce:
3 tablespoons dry white wine or dry cider
6 tablespoons soy sauce
1 clove garlic
1 rounded tablespoon tomato purée
1 teaspoon English mustard powder
1 level tablespoon soft brown sugar
A few drops of tabasco sauce
Freshly-milled black pepper

First crush the garlic in a bowl, and pour in the wine (or cider) and soy sauce. Then stir in the tomato purée, followed by the mustard powder and sugar. Next add a few drops of tabasco, then give it all a good stir and season with pepper—no salt is needed.

Leave the sauce a few moments for the flavours to develop, then when the meat is ready to be cooked, brush each side generously with the barbecue sauce. Grill or barbecue the meat for about 15 minutes on each side, basting now and then with the extra sauce.

Picnics and food for travelling

When it comes to picnics nothing will budge me an inch from my keep-it-simple philosophy. In Edwardian days it was all very well, when butler, maid, bar and fully-equipped hamper could be transplanted into the country. And if you're very rich, I suppose you can still pick up a Henley or an Ascot Hamper from one of the smart London food establishments (though whether the contents will warrant the price is debatable). For less grand affairs I feel many people go wrong by trying to transport the sort of meal they would eat at home: it just doesn't taste the same on squashy paper plates with plastic knives and forks in sizes fit only for 4-year-olds.

Rough outdoor living demands rough outdoor food. Some of the nicest picnics I've had have been in Italy—crusty bread, chunks of salami, ripe plum tomatoes, cheese, olives, pickled pimentoes, peaches and huge black cherries, and of course quantities of something Italian to drink. All we had to pack on these occasions was pepper and salt, an insulated dish for butter, knives, plates and glasses. No cooking was involved, you will note. Even in this country you can approximate this kind of ready-made picnic by stopping at a chain-store with a good food department and buying bread, pork pies, salads in tubs, good fruit and a cake.

However if you're not pushed for time and want to plan and

prepare a picnic, all the recipes in this section will serve you well
out of doors or, if there's a last minute change of weather, inside.

Equipment
Our picnic equipment, such as it is, is not very elegant: I have found
that a few old china plates and mugs, and odd knives and forks, are
infinitely preferable to anything in the plastic line. We also have
some thick chunky glasses which may not look very sophisticated
but are far nicer—especially if you're drinking wine—than paper
cups. In fact the only 'special' equipment I have is a thermos flask
and a wide thermos jug (for soup in cold weather), an insulated
butter dish (if you put very cold butter in it, it keeps cool all day),
and an insulated bag with a little freezer pad (which also keep
things cool when it is frozen and placed inside). Oh, and two other
important items: a pepper mill and a corkscrew!

To keep things like cakes and rolls fresh, I think the best thing is
to wrap them first in greaseproof paper, then in foil and place them
in plastic bags. Polythene boxes are all right, but in our house by the
time we've found the right lid to fit the right box, there's no time for
a picnic.

Picnic foods
French bread This is excellent for picnics, sliced diagonally, split,
buttered and filled with slices of strong Cheddar cheese and sliced
raw onion, then sandwiched together again.

Bap rolls These are delicious filled with the following mixture (for
6 people): mash 6 boiled eggs while they're still warm with a good
knob of butter, 4 teaspoons mayonnaise, salt and pepper. Stir in
2 heaped tablespoons of fresh snipped chives.

Crusty rolls Buy garlic sausage or salami in one piece, so that you can
slice it more thickly. Fill the rolls with this plus some thin slices of
(drained) dill pickled cucumbers.

Garlic butter If you mash a clove of garlic into 8 oz (225 g) butter
along with 2 tablespoons of chopped parsley, then chill it all well
and place in an insulated butter dish, this will be lovely to spread on
French bread or rolls.

Rice salad This is a handy salad to take on a picnic, because it is
dressed beforehand (see page 490). I pack it in individual foil
containers with lids, and find it travels very well.

Crunchy things are nice at picnics—for instance, radishes and crisp spring onions. Firm tomatoes are a good idea, but it goes without saying that they should be taken whole: never slice them or put them in sandwiches, they're too soggy (and that goes for cucumbers too). Some of my favourite picnic recipes are included in this chapter but other parts of the book also contain several that are suitable for travelling.

Let me mention a few (these, and others, are listed at the end of this chapter). *Boeuf en croûte* is rather extravagant perhaps, but left to cool, then cut in slices, it's a super idea for a special picnic. *Shoulder of lamb with rice and kidney stuffing* also cuts very well into thick slices. *Sausage rolls* are picnic perennials that never fail. *Quick wholewheat pizza*, cut into sections and wrapped carefully, tastes marvellous in the open air. *Mustard-and-herb coated chicken* needs no plates or knives and forks, so is good for car journeys. *Cold chicken pie* should be taken in the tin it was cooked in, double wrapped, then cut when you arrive. *Date, apple and walnut loaf* is a nice moist cake with a crunchy crust.

Scotch eggs with fresh herbs
(makes 4)

Scotch eggs are marvellous for travellers or picnickers. Take some spring onions to go with them and, if you've got plates (paper or otherwise), some chutney.

4 hard-boiled eggs
8 oz sausagemeat (225 g)
2 spring onions, finely chopped
1 teaspoon fresh thyme, finely chopped
3 teaspoons chives, snipped
1 tablespoon parsley, finely chopped
Some toasted breadcrumbs
Seasoned plain flour
1 small egg, beaten
Salt and freshly-milled black pepper
Oil for frying

Hard-boil the eggs by covering them in cold water, bringing it to the boil, simming gently for 9 minutes and cooling them under cold running water. Next mix the sausagemeat with the spring onions and herbs and season well. Then shell the cooled eggs and coat each one with some seasoned flour. Divide the sausagemeat into four portions and pat each piece out on a floured surface to a shape roughly 5 × 3 inches (13 cm × 7·5 cm). Now place an egg in the centre of each piece and carefully gather up the sausagemeat to cover the egg completely. Seal the joins well, and smooth and pat into shape all over. Next coat them one by one, first in beaten egg and then thoroughly and evenly in toasted breadcrumbs.

Now heat 1¹/₂ inches (4 cm) of oil in a deep frying-pan up to a temperature of 350°–375°F (180°–190°C). (If you don't have a thermometer, you can easily test the temperature by frying a small cube of bread—if it turns golden brown within 1 minute the oil is hot enough.) Put the eggs into the oil and fry for 6–8 minutes, turning frequently until they have turned a nice brown colour. Drain on crumpled greaseproof paper.

When they're absolutely cold, wrap in clingfilm and store in the lower part of the fridge.

Bacon and egg pie

(serves 4–6 people)

A home-made bacon and egg pie makes a very good and easily transportable picnic dish, I find. Alternatively, it's nice served warm after the 'picnic' if the weather wasn't up to scratch!

4 large eggs
6 rashers lean, streaky bacon
5 fl oz milk (150 ml)
Salt and freshly-milled black pepper

Shortcrust pastry made with:
6 oz plain flour (175 g)
3 oz lard (75 g)
Pinch of salt and pepper
Cold water (to mix)

Pre-heat the oven (and a baking sheet) to gas mark 6, 400°F (200°C)

An 8 inch (20 cm) flan tin, rimmed if possible and 1¹/₂ inches (4 cm) deep.

Hard-boil three of the eggs—which I do by putting them in a saucepan, covering them with cold water, bringing to the boil and simmering gently for 9 minutes. Cool them quickly by running cold water from the tap over them. Then, while they're cooling, grill (or fry) the bacon gently until the fat begins to run, and make up the shortcrust pastry. Now divide the pastry in half, using one half to line the flan tin.

Peel and chop the hard-boiled eggs quite small, chop the bacon fairly small too and arrange them both in the flan. Season with freshly-milled pepper and a very little salt. Beat the remaining egg together with the milk, then pour the mixture over the contents of the pie. Roll out the rest of the pastry to form a lid, dampen the edges and seal well all round, using any trimmings to decorate. Make a small hole in the centre of the pastry, brush the top with milk, then put on the baking sheet on a high shelf in the oven and bake for 10 minutes. After that reduce the heat to gas mark 4, 350°F (180°C) and bake for a further 30 minutes.

Little bacon and egg pies
Alternatively you can make individual pies in 2½ inch (6 cm) patty tins, using 3 inch (7·5 cm) and 3½ inch (8 cm) cutters.

For 11–12 little pies you'll need: the quantity of pastry as above, 2 hard-boiled eggs, 4 rashers back bacon, 1 egg and 4 fl oz (100 ml) milk beaten together.

Use the larger rounds of pastry to line the patty tins, divide the chopped eggs and bacon between the pies, then pour in the egg-and-milk mixture, and top with the smaller pastry rounds. Brush the tops with any left-over egg-and-milk mixture, and bake on a pre-heated baking sheet in the oven at gas mark 6, 400°F (200°C) for 10 minutes, then reduce the heat to gas mark 5, 375°F (190°C) and cook for a further 25 minutes.

Spanish tortilla
(serves 2–4 people)

This is an omelette which is just as nice served cold as it is hot—and excellent therefore for taking on a picnic, where you can cut it up into wedges.

4 large eggs
2 medium-sized potatoes, peeled and diced small
1 small green pepper, deseeded and chopped

1 medium onion, chopped
2 oz piece Spanish chorizo sausage (or similar), cut into small dice (50 g)
3 tablespoons olive oil
Salt and freshly-milled black pepper

Begin by heating 2 tablespoons of the oil in a frying-pan, add the potatoes and cook them for 8–10 minutes (stirring them from time to time) until they're evenly browned. Then add the onion, pepper and sausage. Give them all a good stir and carry on cooking for another 6–8 minutes.

Now beat the eggs and season them well with salt and pepper, and pour them into a frying-pan over the vegetable mixture. Cook over a medium heat for 3 minutes or so, drawing the cooked egg into the centre of the pan with a palette knife and letting the liquid egg run into the gaps. When the omelette is firm—but still slightly moist—turn it upside down onto a plate. Then heat the remaining tablespoon of oil in the pan and slide the omelette back into the pan (other side up). Cook it for a further 3 minutes. You can of course serve this straightaway; otherwise leave to get cold, cover and keep in a cool place until needed.

Meat loaf
(serves 6–8 people)

This is a good idea for a picnic as, once cold, it can be cut into firm slices. However, it's also very good served hot with a fresh tomato sauce.

1 lb lean minced beef (450 g)—from a reliable butcher
8 oz minced pork, or pork sausagemeat (225 g)
2 medium-sized onions, minced
1 small green pepper, finely chopped
1 dessertspoon tomato purée
1 fat clove garlic, crushed
1 level teaspoon dried mixed herbs
2 tablespoons fresh chopped parsley
2 slices white bread from a large loaf
3 tablespoons milk
1 egg, beaten
Salt and freshly-milled black pepper

Pre-heat the oven to gas mark 5,
375°F (190°C)

A 2 lb loaf tin (900 g).

Put the minced beef in a large mixing bowl with the pork, onion,
chopped pepper, tomato purée and garlic and give everything a
thorough mixing, seasoning well with salt and freshly-milled
pepper. Cut the crusts off the bread, soak it in the milk, then squeeze
the excess milk out of it and add it to the rest of the ingredients,
along with the mixed herbs and parsley. Now give the mixture
another thorough mixing, and finally stir in the beaten egg to bind it
all together.

Press the mixture into a 2 lb (900 g) loaf tin, spreading evenly, then
bake it in the oven for 1¼ hours. When it's cooked it will have
shrunk and begun to come away from the sides of the tin. Allow it to
get cold in the tin, wrap it in a double sheet of foil and take it to the
picnic wrapped in a cloth or in an oblong plastic box.

Note: meat loaf is delicious served cold with pickles and salad. It also
goes very well sliced and put into sandwiches or rolls.

All-in-one banana and walnut loaf

This is an extremely easy cake, ideal for
picnics as it has a pronounced flavour.

3 oz soft margarine (75 g)
4 oz caster sugar (110 g)
1 large egg, beaten
The grated rind of 1 orange
The grated rind of 1 lemon
8 oz plain flour (225 g)
2 level teaspoons baking powder
4 medium bananas, peeled
2 oz walnuts (50 g), roughly chopped

Pre-heat the oven to gas mark 4,
350°F (180°C)

A loaf tin, base measuring
3½ × 7½ inches (8·5 × 19 cm),
greased, with the base lined with
greasproof paper also greased.

Start off by placing the margarine, sugar and the beaten egg in a large mixing bowl, then sift in the flour and baking powder. In another bowl slice the bananas and mash them to a pulp with a fork. Now, use an electric mixer to whisk the sugar, fat and flour together until they are thoroughly combined—don't worry if the mixture looks rather dry at this stage. Next add the orange and lemon rinds, followed by the mashed bananas and chopped walnuts, and whisk again thoroughly. Then transfer the mixture to the prepared tin and level the top off.

Bake in the centre shelf of the oven for 50–55 minutes, until the loaf is golden, well-risen and springs back when pressed with a finger. Leave to cool in the tin for 10 minutes, then loosen around the edges and turn out onto a wire cooling tray to finish cooling. This cake is nice sliced and spread with butter.

Honey and spice cake

This cake has a tangy, citrus flavour. Because it has a lemon icing, it is best transported in a polythene box.

8 oz plain flour (225 g)
4 oz butter (110 g)
3 oz caster sugar (75 g)
1 level teaspoon ground ginger
1 level teaspoon ground cinnamon
¼ teaspoon ground cloves
Finely grated zest of 1 small orange
Finely grated zest of 1 small lemon
1 large egg, beaten
3 oz clear, runny honey (75 g)
1 level teaspoon bicarbonate of soda
2 oz finely chopped mixed candied peel (50 g)

For the icing:
4 oz sifted icing sugar (110 g)
1½ tablespoons lemon juice
2 tablespoons warm water

To decorate:
6 pieces crystallised ginger, chopped

Pre-heat the oven to gas mark 3,
325°F (170°C)

One 7 inch (18 cm) square tin, lightly
buttered.

First of all weigh a cup or small basin on the scales then weigh 3 oz
(75 g) of honey into it. Now place the basin into a saucepan
containing barely simmering water and warm the honey a little but
be careful, it mustn't be too hot, just warm. Next sift the flour and
spices into a large mixing bowl, then add the sugar and the orange
and lemon zest. Now add the butter in small pieces, then rub it
lightly into the flour, using your fingertips, until the mixture
becomes crumbly. Next, lightly mix in the beaten egg, using a large
fork, followed by the warm honey. Then in a small basin, mix the
bicarbonate of soda with 3 tablespoons of cold water, stir until
dissolved, then add it to the cake mixture and beat, quite hard, until
the mixture is smooth and soft. Then, finally, stir in the mixed peel
and spoon the mixture into the prepared tin, spreading it out
evenly. Bake the cake just above the centre of the oven for about
30 minutes or until well risen and springy to the touch. Cool it for
10 minutes, then turn it out onto a wire rack to get quite cold.

Meanwhile prepare the icing by sifting the icing sugar into a bowl,
then add 2 tablespoons of warm water along with the lemon juice
and mix to a thin consistency that will coat the back of a spoon. If
you don't think it's thin enough add a little more water. Now place
the cake on a wire rack, with a large plate underneath, and pour the
icing all over, letting it run down and coat the sides a bit. Then
decorate the top with chopped ginger and store in an airtight tin.

See also:
Asparagus and cheese tart
Boeuf en croûte
Cheese and onion quichelets
*Cheese tartlets with
   mushroom pâté*
Cold chicken pie
Cornish pasty pie
Date, apple and walnut loaf

Fish kebabs
Indian kebabs
Mustard-and-herb-coated chicken
Omelette savoyard
Quick wholewheat pizza
Sausage rolls
*Shoulder of lamb with rice and
   kidney stuffing*
Spinach and cream cheese quiche

Cream, ice cream and yoghurt

Including recipes for:

Eggs en cocotte with soured cream and
  asparagus
Leek and soured cream flan
Pork chops with cream and mushrooms
Pheasant with cream and apples
Eighteenth-century creamed apple flan
Plum and soured cream flan
English rhubarb fool
Rich lemon cream with frosted grapes
Crème caramel

Crème brûlée
Vanilla ice cream
Praline ice cream
Blackcurrant ice cream
Black Forest gateau
Home-made yoghurt
Home-made curd cheese
Yoghurt seafood sauce
Chilled yoghurt and cucumber soup
Cucumber raita
Dried fruit salad with yoghurt and nuts

Since the western world has become involved in a seemingly endless dialogue on fats and their contribution to the causes of coronary disease, cream (along with butter, oils and other fatty foods) has inevitably come in for quite a battering. It goes without saying, however, that this chapter is not an invitation to everyone to eat lashings of cream regardless: moderation is always the last word. The fact is that cream is a natural food, and an ingredient to be used (with restraint) in cooking for which there is no really acceptable substitute. I would, for instance, rather have just one ice cream per year made from (guess what!) ice *cream*, than dozens made from synthetic, over-sweetened non-milk fat. For those who are forbidden cream, or are cutting down on their calories, then I would recommend they replace it with home-made yoghurt (see page 534)—which is utterly delicious and very different from the commercially-made kinds.

Cream

Without being too scientific about the subject, let's first consider the difference between the various types of cream. Butterfat is the name given to small globules present in milk, though not visible to the naked eye. Each one of these is surrounded by a layer made up of some of the other solid components in the milk. These little globules tend to gather together and rise to the surface of the milk, forming a layer. This layer is then skimmed off to become cream or butter.

The various types of cream are graded according to the amount of butterfat they contain. Thus *double cream* has to contain no less than 48% butterfat, *single cream* no less than 18%, and *half cream* no less than 12%.

Whipping (or ready-whipped) cream must contain not less than 35% butterfat. This, in fact, is the minimum requirement for whipping ability, which is the reason why single cream is unsuitable for whipping.

Clotted cream has the highest butterfat content of all (55%), and the clotting is achieved by a special treatment. The milk is scalded at a temperature of 180°F (82°C) and allowed to cool overnight before being skimmed. It is, as anyone who has had a holiday in the West Country knows, a real luxury.

There are of course other types of cream available: for instance, *UHT (ultra heat treated) cream*, packed in foil-lined containers, which keeps much longer than fresh cream, and *sterilised cream*, marketed in glass bottles, which lasts even longer. However the treatment that these products undergo to ensure their long life does affect their flavour. Unless there is absolutely no alternative, it is my opinion they are not worth using.

Soured (or cultured) cream

This is single cream (not less than 18% butterfat) which, when commercially-made, is heated and then inoculated with a culture. The temperature is controlled, and when the acidity reaches a certain level, clotting takes place. In Russia and some northern European countries cream was allowed to sour naturally for use in cooking, and many people have asked me if it is possible to sour cream at home. It's not, unfortunately, because all our bottled milk and cream is pasteurised, but it is possible to simulate it.

If you can't get soured cream you can simulate it by adding 1 teaspoon of lemon juice to 5 fl oz (150 ml) of single or double cream, depending on how creamy you want it. Leave it for half an hour or so, and it will have begun to thicken. Another, quicker, way is simply to combine in equal quantities cream (single or double) and natural yoghurt.

Soured cream is particularly useful in recipes, giving them a distinctive flavour (sharper than cream, but creamier than yoghurt). When you're buying it, it's important to look carefully at the date stamp, and make sure the expiry date is as far off as possible. Soured cream becomes more acid the older it gets. It *will* keep for about a week in the refrigerator, but bear in mind the flavour will be that much sharper.

Eggs en cocotte with soured cream and asparagus	This is a lovely way to make a little asparagus go a long way, and its delicate flavour is just right with soft creamy eggs.

(serves 6 people)

8 oz asparagus (225 g)
6 large fresh eggs
1 oz butter (25 g)
½ pint soured cream (225 ml)
6 heaped teaspoons freshly-grated Parmesan cheese
Salt and freshly-milled black pepper

Six 3½ inch (9 cm) ramekin dishes, well buttered

Pre-heat the oven to gas mark 4,
350°F (180°C)

Steam the asparagus (see page 256) for just 4 minutes—it needs to
be only half-cooked. Then when it's cool enough to handle, chop it
into 1 inch (2·5 cm) lengths and arrange the pieces in the bases of the
dishes—making sure each one gets its fair share of the tips, but also
reserving six for the garnish.

Now carefully break an egg into each little dish, season it with salt
and freshly-milled black pepper, then gently spoon approximately
1 tablespoon of soured cream over each egg, spreading it out with
a knife so that it covers the top completely.

Dot them with flecks of butter and sprinkle each one with a teaspoon
of Parmesan cheese and place an asparagus tip in the centre (all this
can be done well in advance if you like).

To cook, pour about an inch (2·5 cm) of boiling water into a meat
roasting tin, place the dishes in it, pop the whole lot in the oven and
bake for about 15–18 minutes. Bear in mind, however, that the eggs
will go on cooking in the heat from the dishes on the way to the table.
Serve with buttered wholemeal bread and chilled white wine.

Leek and soured cream flan

(serves 4–6 people)

This flan has a very crisp, cheese,
wholewheat pastry and makes a very
good lunch dish with a salad.

For the pastry:
3 oz self raising flour (75 g)
3 oz wholewheat flour (75 g)
¾ teaspoon mustard powder
A pinch of salt
1½ oz lard (40 g)
1½ oz margarine (40 g)
2 oz Cheddar cheese, finely grated (50 g)

For the filling:
3 lb leeks (1 kg 350 g), trimmed with 1½ inches (4 cm) of green left on, then sliced thinly
1 clove garlic, crushed
2 oz butter (50 g)

1 large egg, beaten
5 fl oz soured cream (150 ml)
2 tablespoons double cream
2 oz grated Cheddar cheese (50 g)
Salt and freshly-milled black pepper

A 10 inch (25·5 cm) loose-based flan tin, greased

To make the pastry, sieve the flours, salt and mustard into a large bowl, then rub in the fats until the mixture resembles fine breadcrumbs. Now stir in the cheese, and add enough cold water to make a dough that leaves the bowl clean. Pop the pastry into a polythene bag and leave to rest in the fridge for half an hour.

Meanwhile pre-heat the oven to gas mark 4, 350°F (180°C), and put in a baking sheet to pre-heat as well. Roll out the pastry and line the flan tin, using any surplus pastry to reinforce the sides and base, carefully smoothing it into place. Prick the base all over with a fork, then bake the flan case in the centre of the oven on the baking sheet for 15 minutes. After that, remove from the oven and brush all over with a little of the beaten egg (from the filling ingredients). Return to the oven for 5 minutes more, then remove and turn the heat up to gas mark 5, 375°F (190°C).

Now for the filling: melt the butter in a large pan, add the leeks and garlic, and some seasoning. Cover and cook gently, without browning, for 10–15 minutes until they're sufficiently reduced to fill the flan case comfortably. Drain in a colander and return to the pan. Meanwhile combine the creams with the beaten egg and stir this into the leek mixture, seasoning to taste. Spread the mixture over the pastry case, sprinkle with the cheese and bake in the centre of the oven for 40 minutes, until brown and crispy.

Pork chops with cream and mushrooms

(serves 6 people)

This recipe is one of the most popular ones I've ever given. It's excellent for a dinner party because it doesn't need last minute attention.

6 large pork chops, trimmed of excess fat
12 oz mushrooms (350 g)
5 fl oz double cream (150 ml)

Juice of a large lemon
1½ tablespoons plain flour
2 teaspoons fresh chopped thyme (or 1 level teaspoon dried)
2 oz butter (50 g)
Salt and freshly-milled black pepper

Pre-heat the oven to gas mark 4, 350°F (180°C)

Place a large double sheet of cooking foil on a meat roasting tin, bearing in mind it must be large enough to wrap the chops in.

Now in a frying-pan, brown the chops nicely on both sides in butter, and then transfer them onto the foil. Season each one with salt and freshly-milled black pepper and a little thyme.

Now chop the mushrooms roughly and fry them in the same pan in which the meat was browned, adding a little more butter if you think it needs it. Then pour in the lemon juice, let it bubble for a minute, then sprinkle in the flour and stir with a wooden spoon until you have a rather soggy-looking mushroom mixture. Don't worry— it always looks awful at this stage.

Spoon the mixture over the pork chops, some on each, then spoon a little of the double cream over each one. Now wrap up loosely in foil, sealing it very securely, and bake them for 1 hour. Serve the chops with the delicious juices poured over. Since this is very rich, keep the accompanying vegetables fairly simple. A sprig or two of watercress beside each chop gives extra colour.

Note: When this is cooked the cream takes on a slightly curdled appearance, but this doesn't in any way spoil the delicious flavour.

Pheasant with cream and apples

(serves 2 people)

A hen pheasant is best for this recipe, which will only serve two, but you can, of course, double or treble the list of ingredients for more people.

1 plump young pheasant (oven-ready)
1 tablespoon butter
1 tablespoon oil
Half an onion, chopped small

3 medium-sized Cox's apples
About 6 fl oz dry cider (170 ml)
5 fl oz double cream (150 ml)
Salt and freshly-milled black pepper

First, heat the butter and oil together in a casserole. Then season the pheasant with pepper and salt and brown in the hot fat, turning it frequently so it browns evenly all over. Add the onion and let it soften gently whilst you quarter, core, and peel the apples. Slice them, not too thinly, and stir them into the casserole. Then add the cider, turn the bird onto its side and cover the casserole. Cook over a very low heat for about 1 hour or so, remembering that halfway through the cooking time you will have to turn the bird onto its other side.

Then, when the bird is cooked, remove it to a warmed serving dish. Simmer the apples remaining in the casserole until almost all the liquid has evaporated. Stir in the cream and season with salt and freshly-milled black pepper. Heat gently, then pour the apples and cream over the pheasant and serve.

Eighteenth century creamed apple flan

(serves 6 people)

This recipe is a nostalgic one for me as it's one of the first I tried after some research at the British Museum into 18th century British cooking, and it prompted me to do a whole lot more!

For the pastry:
4 oz plain flour, sifted (110 g)
1 oz margarine (25 g)
1 oz lard (25 g)
Water to mix

For the filling:
4 large cooking apples, peeled, cored and sliced
2 tablespoons water
2 oz butter (50 g)
2 tablespoons caster sugar
3 digestive biscuits, crushed into crumbs with a rolling pin

2 tablespoons brandy
The grated peel of a small lemon
2½ fl oz double cream (65 ml)
3 egg yolks
Freshly-grated nutmeg

Pre-heat the oven to gas mark 4, 350°F (180°C)

An 8 inch (20 cm) flan tin, lightly greased.

Make up the pastry by rubbing the fats into the sifted flour until the mixture resembles breadcrumbs. Then add enough water to make a dough that leaves the bowl clean. Pop the pastry in a polythene bag and leave to rest in the fridge for 20 minutes or so, then roll it out and use to line the flan tin. Prick the base all over with a fork, and bake for 20 minutes.

Meanwhile put the sliced apples in a saucepan with the water and cook until they are pulpy. Transfer them to a large mixing bowl and beat until you have a smooth purée. Then whisk in the butter and the caster sugar, followed by the biscuit crumbs, lemon peel and brandy, and a good grating of nutmeg. Combine everything thoroughly and leave the mixture to cool. Next whisk the egg yolks together with the cream—don't over-do it, you just want to thicken it slightly. Then when the apple mixture has cooled, stir the eggs and cream into it. Pour the whole lot into the partly cooked flan case, then bake in the oven for a further 30 minutes.

Note: you can, if you like, substitute cider for the brandy.

Plum and soured cream flan

(serves 4–6 people)

Since I've been writing recipes, this is one I've found to be most popular with everyone who makes it.

6 oz shortcrust pastry (175 g) i.e. made with 6 oz (175 g) flour and 3 oz (75 g) fat
1 lb dessert plums (450 g)
½ pint soured cream (275 ml)
1 oz caster sugar (25 g)
3 egg yolks

| ½ teaspoon mixed spice |
| 2 oz demerara sugar (50 g) |
| 1 teaspoon ground cinnamon |

Pre-heat the oven, and a baking sheet, to gas mark 6, 400°F (200°C)

A 10 inch fluted flan tin (25·5 cm), greased.

Roll out the shortcrust pastry and line the flan tin, then halve the plums and remove the stones. Now beat the soured cream together with the caster sugar, egg yolks and mixed spice, then pour this into the flan case and arrange the plums over the top (flat side up). Place the flan on the baking sheet and bake for 20 minutes.

Then mix the cinnamon with the demerara sugar and sprinkle it all over the top. Bake for a further 20 minutes, turning the heat right up to gas mark 8, 450°F (230°C) for the final 5 minutes so that the top can brown nicely. Serve warm or cold.

English rhubarb fool

(serves 4 people)

Rhubarb fool has always been one of my favourite English puddings. You'll find all manner of recipes for it—but it's best of all when it's made with a proper custard, like this one.

| 2 lb rhubarb, washed and cut into chunks (900 g) |
| 2 oz caster sugar (50 g) |
| 1 teaspoon ground ginger |

| *For the custard:* |
| 8 fl oz double cream (225 g) |
| 3 egg yolks |
| 1 tablespoon caster sugar |
| 1 teaspoon cornflour |
| 2 drops vanilla essence |

| *To decorate:* |
| 4 pieces of preserved ginger cut into tiny chunks |

First of all put the chunks of rhubarb together with the caster sugar into a saucepan, then sprinkle in the ginger. Cover the saucepan and cook the rhubarb very gently for 15–20 minutes, stirring frequently (you want the rhubarb to be tender but not mushy). Then place the cooked rhubarb in a sieve over a bowl to drain off some of the juice.

Meanwhile make the custard. Bring the double cream up to boiling point in a small saucepan. Mix the cornflour, sugar, egg yolks and vanilla essence together in a basin until smooth. Pour the boiling cream into the mixture, whisk thoroughly, then return the whole lot to the saucepan and back onto a medium heat. Carry on whisking until it has thickened, then immediately pour the custard into a bowl to cool (if it looks a little granular you can get it smooth again by beating). Now mash the drained rhubarb until smooth and combine it evenly with the custard. Pour this mixture into four serving dishes (stemmed glasses look nice), top with pieces of preserved ginger, cover with clingfilm and chill slightly before serving.

Rich lemon cream with frosted grapes

(serves 12 people)

This is the very nicest lemon dessert I've ever come across. It serves about 12 people, so is very good for a party. For a smaller quantity, use a 6 inch (15 cm) tin, 1 level dessertspoon gelatine, 1 egg yolk and half the remaining ingredients.

5 fl oz milk (150 ml)
4 level tablespoons caster sugar
Grated rind and juice of 4 lemons
1 level tablespoon powdered gelatine
1 egg yolk
1¼ pints double cream (700 ml)
4 large egg whites

To decorate:
4 oz white grapes (110 g)
1 egg white
Caster sugar

An 8 inch (20 cm) round cake tin, lightly oiled.

Place the milk, sugar, grated lemon rind, gelatine and egg yolk together in a blender or liquidiser. Blend for half a minute at top speed, then pour the mixture into a small saucepan and stir over a very gentle heat for 3 or 4 minutes until fairly hot but *not* boiling. Now return the mixture to the liquidiser and whizz round again, adding the lemon juice and ½ pint (275 ml) of the cream. When all is thoroughly blended, pour the mixture into a bowl, cover with foil and chill, stirring occasionally until the mixture is syrupy.

Whip the remaining cream lightly until it just begins to thicken, then in another very large bowl whisk the egg whites until stiff and carefully fold them into the lemon mixture, followed by the cream. Pour the mixture into the cake tin, cover and chill until firm.

To make the frosted grapes: first of all whisk up the egg white. Then break the grapes into little clusters of 2 or 3 grapes each and dip each bunch first in the egg white, then in a saucer of caster sugar. Leave them spread out on greaseproof paper for a couple of hours before using them.

Before serving, dip the cake tin for a moment in hot water, and turn the lemon cream over onto a plate. Decorate with the frosted grapes and serve the cream cut in slices rather like a cake.

Crème caramel

(serves 4–6 people)

A standard favourite with everyone from tiny babies to 90-year-olds.

5 fl oz milk (150 ml)
½ pint single cream (275 ml)
4 large eggs
1½ oz soft brown sugar (40 g)
1 tablespoon water, tap hot
4 oz granulated or caster sugar (110 g)
Vanilla essence

Pre-heat the oven to gas mark 2, 300°F (150°C)

A 1½ pint (850 ml) oval or round shallow baking dish.

First put the granulated (or caster) sugar in a medium size saucepan and heat. When the sugar begins to melt, bubble and darken, stir and continue to cook until it has become a uniform liquid syrup, about two shades darker than golden syrup. Take the pan off the heat and cautiously add the water—it will splutter and bubble quite considerably but will soon subside. Stir and, when the syrup is once again smooth, quickly pour it into the base of the dish, tipping it around to coat the sides a little.

Now pour the milk and cream into another pan and leave it to heat gently while you whisk together the eggs, brown sugar and a few drops of vanilla essence in a large bowl. Then, when the milk is steaming hot, pour it onto the egg and sugar mixture, whisking until thoroughly blended. Then pour the liquid into the dish and place it in a large roasting tin. Transfer the tin carefully to the oven, then pour cold water into it to surround the dish up to two-thirds its depth. Bake for 1 hour. Cool and chill the crème caramel, until you're ready to serve it. Free the edges by running a knife around before inverting it onto a serving plate.

Crème brûlée

Crème brûlée has its origins in England—it was invented at Trinity College, Cambridge where it was known as Burnt Cream. This could be called a cheat's version, but really it isn't. It has merely been adapted to help those who (like me) have never had a domestic grill that is suitable for fast caramelising of sugar. So here the caramel is made separately and simply poured over.

1 pint double cream (570 ml)
6 egg yolks
2 tablespoons caster sugar
4 level teaspoons cornflour
A few drops pure vanilla essence
6 oz granulated sugar (175 g)

Six ramekins, 3 inches (7·5 cm) diameter.

You need to start the recipe the day before, so that the custard can be well chilled and firm. Heat the cream until it reaches boiling point, and while it's heating blend the egg yolks, cornflour, caster sugar and vanilla essence in a bowl. Then pour the hot cream in, stirring all the time with a wooden spoon, then return the mixture to the saucepan. Heat very gently (still stirring) until the sauce has thickened—which should only take a minute or two. (If it does overheat, don't worry—if you remove it from the heat and continue to beat it *will* become smooth again as soon as it cools.) Divide the custard between the six ramekins and leave to cool. Then cover each dish with clingfilm and refrigerate overnight.

About an hour before serving make the caramel. Place the granulated sugar in a heavy pan, then place the pan over a very low heat to dissolve the sugar gently and caramelise it (to get all the sugar to melt, just shake and tilt the pan from side, but don't stir). When all the sugar has dissolved and you have a clear syrup (about 10–15 minutes) remove the pan from the heat and pour immediately over the custards, covering the surface of each one. Now just leave them for a few minutes for the caramel to harden. Before eating the crème brûlée, tap the surface of the caramel with a spoon to crack and break it up.

Note: to remove any hardened caramel from your pan, fill it with hot water and bring it to the boil.

Vanilla ice cream

You can of course buy electric ice cream gadgets and sorbetiers, but I don't think they're worth the extra expense. The freezing compartment of the fridge will do, provided it is turned down to its coldest setting about half an hour before you start to freeze the ice cream.

10 fl oz single cream (275 ml)
10 fl oz double cream (275 ml)
1½ oz caster sugar (40 g)
2 slightly rounded teaspoons custard powder
3–4 drops pure vanilla essence
4 egg yolks

1 polythene box, approximately 1½ pints (850 ml) capacity, with lid.

First of all whip the double cream until it reaches the 'floppy' stage but isn't too thick, then pop it into the fridge to chill. At the same time put the polythene box into the freezer to chill as well.

Now make the custard by first pouring the single cream into a saucepan and then heating it up to boiling point. While that's happening beat together the egg yolks, vanilla essence and custard powder and sugar until absolutely smooth. Next pour the hot cream onto this mixture, whisking with a fork as you pour. Now return the custard to the pan and continue to whisk it over a medium heat until it has thickened and comes up to boiling point again. (Ignore any curdled appearance, which may come about if you don't keep stirring and have the heat too high. The custard powder will stabilise it provided you beat it off the heat: poured into a bowl it *will* become quite smooth again.)

Now place the bowl of custard in a bowl of cold water, and stir it now and then until absolutely cold. Then fold in the chilled whipped cream. Pour the whole lot into the chilled polythene box, cover and freeze for a couple of hours or until it is just beginning to set. At the same time place a mixing bowl in the freezer to chill, then as soon as the mixture does begin to set, tip it into the chilled bowl and whisk (with an electric hand-whisk or a rotary whisk) very thoroughly. Then return the ice cream to the polythene box, put it back in the freezer (covered) and leave until frozen (about 3 hours). Before serving, remove the ice cream to the main body of the fridge for 45 minutes to get a smooth, not-so-hard texture.

Praline ice cream	1 quantity of vanilla ice cream (page 529)
	2 oz unblanched almonds (50 g)
	2 oz caster sugar (50 g)

Place the sugar and almonds together in a pan over a low heat, and leave them until all the crystals of sugar have completely dissolved to a liquid. Then cook until the liquid has turned a rich brown colour.

Then pour this mixture onto a well-oiled baking sheet, spreading the almonds out in a single layer. Leave the mixture to cool and become brittle, then, using a palette knife, lift it off the baking tray onto a flat surface. Break it up with a few bashes from a rolling pin, then crush it fairly finely with the rolling pin.

Stir the crushed praline thoroughly into the ice cream about half an hour before serving. You can, if you like, make the praline at any time and store it in a screwtop jar, which will keep it crunchy.

Note: if you are short of time, the praline is also good just sprinkled over ice cream.

Blackcurrant ice cream

(serves 6–8 people)

I think blackcurrants make the very nicest ice cream, smooth, rich and velvety. However this same recipe works very well with loganberries, or even raspberries, if you prefer.

1 lb blackcurrants (450 g)
6 oz sugar (175 g)
5 fl oz water (150 ml)
½ pint double cream (275 ml)

A freezer-proof polythene box with a lid and a nylon sieve (a metal one can discolour the fruit).

There's no need to take the stalks off the blackcurrants; just pile them—about one-third of a pound (150 g) at a time—into the sieve set over a mixing bowl, and mash like mad with a wooden spoon until you have extracted all the pulp and only the stalks, pips and skin are left in the sieve. Loganberries or raspberries should be sieved in the same way.

Now place the sugar and water in a saucepan over a medium heat, stir until all the sugar crystals have dissolved, then let it come to the boil, and boil for 3 minutes exactly. Then remove from the heat and stir the syrup into the fruit pulp. Whip the cream until it *just* begins to thicken. Be careful not to overwhip—it mustn't be thick, just floppy. Fold the cream into the fruit mixture until thoroughly blended. Pour it into the polythene box, and freeze in a freezer or in the ice-making compartment of a refrigerator turned to its coldest setting.

As soon as the mixture begins to set (about 3 hours) turn it out into a bowl and beat thoroughly. Then return it to the freezer (in the box) until set—about another 3 hours. Remove to the main part of the fridge about an hour before serving.

Note: this ice cream should be eaten within 3 weeks.

Black Forest gateau

This is wickedly rich but not heavy at all. I think it makes a really lovely birthday cake for someone special.

6 large eggs
5 oz caster sugar (150 g)
2 oz cocoa powder, sieved (50 g)
½ pint double cream (275 ml)
1 level tablespoon caster sugar
1 lb tin (or jar) morello cherries (450 g)
2 oz plain chocolate (50 g)
1 or 2 tablespoons kirsch (or rum)

Pre-heat the oven to gas mark 4, 350°F (180°C)

Two 8 inch (20 cm) sandwich tins, oiled with groundnut oil and the bases lined with greaseproof paper, also oiled.

Start off by separating the eggs and placing the whites in a clean grease-free bowl. Put the yolks in another bowl and whisk them with the caster sugar until they just begin to pale and thicken (be careful not to thicken them too much, though). Now fold in the sieved cocoa powder.

Next, with a clean whisk, beat the egg whites until stiff but not too dry. Stir a heaped tablespoon of the egg white into the chocolate mixture to loosen it up a little bit. Then, using a metal spoon, carefully and gently fold in the rest of the egg white (trying not to lose any air). Divide the mixture equally into the prepared sandwich tins and bake them near the centre of the oven for about 15–20 minutes. They won't appear to be cooked exactly, just set and slightly puffy, and when they're taken out of the oven they will shrink (but that's normal). Leave the cakes to cool in the tins, but turn them out while they're still faintly warm and strip off the base papers.

Now whip the cream with the tablespoon of caster sugar until it is a floppy, spreadable consistency. Next empty the tin of cherries into a sieve set over a bowl and combine 2 tablespoons of the juice with the kirsh or rum. Sprinkle this over the cake layers and, using a palette knife, spread about a third of the whipped cream over one cake.

Then slice the cherries and de-pip them (if they have any pips). Leave about a dozen whole ones for the decoration. Now arrange the sliced cherries all over the cake spread with cream. Next, carefully place the other cake on top and cover the entire cake with the remaining cream, again using a palette knife. Finish off by arranging the whole cherries around the edge, then grate the chocolate and sprinkle it all over.

Yoghurt

It's hard to believe that yoghurt—once a rather obscure substance to be found only in equally obscure healthfood shops—has become the staple snack of the 1980s. There appears to be no limit to the flavours of the month which turn up on the supermarket shelves; but it is just this that disappoints me about the many commercial brands. Despite all the invention which has been lavished on the sweetened flavoured varieties, they have failed to come up with a true *natural* yoghurt that bears much resemblance to what yoghurt should taste like. Let's look at the reasons for this.

What is yoghurt? It is a substance made from milk (whole, skimmed, evaporated or dried) which is first sterilised by heating to 190°–221°F (88°–105°C), then cooled to 106°–114°F (41°–45·5°C) and inoculated with a specially prepared culture. It is then incubated at a warm temperature until the acidity reaches a certain level and clotting takes place. After that it is cooled again, and is ready to eat or be stored.

In the Balkans and the Middle East yoghurt is made naturally from whole milk. This is boiled in open containers, which enable the milk to evaporate and reduce down to about two-thirds, or even half, its original volume. When it is made into yoghurt it is therefore thick, with a natural layer of cream on the surface. It also has a natural sweetness, like the sweetness of fresh milk, which it only loses as it ages and grows more acid. Commercially produced yoghurt is usually made with skimmed (low fat) milk and then thickened by the addition of powdered skimmed milk, rather than by reducing. So it doesn't have the creaminess of home-made natural yoghurt and the time taken in distribution means that it is fairly acid by the time it reaches our homes.

Home-made yoghurt I have already hinted that flavour is one reason for making your own yoghurt at home, but there are others. For one thing it is a great saving on the household bill (especially if you have a family that likes yoghurt), since the cost of making it at home is a third or a quarter of the shop version. You can also be sure that the ingredients you use—and the flavours you add—are pure and natural. And equally important, it is so easy.

Making your own yoghurt

After quite a number of hit-and-miss yoghurt-making sessions (involving airing cupboards, warm blankets and the like) I was lucky enough to come across a method of making it at home— adapted by a man called Peter Bradford from the various methods he had studied in the Middle East—which involves just three items of equipment: a milk saver to prevent the milk boiling over, a cooking thermometer, and a wide-necked insulated jar. These items of equipment can be purchased as a yoghurt-making kit complete with a special yoghurt thermometer.

No electricity is needed, no warm cupboards and, best of all, after the initial stages, no effort on your part. The process works all by itself! The only ingredients required are 1 pint (570 ml) of milk and 1 teaspoon of natural yoghurt (as a 'starter' on the first occasion). This is the method:

Place 1 pint (570 ml) of milk in a fairly large, wide saucepan along with the milk saver (basically a small glass disc). Bring it up to the boil, then let it simmer very gently for about 30 minutes, or until the milk has reduced to about 14 fl oz (400 ml), or roughly two-thirds of its original volume. Now tip the reduced milk into a clean jug and place the jug in a bowl of cold water. Let the milk cool for 5 minutes, then place a clean dry thermometer in the milk. If you're using a special yoghurt kit thermometer, wait until the mark reaches the red line: if you're using an ordinary cooking thermometer, wait until the temperature falls to 120°F (49°C). Now place ½ teaspoon of natural unsweetened yoghurt—a commercial brand will be all right—in the insulated jar, add a little of the milk, stir well, then add the rest of the milk, still stirring. Next place the lid on the jar, and leave it like that for not less than 6 hours (or longer won't hurt). Unscrew the lid, and inside you will have almost ¾ pint (425 ml) of delicious natural yoghurt for the price of 1 pint (570 ml) of milk. Replace the inner lid and store in the refrigerator.

Some important points Everything must be as clean as possible. And when you are washing out the jar before use, make sure it isn't still warm from the washing water: it must be room temperature.

Never use sweetened or flavoured yoghurt as a starter: it must be natural yoghurt. If you're making yoghurt continuously, you can in fact set aside $^1/_2$ teaspoon of the previous batch to start the next, but every three months or so it is best to start with commercially made yoghurt (as this will have the right balance of culture). Home-made yoghurt can be made with long life, skimmed milk or even powdered milk, but I think whole fresh milk makes the best.

Home-made curd cheese

This can be made from fresh yoghurt, and indeed the yoghurt kit mentioned above can be bought with a cheese-making nylon bag and stand. However, you can also assemble your own cheese-maker simply by placing a nylon sieve over a bowl and lining the sieve with a double piece of gauze. This is the method:

Tip the freshly-made yoghurt into the nylon bag (or sieve) and allow the whey—the liquid content—to drain into the bowl beneath, leaving just the curd, or solid content, in the bag. After about 6 hours you will have a soft, creamy curd cheese which can then be used in exactly the same way as any other curd cheese or cottage cheese. You can, for instance, add some seasoning, garlic and fresh chopped herbs to it. I like it eaten Greek-fashion, chilled as a dessert with a spoonful of runny honey poured over.

Cooking with yoghurt

There are many recipes throughout the Cookery Course which make use of yoghurt. It does have a tendency to separate when subjected to heat and cooking, but this in no way affects the flavour (and myself, I'm not the least bothered about the slightly granular appearance). If, however, you want to stabilise yoghurt for cooking, blend 1 teaspoon cornflour with a little cold water, mix this with 5 fl oz (150 ml) of yoghurt, and simmer it for 10 minutes, stirring all the time.

Serving yoghurt

Yoghurt with honey and wheatgerm
Serve thick yoghurt well chilled in stemmed glasses, with runny honey dribbled over the top and a generous sprinkle of wheatgerm.

Yoghurt with muesli
Place 2 tablespoons of muesli per person in bowls, cover completely with 2 tablespoons of thick yoghurt, and top with runny honey.

Home-make fruit yoghurt
For the best results, use equal quantities of thick yoghurt and chopped fruit—strawberries, raspberries, blackcurrants or loganberries are all good. Add enough caster sugar or honey to sweeten according to your taste.

Dried fruit yoghurt
This is nicest of all made with prunes or dried apricots (or a mixture of both). Soak 4 oz (110 g) of apricots or prunes—or 2 oz (50 g) of each—overnight. Add 2 tablespoons of brown sugar and cook them for 10 minutes. Drain well in a sieve, then chop the flesh of the fruit and combine it with ½ pint (275 ml) of thick yoghurt.

Yoghurt seafood sauce

(serves 4–6 people)

This is a lovely, piquant but very easy sauce for shellfish—for instance, *Avocado and seafood salad* on page 78.

2 rounded tablespoons mayonnaise (see page 483)
4 tablespoons natural yoghurt, about 5 fl oz (150 ml)
1 tablespoon tomato purée
1 tablespoon Worcestershire sauce
2 level teaspoons horseradish sauce
2 tablespoons lemon juice
1 clove garlic, crushed
Cayenne pepper
Salt

This recipe is unbelievably easy, because all you do is combine all the above ingredients with a seasoning of salt and a pinch of cayenne, and stir well to blend them together thoroughly. Store, covered, in a cool place until needed.

Chilled yoghurt and cucumber soup

(serves 6–8 people)

This deliciously light and subtle soup is incredibly easy and quick to make. However it *does* need some fresh British cucumbers and not the rather tasteless imported ones.

| 1 medium-sized firm, young cucumber |
| 5 fl oz natural yoghurt (150 ml) |
| 2½ fl oz soured cream (65 ml) |
| A little milk |
| 1 small clove garlic, crushed |
| 1 teaspoon fresh lemon juice |
| 1 level teaspoon fresh chopped mint |
| A few slices of lemon, cut very thinly |
| Salt and freshly-milled black pepper |

First of all peel the cucumber thinly with a potato peeler so as to leave some of the green, then slice it. Reserve a few slices to garnish the soup, then place the rest in a liquidiser along with the yoghurt, soured cream and crushed garlic. Switch on and blend at the highest speed until smooth. Add a seasoning of salt and pepper and lemon juice, then pour the soup into a tureen and if it seems to be a little too thick, thin it with some cold milk. Now stir in the fresh chopped mint, cover with foil or with a lid and chill very thoroughly for several hours before serving.

To serve, ladle the soup into individual soup bowls and float a few thin slices of cucumber and a thin slice of lemon on each one.

Cucumber raita

(serves 4 people)

This is a side dish for curries. The idea is that the coolness of the yoghurt and the cucumber will counteract the hotness of the curry and so it does—much more effectively than cold drinks.

| 2 oz peeled cucumber (50 g) |
| 1 spring onion, finely chopped |
| ½ clove garlic, crushed |
| 5 fl oz natural yoghurt (150 ml) |
| 2 pinches cayenne pepper |
| 1 pinch cumin seeds |
| Salt and freshly-milled black pepper |

First slice the cucumber thinly, then cut the slices in half, put into a basin and sprinkle with salt. Leave it for an hour, by which time a lot of the liquid will have been drawn out of it, so drain off the liquid and dry the cucumber in some kitchen paper.

Now combine the cucumber, yoghurt, spring onion and garlic, mixing them thoroughly. Season with salt and freshly-milled pepper. Pour the mixture into a serving bowl, sprinkle with cayenne and cumin, cover and chill thoroughly before serving.

Dried fruit salad with yoghurt and nuts

(serves 4–6 people)

If you're wholefood minded, you'll love this, which is full of good natural things.

4 oz prunes (110 g)
4 oz dried apricots, separated (110 g)
4 oz dried figs (110 g) —cut out the hard stalk ends
4 oz large raisins, separated (110 g)
Zest and juice of 1 orange
2 oz demerara sugar (50 g)
2 oz chopped, toasted hazelnuts (50 g)
15 fl oz natural yoghurt (425 ml)

The night before, place the four dried fruits in a deep 2½ pint (1·5 litre) bowl and cover with 1¼ pints (700 ml) cold water. Make quite sure *all* the fruit is immersed and leave to soak overnight.

The next day, drain off 3 fl oz (75 ml) of the water, then place the fruits, sugar and the remaining water in a small pan. Cover and bring to simmering point, and leave to simmer gently for about 10 minutes or until all the fruit feels tender when tested with a skewer. Next stir in the orange zest and juice, then tip the whole lot into a shallow serving bowl to cool. Cover with clingfilm and chill. Just before serving, spread the yoghurt carefully all over the fruit and sprinkle on the hazelnuts.

See also:
Chocolate and soured cream cake filling
Coeur à la crème
Cream puffs
Creamed potatoes with soured cream and chives
Cucumber and yoghurt salad
Gratin dauphinois

Jacket potatoes with soured cream and chives
Liver in yoghurt and juniper sauce
Simple Stroganoff
Soured cream soda bread
Sweetbreads with soured cream and onion sauce
Vegetarian goulash

Pastry

Including recipes for:
Basic shortcrust pastry
Apple and blackberry pie
English gooseberry pie
Fresh cherry pie
Damson plum pie
Spiced apple and raisin pie
Apple pie
Rhubarb pie
Summer fruits pie
Mince pies
Lancaster lemon tart
Lemon meringue pie
Wholewheat treacle tart
Cornish pasty pie
Quiche pastry
Mushroom and onion quiche
Courgette and cheese quiche
Kipper quiche
Basic suet crust pastry
Beefsteak and kidney pie

Beefsteak and kidney pudding
Old English rabbit pie
Quick flaky pastry
Sausage rolls
Bœuf en croûte
Eccles cakes
John Tovey's rough puff pastry
Basic val-au-vents
Hot mushroom and bacon filling
Cream cheese and herb filling
Cream puffs
Richmond maids of honour
Creme patissière
Rich flan pastry
Crisp cinnamon flan
Linzertorte
Basic choux pastry
Profiteroles
Chocolate and hazelnut choux buns
Coffee éclairs
Gougère with cheese

Of all the cooking skills pastry-making, it seems, is the one that causes most problems. Pondering on why this should be, I think I detect two main reasons: first there are too many conflicting and confusing rules, and secondly pastry-making is one of those skills that needs to the *taught*. It's not an instinct you're either born with or not—it's a technique that needs proper explanation and a little bit of patience and practice. Unfortunately practice is rarely something that is allowed for in cooking. People spend money on driving lessons or learning a foreign language, but when it comes to food, if it doesn't work the first time, it's a 'wicked waste'.

Pastry psychology

Yes, there is a sort of psychology involved. Attitude is the word I think sums it up, your attitude towards pastry-making. Once you've been shown how to do it, you must be bold and self-assertive! Go to it with confidence—I almost think that pastry dough can sense anxiety and then start to play up! True, you need to be light-handed, but in this section you'll learn how to be light-handed. Also true, pastry must not be overhandled, and overhandling is a symptom of nervousness: just as people who lack confidence insist on stirring, prodding or peeping at things, so it is with pastry. So approach this subject with a confident attitude, and I'm sure perfect pastry is just a few pages away.

Pastry perversity

Although there is a set of basic rules for making pastry, there will always be those infuriating people who appear to break or ignore the rules and still turn out perfect pastry. Well . . . other people's cooking often tastes better than your own, if only because you haven't had to do it. If you are a beginner, don't be side-tracked away from the basic ground rules: a hundred and one versions from friends and family will only confuse you.

There are quite a number of different pastries: shortcrust, quick flaky, and suet crust will suit most purposes for beginners, while choux and proper puff pastry are for slightly more advanced cooks.

Shortcrust pastry

What is shortcrust? There is no such thing—in answer to an 8-year-old who once asked me—as longcrust. Short in this context actually means friable or easily crumbled, so the shorter the pastry the crumblier it it. It is the most useful and versatile of all pastries (the kind that crops up in your apple pies or jam tarts), and once this one is mastered the various other kinds will be relatively easy to learn.

Flour

Ordinary plain flour is best for shortcrust pastry. Self-raising flour is used by some people, but I think it produces a more 'cakey' texture, being slightly aerated:. the finished pastry is softer, less crisp than with plain flour. Air, however, is a vital ingredient, and all flour must be sifted. Sifting is done not only to disperse the lumps, but also to give the flour an airing—so the higher you hold your sieve over the bowl, the further the flour travels and the more air it incorporates. (Because I always sift white flour, I never pay the extra money for superfine or supersifted flours: the ordinary 'own-brand' in a reliable supermarket is perfectly good, so sifting yourself saves money.)

Wholewheat flour can also be used for shortcrust. Because this flour is coarse-textured, the pastry can sometimes seem heavy or difficult to roll. Therefore to combine the flavour of the wholewheat with a lightness of texture, I use the proportion of half wholewheat flour to half white self-raising.

Salt

I have included a generous pinch of salt in many pastry recipes. For my own part I only use it in savoury ones, in which case I season with salt *and* freshly-milled pepper.

Fats

The choice of fat will determine the flavour as well as the texture of your pastry, and here any differences of opinion can probably only be resolved in the end by personal taste, and the type of recipe the pastry is intended for (for instance, to me in a bacon-and-egg pie or a Cornish pasty lard seems to give the 'right' flavour). Below are my own comments of different combinations:

All margarine (block, not soft margarine which is not suitable). This gives a fairly flaky texture, but cooked at a high temperature, gas mark 7, 425°F (220°C), it has a pronounced margarine flavour.

All butter This produces the crunchiest, crispest shortcrust, but although the flavour is good it is also rich and rather more fatty. So I wouldn't choose this for a recipe with a rich, creamy filling. Butter is also a little more difficult to rub in.

All lard makes a shorter and flakier pastry, but it does have a distinctive flavour which is good for savoury recipes and not so good for sweet. Because lard reaches room temperature more quickly than butter or marge, if too soft it can be more difficult to rub in. All-lard pastry also needs less water for mixing.

Half butter: half lard This is very easy to rub in and handle. The pastry has a good texture with the right amount of crispness, and a good flavour.

Half margarine: half lard Again easy to rub in and roll out—and my personal favourite for most of my own pastry-making. A few experiments will soon reveal your own preferences.

As a rule fat should be used at room temperature. If it is too cold, it will be inconvenient to rub in: if it is too warm, it will be already slightly oily and the additional heat of your hands will make it too soft to rub in correctly (this will only worry you in a heat-wave or a particularly hot kitchen, in which case don't take it out of the fridge too soon). Fat removed from the refrigerator 2 hours before needed is generally about right.

Liquid
Cold water, as cold as possible in fact, is best for shortcrust pastry. The amount you use can vary enormously, because (as we discovered with bread) different flours absorb different amounts. It is best to add a little at first, and a little more as you need to. What you are aiming for in the end is a dough that's smooth without any dryish bits or cracks in it, moist enough to incorporate all the flour and fat and leave the bowl fairly cleanly. Remember that too much water will produce a hard crust, and too little will make the dough difficult to roll out—but having said that, you will find it easy enough to get the right balance.

Shortcrust pastry—basic principles
(1) *Making the dough: keeping cool* It is true everything should be as cool as you can manage for pastry-making, because if the ingredients—and your hands—are too warm the fat becomes too soft, even oily, and it coats more flour grains than it should. The flour is then unable to absorb enough water and the pastry will be too crumbly. However, don't be put off if your kitchen is typically hot and steamy. Open a window and make the pastry as near to the window as possible.

(2) *Rubbing in* Once the flour is sifted into a bowl, you then divide the fat into smallish lumps and add them to the flour. Start off with a knife and 'cut' the fat into the flour. Then use your finger-tips only: start to lift the pieces of fat up with the flour and rub them gently through your fingers. Now it's well known that light hands make good pastry—that means, in a word, be as *gentle* as you can. Keep lifting your hands high above the bowl and let in the air and, therefore, lightness. Although this process is called 'rubbing in', I'd prefer to call it 'mingling in', which is nearer what it should be.

(3) *Mixing* We've established that coolness is important, so here speed is what is needed. The less you handle it, the less likely the warmth of your hands will affect it. Once the fat has been evenly distributed and the mixture looks crumbly, you can start to add the water. Run the cold tap for a minute to get it really cold, half-fill a jug and sprinkle in the water all over (for 4 oz of flour start with 3

tablespoons of water). Now use a round-bladed knife to start to mix to a dough, and finish off with your hands to bring it all together, adding more water till you have enough. (I find *sprinkling* the water all over brings it together more quickly than pouring it into the centre and having to work the wet out towards the dry edges.)

(4) *Resting* It's a bore, but if you don't want your pastry to break as you roll it out or shrink while it is cooking, you must allow it at least 20–30 minutes before you roll it out. Why? Because, as we discovered with bread, the gluten in the flour reacts to water and develops in time, becoming more pliable and elastic (and so easier to roll and less likely to shrink). Wrap the dough carefully in foil or a polythene bag, and leave it to rest in the refrigerator to keep it cool—this covering is important, to prevent the pastry acquiring a tough skin which will break and crack as you start to roll it out.

(5) *Rolling* What you need for this is a flat surface, a table-top, laminated work-surface or a proper pastry board. Also the length of the rolling-pin is important: the longer it is, the more evenly it

will roll (I find the 18 inch one ideal, and without handles it is far easier to control). A flour dredger is not an expensive item and will sprinkle flour lightly and evenly. Place the dough on a lightly-floured surface, and first shape it with your hands (to a round, or oblong, or whatever your final shape must be).

Give the rolling-pin a dusting of flour, and start to roll with both hands positioned flat at each end of the pin (see illustration), keeping the pressure even and being *gentle*. Save all your aggressions for making bread dough! If the pastry starts sticking to the pin, dust the pin (rather than the pastry) with more flour.

Don't turn the pastry over while you're rolling, it is totally unnecessary and the pastry you've rolled out will only shrink back and possibly break. When you are rolling a specific shape, always revolve the pastry rather than the rolling-pin. To roll out to a round shape, all you do is keep giving the pastry a quarter-turn after each rolling. Any shape should be rolled fractionally larger than you actually require to line the tin.

(6) *Transferring pastry to a tin*
The best way is to place the rolling-pin at either end of the pastry, and lightly roll the pastry round the pin, then transfer it to the waiting tin—place the tip of the pastry over one edge of the tin and unroll. Now start to ease the pastry gently into position to line the tin (what you need to keep in mind at this stage is that it is better for the pastry to shrink at the lining stage than to be stretched (otherwise it will shrink in the oven). So ease back any overlapping bits into the tin, leaving yourself as little to trim off as possible. Take care, as well, to press it into position firmly so that no air can be trapped underneath.

Right: Bœuf en croûte, page 566

Cutting out

Whenever you need to cut out tartlets or pastry shapes, remember to dust the edge of the cutter with flour first. Then place it on the pastry and give it a sharp *tap*. It's very tempting to want to twist the cutter, but my advice is don't, unless you want your round tartlet shapes to turn out oval.

Baking blind

Baking something 'blind' means cooking the pastry on its own in the oven, before the filling goes in. There is a tendency, when this is done, for the base to balloon up during the cooking if there is any air trapped under the pastry. Various remedies for this are used, like lining papers and baking beans to weight the pastry down—but if you have lined the tin properly (see above) these things are redundant. And an extra precaution is to prick the base all over with a fork to release any trapped air (no, the filling won't run through the holes, because as the pastry sets they'll close up again). A final way of making sure is simply to open the oven after 7–8 minutes, have a look and, if the pastry is puffing up, press it back down and prick it once more.

Oven temperatures

These will vary according to the recipe, but most need a pre-heated oven (gas mark 5–7, 375°–425°F, 190°–220°C). A pre-heated baking sheet, too, is essential for anything that needs a crisp base, as this will conduct the heat more efficiently under the tin.

Baking tin, trays, etc.

I cannot stress enough that metal is so much better a conductor of heat than either glass or porcelain. I admit those white fluted porcelain dishes look extremely pretty and many women's magazines show tempting pictures of quiches and flans made in them. But alas, what looks good from the outside is often watery and soggy within—so for crisp, evenly cooked pastry, use metal.

Using shortcrust pastry

So far I have been setting out my own personal notes on ingredients and preferences. However, in the following recipes, the type of fat you use is up to you. If you're a vegetarian, for instance, you will obviously want to use vegetable fat or margarine: similarly any recipe for shortcrust pastry can easily be changed to wholewheat shortcrust if you prefer it.

Left: Eccles cakes, page 567; Wholewheat treacle tart, page 556; Fresh cherry pie, page 550.

Basic shortcrust pastry

Since confusion regularly arises over the term '4 oz of shortcrust pastry' (does it mean 4 oz total weight of pastry, or shortcrust made with 4 oz flour?) I have given the required quantities of flour *and* fat.

4 oz flour (110 g)
1 oz margarine at room temperature (25 g)
1 oz lard at room temperature (25 g)
A pinch salt
Cold water

Sift the flour and salt into a large mixing bowl, holding the sieve up as high as possible to give the flour an airing. Then cut the fat into small cubes and add them to the flour. Now, using your fingertips, lightly and gently rub the pieces of fat into the flour—lifting your hands up high as you do this (again to incorporate as much air as you can) and being as quick as possible.

When the mixture looks uniformly crumbly, start to sprinkle roughly 2 tablespoons of water all over. Use a round-bladed knife to start the mixing, cutting and bringing the mixture together. Carefully add more water as needed, a little at a time, then finally bring the mixture together with your hands to form a smooth ball of dough that will leave the bowl clean. (If there are any bits that won't adhere to it, you need a spot more water.) Now rest the pastry, wrapped in foil or polythene, in the refrigerator for 20–30 minutes before rolling out.

For *wholewheat pastry*, follow the method above, using 2 oz (50 g) of wholewheat flour and 2 oz (50 g) of white self-raising flour.

Clearly these quantities will vary with each recipe (i.e. you may find you need 8 oz (225 g) of flour and 4 oz (110 g) of fat), but generally speaking the proportion of fat is always half that of flour.

Deep fruit pies

These are made in the traditional deep, oval, rimmed pie-dishes and only have a crust over the top. The advantage with this type of pie is that you retain all the fragrant juices of the fruits, leaving the top crust crisp and separate.

Apple and blackberry pie

(serves 6 people)

This is best of all made with wild brambles, which seem to have twice as much flavour as the cultivated kind.

For the filling:
1 lb cooking apples (4 medium-sized apples) (450 g)
½ lb brambles, (225 g) washed
3 oz sugar (75 g)

For the shortcrust pastry:
6 oz plain flour (175 g)
1½ oz lard (40 g)
1½ oz margarine (40 g)
A pinch of salt
Cold water to mix

For the glaze:
Milk and caster sugar

Pre-heat the oven to gas mark 7, 425°F (220°C)

A 1½ pint (845 ml) rimmed pie-dish.

Start by making the pastry, then leave it to rest while you peel and slice the apples straight into the pie-dish. Then sprinkle in the brambles and the sugar.

Now roll out the pastry, about 1 inch (2·5 cm) larger than the pie-dish, then cut out a 1 inch (2·5 cm) strip to fit the edge of the dish. Dampen the edge, then fit on the strip of pastry, pressing it firmly, and dampen that too. Then press the rest of the pastry over that to form a lid, knock up and flute the edges and make a steam hole in the centre.

Now brush the pastry with milk and sprinkle on a light dusting of caster sugar. Place the pie on a baking sheet on a high shelf and bake for 10 minutes, then reduce the heat to gas mark 5, 375°F (190°C), and continue baking for a further 30 minutes. Then, using a skewer, take out a piece of apple from the centre to test if it's cooked—if it still feels very firm, give it another 5 minutes or so.

Serve hot with chilled pouring cream to mingle with the juices.

Alternatives for deep fruit pies

Here are three different fillings, bearing in mind that the pastry method and cooking times are as in the previous recipe.

English gooseberry pie
For this you'll need 2 lb (900 g) young green gooseberries, 6 oz (175 g) caster sugar and a 1½ pint (845 ml) pie-dish.

Fresh cherry pie
1½ lb (700 g) fresh cherries, 3 level tablespoons Demerara sugar, ½ teaspoon ground cinnamon and a 1½ pint (845 ml) pie-dish.

Damson plum pie
1½ lb (700 g) damsons or damson plums, 4 oz (110 g) sugar and a 1½ pint (845 ml) oval pie-dish.

Basic double-crust fruit pie

The quantities for the recipe below are for any basic fruit pie with a double crust using either pie or wholewheat shortcrust. That is to say the pastry for a 9½ inch (24 cm) enamel pie-plate is always 8 oz (225 g) flour and 4 oz (110 g) fat. The filling is usually 1½ lb (700 g) fruit (see below).

Spiced apple and raisin pie

(serves 6 people)

For the pastry:
4 oz wholewheat flour (110 g)
4 oz self-raising flour (110 g)
2 oz margarine (50 g)
2 oz lard (50 g)
A pinch salt
Cold water

For the filling:
1½ lb Bramley apples (700 g)
1 oz soft brown sugar (25 g)
¼ teaspoon ground cloves
½ teaspoon ground cinnamon
3 oz raisins (75 g)
2 tablespoons water
¼ whole nutmeg, grated

For the glaze:
Milk and caster sugar

Pre-heat the oven to gas mark 6, 400°F
(200°C)

A 9¹/₂ inch (24 cm) enamel pie-plate,
lightly greased.

First quarter, core and peel the apples, then slice them thinly into a
saucepan and mix them with the sugar, spices and raisins. Next
sprinkle in the water and cook gently (with a lid on) for about 10
minutes or until the apples are soft and fluffy. Then empty the
mixture into a bowl to cool.

Next make up the pastry and leave it to rest whilst you pre-heat the
oven—putting in a baking sheet—and lightly grease the pie-plate.

Roll out a *little more* than half the pastry to a round, then transfer it
to line the plate, pressing it gently and firmly all round. Now spoon
in the filling, then roll out the other half of the pastry to form a lid.
Dampen the bottom layer of pastry round the edge with water,
then fix the lid into position, pressing it very firmly all around. Now
trim the edges with a knife and use the broad edge of the blade to
knock the edges all round, making a layered effect. Then flute the
edges by making an impression with your thumb and, using the
back of the knife, draw in the edges of the pastry to make a fluted,
scalloped effect. Now decorate with the trimmings made into
leaves and make a hole in the centre (alternatively, just snip the pie
all along the centre with a pair of scissors to make holes) for the
steam to escape.

Brush with milk next, then sprinkle on a dusting of caster sugar,
which will give a nice crisp sugared surface when the pie is baked.

Place the pie on the baking sheet and bake for 30 minutes.

Alternative fillings for double-crust pies
To get the correct balance of filling, I find it's always best to cook it a
little first as the ripeness and sharpness in fruit varies. You can then
gauge just the right amount of sugar. Also I've found that cooking
the fruit first allows you to get rid of some of the excess juice, e.g.
with rhubarb or plums. Alternatively, as with apples, water can be
added to make a moister filling.

Apple pie
For the very best flavour use 1 lb (450 g) Bramleys and ¹/₂ lb
(225 g) Cox's, 1 oz (25 g) sugar and 2 tablespoons water.

Rhubarb
A little ginger always brings out the flavour of rhubarb, so place
2¹/₂ lb (1 kg 125 g), cut in chunks, in a saucepan with 1 rounded
teaspoon ground ginger and 3 oz (75 g) dark brown sugar but *no*
water. Then cook gently, stirring now and then, for about 10
minutes and drain well in a sieve set over a bowl before using.

Summer fruits
A delicious combination: ³/₄ lb (350 g) raspberries, ¹/₄ lb
(110 g) redcurrants, ¹/₄ lb (110 g) blackcurrants, 5 oz (150 g)
caster sugar. Place the fruits and sugar in a saucepan and cook, very
gently, for just 4 minutes, then drain in a sieve set over a bowl.

Mince pies
(makes 3 dozen)

One tip I may be able to pass on, as a result of years of fraught Christmas preparations—that is, to invest in at least 4 tins which make a dozen tarts each. It's infuriating when a tin only holds nine and it's impossible to place them both on the same shelf. What I now do is bake 2 dozen, a dozen on each shelf, changing over at half-time, and prepare another 2 dozen while they're cooking.

For the pastry:
12 oz plain flour (350 g)
3 oz lard (75 g)
3 oz margarine (75 g)
A pinch of salt
Cold water

Filling:
1½ lb mincemeat (700 g)

For the top:
Milk
Icing sugar

Pre-heat the oven to gas mark 6, 400°F (200°F)

For the normal 2¹/₂ inch (6 cm)
patty tins you'll need one fluted 3 inch
(7·5 cm) pastry cutter, and one fluted
2¹/₂ inch (6 cm) cutter.

Make up the pastry and allow it to rest for 20–30 minutes. Then roll
half of it out to about ¹/₈ inch (3 mm) thick and cut it out into 3
dozen 3 inch (7·5 cm) rounds, gathering up the scraps and re-rolling
again. Then do the same with the other half of the pastry, this time
using the 2¹/₂ inch (6 cm) cutter.

Now grease the patty tins lightly and line them with the large
rounds; fill these with the mincemeat (not too much—only to the
level of the edges of the pastry).

Now dampen the edges of the smaller rounds of pastry with water
and press them lightly into position to form lids, sealing the edges.
Brush each one with milk and make about three snips in the top
with a pair of scissors.

Bake near the top of the oven for 25–30 minutes until they're a light
golden-brown. Then cool them on a wire tray and sprinkle with
sifted icing sugar. Store the cooled mince pies in an airtight tin and
warm them slightly before serving.

Lancaster lemon tart

(serves 4–6 people)

This is a first cousin of a Bakewell tart,
using home-made lemon curd instead of
jam, which I think goes very well with
the flavour of almonds.

Shortcrust pastry made with 3 oz (75 g) flour and 1½ oz (40 g) fat

For the filling:
3 rounded tablespoons lemon curd
3 oz butter (room temperature) (75 g)
4 oz self-raising flour (110 g)
3 oz caster sugar (75 g)
1 egg, beaten lightly
1 oz ground almonds (25 g)
The grated zest and juice of a large lemon
1 oz whole almonds (25 g), peeled and halved

Pre-heat the oven to gas mark 6, 400°F (200°C)

A 7 or 8 inch (18 or 20 cm) enamel pie-plate, lightly greased.

First roll out the pastry and line the pie-plate, crimping the edges, then spread the lemon curd all over the pastry.

Now cream the butter and sugar together till pale and fluffy, then gradually beat in the egg about a teaspoonful at a time. Gently and carefully fold in the ground almonds and flour, followed by the lemon juice and grated zest.

Now spread this mixture evenly over the lemon curd, smoothing it out with a palette knife. Then sprinkle the halved almonds over the surface. Bake it, on a baking sheet, in the centre of the oven for 15 minutes, then reduce the heat to gas mark 2, 300°F (150°C), and continue cooking for a further 25–30 minutes.

This can be served either warm or cold with cream.

Lemon meringue pie

(serves 6 people)

This is one sweet, with its three distinct elements, that needs a careful balance of textures and quantities. The filling has to be lemony enough, neither too stiff nor too oozy. The meringue should be wafery crisp on the outside and soft and marshmallowy within.

For the pastry:
4 oz plain flour (110 g)
1 oz margarine (25 g)
1 oz lard (25 g)

For the filling:
2 large lemons (the grated rind and the juice)
½ pint cold water (275 ml)
3 level tablespoons cornflour
1½ oz butter (40 g)
2 large egg yolks
2 oz caster sugar (50 g)

For the meringue
2 large egg whites
4 oz caster sugar (110 g)

Pre-heat the oven to gas mark 5, 375°F (190°C)

The best dish for this recipe is a deep enamel pie-plate with sloping sides and a rim, measuring 6 inches (16 cm) at the base and 8 inches (20 cm) at the top. Start by making up the pastry and chilling it in the fridge for 20 minutes. Then roll it out to a round about $^1/_3$ inch larger all round than the rim of the tin. Cut away a narrow ($^1/_3$ inch) strip all round, dampen the rim of the tin with water and fix this pastry strip on it all round, pressing down well. Next dampen the pastry strip and transfer the pastry round to line the tin—making sure you don't trap any air underneath it. Then flute the edge of the pastry and prick the base all over with a fork. Bake on a high shelf of the oven for 20–25 minutes or until cooked through.

Remove the pastry case from the oven, and immediately lower the heat to gas mark 2, 300°F (150°C) for the meringue.

Next the filling: measure $^1/_2$ pint of cold water into a jug and spoon the cornflour and sugar into a bowl. Add enough of the measured water to mix the cornflour to a smooth paste, then pour the rest of the water along with the grated lemon into a small saucepan. Bring this up to the boil, then pour it onto the cornflour paste and mix till smooth.

Transfer the mixture back to the saucepan and bring back to the boil. Then simmer gently for 1 minute—stirring all the time to prevent it from catching. Remove the pan from the heat and beat in the egg yolks, lemon juice and finally the butter. Pour the lemon mixture into the pastry shell and spread it out evenly.

Finally the meringue: for this use a large roomy bowl and in it whisk the egg whites till they form stiff peaks. Beat in a quarter of the caster sugar at a time until it is all incorporated, then spread the meringue mixture all over the filling. Use a broad-bladed knife to spread the meringue to the very edge of the pastry rim, so it seals the top completely. (With your knife you can also make a few decorative swirls.) Cook in the oven for 45 minutes, by which time the meringue will have turned pale beige, and be duly crisp on the outside and squashy within. Serve warm or cold.

Wholewheat treacle tart

(serves 6 people)

I think the crunchiness of wholewheat pastry, and wholewheat breadcrumbs too, make a nicer treacle tart than the traditional version.

For the pastry:
2 oz wholewheat flour (50 g)
2 oz self-raising flour (50 g)
A pinch salt
1 oz lard (25 g)
1 oz margarine (25 g)
Water to mix

For the filling:
4 oz wholewheat breadcrumbs (110 g)
5 tablespoons golden syrup
1 tablespoon black treacle
Some milk

Pre-heat the oven to gas mark 5, 375°F (190°C)

An 8 inch (20 cm) fluted flan tin with a loose base (lightly greased).

If you place the syrup and treacle tins in the oven whilst it's pre-heating, you'll find them easier to measure.

Meanwhile make the pastry and allow it to rest for 20–30 minutes. Then roll it out thinly and line the flan tin with it, cutting off the pastry trimmings and keeping them on one side.

Then measure out the warmed treacle and syrup into a bowl, and stir in the breadcrumbs quite thoroughly before pouring the whole lot into the prepared pastry case.

Now roll out the pastry trimmings and cut strips long enough to make a criss-cross pattern all over the surface of the tart. Then brush the strips and edges lightly with milk and place the tart on a baking sheet in the oven. Bake it for about 30–35 minutes. Serve still warm with some chilled whipped cream.

Cornish pasty pie

(serves 6 people)

I find Cornish pasties often have too much pastry and not enough filling. However, the traditional filling of steak, potato and turnip is so delicious I now make one big pie using this filling—which is also a lot quicker than making individual pasties.

For the pastry:
6 oz lard (175 g)
12 oz plain flour (350 g)
Water to mix
Salt and freshly-milled pepper

For the filling:
1¼ lb chuck steak (560 g)
1 medium to large turnip
1 medium to large potato
1 large onion, finely chopped
½ teaspoon mixed herbs
1 tablespoon water
Salt and freshly-milled pepper

To glaze:
Beaten egg

Pre-heat the oven to gas mark 6, 400°F (200°C)

A well-greased 10 inch (25·5 cm) fluted metal quiche tin.

Make the pastry first, adding a little salt and pepper to season it, then pop it into a plastic bag and leave it in the fridge for 10–15 minutes. Meanwhile, slice the meat into very thin strips about 2 inches (5 cm) long (it's important to keep them very thin—in order that they cook in the time given).

Place the meat in a mixing bowl, with the chopped onion and mixed herbs. Then peel the potato and turnip and slice these as thinly as possible too (the slicing edge of a four-sided grater does this thin slicing job in moments). Now add the turnip and potato to the meat, season with salt and pepper, and mix very thoroughly.

Next roll out half the pastry, large enough to line the tin with about
¹/₂ inch (1 cm) overlapping. Spoon the filling in, spreading it
evenly all over, then sprinkle in 1 tablespoon of water.

Roll out the other half of the pastry, dampen the edge all round,
then fit it over the top of the pie. Then seal the edges, folding them
inwards and pressing gently to make a rim just inside the edge of the
tin. Make a steam-hole in the centre (about the size of a 10p piece),
brush the surface with beaten egg, and bake the pie on a baking
sheet, on a high shelf, for 15 minutes. Then turn the heat down to
gas mark 4, 350°F (180°C), and continue to cook on the centre
shelf for a further 1¹/₂ hours. This is still very good eaten cold,
so it's a good idea for a picnic.

Quiches and open tarts

For years I've been experimenting with this type of recipe to
eliminate—for ever—the problem of the soggy pastry base that
seems to plague so many people, myself included. I'm happy to
announce that the problem seems largely solved by (a) pre-baking
the pastry case, (b) *always* using a baking sheet underneath the tin,
(c) painting the inside of the pre-baked pastry shell with beaten egg
and allowing it to rest for 5 minutes in the oven before the filling goes
in. I have already said (but will stress again) that the container
must be *metal*, not porcelain or glass.

Quiche pastry

4 oz plain flour (110 g)
Pinch of salt
1 oz lard (25 g)
1 oz margarine (25 g)
Cold water

This will be enough for a lightly-
greased 8 inch (20 cm) quiche or flan tin
with fluted edges and a removable base.

Make up the pastry, then rest it for 20–30 minutes in a polythene
bag in the fridge.

Meanwhile, pre-heat the oven to gas mark 4, 350°F (170°C),
with a baking sheet placed on the centre shelf.

Then roll out the pastry and line the tin with it, easing any overlapping pastry back into the sides if you can. Be careful to press firmly on the base and sides, then prick with a fork all over. Bake the pastry case for 15 minutes on the centre shelf, then remove it from the oven and paint the inside of it, all over, with some of the beaten egg in the filling ingredients, and pop it back into the oven to set for a further 5 minutes.

Now add the filling and bake for a further 30–40 minutes until the quiche is set in the centre and has turned golden-brown and looks puffy.

Mushroom and onion quiche

This is made with what the French called *duxelles*, a paste made with chopped mushrooms and onion. For the lightest and best quiche filling use double cream or single. If you're economising, milk will do.

½ lb flat mushrooms (225 g) chopped very, very small
1 medium onion, also chopped very small
2 large eggs
½ pint double cream (275 ml)
1 oz butter (25 g)
Freshly-grated nutmeg
Salt and freshly-milled black pepper

Heat the butter in a saucepan and soften the onion in it for 5 minutes or so. Now stir in the chopped mushrooms and let it all cook gently (uncovered) for half an hour or until most of the juice has evaporated—giving it a stir quite often. Transfer the filling to the tart with a draining spoon, and arrange it evenly over the base.

Beat the eggs thoroughly, then whisk the cream into them and season with salt, pepper and a small grating of nutmeg. Pour this mixture over the filling, put the flan on the baking sheet in the oven and bake for 35–40 minutes, or until the centre is set and the filling golden and puffy.

Serve straight from the oven, if possible (though this does reheat quite well).

Courgette and cheese quiche	½ lb courgettes (225 g)
	1 oz butter (25 g)
	2 oz grated cheese (preferably Gruyère) (50 g)
	1 small onion, finely chopped
	2 large eggs
	½ pint single or double cream (275 ml)
	1 tablespoons grated Parmesan cheese
	Salt and pepper

Slice the courgettes fairly thinly. Soften the onion in the butter in a frying-pan for 5 minutes, then add the courgettes and brown them a little, turning them frequently. Now transfer both onions and courgettes to the pastry case, sprinkle the grated cheese over them, and proceed as in the previous recipe (sprinkling the Parmesan over the top before baking).

Kipper quiche
Use 8 oz (225 g) cooked, flaked kippers, add 2 teaspoons mustard, some freshly-grated nutmeg and a couple of pinches of cayenne pepper to the egg and cream mixture and proceed as above.

Suet crust pastry
If you've never tried this pastry, then it's a must next time you make steak and kidney pie. Because it is made with shredded beef suet it has the best possible flavour for a beefsteak pie. But more than that—it is beautifully easy to make since there is no rubbing-in. It is resilient and easy to roll out, and it is deliciously light and crusty.
   Important note: Suet crust is always made with self-raising flour, because suet being a heavy fat the pastry needs a raising agent to aerate it and make it lighter. And as it is made with self-raising flour, it follows that suet crust should always be rolled out and used *immediately*—because once the raising agent in the flour becomes damp it will begin to lose its raising power. This pastry can't be made in advance, but it is easy to make so this should not be a problem.

Butcher's suet
This can be used, but it's tedious separating suet from skin and membrane and grating it finely. Packet suet is quite pure, with a coating of flour (or rice flour) to separate the grains.

Basic suet crust pastry

These quantities will be enough to top a 1½ pint (1 litre) rimmed pie-dish. (For a 2½ pint pie-dish use 12 oz self-raising flour and 6 oz suet.)

8 oz self-raising flour (225 g)
4 oz shredded suet (110 g)
Cold water
Salt and freshly-milled pepper (for a savoury crust)

Sift the flour into a bowl, then sprinkle the suet in and just mix it in lightly with your hands to distribute it evenly. Now sprinkle in some cold water (you'll find you need more for this pastry than for shortcrust). Begin mixing with a round-bladed knife, and then use your hands at the end to bring it all together to a smooth elastic dough that leaves the bowl clean. Suet crust should be left for 5 minutes, then rolled out immediately. Remember, too, that you always roll it out rather more thickly than shortcrust (approximately ½ inch (1 cm) thick).

Beefsteak and kidney pie

(serves 4 people)

Once you've eaten this, I'm sure you will never want to make it with anything but suet crust again.

Suet crust pastry made with 8 oz flour and 4 oz suet as above

For the filling:
1½ lb chuck steak (700 g) in 1 inch cubes
6 oz ox kidney (175 g), chopped
½ lb dark-gilled mushrooms (225 g)
2 medium onions, roughly chopped
1½ tablespoons flour
1 tablespoon beef dripping
¾ pint beef stock (425 ml)
½ teaspoon Worcestershire sauce
2 teaspoons mushroom ketchup
½ teaspoon dried mixed herbs
Salt and freshly-milled black pepper

A 2 pint (1 litre) pie dish.

In a large saucepan fry the chopped onion in the dripping for a few minutes, then add the cubes of steak and the kidney. Continue to cook (stirring now and then) till the meat is nicely browned, then add the flour and stir it in well. Add the herbs next, followed by the Worcestershire sauce and the ketchup: season with salt and pepper and gradually stir in the stock. Finally add the mushrooms (sliced), bring the whole lot to simmering point, and simmer gently for about 2 hours or until the meat is tender. Check the seasoning and pour everything into the pie-dish. Pre-heat the oven to gas mark 7, 425°F (220°C).

Mix the pastry to a smooth elastic dough, and roll it out on a lightly-floured surface to a shape about 1 inch (2·5 cm) larger than the rim of the pie-dish. Now cut a 1 inch (2·5 cm) strip all round, dampen the edge of the pie-dish and press this pastry strip on. Then dampen the strip and lay the pastry lid on top, pressing it down and sealing it around the edge. Flute the edge, make a small steam-hole in the centre, and bake in the oven for 30–40 minutes, until the pastry is golden-brown.

Note: To make a pie for 6 people, use a 3 pint (1·5 litre) dish, and the ingredients will be 2½ lb (1 kg) chuck steak, ¾ lb (350 g) ox kidney, ½ lb (225 g) mushrooms, 2 tablespoons flour, 1 pint (570 ml) stock; and for the pastry: 12 oz (350 g) self-raising flour, 6 oz (175 g) shredded suet.

Beefsteak and kidney pudding

(serves 4 people)

Properly made, I think this is one of the glories of real British cooking! For notes on steaming see page 649.

For the suet crust pastry:
12 oz self-raising flour (350 g)
6 oz shredded suet (175 g)
Salt, pepper and cold water

For the filling:
1 lb chuck steak (450 g)
½ lb ox kidney (225 g)
1 medium onion, sliced
2 level tablespoons well-seasoned flour
Worcestershire sauce

Cold water
Salt and freshly-milled pepper

A 2 pint (1 litre) pudding basin.

Make up the pastry to form an elastic dough that leaves the bowl clean, keep a quarter of it (for a lid), roll the rest out and line the well-buttered pudding basin with it. Next chop the steak and the kidney into fairly small cubes, toss them in the seasoned flour, then add them to the pastry-lined basin. Pop the slices of onion in here and there, then add enough cold water to reach almost to the top of the meat and sprinkle in a few drops of Worcestershire sauce and season.

Roll out the pastry lid, dampen its edges and put it in position on the pudding. Seal well and cover with a double sheet of foil—pleated in the centre to allow room for expansion while cooking—secure with string, and place it in a steamer over boiling water. Steam for 5 hours—you may find you need to add more boiling water halfway through.

Old English rabbit pie

(serves 4–6 people)

This is a really delicious pie, good for a dinner party—and if you can get hold of a wild rabbit for it so much the better.

For the suet crust pastry:
12 oz self-raising flour (350 g)
6 oz shredded suet (175 g)
Cold water to mix
½ teaspoon salt
Freshly-milled black pepper

For the filling:
1 rabbit approx. 3 lb (1 kg 350 g), cut into joints
2 medium onions, chopped fairly small
½ lb unsmoked streaky bacon (225 g), in one piece
1 medium cooking apple, peeled and sliced
¼ lb pitted prunes (110 g) (weighed after the stones have been removed), chopped
½ pint dry cider (275 ml)

¾ pint stock (or water) (425 ml)
½ whole nutmeg, grated
1 bayleaf
1½ oz plain flour (40 g) *and* 1½ oz butter (40 g) mixed together to a smooth paste
Salt and freshly-milled black pepper

Pre-heat the oven to gas mark 7, 425°F (220°C)

A 2½ pint (1·5 litre) pie-dish.

Wash the rabbit joints first of all, and place them (apart from the ribs, which don't carry much meat) in a large saucepan. Tuck in the onion and apple amongst the meat. Now remove the rind from the bacon, chop the meat up into 1 inch (2·5 cm) cubes and add that to the saucepan along with the bayleaf, a little salt and some freshly-milled pepper. Pour in the cider and the stock, bring to simmering point, skim off any bits of scum, then put a lid on and leave to simmer gently for about an hour or until tender.

When it's cooked remove the rabbit pieces together with the bacon, apple and onion (with a draining spoon) and transfer them to the pie-dish, sprinkling in the chopped prunes as well. Now add the butter-and-flour mixture to the stock in the saucepan, adding it in tiny (peanut-size) pieces, stir them round over a medium heat to melt and thicken the sauce. Sprinkle in the nutmeg and when the sauce reaches simmering point pour it over the rabbit.

Now make up the suet crust pastry. Mix the flour, salt, pepper and suet together, then add enough cold water to form a fairly soft, elastic dough that leaves the bowl cleanly. Roll the dough out to a shape 1 inch (2·5 cm) wider than the top of the pie-dish, and cut a 1 inch (2·5 cm) wide strip all round. Dampen the edge of the dish and press this strip around the rim of the dish. Now dampen the rim of the pastry, and place the pastry lid in position on top, pressing well all round to seal the edges, which can be decorated with fluting if you like. Make a small hole for steam to escape, then bake for 30 minutes or until golden-brown.

Quick flaky pastry
This pastry is surely heaven-sent. It's uncomplicated, no trouble to
roll out and handle, and tastes really crisp and flaky. That doesn't
sound like the flaky pastry you've heard about? Probably not—the
advanced version certainly calls for time and effort, which few of us
can spare (though if you do have the time, there is a recipe for puff
pastry on page 570). In this one, a much higher percentage of fat
than in shortcrust is *grated* directly into the flour, so eliminating the
repeated processes of rolling out, folding over and half-turning
which make the traditional flaky pastry so time-consuming. The
results, I'm quite certain, will speak for themselves.

Quick flaky pastry	8 oz plain flour
	6 oz margarine
	A pinch of salt
	Cold water

The margarine has to be block (not soft 'tub' margarine, which is
not suitable). Take it hard from the fridge, weigh out the required
amount, then wrap it in a piece of foil and return it to the freezing
compartment of the refrigerator for half an hour. Meanwhile sift the
flour and salt into a mixing bowl.

When you take the margarine out of the freezer hold it in the foil, dip
it into the flour, then grate it on a coarse grater placed in the bowl
over the flour. Keep dipping the margarine down into the flour to
make it easier to grate. At the end you will be left with a lump of
grated fat in the middle of the flour, so now take a palette knife and
start to cut it into the flour—don't use your hands—until the
mixture is crumbly. Now add enough water to form a dough that
leaves the bowl clean, using your hands. Pop the dough into a
polythene bag and chill it for half an hour—this time in the main
body of the fridge.

Sausage rolls with quick flaky pastry (makes about 24)	Quick flaky pastry made with 8 oz flour and 6 oz margarine
	1 lb good pork sausage meat (450 g)
	1 medium onion, grated
	1 teaspoon sage
	1 egg beaten with 1 tablespoon milk

Pre-heat the oven to gas mark 7, 425°F
(220°C)

Make up the pastry as above, and leave it to rest in the refrigerator
for half an hour. Mix the sausage meat, onion, and sage together
thoroughly in a mixing bowl, then on a floured surface roll out the
pastry to form an oblong (as thin as you can). Cut this oblong into
three, then divide the sausage-meat mixture also into three, making
three long rolls the same length as the pastry (if it's sticky sprinkle
on some flour).

Place one roll of sausage meat onto one strip of pastry. Brush the
beaten egg mixture along one edge, then fold the pastry over and
seal it as carefully as possible. Lift the whole thing up and turn it, so
that when you put it down the sealed edge is underneath. Press
lightly, then cut into individual rolls each about 2 inches long. Snip
three V-shapes in the top of each roll with scissors, and brush with
beaten egg. Then repeat all this with the other portions of pastry
and meat. Place all the rolls on a baking-sheet and bake high in the
oven for 20–25 minutes. Store the cooled sausage rolls in a tin, and
warm them slightly before serving.

Bœuf en croûte

(serves 6 people)

Fillet steak is overwhelmingly expensive,
but for a very special occasion it does
make a most attractive and delicious
main course, wrapped in pastry with a
mushroom stuffing.

For the quick flaky pastry:
6 oz plain flour (175 g)
4 oz margarine (110 g)
Cold water

For the rest of the ingredients:
1¾ lb thick end fillet steak (800 g)
1 Spanish onion
¾ lb mushrooms (350 g)
2 oz butter (50 g)
A little brandy
Beaten egg
Salt, freshly-milled pepper, and nutmeg

Pre-heat the oven to gas mark 5, 375°F
(190°C)

First of all make up the pastry, pop it into a polythene bag and chill
it in the body of the fridge for half an hour. Meanwhile you can be
trimming the meat, removing any exess fat and bits of sinew. Brush
it all over with some brandy, rub ½ oz (10 g) of butter over it,
place it in a roasting tin and cook for 40 minutes (basting it now and
then with the juices). Then remove from the oven and leave to get
quite cold.

Chop the onion and mushrooms as finely as possible, then melt the
remaining 1½ oz (40 g) of butter in a small saucepan. Stir the
onion into it, allow it to cook for 5 minutes, then stir in the
mushroom and continue to cook the mixture over a gentle heat
(without a lid) for about 20–25 minutes, so that the juices will be
drawn out of the mushrooms and onion and evaporate, leaving you
with a concentrated mixture. The final mixture *mustn't* be too liquid.

Season it then with salt, pepper and a grating of nutmeg. When both
the meat and mushroom mixture are ready, pre-heat the oven to gas
mark 8, 450°F (230°C). Take the pastry from the fridge and roll it
out to a rectangle approx. 14 × 10 inches (35·5 × 25·5 cm). Trim the
edges (keep the trimmings for decoration), then spread half the
mushroom and onion mixture over the centre. Place the fillet on top
and the rest of the mixture on top of that: pat it down into a good
shape. Now brush the edges of the pastry with beaten egg, and wrap
the pastry like a parcel around the meat—if necessary brush the
edges at each end and fold them over again.

Place the whole lot on a baking sheet, brush all over with beaten egg
(including any decorations you have added), and bake in the oven
for a further 30 minutes. This should be served cut into thick slices,
together with some gravy made with the meat juices left in the
roasting tin and some red wine.

Eccles cakes

(makes about 18–20)

These spicy currant pastries are,
predictably, a northern delicacy—which
are never better than when homemade.

For the quick flaky pastry:
8 oz plain flour (225 g)
6 oz margarine (175 g)

| **A good pinch of salt** |
| **Cold water to mix** |

| *For the filling:* |
| **3 oz butter (75 g)** |
| **5 oz soft brown sugar (150 g)** |
| **5 oz currants (150 g)** |
| **1 teaspoon cinnamon** |
| **½ teaspoon freshly-grated nutmeg** |
| **The grated rind of 1 large orange** |
| **2 oz finely-chopped peel (50 g)** |

| *To finish off:* |
| **Milk and caster sugar** |

A greased baking sheet.

To make the pastry, weigh the margarine (hard from the refrigerator), then wrap it in a piece of foil and place it in the freezing compartment of the fridge for half an hour.

Meanwhile sift the flour and salt into a bowl, then when you take the margarine out of the freezer hold it with the foil, dip it into the flour, then grate it on a coarse grater placed in the bowl over the flour. Carry on dipping the margarine down into the flour to make it easier to grate. When you have finished you will have a lump of grated margarine sitting in the middle of the flour. Then take a palette knife and start to cut the fat into the flour (don't use your hands) until the mixture is crumbly. Now add enough water so that it forms a dough that leaves the bowl clean (you *can* use your hands for the dough), then place it in a polythene bag and chill it in the main part of the refrigerator for half an hour.

Meanwhile, prepare the filling by first melting the butter in a small saucepan. Then take it off the heat and stir in all the filling ingredients quite thoroughly and leave it to cool.

Next turn the dough out onto a lightly-floured surface. Roll it out to about ⅛ inch (3 mm) thick, then using a plain 3½ inch (8 cm) cutter, cut the pastry into rounds. Put a teaspoon of filling onto each round, then brush the edge of half the circle of pastry with water, and bring the other side up to seal it. Then bring the corners up to the centre and pinch to seal well. Now turn your sealed pastry parcel over, so that the seam is underneath, then gently roll

it flat to about ¼ inch thick (½ cm) and pat it into a round
shape. Place them all onto the greased baking sheet and gash each
cake diagonally across three times, using a sharp knife. Now brush
them with milk and sprinkle with caster sugar and bake them in the
oven pre-heated to gas mark 7, 425°F (220°C), for about 15
minutes or until golden-brown. Then transfer them to a wire rack
to cool.

Puff pastry

Some time ago I had almost given up on traditional puff pastry. It
wasn't that I couldn't make it well, it was just that I couldn't spare
the *time* to make it well! All that long resting and rolling never
seemed to fit in with the rest of my life, and I would either leave it too
long in the fridge (so that I couldn't roll it), or I would be impatient
and not leave it long enough.

Then, a few years ago, my friend John Tovey showed me his
method, which takes 30 minutes flat. Because his is the best I've
ever tasted (invariably light and crisp), I no longer persevere with
any of the other methods. His recipe follows, but first some general
points about puff pastry.

What is puff pastry? It is the pastry used for vol-au-vents, sausage
rolls, mince pies, jam puffs, and toppings for savoury and fruit pies.
Unlike shortcrust or suet crust pastries, both of which can be
described as granular in texture, puff pastry is made up of a number
of thin layers (although they're close together, they are in fact quite
separate). This is achieved by layering the fat into the flour, rather
than rubbing it in. The dough is also folded (more layering), and
after folding sealed at the edges, so that air is trapped inside. During
the baking the expansion of steam forces the layers up, and the
pastry rises (hence the French name for puff pastries, *mille feuilles* or
thousand leaves).

Finally a few points to bear in mind when making puff pastry:

Always use strong flour.

The fat should be at room temperature when making the pastry, but
the finished pastry should be thoroughly chilled before using
(preferably overnight).

Allow the pastry to come back to room temperature before rolling
out for use.

Once rolled and cut out, the pastry should be allowed to chill again
(15–20 minutes) before going into the oven.

Dampen the baking sheet with cold water—to create a steamy atmosphere in the oven which encourages the pastry to rise.

The oven *must* be hot: gas mark 8, 450°F (230°C). Use the shelf just above the centre of the oven.

Warning! Having assembled a quantity of beautifully layered puff pastry, remember that the trimmings you have left after rolling out and cutting will not be layered together laterally. So re-rolled trimmings will not rise up and layer in quite the same way as the pastry from the first rolling. I think it is best to keep the trimmings (in a polythene bag in the fridge) for later use as a pie crust or for *Richmond maids of honour* (see page 573).

John Tovey's rough puff pastry

This, unlike my quick flaky pastry on page 565, is the real thing—perfect, puffy, flaky layers, which are very light and crisp.

1 lb strong plain flour (450 g), sifted with a pinch of salt
8 oz margarine (225 g), cut into ½ oz (10 g) pieces (i.e. 16 pieces)
8 oz lard (225 g), cut into ½ oz (10 g) pieces
½ pint iced water (275 ml), less 1 tablespoon
1 tablespoon lemon juice

Sift the flour and salt into a bowl, then add the pieces of fat. Now just flick them around to get them all coated with flour, but don't 'work' the pastry yet or attempt to mix them in. Make a well in the centre and pour in the iced water mixed with the lemon juice. Take a palette knife and make cuts across and across, turning the bowl around as you go so that you gently bring all the ingredients together. Work quickly, and as soon as you have a reasonable lump of mixture, turn it out onto a floured board—along with all the loose flour that's left.

Now, using your hands, lightly and gently shape the mixture into a brick shape, then take a large, long rolling-pin and (holding it right at the ends) make three quick depressions widthwise, to trap the air. Then, still keeping your hands at the ends of the pin (the pressure should not be directly over the pastry) roll the brick shape into an oblong roughly 13 inches (32·5 cm) long and 8 inches (20 cm) wide.

Fold one-third over to the centre, then the other third over that. Use your pin to press the edges firmly and again trap the air. Now rest the pastry for 5 minutes, then lift it and flour the board. Give the pastry a quick quarter-turn and make three depressions again. Repeat the whole process three more times, remembering to keep your board and pin well floured throughout. Wrap the pastry in foil or polythene and chill well before using, preferably overnight.

Note: before attempting to roll the pastry out for use, do make sure you allow it to come back to room temperature.

Vol-au-vents

Traditional vol-au-vents are rather fiddly things to make: they require a certain thickness of pastry to make room for the fillings, and then quite a bit of the soggy centre has to be scraped out and wasted. John Tovey has come up with the brilliant idea of simply baking small rounds of pastry, halving them, and sandwiching them together with a filling. The results are far crisper, with less pastry and more filling—a lighter, tastier product altogether.

Basic vol-au-vents

(makes 12)

1 lb John Tovey's rough puff pastry (half the quantity in the recipe opposite)

Pre-heat the oven to gas mark 8, 450°F (230°C)

Roll the pastry out to about ⅛ inch (3 mm) thick as evenly as possible, then using a 3½ inch (8·5 cm) fluted cutter cut out twelve rounds. Place these on a damp baking sheet, and leave them to rest for 10 minutes in a cool place or in the fridge. Brush each one with a little milk or beaten egg, and bake on a high shelf in the oven for 10–15 minutes.

When they are a good rich golden colour, remove them from the oven and transfer to a wire cooling tray. Slice each one in half horizontally (making sure you keep them in pairs, ready for re-assembling). If there is any uncooked pastry in the centre, scrape it out—but there should be only very little.

If you use the hot mushroom filling (see following recipe) you can fill and serve the vol-au-vents straightaway, or else warm them through and fill when you are ready. For cold fillings such as the cream cheese one on the next page, fill and sandwich them together just before serving.

You can serve the vol-au-vents as a lunch-time snack with a salad (2 per person) or as a first course (1–2 per person). For buffet parties, or for serving with drinks, you can make small, bite-sized versions, using a 2 inch (5 cm) cutter. Remember that they shrink in width during cooking.

Note: for the hot vol-au-vents, a little melted butter brushed over the surface before serving gives them a lovely sheen.

Hot mushroom and bacon filling

2 oz butter (50 g)
Half a medium-sized onion, chopped fairly small
2 rashers back bacon, chopped
1 oz flour (25 g)
8 oz mushrooms, roughly chopped (225 g)
8 fl oz single cream (220 ml)
Freshly grated nutmeg
Salt and freshly-milled black pepper

Melt the butter gently in a pan, and soften the onion and bacon in it for about 5 minutes. Then stir in the mushrooms and cook over a gentle heat for about 6 more minutes, stirring now and then. Next sprinkle in the flour, and stir well to soak up all the juices. Add the cream, a little at a time, stirring well after each addition. Cook the mixture for about 5 minutes (still giving it the odd stir). Taste and season with as much salt, pepper and nutmeg as you think it needs. Finally spoon the filling onto the warm vol-au-vents and sandwich them together.

Cream cheese and herb filling

6 oz cream cheese (225 g)
2 cloves garlic, crushed
2 tablespoons finely chopped parsley
2 tablespoons snipped chives
Salt and freshly-milled black pepper

Simply mash the ingredients together, blending them thoroughly. Taste to check the seasoning, then use the mixture to sandwich the cold vol-au-vents together (being fairly generous with the filling) just before serving.

Cream puffs
(makes 12)

These are a sweet 'afternoon tea' version of the basic vol-au-vent recipe.

1 lb John Tovey's rough puff pastry (half the quantity on pages 570–1)
2 tablespoons granulated sugar
A little milk

For the filling:
6 heaped teaspoons strawberry jam (or any other flavour)
5 fl oz (150 ml) whipped cream

Pre-heat the oven to gas mark 8, 450°F (230°C

Roll and cut the pastry as in the basic recipe on page 571. Brush each round on one side with milk, place it milk-side down on a saucer of granulated sugar, then bake on a baking sheet (sugar-side uppermost) to get a nice, sugary, crusty topping. Bake on a high shelf in the oven for 10 to 15 minutes, then split them, cool and sandwich together with jam and whipped cream. If you don't want to bother with a sugar-crusted topping, leave them plain and simply dust them with icing sugar before serving.

Richmond maids of honour
(makes about 16)

These little puff pastry cheese cakes were said to have been created by the maids of honour at Richmond Palace in the 16th century.

8 oz puff pastry (225 g) (quarter the quantity on pages 570–1)
A little apricot jam
8 oz curd cheese (225 g), (or cottage cheese sieved)
1 large egg

1 extra yolk
1½ oz caster sugar (40 g)
The grated rind of 1 lemon
1 oz ground almonds (25 g)
1 rounded tablespoon currants
A little icing sugar

Pre-heat the oven to gas mark 6,
400°F (200°C)

Start by rolling out the pastry to ⅛ inch (3 mm) thick, then
using a 3¼ inch (8 cm) fluted cutter cut out little circles and
place them in tartlet tins.

Combine the cheese, caster sugar, lemon rind, ground almonds and
currants in a bowl, then beat the egg and egg yolk together and add
this as well. Mix, very thoroughly, with a fork until everything is
evenly blended. Next, spoon the merest trace of jam into the base of
each pastry case, and fill each one about two-thirds full with the
cheese mixture. Bake them in the centre of the oven for about 25–30
minutes, by which time the mixture will have puffed right up and
turned a lovely golden brown.

Take them out of the oven and transfer them onto a wire rack to
cool. Don't worry as you see the centres starting to sink down
because that's absolutely correct and normal. When they're cool
they'll look nice with a faint dusting of icing sugar sifted over.

Crème patissière

(makes 15 fl oz)

This delicious custard cream makes an
alternative—almost better—filling than
fresh cream for all kinds of pastries.

15 fl oz milk (425 ml)
1 vanilla pod
4 oz caster sugar (110 g)
5 egg yolks
2 level tablespoons plain flour
1 level tablespoon cornflour
½ oz butter (10 g)

Pour the milk into a pan, and pop in the vanilla pod. Bring to the
boil, then take the pan off the heat and leave for the milk to infuse.

Whisk the egg yolks together with the caster sugar in a bowl, until the mixture is thick and creamy-coloured. Then gradually whisk in the flour and the cornflour. Remove the vanilla pod from the milk, and pour the infused milk into the egg yolk mixture—stirring vigorously as you pour. Return the whole lot to the rinsed-out pan and bring to the boil over a medium heat (still stirring all the time). Simmer for 3 minutes and continue to beat briskly. As the mixture thickens lumps may form, but these will eventually beat out. Take the pan off the heat, and finally beat in the butter. Transfer the cream to a bowl, and cover closely with a buttered sheet of greaseproof paper over the surface, to prevent a skin forming. Leave to get cold—but use the cream within 2–3 days.

Note: after the cream has thickened you could add a little liqueur!

Rich flan pastry

I like a light, crunchy, nutty-flavoured pastry for 'special' open fruit flans. When making either of the two recipes that follow, I make a 6 oz (175 g) quantity of pastry which is enough to line an 8 inch (20 cm) flan tin and also make a lattice-work top.

Crisp cinnamon flan (serves 6 people)	
	6 oz plain flour (175 g)
	3 oz butter (75 g)
	3 tablespoons caster sugar
	3 egg yolks
	1 teaspoon cinnamon
	For the filling:
	1 lb blackcurrants, gooseberries or loganberries (450 g)
	2 tablespoons granulated sugar
	1 rounded teaspoon arrowroot
	For decorating:
	A little caster sugar

Pre-heat the oven to gas mark 6, 400°F (200°C)

An 8 inch (20 cm) flan tin, lightly greased.

First prepare the pastry. Sieve the flour with the cinnamon into a mixing bowl, then rub in the fat, stir in the sugar and use the egg yolks in place of liquid to mix the pastry to a dough. Pop it into a polythene bag and chill for one hour in the fridge before using.

Meanwhile prepare the filling, by sprinkling the sugar over the fruit in a saucepan and heating gently until the juice begins to run. Then mix the arrowroot with enough cold water to make a smooth paste, mix this with the fruit and simmer till thickened.

To make the flan, roll out three-quarters of the pastry and line the flan tin with it, pricking the base with a fork. Now fill with the fruit mixture and arrange the remaining pastry in a lattice pattern over the top. Brush the top with cold water, dust with a little caster sugar, then bake on a baking sheet for 10 minutes. Reduce the heat to gas mark 5, 375°F (190°C) and cook for a further 35 minutes. Serve (warm or cold) with whipped cream.

Linzertorte

(serves 6 people)

This is a famous Austrian torte named after the town of Linz. The rich pastry flan is made with ground hazelnuts. If you can't get hold of cranberry jelly, redcurrent could be used.

6 oz plain flour (175 g)
3 oz ground hazelnuts (75 g)
2 oz icing sugar, sifted (50 g)
The finely grated rind of 1 lemon
¼ teaspoon cinnamon
Freshly grated nutmeg
4 oz butter (110 g)
2 egg yolks
12 oz cranberry jelly (350 g)
2 teaspoons lemon juice
A little icing sugar

Pre-heat the oven to gas mark 5, 375°F (190°C)

A 9 inch (23 cm) round, fluted flan tin with a removable base, well buttered.

First combine the flour, ground hazelnuts, icing sugar, lemon rind, cinnamon and a few gratings of whole nutmeg in a bowl, then rub in the butter until the mixture is crumbly. Stir in the egg yolks and form the mixture into a dough. Weigh a 5 oz (150 g) piece of the pastry dough and put it on one side. Roll out the rest on a floured surface to a 10 inch (25·5 cm) round. Place this in the base of the tin and, using your fingers, gradually ease the dough up the side of the tin so that it stands up above the edge. Smooth the base out with your hands.

Next, mix the jelly with the lemon juice and spoon all but 2 tablespoons onto the pastry, smoothing it out evenly to the edge. Use the rest of the dough to make a lattice-work pattern on the top, with strips about ⅓ inch (½–1 cm) wide. Then go round the pastry edge with a fork, turning it over inside the edge of the tin to give about a ½ inch (1 cm) border all round.

Bake on a high shelf for 30 minutes, or until the pastry is golden brown. Then, as soon as the flan comes out of the oven, use the reserved jam to fill up the squares formed by the lattice. Sift icing sugar over the top and serve it warm or cold with whipped cream.

Choux pastry

This is the light, crisp, airy pastry which is used to make éclairs, profiteroles, or savoury gougères. It puffs up in the oven until it is eventually set by the heat of the cooking. The airiness, in fact, is caused because choux has a high water content which in cooking is turned into steam, which forces the pastry shell outwards, and gives it some volume.

What's so good about choux is that it doesn't call for any particular pastry skills (like lightness of hand or careful rolling). Of course some people make hard work of it by recommending that it always has to be piped through piping bags. But personally—quite apart from the fact that piping requires experience and a steady hand—I find it a wasteful method; and I'm convinced that a freshly-baked golden profiterole looks to much crustier if it's spooned, rather than piped, onto a baking sheet.

My own advice on choux pastry can be summarised as follows:

Try to use strong plain flour, which (with its higher gluten content) gives crisper results than ordinary soft plain flour.

Raising the oven temperature during the cooking, I have found, gives really crisp, well-risen choux.

Choux pastry doesn't keep well, and it is best eaten as soon as possible. It will stay crisp for up to 4 hours, though I prefer to have mine ready just 2 hours before it is needed.

Fillings, if put in too far in advance, make the pastry soggy. So it is advisable to fill the cakes, buns or whatever as near as possible to the time they are to be eaten.

Basic choux pastry

2½ oz strong plain flour (60 g)
2 oz butter, cut into small pieces (50 g)
1 teaspoon sugar (only for sweet choux pastry, otherwise use a seasoning of salt and pepper)
2 eggs, well beaten
5 fl oz cold water (150 ml)

Pre-heat the oven to gas mark 6, 400°F (200°C)

First of all, put the water in a medium-sized saucepan together with the pieces of butter, and leave on one side while you weigh out the flour.

As you are going to need to 'shoot' the flour quickly into the water and melted butter, fold a sheet of greaseproof paper to make a crease, then open it up again. Sift the flour straight onto the square of greaseproof. If the end product is going to be sweet, add the sugar to the flour; if it is to be savoury, season the flour well with salt and pepper instead.

Next, place the saucepan of water and butter over a moderate heat, and stir with a wooden spoon. As soon as the butter has melted and the mixture comes up to the boil, turn off the heat and tip the flour in—all in one go—with one hand, while you beat the mixture vigorously with the other (you can do this with a wooden spoon, though an electric hand-whisk will save you lots of energy).

Beat until you have a smooth ball of paste that has left the sides of the saucepan clean (probably this will take less than a minute). Then beat the beaten eggs in—a little at a time—until you have a smooth glossy paste.

Left (from top to bottom): All-in-one sponge, page 594; Squidgy chocolate log, page 602; Traditional Dundee cake, page 605; Lemon cheesecake with frosted grapes, page 476.

At this stage grease a baking sheet lightly, then hold it under cold running water for a few seconds, and tap it sharply to get rid of excess moisture (this will help create a steamy atmosphere, which in turn helps the pastry to rise). Your choux pastry is then ready for any of the following recipes.

Profiteroles

(makes about 18)

Profiteroles—little choux buns filled with cream and covered in a chocolate sauce—make a rather special ending to a dinner party.

1 quantity choux pastry (see page 578)
½ pint double cream, whipped thick (275 ml)
8 oz plain chocolate (225 g)
3 tablespoons water

Pre-heat the oven to gas mark 6, 400°F (200°C)

A large baking sheet, greased and dampened.

Place teaspoons of choux pastry on the baking sheet, and then bake in the pre-heated oven for 10 minutes. After that, increase the heat to gas mark 7, 425°F (220°C) and bake for a further 15–20 minutes until the choux buns are crisp, light and a rich golden colour. Pierce the side of each one (to let out the steam), then cool them on a wire rack.

To make the chocolate sauce, melt the chocolate together with the water in a basin fitted over a saucepan of simmering water, stirring until you have a smooth sauce (see my note on chocolate, page 632). Just before serving, split the choux buns in half, fill each one with a teaspoon of whipped cream, then join the halves together again. Pour the melted chocolate over them (see the photograph opposite) and serve immediately.

Note: don't be tempted to put the cream in too far in advance, because this tends to make them soggy.

Left: Profiteroles, this page.

Chocolate and hazelnut choux buns

(makes 8 or 9)

These lovely, light, airy choux buns are filled and topped with a squidgy chocolate mousse mixture and coated with chopped nuts.

1 quantity of choux pastry (see page 578)

For the filling:
6 oz plain dessert chocolate (175 g)
3 large eggs, separated)

For the topping:
2 level tablespoons chopped, toasted hazelnuts

The mousse filling should be made several hours in advance. Melt the chocolate in a heat-proof bowl set over a pan of barely simmering water. Then beat the egg yolks into the chocolate and allow the mixture to cool. Whisk the egg whites to the soft peak stage. Stir one tablespoon of egg white into the chocolate mixture to loosen it, then carefully fold in the remainder. Cover the bowl and chill in a refrigerator for about 3 hours.

Pre-heat the oven to gas mark 6, 400°F (200°C). Place rough dessertspoons of the choux pastry on a greased and dampened baking sheet and bake, on a high shelf, for 10 minutes. Then increase the heat to gas mark 7, 425°F (220°C) for a further 20–25 minutes until the buns are nicely brown and puffy. Pierce the side of each one and cool on a wire cooling tray.

It's best not to put in the filling until about an hour before serving. All you do is slice the choux buns horizontally, but not quite in half, then place a spoonful of the chocolate mousse inside, spread a little over the top using the back of the spoon, and finally, sprinkle each one with chopped hazelnuts.

Coffee éclairs

(makes 8 or 9)

You can, of course, make these as the choux buns in the last recipe, but if you want to serve the classic éclair shape you'll need to use a piping bag.

1 quantity of choux pastry (see page 578)

For the filling:
½ pint double cream (275 ml)
1 tablespoon instant coffee
2 teaspoons boiling water
1 tablespoon caster sugar

For the icing:
5 oz sieved icing sugar (150 g)
2 teaspoons instant coffee
1 tablespoon boiling water

Pre-heat the oven to gas mark 6, 400°F (200°C)

Spoon the choux pastry into a large nylon piping bag, fitted with a plain ½ inch (1 cm) piping nozzle. Pipe the mixture onto rinsed baking sheets (see the recipe on page 578) in lengths just over 3 inches (7·5 cm).

Bake the éclairs on a high shelf for 10 minutes, then increase the heat to gas mark 7, 425°F (220°C) for a further 10 minutes. Remove them from the oven to a wire cooling tray and make a slight hole in the side of each one.

For the filling, dissolve the coffee and sugar in the boiling water. Beat the cream till thickened and add the coffee mixture to it, stirring to blend it evenly. Now wash and dry the piping bag and nozzle thoroughly; spoon the coffee cream into it. Slit the éclairs along one side, pipe in the cream and carefully press the tops gently back over the cream.

Next prepare the icing. In a small basin dissolve the coffee in the boiling water, sift the icing sugar into it and stir. It should now be the consistency of thick cream. Finally, dip the tops of the éclairs into the icing and let the excess drip back into the bowl before returning each one to the wire rack.

Note: as an alternative filling for choux buns, profiteroles or éclairs you could use the *Crème patissière* on page 574. For coffee flavour, add 1 dessertspoon of instant coffee dissolved in 1 teaspoon warm water, and for a chocolate filling combine the cream with 2 oz (50 g) melted dessert chocolate.

Gougère with cheese

(serves 2 people)

This is a ring of cheese-flavoured choux pastry, crisp on the outside and slightly squidgy inside. It is nice served with a salad for a lunch dish.

1 quantity of choux pastry (see page 578)
2½ oz Cheddar cheese, grated (60 g)
½ teaspoon mustard powder
A good pinch cayenne pepper
Salt and freshly-milled black pepper to season

Pre-heat the oven to gas mark 6, 400°F (200°C)

Make the choux paste in exactly the same way as outlined on page 578—seasoning with salt and pepper—except that immediately after you have added the beaten eggs, also add 2 oz (50 g) of the cheese, the mustard and the cayenne pepper.

Now spoon dessertspoons of the mixture onto a greased and ready-dampened baking sheet, so that they touch each other and form a circle that is approximately 7 inches (18 cm) in diameter.

Brush the choux circle with some beaten egg, then sprinkle the remaining grated cheese all round the top. Bake in the pre-heated oven for 10 minutes, then increase the heat to gas mark 7, 425°F (220°C) and cook for a further 20–25 minutes. Serve it hot and puffy, straight from the oven.

Note: to make this recipe extra special, you could use Swiss Gruyère cheese instead of Cheddar.

See also:
Bacon and egg pie
Caramelized apple flan
Cheese and onion quichelets
Eighteenth-century creamed apple flan

Flaky fish pie
Plum and soured cream flan
Spinach and cream cheese quiche
Thick onion tart

Cakes

Including recipes for:
Classic Victoria sponge
All-in-one sponge
All-in-one chocolate sponge
All-in-one coffee and walnut sponge
All-in-one orange or lemon sponge
All-in-one orange or lemon layer cake
All-in-one wholewheat sponge
Whisked fatless sponge
Lemon curd butterfly cakes
Fresh lemon curd
Coffee cream mousseline

Chocolate and soured cream filling
Chocolate fudge filling and topping
Oatmeal parkin
Date, apple and walnut loaf
Squidgy chocolate log
Sticky date cake
Marmalade cake
Traditional Dundee cake
Rich fruit cake
Almond paste
Royal icing
Modelling paste

One of the cheapest ways to add a touch of luxury to our everyday eating, I think, is to indulge in a little home baking now and then. Some of the chief contributors to the boredom of our modern synthetic diet are those dull factory-made cakes and flavourless biscuits which come so prettily wrapped on our supermarket shelves. Eating of course is for sustenance—but surely for enjoyment too: and hasn't the sheer blandness of mass production taken away some of the joy?

If you have never done any home baking, or have lapsed for some time, I do hope you'll revive the art. There's so much personal pleasure in it and a sort of wholesomeness about a kitchen filled with the aroma of baking—a lovely way to make your family feel spoiled.

I've never believed, as some people seem to, that you either have a gift for cake-making or you don't. Confidence is the key and nothing can shake one's confidence like having a failure with a cake into which so much care has gone. So perhaps the first thing we ought to do is to try to understand what is actually happening when a cake is being baked—because any interference with this process could end in the failure we all want to avoid!

What happens when you bake a cake?
When fat and sugar are mixed together—the process is called creaming—little bubbles of air are being trapped in the mixture, each one surrounded by a film of fat (which is why the mixture changes colour during creaming as the trapped air creates a foam). It is this air which produces the lightness in the finished cake, but unless beaten egg is added to the mixture the fat would collapse and the air escape during cooking. The egg white conveniently forms a layer around each air bubble, and as the temperature of the cake rises in the heat of the oven this layer coagulates and forms a rigid wall round each bubble, preventing it from bursting and ruining the texture of the cake.

During the baking the bubbles of air will expand and the cake will 'rise'. At the same time the stretchy gluten in the flour—which has formed an elastic network round the air bubbles—will stretch until, at a higher temperature, it loses its elasticity and the shape of the cake becomes fixed.

But until that moment is reached the expansion process must be allowed to continue uninterrupted. Which is why a) the cake should be baked as soon as it is mixed and b), even more importantly, the oven door should *never* be opened in the early stages of cooking:

the temperature will drop suddenly and the air in the cake will stop expanding and actually contract. The whole structure of the cake will then sink back because there's nothing to prop it up. So, remember, never look at a cake until three-quarters of the cooking time has elapsed.

Cake tins

Here we have another possible cause of failure. There are so many differing sizes of cake tin available, and even a half-inch difference all round can often upset both the timing of a recipe and the finished size of the cake. It is therefore *important* to use the correct sized tin. In my recipes I usually try to keep to 7 or 8 inch tins (which metrically are approximately 18 or 20 cm—the difference in volume is minimal). These are fairly standard sizes, though some manufacturers come up with some very strange alternatives in the name of metrication.

Sponge sandwich tins To get a properly risen cake it is most important to use a sponge tin that is at least 1¹/₂ inches (4 cm) deep. The cause of many a flat sponge cake is a sponge tin that is too shallow.

Loaf tins These too come in a confusing array of sizes, and again I have kept all my recipes to two sizes—either the 2 lb (900 g) capacity loaf tin, or else a slightly narrower tin with a base measurement of 7¹/₂ inches (19 cm) by 3¹/₂ inches (8·5 cm).

Non-stick surfaces Normally I use non-stick bakeware simply as an extra aid, never relying on it exclusively. In practice I use it as I would normal bakeware, greasing and lining it by the traditional method. I just find this more reliable.

Cake ingredients

Plain flour Unless yeast is used in a recipe (e.g. *Hot cross buns* on page 62) ordinary soft flour is always best for cake recipes requiring plain flour. This has a lower protein content than strong flour, and therefore produces that finer, shorter texture suitable for cakes, biscuits and scones.

Self-raising flour On those occasions when a raising agent is called for, it is usually more convenient to use self-raising flour since this has a standard amount of raising agent already added to it. From time to time a recipe might need rather more (or less) raising power, in which case plain flour plus the appropriate quantity of baking powder is used.

Wholewheat flour Nowadays most food scientists are agreed about the lack of fibre in our diet, and even the commercial giants are replacing the bran which was milled out of flour in the first place (thus we see 'bran' finding its way into countless breakfast cereals, biscuits and cakes). To meet the problem at home I find it better to switch over completely to wholewheat flour in baking. I'm delighted to report that most of my wholewheat experiments with cakes have been very successful, which I hope some of the following recipes will prove.

Baking powders These are normally a mixture of bicarbonate of soda and another acid-acting chemical, like cream of tartar. Very often, though, one needs far less raising power than these mixtures give—which explains why some recipes require bicarbonate of soda on its own.

Fats Flavour-wise it is said you can't beat butter in baking. And certainly for purists that's probably true—I see one leading chain-store proudly advertises 'made with all butter' on its wrappings! My own opinion is that margarine—now it has improved so much in flavour—is very good for baking, and with the advent of soft margarine and the all-in-one method of making sponges (see recipes), I actually hardly ever use butter for baking. Very occasionally I use lard, as in the *Marmalade cake* recipe (see page 604).

Fats should usually be at room temperature for cake-making. Allow 1 hour to soften butter, block margarine and lard. Soft or whipped margarines can be used straight from the fridge (although in practice I usually allow half an hour at room temperature), but it is vital that any margarine that is high in polyunsaturated fats is always used straight from the fridge.

Sugar I believe caster sugar is worth paying the extra for in baking (especially for sponges), since it does give a finer texture. Some people manage successfully to make granulated sugar into caster sugar in a liquidiser and to save money, but be warned; if you over-do it you can finish up with a powdery 'icing' sugar and won't have saved anything! In wholefood cakes, soft brown sugar (or sometimes demerara) can be used and indeed is preferable.

Eggs As discussed on page 25, eggs for all cooking purposes should be at room temperature. If they are too cold or used straight from the fridge, they curdle more easily. So remember to remove from the fridge a couple of hours before beginning baking.

Air Yes, another all-important ingredient. Air means lightness in your cakes, and to incorporate it you need (i) large and roomy mixing bowls, and (ii) always to sift the flour, holding your sieve up high to give the flour a good airing on its way to the bowl. Careful folding with a metal spoon, which cuts cleanly into the mixture, enables you to retain the precious air incorporated at the mixing stage.

What went wrong?

I hope you're not reading this section because things *have* gone wrong! It's really here to try to prevent that happening, or at least to reassure you.

Hit or miss One of the primary reasons why cakes sometimes fail is the recipe itself. It might be wrong or simply too vague, like some of grandma's hand-me-downs which never mention details like tin sizes or oven temperature. Be suspicious of any recipe that does not offer you all the information you need. But if it is precise, then follow it precisely: if it calls for an 8 inch (20 cm) square tin and you've only got a 6 inch (15 cm) round tin, it *does* matter.

Over-anxiety It is always tempting to take a peep in the oven to see how your creation is getting on. As I mentioned before, impatient cooks are inviting disaster.

Curdling If you are using a creaming method (see page 591), it can sometimes happen that the beaten eggs are added to the sugar-and-fat mixture too quickly, causing the whole mixture to separate. This 'breaking up' means that some of the air incorporated at the creaming stage will escape and the finished cake will be slightly heavier. For beginners the way to avoid this is to add the beaten eggs just a teaspoonful at a time, whisking preferably with an electric hand-whisk. If it does curdle, don't worry: the cake won't be as light but it's not a disaster.

Fruit sinking This is usually a fault in the recipe. It means the mixture is too slack (too liquid) to hold the fruit. Fruit cakes need a larger proportion of flour in order to hold the fruit evenly. Glacé cherries and other sugar-coated fruit should be rinsed and dried (and chopped if large) before adding to a cake mixture. Both the size of the fruit and sugar coating can cause sinking.

Over-browning Sometimes the top of a cake becomes brown before the centre is cooked. To prevent this, check the cake three-quarters of the way through the cooking time and, if necessary, fit a protective circle of double greaseproof paper (with a hole about the size of a 50p piece in the centre) over the top of the cake.

But above all don't be daunted. Always remember the good things that go into a home-made cake, and even if the finished product does happen to have sunk a bit, it will still taste delicious.

Notes on preparation

Lining tins Where a recipe asks you to line a tin, always do so. It may seem like an extra bother, but it only takes a few moments and it makes turning out the cake far easier. Greaseproof paper is used in most cases, but for delicate cakes like sponges I use silicone paper (from good stationers) for a base lining, as it *never* sticks. It is important to allow an extra couple of inches (5 cm or so) so that the lining paper extends above the rim of the cake tin.

For a round tin: cut a strip of paper slightly longer than the circumference of the tin, and fold back about an inch (2·5 cm) along its length. Snip this at intervals with scissors, cutting at a slight angle right up the fold (A). Grease the tin, then press the paper around the sides. You will find the snipped edge will overlap on the base of the tin to give a snug fit (B). Finally, cut a circle of paper—using the tin as a template—to fit over the base.

For a square tin: cut a piece of paper to size by measuring the length and width of the tin and adding twice its depth. Centre the tin on the paper, then make four cuts from the paper's edge right up to the corners of the tin (C). Grease the tin and fit the paper inside, folding and overlapping at the corners (D).

Greasing tins In my experience so-called non-stick tins sometimes do! So I recommend that you always grease cake tins regardless. The best thing is to use some of the same sort of fat as is used for the cake mixture. Smear it evenly all over the inside of the tin (making sure you get into the corners) using a piece of absorbent kitchen paper.

Flouring tins Some recipes state that the tins should also be lightly dusted with flour. This is unnecessary unless for some reason the cake needs to be extra crisp at the edges.

How to store cakes

Cake tins are definitely better than plastic boxes for storage, because metal is non-porous. However carefully you wash plastic, smells linger on. The previous occupant of a plastic container can taint the next, and mould can develop. Also never store cakes and biscuits in the same tin, as the moisture from the cake will make the biscuits soggy. For short-term storing an aluminium foil wrapping can be used, but if you're storing a rich fruit cake for a longer period, then use a double layer of greaseproof paper on the inside and foil on the outside—because the acid in the fruit can corrode the foil if it comes into direct contact with it and a mould will develop.

Some different methods of cake-making

Creaming This is the term used when a cake is made with butter or block margarine (soft or whipped margarines are unsuitable). It means that the fat and sugar are beaten together till creamy and pale: the eggs are then beaten into this mixture, bit by bit. This method is explained in the *Classic Victoria sponge* recipe (page 592).

Rubbing-in A cake made by this method starts off with the fat being rubbed into the flour—exactly the same as for shortcrust pastry. Butter, block margarine and lard can all be used. It is a very easy method—see the *Marmalade cake* recipe (page 604).

Boil-and-bake In recipes of this kind the fat and liquid are boiled together before the flour is added. Again, a very straightforward method, as in the *Sticky date cake* recipe (page 603).

All-in-one Exactly as the name suggests, these cakes are mixed all in one go. All the ingredients go into the bowl together and the mixing is done in seconds. Soft margarine is tailor-made for this method.

Sponge cakes

I have to admit that since soft margarine came onto the market and sponge cakes can be made simply by combining all the ingredients in the bowl at once, I very rarely make the classic Victoria sponge, which is a lot more work. However there will probably always be those who prefer cakes made with butter for that bit of extra flavour. Anyway, for those who are new to cake-making or those who would like to experiment, here are my own notes on the differences between the three main methods of sponge-making:

1 Classic (Victoria) sponge Provides a good flavour and, if skilfully made, should have a light texture; but not quite as moist as an all-in-one sponge especially after storing.

2 All-in-one sponge This does have a very light texture—it really melts in the mouth. It keeps better than any other type of sponge I've made. The flavour is slightly less rich than the Victoria.

3 Whisked fatless sponge Extremely light in texture but the absence of fat can give a hint almost of rubberiness. This one must be eaten as fresh as possible: it can become stale by the next day.

There are of course other, rather more complicated sponge recipes, such as a Genoese or an oil-based sponge. But as this is essentially a basic cookery course I have not included them here. Recipes for them can be found in *Delia Smith's Book of Cakes* (Coronet Books).

Classic
Victoria sponge

I find a 4 oz mixture (i.e. 4 oz or 110 g) each of flour, sugar and butter to 2 eggs) gives just the right depth and balance between cake and filling, if 7 inch (18 cm) tins are used. However if you like your sponges to have more depth, you can increase this mixture to 6 oz (175 g) each of flour, sugar and butter and use 3 eggs. Allow an extra 5–10 minutes cooking time in that case.

4 oz butter, at room temperature (110 g)
4 oz caster sugar (110 g)
2 large eggs
4 oz self-raising flour, sifted (110 g)

| A few drops of vanilla essence |
| Some hot water, if required |

| *To finish:* |
| Jam and sifted icing sugar |

Pre-heat the oven to gas mark 3, 325°F (170°C)

Two 7 inch (18 cm) sponge tins at least 1¹/₂ inches (4 cm) deep, greased, and the bases lined with greaseproof paper.

In a medium-sized mixing bowl, cream the butter and sugar together until you get a pale, fluffy mixture that drops off the spoon easily (an electric hand-whisk speeds this up considerably, but a wooden spoon will do). Then in a separate jug or bowl beat the eggs together thoroughly, then add them a little at a time, beating well after each addition. For a beginner I recommend just a teaspoonful at a time: if you add it like this, just a little at a time and beating after each addition, the mixture won't curdle.

When the eggs have been incorporated, stir in a few drops of vanilla essence, then take a metal spoon (which will cut and fold the flour in much better than a wooden spoon). Have the flour in a sieve resting on a plate, then lift the sieve high above the bowl and sift about a quarter of the flour onto the mixture. Then replace the sieve on the plate, and lightly and gently fold the flour into the mixture (if you beat the flour in, you'll lose some precious air). Then repeat until all the flour is incorporated: lifting the sieve high above the bowl will ensure the flour gets a good airing before it reaches the mixture.

Now that the flour has been added you should have a mixture that will drop off the spoon easily when you tap it on the side of the bowl (this is what is called a good 'dropping' consistency). If the consistency is not right, add one or two teaspoons of hot water.

Now divide the mixture equally between the two tins—if you want to be very precise you could place both tins on balance scales (I've never bothered, though, because I don't mind if one sponge is fractionally larger than the other). Place them on the centre shelf of the oven, and they'll take about 25–30 minutes to cook. When they are cooked the centres will feel springy when lightly touched with a little finger-tip and no imprint remains.

When you are satisfied that the sponges are cooked, remove them from the oven, then after about one minute turn them out onto a wire cooling tray, loosening them around the edges with a palette knife first. Then carefully peel off the base papers and leave the cakes to cool completely before sandwiching them together with jam and sifting a little icing sugar over the surface.

Note: for 8 inch (20 cm) sponge sandwich tins, use 6 oz (175 g) each of flour, sugar and butter and 3 large eggs.

All-in-one sponge

For me this is the best sponge of all, and should work even if you've never made a cake before in your life.

4 oz self-raising flour, sifted (110 g)
1 teaspoon baking powder
4 oz soft margarine, at room temperature (110 g)
4 oz caster sugar (110 g)
2 large eggs
2–3 drops vanilla essence

To finish:
Icing sugar, jam and/or fresh cream

Pre-heat the oven to gas mark 3, 325°F (170°C)

Two 7 inch (18 cm) sponge tins, no less than 1½ inches (4 cm) deep, lightly greased and lined with greaseproof paper (also greased) or silicone paper.

Take a large roomy mixing bowl, and sift flour and baking powder into it, holding the sieve high to give the flour a good airing. Then simply add all the other ingredients to the bowl, and whisk them— preferably with an electric hand whisk—till thoroughly combined. If the mixture doesn't drop off a wooden spoon easily when tapped on the side of the bowl, then add 1 or 2 teaspoons of tap-warm water, and whisk again.

Now divide the mixture between the two prepared tins, level off and bake on the centre shelf of the oven for about 30 minutes. When cooked leave them in the tins for only about 30 seconds, then loosen the edges by sliding a palette knife all round and turn them out onto a wire cooling rack. Peel off the base papers carefully and, when cool, sandwich them together with jam or lemon curd (or jam and fresh cream), and dust with icing sugar.

All-in-one chocolate sponge
Add 1 tablespoon of cocoa powder to the basic ingredients. Omit the vanilla essence.

All-in-one coffee and walnut sponge
Add 2 oz (50 g) of finely chopped walnuts, plus 1 tablespoon of instant coffee mixed with 1 dessertspoon of hot water, to the basic ingredients. Omit the vanilla essence. For filling and topping use *Coffee cream mousseline* (page 598).

All-in-one orange or lemon sponge
Add the grated rind of a medium orange or lemon, plus 1 dessertspoon of the juice, to the basic ingredients. Omit the vanilla essence.

All-in-one orange or lemon layer cake
Use 6 oz (175 g) flour, margarine and sugar to 1½ teaspoons baking powder and 3 large eggs, together with the orange or lemon flavour as above, in two 7 inch (18 cm) tins. Bake for 30 minutes, then when the cakes are cold, slice each one carefully in half horizontally. Use a lemon or orange curd filling (page 598) to sandwich the layers together, and dust the top with icing sugar.

All-in-one wholewheat sponge
This works surprisingly well using 4 oz (110 g) of plain wholewheat flour and adding 2½ teaspoons of baking powder. You could also use soft brown sugar, but I find the texture is better with caster sugar. In short, any recipe for an all-in-one sponge cake can be made with wholewheat flour so long as the extra amount of baking powder is also used.

Whisked fatless sponge

This is a very good recipe for those attempting to cut the fat content in their diets—and one or two slices will not contain a great deal of egg.

3 oz plain flour, sifted (75 g)
½ teaspoon baking powder

| 3 large eggs |
| 3 oz caster sugar (75 g) |

| *To finish:* |
| A little caster sugar, jam and icing sugar |

Pre-heat the oven to gas mark 4, 350°F (180°C)

Two 7 inch (18 cm) sandwich tins, liberally brushed with melted fat and the bases lined with greaseproof paper (also greased).

First separate the eggs, placing the whites in a very large grease-free bowl and the yolks in a separate one. Now add the sugar to the yolks and whisk, either with an electric hand-whisk or by hand, until the mixture is very pale and fluffy and has thickened—about 5 minutes with an electric whisk. Now wash and dry the whisk very thoroughly and use it to beat the whites until stiff but not dry.

Next with the aid of a large metal spoon fold the egg whites into the yolk-and-sugar mixture alternately with the sifted flour and baking powder, starting and finishing with egg whites. Then spoon an equal quantity of the mixture into the prepared tins and bake in the centre of the oven for 20–25 minutes. The sponges are cooked when they feel firm and springy in the centre and have begun to shrink slightly away from the sides of the tins.

Leave to cool in the tins for 3 minutes, then have ready a sheet of greaseproof paper, sprinkled with a little caster sugar. Turn the cakes out onto this before transferring to a wire rack to finish cooling. Then sandwich them together with jam, and dust the top with icing sugar.

Note: it's important to eat a fatless sponge as fresh as possible.

Lemon curd
butterfly cakes

(makes 12–13 cakes)

These little cakes are baked in small paper baking cases, which can usually be bought at good stationers.

6 oz self-raising flour (175 g)
A pinch of salt
4 oz soft margarine, at room temperature (110 g)
4 oz caster sugar (110 g)
2 large eggs
1 dessertspoon lemon juice
The grated rind of 1 lemon

For the lemon curd filling:
1 quantity of lemon curd (see page 598)

Pre-heat the oven to gas mark 5, 375°F (190°C)

A patty tin, greased, and some paper baking cases.

First of all make up the filling, and leave to get quite cold.

To make the cakes combine all the ingredients together in a bowl and beat till absolutely smooth (1–2 minutes). Then drop an equal quantity of the mixture into the paper cases, and sit the cases in the patty tin—give it two or three light taps to settle the cake mixture. Then bake on the shelf just above the centre of the oven for 15–20 minutes or until the cakes are well risen and golden. Then remove them to a wire rack and leave to cool.

When they're cool, take a sharp knife and cut the top of each at an angle in a circle about ¹/₂ inch (1 cm) from the edge of the cake, so that you remove a cone-shaped round, leaving a cavity in the centre. Cut each cone in half (top to bottom) and set aside. Now fill the cavity of each cake with the lemon curd then sit the two cone-shaped pieces of cake on top like butterfly wings.

Sponge toppings and fillings
These are an important part of a finished sponge, and while jam in the centre and icing sugar on top are delicious, there are a great many possible alternatives. What starts out as an ordinary sponge can be made into something really special.

One of the little campaigns that runs through my cooking is to try to reduce the amount of sugar in recipes, wherever possible and desirable. Consequently I have avoided those sticky sweet icings and butter creams (which taste even worse made with margarine) in this section. Instead here are several delicious alternatives, that aren't too much bother and taste far better. Quantities are for the standard sponge recipes on the previous pages.

Fresh lemon curd

Home-made lemon curd is so easy a child can make it, and it is a beautifully fresh-tasting filling. The quantity here is enough to sandwich a layer cake.

3 oz caster sugar (75 g)
1 large, juicy lemon (grated rind and juice)
2 large eggs
2 oz unsalted butter (50 g)

Place the grated lemon rind and sugar in a bowl. In another bowl whisk the lemon juice together with the eggs, then pour this mixture over the sugar. Add the butter cut into little pieces, and place the bowl over a pan of barely simmering water. Stir frequently till thickened—about 20 minutes. Then cool the curd and use it to sandwich the sponges together, spreading it thickly.

Note: for *orange curd* replace the lemon with 1 large orange.

Coffee cream mousseline

This is a soft, fluffy, not-too-sweet creamy filling; it goes very well with the *Coffee and walnut sponge* page 595.

5 oz unsalted butter, at room temperature (150 g)
2½ oz caster sugar (60 g)
2 large egg yolks
4 tablespoons water
1 tablespoon instant coffee dissolved in 1 tablespoon hot water

Place the sugar and water together in a small saucepan and slowly bring it to the boil—keep an eye on it and make sure the sugar has dissolved completely before it comes to the boil. Then let it simmer gently for about 10–15 minutes or until the mixture forms a 'thread' when pressed between thumb and forefinger (to do this take some on a teaspoon, cool it a little, and dip your finger in cold water before testing). If you have a cooking thermometer the temperature should be between 218°F (103°C) and 220°F (105°C).

Now whisk the egg yolks in a bowl, place the bowl on a damp tea towel to steady it, then pour the sugar syrup onto the egg yolks in a steady stream, whisking all the time. Then whisk the butter in, about 1 oz (25 g) at a time, till you have a smooth fluffy cream. Now whisk in the dissolved coffee, and use the cream to sandwich the cake and to decorate the top (along with some walnut halves perhaps). This fills and tops a 7 or 8 inch (18 or 20 cm) sponge.

Chocolate and soured cream filling

This has a sophisticated, dark bitter chocolate flavour and is not at all sweet (should you want it sweeter, add 1 dessertspoon of caster sugar).

5 oz plain dessert chocolate (150 g)
5 fl oz soured cream (150 ml)

Break the chocolate into a basin fitted over a pan of barely simmering water, add the soured cream too, and stir—keeping the heat low until the chocolate has melted. Then remove the pan from the heat and as soon as the mixture has cooled, spread it over the centre and top of a 7 or 8 inch (18 or 20 cm) chocolate sponge. A few walnuts or hazelnuts are nice for decoration.

Chocolate fudge filling and topping

This makes enough to fill and top a 7 or 8 inch (18 or 20 cm) cake.

3 oz granulated sugar (75 g)
1½ oz butter or margarine (40 g)
4 oz unsweetened cooking chocolate, or plain dessert chocolate (100 g)
3 fl oz evaporated milk (75 ml)
2 drops vanilla essence

To start with combine the sugar and evaporated milk in a heavy saucepan. Place the pan over a low heat and allow the sugar to dissolve, stirring frequently. When all the granules of sugar have melted, bring the mixture to the boil and simmer very gently for 6 minutes—this time without stirring.

Take the pan off the heat, stir in the chocolate (broken into small pieces) and keep stirring until the chocolate has melted. Finally stir in the butter and vanilla essence.

Now transfer the mixture to a bowl, cool, then cover with clingfilm and chill for a couple of hours until it has thickened to a spreadable consistency.

Family cakes
In the section that follows I have selected some of my own favourite cake recipes, and have attempted at the same time to cover a variety of cake-making methods.

Oatmeal parkin

One of the fascinating things about this traditional Northern recipe is that it's nothing out of the ordinary when it's freshly made—but if kept in an airtight tin it matures to a lovely chewy consistency. One week's keeping is enough, but two weeks is even better!

6 oz medium oatmeal (175 g)
3 oz self-raising flour, sifted (75 g)
A pinch of salt
4 oz golden syrup (110 g)
1 oz black treacle (25 g)
3 oz margarine (75 g)
3 oz soft brown sugar (75 g)
1½ teaspoons ground ginger
1 small egg, beaten
1 dessertspoon milk

Pre-heat the oven to gas mark 1, 275°F (140°C)

One 6 inch (15 cm) square cake tin, lightly greased.

First weigh a saucepan on the scales, then weigh the syrup and treacle into it. Then add the margarine and sugar to the saucepan and place it over a gentle heat until the margarine has melted down—don't go away and leave it unattended, because for this one you do not want it to boil.

Meanwhile measure the oatmeal, flour and ginger into a mixing bowl, add a pinch of salt, then gradually stir in the warmed syrup mixture until everything is thoroughly blended. Next add the beaten egg and lastly the milk. Now pour the mixture into the prepared tin and bake in the centre of the oven for about 1¹/₂ hours or until the centre feels springy to the touch.

Then cool the parkin in the tin for 30 minutes before turning out. Don't worry too much if the parkin sinks slightly in the middle—it sometimes happens in Yorkshire too, I'm told.

Date, apple and walnut loaf

A very easy and deliciously wholesome cake—which I particularly like to make for a picnic or a packed lunch.

1 small cooking apple
4 oz soft margarine (110 g)
6 oz soft brown sugar (175 g)
2 eggs, lightly beaten
4 oz wholewheat flour (110 g)
4 oz plain flour (110 g)
A pinch of salt
1¹/₂ teaspoons baking powder
4 oz walnuts, roughly chopped (110 g)
3 oz pitted dates, roughly chopped (75 g)
3 or 4 tablespoons milk

Pre-heat the oven to gas mark 4, 350°F (180°C)

A loaf tin with base measurements of 3¹/₂ × 7¹/₂ inches (8·5 × 19 cm), well buttered.

Put the margarine, sugar, eggs, flours, salt and baking powder into a large mixing bowl (sifting the flours in) then whisk them together with an electric hand-whisk until thoroughly combined. Next add the apple, peeled and cored and roughly chopped, followed by the walnuts and pitted dates. Finally add the milk, then mix it all well before transferring the mixture to the prepared tin. Spread it out evenly, then bake for 1 hour or until the loaf feels springy in the centre and a skewer inserted in the middle comes out clean.

Let the cake cool for a minute or two in the tin, then turn it out onto a wire tray. Store in an airtight tin as soon as cold.

Squidgy chocolate log

This is a cake that has no flour in it—so it's extremely light and moist. It's also a bit wicked, with its chocolate mousse and whipped cream filling!

5 oz caster sugar (150 g)
6 large eggs, separated
2 oz cocoa powder (50 g)

For the filling:
8 oz plain chocolate (225 g)
2 large eggs, separated
8 fl oz double cream (225 ml)
Icing sugar

Pre-heat the oven to gas mark 4, 350°F (180°C)

A tin 11½ × 7 inches (29 × 18 cm) and about 1 inch (2·5 cm) deep, oiled and lined with greaseproof paper (also lightly oiled).

Begin by making the chocolate filling. Break the plain chocolate in pieces into a basin and add 2 tablespoons of water. Now place the basin over a saucepan of barely simmering water and wait for the chocolate to melt. After that, remove from the heat and beat it with a wooden spoon until smooth. Next separate two large eggs and beat the yolks, first on their own, then into the warm chocolate mixture. Let it cool a bit then whisk the egg whites till stiff and fold them into the chocolate mixture. Cover the bowl and chill in the refrigerator for about an hour.

Meanwhile you can get on with the cake. First place the egg yolks in a basin and whisk until they start to thicken, then add the caster sugar and continue to whisk until the mixture thickens slightly— but be careful not to get it *too* thick. Now mix the cocoa powder into the egg yolk mixture, then, using a clean whisk and bowl, beat up the egg whites to the soft peak stage. Next carefully cut and fold the egg whites into the chocolate mixture—gently and thoroughly—then pour the mixture into the prepared tin.

Bake the cake on the centre shelf for 20–25 minutes until springy and puffy. When the cake is cooked, remove it from the oven but leave it in the cake tin to cool (it will shrink quite a bit as it cools but don't worry, that's normal).

Then when the cake is quite cold, turn it out onto an oblong of greaseproof paper which has been liberally dusted with icing sugar. Peel away the cake tin lining paper from the bottom of the cake (which is now facing upwards), then spread the chocolate mousse filling over the cake. Next whip the cream softly and spread it over the chocolate filling. Finally, gently roll up the cake to make a log shape. This will serve 8 people and, although it's unlikely that there will be any left, you can cover any remaining cake with an upturned basin and keep it in the refrigerator. As an alternative, an 11 oz tin of sweetened chestnut purée (*crème de marrons*) can replace the chocolate mousse.

Note: during the rolling up, the cake will crack, but this is quite normal and looks most attractive.

Sticky date cake

This is an example of what I call 'boil-and-bake'. There's no sugar in it, but the boiled condensed milk gives a lovely dark toffee flavour.

4 oz raisins (110 g)
8 oz chopped dates (225 g)
6 oz sultanas (175 g)
4 oz currants (110 g)
10 oz margarine (275 g)
½ pint water (275 ml)
1 large tin condensed milk
5 oz plain flour (150 g)
5 oz wholemeal flour (150 g)
¾ teaspoon bicarbonate of soda
A pinch of salt
1 generous tablespoon chunky marmalade

Pre-heat the oven to gas mark 3, 325°F (170°C)

An 8 inch (20 cm) square cake tin,
greased and lined.

Place all the fruits in a saucepan, together with the margarine,
water and condensed milk and bring to the boil. Stir frequently to
avoid sticking. Simmer the mixture for exactly 3 minutes and stir
occasionally. Now transfer the mixture to a large mixing bowl and
let it cool for approximately 30 minutes.

While it's cooling, weigh the flours and sift them into a bowl
together with the salt and bicarbonate of soda. (When sieving
wholemeal flour, you frequently find small quantities of bran left in
the sieve; these can be tipped on to the already sieved flour.)

When the fruit mixture has cooled stir into it the flour, salt and
bicarbonate of soda and add a good round tablespoon of
marmalade. Now spoon the mixture into the prepared tin and bake
the cake on the centre shelf of the oven for $2^1/2$–3 hours. This
cake does get rather brown on top if not protected. You should
therefore cover it from the beginning of the cooking with a double
square of greaseproof paper (with a hole the size of a 50p piece in the
centre).

After removing the cake from the oven let it cool in the tin for
5 minutes before turning it out onto a wire tray. This is quite a
large cake which will keep well for several weeks in an airtight tin
and, I think, even improves with keeping.

Marmalade cake   It's hard to beat the flavour of this cake,
although it looks quite ordinary when it's
cooked. It's made by the 'rubbing-in'
method, which is very easy.

8 oz self-raising flour, sifted (225 g)
4 oz caster sugar (110 g)
2 oz butter, at room temperature (50 g)
2 oz lard, at room temperature (50 g)
1 rounded tablespoon thick marmalade
Grated rind of half a large lemon
Grated rind of half a large orange
1 teaspoon mixed spice
1 teaspoon vinegar
A pinch of salt

6 fl oz milk (175 ml)
4 oz mixed dried fruit (110 g)
1 tablespoon demerara sugar

Pre-heat the oven to gas mark 4, 350°F (180°C).

A loaf tin 7¹/₂ × 3 inches (19 × 8·5 cm), greased and base lined with lightly greased greaseproof paper.

First rub the butter and lard into the flour until crumbly, then add the sugar, salt, mixed fruit, spice, lemon and orange rinds. Now stir in the milk a little at a time, add the vinegar and mix until the ingredients are well combined. Next stir in the marmalade and now the mixture should be of a good dropping consistency. (This means that when you tap a spoonful of the mixture on the side of the bowl it drops off easily.)

Now spoon the mixture into the prepared tin and spread it out evenly. Sprinkle the surface with the demerara sugar and bake for 1–1¹/₄ hours. The cake, when cooked, will have shrunk away from the side of the tin and the centre will be firm and springy to the touch. Leave the cake in its tin for 15 minutes, then turn it out onto a wire cooling rack. When cold, store in an airtight tin. I think this cake improves after a couple of days' keeping.

Traditional Dundee cake

This is a really good fruit cake for those who don't like the heavy, rich sort (see the following recipe). It does have an excellent flavour and a light crumbly texture.

5 oz butter, at room temperature (150 g)
5 oz caster sugar (150 g)
3 large eggs
8 oz plain flour, sifted (225 g)
1 teaspoon baking powder
6 oz currants (175 g)
6 oz sultanas (175 g)
2 oz glacé cherries, rinsed, dried and cut into halves (50 g)

| 2 oz mixed whole candied peel, finely chopped (50 g) |
| 2 tablespoons ground almonds |
| The grated rinds of 1 small orange and 1 small lemon |
| 2 oz whole blanched almonds (50 g) |

Pre-heat the oven to gas mark 3,
325°F (170°C)

A 7–8 inch (18–20 cm) round tin, greased
and lined with greaseproof paper.

Put the butter and sugar in a mixing bowl and beat with a wooden
spoon until light and fluffy—or an electric mixer will do this much
more quickly.

Whisk the eggs separately then, a little at a time, beat them into the
creamed butter and sugar. Next, using a large tablespoon, carefully
fold in the flour and baking powder. Your mixture needs to be of a
good, soft dropping consistency so, if it seems too dry, add a
dessertspoon of milk.

Now carefully fold in the currants, sultanas, cherries, mixed peel,
ground almonds and orange and lemon rinds. Then spoon the
mixture into the prepared cake tin, smoothing it out evenly with the
back of the spoon. Next arrange the whole almonds in circles on top
of the mixture, but do this carefully and lightly; if they are pressed in
they will sink during the baking.

Place the cake in the centre of the oven and bake for 2–2½ hours
or until the centre is firm and springy to the touch. Let it cool before
taking it out of the tin. This cake keeps very well in an airtight tin
and tastes all the better if kept for a few days before cutting.

Rich fruit cakes

My recipe is the one I always make for a 'celebration' cake. It is
more or less my mother's recipe and I have made it for Christmas,
birthdays and weddings. It is very rich and if you prefer a fruit cake
with a lighter, crumblier texture I recommend the *Traditional Dundee
cake* on the previous page.

Rich fruit cakes are best made about eight weeks before they are
needed, but if you can't manage this, it's not a disaster: they just
taste better if they mature a little.

The recipe which follows is for an 8 inch (20 cm) round cake or a 7 inch (18 cm) square one—just the right size for Christmas and I have given the directions for a simple and *quick* decoration using almond paste and royal icing.

Rich fruit cake

1 lb currants (450 g)
6 oz sultanas (175 g)
6 oz raisins (175 g)
2 oz glacé cherries, rinsed and finely chopped (50 g)
2 oz mixed peel, finely chopped (50 g)
3 tablespoons brandy
8 oz plain flour (225 g)
½ teaspoon salt
¼ teaspoon freshly grated nutmeg
½ teaspoon mixed spice
2 oz almonds, chopped (50 g)—the skins can be left on
8 oz soft brown sugar (225 g)
1 dessertspoon black treacle
8 oz unsalted butter (225 g)
4 eggs
The grated rind of 1 lemon
The grated rind of 1 orange

Pre-heat the oven to gas mark 1, 275°F (140°C)

An 8 inch (20 cm) round cake tin, or a 7 inch (18 cm) square tin, greased and lined with greaseproof paper.

The night before you make the cake, place all the dried fruit and peel in a bowl and mix in the brandy. Cover the bowl with a cloth and leave to soak for at least 12 hours.

It is quite a good idea before you measure the treacle to place the tin in the warming drawer of the oven, so that it melts a little which makes things easier.

Sieve the flour, salt and spices into a large mixing bowl, and in a separate bowl cream the butter and sugar together until the mixture's light and fluffy (this in fact is the most important part of the cake, so don't cut any corners). Next beat up the eggs and —a tablespoon at a time—add them to the creamed mixture, beating thoroughly after each addition. If it looks as if it might start to curdle, you can prevent this happening by adding a little of the flour.

When all the egg has been added, fold in the flour and spices (fold, don't beat). Now stir in the fruit and peel that has been soaking, the nuts, the treacle and the grated lemon and orange rinds.

Spoon the mixture into the prepared cake tin, and spread it out evenly with the back of a spoon. (If you are not going to ice the cake, at this stage you can arrange some whole blanched almonds over the surface—but do it lightly, or else they disappear for ever into the cake!)

Tie a band of brown paper around the outside of the tin, and cover the top of the cake with a double square of greaseproof paper (with a hole in the middle approximately the size of a 50p). Bake the cake on the lower shelf of the oven for $4^{1}/_{2}$–$4^{3}/_{4}$ hours, and don't open the door to peek at it until at least 4 hours have passed. When the cake is cold, wrap it well in double greaseproof paper and store in an airtight tin. I like to 'feed' it at odd intervals with brandy during the storage time. To do this, strip off the lining papers, make a few extra holes in the top with a thin darning needle and pour a few teaspoons of brandy in to soak into the cake. Repeat this at intervals for a week or two.

Christmas cake   For a basic and uncomplicated icing, I've chosen a layer of almond paste topped with a semi-rough royal icing, decorated with almond paste flowers (in this case poinsettias). Ideally the cake should be almond iced at least seven days before the royal icing is put on—to give it a chance to dry out. Otherwise the almond oil may seep through and discolour the royal icing. The thick 'snowy' icing in this recipe, however, should keep the oil at bay even if you (like me) find that sometimes you still have the cake decorating to do on Christmas Eve!

An 8 inch (20 cm) round cake or a 7 inch (18 cm) square cake, made from the rich fruit cake recipe, page 607

For the almond paste:[*]

1 lb ground almonds (450 g)

8 oz caster sugar (225 g)

8 oz icing sugar (225 g)

2 eggs

2 egg yolks—reserve the whites for the royal icing (see below)

½ teaspoon almond essence

1 teaspoon brandy

1 teaspoon lemon juice

Red, green and yellow food colouring

[*] Part of this is used to ice the cake, the rest is used to model the flower decorations

---

For the royal icing:

4 egg whites—combine three but keep one separate

Approximately 1 lb 2 oz sifted icing sugar (500 g)

1 teaspoon glycerine

To make the almond paste, begin by sieving the two sugars into a large bowl and stirring in the eggs and egg yolks. Put the bowl over a pan of barely simmering water and whisk for about 12 minutes until the mixture is thick and fluffy. Then remove the bowl from the heat and sit the base in a couple of inches of cold water.

Next whisk in the essence, brandy and lemon juice and carry on whisking until the mixture is cool. Stir in the ground almonds and knead to form a firm paste. Weigh out 6 oz (175 g) of the paste and reserve this (in a bowl covered with clingfilm) for makng the flower decoration.

Divide the rest of the paste in half and roll out one piece into a shape approximately 1 inch (2·5 cm) larger than the top of the cake (your working surface should be kept dusted with some sifted icing sugar so that the paste doesn't stick to it). Brush the top of the cake with egg white, then invert the cake to sit centrally on the almond paste and with a palette knife press the paste up around the edge of the cake. Now turn the cake the right way up and brush the sides with egg white.

Roll out the other half of the paste into a rectangle and trim it so that it measures half the circumference of the cake by twice the height of the cake (use a piece of string to measure this). Now cut the paste rectangle in half lengthwise, and lightly press the two strips onto the sides of the cake. Smooth over the joins with a knife, and leave the cake covered with a cloth to dry out.

To make the almond paste poinsettias, take out the paste reserved for decoration. Now using a skewer (so as not to overdo it) colour yellow a small piece about the size of a walnut. Divide the remaining paste in half, colouring one half of it green, the other red. Using the drawings on the left as a guide, cut out templates in stiff paper or card. Roll out both colours of paste to about $1/8$ inch (3 mm) thick, then with the aid of the templates cut out 6 red leaves and 6 green. Trace a suggestion of veins on the surface with the back of the knife. Let the leaves dry, face upwards over a rolling pin. Model the yellow paste into some small pea-sized balls and leave everything to dry overnight.

To make the royal icing, place the three egg whites in a grease-free bowl. Then stir in the icing sugar, a spoonful at a time, until the icing falls thickly from the spoon. At that point, stop adding any more sugar and whisk with an electric mixer for 10 minutes or until the icing stands up in stiff peaks, then stir in the glycerine. Now spoon half the icing into a screw-top jar and put aside in the fridge. Beat about 2 teaspoons more egg white into the remaining half of the icing.

Next use a dab of icing to fix the cake to a 10 inch (25·5 cm) cakeboard, then spread about two-thirds of the remainder on top of the cake. Work the icing back and forth to get rid of any tiny air bubbles, then take a clean plastic ruler and holding it at each end, glide it once over the surface of the cake to give a smooth finish.

Hold the ruler vertically and remove any surplus icing from the top edges of the cake, then spread the remaining icing onto the sides of the cake. Keeping your ruler vertical, turn the cake round in one sweep to smooth the sides—a turntable is ideal for this, but two plates set base to base will also do the job. Now leave the cake for 24 hours for the icing to dry.

To finish off: mark the centre of the cake with a 3¼ inch (8 cm) plain circular cutter, then taking your reserve icing from the screw-top jar, spread it thickly outside the marked circle. Use a broad-bladed knife to 'spike' the icing into snow-like peaks. At the edge, bring the peaks over and down to give the effect of hanging snowy icicles (see the drawing below). Lastly lay the green almond paste leaves in the centre of the cake, then the red leaves on top of them. Place the small yellow 'berries' in the centre, fixing them in place with a little icing. Set the whole effect off with red ribbon, tied in a bow around the cake.

Quantities and cooking times for other sizes of cake

The size of your cake will obviously depend on the number of people you need to cater for. You may need more than one tier for a very special occasion such as a wedding. As a guide, I estimate that the 8 inch (20 cm) cake on page 607 would be sufficient for between 25 and 40 people. The easiest way for me to give you the ingredients and cooking times for the different sizes of cake is in a chart. The method in all cases is the same as on pages 607–8.

	6 inch (15 cm)	9 inch (23 cm)	11 inch (28 cm)
Currants	8 oz (225 g)	1 lb 4 oz (560 g)	2 lb (900 g)
Sultanas	3 oz (75 g)	8 oz (225 g)	12 oz (350 g)
Raisins	3 oz (75 g)	8 oz (225 g)	12 oz (350 g)
Glacé cherries, rinsed and finely chopped	1$^{1}/_{2}$ oz (40 g)	2$^{1}/_{2}$ oz (60 g)	4 oz (110 g)
Mixed peel, finely chopped	1$^{1}/_{2}$ oz (40 g)	2$^{1}/_{2}$ oz (60 g)	4 oz (110 g)
Brandy	3 tablespoons	4 tablespoons	6 tablespoons
Plain flour	4 oz (110 g)	10 oz (275 g)	1 lb (450 g)
Salt	Pinch	$^{1}/_{2}$ teaspoon	$^{1}/_{2}$ teaspoon
Freshly-grated nutmeg	$^{1}/_{4}$ teaspoon	$^{1}/_{2}$ teaspoon	$^{1}/_{2}$ teaspoon
Mixed spice	$^{1}/_{4}$ teaspoon	$^{3}/_{4}$ teaspoon	1 teaspoon
Almonds, chopped	1$^{1}/_{2}$ oz (40 g)	2$^{1}/_{2}$ oz (60 g)	4 oz (110 g)
Soft brown sugar	4 oz (110 g)	10 oz (275 g)	1 lb (450 g)
Black treacle	1 teaspoon (rounded)	1 tablespoon	2 dessertspoons
Unsalted butter	4 oz (110 g)	10 oz (275 g)	1 lb (450 g)
Eggs	2	5	8
Grated lemon rind	$^{1}/_{2}$ lemon	1 large lemon	2 lemons
Grated orange rind	$^{1}/_{2}$ orange	1 large orange	2 oranges
Cooking times (approximate)	3$^{1}/_{2}$ hours	4$^{3}/_{4}$ hours	5$^{1}/_{2}$ hours

Almond paste for different sizes of cake

The ingredients below differ slightly from my quick almond paste on page 609, and to fix this paste to the cake I use apricot jam instead of egg white. In this case, I think it is essential to let the almond-iced cake dry for at least a week before applying any royal icing, especially if the iced cake is going to be kept a while before being eaten. If you are going to ice it and eat it very soon afterwards, 2 days' drying will be enough.

	6 inch (15 cm)	9 inch (23 cm)	11 inch (28 cm)
Ground almonds	8 oz (225 g)	1 lb (450 g)	1 lb 8 oz (675 g)
Icing sugar, sifted	4 oz (110 g)	8 oz (225 g)	12 oz (350 g)
Caster sugar	4 oz (110 g)	8 oz (225 g)	12 oz (350 g)
Almond essence	2 drops	1/2 teaspoon	1 teaspoon
Lemon juice	1/2 teaspoon	1 teaspoon	2 teaspoons
Sherry	1 dessertspoon	1–2 tablespoons	2–3 tablespoons
Egg yolks	3	5	8
Apricot jam (warmed)			

Mix all the dry ingredients together first, then stir in the almond essence, sherry, lemon juice and egg yolks and combine everything to form a stiff paste. Transfer the paste to a pastryboard (dusted with icing sugar) and knead it into a ball. Try not to handle it *too* much—the heat of your hands might make it oily. Warm the apricot jam and brush it over the top and sides of the cake. Now take about half the paste and roll it out to a shape approximately 1 inch (2·5 cm) larger than the top of the cake. Then invert the cake on the paste shape and trim around the edges if you need to.

Next roll out the rest of the paste into an oblong which is half the circumference and twice the height of the cake (use some string or a tape measure to get these measurements), then cut the oblong in half lengthwise. Roll up one strip. Lightly place one end against the side of the cake and unroll the paste, pressing firmly to the cake as you go. Repeat with the other strip to complete the sides of the cake and press the joins together. Turn the cake the right way up, even the surfaces with a rolling pin and store in a double sheet of greaseproof paper for at least a week before applying royal icing.

Royal icing for different sizes of cake

If your cake is in tiers, then in order to support the weight of one tier on top of another, you are going to need *three* layers of this hard-set icing. If it is only one tier, then a single thick layer with the quantities below will be all right (you can also add 2–3 teaspoons of glycerine to give a softer texture, if preferred). The cake boards for a tiered cake in each case need to be 2–3 inches wider than the width of the cake itself. Useful items of equipment would be a turntable, palette knife and plastic icing scraper.

	6 inch (15 cm)	9 inch (23 cm)	11 inch (28 cm)
Icing sugar	1 lb (450 g)	1 1/2 lb (700 g)	2 lb (900 g)
Egg whites	2–3	4	6

Place the egg whites in your largest bowl (and make sure it is grease-free), then stir in the sifted icing sugar, two spoonfuls at a time. When it is all stirred in, take an electric mixer and whisk at top speed for about 10 minutes, by which time the icing should be standing up in peaks at least 2 inches (5 cm) high. As soon as you reach this stage, cover the bowl with a damp cloth to prevent the icing drying out.

Use a little icing to stick the cake to the board, then place the board on the turntable and give the cake one coat of icing—using one-third of the quantity. Ice the top of the cake first, and then the sides with the aid of a palette knife. Get the sides smooth with a plastic scraper, and the top with a palette knife dipped into hot water and shaken. Smooth the icing right up to the edge of the board too. Store the rest of the icing in a plastic container, and leave the cake to dry overnight. Then give it the second and third coats, leaving each coat to dry overnight.

Decoration
Even for a special occasion cake, I find the simpler the design the better, keeping piping to an absolute minimum and using roses made from modelling paste. These roses can be tinted in various colours and offset by golden or silver paper leaves. Finish off with satin ribbon tied around the cake or around each tier.

Modelling paste

2 oz lard (50 g)
2 tablespoons lemon juice
1½ lb sifted icing sugar (700 g)
Food colouring (according to your design)

Heat the lard and lemon juice with 2 tablespoons of water until the fat melts. Then stir in ½ lb (225 g) of the icing sugar, and cook over a very low heat until the sugar dissolves and turns a semi-opaque colour (about 2 minutes). Then remove the pan from the heat and stir in the rest of the sugar which will eventually give you a mixture the consistency of dough.

Turn it out onto a working surface dusted with sugar, knead for a few seconds, then divide it in half and work in whatever colours you have chosen. Add the colour with a skewer in *small* drops until you arrive at the right shade. The paste should be stored in a plastic bag, and when you're ready, roll out the paste and cut out some small, circular shapes the size of a 10p piece, and some slightly smaller than 5p pieces. Make up the roses as in the drawings on the left, curving the circular pieces around and pinching them gently into shape. Leave them to dry on a tray overnight.

Arrange the roses how you like, with some gold or silver paper leaves here and there, sticking them on to the cake with small amounts of icing. To neaten the edges of the cake at the base and top, you could pipe a tiny row of beads (using an icing bag fitted with a large, plain no. 1 nozzle). Finally tie bands of ribbon in place around the cake or around each of the tiers.

See also:

All-in-one banana and walnut loaf
American brownies
Black Forest gateau
Chocolate and hazelnut choux buns
Coffee eclairs
Cream puffs
Curd cheesecake with fruit topping

Eccles cakes
Fresh lemon cheesecake with
*   frosted grapes*
Honey and spice cake
Linzertorte
Orange cheesecake
Richmond maids of honour
Strawberry shortcake

Scones and biscuits

Including recipes for:
Plain scones
Wholewheat fruit scones
Wholewheat cheese-crusted scones
Wholewheat girdle cakes
Crumpets
Shortbread biscuits
Scottish shortbread
Strawberry shortcake
Wholewheat shortbread
Whole oat crunchies
Oatmeal biscuits
American brownies
Gingernuts
Cheese savouries

In the days when households had such things as 'baking' days, bread and cakes would be baked in batches to last a week or even longer. The kitchen range was brought up to heat and kept topped up all day, and not an inch of space or minute of fuel time was wasted. Girdle cakes or crumpets used the heat on the top of the stove, scones fitted in alongside the bread, and biscuits were dried out at the end of the day as the heat died down in the range. The results, I'm sure, must have been enough to feed an army.

Nowadays few of us have the time or inclination to bake on such an organised scale, and inevitably the main casualties have been those items which form the subject of this chapter. We have come to rely very largely on bakeries and supermarkets for our scones and biscuits, but we are paying very dearly for this convenience (as a quick comparison between the weight and prices of almost any packet of biscuits will confirm). Yet this branch of baking is the easiest of all, using ingredients that most people keep regularly in their store-cupboard. I hope the recipes in this section will inspire you to re-discover some of the pleasures of 'batch' baking, and save lots of money at the same time!

Scones

The modern scone seems to have evolved from something rather similar to the girdle cake (see recipe page 621): it was only when raising agents were introduced to flour that scones began to be oven-baked and well-risen as we know them today. And that straightaway brings me to one of the most persistent queries I get from readers: why don't their scones ever rise to a proper height?

Now some problems are difficult to answer specifically, particularly when you can't see what people are doing wrong. But on the subject of scones I can nearly always put them right by suggesting that perhaps they are rolling the dough out too thinly—the major cause of failure. The dough for a perfect scone whould never be rolled out to anything less than 3/4 inch (2 cm). And there's another minor cause for concern which can be tracked down to the rolling too—that's scones which emerge uneven in shape. This is caused by uneven pressure on the rolling pin, which tends to make the dough (and therefore the scones) slanted. Hardly a disaster, in fact it can be quite appealing by giving them that home-made air in contrast to the clinical perfection of the shop-bought variety!

Plain scones

(makes about 12)

Eat these with butter, home-made jam and, if you can get it, clotted cream.

8 oz self-raising flour (225 g)
1½ oz butter (or margarine) at room temperature (40 g)
¼ pint milk (150 ml)
1½ tablespoons caster sugar
A pinch of salt
A little extra flour

Pre-heat the oven to gas mark 7, 425°F (220°C)

A baking sheet, greased.

First of all, sift the flour into a bowl and rub the butter into it rapidly, using your fingertips. Next stir in the sugar and salt, then take a knife and use it to mix in the milk little by little. Now flour your hands a little and knead the mixture to a soft dough—adding a drop more milk if it feels at all dry.

Then turn the dough out onto a floured pastry board and roll it out to a thickness of not less than ¾ inch (2 cm) using a lightly floured rolling pin. Take a 1½ or 2 inch (4 or 5 cm) pastry cutter (either fluted or plain) and place it on the dough, then tap it sharply so that it goes straight through the dough— don't twist it or the scones will turn out a peculiar shape! After you have cut out as many scone shapes as you can like that, knead the dough trimmings together again and repeat until you have used it all.

Then place the scones on the greased baking sheet, dust each one with a little extra flour and bake near the top of the oven for 12–15 minutes. When cooked the scones will have turned a crisp golden brown. Cool on a wire rack and eat them slightly warm, still crisp on the outside and soft and light inside. In fact, always eat scones as fresh as possible as they can go stale very quickly.

Wholewheat fruit scones

(makes 7 or 8)

It took several tests and a few brick-like results before I got the right combination of ingredients for these, and I think it is most important to have the oven really hot before you bake them in order to raise them properly.

3 oz wholewheat flour (75 g)
3 oz self-raising flour (75 g)
1 teaspoon baking powder
½ teaspoon ground cinnamon
1 oz soft brown sugar (25 g)
1 oz butter or margarine at room temperature (25 g)
1½ oz mixed dried fruit (40 g)
1 large egg
2–2½ tablespoons milk
Extra milk and wholewheat flour

Pre-heat the oven to gas mark 8,
450°F (230°C)

A baking sheet, well-greased.

In a mixing bowl sift the flours and combine with the bran left in the sieve, baking powder, cinnamon and sugar. Then rub in the fat and mix in the dried fruit. Now beat the egg with 2 tablespoons of milk and add this, mixing it to a smooth dough using a palette knife. If you need to, add a spot more milk.

Next roll out the dough to ¾ inch (2 cm) thick and, using a 2¼ inch (6 cm) cutter cut out the scones. Place them on the baking sheet, brush the tops with milk and dust them with wholewheat flour. Bake on a high shelf in the oven for 15–20 minutes. Cool on a wire tray and serve warm, spread with butter.

Wholewheat cheese-crusted scones

(makes 6 to 8)

If you can't think of anything for a quick snack lunch or late supper, these are quick to make and quite irresistible served warm and spread with butter.

3 oz wholewheat flour (75 g)
3 oz self-raising flour (75 g)
1 oz butter (room temperature) (25 g)
1 teaspoon baking powder
2–3 tablespoons milk
3 oz finely grated strong Cheddar cheese (75 g)
1 large egg
½ teaspoon salt

| ½ teaspoon mustard powder |
| 2 good pinches cayenne pepper |
| A little extra milk |

Pre-heat the oven to gas mark 7,
425°F (220°C)

A baking sheet, well-greased.

First sift the flours into a mixing bowl, add the bran remaining in
the sieve, the mustard powder, salt and one good pinch of cayenne
pepper. Mix them together well, then rub in the butter—using your
fingertips—until the mixture is all crumbly. Now mix in most of the
grated cheese, leaving about 1 tablespoon.

Next, in a small bowl, beat the egg together with 2 tablespoons of
milk. Add this to the mixing bowl to make a soft dough—what you
are after is a smooth dough that will leave the bowl clean, so add just
a few more drops of milk if it is too dry.

Now roll out the dough on a floured surface to a thickness of about
¾ inch (2 cm) and use a 2¼ inch cutter (6 cm) to cut out
the scones. Place the scones on the baking sheet, brush the tops with
milk, then sprinkle the remaining grated cheese over the top of each
scone, with a faint dusting of cayenne. Bake on a high shelf for
15–20 minutes, cool them slightly on a wire tray, and serve warm.

Wholewheat girdle cakes

(makes about 25)

Unlike oven-baked scones, girdle cakes
are cut quite thin and cooked on top of
the stove. Traditionally cooked on a
heavy iron girdle, we can now make them
in a thick-based, heavy frying pan
(though iron girdles are still available at
good kitchen shops).

| 4 oz wholewheat flour (110 g) |
| 4 oz self-raising flour (110 g) |
| 1 teaspoon baking powder |
| 3 oz mixed dried fruit (75 g) |
| 3 oz caster sugar (75 g) |
| 1 large egg |
| ½ teaspoon mixed spice |
| 4 oz butter or margarine, at room temperature (110 g) |

Begin by sifting the dry ingredients (except the fruit) together into a mixing bowl, add any bran remaining in the sieve then rub in the butter until the mixture becomes crumbly. Then add the fruit and mix it in thoroughly. Next beat the egg lightly, add it to the mixture, and mix to a dough (if it seems to be a little too dry, you can add a spot of milk).

Transfer the dough onto a lighly floured surface and roll out to a thickness of about $1/4$ inch (5 mm). Then, using a $2^1/2$ inch (6·5 cm) plain cutter, cut the dough into rounds—re-rolling and cutting the trimmings until you have used all the dough.

Now lightly grease your pan and heat it over a medium heat, then cook the girdle cakes, a few at a time, for about three minutes on each side. If they look as if they are browning too quickly, turn the heat down because they must be cooked all through and still be fairly brown and crisp on the outside. Serve warm with lots of butter and perhaps some home-make jam.

Crumpets
(makes about 12)

Although you can buy quite good crumpets, I do think they're fun to make—especially on a cold snowy day when everyone's housebound. Once upon a time you could buy special crumpet rings, but egg cooking rings will do equally well provided you grease them really thoroughly.

8 oz strong plain flour (225 g)
1 teaspoon salt
1 tablespoon dried yeast
1 teaspoon caster sugar
$1/2$ pint milk (275 ml)
2 fl oz water (55 ml)

A thick-based frying-pan, some egg cooking rings, and a little lard.

First of all heat the milk and water together in a small saucepan till they are hand-hot. Then pour into a jug, stir in the sugar and dried yeast and leave it in a warm place for 10–15 minutes till there is a good frothy head on it.

Meanwhile sift the flour and salt into a mixing bowl, make a well in the centre and, when the yeast mixture is frothy, pour it all in. Next use a wooden spoon to work the flour into the liquid gradually, and beat well at the end to make a perfectly smooth batter. Cover the basin with a tea-towel and leave to stand in a warm place for about 45 minutes—by which time the batter will have become light and frothy.

Then to cook the crumpets: grease the insides of the egg rings well, and grease the frying-pan as well before placing it over a medium heat. Arrange the rings in the frying-pan, and when the pan is hot spoon one tablespoon of the crumpet batter into each ring. Let them cook for 4 or 5 minutes: first tiny bubbles will appear on the surface and then, suddenly, they will burst leaving the traditional holes. Now take a spoon and fork, lift off the rings and turn the crumpets over. Cook the crumpets on the second side for about 1 minute only. Re-grease and reheat the rings and the pan before cooking the next batch of crumpets.

Serve crumpets while still warm, generously buttered. If you are making crumpets in advance then reheat them by toasting lightly on both sides before serving.

Biscuits

The origins of the biscuit are described in the word itself. 'Twice-cooked' it means in French, and that goes back to the days when bakers were in the habit of putting slices of newly-baked bread back into the cooking oven, so that they dried out completely. The result was something like a rusk, and was used as ships' biscuits for long voyages.

For a long time housewives continued to dry their biscuits with a second baking: the practice only died out at the beginning of the last century, but when it did the quality and variety of biscuits improved no end. There's almost no limit to the kind of biscuit that can be easily baked at home today. Here are some favourites using a range of basic biscuit ingredients.

Shortbreads

One thing that distinguishes the several 'rules' about making shortbread that have been handed down is their conflicting advice. Thus one old Scottish cookbook of mine suggests that it should be 'browned to taste': a more modern one recommends no colouring at all on the surface. There is a consensus that butter—and only butter—should be used: yet I have a friend who makes hers with margarine and I have to admit that it tastes very good.

For my part I would say that shortbread mixture should *not* be overcooked: it ought to be a pale golden colour and not golden brown. And I certainly think that the mixture shouldn't be over-worked, because the heat in your hands can turn the fat oily. To overcome this the method I now use involves beating the fat with a wooden spoon to soften it, then gradually working it into the other ingredients. This way it is only handled at the end. When it is mixed, you can then either just pat and spread the dough straight into a prepared tin, or else roll out the dough and cut the biscuits out. Some say the latter method makes the shortbread tough because it involves extra handling, but I've not found this.

Shortbread biscuits

(makes about 15)

6 oz plain flour (175 g)
4 oz butter or margarine, at room temperature (110 g)
2 oz caster sugar (50 g)
Extra caster sugar for dusting

Pre-heat the oven to gas mark 2, 300°F (150°C)

A baking sheet, lightly greased.

Begin by first beating the butter with a wooden spoon to a soft consistency, then beat in first the sugar and then the sifted flour. Still using the wooden spoon, start to bring the mixture together, then finish off with your hands to form a paste. Now transfer this to a board lightly dusted with caster sugar, then quickly and lightly roll it out to about ⅛ inch (3 mm) thick (dusting the rolling pin with sugar if necessary). Use a 3 inch (7·5 cm) fluted cutter to cut the biscuits out, then arrange them on the baking sheet and bake on a highish shelf in the oven for 30 minutes. Cool the biscuits on a wire rack, dust them with some caster sugar, and store in an airtight tin to keep them crisp.

Scottish shortbread

(makes 12 wedges)

This shortbread is made in one piece in a tin, then cut into wedges after baking. The addition of fine semolina gives it a crunchier texture.

6 oz plain flour (175 g)
6 oz butter or margarine, at room temperature (175 g)
3 oz caster sugar (75 g)
3 oz fine semolina (75 g)

Pre-heat the oven to gas mark 2, 300°F (150°C)

An 8 inch (20 cm) fluted flan tin with a loose base.

First of all beat the butter in a bowl with a wooden spoon to soften it, then beat in the sugar followed by the sifted flour and the semolina. Work the ingredients together with the spoon, pressing them to the side of the bowl, then finish off with your hands till you have a dough that doesn't leave any bits in the bowl.

Next transfer the dough to a flat surface and roll it out lightly to a round (giving it quarter turns as you roll), then transfer the round to the tin. Lightly press the mixture evenly into the tin, right into the fluted edges (to make sure it's even you can give it a final roll with a small glass tumbler). Now you *must* prick the shortbread all over with a fork or it will rise up in the centre while it's baking.

Bake the shortbread for about 1 hour on the centre shelf, then using a palette knife mark out the surface into 12 wedges while it's still warm. Leave it to cool in the tin, then remove the rim of the tin, cut the shortbread into wedges and store in an airtight tin.

For *Strawberry shortcake* In the summer a round of shortbread made as above and left whole can be spread with whipped cream, and topped with strawberries just before serving. This makes a really delicious pud for a summer dinner party, or tea in the garden.

Wholewheat shortbread

(makes 12 wedges)

This is similar to the previous recipe, but I've used half wholewheat flour for more of a wheaty flavour, and ground rice in place of semolina for crunchiness.

3 oz wholewheat flour (75 g)
3 oz plain flour (75 g)
2 oz ground rice (50 g)
2 oz caster sugar (50 g)

| **6 oz butter or margarine, at room temperature (175 g)** |
| **A little extra sugar** |

Pre-heat the oven to gas mark 2, 300°F (150°C)

An 8 inch (20 cm) fluted flan tin with a removable base, lightly greased.

Start by beating the butter in a bowl with a wooden spoon to soften it, then beat in the sugar followed by the flours and ground rice. Work it together as much as you can with the wooden spoon, then finish off with your hands lightly and quickly. Now roll out the dough to approximately an 8 inch (20 cm) round, giving it quarter turns as you roll. Transfer it to the tin and press it evenly into the edges. If it seems uneven on top, just roll lightly over the surface with a glass tumbler.

Now prick the dough all over to prevent it rising, then bake it for 80 minutes on a high shelf. Remove the shortbread from the oven and cut it into 12 portions while it's still warm. Then cool it in the tin, remove the portions and store them in an airtight tin.

Oat biscuits
Oats have long been used in Scotland and the north of England for biscuit-making: they give a lovely crunch to the biscuit as well as a characteristic nutty flavour. Prepared oats come in a variety of forms, all of them suitable for baking.

Oatmeal This means that the oats have been milled, in the same way as wheat is milled into flour. Oatmeal comes in different grades, most commonly as *fine* or *medium* (either of which can be added to bread dough or used for biscuits—see oatmeal biscuit recipe below) or *coarse* which is often used for porridge.

Oat flakes These are also known as *rolled oats* and are the husked grains which have been rolled mechanically into flakes. Very good for porridge and biscuits.

Whole oats Also referred to as *jumbo oats*, these are flakes as well, but large and coarse. They also have more of a nutty flavour and are excellent for biscuits.

Quick cooking oats These so-called 'instant oats' have been treated in some way and are not really suitable for baking.

Whole oat crunchies

(makes 12)

These are the quickest and easiest biscuits I've ever made: they have a nice crunchy, toffee taste. If you can get hold of jumbo oats from a health food shop so much the better, otherwise all ordinary porridge oat flakes will do.

2 oz whole (jumbo) oats (50 g)
2½ oz porridge oats (70 g)
4 oz margarine (110 g)
3 oz demerara sugar (75 g)

Pre-heat the oven to gas mark 5, 375°F (190°C)

A shallow baking tin measuring 11 × 7 inches (28 × 18 cm), well greased.

First weigh out the oats and sugar, place them in a bowl and mix them together as evenly as possible. Then gently melt the margarine in a saucepan—only just melt it, be careful not to let it brown. Next pour the melted margarine into the bowl with the oats and sugar and mix until everything is well and truly blended.

Now all you have to do is to tip the mixture into the prepared tin and to press it out evenly all over using your hands.

Bake on the centre shelf of the oven for 15 minutes or until it's a nice pale gold colour. Then remove the tin from the oven and cut the mixture into 12 portions while it's still warm. Leave it in the tin until cold and crisp before storing the biscuits in an airtight tin.

Oatmeal biscuits

(makes 24)

I think it's really nice to be able to offer home-made biscuits with cheese and these are lovely with some Stilton or strong Cheddar and crisp celery.

6 oz wholewheat flour (175 g)
2 oz medium oatmeal (50 g)
4 oz butter or margarine, at room temperature (110 g)
4 teaspoons soft brown sugar
1 teaspoon baking powder
½ teaspoon salt

| ¼ teaspoon hot curry powder |
| About 1 tablespoon milk, for binding |

Pre-heat the oven to gas mark 4,
350°F (180°C)

A baking sheet, lightly greased.

Simply combine all the ingredients (except the milk) together in a
bowl, then rub the fat evenly into the ingredients and add just
enough milk to give you a slightly wetter dough than you would
require normally (say, for shortcrust pastry)—since this pastry is
prone to breaking, a little extra moisture is deliberately used to help
to hold it together.

Next, turn the dough out onto a floured working surface and roll out
to about ⅛ inch (3 mm) thick. Use a 2¾ inch (7 cm) cutter
to cut out the biscuit rounds—re-rolling the trimmings and adding
a drop of milk if the dough happens to become a little dry.

Place the biscuits on the baking sheet and bake them for 15–20
minutes until firm and lightly browned. Leave them to cool on the
baking sheet for 5 minutes before transferring them to a wire rack to
cool. Store in an airtight tin.

American brownies

(makes 15 squares)

These are squidgy, nutty chocolate
bars—delicious if you want to be really
self-indulgent once in a while.

| 2 oz American unsweetened chocolate (available at specialised food shops) or plain dessert chocolate (50 g) |
| 4 oz butter (110 g) |
| 2 eggs, beaten |
| 8 oz granulated sugar (225 g) |
| 2 oz plain flour, sifted (50 g) |
| 1 teaspoon baking powder |
| ¼ teaspoon salt |
| 4 oz chopped nuts—these can be walnuts, almonds, hazelnuts or Brazils or a mixture (110 g) |

Pre-heat the oven to gas mark 4,
350°F (180°C)

An oblong tin measuring 7 × 11 inches
(18 × 28 cm) well-greased and lined with
greaseproof paper. Bring the paper up a
good 2 inches (5 cm) above the rim of
the tin.

First of all melt the butter and the chocolate (broken up into small
pieces) together in the top of a double saucepan (or else place in a
basin fitted over simmering water on a very low heat). Away from
the heat, stir all the other ingredients into the butter and chocolate
mixture thoroughly, then spread all this in the lined tin.

Bake in the oven for 30 minutes, or until a knife inserted in the
centre comes out cleanly (but don't overcook—it will firm up as it
cools). Then leave the mixture in the tin to cool for 10 minutes
before dividing into approximately 15 squares and transferring
them to a wire rack to finish cooling.

Gingernuts
(makes 16)

These are, like most biscuits, extremely
simple to make at home and you'll
wonder why you ever bought them!

4 oz self-raising flour (110 g)
1 slightly rounded teaspoon ground ginger
1 teaspoon bicarbonate of soda
1½ oz granulated sugar (40 g)
2 oz margarine (50 g)
2 oz (or 2 tablespoons) golden syrup (50 g)

Pre-heat the oven to gas mark 5,
375°F (190°C)

One large (or two small) baking sheets,
lightly greased.

Begin by sifting the flour, ginger and bicarbonate of soda into a
mixing bowl, add the sugar, then lightly rub in the margarine until
the mixture is crumbly. Next add the syrup and mix everything
together to form a stiff paste.

Now divide the mixture into sixteen pieces about the same size as
each other, and roll each piece into a little ball. Place them on the
baking sheet(s), leaving plenty of room between them because
they spread out quite a bit while they're cooking. Then simply

flatten each ball slightly with the back of a spoon and bake just above the centre of the oven for 10–15 minutes, by which time they will have spread out and cracked rather attractively. Cool on the baking sheet(s) for 10 minutes then transfer to a wire rack to finish cooling, and store in an airtight tin.

Cheese savouries

(makes about 30)

I like to make batches of these, cut out quite small, to serve with drinks at a party. They can be sprinkled with different toppings to vary the flavours.

2 oz wholewheat flour (50 g)
2 oz grated Cheddar cheese (50 g)
2 oz grated Cheshire cheese (50 g)
2 oz butter, at room temperature (50 g)
¼ teaspoon salt
1 pinch cayenne pepper
1 twist ground black pepper

Optional toppings: **garlic salt, celery salt, mild curry powder, or cayenne pepper**

Pre-heat the oven to gas mark 5, 375°F (190°C)

A baking sheet, lightly greased.

First of all sift the flour and salt into a mixing bowl, and add the cayenne and black pepper. Next add the two cheeses along with the butter and rub the mixture to the crumbly stage, then bring the mixture together—it shouldn't need any liquid, but if it does add just a drop of milk.

Now roll out the dough to a thickness of about ⅛ inch (3 mm) then use a 1 or 1½ inch (2·5 or 4 cm) cutter to cut out the biscuits. Arrange them fairly close together on the baking sheet, sprinkle the selected topping (if any) on them, then bake on a high shelf in the oven for 10–12 minutes, before removing to a wire rack to cool and crisp. Store them in an airtight tin.

See also:
Scone pizza

Fruits and puddings

Including recipes for:
Summer pudding
Pavlova
Strawberries in raspberry purée
Cardinal peaches
Fresh fruit salad
Dried fruit jelly
Apricot hazelnut meringue
Traditional trifle
Rich chocolate mousse
Chocolate orange mousse
Cold chocolate orange soufflé
Caramelised apple flan
Baked apple and almond pudding
Spiced apple and raisin crumble
Rhubarb and ginger crumble
Gooseberry crumble
Damson and cinnamon crumble
Dried fruit crumble
Blackcurrant crumble
Raspberry crumble
Steamed raisin pudding
Christmas pudding
St Stephen's pudding
Apple and orange crunch
Chocolate and walnut pudding
Lemon surprise pudding
Wholewheat treacle sponge
Spiced fig pudding with rum butter
Eliza Acton's rich rice pudding
Cider baked apples with toasted muesli
Queen of puddings
Rich bread and butter pudding
Hot chocolate rum soufflé
Traditional apple charlotte

If this chapter seems at variance with my continuing war on sugar consumption, let me say I am all in favour of delicious puddings and sweet dishes—but *not* too often. I happen neither to eat sweets and confectionery nor drink soft drinks, but I do think a really mouth-watering cake or pudding is something to be enjoyed on all feast days and holidays. Very often sweet recipes contain what I would consider an excessive amount of sugar, but even in this chapter you won't find anything with low calories or artificial sweeteners (or any other type of slimmers' aid). Let's first consider some of the ingredients that will be used for cold puddings.

Gelatine Cold mousses, soufflés and jellies need flavourless gelatine to get them to set. One detail worth paying close attention to is to make sure your gelatine has dissolved properly: failure to do so is perhaps the commonest cause of problems.

There are two kinds of gelatine. One (not very widely available) is transparent leaf gelatine. The other is powdered gelatine, which comes in packets of ½ oz (10 g) each. This amount of powdered gelatine is usually enough to stiffen 1 pint (570 ml) of liquid (or use three sheets of gelatine per pint).

The best way to dissolve gelatine is to sprinkle it into a cup or small basin containing 3–4 tablespoons of some hot or cold liquid. Stir it, and when the gelatine has soaked up the liquid place the cup in a pan of barely simmering water and leave until it has dissolved completely and turned transparent. To test this, dip a teaspoon in, turn it over and you'll soon see if there are any undissolved granules. It's important not to let the liquid boil—so keep the heat under the pan gentle, and before you use it pass the gelatine through a strainer, to extract any bits of skin that may have formed. Another tip (that appears on the back of some packets) is that you should sprinkle the gelatine granules onto the liquid, and not the other way round.

Cream Only double cream (or whipping cream) is suitable for whipping. Take care, though, because over-whisking can cause the cream to take on a curdled appearance, so that it won't fold into anything nor go through a piping bag. So if you have to fold cream into anything, beat it only to the thickened 'floppy' stage. For piping it has to be stiffer: beat it until stiff peaks are left when you lift the whisk from the cream (but again, don't overdo it).

Chocolate Buy eating chocolate rather than cooking chocolate: it looks and tastes better. Melting chocolate can be a tricky affair.

Overheating, or leaving it near the heat too long, makes it granular, when other ingredients are added, and the chocolate loses all its gloss. But if you deal with it carefully you'll never have any problems. Just break the chocolate up into small squares, place them in a basin fitted over a pan of barely simmering water (if it's boiling too fast turn the heat out, so that you just have very hot water), and the chocolate will soon start to melt round the edge. Then stir it with a wooden spoon, and in 3–5 minutes it will all have melted and become smoothly liquid.

Summer pudding

(serves 6 people)

Maybe the reason why this pudding is such a favourite is because we only have these particular fruits for a short time each year—anyway in our house it's become a sort of annual event.

1 lb raspberries (450 g)
8 oz redcurrants (225 g)
4 oz blackcurrants (110 g)
5 oz caster sugar (150 g)
7–8 medium slices white bread from a large loaf

A 1½ pint (850 ml) pudding basin, lightly buttered.

Separate the redcurrants and blackcurrants from their stalks by holding the tip of each stalk firmly between finger and thumb and sliding it between the prongs of a fork—pushing the fork downwards, so pulling off the berries as it goes. Rinse all the fruits, picking out any raspberries that look at all musty.

Place the fruits with the sugar in a large saucepan over a medium heat and let them cook for about 3–5 minutes, only until the sugar has melted and the juices begin to run—don't overcook and so spoil the fresh flavour. Now remove the fruit from the heat, and line a 1½ pint (850 ml) pudding basin with the slices of bread, overlapping them and sealing well by pressing the edges together. Fill in any gaps with small pieces of bread, so that no juice can get through when you add the fruit.

Pour the fruit in (except for a cupful of juice), and cover the pudding with another slice of bread. Then place a small plate or saucer (one that will fit exactly inside the rim of the bowl) on top, and on top of that place a 3 lb or 4 lb (1·4 kg or 1·8 kg) weight, and leave in the refrigerator overnight.

Just before serving the pudding, turn it out on to a large serving dish and spoon the reserved juice all over, to soak any bits of bread that still look white. Serve cut into slices, with a bowl of thick cream on the table.

Pavlova
(serves 6 people)

This is a delicious pudding from New Zealand, which is very difficult to make if you don't have the right recipe but dead easy if you do!

3 large fresh egg whites
6 oz caster sugar (175 g)
½ pint whipped cream (275 ml)
12 oz soft fruits (350 g)—raspberries, strawberries and redcurrants mixed
A little icing sugar

Pre-heat the oven to gas mark 2, 300°F (150°C)

A lightly-oiled baking sheet, lined with greaseproof paper (which should also be oiled lightly) or silicone paper, which peels off very easily.

Place the egg whites in a large clean bowl and have the sugar measured and ready. Now whisk the egg whites until they form soft peaks and you can turn the bowl upside down without them sliding out (it's very important, though, not to over-beat the eggs because, if you do, they will start to collapse).

When they're ready, start to whisk in the sugar, approximately 1 oz (25 g) at a time, whisking after each addition until all the sugar is in. Now take a metal tablespoon and spoon the meringue mixture onto the prepared baking sheet, forming a circle about 8 inches (20 cm) in diameter. Make a round depression in the centre and, using the tip of a skewer, make little swirls in the meringue all round the edge, lifting the skewer up sharply each time to leave tiny peaks.

Now place the baking sheet in the oven, then immediately turn down the heat to gas mark 1, 275°F (140°C) and leave it to cook for 1 hour. Then turn the heat right off but *leave* the Pavlova inside the oven until it's completely cold. I always find it's best to make a Pavlova in the evening and leave it in the turned-off oven overnight to dry out. It's my belief that the secret of successful meringues of any sort is to let them dry out completely, which is what this method does perfectly.

To serve the Pavlova, lift it from the baking sheet, peel off the paper and place it on a serving dish. Then just before serving, spread the whipped cream on top, arrange the strawberries, etc., on top of the cream and dust with a little sifted icing sugar. Serve cut into wedges.

Note: of course, this can be made with just one kind of fruit—for instance strawberries. In the winter, when there are no soft fruits available, sliced bananas and chopped preserved ginger make a nice alternative filling.

Strawberries in raspberry purée

(serves 4–6 people)

This is one of the simplest and most delicious sweet dishes I know and proves it's not always necessary to spend hours in the kitchen to make something spectacular.

1 lb firm strawberries (450 g)
8 oz raspberries (225 g)
2½ oz sieved icing sugar (60 g)
3 or 4 macaroon biscuits, crushed
5 fl oz double cream (150 ml), whipped

Hull the strawberries, but don't wash them—just gently wipe them with a piece of damp kitchen paper. The raspberries should then be pressed to a pulp through a nylon sieve, and mixed with the icing sugar. Now arrange the strawberries in a bowl (a glass one would show off the attractive colour of this dish), and sit the bowl on some ice-cubes which you have arranged in the bottom of another bowl.

Mix the raspberry purée into the strawberries, then just before serving top with the whipped cream and sprinkle all over with the crushed macaroons.

Cardinal peaches

(serves 6 people)

These look and taste stunning served in stemmed glass dishes—a really fresh and fragrant way to end a meal.

6 large, ripe peaches
1½ tablespoons caster sugar
2–3 oz icing sugar (50–75 g)
1 vanilla pod
12 oz fresh raspberries (350 g)
1 tablespoon flaked almonds

First wash the peaches and place them, whole and unpeeled, in a large saucepan. Pour in just enough water to cover them, add the caster sugar and the vanilla pod, bring it up to simmering point, then put a lid on and simmer gently for about 10 minutes. Then drain the peaches, and when they're cold slip the skins off.

Meanwhile sprinkle the raspberries with icing sugar and leave them for 20 minutes. Then press them through a nylon sieve to make a purée. Now place the peaches in a bowl and pour the raspberry purée over. Cover with clingfilm and chill thoroughly for several hours. To serve them, place on one large serving dish or in six individual dishes and sprinkle with flaked almonds.

Fresh fruit salad

(serves 8 people)

Any fresh fruit salad may be varied according to whatever fruits are in season but this one seems to have just the right balance. If you don't have rum—or don't like it—you can replace it with fresh orange juice.

1 pineapple
2 bananas
2 Cox's apples
2 Comice pears
2 oranges
8 oz black grapes (225 g)

For the syrup:
4 oz caster sugar (110 g)
½ pint water (275 ml)

| The juice of 1 lemon |
| 6 tablespoons rum |

Begin by making the syrup. To do this, place the sugar and water in a small pan, and let the sugar dissolve over a gentle heat. Then bring to the boil and simmer for a minute, remove from the heat and add the lemon juice, then tip into a serving bowl to cool. When cold, add the rum.

Now prepare the fruits: peel the oranges and divide into segments, then add all the segments to the syrup in the bowl, and toss well. Rinse and drain the grapes, then cut each one in half and remove the pips before adding to the syrup. Slice the top off the pineapple and cut away the sides and the base: then slice the pineapple across and cut the slices into segments, and add to the syrup. The apples and pears need to be cored but leave the peel on, and slice directly into the syrup. Leave the bananas to last—they discolour the quickest—and slice straight into the bowl. When all the fruit is in, toss everything well, cover the bowl with clingfilm and chill in the fridge before serving.

Dried fruit jelly
(serves 6 people)

This is cool and light and is good after a rich meal. It goes beautifully served with home-made natural yoghurt.

| 4 oz dried prunes (110 g) |
| 4 oz dried apricots (110 g) |
| 1 strip of orange peel |
| Juice of 1 orange |
| 1 small piece cinnamon stick |
| 2 oz sugar (50 g) |
| 1 level tablespoon powdered gelatine |

Start this off the night before by putting the dried prunes and apricots to soak in a pint (570 ml) of cold water. Then, when you are ready to make the jelly, pour the fruits (and the water they were soaked in) into a saucepan, adding the sugar, cinnamon and orange peel, and simmer gently for 20 minutes. Next fit a sieve over a bowl, pour the fruits into it and let them drain thoroughly. Then pour the liquid into a measuring jug, and add the orange juice and enough water to make it up to a pint (570 ml). At this stage taste to check there's enough sugar.

Now put 3 tablespoons of the liquid into a small bowl, sprinkle in the gelatine and, when it has absorbed all the liquid, fit the bowl over a saucepan of barely simmering water. Stir now and then, and when the gelatine has dissolved and become transparent, strain it back into the rest of the mixture, mixing it in thoroughly.

Take the stones out of the prunes and chop all the flesh of the fruits roughly and arrange in the base of a 2 pint (1·25 litre) mould. Pour the gelatine mixture over the fruit and leave in a cool place to set.

Apricot hazelnut meringue

(serves 6 people)

A light and delicious—and rather special—sweet. You can buy ready-ground hazelnuts at wholefood shops and delicatessens, or if you're grinding your own, brown them first in the oven (gas mark 4, 350°F (180°C) and grind them in a food processor or liquidiser.

3 large egg whites
6 oz caster sugar (175 g)
3 oz ground hazelnuts (75 g)
½ pint double cream (275 ml)
A few whole toasted hazelnuts

For the filling:
4 oz dried apricots, soaked overnight (110 g)
The juice of 1 small orange
A small strip of orange peel
½ inch cinnamon stick (1 cm)
2 teaspoons arrowroot
1 tablespoon brown sugar

Pre-heat the oven to gas mark 5, 375°F (190°C)

Two 7 inch (18 cm) sandwich tins, lightly oiled and the base lined with silicone or greaseproof paper, also lightly oiled.

First whisk the egg whites in a bowl until they form stiff peaks, then whisk in the caster sugar, a little at a time. Then, using a metal spoon, lightly fold in the ground hazelnuts. Now divide the mixture equally between the two tins and level them out. Bake the meringues on the centre shelf of the oven for 20–30 minutes. Leave them in the tins to cool for 30 minutes before turning out (the surface will look uneven, but don't worry). When they've cooled, loosen round the edges, turn them out onto wire racks and strip off the base papers.

While the meringues are cooking, you can prepare the apricot filling. Drain the soaked apricots in a sieve over a bowl, then transfer the apricots to a small saucepan and add the orange juice, peel, cinnamon and sugar plus 2 tablespoons of the soaking water. Simmer gently for 10–15 minutes until they are tender when tested with a skewer, then remove the cinnamon stick and orange peel. Mix the arrowroot with a little cold water and add this to the apricot mixture, stirring over a fairly low heat, until the mixture has thickened. Then leave it to get quite cold.

To serve the meringue: whip the cream, then carefully spread the cold apricot mixture over one meringue, followed by half the whipped cream. Place the other meringue on top, spread the remaining cream over that and decorate the top with some whole toasted hazelnuts.

Traditional trifle

(serves 6–8 people)

This is a real trifle made with proper custard—a bit extravagant but well worth it.

3 egg yolks
1 pint double cream (570 ml)
1 oz caster sugar (25 g)
1 level teaspoon cornflour
5 trifle sponge cakes
2 oz flaked almonds, lightly toasted (50 g)
Some raspberry jam
2 fl oz sherry (55 ml)
8 oz frozen raspberries (225 g)—no need to defrost
2 small bananas, peeled and sliced thinly

Break the sponge cakes in pieces and spread a little raspberry jam on each piece. Then put them into a large glass bowl and sprinkle the raspberries and sherry over them, giving everything a good stir to soak up the sherry.

To make the custard, heat ¹/₂ pint (275 ml) of the double cream in a small saucepan. Blend the egg yolks, sugar and cornflour together thoroughly in a basin, and when the cream is hot, pour it over the egg mixture stirring the whole time. Now return the custard to the saucepan and stir over a very low heat until thick, then remove it and allow it to cool. Slice the bananas, sprinkle them in amongst the raspberries and pour the custard over the sponge cakes. Whip up the remaining ¹/₂ pint (275 ml) of cream and spread it over the top. Decorate with the flaked almonds. Cover and chill for 3 or 4 hours before serving.

Rich chocolate mousse

(serves 2 people)

This one is definitely amongst my top ten favourite puds. It can be made for any number of people if you remember to use 1 egg and 2 oz (50 g) of chocolate per person.

4 oz plain dessert chocolate (110 g)
2 eggs, separated
1 tablespoon rum (or brandy)
2 heaped teaspoons whipped cream
Grated chocolate and/or chopped, toasted nuts

2 stemmed wine glasses or ramekins.

Melt the chocolate as described on page 632. When it is smooth and liquid, remove it from the heat. Beat the egg yolks and add them to the chocolate while it's still hot, beating thoroughly (this cooks the egg yolks slightly).

Now leave the mixture to cool for about 15 minutes. Then beat up the egg whites—not too stiffly, just to the soft peak stage—then fold them into the chocolate mixture. Next spoon the mixture into the glasses, cover each one with foil or clingfilm and chill until firm (about 2 hours).

When you're ready to serve, make a few holes in the top of each mousse (using a small skewer or darning needle) and spoon some rum or brandy over the surface to soak in. Then top with a blob of whipped cream and some grated chocolate or chopped nuts. This mousse is very nice served with *langue de chat* biscuits.

Note: for a *Chocolate orange mousse* add the grated zest and the juice of half an orange to a 4 oz (110 g) quantity of chocolate at the melting stage.

Cold chocolate orange soufflé

(serves 4—6 people)

I have a weakness for anything 'chocolatey' and this is one of my most favourite chocolate puddings.

7 oz plain chocolate (200 g)
3 whole eggs
2 eggs separated
3 oz caster sugar (75 g)
Grated zest and juice of 1 large orange
2 fl oz water (55 ml)
½ oz powdered gelatine (10 g)
3 fl oz double cream (75 ml), lightly beaten until floppy but not thick

For the decoration:
5 fl oz double cream, whipped (150 ml)
1 tablespoon grated chocolate

Start off by soaking the gelatine in the orange juice in an old cup, then place it in a pan of barely simmering water until it has dissolved and become completely transparent.

While that is happening, place the 2 egg yolks, 3 whole eggs and the sugar in a largish mixing bowl and place this over another pan of barely simmering water. Now, using an electric hand or rotary whisk, whisk until the mixture has become thick and creamy which should be in approximately 10 minutes. Then remove the mixing bowl from the heat and place another bowl over the hot water and break the chocolate into it, add the water and stir until the chocolate has melted and become a smooth liquid. Remove it from the heat, stir in the grated orange zest, and leave it to cool for about 15 minutes. Now stir and fold the chocolate mixture into the egg mixture along with the gelatine, which should be put through a strainer.

Now whisk the egg whites—not too stiffly, just to the soft peak stage—and fold them into the mixture gently and carefully. Finally, fold in the whipped cream.

Next pour the mixture into a straight-sided 2 pint (1 litre) soufflé dish, cover and chill for several hours. Serve decorated with blobs— or piped rosettes—of cream and sprinkle with a little grated chocolate.

Caramelised apple flan

(serves 4–6 people)

This is from a French recipe called 'Tarte Tatin'–it's baked, chilled and then served upside down.

1 lb cooking or dessert apples, peeled, cored and thinly sliced (450 g)
4 oz soft dark brown sugar (110 g)
1 teaspoon ground cinnamon
Shortcrust pastry, made with 4 oz plain flour (110 g) and 2 oz butter (50 g)
1 tablespoon melted butter (for greasing)

Pre-heat the oven to gas mark 4, 350°F (180°C)

An 8 inch (20 cm) sponge tin with no rim and straight sides, brushed with the melted butter, with a circle of greaseproof paper, also brushed with melted butter, covering the base.

Begin by covering the base of the prepared tin with brown sugar, pressing it down evenly and well. Now sprinkle on the ground cinnamon, and then arrange the sliced apples neatly, making sure they're pressed well down.

Roll out the pastry to a thickness of approximately ½ inch (1 cm) and cut out a circle that will fit the top of the tin. Cover the apples with the pastry, pressing it down gently. Place in the centre of the oven for 40 minutes until the pastry is golden.

When the tart is quite cold, loosen it round the edges, cover with a plate and carefully turn it all upside down, then remove the tin and the greaseproof paper. Serve with or without cream.

Hot puddings

If there is a gap in the repertoire of Haute Cuisine then it is surely in the area of what I'd call 'proper puddings'. You'd have thought it would have taken a really exotic dish to get a Frenchman beside himself with admiration for the cooking of any other country but his own: yet at the end of the 17th century M. de Valbourg, a French traveller in England, wrote this:

Ah! What an excellent thing is an English pudding! It is manna that hits the palate of all sorts of people, better than that of the wilderness.

But our puddings didn't stop there: throughout the 18th century and into Victorian times the British pudding was unsurpassed. George I (Pudding George—hence the nursery rhyme about Georgy-Porgy) was particularly partial to the boiled variety, and later Prince Albert became a champion of our puddings. Up at the Palace the royal chefs were very busy creating new temptations for the royal palate: Queen's pudding, Windsor pudding, Empress pudding, Albert pudding. If he had lived 150 years later how much more ecstatically would that nice Frenchman have written 'To come at pudding time is to come in the most lucky moment in the world!'

Nowadays of course he'd be hard pushed to find a traditional pudding on a restaurant menu. It has become a casualty of affluence and our national preoccupation with dieting and calorie-counting. However, our memories are not so easily dimmed as one might imagine, and people's eyes often light up at the mention of something steamy, curranty or syrupy. It would seem to me the height of irony if our figure-conscious generation should be the one that lets the traditional pudding die of neglect—even as it continues to push up the sales of confectionery, bars of chocolate, synthetic packaged desserts and artificial ice-creams.

Baked apple and almond pudding

(serves 4–6 people)

1 lb cooking apples, peeled and sliced (450 g)	
2 oz soft brown sugar (50 g)	
4 oz ground almonds (110 g)	
4 oz butter at room temperature (110 g)	
4 oz caster sugar (110 g)	
2 large eggs, beaten	

Pre-heat the oven to gas mark 4,
350°F (180°C)

A buttered pie dish approximately
1¹/₂ pint (850 ml) capacity.

Place the apples in a saucepan with the brown sugar and
approximately 1 tablespoon water, simmer gently until soft, and
then arrange them in the bottom of the prepared pie dish.

In a mixing bowl, cream the butter and caster sugar until pale and
fluffy and then beat in the eggs a little at a time. When all the egg is
in, carefully and lightly fold in the ground almonds. Now spread
this mixture over the apples, evening out the surface with the back
of a tablespoon. Then bake on a 'highish' shelf in the oven for
exactly 1 hour.

This pudding is equally good served warm or cold—either way it's
nice with some chilled pouring cream. It will keep in the refrigerator
for 3 or 4 days.

Fruit crumbles
Crumbles are a good all-round family sweet dish, which can be
varied not just by using fruits in season, but also by ringing the
changes with the crumble topping. Whatever problems you may
have with your pastry-making technique, you're absolutely safe
with a crumble because there is no resting or roll-out involved.

Basic
crumble topping

(serves 6 people)

8 oz plain flour (225 g) or—and I prefer it—wholewheat flour
5 oz soft brown sugar (150 g)
3 oz butter at room temperature (75 g)
1 level teaspoon baking powder

Pre-heat the oven to gas mark 4,
350°F (180°C)

Place the flour in a large mixing bowl, sprinkle in the baking
powder, then add the butter and rub it into the flour lightly, using
your fingertips. Then when it all looks crumbly, and the fat has been
dispersed fairly evenly, add the sugar and combine that well with
the rest.

*Right: Steamed raisin pudding, page 652; Cider baked apples with toasted muesli,
page 659.*

Now sprinkle the crumble mixture all over the fruit in a pie dish, spreading it out with a fork. Place the crumble on a high shelf in the oven and bake it for 30–40 minutes or until the top is tinged with brown.

Variations on the crumble topping
1 Instead of all flour use 4 oz wholewheat flour (110 g) and 4 oz jumbo or porridge oats (110 g).
2 Instead of all flour, use 4 oz wholewheat flour (110 g) and 4 oz muesli (110 g).
3 For a nut crumble topping, use 6 oz (175 g) wholewheat flour and 3 oz chopped nuts (75 g). You will need to use only 3 oz of soft brown sugar (75 g) with the 3 oz of butter (75 g).

Spiced apple and raisin crumble

(serves 6 people)

2 lb Bramley apples, peeled and sliced (900 g)
1 oz soft brown sugar (25 g)
¼ teaspoon ground cloves
1 level teaspoon ground cinnamon
3 oz raisins (75 g)
2 tablespoons water

Pre-heat the oven to gas mark 4, 350°F (180°C)

A 3 pint (1·75 litre) pie dish.

Place the sliced apples, raisins, sugar and spices in a saucepan, sprinkle with the water, then cook gently until the apples are soft and fluffy. Spoon the mixture into the pie-dish and sprinkle with any of the crumble toppings above. Use a fork to even it out, but don't press it down at all. Cook for 30–40 minutes until the topping is tinged with brown.

Alternative crumble fillings
All the recipes that follow are cooked at the same temperature as the *Spiced apple and raisin crumble* recipe above and are all cooked in the same size dish (3 pint or 1·75 litre). They all serve 6 people also.

Left: Rich chocolate mousse, page 640; Cardinal peaches, page 636; Blackcurrant ice cream, page 531.

Rhubarb and ginger crumble

Use 2 lb rhubarb (900 g), 3 oz soft brown sugar (75 g) and 1 level teaspoon powdered ginger.

Cut the rhubarb into chunks, then place in a saucepan together with the sugar and ginger. Cook over a gentle heat (covered) for 15 minutes, stirring to get the uncooked pieces at the top down into the heat. Try not to overcook it, though—it should be chunky, not mushy. When it's cooked, drain off about half the juice, then transfer the fruit to a pie-dish, sprinkle with a crumble topping (page 647), and bake for 30–40 minutes.

Gooseberry crumble

Use 2 lb gooseberries (900 g) and 6 oz caster sugar (175 g).

Just top and tail the gooseberries, place them in the dish, and sprinkle in the caster sugar. Top straightaway with one of the crumble mixtures (page 647), and bake on the centre shelf of the oven for 40–45 minutes.

Damson (or plum) and cinnamon crumble

Use 2 lb damsons or plums (900 g), 4 oz demerara sugar (110 g) and 1 teaspoon powdered cinnamon.

Wash the damsons or plums, then place them whole in the pie-dish. Sprinkle them with the sugar and cinnamon, then spread with the crumble topping (page 646). I think the nut crumble mixture is the nicest for this. Bake for 30–40 minutes until the topping is tinged with brown. *Note:* plums should be stoned and halved, but damson stones are easier left for the diners to extract!

Dried fruit crumble

For this you can use any combination of dried fruits: prunes, apricots, figs, raisins etc. You need 1 lb mixed dried fruits (450 g), the zest and juice of 1 large orange and 2 oz demerara sugar (50 g). Soak the fruit overnight in a deep bowl, covered with about 1¼ pints (720 ml) of water. Next day drain off ¼ pint of the water, then place the rest of the water, the fruit and the sugar in a saucepan, bring to simmering point and simmer for 10 minutes or until the fruit is tender. Then stir in the orange juice and zest, pour the whole lot into the pie dish and top with the basic or the oat crumble (see page 647), and bake for 30–40 minutes.

Blackcurrant crumble

1 lb fresh blackcurrants (450 g)
2 tablespoons caster sugar

(serves 4–6 people)

Pre-heat the oven to gas mark 4, 350°F (180°C)

I think this particular crumble is nicest baked in a shallow 9 inch (23 cm) baking dish (or something similar). Strip the blackcurrants from their stalks, arrange them in the tin, sprinkle with the sugar, top with your choice of crumble (see page 647), and bake for 30–40 minutes.

Raspberry crumble
This is made in the same way as the blackcurrant crumble, but with 1 instead of 2 tablespoons of caster sugar sprinkled over.

Steamed puddings

A steamed pudding is far easier to make and serve than most people seem to think. The mixing makes little demand on your time, needs no particular skill, and once the pudding is on the stove it requires very little attention. Extra steaming does no harm at all: so if you want to serve it an hour later than planned, say, it will be just as good.

Steamer Not a very costly piece of equipment but, I think, an essential one. Over the years it will earn its keep, even if it's only

for making your own Christmas puddings. Modern steamers are made to fit most sizes of saucepan. Because the pudding cooks only in the steam that rises from the water boiling in the saucepan underneath, there's no danger here of the water itself bubbling in to swamp the pudding. Filled three-quarters full, the water should not need topping up for most steaming recipes— but if it does look like getting a bit low, always top up with boiling water. I should add that one of the beauties of steaming is, if you possess more than one steamer (I find I need four at Christmas!), you can steam two puddings over one pan of water—change the position of the steamers over at half-time.

An alternative form of steaming, if you don't have a steamer, is to sit the pudding basin on a small upturned plate or perhaps a wad of crumpled foil inside a saucepan (so it can sit above the water-line). The saucepan is then filled with boiling water but *only* up to a third of its capacity. There are snags: if the heat is too high, the water can boil up too fiercely and into the pudding—and it is liable to boil away rather quicker than with a steamer. The answer is to keep a vigilant eye on it.

Lids Whether you are using a steamer or a saucepan, it is essential to have a well-fitting lid, to prevent the steam escaping and water drying up completely. Inevitably *some* steam will escape, but it won't be a problem if your lid fits properly.

Coverings Old-fashioned boiled puddings were sometimes made directly inside pudding-cloths. Nowadays china pudding-basins are much more convenient, and whereas once even these would be covered with greaseproof paper and linen cloth, today modern foil does the job on its own. The basin should be covered with double foil for extra strength, and this should be pleated in the centre (to allow room for expansion when the pudding is cooking). Before placing the foil over the basin, butter the side that will come into contact with the pudding—to prevent it sticking—then tie the foil all around the edge of the basin as tightly as you can with string. And if you can make a little handle with the string at the same time, it will make it easier to lift the basin out of the saucepan at the end.

Pressure-cooking puddings

A pressure-cooker is ideal for steaming puddings, as it cuts the steaming time considerably. If you own one, the manufacturer's instruction booklet will explain the general principles. But first a couple of important points.

The preparation of the pudding is the same as for ordinary steaming, and the basins are covered and tied down in a similar way. Place the trivet inside the pressure-cooker, add $1\frac{1}{2}$ pints (800 ml) of water and bring this up to simmering point. Then lower the pudding in, to stand on the trivet, and put the lid on but leave the vent open—so that the pudding gets 15 minutes' gentle steaming before the pressure is brought up (keep the heat very low for this, to prevent too much steam escaping, thus reducing the correct water level inside). Then after 15 minutes, start the pressure at low (5 lb) and give the pudding 35 minutes if the ordinary steaming time was 1½–2 hours, or 60 minutes if the ordinary steaming time was 2–3 hours.

Some notes on hot pudding ingredients

Flour Self-raising flour must be used in all suet and sponge recipes. Plain flour plus baking-powder can be used, but self-raising is preferable because it already contains just the right balance of raising agent. Where an all-in-one sponge method is used an extra amount of raising agent is needed.

Fats I find packet shredded suet is actually better, as well as more convenient, for suet puddings than butcher's suet because it is shredded to exactly the right size and is competely free of skin and membrane.

Dried fruits One tip I can pass on when buying dried fruit, and that is always buy it in cellophone packets or else loose. The important thing is to be able to *see* what your're buying. Those enclosed cardboard packets only too often carry last season's dried fruit with a very dry and musty look to it.

Pudding spices The mixed ground spices used in puddings can go stale and lose their strength if they're stored too long. So buy them in small quantities, and better discard any you have had for as long as a year. Nutmeg really should be *freshly grated* at all times: once ground its fragrance vanishes extremely quickly.

Candied peel The same tendency is to be found with this. Buy your candied peel whole and you'll find it has a great deal more flavour than the ready-cut peel (and only cut the peel as and when you need it). It will keep almost indefinitely in a screw-top jar, so it is worth buying in a stock of it when it's readily available at Christmas time. If at other times it is not to be found at your local shops or supermarket, you will probably be able to get some at a specialised food shop or health food store.

Chocolate can be tricky to work with if not handled carefully. As I mentioned before use 'proper' chocolate rather than 'cooking' chocolate and follow the instructions on page 632.

Steamed raisin pudding

(serves 4 people)

This is a very special steamed pudding, suitable for a dinner party. Don't worry about the absence of sugar—the raisins provide enough sweetness.

2 oz brown breadcrumbs (50 g)
2 oz self-raising flour (50 g)
4 oz shredded suet (110 g)
8 oz prepared stoned raisins (225 g)
1/8 teaspoon salt
1/2 nutmeg, grated
1/2 teaspoon ground ginger
1/8 teaspoon ground mace
1 oz whole candied peel (25 g), finely chopped
The grated zest of an orange
3 eggs
3 tablespoons brandy

You will need a 1½ pint (845 ml) pudding-basin well buttered.

In a large bowl mix together the breadcrumbs, flour and suet. Add the raisins, making sure there are none stuck together. When these ingredients are well mixed, add the salt, nutmeg, mace, ginger, candied peel and orange zest and again mix thoroughly.

Now in a small basin beat the eggs well and add them and the brandy to the mixture and stir for at least 5 minutes to amalgamate everything thoroughly and evenly. Pack the pudding basin with the mixture, cover with greaseproof paper and foil, and tie down with string. Steam for 4 hours, making sure that the saucepan doesn't boil dry. When ready to serve, loosen the pudding all round the sides with a palette knife and turn out onto a heated dish. Serve with *Port wine sauce* on page 449.

Christmas pudding

For 2 puddings in 2 pint (1 litre) basins, or 4 in 1 pint (570 ml) basins.

This has proved to be one of the most popular recipes I've ever produced and, if you're making it for the first time, I hope you'll agree.

8 oz shredded suet (225 g)
1 heaped teaspoon mixed spice
½ teaspoon grated nutmeg
¼ teaspoon ground cinnamon
4 oz self-raising flour (110 g)
1 lb soft brown sugar (450 g)
8 oz white breadcrumbs (225 g), grated from a stale loaf
8 oz sultanas (225 g)
8 oz raisins (225 g)
1¼ lb currants (560 g)
2 oz almonds (50 g), blanched, skinned and chopped
2 oz mixed peel (50 g), finely chopped whole candied and citron peel (if available)
The grated rind of 1 orange and 1 lemon
1 apple, peeled, cored and finely chopped
4 standard eggs
5 fl oz barley wine (150 ml)
5 fl oz stout (150 ml)
4 tablespoons rum

Put the suet, flour, breadcrumbs, spices and sugar in a bowl, mixing in each ingredient thoroughly before adding the next. Then gradually mix in all the fruit, peel and nuts and follow these with the apple and the orange and lemon peel.

In a different bowl beat up the eggs, and mix the rum, barley wine and stout into them. Empty all this over the dry ingredients—and then stir very hard indeed (it's vital this mixing, so recruit some help if necessary). You may find you need a bit more stout—it's not possible to be exact with the liquid quantities, but the mixture should be of a good dropping consistency (that is, it should fall from the spoon when tapped sharply against the side of the bowl).

After the mixing, cover the bowl with a cloth and leave it overnight. The next day, grease 2 (or 4) pudding basins and pack the mixture into them right to the top. Cover each basin with a square of greaseproof paper, with a square pudding-cloth on top. Tie these round the rims of the bowls with string, then tie the corners of the cloth together on top.

Steam the puddings for 8 hours—keeping an eye on the water now and then to make sure it doesn't boil away. When cooked and

cooled, remove the paper and cloths and replace with a fresh lot.
Store in a cool dry place and, when ready to eat, steam for 2 hours.

St Stephen's pudding

(serves 4–6 people)

This pudding was sent to me by a
television viewer in East Anglia and is a
very good alternative pudding for those
who prefer a less rich pudding for
Christmas.

4 oz breadcrumbs (110 g)
2 oz self-raising flour (50 g), sifted
2 oz soft brown sugar (50 g)
3 oz suet (75 g)
Pinch of salt
4 oz seedless raisins (110 g)
2 medium-sized cooking apples
Grated rind of 1 lemon
1 egg
3 tablespoons milk

A 2 pint (1 litre) pudding-basin, well
greased.

In a large mixing bowl first combine all the dry ingredients, then
add the raisins, the apples (peeled and then grated) and the grated
lemon rind. Stir thoroughly to combine everything well. Now beat
the egg into the milk and stir the whole lot into the mixture.

Pack the mixture into the pudding-basin, cover the basin tightly
with a sheet of greaseproof paper, then with a sheet of foil, and
secure with string. Steam the pudding for 2 hours. Serve with *Proper
custard sauce* (page 447) or with *Brandy butter* (page 452).

Apple and orange crunch

(serves 4 people)

I like this crunchy pudding served with
Proper custard sauce (page 447) or, failing
that, a thick pouring cream.

Approximately 12 thinnish slices of bread from a small brown or white loaf

4 oz butter (110 g)
1 small orange **(half the rind and all the juice)**
3 oz demerara sugar (75 g)
3 medium cooking apples, peeled and sliced **thinly**

Pre-heat the oven to gas mark 4, 350°F (180°C)

A 1½ pint (845 ml) baking dish.

Melt the butter in a saucepan over a low heat. Cut the crusts off the bread slices, and spread 6 or 7 on both sides with melted butter, using a pastry brush. Place them in a well buttered baking dish, covering the base and sides as a lining. Press them down firmly, then sprinkle in a layer of sliced apple, a little grated rind and juice, and a layer of sugar. Carry on like this until all the apple is used, but keep back a tablespoon of sugar. Bush melted butter on the other slices and press them on top. Sprinkle on the remaining sugar and add any melted butter left.

Bake the pudding for 45 minutes or until the top is crisp, golden and crunchy and the apples inside are soft.

Chocolate and walnut pudding

(serves 4 people)

This is a pudding popular with children, as when it's cooked it's surrounded with its own pool of chocolate sauce.

2 oz caster sugar (50 g)
1 oz cocoa powder (25 g)
½ teaspoon ground cinnamon
2 oz fine semolina (50 g)
1 teaspoon baking powder
1 oz butter (25 g) melted
¼ teaspoon vanilla essence
2 eggs, beaten
1 oz walnuts (25 g), finely chopped
½ pint hand-hot water (275 ml)
3 oz dark brown sugar (75 g)
½ oz plus 2 teaspoons cocoa powder **(10 g plus 2 teaspoons)**

Pre-heat the oven to gas mark 4, 350°F (180°C)

A 1³/₄ pint (1 litre) deep, oval baking dish, buttered.

Start by sifting the first 5 ingredients into a mixing bowl and, in a separate bowl, whisk together the melted butter, eggs and vanilla essence. Then stir this into the dry ingredients together with the chopped walnuts and pour this mixture into the buttered baking dish.

Now mix together the brown sugar and cocoa powder and, with a fork, gradually whisk in the hot water, then pour this all over the pudding (you may think this sounds unusual, but it's correct).

Place the pudding in the pre-heated oven and bake for 30 minutes or until the pudding has risen and is firm in the middle. Before serving sprinkle the top with some icing sugar.

Lemon surprise pudding

(serves 4 people)

In this pudding the 'surprise' is that after it is cooked you'll find that underneath the light sponge topping there's a delicious pool of lemony sauce.

2 eggs, separated
2 oz butter (50 g)
4 oz caster sugar (110 g)
2 large lemons (the rind and juice)
2 oz self-raising flour (50 g), sifted
¼ pint milk (150 ml)

Pre-heat the oven to gas mark 4, 350°F (180°C)

1¹/₂ pint (845 ml) buttered deep baking dish.

First beat the butter, sugar and lemon rind together until well softened (it won't go light and fluffy because there's more sugar than butter). Then beat in the egg yolks, a little at a time. Next fold in the flour, alternately with the milk and lemon juice. Finally whisk the egg whites and fold them in as well (the mixture will look a bit curdled at this stage, but that's normal). Pour the mixture

into the baking dish and bake in the centre of the oven for 40–45
minutes or until golden-brown. It's usual to serve this pudding hot
from the oven, but as a matter of fact it's just as nice served cold.

Wholewheat treacle sponge
(serves 4 people)

This is much lighter than it actually
sounds and it's lovely served on a cold
day with extra warmed syrup poured
over.

4 oz wholewheat flour (110 g)
2 tablespoons golden syrup
2½ teaspoons baking powder
2 large eggs
4 oz soft brown sugar (110 g)
4 oz soft margarine (110 g)

You'll need a 1½ pint (845 ml)
basin, well buttered.

Begin by putting the golden syrup in the base of the pudding basin.

Next place all the remaining ingredients in a bowl and beat well for
2 or 3 minutes until thoroughly mixed. Now spoon this mixture on
top of the golden syrup and, using the back of the spoon, spread it
out evenly. Cover this with a double piece of buttered foil, pleated in
the middle (to allow for expansion) and press down over the rim of
the basin and tie round with string. Cut off any extra foil about an
inch from the string.

Place in a steamer over boiling water and steam for 1½ hours.
Make sure that the saucepan does not boil dry or the water go off the
boil and, when necessary, use *boiling water* to top up. When cooked,
turn onto a warmed plate and serve hot with custard or extra syrup.

Note: If using a pressure cooker the cooking time will be 20 minutes
steaming and 45 minutes at 5 lb pressure.

Spiced fig pudding with rum butter
(serves 6 people)

8 oz dates (225 g), stoned and chopped
6 oz dried figs (175 g), chopped
3 oz raisins (75 g)
2 oz preserved ginger (50 g), chopped
6 oz fresh white breadcrumbs (175 g)

4 oz shredded suet (110 g)
2 oz self-raising flour (50 g)
2 tablespoons brandy
2 large eggs
Grated rind and juice of an orange
½ teaspoon mixed spice
Generous quantity freshly-grated nutmeg

You'll need a generously buttered
1½ pint (845 ml) pudding basin.

Place the measured flour, breadcrumbs and suet in a mixing bowl.
Add the fruits, spices and the orange peel and mix together very
thoroughly.

Next beat the eggs with the brandy and orange juice and add this to
the mixture, stirring well to make sure all the ingredients are
thoroughly mixed, then pack the mixture into the basin. Cover with
a double piece of buttered foil, pleated in the middle, and tie it under
the rim of the basin with string. Steam the pudding over boiling
water for 4 hours.

This is delicious served with some ice-cold rum butter made as
follows: Take 4 oz (110 g) unsalted butter and into it gradually beat
4 oz (110 g) dark brown sugar until you have a pale cream mixture.
Then beat in—a little at a time—2–3 tablespoons of rum and chill
the butter for several hours.

Eliza Acton's rich rice pudding

(serves 4 people)

Tinned rice pudding might be
convenient, but it bears no resemblance
to the proper kind, which always has a
dark caramelised skin on top, covering
just the right amount of creaminess and
stickiness inside.

4 oz short-grain rice (110 g)
1½ pints milk (845 ml)
2 oz butter (50 g)
3 oz caster sugar (75 g)
3 eggs
Grated rind of half a lemon
Whole nutmeg

Pre-heat the oven to gas mark 2, 300°F (150°C)

For this you'll need a 2 pint (1 litre) baking dish, well buttered.

First put the rice into a saucepan, add the milk and bring it slowly almost to simmering point, then let it cook very gently until the rice is practically tender, which should take about 10 minutes.

Next add the sugar and butter and stir until they have dissolved and melted. Now take the saucepan off the heat and let the mixture cool a little, then stir in the eggs—well beaten—with the lemon peel.

Pour the mixture into the baking dish, sprinkle on some freshly-grated nutmeg and bake for 30–40 minutes—or longer if you prefer a thicker consistency. Serve with pouring cream.

Cider baked apples with toasted muesli

(serves 4 people)

This is a very simple recipe but really delicious when the first Bramley apples come into season.

4 Bramley apples (medium sized)
½ pint dry cider (275 ml)
A little butter
4 tablespoons of any muesli

Pre-heat the oven to gas mark 5, 375°F (190°)

Begin by wiping and coring the apples—if you have an apple corer this is quite a simple job. Next, with a sharp knife, cut just through the skin around the centre of each apple.

Pour the cider into a shallow baking tin, then lightly grease each apple—wiping them with a buttered piece of kitchen paper is a good way of doing this. Now stand the apples upright in the cider.

Bake them for about 40 minutes or until they're tender when tested with a skewer, and baste them occasionally with the cider during the cooking time.

After 15 minutes put the muesli in the oven in an uncovered baking dish so that it will heat through and have a slightly toasted appearance.

When the apples are cooked, place them on top of the muesli, pour the juices over and serve with some cold pouring cream.

Note: There is no need to add sugar to the apples if the muesli is sweetened. Wholefood shops usually stock excellent muesli.

Queen of puddings
(serves 4 people)

This, with a cloud of meringue on top, is probably one of the lightest of puddings.

1 pint milk (570 ml)
4 oz fresh white breadcrumbs (110 g)
½ oz butter (10 g)
2 oz caster sugar (50 g)
The grated rind of a small lemon
2 eggs
3 level tablespoons raspberry jam

Pre-heat the oven to gas mark 4, 350°F (180°C)

You'll need a generously buttered 1½ pint (845 ml) oval pie-dish.

First pour the milk into a saucepan and bring to the boil. Remove from the heat and stir in the butter, breadcrumbs, 1 oz (25 g) of the sugar and the lemon rind, and leave for 20 minutes to allow the breadcrumbs to swell.

Now separate the eggs, beat the yolks and add them to the cooled breadcrumb mixture. Pour it all into the pie-dish and spread it out evenly. Bake in the centre of the oven for 30–35 minutes, or until set.

Meantime, in a small saucepan melt the jam over a low heat and, when the pudding is ready, remove it from the oven and spread the jam carefully and evenly all over the top.

Next beat the egg whites until stiff, then whisk in 1 oz (25 g) of caster sugar and spoon this meringue mixture over the pudding. Finally, sprinkle a teaspoon of caster sugar over it all and bake for a further 10–15 minutes until the topping is golden-brown.

Rich bread and butter pudding

(serves 4–6 people)

Never fear if you have some stale bread that needs using up. This is a light delicious pudding with a lovely dark toasted nutmeg crust.

½ pint milk (275 ml)
⅛ pint double cream (70 ml)
Grated rind of half a small lemon
2 oz caster sugar (50 g)
3 eggs
8 slices of bread (from a small loaf), buttered
½ oz candied lemon or orange peel (10 g), finely chopped
2 oz currants (50 g)
Freshly-grated nutmeg

Pre-heat the oven to gas mark 4, 350°F (180°C)

Begin by buttering well a 2 pint (1 litre) enamel baking dish (one of the oblong kind). Then slice the bread, not too thickly, butter it, then cut each slice in half—leaving the crusts on. Now arrange one layer of buttered bread over the base of the baking dish, sprinkle the candied peel and half the currants over, then cover with another layer of the bread slices and the remainder of the currants.

Next, in a glass measuring jug, measure out ½ pint of milk (275 ml) and add ⅛ pint (70 ml) of double cream. Stir in the caster sugar and lemon peel, then whisk the eggs, first on their own in a small basin and then into the milk mixture. Pour the whole lot over the bread, sprinkle over some freshly-grated nutmeg, and bake in the oven for 30–40 minutes. Serve warm.

Hot chocolate rum soufflé

(serves 4 people)

4 oz plain chocolate (110 g)
2 tablespoons rum
4 egg yolks
6 large egg whites
½ pint double cream (275 ml)
Icing sugar

Pre-heat the oven and a baking sheet to gas mark 6, 400°F (200°C)

First of all well butter a 2 pint (1 litre) soufflé dish. Next break the chocolate into a mixing bowl, add the rum and place the bowl in the bottom of the oven for 5–10 minutes or until the chocolate is soft, then beat, using a wooden spoon, until it's smooth.

In a small basin whisk the egg yolks thoroughly and stir them into the chocolate. In another bowl—and making sure your beater is clean and dry—whisk the egg whites until stiff, then fold them gently and carefully into the chocolate mixture, using a metal spoon. Next pour it all into the prepared soufflé dish and bake, on the baking sheet, for approximately 20 minutes or until the soufflé is puffy and springy to touch.

Serve straight from the oven, dusting the top with some sieved icing sugar and with the double cream in a jug to pour over separately. (It's much better to serve pouring cream with this rather than whipped cream.)

Traditional apple charlotte

(serves 4 people)

This is a real apple charlotte, moulded in a basin, so that when it's turned out the outside is crisp and buttery with the apples cooked to a pulp inside.

1 lb apples (half Bramley and half Cox's if possible) (450 g)
1 tablespoon caster sugar
1 oz butter (25 g)
1 egg yolk
6 slices bread from a large loaf (about ¼ inch (½ cm) thick with crusts removed)
3 oz (extra) butter (75 g)

Peel, core and thinly slice the apples first of all: rinse them in cold water and put them in a saucepan with 1 tablespoon of sugar and 1 oz (25 g) butter. Cook them over a low heat until they are soft enough to beat into a purée. Beat them and leave on one side to cool. Meanwhile melt the 3 oz (75 g) of butter gently, and cut each slice of bread into 6 rectangles.

Next brush each piece of bread with melted butter (both sides), being careful not to leave any unbuttered patches, then line a 1 pint (570 ml) pudding basin with approximately three-quarters of the bread (or as much as you need). Don't leave any gaps between the pieces—overlap them and press firmly. When the apple purée has cooled, beat the egg yolk into it and fill the lined basin with the mixture. Finally seal the top with overlapping slices of the remaining bread.

Place a suitably-sized plate on top of the pudding and weigh it down with a 2 lb (900 g) weight.

Meanwhile pre-heat the oven to gas mark 6, 400°F (200°C).
After half an hour place the basin (with the weight still on it) in the oven to bake for 35 minutes. Then, with an oven cloth, remove the plate and weight, and bake the pudding for another 10 minutes to brown on top. Leave the pudding to settle in the basin for a minute after removing from the oven, then carefully invert it onto a warmed plate to serve.

See also:
Apple and blackberry pie
Apple and cinnamon crêpes
Apple pie
Basic pancakes
Blackcurrant ice cream
Black Forest gateau
Brown rice pudding with prunes and apricots
Chocolate and hazelnut choux buns
Cœur à la crème
Coffee eclairs
Crème brûlée
Crème caramel
Crêpes Suzette
Crisp cinnamon flan
Curd cheesecake with fruit topping
Damson plum pie
Dried fruit salad with yoghurt and nuts
Eighteenth-century creamed apple flan
English gooseberry pie
English rhubarb fool
Fresh cherry pie

Fresh fruit and mint vinaigrette
Fresh lemon cheesecake with frosted grapes
Lemon meringue pie
Lemon soufflé omelette
Linzertorte
Mince pies
Old-fashioned bread pudding
Orange cheesecake
Plum and soured cream flan
Praline ice cream
Profiteroles
Rhubarb pie
Rich lemon cream with frosted grapes
Spiced apple and raisin pie
Spiced pears in cider
Squidgy chocolate log
Strawberry shortcake
Summer fruits pie
Vanilla ice cream
Wholewheat treacle tart
Zabaglione

Preserving

Including recipes for:

Green tomato chutney
Spiced plum chutney
Old Doverhouse chutney
Sweet piccalilli
Victoria plum or damson ketchup
Cranberry and orange relish
Quick pickled onions
Pickled red cabbage
Strawberry jam

Loganberry jam
Damson jam
Plum jam
Blackcurrant jam
Seville orange marmalade
Quick bramble jelly
Redcurrant jelly
Home-made Christmas mincemeat
Uncle Billy's toffee

The British have always been particularly good at preserving and pickling (just as we have excelled at smoking and curing). We have always been fortunate in this country to be able to grow a wide range of fruits and vegetables, beyond our immediate needs, and so have mastered the arts of storing up produce for the dreary winter months. We even exported our enthusiasm abroad—to India, for example—and came back with all manner of chutneys. You can still see the legacy of this passion at our local flower show—and doubtless at shows all over the country—where multi-coloured mountains of neatly-labelled jars stand awaiting inspection and judgement.

Perhaps the necessity to preserve food is no longer so pressing, but the pleasure remains. There's no doubt that strawberry jam spread on a crumpet or fresh-baked scone does bring the memory of a sunny June into the greyness of January, and some dark, spicy plum chutney served with cold ham can remind us that the fruitfulness of autumn can be savoured throughout the year. Most shop-bought jams, with their decided lack of fruit and surfeit of sweetness, or blandly uniform pickles, somehow fail to evoke any such pleasurable dream. All this combined with soaring prices in the shops provides good reasons for making these items at home. And anyone who cares about real food and real flavour won't grudge the time spent on preserving, when a spoonful of faintly sharp and fruity damson jam can put bread-and-jam into the luxury class, or some spicy home-made plum sauce can utterly transform a modest meal of bangers and mash.

General equipment

Contrary to what you might think, preserving at home does not call for a whole battery of special equipment. Below is a list of the general items which will come in very useful.

Preserving pans A heavy-gauge aluminium preserving pan is a good investment—it's large, sturdy, and will last a lifetime. Its biggest asset is its size, since it will hold more than most family-sized saucepans. It is also very wide and open at the top which means (in the case of chutney-making) the vinegar can reduce more effectively. Perhaps I ought to emphasise 'open' here, because I recall one distressed reader phoning the paper I worked for, saying she had been simmering her chutney for a whole day and it still hadn't reduced. On phoning her back I discovered she had used a large saucepan, instead of a preserving pan, and because I hadn't said otherwise in the recipe, she had kept the lid on! Don't let the lack of a preserving pan stop you from making jams and pickles, but don't ever put the lid on your saucepan.

Jars Ideally, preserving jars are what you need to make life simple, since they seal down with their own proper lids, and can be bought in a variety of sizes. But for economy, if you get into the habit of saving up all the jars that come into your possession, you'll soon build up quite a collection. At the time of writing most of these are of 1 lb (450 g) capacity, which works well for most things (except pickled onions), so I have kept to this size as a guideline in most recipes. But it's really not important—other sizes of jar can be used; if each one is filled to capacity, then any left-overs can be stored in small jars or used up quickly. You must bear in mind that the vinegar in pickles and chutneys can corrode metal, so for these plastic coated lids are essential. *Warning:* never use paper or cellophone covers for pickles and chutneys. They are fine for jams, but vinegar will evaporate during long storage if the jars aren't completely airtight (which paper covers never are). This is why chutney shrinks and dries out when covered with paper.

All jars and lids for preserving must be washed in warm, soapy water, rinsed thoroughly in warm water, then well dried with a clean towel. As an extra precaution I always place the jars in a moderate oven for 5 minutes, and pour the contents in while the jars are very hot. If you want to use for something else a jar that once contained pickled onions, soak it overnight in cold water with a teaspoonful of bicarbonate of soda stirred in. This should remove any evidence of pickled onions by the next day!

Gauze In my early days of cooking I used to get infuriated when cookery books demanded muslin bags to hold the spices, because I never had such a thing as muslin lying around. However I then discovered that ordinary gauze from the chemist was perfect for the job of holding spices for pickles (or pips for jam-making).

Waxed paper discs Circles of waxed paper are placed over chutneys and jams (wax-side down) to provide a seal. These can be made from the waxed paper found in breakfast cereal packets, or bought from stationers ready-made.

Ingredients for preserving
The vital point to remember is that all ingredients like fruit and vegetables for preserving must be sound. Anything that looks damaged or decayed in the slightest way should not be used.

Chutney-making

Chutney is derived from a Hindu word, and in fact reveals the origin of this particular form of preserving—namely India. In the first place, chutneys were attempts to reproduce in Britain the exotic recipes brought back by our Indian traders in the 18th and 19th centuries: but these efforts very soon brought forth a large range of home-grown preserves—of which piccalilli is one of the best-known examples. Our own native fruits, like plums, damsons and unripe tomatoes, proved excellent for this form of preserving, which is basically simmering slowly in vinegar.

A chutney is ready when the vinegar has reduced sufficiently. The way to tell this is to make a channel with a wooden spoon right across the surface of the chutney. If the spoon leaves a channel imprinted for a few seconds—without it being filled with vinegar— then the chutney is ready.

All chutneys should be stored for at least three months before using. This causes them to mature and mellow in flavour (a really freshly-made chutney, if you were to taste it, could be too harsh and vinegary). A cool, dark place is usually recommended for storage, and in these days of central heating I have found under the bed in the spare bedroom as good a place as any! Failing that, a covered cardboard box in the garage or garden shed will do.

Green tomato chutney

(makes about 8 lb or 3·65 kg)

Originally I thought this was a good recipe for using up all those stubborn green tomatoes that never seemed to ripen, but now we all love this chutney so much I don't even want half my tomatoes to ripen—just so I'll be able to make plenty.

2½ lb green tomatoes (1 kg)
2½ lb cooking apples (1 kg)
2 lb onions (900 g)
6 large cloves garlic, crushed
1 lb raisins (450 g)
1 lb 6 oz soft brown sugar (or demerara) (625 g)
1 oz pickling spice (25 g)
½ tablespoon cayenne pepper
2 level dessertspoons ground ginger

| ½ tablespoon salt |
| 3 pints genuine malt vinegar (1·75 litres) |

A small preserving pan, 8 × 1 lb (450 g) preserving jars, a mincer, string and some gauze.

Wash the tomatoes and cut them into quarters; peel the onions and quarter them; and peel and core the apples, keeping them in water to prevent browning.

Using the medium blade of a mincer, mince the tomatoes and place them in the pan, next the onions, then the raisins followed by the apples (don't worry if they have turned brown). Now add the garlic, the cayenne, salt, ginger and sugar, blending everything thoroughly. Next tie the pickling spice in a small piece of double-thickness gauze and attach it to the handle so that it hangs down into the other ingredients. Now pour in the vinegar, bring to simmering point, remove any scum from the surface, then let it simmer very gently for about 3½ hours without covering. Stir now and then, especially towards the end, to prevent sticking. It's ready when the vinegar has been almost absorbed and the chutney has thickened to a nice soft consistency and the spoon leaves a trail. Do be careful not to overcook, and remember it does thicken up quite a bit as it cools.

Pour the hot chutney into hot jars, filling them as full as possible. Cover with waxed sealing discs and seal with a tight lid at once. Label the jars when the chutney is cold.

Spiced plum chutney

(makes about 6 lb or 2·75 kg)

When the preserving season comes around, this plum chutney is an automatic choice with us. You can also make it with damsons, stewed in their own juice to remove the stones.

| 3 lb plums (1·35 kg), the small dark ones are best |
| 3 largish onions |
| 1 lb cooking apples (450 g) |
| 1 lb seedless raisins (450 g) |
| 1 lb dark soft brown sugar (450 g) |

| 1 lb demerara sugar (450 g) |
| 1 dessertspoon whole cloves |
| 2 pints malt vinegar (1·25 litres) |
| 3 cloves garlic |
| 2 heaped teaspoons ground ginger |
| 2 tablespoons salt |
| 2 small cinnamon sticks |
| 1 oz whole allspice berries (25 g) |

A preserving pan (or very large pan), a 12 inch (30 cm) square piece of gauze (which can be brought from chemists), some string and 6 × 1 lb (450 g) preserving (Kilner) jars or jars with plastic-lined screw-top lids.

First of all wash and dry the plums, then slit them down the natural line of the fruit with a sharp knife and remove the stones—putting the halved plums into the pans as you go. Next peel, core and mince the apples and add them to the pan, and do the same with the onions.

Now crush the garlic and add that, followed by the ginger and raisins, the sugars and the vinegar. Sprinkle in the salt and stir everything thoroughly. The cinnamon, allspice berries and cloves should be wrapped in the gauze and tied loosely to form a little bag, which should then be tied onto the handle of the pan and suspended into the middle of the rest of the ingredients.

Bring everything to the boil, then lower the heat and let the chutney simmer very gently for 2–3 hours, stirring it occasionally and rather more often towards the end to prevent it sticking to the bottom. When almost all the vinegar has disappeared and the chutney has thickened to a soft consistency, it's ready. It *will* thicken more when it has cooled, so be careful not to overcook it (and remember the narrower the top of the pan the longer the chutney will take to reduce).

While it is still warm, pour it into the jars (washed, dried and put into a moderate oven to warm through first). Cover with waxed discs and seal down with a screw lid. Label when cold and store in a cool, airy cupboard. Leave to mellow for at least three months before eating.

Old Doverhouse chutney

(makes 8 lb, 3·65 kg)

This is a very old recipe given to me hand-written on a yellowing page from a cookbook belonging to someone's great-grandmother. Where the name came from I've no idea but the chutney is delicious.

1½ lb plums, preferably Victorias (700 g)
1½ lb cooking apples, weighed after peeling (700 g)—about 2 lb (900 g) to start with
8 oz green or red tomatoes (225 g), whatever's available
1 lb stoned raisins (450 g)
8 oz onions (225 g)
1½ lb demerara sugar (700 g)
4 oz preserved ginger (110 g)—the sort that's preserved in syrup
¼ oz garlic, finely chopped (5 g)
¼ oz whole chillies (5 g)
1½ tablespoons cooking salt
1 pint malt vinegar (570 ml)

A preserving pan or very large saucepan, a small square of gauze, and some string. Eight 1 lb (450 g) jars.

First, pick over the plums and wash them, then cut them in half, remove the stones and cut the halves into two (or if very large into three). Then chop the tomatoes roughly into not-too-small pieces, and place both plums and tomatoes into a preserving pan.

Now pass the onions, apples, raisins and preserved ginger through the coarse blade of a mincer, or chop them finely in a food processor, and add these to the pan together with the chopped garlic, vinegar, sugar and salt. Tie the chillies in the gauze with string and suspend them from the handle of the pan. Now cook the chutney very slowly for about 1–1½ hours, or until most of the liquid has evaporated and you've given it the 'channel' test as described on page 668. Also, have a few good stirs during the cooking—and especially towards the end to prevent the mixture sticking to the base of the pan. Pot the chutney when it is still hot into hot jars. Seal with waxed discs and tight lids. Label the jars when the chutney is cold.

Sweet piccalilli

(makes about 5 lb
or 2·25 kg)

There's nothing like a few home-made pickles and chutneys for brightening up left-over meat, sausages or other winter economy dishes. When there are no runner beans left, this one can be made with frozen string beans (sometimes called *haricots verts*).

1 lb runner beans (450 g), cut into largish slices for cooking
2 medium-sized cauliflowers, divided into 1 inch (2·5 cm) florets
1 lb small onions (450 g), quartered and cut across
2 cloves garlic, crushed with 3 teaspoons salt
1 cucumber, peeled, cut into ¼ inch (½ cm) rounds, then each round quartered
2 pints malt vinegar (1·25 litres)
12 oz caster sugar (350 g)
2 oz English mustard powder (50 g)
6 tablespoons plain flour
1 oz turmeric powder (25 g)
Half a whole nutmeg, grated
½ teaspoon powdered allspice
5 additional tablespoons malt vinegar
3 tablespoons water

5 × 1 lb jars (450 g).

First place the cauliflower florets, onions and vinegar together in a large saucepan, then add the nutmeg and allspice and bring to the boil. Cover and simmer for 8 minutes. Now take the lid off and stir in the cucumber, runner beans and sugar. Crush the garlic in the salt and stir this in as well. Bring the mixture up to simmering point again, cover and cook for a further 5 minutes. The vegetables should still all be slightly crisp—so don't go away and forget them.

Now set a large colander over a large bowl and pour the contents of the saucepan into it and leave it all to drain (reserving the vinegar). Then mix the mustard powder, turmeric and flour together in a bowl. Gradually work in 5 additional tablespoons of vinegar and 3 of water so that the mixture becomes a fairly loose paste. Next add a ladleful of the hot vinegar liquid, drained from the vegetables, stir and transfer the blend to a saucepan.

Bring to the boil, whisking with a balloon whisk, and gradually adding the remaining hot vinegar. Boil gently for 5 minutes, then transfer the vegetables from the colander to the large bowl, and pour over the sauce. Stir well to mix, then spoon the piccalilli into heated, warmed and dried screw-top jars. Keep for three months before eating.

Note: if you get lumps in the sauce, whisk with a rotary whisk to disperse them.

Victoria plum or damson ketchup

(makes 3½ pints or 2 litres)

This is delicious served with cold meats or sausages and will keep indefinitely. Use bottles that have contained shop-bought ketchup or you can buy the old-fashioned type 'pop' bottles from good kitchen shops.

8 lb plums or damsons (3 kg 600 g)
8 oz currants (225 g)
1 lb onions, chopped small (450 g)
2 oz coarse salt, grated (50 g)
1 lb demerara sugar (450 g)
2 pints distilled white vinegar (1·25 litres)

Tie the following spices in a piece of gauze:
6–8 dried chillies
1 tablespoon black peppercorns
1 tablespoon mustard seeds
½ oz dried root ginger, crushed a bit first (10 g)
½ oz allspice berries (10 g)
2 whole garlic cloves

First slit the plums with a sharp knife and remove the stones, then place the fruit in a large pan and add the currants, onions and the bag of spices. Add 1 pint (570 ml) of the vinegar, bring to the boil and simmer gently, uncovered, for about 30 minutes or until the mixture is soft.

Now remove the bag of spices, place the contents of the pan in a liquidiser and blend until perfectly smooth—if necessary sieve as well. Then rinse out the pan and return the purée and bag of spices to it, adding the salt, sugar and the remaining 1 pint (570 ml) of vinegar. Bring to simmering point and cook gently, uncovered, for 1½–2 hours or until the ketchup has reduced to approximately 3½ pints (2 litres). Stir now and then to prevent sticking.

In the meantime prepare the containers by boiling the bottles and their tops. When the ketchup is ready pour it into the bottles while they're still hot, filling them to within an inch (2·5 cm) of the top. Put on the tops immediately but screw them only half-way and if you're using the 'pop' type bottles push the top in but leave the lever up.

Next place the bottles in a pan (standing them on an upside down plate) and add warm water to within 1½ inches (4 cm) from the tops. Bring the water to the boil and after 10 minutes transfer the bottles to a wooden surface and complete the sealing.

Note: although it has never happened to me, I have heard of the upside down plate sometimes breaking—so perhaps an enamel plate would be safer.

Cranberry and orange relish

(serves 8 people)

This cranberry sauce is an excellent accompaniment to the Christmas turkey, but there is no need to confine it to that: it goes just as well with many poultry, pork or ham dishes too,

1 lb fresh cranberries (450 g)
The zest and juice of 1 orange
Piece of cinnamon stick
3 oz sugar (75 g)
4 cloves
½ teaspoon ginger
2 tablespoons port

Begin by mincing the cranberries finely, then put them into a saucepan. Remove the outer zest of the orange (with a potato peeler if you like) and cut into very thin strips. Now add these strips of zest together with the juice of the orange to the minced cranberries, followed by the cinnamon stick, cloves, ginger and the sugar. Bring the whole lot to boiling point, put a lid on and cook gently for about 5 minutes. Then take the pan off the heat and stir in the port. Pour everything into a serving bowl, cover it and leave in the refrigerator until required (remembering to remove the cinnamon and cloves before serving).

Pickling

I'm afraid I have neither the stamina nor the patience to endure long pickling sessions (especially with onions). So I always use the method in the recipe below, which cuts out the normal salting and brining process. The results are excellent, except that the vegetables pickled in this way do need to be eaten within three or four months. I actually find that no hardship—a batch made in October ensures a good supply for Christmas, and after that another batch can be made. The whole thing takes about 45 minutes from start to finish. (For those who require longer-keeping pickles, may I refer you to the specialised books on preserving in the book list, page 699).

Quick
pickled onions

In this recipe I put the spices in with the onions, which gives them a lovely, hot spicy flavour. Just the thing to serve with strong Cheddar cheese, real bread and real ale.

4¾ lb pickling onions (2 kg 150 g)
3¼ pints malt vinegar (1 litre 850 ml)
1 oz pickling spice (25 g)

4 × 1¾ pint (1 litre) preserving jars (or the equivalent).

Peel the onions—preferably while you listen to some good music on the radio to take your mind off the job. Then pack the jars half-full with the onions and sprinkle a level dessertspoon of pickling spice into each jar. Then fill up each jar with more onions, followed by another dessertspoon of pickling spice.

Now pour the vinegar over the onions, right up to the top so that it covers them completely, and fix on the lids. Store in a cool, dark place for at least 8 weeks before eating.

Note: if you don't have proper preserving jars, any other jars will do, provided they have plastic-coated lids. Paper covers will *not* do—see notes on jars, page 667.

Pickled red cabbage   This, again, is made by a quick no-salting method; and the cabbage keeps perfectly crisp for up to four months.

1½ lb red cabbage, cleaned and shredded (700 g)
1¾ pints malt vinegar (1 litre)
1 oz pickling spice (25 g)
1 level tablespoon coriander seeds

5 × 1 lb (450 g) preserving jars, washed and dried.

Place the pickling spice in a saucepan with the vinegar, cover with a lid, and bring to simmering point very slowly over a gentle heat. Then remove the pan from the heat, and allow the vinegar to infuse the spicy flavours for about 4 hours.

After that strain the vinegar into a large mixing bowl (reserving the spices), stir in the red cabbage and the coriander seeds, and mix thoroughly. Now spoon this mixture into the prepared jars, making sure each jar has enough vinegar to come right up to the top. Extract some pieces of red chilli (or whole ones) from the pickling spices, and place them amongst the red cabbage. Seal down the jars and store for about 2 months before opening.

Jam and marmalade making

The great advantage of home-made jams is that they are pure, made from fruit and sugar only—unlike their shop-bought cousins which often list several other ingredients as well. It is true you *can* buy the more expensive brands which proudly display the fact that they contain no preservative or colouring, but (being an avid jam label studier) I have rarely come across a jam—or a marmalade—that is made only from fruit and sugar, whatever the price. The answer, both in terms of quality and economy, is to make them at home and add a touch of luxury to everyday eating.

What is jam? Essentially it's preserved fruit. The fruit, if it is in good condition and slightly under-ripe, contains in its cell walls a natural setting agent called pectin. This, together with the natural acid from the fruit, is released when the fruit is boiled with sugar. As the mixture boils, the sugar concentrates and all three (sugar, acid and pectin) combine to form a mass that eventually reaches 'setting point'.

Ingredients
Fruit First of all, this should be dry since the water content in the damp fruit will dilute the pectin and the acid, and render them less active. Very dusty fruit should be wiped with damp kitchen paper, but normally the boiling process will effectively purify the fruit. Research has shown that slightly under-ripe fruit contains a lot more pectin and fruit acid than over-ripe fruit (which should be avoided). With those fruits that contain less acid than others, this deficiency is made up by adding lemon juice.

Sugar The proportion of sugar to fruit varies according to the type of fruit used. For me, the really sharp fruits—like damsons or loganberries—make the best jams because they are not over-powered by the sweetness of the sugar. In other words, the fruit flavour is stronger. This is also why I believe the bitter Seville oranges make the best marmalade: tasting of oranges rather than sugar. I don't find that special preserving sugar is essential, and in fact never use it because it's so much more expensive.

Equipment
The equipment for jam-making is the same as that outlined at the beginning of the chapter, except you will find some recipes advise the use of jam thermometers. These are clipped to the side of the preserving pan, and when the mixture reaches 220°F (104°C) setting point should be reached. However I must say I have never had much success with thermometers, perhaps because the steam caused by fast-boiling makes it impossible to see the temperature clearly (and if you take the thermometer out, the temperature marking drops immediately). I would recommend you use the 'cold plate' test, see page 678.

Jars They need the same treatment as outlined on page 667, except that in this case the coverings can be cellophane discs kept in place by elastic bands. These are sold in packets, which also contain the waxed discs. Many people say cellophane is the best covering, though it must be admitted that proper lids are a lot more convenient when you start to eat the jam!

Important points for jam-making
(1) Tough-skinned fruits should be simmered and softened before the sugar is added, as the sugar has a hardening effect.
(2) Soft-skinned fruits (like strawberries) that tend to disintegrate when cooked should be soaked in sugar first to harden them—and

so help to keep the fruit in the finished jam whole.

(3) The sugar must be dissolved completely before the jam is boiled, otherwise it will be difficult to set and the finished jam will be sugary. To test if the sugar has dissolved, dip a wooden spoon in, turn it over, and if no sugar crystals are visible on the liquid that coats the spoon, it has indeed dissolved. (But be sure to stir well and try this test two or three times.) To speed up the dissolving process, you can warm the sugar in a bowl in the oven before adding it.

(4) Never try to make jam in too large quantities. It will take far too long to come to the boil, and then will not boil rapidly enough to produce a good set.

(5) *How to test for a set:* when you start to cook the fruit place about four small plates in the freezing compartment of the fridge. Then, when you have boiled the jam for the given time, remove the pan from the heat, and place a teaspoonful of the jam onto one of the chilled plates. Allow it to cool for a few seconds, then push it with your finger: if a crinkly skin has formed on the jam, then it has set. If it hasn't set, boil it again for another 5 minutes and then do another test.

(6) Ignore any scum that rises to the surface while the jam is boiling. If you keep skimming it off, you'll find you have no jam left! Instead, wait until you have a set, then remove the jam from the heat and stir in a small lump of butter which will disperse the scum.

(7) After the jam has set, allow it to settle for 15 minutes (specially necessary for jam containing whole fruit—such as strawberry or damson or even chunky marmalade—to prevent the fruit rising to the top when it's poured into the jar). Then pour into dry, clean, warmed jars, filling them as far up to the neck as possible. Then immediately place a waxed disc over the surface, and tie down straightaway with cellophane covering (to do this, wipe the cellophane with a damp cloth and place it on the jar damp side up). Wipe the jars with a hot damp cloth.

(8) Don't put the labels on until the jam is cold, since the heat will prevent them sticking properly and they will very soon peel off.

(9) Store in a cool, dry, and preferably dark, place. Too much light is not good for storage, while a damp or steamy atmosphere can cause mould to develop on the surface of your jam.

(10) If things go wrong. . . . If the jam hasn't set after cooling and potting, tip it all back into the pan and boil again adding the juice of a small lemon. If a mould develops on the surface, remove it

Right: Cold pressed ox tongue, page 248; Damson ketchup, page 673; Spiced plum chutney, page 669; Quick pickled onions, page 675; Sweet piccalilli, page 672.

plus about half an inch of the jam underneath. The rest of the jam will not be affected.

(11) There is no need to use commercially produced pectin. It's expensive and shouldn't ever be necessary.

Strawberry jam

(makes 6 lb or 2·75 kg)

The way to keep strawberries whole in jam is to cover them with the sugar and leave them overnight. The sugar will then draw out the juices and firm the fruit.

4 lb slightly under-ripe dry strawberries (2 kg)
3 lb sugar (1·35 kg)
The juice of 2 large lemons

A preserving pan with a lightly buttered base. 4 small plates chilled in the ice-making compartment of the refrigerator

Hull the strawberries and wipe with some damp kitchen paper, then layer them in the preserving pan, sprinkling them with the sugar as you go. Leave them like this overnight, by which time the sugar should have almost dissolved.

To make the jam, place the pan over a lowish heat just to melt the rest of the sugar and draw some of the juice out of the strawberries—don't stir too much, just shake the pan now and then to keep the fruit as whole as possible. When the sugar has completely dissolved, add the lemon juice, turn up the heat and as soon as the jam is really bubbling, time it for 8 minutes and then remove it from the heat. Spoon a little onto a chilled plate, allow it to cool, then push with your little finger: if it forms a crinkly skin, it's set. If not, boil it up for a further 3–4 minutes. Repeat the test, removing the pan from the heat three or four times if necessary until you have a set.

Then remove from the heat, stir in a small lump of butter to disperse any scum, and allow the jam to settle for 15 minutes before pouring it into dry clean jars (heated in a moderate oven for 5 minutes). Seal immediately with waxed discs and tie down while still warm. Label when cold.

Left: Plain scones and Wholewheat fruit scones, page 619; Whole oat crunchies, page 627; Shortbread biscuits, page 624; Gingernuts, page 629.

Note: try not to wash strawberries or attempt to make jam after it has rained heavily and the fruit is wet—it must be as dry as possible. If you are forced to wash the fruit, dry it and spread it out on clean teacloths to dry further before using. Any extra moisture will dilute the pectin and make setting more difficult.

Loganberry jam

(makes 5 lb or 2·25 kg)

You can make this in any quantity, using 1 lb (450 g) of sugar for each pound of loganberries.

3 lb loganberries, preferably under-ripe (1 kg 350 g)
3 lb granulated sugar (1 kg 350 g)

Pre-heat the oven to gas mark 4, 350°F (180°C)

5 × 1 lb (450 g) jars, washed, dried and heated in a moderate oven for 5 minutes.

Put 4 small plates into the freezer compartment of the fridge to get them really cold.

Pick over the fruit, discarding any stalks or leafy bits, then put them into a pan. Don't wash them as the heat from the cooking will purify them. Place the pan on a fairly low heat—don't stir at all, just leave it on the heat until the juices start to run.

Then, gently, shake the pan from side to side, to get the top loganberries down to the bottom; or you can stir, but be careful and try not to break the fruit too much—it's nice to get some whole fruits in the finished jam. Now leave it to cook very slowly for about 30 minutes or until the fruit is cooked and all the berries are tender.

While all that's happening—in fact as soon as you've put the fruit on to cook—tip the sugar into a bowl and place it in the pre-heated oven. When the fruit is cooked, add the hot sugar, tipping the pan and stirring gently. Then leave it again on a low heat for a further 15 minutes or so until the sugar has dissolved completely—it's very important no sugar crystals should be left or the finished jam will go sugary. The way to test this is by coating the back of a wooden spoon with the mixture and you will be able to see if the sugar hasn't dissolved.

As soon as it has dissolved, turn the heat right up as high as it will go, and boil the jam rapidly for 10 minutes. Then remove it from the heat, spoon a little onto one of your cooled plates, and when it's cool push the jam with your little finger. If a crinkly skin has formed, it's set. If not boil it rapidly again for 5 minutes, test again and carry on like this until the jam has set.

Ignore any scum while the jam is boiling, but as soon as it's set, add a little knob of butter which will get rid of most of it (you can skim off any that's left with a slotted spoon). Leave the jam for 15 minutes to settle, then pour it into the hot jars, filling them right to the top. Cover straight away with waxed discs, and seal with tight-fitting lids or cellophane. Label the jars when the jam is cold.

Other varieties of jam
Damson jam
Use 2¼ lb (1 kg 60 g) of sugar to 3 lb (1 kg 350 g) of fruit. Simmer the fruit in ¾ pint (425 ml) of water until soft, then proceed as for *Loganberry jam* opposite.

Plum jam
Use 2 lb (900 g) stoned, halved fruit and 1½ lb (700 g) sugar. Simmer the fruit in 8 fl oz (225 ml) of water until tender, then proceed as for *Loganberry jam*.

Blackcurrant jam
Use 2 lb (900 g) of fruit simmered in 1 pint (570 ml) of water until tender. Add 2½ lb (1 kg 125 g) of sugar and continue as for *Loganberry jam*.

Seville orange marmalade
(makes 6 lb or 2·75 kg)

I find it hard to make in one go larger quantities than are given in the recipe below.

2 lb Seville oranges (900 g)
1 lemon
4 lb granulated sugar, warmed (1·8 kg)
4 pints water (2·25 litres)

6 × 1 lb (450 g) jars, 9 inch
(23 cm) square of gauze, string,
3 or 4 tea-plates.

Begin by measuring the water into a preserving pan, then cut the lemon and oranges in half and squeeze the juice out of them. Add the juice to the water, and place the pips and any bits of pith that cling to the squeezer on the square of muslin (laid over a dish or cereal bowl first). Now cut the orange peel into quarters with a sharp knife, and then cut each quarter into thinnish shreds. As you cut add the shreds to the water and any pips or spare pith you come across should go onto the muslin. Remember that the pith contains a lot of pectin so don't discard any.

Now tie the pips up loosely in the muslin to form a little bag, and tie this onto the handle of the pan so that the bag is suspended in the water. Then bring the liquid up to simmering point, and simmer gently, uncovered, for 2 hours or thereabouts until the peel is completely soft—test a piece carefully by pressing it between your finger and thumb. At this point pop the tea-plates into the freezing compartment of the fridge.

Next remove the bag of pips and leave it to cool on a saucer. Then pour the sugar into the pan and stir it now and then over a low heat, until all the crystals have melted (check this carefully, it's important). Now increase the heat to very high, and squeeze the bag of pips over the pan to extract all of the sticky, jelly-like substance that contains the pectin. As you squeeze you'll see it ooze out. You can do this by placing the bag between two saucers or using your hands. Then stir or whisk it into the rest.

As soon as the mixture reaches a really fast boil, start timing. Then after 15 minutes spoon a little of the marmalade onto one of the cold plates from the fridge, and let it cool back in the fridge. You can tell—when it has cooled—if you have a 'set' by pushing the mixture with your little finger: if it has a really crinkly skin, it is set. If not, continue to boil the marmalade and give it the same test at about 10-minute intervals until it does set.

After that remove the pan from the heat (if there's a lot of scum, most of it can be dispersed by stirring in half a teaspoon of butter, and the rest can be spooned off). Leave the marmalade to settle for 20 minutes.

In the meantime the jars (washed, rinsed and dried first) should be heated in a moderate oven for 5 minutes. Pour the marmalade, with the aid of a funnel or a ladle, into the jars and cover with waxed discs and seal while still hot. Label the jars when quite cold.

Quick bramble jelly
(makes 1 lb or 450 g)

This is not a jelly that will keep for long—perhaps only a month—but if you've been for a long walk in the autumn and returned with a harvest of brambles from the hedgerows, this recipe is so easy and quick to make and it does taste delicious spread on hot crumpets or scones.

1 lb ripe blackberries (450 g)
1 lb granulated sugar (450 g)
6 fl oz water (170 ml)
Juice of 1 lemon

A large nylon sieve and a piece of chemist's gauze about 14 inches (35 cm) square.

Wash the blackberries and place in a thick-based saucepan with the water, then stew them very gently with a lid on for about 20–25 minutes. Now and then give them a good mash to reduce them to pulp and squeeze as much juice out of them as possible. After that add the sugar and lemon juice to the pan and allow the sugar to dissolve completely, with the heat still low. There must not be any whole granules of sugar left. This takes about 10–15 minutes. Now turn the heat right up and boil fairly rapidly for 8 minutes, stirring now and then to prevent sticking.

Meanwhile warm a large bowl and a 1 lb (450 g) jam jar in the oven—get them nice and hot—and then place the sieve, lined with gauze, over the bowl and pour the blackberry mixture into the lined sieve. Then, using a wooden spoon, get all the liquid through as quickly as possible, squeezing the remaining pulp as much as you can—but do be quick as the jelly sets if you take too long. Now pour the jelly into the warmed jar, cover with a waxed disc, cool and tie down.

Note: if it begins to set before you've had a chance to pour it into the jar, just reheat it gently.

Redcurrant jelly

(makes 2 lb or 900 g)

One preserve that has suffered bitterly from commercialism is redcurrant jelly: so often it is sickly sweet and the flavour of the redcurrants is lost amongst other ingredients. Luckily I've found an extremely easy recipe for making it from Eliza Acton's *Modern Cookery for Private Families* (1840). Her name for it was 'Superlative Reducrrant Jelly'.

---
2 lb redcurrants (900 g)
---
2 lb sugar (900 g), warmed
---

1 packet gauze from the chemists, 1 large nylon sieve, 2 × 1 lb (450 g) jars, washed, dried and heated in a moderate oven for 5 minutes.

The first easy thing is that there's no need to go through the tedious business of stripping the currants from the stalks. Just place the washed fruit—stalks and all—in a preserving pan, bring slowly to the boil, and stir and press the redcurrants to break down the fruit and release the juice. As soon as the fruit is cooked (about 10 minutes), add the warmed sugar, stir until absolutely dissolved, then bring the mixture up to a rapid boil, and boil for 8 minutes.

Meanwhile place a large nylon sieve over a bowl and line it with a double layer of gauze. Then, when the 8 minutes are up, tip the whole lot into the sieve and let it drip through. If you don't mind not having a completely clear jelly, you can press to extract as much as possible. Then pour the jelly into warmed jars, cover with waxed discs and tie down.

Note: this makes 2 lb (900 g), but the process is exactly the same for a larger quantity.

Home-made Christmas mincemeat

(makes 6 lb or 2·75 kg)

I give you a warning here. Once you've tasted home-made mincemeat in mince pies, you'll never again be able to revert to shop-bought!

---
1 lb cooking apples, peeled, cored and finely chopped (450 g)
---

8 oz shredded suet (225 g)
12 oz raisins (350 g)
8 oz sultanas (225 g)
8 oz currants (225 g)
8 oz whole mixed peel, finely chopped (225 g)
12 oz soft dark brown sugar (350 g)
The grated rind and juice of 2 oranges
The grated rind and juice of 2 lemons
2 oz whole almonds, cut into slivers (50 g)
4 teaspoons mixed spice
½ teaspoon ground cinnamon
Half a nutmeg, grated
6 tablespoons brandy

Just mix all the ingredients, except for the brandy, together in a large bowl very thoroughly. Then cover with a cloth and leave for 12 hours. To prevent fermentation place the mincemeat in a cool oven, gas mark ¼, 225°F (120°C) for 3 hours. Then allow it to get quite cold, stir in the brandy and spoon into clean dry jars. Cover with waxed discs, then seal.

Uncle Billy's toffee

(makes about 1¼ lb or 575 g)

For years my Uncle Billy (from Wales) cherished the secret of his home-made toffee—which is the best I've ever tasted, I swear. Now he has relented, and I can pass on to you the recipe for this buttery, chewy delicacy!

1 lb soft brown sugar (450 g)
12 oz salted butter (350 g)
1 teaspoon malt vinegar
5 fl oz water (150 ml)

A shallow tin 7½ inches (19 cm) square, lightly oiled.

First take your very largest saucepan—toffee tends to boil over if it doesn't have much room, so a 4½ or 5 pint (2·5 or 3 litre) one would be ideal. Put all the ingredients in the saucepan, and bring them *slowly* to the boil over a low heat (about 10–15 minutes), stirring occasionally. When the sugar has completely dissolved, turn the heat up a little, insert a cooking thermometer and let the mixture bubble away (without stirring) until the temperature reaches 250°F (130°C)—which will take about 10 minutes. Then pour it into the prepared tin and leave to set.

When it has set, turn the toffee out onto a board and break it up with a small hammer (or other heavy object), then store the pieces in a polythene bag tied at the neck.

Note: if you do not possess a cooking thermometer, test the toffee by dropping a teaspoonful into a saucer of cold water: if it sets immediately into a soft, pliable ball, the toffee is ready.

See also:
Lemon curd

Left-overs

Including recipes for:
Rissoles
Fish cakes
Special cottage pie
Baked stuffed courgettes
Creamy chicken curry
Ham, egg and cheese risotto
Bubble and squeak
Ham croquettes
Old-fashioned bread pudding

Here, at the very end of the Cookery Course, it seemed appropriate to look at what to do with left-overs. However well we plan, and however meticulous we are, we all have food left over at times and it would be criminal not to put it to good use. A recent study in one American city showed that about 15% of the food bought in most households was thrown away—all of it perfectly usable meat, bread and so on. A far cry from the traditional 'Vicarage mutton' which Dorothy Hartley quotes as being served 'hot on Sunday, cold on Monday, hashed on Tuesday, minced on Wednesday, curried on Thursday, broth on Friday, cottage pie on Saturday'.

That must have been quite some joint! But there's a lot to be said for the idea, with the price of meat being what it is. At home, when we do have a joint I like to buy a decent cut, so that it can provide two or three meals. The same goes for poultry or the end of a bacon joint—there's always something that can be made from it.

So here are a few ideas—even for left-over stale bread, which, if you don't own a freezer, can become an enormous problem. Quite simply, make it into an old-fashioned bread pudding, which will disappear in seconds.

Rissoles

My family have a definite weakness for rissoles. We don't eat great quantities of meat, but we *do* have a joint at weekends and that means lots of lovely left-over bits to make rissoles the next day.

The recipe below is my standard one, but in fact the ingredients are by no means invariable. I like to vary them slightly. For something really spicy (with either lamb or beef) I add ¼ teaspoon of chilli powder and half a green or red pepper very finely chopped or minced. For a Middle Eastern flavour to your rissoles, try adding ½ teaspoon of ground cumin plus ½ teaspoon ground coriander. Or for an Indian influence, add 1 level teaspoon of curry powder, ½ teaspoon of ginger and ½ teaspoon ground turmeric. Whichever combination you choose, home-made rissoles are quite delicious!

Rissoles

(serves 2–3 people)

8 oz cooked lamb or beef (225 g)
1 small onion
1½ oz fresh breadcrumbs (40 g)
¼ teaspoon ground cinnamon
2 level tablespoons chopped parsley
1 clove garlic, crushed

| 1 small egg, beaten |
| Salt and freshly-milled black pepper |

| *For the coating and frying:* |
| Seasoned wholewheat flour |
| Oil, for shallow frying |

Either mince both the onion and the meat through the finest blade of a mincer, or else chop them finely in a food processor. Then place them in a mixing bowl and add the rest of the ingredients. Now just mix and mix until everything is thoroughly blended.

Divide the mixture into six portions, and shape each into a round cake shape with your hands. Then coat each rissole all over with some seasoned wholewheat flour.

All this can be done in advance, and the rissoles can be covered and chilled in the fridge. When you're ready to cook, heat some oil in a frying-pan (just enough to cover the base) and when it's very hot fry the rissoles for 5 minutes on each side.

Fish cakes

(serves 2–3 people)

I think it's actually worth cooking more fish than you need for a meal, just so that you have some left over to make these delicious little fish cakes.

| 8 oz cooked cod (225 g) |
| 8 oz creamed mashed potatoes (225 g) |
| 1 tablespoon chopped parsley |
| ½ teaspoon anchovy essence |
| 1 level teaspoon capers, chopped |
| 1 small egg, beaten |
| ½ oz butter (10 g) (room temperature) |
| 1 teaspoon lemon juice |
| 1 clove garlic, crushed |
| A pinch cayenne pepper |
| A little grated nutmeg |
| Salt and freshly-milled black pepper |

| *For the coating:* |
| 1 egg, beaten |
| 3 oz (approx) dry white breadcrumbs (75 g) |

In a large mixing bowl combine all the ingredients for the fish cakes together thoroughly, then taste and season as required with salt and pepper. (If the fish and potatoes are freshly cooked, you will need to chill the mixture at this stage for an hour or two to get it nice and firm.)

When you're ready to cook, lightly flour a working surface, turn the fish mixture out onto it and form it into a long roll 2–2½ inches (5 cm) in diameter. Cut the roll into 12 round fish cakes. Pat each cake into a neat flat shape, and dip each one first into beaten egg and then in the dry white breadcrumbs. Now shallow fry the cakes in equal quantities of oil and butter until golden brown on both sides. Drain on crumpled kitchen paper and serve immediately.

Special cottage pie

(serves 4 people)

This is 'special' because it has a topping of potatoes and leeks which really adds an extra dimension. If you want to make it with raw minced meat, extend the initial cooking time to about 45 minutes (after the stock has gone in) instead of 10 minutes.

1 lb cooked minced beef (450 g)
2 medium-sized onions, chopped
1 large carrot, chopped very small
1 level tablespoon flour
½ teaspoon mixed herbs
½ teaspoon ground cinnamon
1 tablespoon fresh chopped parsley
½ pint hot beef stock (275 ml)
1 tablespoon tomato purée
Some beef dripping
Salt and freshly-milled black pepper

For the topping:
2 lb potatoes (900 g)
2 medium leeks, chopped
2 oz butter (50 g)
Salt and freshly-milled black pepper

Pre-heat the oven to gas mark 6, 400°F (200°C)

First of all fry the onions in the dripping until they are soft, then add the carrot and minced meat, continuing to cook for about 10 minutes until the meat and carrot has browned a little. Now season with salt and pepper and add the cinnamon, mixed herbs and parsley. Stir in the flour, mix the tomato purée with the hot stock, add to the meat mixture and bring to simmering point.

To make the topping: boil the potatoes in salted water and cook the leeks gently in the butter. When the potatoes are done, cream them and then stir in the cooked leeks together with their butter and season to taste.

Put the meat mixture into a well-greased baking dish, spread the potato mixture over the top and bake for about 25 minutes.

Baked stuffed courgettes

(serves 2 people)

This is a Greek-inspired recipe, very good for using up a little left-over lamb.

4 large courgettes
White or brown rice measured to the 3 fl oz (75 ml) level in a measuring jug
1 medium-sized onion, finely chopped
1 clove garlic, crushed
6 oz minced cooked lamb (175 g)
3 tablespoons oil
¼ teaspoon ground cinnamon
1 heaped tablespoon fresh, chopped parsley
12 oz ripe tomatoes, peeled and chopped (350 g)
1 dessertspoon tomato purée
Salt and freshly-milled black pepper

Pre-heat the oven to gas mark 4, 350°F (180°C)

Wipe the courgettes, but don't peel them. Cut each one widthwise into 3 pieces, then using a small knife, flat skewer, or apple corer, hollow out the centre of each piece. You should then end up with 12 hollowed-out little barrel shapes. Now, sprinkle the insides with salt and leave them to drain for about 30 minutes.

While that is happening, cook the rice in double its volume of boiling salted water, until all the water has been absorbed and each grain is separate (this will take about 15 minutes for white rice,

40 minutes for brown). Heat 2 tablespoons of the oil in a frying-pan, soften the chopped onion in it for 5 minutes, then stir in the garlic followed by the minced lamb and, finally, the rice. Stir well so that everything gets a good coating of oil. Then sprinkle in the parsley and cinnamon and some seasoning and remove the pan from the heat.

Now wipe the insides of the courgettes with kitchen paper and fill each one with the stuffing, packing it in as tightly as possible. As each one is filled, lay it in a casserole and, when they're all in, tuck any left-over stuffing in between them. Sprinkle another tablespoon of oil all over.

Next beat the tomatoes to a pulp, stir in the tomato purée, season with salt and pepper, and pour the mixture all over the courgettes. Bake with a lid on the casserole for 45 minutes and for a further 15–30 minutes without the lid until the courgettes are tender. Serve with extra rice and perhaps a green salad.

Creamy chicken curry
(serves 4 people)

This is good for either left-over chicken or turkey. It has a fairly mild curry flavour but you can 'hot it up' if you like by adding a little more curry powder.

1 lb cooked chicken, cut into 1 inch (2·5 cm) pieces (450 g)
2 tablespoons groundnut oil
1 large onion, roughly chopped
2 sticks celery, chopped
1 large green pepper, chopped
1 heaped tablespoon flour
1 rounded teaspoon Madras curry powder
1 level teaspoon ginger
1 level teaspoon turmeric
1 pint chicken stock (570 ml)
1 clove garlic, crushed
2 tablespoons double cream
Salt and freshly-milled black pepper

In a large flameproof casserole heat up the oil and soften the onion in it for 5 minutes, then add the chopped celery and green pepper and soften these for 5 minutes more. Next add the prepared chicken pieces and toss them around with the other ingredients.

Now stir in the spices, curry powder and crushed garlic, add the flour and continue to stir to soak up the juices. Next, gradually add the stock, a little at a time, stirring well after each addition. Season with salt and pepper, put a lid on and simmer very gently for 20–25 minutes or until the vegetables are just tender. Remove the curry from the heat, stir in the cream and serve with spiced pilau rice and mango chutney.

Ham, egg and cheese risotto

(serves 3–4 people)

This is a good recipe for using up the remains of a bacon joint.

6 oz boiled bacon, cut into ½ inch (1 cm) cubes (175 g)
Long grain brown rice measured to the ½ pint (275 ml) level in a measuring jug
1 pint boiling water (570 ml)
1½ tablespoons olive oil
2 medium onions, roughly chopped
2 hard-boiled eggs, sliced
2 oz strong Cheddar cheese, grated (50 g)
1 tablespoon breadcrumbs
8 fl oz milk (225 ml)
¾ oz plain flour (20 g)
¾ oz butter (20 g)
Cayenne pepper
Salt and freshly-milled black pepper

In a small flameproof casserole, heat the olive oil and fry the onion for 5 minutes. Then add the bacon cubes, stir in the rice, season with a little salt and pour in the boiling water. Simmer gently—with a lid on—for 45 minutes or until the water is absorbed and the rice tender.

While that's happening, put the flour, butter and milk in a saucepan, then—whisking continuously—bring to simmering point, by which time the mixture will have thickened. Add a seasoning of salt and freshly-milled black pepper and simmer for 6 minutes. Remove from the heat and stir in half the grated cheese.

A few minutes before the rice is cooked, turn on the grill. Remove the lid from the casserole and, using a skewer, fluff up the rice gently. Then place the sliced eggs over the top and pour on the cheese sauce. Next sprinkle on the rest of the grated cheese and the breadcrumbs and add a dusting of cayenne pepper. Place the dish under a heated grill and serve when the top is brown and bubbly. A fresh crunchy salad goes well with this.

Bubble and squeak
(serves 2 people)

An old-fashioned favourite for using up left-over potatoes and cabbage or you could, of course, use Brussels sprouts.

1 lb cooked potatoes (450 g)
1 small cabbage
1 heaped tablespoon seasoned flour
1 oz butter (25 g)
Beef dripping, for frying
Salt and freshly-milled black pepper

First cut the cabbage into quarters, remove the hard stalk and shred the rest. Wash it thoroughly, then plunge it into fast-boiling water, put a lid on and boil for about 6 minutes. Then transfer the cabbage to a colander and let it drain thoroughly (by putting a plate with a weight on it on top).

Mash the potatoes with the butter and a good seasoning of pepper (preferably with an electric hand whisk). When smooth mix the potatoes with the drained cabbage, then take tablespoons of the mixture and shape them into round cakes. Dust these with seasoned flour, then fry them in hot dripping to a good, crisp, golden brown on both sides. Drain on crumpled greasproof paper, and serve straightaway.

Ham croquettes
(serves 4 people)

This is obviously a good way to use up left-over ham, but it's also worth buying some ham just to make them.

12 oz cooked ham (350 g)
1 large onion
2 slices wholemeal bread, soaked in a little milk and then squeezed out
1 clove garlic, crushed
1 tablespoon parsley, chopped

2 teaspoons Dijon mustard
1 egg
Some plain flour
Olive oil
Salt and freshly-milled black pepper

Mince the cooked ham, using the coarse blade of your mincer, and put the onion through the mincer also. Then, in a large mixing bowl, combine the ham and onion. Break up the soaked bread and stir this in, together with the garlic, parsley and mustard. Season with pepper, but be sparing with the salt—as the ham may be salty. Add the beaten egg and stir thoroughly.

Now mould the mixture into 8 large—or 12 smallish—croquettes or rolls, pressing firmly to bind them together. Sprinkle some flour onto a pastry board and roll each croquette in it so that they're all lightly dusted with flour. Shallow fry them in olive oil to a light brown colour. Fried eggs make a nice accompaniment.

Old-fashioned bread pudding

(serves 4 people)

This is a lovely spicy cross between a cake and a pudding—perfect for using left-over bread.

8 oz bread (225 g)—it doesn't matter whether this is brown or white but cut off the crusts
½ pint milk (275 ml)
2 oz butter, melted (50 g)
3 oz soft brown sugar (75 g)—if you don't have any brown sugar, you can use white
2 level teaspoons mixed spice
1 egg, beaten
6 oz mixed fruit (175 g)—currants, raisins, sultanas, candied peel
Grated rind of half an orange
Freshly grated nutmeg

Pre-heat the oven to gas mark 4, 350°F (180°C)

A 2–2½ pint (1·25–1·5 litre) baking dish, buttered.

Begin by breaking the bread into suitable-sized pieces and place them in a bowl. Pour over the milk, then give the mixture a good stir and leave it for about 30 minutes so that the bread becomes well soaked with the milk.

Now add the melted butter, the sugar, mixed spice and beaten egg. Using a fork, beat the mixture well, making sure that no lumps remain, then stir in the mixed fruit and orange rind. Next spread the mixture in the prepared baking dish and sprinkle over some freshly grated nutmeg. Bake in the pre-heated oven for about 1¼ hours. This is nice served with hot custard but some people are particularly partial to eating it cold.

For a richer version of this pudding see below.

See also:
Rich bread and butter pudding
Turkish stuffed peppers

Recommended books

There are so many cookbooks, on every conceivable aspect of cookery, that one hardly knows where to begin. But the following list is a selection of my own favourites, ones which I have found useful. Anyone who has followed the Cookery Course should have a working knowledge of the basics of cooking, but for those who want to take the subject further here is a short list of further reading.

Acton, Eliza, *Modern Cookery for Private Families*, 1845, reprinted as *The Best of Eliza Acton's Modern Cookery for Private Families* by Longman in 1968, and Penguin Books 1980. Several of her recipes have appeared in the Cookery Course.

Carrier, Robert, *Food, Wine and Friends*, Sidgwick and Jackson, 1980.

Child, Julia, *From Julia Child's Kitchen*, Cape, n.e. 1978.

Cleave, T. L., *The Saccharine Disease*, Wright, 1974.

Costa, Margaret, *Four Seasons Cookery Book*, Nelson, 1971, and Sphere, 1972.

David, Elizabeth. I have found all her books invaluable. All are published by Penguin Books, and are as follows: *French Provincial Cooking*, 1970; *French Country Cooking*, 1970; *Italian Food*, 1970; *Mediterranean Food*, 1970; *Salt, Spices and Aromatics in the English Kitchen*, vol. 1 of *Ancient and Modern English Cooking*, 1970; and *English Bread and Yeast Cookery*, 1980.

Grant, Doris, *Your Daily Food*, Faber, 1973.

Grigson, Jane, *The International Wine and Food Society's Guide to Fish Cookery*, David and Charles, 1973, and Penguin Books, 1975; *The Vegetable Book*, Michael Joseph, 1978, and Penguin Books, 1980.

Hartley, Dorothy, *Food in England*, Macdonald 1955, and paperback 1975. The standard reference work on the subject.

Hazan, Marcella, *The Classic Italian Cook Book*, W. H. Allen, 1975.

Home and Freezer Digest, *Will It Freeze?* Jill Norman, 1980.

Leith, Prue and Waldegrave, Caroline, *Leith's Cookery Course* (3 vols), Fontana, 1980.

Liddell, Caroline, *The Wholefood Cook Book*, Coronet, 1980.

Loewenfeld, Claire, *Herb Gardening*, Faber, 1964.

Lyon, Ninette, *Meat at any Price*, Faber, paperback 1969.

Ministry of Agriculture, *Home Preservation of Fruit and Vegetables*, HMSO, 1972.

MacNeill, F. Marian, *The Scots Kitchen*, Mayflower, 1974.

Rubinstein, Helge and Bush, Sheila, *Ices Galore*, Deutsch, 1977.

Smith, Delia. More of my own recipes may be found in the following books, all published by Coronet: *How to Cheat at Cooking*, 1973; *Frugal Food*, 1976; *The 'Evening Standard' Cook Book*, 1978; and *Delia Smith's Book of Cakes*, 1978. Other recipes from some of the leading restaurateurs in England can be found in *Recipes from Country Inns and Restaurants*, Ebury Press, 1973, o.p.

Smith, Michael, *Fine English Cookery*, Faber, 1977.

Stewart, Katie, *'The Times' Cookery Book*, Collins, 1972; and *'The Times' Calendar Cook Book*, Pan, 1977.

Stobart, Tom, *Herbs, Spices and Flavourings*, Penguin Books, n.e. 1977.

Tovey, John, *Entertaining with Tovey*, Macdonald and Jane's, 1979.

Index

A

Aduki beans
    generally 342
    brown rice salad, and 344
Aioli sauce 484
All-in-one
    banana and walnut loaf 514
    sponge 594
Allspice 411
Almond
    baked apple and almond pudding
        643
    paste 609, 612
Alpine eggs 473
American
    brownies 628
    hamburgers 502
Anchoiade 504
Anchovy
    anchoiade 504
    butter 451
    lentil bean and anchovy salad 348
    starter, for 75
Apple
    and cinnamon crêpes 377
    baked apple and almond pudding
        643
    blackberry and apple pie 549
    braised red cabbage with 262
    caramelised apple flan 642
    charlotte 662
    cider baked, with toasted muesli
        659
    date, apple and walnut loaf 601
    eighteenth-century creamed apple
        flan 523
    Normandy pork with cream and
        196
    orange and apple crunch 654
    pheasant with cream and 522
    pie 551
    pork with apples and cider 197
    pork chops with sage and 400
    prune and apple sauce 231
    spiced apple and onion sauce 441
    spiced apple and raisin crumble
        647
    spiced apple and raisin pie 550
    tomato, apple and celery cream
        soup 110
Apricot hazelnut meringue 638
Arrowroot 431
Artichoke
    carrot and artichoke soup 109
    globe 269
    Jerusalem 270
    starter, for 74
    vinaigrette 72
Asparagus
    generally 256
    cheese tart, and 81
    eggs en cocotte with soured cream
        and 519
    starter, for 74
    vinaigrette 72

B

Aubergine
    generally 256
    baked aubergines with tomatoes
        257
    Italian stuffed 505
Avocado
    four star salad 496
    guacamole 426
    mousse with prawns and
        vinaigrette 78
    sauce 446
    seafood salad, and 78
    soup 99
    vinaigrette 72, 77

B

Bacon
    generally 172
    cauliflower with garlic and 264
    egg pie, and 511
    fried cabbage with 261
    halibut with 125
    hot mushroom and bacon vol-au-
        vent filling 572
    macaroni with leeks and 368
    mashed swedes with 291
    pot roast 173
    smoked bacon and lentil soup 100
    thick bean and bacon soup 352
Baked
    meat and macaroni pie 367
    stuffed courgettes 693
Banana
    all-in-one banana and walnut loaf
        514
Baps, breakfast 58
Bara brith 61
Barbecue
    generally 500
    charcoal 501
    equipment 502
    laying the fire 501
    lighting-up 501
    sauce 219, 507
Barley 314
Basil
    generally 382
    fresh tomato soup with 107
    Pesto alla Genovese 394
Batter, fish 136
Bayleaves 382
Beans
    haricot bean and salami salad 494
    Italian bean and pasta soup 347
    lentil, bean and anchovy salad 348
    oxtail with haricot 250
    thick bean and bacon soup 352
    white bean and tuna fish salad 80
    see also individual beans e.g. aduki,
        runner
Béarnaise sauce 440
Béchamel sauce 434
Beef
    generally 159
    beer, in 187
    bœuf Bourguignonne 190
    bœuf en croûte 566

bœuf en daube 162
boiled beef with dumplings 164
braised meatballs with peppers
    and tomatoes 203
braised steak and onions in stout
    191
braised steak with green
    peppercorn sauce 417
chilli con carne 346
curry with whole spices 419
English pot roast 163
Hungarian goulash 189
meat loaf 513
moussaka 422
simple Stroganoff 188
special cottage pie 692
steak and kidney pie 561
steak and kidney pudding 562
steak au poivre 416
stewed shin of beef with mushroom
    dumplings 192
stock
    brown 92
    light 93
    pressure-cooked 93
Beetroot
    chilled consommé 101
    salads, in 486
Biscuits
    American brownies 628
    cheese savouries 630
    gingernuts 629
    oatmeal 627
    origins 623
    shortbread 624
    whole oat crunchies 627
Bitter orange sauce 444
Black beans 342
Black-eyed beans 342
Black Forest gateau 532
Blackberry and apple pie 549
Blackcurrant
    crumble 649
    ice cream 531
    jam 683
Bloater 139
    paste 140
Bœuf Bourguignonne 190
Bœuf en croûte 566
Bœuf en daube 162
Braised
    celery with cheese and onion sauce
        265
    meatballs with peppers and
        tomatoes 203
    peas with lettuce and spring onions
        288
    red cabbage with apples 262
    steak and onions in stout 191
    steak with green peppercorn sauce
        417
Braising 189
Bramble jelly 685
Brandy
    butter 452
    sauce 449
Bread
    generally 42

butter pudding, and 661
chapattis 59
oatmeal 53
old-fashioned bread pudding 697
poppy seed rolls 57
quick and easy wholewheat 50
quick wheatmeal rolls 55
sauce 441
soured cream soda 54
wheatmeal 42, 44
white 52
wholewheat 42
Breakfast baps 58
Broad beans
generally 258
baby broad beans in parsley sauce 259
purée 258
salad 497
Broccoli
generally 259
cheese soufflé 471
fritters 260
Broth, Scotch 102
Brownies, American 628
Brussels sprouts 260
Bubble and squeak 696
Buckling, smoked 140
Buckwheat
flour 317
vegetable and buckwheat pie 319
whole 317
Buns
chocolate and hazelnut choux 582
hot cross 62
Butter
anchovy 451
brandy 452
flavoured 450
garlic 509
green 169
herb 450
hot lemon 451
rum 658
Butter beans 341
Butterfly cakes 596
Butterscotch sauce 448

C
Cabbage
generally 261
bubble and squeak 696
fried, with bacon 261
garlic and juniper, with 262
leaves stuffed with rice 332
red cabbage and coriander salad 492
red cabbage braised with apples 262
red cabbage, pickled 676
salads, in 486
Cakes
all-in-one 591
baking process 586
Black Forest gateau 532
boil-and-bake 591

Christmas 608
creaming 591
date, apple and walnut loaf 601
Dundee 605
family 600
fruit sinking 589
honey and spice 515
ingredients 587
lemon curd butterfly 596
marmalade 604
methods of making 591
oatmeal parkin 600
over-browning 589
problems 589
rich fruit 606
quantities and cooking times 612
rubbing in 591
sponge see Sponge cakes
squidgy chocolate log 602
sticky date 603
storage 591
tins, preparation 587, 590
Cannelloni, pancake 374
Capers 125, 134, 144, 411
Capsicums 407
Caramelised apple flan 642
Caraway seeds 411
Cardinal peaches 636
Cardamom 412
Carrot
generally 263
Artichoke soup, and 109
spring carrots with tarragon butter 263
spring onions and cream, with 263
tarragon soup, and 392
Casseroles
generally 13, 183, 186
electric slow cookers 186
pressure cookers 186
principles 183
Cassoulet 349
Cauliflower
generally 264
garlic and bacon, with 264
sautéed cauliflower with coriander 427
Cayenne pepper 408
Celery
generally 265
braised celery with cheese and onion sauce 265
cream of celery soup 109
sauce 439
tomato, apple and celery cream soup 110
Cevapcici 503
Chapattis 59
Charcuterie 73
Cheese
Alpine eggs 473
asparagus tart, and 81
baked spinach with brown rice and 289
blue-veined 457
British 459
broccoli cheese soufflé 471
buying 459

and herb sausages 465
cœur à la crème 478
continental 461
cottage 457
courgette and cheese quiche 560
courgettes and tomatoes au gratin 268
cream 458
cream cheese and herb vol-au-vent filling 572
cream cheese with herbs 402
curd
generally 457
home-made 535
Dutch 462
omelette 470
eggs and leeks au gratin 32
factory 458
farmhouse 458
Feta 469
fillets of sole gratiné 469
French 461
goat's 462
gougère with 584
grading 458
Greek 462
Greek salad 469
ham, egg and cheese risotto 695
hard 457
Italian 462
making 456
Mozzarella 73
onion quichelets, and 463
onion sauce with braised celery, and 265
pan-fried pizza 464
pastry 467
pizza with Mozzarella 65
Richmond maids of honour 573
Roman gnocchi 465
sauce 436
savouries 630
soft paste 456
soufflé 35
soufflé pancakes 376
soupe à l'oignon gratinée 104
spinach and cream cheese quiche 466
starter, for 73
storing 459
Swiss 462
tartlets with mushroom pâté 473
toasted cheese with ale 468
Welsh rarebit soufflé 468
wholewheat cheese-crusted scones 620
wholewheat macaroni 369
Cheesecake
curd, with fruit topping 475
fresh lemon, with frosted grapes 476
orange 475
Cherry pie 550
Chervil 383
Chestnut and apple stuffing 228
Chick pea
generally 342
hummus bi tahina 354

salad 493
spiced lamb with 355
Chicken
  generally 206
  barbecue sauce, in 219
  boning 209
  carcass stock 94
  carving 211
  chill-fresh 207
  choosing 208
  cold chicken pie 221
  coq au vin 214
  creamed chicken with avocado 214
  creamy chicken curry 694
  free-range 207
  fried mustard-and-herb-coated 217
  frozen 207, 209
  giblet stock 94
  grape stuffing, with 222
  in the pot 216
  jointing 209
  lemon sauce, with 218
  liver pâté 84
  New York dressed 207
  paprika 421
  pressure-cooked chicken stock 94
  roast 211
  salad with tarragon and grapes 396
  spiced 420
  stuffing 210, 211
  trussing 210
  whole spices, with 220
Chicory in salads 486
Chilladas 350
Chilled
  avocado soup 99
  beetroot consommé 101
  Spanish gazpacho 106
Chilli
  generally 407
  con carne 346
  eggs 37
  sauce, pork kidneys in 247
Chinese
  beansprout salad with soy dressing 495
  leaf 486
  mushroom soup 108
Chips 280
Chives
  generally 383
  trout with butter, cream and 398
Chocolate
  American brownies 628
  cold chocolate orange soufflé 641
  fudge filling and topping 599
  hazelnut choux buns, and 582
  hot rum soufflé 661
  melting 632
  mousse 640
  orange mousse 641
  puddings, for 632
  soured cream and chocolate filling 599
  sponge, all-in-one 595
  squidgy chocolate log 602
  walnut and chocolate pudding 655
Cholesterol, 23

Christmas
  cake 608
  pudding 652
Chutney
  generally 668
  cranberry and orange relish 674
  damson ketchup 673
  green tomato 668
  Old Doverhouse 671
  spiced plum or damson 669
  sweet piccalilli 672
  Victoria plum ketchup 673
Cider
  baked apples with toasted muesli 659
  spiced pears in 427
  vinegar 410, 480
Cinnamon
  generally 412
  damson (or plum) and cinnamon crumble 648
  flan 575
Cloves 412
Cod 120
Cod's roe
  smoked 86, 138
  taramasalata 86, 138
Cœur à la crème 478
Coffee
  all-in-one walnut and coffee sponge 595
  cream mousseline 598
  éclairs 582
Coley 120
Consommé, chilled beetroot 101
Conversion tables 6
Coq au vin 214
Coriander
  generally 413
  baked lamb with 178
  baked marrow with tomatoes and 272
  marinaded pork with 422
  sautéed cauliflower with 427
Cornflour 431
Cornish pasty pie 557
Corn-on-the-cob 267
Cottage pie, special 692
Country pâté 82
Courgettes
  generally 267
  baked stuffed 693
  cheese and courgette quiche 560
  fritters 267
  tomatoes and courgettes au gratin 268
Crab
  hot crab soufflé 154
  how to dress 152
Crackling 168, 169, 171
Cranberry and orange relish 674
Cream
  clotted 518
  cœur à la crème 478
  and egg sauce 142
  double 518
  eighteenth-century creamed apple flan 523

half 518
  ice see Ice cream
  pheasant with apples and 521
  poached eggs with cream and watercress 31
  pork chops with mushrooms and 521
  puddings, for 632
  puffs 573
  ready-whipped 518
  rich lemon cream with frosted grapes 526
  single 518
  soured see Soured cream
  sterilised 518
  ultra heat treated 518
  whipping 518, 632
Cream cheese with herbs 402, 572
Creamed chicken with avocado 214
Crème
  brûlée 528
  caramel 527
  patissière 574
Crêpes Suzette 273
Crudités 74
Crumble
  blackcurrant 649
  damson and cinnamon 648
  dried fruit 648
  gooseberry 648
  plum and cinnamon 648
  raspberry 649
  rhubarb and ginger 648
  spiced apple and raisin 647
Crumble topping
  basic 644
  variations 647
Crumpets 622
Cucumber
  chilled yoghurt and cucumber soup 536
  raita 537
  salads, in 486
  sauce 439
  soured cream and dill, with 399
  yoghurt and cucumber salad 331
Cultured cream see Soured cream
Cumberland sauce 442
Cumin 413
Curd cheesecake 475
Curry
  beef curry with whole spices 419
  creamy chicken 694
  egg and lentil 30
  Indian kebabs 418
  lambs' kidneys 243
  nut roast 326
  ox kidneys 245
  paste 413
  powder 413
Custard
  patissière 574
  sauce 447

D
Dab 121
Damson
  cinnamon crumble, and 648

jam 683
ketchup 673
plum pie 550
Date
  apple and walnut loaf 601
  sticky date cake 603
Dill
  generally 384
  cucumber with soured cream and 399
Dogfish 119
Dolmades 329
Dover sole 118, 126
Dressing, vinaigrette 481
Dried fruit
  crumble 648
  jelly 637
  salad with yoghurt and nuts 538
Duck
  generally 224
  buying 224
  cooking times 225
  drying 224
  gravy 226
  roast 225
  sauces for 226
  stuffing 225
Dumplings
  boiled beef with 164
  mushroom 192
  parsley 193
Dundee cake 605
Dutch omelette 470
Duxelles 273
Dwarf Beans 258

E
Eccles cakes 567
Eclairs, coffee 582
Eel, smoked 138
Eggs
  generally 22
  Alpine 473
  bacon and egg pie 511
  baked 28
  boiled 26
  cheese soufflé 35
  chilli 37
  cream and egg sauce 142
  en cocotte with soured cream and asparagus 519
  Florentine 290
  frying 28
  ham, egg and cheese risotto 695
  hard-boiled 26
  hollandaise sauce 437
  hot chocolate rum soufflé 661
  leeks au gratin, and 32
  lentil curry, and 30
  mayonnaise 72
  omelettes 28, 29, 30, 39
  piperade 36
  poached 27
    with cream and watercress 31
  sauce béarnaise 440
  sauce sabayon 448
  Scotch eggs with fresh herbs 510

scrambled 27
Spanish tortilla 512
storing 25
whisking 25
zabaglione 38
Egyptian beans 343
Eighteenth-century creamed apple flan 523
Electric slow cookers 186
Eliza Acton's
  English salad sauce 484
  rich rice pudding 658
  vegetable mulligatawny 105
English
  pot roast 163
  rhubarb fool 525
Equipment 11
  baking 13
  casseroles 13, 186
  chopping 16
  cutting 16
  food processor 20
  frying-pans 13
  grating 17
  grinding 18
  jam jars 677
  liquidising 20
  measuring 19
  meat roasting tins 13
  mincing 18
  mixing 14
  pastry-making 13, 543
  pressure cooker 186
  saucepans 11
  sieving 19
  sifting 19
  skewers 20, 255, 502
  slow cooker 186
  steamer 649
  straining 19
  temperature 20
  testing 20
  timing 20
  whisking 14

F
Faggots and peas 241
Fennel
  generally 268, 384, 486
  braised 268
  salads, in 486
Fig pudding, spiced 657
Fish
  baked, with mushrooms 126
  baked, with soured cream and capers 125
  baking 117
  batter 136
  cakes 691
  cod 120
  coley 120
  dab 121
  deep-frying 116
  dogfish 119
  en papillote 117
  fisherman's pie 123
  flake 119

flounder 121
foil, in 117
frying 115
garlicky fish soup 111
grilling 116
haddock 120
hake 120
halibut 120
herring 128
huss 119
Italian baked 121
kebabs 124
mackerel 131
Norwegian red 120
oily 128
plaice 121
poaching 117
preparation 114
salmon 135
skate 119
smoked 136
smoked fish pâté 87
smoked fish creams 82
smoked fish pie 142
sole 118
sprat 133
starter, for 74
steaming 117
stock 95
trout 134
turbot 120
whitebait 132
whiting 120
witch sole 118
see also types of fish e.g. Haddock
Fisherman's pie 123
Flageolets 343
Flake 119
Flaky fish pie 122
Flan
  caramelised apple 642
  crisp cinnamon 575
  eighteenth-century creamed apple 523
  leek and soured cream 520
  Linzertorte 576
  plum and soured cream 524
Flounder 121
Flour
  generally 42
  pastry, in 541, 569, 577
  sauces, in 431
Forks, kitchen 15
Four star salad 496
Fresh fruit salad 636
Fruit
  cake 606
  dried fruit crumble 648
  dried fruit jelly 637
  dried fruit salad with yoghurt and nuts 538
  fresh fruit and mint vinaigrette 76
  jam, for 677
  pies, deep 548
  salad 636
  scones, wholewheat 619
Frying
  eggs 28

fish 115
pans 13
Fudge, chocolate, filling and topping 599

G

Gammon
generally 172
sugar-glazed 174
Garam masala 413
Gardeners' soup 100
Garlic
generally 385
bread 504
butter 509
fish soup 111
hot herb and garlic loaf 504
mussels with garlic stuffing 147
plaice fillets with garlic and herbs 127
Gazpacho 106
Gelatine 632
Ginger
generally 414
rhubarb and ginger crumble 648
Gingernuts 629
Girdle cakes 621
Globe artichoke 269
Gnocchi 465
Goose, roast stuffed 231
Gooseberry
crumble 648
pie 550
Gougère with cheese 584
Goujons of sole 118
Goulash
Hungarian 189
vegetarian 328
Grapes
chicken salad with tarragon and 396
frosted, fresh lemon cheesecake with 476
frosted, rich lemon cream with 526
stuffing 222
Gratin dauphinois 284
Graters 17
Gravy 452
Greek salad 469
Green herb and rice salad 394
Green herb soup 392
Green salad 488
Green tomato chutney 668
Green tomato sauce, spiced 445
Green winter salad 488
Grilling fish 116
Guacamole 426

H

Haddock
generally 120
Arbroath smokies 140
Finnan 140
golden cutlets 141
potted haddock with capers 144
smoked 140
smoked fillets 141
smoked fish creams 82
smoked haddock with cream and egg sauce 142
Hake 120
Halibut
generally 120
bacon with 125
Ham
generally 172
croquettes 696
egg and cheese risotto 695
Parma 72, 73
Hamburgers 502
Haricot beans
generally 341
oxtail with 250
salami and haricot bean salad 494
Hazelnut
apricot hazelnut meringue 638
chocolate and hazelnut choux buns 582
vegetable and hazelnut burgers 327
Heart 237
Herb
generally 380
baked mackerel with herb stuffing 398
butter 450
chopping 381
cream cheese and herb vol-au-vent filling 572
cream cheese with 402
dried 381
freezing 380
fresh, cooking with 381
green herb and rice salad 394
green herb soup 392
hot herb and garlic loaf 504
nine herb salad of Hintlesham 395
plaice fillets with garlic and 127
poached trout with 397
storing 380
see also individual herbs e.g. Basil
Herring
generally 128
pickled 75
Russian 75
smoked 139
soused 129
stuffed baked 130
Hollandaise sauce 437
John Tovey's quick 39
Honey and spice cake 515
Hors d'oeuvres 72
Horseradish 161
Hot cross buns 62
Hot herb and garlic loaf 504
Hotpot
ox liver and bacon 240
traditional Lancashire 194
Hummus bi tahina 354
Hungarian goulash 189
Huss 119

I

Ice cream
blackcurrant 531
praline 530
vanilla 529
Icing
modelling paste 614
royal 609, 613
Indian kebabs 418
Irish stew with parsley dumplings 193
Italian
baked fish 121
bean and pasta soup 347
green sauce 446
stuffed aubergines 505

J

Jam
blackcurrant 683
damson 683
fruit for 677
jars 677
loganberry 682
making 676, 677
plum 683
strawberry 681
sugar for 677
testing for set 677
Jelly
dried fruit 637
quick bramble 685
redcurrant 686
Jerusalem artichoke 270
John Tovey's
quick hollandaise sauce 39
rough puff pastry 570
Juniper
generally 414
cabbage with garlic and 262
liver in yoghurt and juniper sauce 239

K

Kebabs
fish 124
Indian 418
lamb 506
Yugoslav 503
Kedgeree, buttery 312
Ketchup, Victoria plum or damson 673
Kidney
generally 235
beefsteak and kidney pie 561
beefsteak and kidney pudding 562
curried ox 245
jacket potatoes, kidneys in 244
lambs' see Lambs' kidneys
ox 235
pork see Pork kidneys
preparation 236
rice and kidney stuffing 177
veal 235
Kipper
generally 139
fish cakes 141
grilled 139
jugged 139

marinaded kipper fillets 144
quiche 560
Knives 16

L
Lamb
generally 175
baked lamb with coriander 178
Irish stew with parsley dumplings
193
kebabs 506
leg of lamb, baked with butter and
herbs 401
moussaka 422
mustard glazed lamb cutlets 506
ragoût of 195
shoulder of lamb with rice and
kidney stuffing 177
spiced lamb with chick peas 355
spring sauce for 393
stuffed breast 176
tongue casserole 249
traditional Lancashire hotpot 194
Lambs' kidneys
generally 235
curried 243
fresh tomato sauce, in 243
jacket potatoes, in 244
red wine, in 242
Lambs' liver
generally 234
paprika 238
peppered 238
yoghurt and juniper sauce, in 239
Lancashire hotpot 194
Lancaster lemon tart 553
Lasagne al forno 366
Leek
generally 271
buttered 271
cream sauce 439
eggs and leeks au gratin 32
macaroni with leeks and bacon 368
onion and potato soup 97
and soured cream flan, 520
turnips and leeks boulangère 293
Lemon
curd 598
curd butterfly cakes 596
fresh lemon cheesecake with
frosted grapes 476
hot lemon butter 451
Lancaster lemon tart 553
layer cake, all-in-one 595
meringue pie 554
rich lemon cream with frosted
grapes 526
salad, for 481
sauce 218
sole 118
soufflé omelette 39
sponge, all-in-one 595
squeezer 18
surprise pudding 656
zester 17
Lentil
generally 342

bean and anchovy salad 348
chilladas 350
egg and lentil curry 30
smoked bacon and lentil soup 100
split 342
vegetarian shepherd's pie 351
Lettuce in salads 485
Lima beans 342
Linzertorte 576
Liquidiser 20
Liver
generally 234
calves' 234
chicken liver pâté 84
faggots and peas 241
frying 235
grilling 235
lambs' see Lambs' liver
ox 234
ox liver and bacon hotpot 240
pigs' 234
Loaf
banana and walnut 514
hot herb and garlic 504
meat 513
non-meat 335
tin 49
Loganberry jam 682
Loin of pork Dijonnaise 171
Lovage 385

M
Macaroni
baked meat and macaroni pie 367
leeks and bacon, with 368
wholewheat macaroni cheese 369
Mace 414
Mackerel
generally 131
baked mackerel with herb stuffing
398
marinaded 131
smoked 138
smoked mackerel pâté 86
Malt vinegar 410
Mange tout 271
Marinade for beef 162
Marinaded
kipper fillets 144
mackerel 131
mushrooms 79
pork with coriander 422
Marjoram 386
Marmalade
cake 604
fruit for 677
jars 677
making 676, 677
Seville orange 683
sugar for 677
testing for set 677
Marrow
generally 272
baked marrow with tomatoes and
coriander 272
Mayonnaise
generally 482

home-made 483
quick 484
Meatballs, braised with peppers and
tomatoes 203
Meat loaf 513
Melon 75
Meringue
apricot hazelnut 638
lemon meringue pie 554
Pavlova 634
queen of puddings 660
Mince pies 552
Mincemeat, home-made Christmas
686
Mincer 18
Minestrone soup with rice 98
Mint
generally 386
fresh fruit and mint vinaigrette 76
redcurrant, orange and mint sauce
443
sauce 176
spring sauce for lamb 393
Mixed spice 415
Mixed vegetables à la Grècque 333
Modelling paste 614
Morello cherry sauce 444
Mortadella 73
Moussaka 422
Moules à la marinière 146
Mousse
chocolate orange 641
rich chocolate 640
Mozzarella and tomatoes 74
Muesli 318
Muffins 59
Mulligatawny, Eliza Acton's
vegetable 105
Mushroom
generally 273
bacon and mushroom vol-au-vent
filling 572
baked fish with 127
Chinese mushroom soup 108
dumplings 192
duxelles 273
four star salad 496
hot garlic butter, in 274
marinaded 79
onion and mushroom quiche 559
pâté 473
pizza with salami and 64
pork chops with cream and 521
pork kidneys in mushroom and
onion sauce 246
Mussels
generally 145
cleaning 145
garlic stuffing, with 147
moules à la marinière 146
Mustard
generally 161, 408
glazed lamb cutlets 506
sauce 435

N
Nine herb salad of Hintlesham 395

Non-meat loaf 335
Normandy pork with cream and apples 196
Nutmeg 415
Nuts
    curried nut roast 326
    dried fruit salad with yoghurt and 538
    hazelnut and vegetable burgers 327

O

Oatmeal
    biscuits 627
    bread 53
    grades 626
    parkin 600
    porridge 319
Oats
    generally 317, 626
    flakes 626
    jumbo 626
    quick cooking 626
    rolled 626
    whole 626
    whole oat crunchies 627
Offal see types of offal e.g. Liver
Oil
    generally 480
    groundnut 481
    olive 481
    soya 481
    sunflower 481
Old Doverhouse chutney 671
Omelette
    generally 28, 39
    Dutch 470
    fines herbes 29
    lemon soufflé 39
    open-faced 29
    savoyard 30
    Spanish tortilla 512
Onion
    generally 274
    buttery onion sauce 438
    cheese and onion sauce with braised celery 265
    crisp-fried onion rings 275
    leek, onion and potato soup 97
    pork kidneys in mushroom and onion sauce 246
    quick pickled 675
    sauce 438
    soupe à l'oignon gratinée 104
    soured cream and onion sauce 251
    spiced apple and onion sauce 441
    thick onion tart 337
Orange
    apple and orange crunch 654
    bitter orange sauce 444
    cheesecake 475
    chocolate orange mousse 641
    cold chocolate orange soufflé 641
    cranberry and orange relish 674
    curd 598
    layer cake, all-in-one 595
    redcurrant, orange and mint sauce 443

sponge cake, all-in-one 595
Ossobuco 201
Oven temperature 7
Ox kidneys, curried 245
Ox liver and bacon hotpot 240
Ox tongue 236, 248
Oxtail
    generally 236
    haricot beans, with 250

P

Pancakes
    generally 370
    apple and cinnamon crêpes 377
    basic 371
    buckwheat 373
    cannelloni 374
    cheese soufflé 376
    crêpes Suzette 373
    honey 373
    keeping hot 371
    lemon 372
    pan for 371
    re-heating 371
    spinach stuffed pancakes with cheese sauce 375
    strawberry jam 372
    syrup 373
Paprika
    generally 408
    chicken 421
    liver 238
Parma ham 72, 73
Parsley
    generally 387
    dumplings 193
    sauce 436
Parsnip
    generally 275
    baked 275
    creamed 275
Pasta
    generally 358
    boiling 362
    cooking 360
    egg 359
    fresh tomato sauce for 363
    green 359
    home-made 359
    ingredients for pasta recipes 361
    quantities 361
    ragù Bolognese 364
    shapes 359
    wholemeal 359
    see also various types of pasta e.g. Macaroni
Pasties, spinach 324
Pastry
    generally 540
    cheese 467
    choux 577, 578
    fats in 541
    flour for 541, 569, 577
    John Tovey's rough puff 570
    puff 569
    quiche 558
    quick flaky 565

rich flan 575
shortcrust 540, 542, 548
suet crust 560, 561
wholewheat 548
Pâté
    chicken liver 84
    country 82
    mushroom 473
    pork 84
    smoked fish 87
    smoked mackerel 86
    taramasalata 86
Pavlova 634
Peaches, cardinal 636
Pears, spiced in cider 427
Pea
    generally 287
    braised peas with lettuce and spring onions 288
    chick pea salad 493
    dried 342
    faggots and 241
    mange tout 271
    pease pudding 356
    thick pea soup 345
Pease pudding 356
Pepper (spice)
    generally 406
    mill 18
    steak au poivre 416
Peppers, Turkish stuffed 307
Peppered liver 238
Pestle and mortar 18
Pesto alla Genovese 394
Pheasant with cream and apples 522
Pickling
    generally 675
    onions 675
    red cabbage 676
Picnics
    generally 508
    equipment 509
    foods for 509
Pie
    apple and blackberry 549
    apple, double-crust 551
    bacon and egg 511
    beefsteak and kidney 561
    buckwheat and vegetable 319
    cold chicken 221
    cherry 550
    Cornish pasty 557
    damson plum 550
    deep fruit 548
    double-crust fruit 550
    fisherman's 123
    flaky fish 122
    gooseberry 550
    lemon meringue 554
    meat and macaroni, baked 367
    mince 552
    rabbit 563
    rhubarb, double-crust 552
    smoked fish 142
    special cottage 692
    spiced apple and raisin 550
    summer fruits 552
    vegetarian shepherd's 351

Piperade 36
Pissaladière 69
Pizza
  dough 63
  Mozzarella, anchovies and olives,
    with 65
  pan fried 464
  pissaladière 69
  quick wholewheat 66
  salami and mushrooms, with 64
  scone 334
Plaice
  generally 121
  baked with mushrooms 126
  fillets with garlic and herbs 127
Plum
  cinnamon crumble, and 648
  jam 683
  soured cream and, flan 524
  spiced plum chutney 669
  Victoria plum ketchup 673
Poaching
  eggs 27
  fish 117
Poppy seed rolls 57
Pork
  generally 167
  apples and cider, with 197
  braised meatballs with pepper and
    tomatoes 203
  cassoulet 349
  chops with cream and mushrooms
    521
  chops with sage and apples 400
  crackling 168, 169, 171
  green butter, with 169
  loin of pork Dijonnaise 171
  marinaded pork with coriander 422
  meat loaf 513
  Normandy pork with cream and
    apples 196
  pâté 84
  sage and onion stuffing 227
  sausages braised with red wine 202
  Spanish pork with olives 198
  spare ribs in barbecue sauce 507
  stuffed tenderloin 170
Pork kidneys
  generally 236
  chilli sauce, in 247
  mushroom and onion sauce, in 246
Porridge 319
Port wine sauce 240, 449
Pot roasting
  generally 158
  bacon 173
  English pot roast 163
Potatoes
  generally 276
  boulangère 283
  bubble and squeak 696
  chips 280
  creamed with nutmeg 278
  creamed with soured cream and
    chives 278
  gratin dauphinois 284
  jacket 279
  jacket, kidneys in 244

jacket, soured cream and chives
    with 279
leek, onion and potato soup 97
mashed 278
new 286
new Jersey potatoes with fresh herb
    butter 286
new potato salad with mint and
    chives 492
roast 278
sauté Lyonnaise 285
sauté Niçoise 286
stuffed potatoes with garlic and
    herbs 280
Potted haddock with capers 144
Poultry see types e.g. Chicken
Praline ice cream 530
Prawns
  generally 150
  avocado mousse with prawns and
    vinaigrette 78
  spiced prawns with tomatoes 151
Preserving
  generally 666
  chutney-making see Chutney
  gauze 667
  ingredients 667
  jam see Jam
  jars 667
  pans 666
  waxed paper discs 667
Pressure-cooked
  beef stock 93
  casseroles 186
  chicken stock 94
  puddings 650
Profiteroles 581
Prosciutto 73
Proteins 323
Provençale vegetable stew 336
Prune, apple and sauce 231
Pudding
  generally 632, 643
  baked apple and almond 643
  beefsteak and kidney 562
  bread and butter 661
  chocolate and walnut 655
  chocolate for 632
  Christmas 652
  crumble see Crumble
  Eliza Acton's rich rice 658
  ingredients for 651
  lemon surprise 656
  old-fashioned bread 697
  pease 356
  pressure cooking 650
  queen of 660
  St Stephen's 654
  spiced fig 657
  steaming 649
  steamed raisin 652
  summer 633
  wholewheat treacle sponge 657
  Yorkshire 161
Pulses
  generally 340
  varieties 341
Punchnep 293

Punchnep soup 103

Q
Queen of puddings 660
Quiche
  generally 558
  courgette and cheese 560
  kipper 560
  mushroom and onion 559
  pastry 558
  spinach and cream cheese 466
Quichelets, cheese and onion 463

R
Rabbit pie 563
Ragoût of lamb 195
Ragù Bolognese 364
Raisin crumble, spiced apple and 647
Raisin pie, spiced apple and 550
Raspberry crumble 649
Raspberry purée, strawberries in 635
Ratatouille 336
Red cabbage see Cabbage
Red kidney bean
  generally 341
  chilli con carne 346
  salad 353
Redcurrant
  jelly 686
  orange and mint sauce 443
Rhubarb
  fool 525
  ginger and, crumble 648
  pie 552
Rice
  generally 298
  Arborio 301
  baked spinach with brown rice and
    cheese 289
  Basmati 300
  brown 299
  brown rice and aduki bean salad
    344
  brown rice and tuna fish salad 491
  brown rice, lentil and mushroom
    salad 306
  brown rice pudding with prunes
    and apricots 313
  brown rice with vegetables and
    cheese sauce 325
  buttery kedgeree 312
  cabbage leaves stuffed with 332
  Carolina 300
  easy-cook 300
  grades 299
  green herb and rice salad 394
  ham, egg and cheese risotto 695
  herb butter, with 305
  kidney and rice stuffing 177
  long grain 299
  medium grain 299
  mushrooms with 304
  onion 304
  Patna 300
  peppers with 304
  perfect 303

pre-cooked 300
prepared 299
products 301
pudding 658
regional varieties 300
risotto *see* Risotto
rules for cooking 301
saffron 305
salad 490
short grain 299
spiced pilau 305
Turkish stuffed peppers 307
white (polished) 300
Rich lemon cream with frosted grapes 526
Richmond maids of honour 573
Rillettes de Tours 84
Risotto
alla Milanese 309
chicken livers and mushrooms with 308
ham, egg and cheese 695
spring, for 310
Rissoles 690
Roasting
generally 159
beef 160
chicken 211
duck 225
lamb 175
pork 168
potatoes 278
stuffed goose with prune and apple sauce 231
turkey 229
Rollmops 75
Rolls (bread)
poppy seed 57
quick wheatmeal 55
Roman gnocchi 465
Rosemary 387
Rough puff pastry 570
Roux 432
Royal icing 609, 613
Rum
butter 658
hot chocolate rum soufflé 661
sauce 449
Runner beans 258
Rye 314

S
Sabayon sauce 448
Saffron 415
Saffron rice 305
Sage
generally 388
pork chops with sage and apples 400
St Stephen's pudding 654
Salad
generally 480
aduki bean and brown rice 344
avocado and seafood 78
basket 19
broad bean 497
brown rice and tuna fish 491

brown rice, lentil and mushroom 306
chick pea 493
chicken salad with tarragon and grapes 396
Chinese beansprout salad with soy dressing 495
cucumber and yoghurt 331
dressings 480, 487
Eliza Acton's English salad sauce 484
four star 496
Greek 469
green 388
green herb and rice 394
green winter 488
haricot bean and salami 494
ingredients and their preparation 485
lemons for 481
lentil, bean and anchovy 348
new potato salad with mint and chives 492
nine herb salad of Hintlesham 395
Niçoise 498
oil for 480
raw spinach and watercress 489
red bean 353
red cabbage and coriander 492
rice 490
tomato 72, 488
vinaigrette dressing 481
vinegar for 480
white bean and tuna fish 80
Salami
haricot bean and salami salad 494
pizza with salami and mushrooms 64
starter, as 73
Salmon
generally 135
foil-baked fresh 135
smoked 137
Salmon trout 136
Salsa verde 446
Salt 405
Sardines
Portuguese 74
stuffed tomatoes 74
Sauce
aioli 484
avocado 446
barbecue 219, 507
basil 394
béarnaise 440
béchamel 434
bitter orange 444
brandy 449
bread 441
butterscotch 448
buttery onion 438
celery 439
cheese 436
cheese and onion 265
cooking time 432
cream and egg 142
cucumber 439
Cumberland 442

curdling, in 430, 431, 438
custard 447
Eliza Acton's English salad 484
fats in 432
flour in 431
fresh tomato 363
green peppercorn 417
hollandaise 39, 437
Italian green 446
leek cream 439
lemon 218
liquid in 431
lumps in 430
mint 176
morello cherry 444
mustard 133, 435
onion 438
parsley 436
port wine 449
prune and apple 231
redcurrant, orange and mint 443
reheating 433
rouille 484
roux 432
rum 449
sabayon 448
spiced apple and onion 441
spiced green tomato 445
spinach and cheese 436
spring sauce for lamb 393
tabasco 408
tartare 484
tomato chilli 364
tomato, fresh 363
white 433, 434
yoghurt 503
Sausage
braised in red wine 202
cheese and herb 465
four star salad 496
rolls 565
Sauté potatoes
Lyonnaise 285
Niçoise 286
Sautéed mixed vegetables 331
Scales, measuring 19
Scallops
generally 147
cream soup 149
in the shell 148
Scampi 151
Scissors, kitchen 17
Scone pizza 334
Scones
generally 618
plain 619
problems 618
wholewheat cheese-crusted 620
wholewheat fruit 619
wholewheat girdle cakes 621
Scotch eggs with fresh herbs 510
Scotch broth 102
Scottish shortbread 624
Scrambling eggs 27
Seafood
avocado and seafood salad 78
yoghurt seafood sauce 536
Sesame and sunflower seeds, toasted 3.

Seville orange marmalade 683
Shallot 274
Shepherd's pie, vegetarian 351
Shortbread
  biscuits 624
  rules for making 623
  Scottish 624
  wholewheat 625
Shortcake, strawberry 625
Shrimps 150
Skate 119
  with black butter 119
Skewers 20, 255, 502
Smoked fish
  generally 136
  pâté 87
  see also types of fish e.g. Salmon
Soda bread 54
Sole
  generally 118
  goujons of 118
  gratiné, fillets of 469
  grilled 118
Sorrel 388
Soufflé
  broccoli cheese 471
  cheese 35
  cheese pancakes 376
  cold chocolate orange 641
  hot chocolate rum 661
  hot crab 154
  lemon soufflé omelette 39
  Welsh rarebit 468
Soup
  generally 95
  à l'oignon gratinée 104
  blending 96
  carrot and artichoke 109
  chilled avocado 99
  chilled beetroot consommé 101
  chilled Spanish gazpacho 106
  chilled yoghurt and cucumber 536
  Chinese mushroom 108
  cream of celery 109
  Eliza Acton's vegetable
    mulligatawny 105
  gardeners' 100
  garlicky fish 111
  green herb 392
  Italian bean and pasta 347
  leek, onion and potato 97
  minestrone with rice 98
  over-salted 96
  over-seasoning 96
  punchnep 103
  puréeing 96
  rescue operations 96
  scallop cream 149
  Scotch broth 102
  smoked bacon and lentil 100
  sweating vegetables for 95
  thick bean and bacon 352
  thick pea 345
  thickening 96
  thinning 97
  tomato with basil 107
  tomato, apple and celery cream 110
  vegetable mulligatawny 105

Vichyssoise 98
  watercress cream 103
Soured cream
  generally 519
  baked fish with soured cream and
    capers 125
  chocolate and soured cream filling
    599
  cucumber with soured cream and
    dill 399
  eggs en cocotte with asparagus and
    519
  leek and soured cream flan 524
  onion sauce, and 251
  plum and soured cream flan 524
  potatoes with chives and 279
  soda bread 54
Soy dressing 495
Soya beans 342
Spaghetti
  alla carbonara 364
  anchovies, mushrooms and olives,
    with 365
Spanish
  pork with olives 198
  tortilla 512
Spiced
  apple and onion sauce 441
  apple and raisin crumble 647
  apple and raisin pie 550
  chicken 420
  fig pudding 657
  green tomato sauce 445
  honey and spice cake 515
  lamb with chick peas 355
  pears in cider 427
  pilau rice 305
  plum or damson chutney 669
  prawns with tomatoes 151
Spices
  generally 404
  see also types of spice, e.g.
    Cardamom
Spinach
  generally 288
  baked spinach with brown rice and
    cheese 289
  cheese sauce, and 436
  cream cheese quiche, and 466
  eggs Florentine 290
  pasties 324
  raw spinach and watercress salad
    489
  stuffed pancakes with cheese sauce
    375
Split peas 342
Sponge cakes
  generally 592
  all-in-one 594
    chocolate 595
    coffee and walnut 595
    lemon 595
    lemon layer 595
    orange 595
    orange layer 595
    wholewheat 595
  classic Victoria 592
  fillings 597

sandwich tins 587
toppings 597
whisked fatless 595
Spoons 15
Sprats
  deep-fried in mustard sauce 133
  smoked 140
Spring onions in salads 487
Spring sauce for lamb 393
Squidgy chocolate log 602
Steak see Beef
Steamed puddings
  beefsteak and kidney 562
  Christmas 652
  raisin 652
  St Stephen's 654
  spiced fig 657
  wholewheat treacle sponge 657
Stewing 189
Sticky date cake 603
Stock
  basic notes 90, 91
  beef
    brown 92
    light 93
    pressure-cooked 93
  chicken
    carcass 94
    giblet 94
    pressure-cooked 94
  reducing 92
  removing fat 91
  simmering 91
  skimming 91
  turkey giblet 94
Strawberry
  jam 681
  raspberry purée, in 635
  shortcake 625
Stroganoff 188
Stuffed
  baked herrings 130
  baked stuffed courgettes 693
  breast of lamb 176
  Italian aubergines 505
  pork tenderloin 170
  tomatoes, Turkish 292
  vine leaves 329
Stuffing
  chestnut and apple 228
  chicken, for 210, 211
  grape 222
  herb 398
  pork, sage and onion 227
  rice and kidney 177
Suet 560
Sugar, jam, for 677
Summer fruits pie 552
Summer pudding 633
Sunflower and sesame seeds, toasted
  332
Swede, with crispy bacon 291
Sweet piccalilli 672
Sweetbreads
  generally 237
  soured cream and onion sauce,
    with 251

T

Tabasco sauce 408
Tahina paste 354
Taramasalata 86, 138
Tarragon
  generally 391
  carrot and tarragon soup 392
  chicken salad with tarragon and
    grapes 396
  spring carrots with tarragon butter
    263
Tart
  asparagus and cheese 81
  Lancaster lemon 553
  thick onion 337
  wholewheat treacle 556
Tartlets, cheese, with mushroom
  pâté 473
Thermometer 20
Thick bean and bacon soup 352
Thick onion tart 337
Thick pea soup 345
Thyme 391
Timer 20
Toasted cheese with ale 468
Toasted sesame and sunflower seeds
  332
Toffee, Uncle Billy's 687
Tomato
  generally 291
  apple and celery cream soup 110
  baked aubergines with 257
  baked marrow with tomatoes and
    coriander 272
  chilli sauce 364
  courgettes and tomatoes au gratin
    268
  fresh tomato sauce 363
  green tomato chutney 668
  kidneys in fresh tomato sauce 243
  salad 72, 488
  sardine stuffed 74
  sauce, fresh 363
  soup with basil 107
  spiced green tomato sauce 445
  spiced prawns with 151
  Turkish stuffed 292
Tongs, kitchen 15
Tongue
  lambs' 236
  lambs' tongue casserole 249
  ox 236
  pressed 248
Treacle
  sponge 657
  tart 556
Trifle, traditional 639
Tripe
  generally 237
  onions, and 252
Trout
  generally 134
  brown 134
  butter, cream and chives, with 398
  caper sauce, with 134
  poached trout with herbs 397
  smoked 138
Tuna
  brown rice and tuna fish salad 491
  starter, for 75
  white bean and tuna fish salad 80
Turbot 120
Turkey
  generally 226
  buying 227
  cooking times 229
  giblet stock 94
  stuffing 227, 228
  traditional roast 229
Turkish
  stuffed peppers 307
  stuffed tomatoes 292
Turmeric 416
Turnips
  generally 293
  buttered 294
  glazed baby 294
  leeks and turnips boulangère 293
  punchnep 293
  punchnep soup 103

U

Uncle Billy's toffee 687

V

Vanilla
  flavouring 416
  ice cream 529
Veal, ossobuco 201
Vegetables
  generally 254
  buckwheat and vegetable pie 319
  hazelnut and vegetable burgers 327
  mixed vegetables à la Grècque 333
  Provençal vegetable stew 336
  sautéed mixed 331
  summer 255
  winter 255
  see also types of vegetable e.g.
    Artichoke
Vegetarian
  goulash 328
  shepherd's pie 351
Vichyssoise 98
Victoria sponge 592
Vinaigrette dressing 481
Vinegar 410, 480
Vol-au-vent
  generally 571
  basic recipe 571
  cream cheese and herb filling 572
  cream puffs 573
  hot mushroom and bacon filling
    572

W

Walnut
  all-in-one banana and walnut loaf
    514
  all-in-one walnut and coffee sponge
    595
  chocolate and walnut pudding 655
  date, apple and walnut loaf 601

Watercress
  cream soup 103
  poached eggs with cream and 31
  raw spinach and watercress salad
    489
  salads, in 487
Welsh rarebit soufflé 468
Wheat 43, 317
Wheatmeal
  bread 42, 44
  flour 44
  quick rolls 55
Whisked fatless sponge 595
Whisking
  eggs 25
  equipment 14
White sauce 433, 434
Whitebait 132
Whiting 120
Whole grain cereals 314
Whole oat crunchies 627
Wholewheat
  bread 42
  cheese-crusted scones 620
  flour 44
  fruit scones 619
  girdle cakes 621
  macaroni cheese 369
  pizza 66
  quick and easy bread 50
  shortbread 625
  sponge cake 595
  treacle sponge 657
  treacle tart 556
Wine vinegar 410, 480
Winter salad, green 488
Witch sole 118

Y

Yeast 45, 47, 50
Yoghurt
  generally 533
  chilled yoghurt and cucumber soup
    536
  cooking with 535
  cucumber and yoghurt salad 331
  cucumber raita 537
  dried fruit 536
  dried fruit salad with nuts and 538
  home-made 533
  home-made yoghurt curd cheese
    535
  home-made fruit 536
  honey and wheatgerm with 535
  liver in yoghurt and juniper sauce
    239
  muesli, with 535
  sauce 503
  seafood sauce 536
Yorkshire pudding 161
Yugoslav kebabs 503

Z

Zabaglione 38